# HUMAN ECOLOGY

# · Contributing Authors

JOHN J. B. ANDERSON,
*Department of Orthopaedic Surgery, School of Medicine,*
*University of North Carolina, Chapel Hill*

JOHN E. BAERWALD,
*Department of Civil Engineering,*
*University of Illinois, Urbana*

ALBERT Z. GUTTENBERG,
*Department of Urban and Regional Planning,*
*University of Illinois, Urbana*

JOSEPH KASTELIC,
*deceased, formerly Department of Animal Science,*
*University of Illinois, Urbana*

S. CHARLES KENDEIGH,
*Department of Zoology,*
*University of Illinois, Urbana*

KENRAD E. NELSON,
*Department of Preventive Medicine and Community Health,*
*University of Illinois at the Medical Center, Chicago*

LAWRENCE I. O'KELLY,
*Department of Psychology,*
*Michigan State University, East Lansing*

CAROL E. STEINHART
*Professional Scientific Writer*

· A number of chapters have been
rewritten or edited by

CAROL E. STEINHART

in order to provide the book
with homogeneity of style and presentation.

# HUMAN ECOLOGY

PRINCIPAL AUTHOR AND EDITOR

## Norman D. Levine

*Director, Center for Human Ecology,*
*University of Illinois, Urbana*

**DUXBURY PRESS** · NORTH SCITUATE, MASSACHUSETTS

A DIVISION OF WADSWORTH PUBLISHING COMPANY, INC.

BELMONT, CALIFORNIA

*Duxbury Press*

A DIVISION OF WADSWORTH PUBLISHING COMPANY, INC.

*Human Ecology* was edited and prepared for composition by Eleanor Gilbert and Margaret Kearney. Interior design was provided by Dorothy Booth and the cover was designed by Patricia Sustendal.

L.C. Cat. Card No.: 72–93413
ISBN 0–87872–048–0

PRINTED IN THE UNITED STATES OF AMERICA

1  2  3  4  5  6  7  8  9  10—79  78  77  76  75

# · Contents ·

# · Preface ·

In recent years the expression "human ecology" has come into fashionable use and frequent abuse. It has become a catchall for a variety of marginally related activities—from picking up beer cans to saving the wilderness to halting industrial pollution. But popular concern with environmental issues can lead to solutions only if we take a holistic view of man's role in nature. The theme of this introduction to *Human Ecology* is that humans, like all living organisms, function in their environment by means of *adaptation*. The most important human adaptive mechanism—and the one whose unforeseen effects have generated the current interest in ecology—is *culture*.

*Human Ecology* has been organized to develop the student's understanding of this theme in three stages. The first part of the book, consisting of chapters 1 through 8, deals with the physical environment, its ecological laws, and the biological functioning of human beings within it. The second part, chapters 9 and 10, introduces culture as an adaptive device. The third part, chapters 11 through 15, explores the cultural institutions we have developed and places the study of human ecology in a present-day context. An epilogue speculates about the human ecology of the future.

This book grew out of an interdisciplinary course which has been taught since 1962 by the Center for Human Ecology at the University of Illinois (Champaign—Urbana). Begun as an informal committee within the Zoology Department in 1959, the Center was formally organized in 1965 and currently has about nineteen members in several departments and campuses of the university.

Most of the authors of *Human Ecology* are members of the Center. Their experience in teaching interdisciplinary, problem-oriented courses has given the book a breadth of coverage and unity of theme lacking in previous introductory texts. The articles have all been written by experts especially for this volume, and have been carefully integrated by Dr. Norman D. Levine, Director of the Center for Human Ecology. Valuable contributions were also received from John E. Baerwald of the Highway Traffic Safety Center of the University of Illinois. Dr. Carol E. Steinhart deserves special appreciation. She contributed an exceptional combination of scientific knowledge and writing ability to the final manuscript. She created some parts of the manuscript and re-wrote many others, thus providing it with a unity of style and outlook.

Acknowledgements are due to all members of the University of Illinois Council on Human Ecology for their contributions to the thinking of the editor and authors, and especially to Dr. Demitri B. Shimkin for his insight into the problems associated with human ecology. Special acknowledgement is given to Mrs. Janet B. Manning, who typed the manuscript and shepherded it through its many drafts.

# ·1·

# The Nature of Human Ecology

The origin of the word ecology is hidden in the past, as most origins are. One of the early recorded uses of the word is in 1858, when naturalist Henry David Thoreau wrote to his cousin that a neighbor was "still in Concord, attending to Botany, Ecology, etc." The concept of ecology was as uncertain as the origin of its name, until the German biologist Ernst Haeckel gave it precision in 1870: "By ecology we mean the body of knowledge concerning the economy of nature — the investigation of the total relations of the animal both to its inorganic and to its organic environment; including, above all, its friendly and inimical relations with those animals and plants with which it comes directly or indirectly into contact — in a word, ecology is the study of all the complex interrelations referred to by Darwin as the conditions of the struggle for existence."

This definition seems clear enough, but ecology continues to mean different things to different people and everything to some. To contemporary American ecologist Eugene Odum, ecology is the all-embracing "study of the structure and function of nature." The concerns of *human* ecology are hardly narrower, because man is in nature and part of it. Everything that happens, including everything that man does, affects everything else.

Is "human ecology," then, an empty phrase, a useless slogan? Must it be divided and subdivided until we are left with only the same old academic "disciplines" into which all knowledge is safely and barrenly pigeonholed? On the contrary! It is the synthesis of these many disciplines, their coming together into the broad, interdisciplinary and multidisciplinary field of human ecology, that is vital to the understanding of ourselves and our eternal predicament. Human ecology is, literally, the science of man in his house, and man's house is the planet Earth.

The study of tsetse flies is entomology; the study of the disease-causing trypanosomes that they carry is protozoology or parasitology; the study of

1

the diseases caused by trypanosomes is human or veterinary medicine. The study of livestock production is animal husbandry or agriculture. The study of weather and climate is meteorology. The study of the physical features of the Rift Valley is geology or geography. The study of the Masai people is anthropology. But bring them all together in a study of the effects of weather and climate and physical features of the land on the epidemiology of trypanosomiasis, and the effects of this disease on domestic animals and man and thus on human culture and human potential, and you have a study in human ecology. Clearly, human ecology is too broad for any one person to master in detail. But an overview of the field gives a framework on which to hang the data and theories of specialized fields, as well as a broad perspective on the nature and limitations of man and his environments, past, present, and future. It is such an overview that this book attempts to present.

## PHYSICAL AND BIOLOGICAL BASIS OF MAN'S ADAPTATION TO HIS ENVIRONMENT

A study of the interrelationships of an organism with its environment involves a study of its adaptation to the environment. Adaptation implies change, both in the organism and in its environment, since change in one may elicit change in the other. Change is the stuff of which evolution is made. The study of human ecology, then, rests on principles of evolution — on the complex and ever changing interactions of organisms with each other and with their physical surroundings. It is difficult to omit the idea of progress from evolution. In fact, that is what the doctrine of emergent evolution is all about. The general trend of evolution is toward increasing complexity, and the properties of complex systems cannot, in our present state of understanding, necessarily be predicted from knowledge of their components. Thus it is not possible to predict the properties of an atom from knowledge of protons and electrons, or of molecules from knowledge of atoms. Aggregates of molecules have properties vastly different from individual molecules because new properties emerge from the association of molecules in groups. The phenomenon of life cannot be predicted from study of inorganic chemistry. The amazing development of the thing we call man's mind is not foreshadowed in brainless forms of life. Finally, any organism that is known only in isolation from its normal surroundings is poorly known. That is why extrapolations from laboratory to field conditions are so risky. It is also why the study of ecology is important.

Adaptive changes in all organisms, including man, are mediated by changes in the information encoded in the hereditary material that is passed on from generation to generation. These changes are random. If they are helpful, the organism survives and produces offspring which are better adapted than organisms without the change. If the changes are harmful, the organisms bearing them are less well adapted and less likely to survive and reproduce. Nature has experimented with many creatures since life began. Only a fraction of them were ever successful, and only a fraction of those successful ones survive today.

## CULTURAL BASIS OF MAN'S ADAPTATION TO HIS ENVIRONMENT

Man has superimposed a new form of adaptation on the slow, inefficient, and often painful process of physical adaptation. It is culture. For the last 500,000 years or so man has adapted to his environment primarily by modifying his habits and behavior. Detailed instructions for how to behave as a human are not encoded in the sperm and egg from which a human being develops, as instructions for how to behave as a worm or a fish are encoded in the sex cells of these animals. In man, such instructions must be transmitted from one generation to the next through the medium of culture. Like ecology, culture has many definitions. A useful one is that culture is learned behavior shared by members of a social group and transmitted from generation to generation. It includes customs, beliefs, technology, and art.

The analogy between men and worms is extreme, as rudiments of culture are to be found in many birds and mammals. Some birds must learn the characteristic songs and calls of their species. If raised with birds of another species they will learn to sing those songs instead. Many birds and mammals, if raised by man, adapt so thoroughly to the ways of man that they later are unable to live with their own kind in the way characteristic of their species. Only casual encounters with man can change animal "culture." Compare the begging bears of the garbage dumps in our popular national parks with their relatives in more remote areas. A worm cannot change in this way.

Not surprisingly, it is among our primate relatives that the beginnings of culture are most evident: a young monkey or ape has much to learn from its peers and other members of its group, and any infant primate deprived of this learning is a pathetic creature indeed. However, the culture gap between man and all other animals is so enormous that it is reasonably safe to say that a quantitative difference has become qualitative. Culture is a unique feature of the animal that is man.

## THE PLAN OF THIS BOOK

We must share the earth with a bewildering variety not only of other people, but of other species; and while the limits of life as we know it are defined rather narrowly, these limits permit a range of physical environments. Part I of this book takes a look at the physical and biological environment in which we find ourselves — the environment which has acted on us and on which we, in turn, have acted for the one or two million years of our history. We are not gods. We can direct even our culture only within limits imposed by climate, soil, and the availability of resources. We are also dependent on plants, animals, and microorganisms, both wild and domesticated, and on the stability of the systems in which they occur.

Similarly, we can never become free from the restrictions imposed by our own biological nature. In Part II we consider some principles of evolution and adaptation and how they are illustrated by the evolution of man. The variability of the human species today results from long years of evolution and adaptation, and in it lurks clues to the possibilities for the future. Change begets change. Organisms adapt to changing environments and changes in organisms may bring about further environmental change.

The human environment is not only external, but internal. The basic unit of growth, differentiation, and biological activity is the cell. In most organisms the information encoded in the cells is necessary but not sufficient to ensure normal development and function of the organism. Interactions with other cells and products of cellular activity are also necessary. Most cells are isolated from the external environment, exposed only to a remarkably constant internal environment which nourishes and protects them and mediates interactions among them. The nineteenth century physician and physiologist Claude Bernard was the first to point this out. He said: "It is as though the organism had enclosed itself in a kind of hothouse where the perpetual changes in external conditions cannot reach it." In Part II we will also look at the life history of a human being from conception through old age and death, and at the nature and regulation of the internal environment that makes that life possible.

During recorded history, changes in organisms, including man, generally have been rather minor. Some species have become extinct. Others are diverging into races or subspecies. Man has directed the evolution of many plants and animals, and the changes thus brought about in domestic animals and crop plants are profound. Rats, pigeons, and English sparrows have learned to live successfully in cities. Some pale-colored moths in Great Britain have become dark in industrial regions. But in general, change is imperceptibly slow even in a time frame of thousands of years. Man today *looks* as he did 1, 10, or 100 thousand years ago.

He looks the same, but he is not the same — nor is his environment the same, because of the evolution of culture. Part III discusses this unprecedented phenomenon, the cultural adaptation and evolution of man. It discusses how, in adapting to and controlling his environment, man changes his environment and himself. It considers the development of various strategies for using energy and resources, and how these strategies —from hunting and gathering to different systems of agriculture to industrialization—influence social, political, and economic structure and the dynamics of populations.

Man has long dreamed of utopia. At first these utopias were in heaven, or someplace akin to it. During the last few centuries, however, some people have not been content to wait for heaven and have tried to create ideal human communities on earth. Today it is becoming increasingly evident that as we mold our culture it molds us, and that many of our problems arise not only from our failures but from our successes in confronting our environment through culture. Part IV considers some aspects of this confrontation of man with his environment. Chief among them is the problem of feeding a rapidly increasing population in the face of cultural, political, and economic roadblocks and the finite resources of the earth. The fact that we have this enormous population to feed testifies to our past success as a species, but in no way promises that our success will continue if we continue to multiply.

Much of our success is attributable to the conquest of disease. However, disease is still very much with us, and an understanding of its ecology is important for an understanding of man, past and present. The ecology of disease, which is the concern of epidemiology, is also discussed in Part IV.

Human activity has always produced unwanted residuals, commonly called "pollution." Even in the distant past, pollution was often locally severe, but not until recently has it become a problem of global dimensions. There are many examples of "natural pollution," not caused by man, which sometimes can poison environments or render them unfit for certain organisms. These include physical phenomena like natural oil seeps in the Santa Barbara Channel and elsewhere, soils with concentrations of particular elements, like selenium, toxic to many plants and animals, ash and gases spewed out in volcanic eruptions, the inhospitable conditions in hot springs, and the naturally-occurring radioactivity around and in us. They also include toxic materials and waste products released by some organisms, which may be harmful to the polluters themselves as well as to other organisms and which help to control population density, predation, and disease. These types of pollution differ from man-made pollution in two important respects. First, they have existed at fairly constant levels, or within fairly constant limits, for millennia, and organisms have evolved in relation to them. Second, they do not, in general, exceed the capacity of the environment to assimilate, dilute, or otherwise render them harmless. Much man-made pollution, in contrast, is on an unprecedented scale that overwhelms the physical and biological cycles of the earth as they now operate. Increasingly, brand new chemical poisons and radioactive elements are being introduced by man. As a result, pollution is forcing living creatures and the earth to grope toward a new equilibrium, and this new equilibrium will not necessarily be consonant with human values.

Are all the changes man has made in the face of the earth harmful by some criterion? Some people think so. They view man as a disease of the earth, as malignant as the extraterrestrial viruses of science fiction, but much larger, spreading rapidly and destroying everything in his path. Others think that earth somehow belongs to man, to do with as he pleases. If grizzly bears hurt him, grizzly bears must be exterminated. If foxes and hawks steal his chickens, then foxes and hawks, too, must go. If there is a wild river, it must be dammed for a hydroelectric plant. If there is petroleum under a wildlife refuge, the wildlife must take refuge elsewhere. Neither attitude is justified. The truth, as usual, lies somewhere in between. There is general agreement, however, that pollution is an undesirable — if inevitable — consequence of human activity. Part IV concludes with a discussion of man-made pollution and waste.

Finally, we look to the future, to the year 3000. Predictions of this sort are both satisfying and frustrating, because those who make them cannot be present to see whether they are fulfilled. But evolution continues; we cannot stop the world no matter how much we want to get off. Crystal-ball gazing of the sort you will find in the Epilogue is valuable, even necessary, because man alone, of all creatures, is able to modify the course of evolution according to his needs and desires. He influences the physical evolution of domesticated plants and animals and of the microorganisms and viruses he grows in the laboratory. He may even influence the physical evolution of himself. (When this is called **eugenics***or genetic engineering, it conjures up visions of bigotry and discrimination, or worse. When it is called genetic counseling it is more respectable.) But more important, perhaps, is that through cultural adaptations man will determine his future environments. So with mixed daring and humility, we will look to the year 3000.

*Boldface words can be found in the glossary.

# PART ONE

## Man's Environment

# · 2 ·

## NORMAN D. LEVINE

# The Physico-Chemical Habitat

The non-living earth imperceptibly gave rise to life between 3 and 3.5 billion years ago. In retrospect it seems as though life arose when and where it could, as if it were inevitable. So many chemical experiments were taking place so rapidly, compared to geologic time, that no matter how small the probability of success that any one experiment might have had, in the end the origin of life was a likely outcome.

A fortuitous combination of circumstances makes life as we know it possible on this planet, and impossible under most other conditions. In a sense this is simply ·a way of saying the obvious: that organisms must be adapted to their environment or perish. But there is more to it than that. Certain conditions are necessary to permit the formation and survival of the molecules from which life could evolve, and the physical and chemical requirements for complex life forms are more exacting still. In this chapter we will consider how the physical and chemical nature of the earth has determined the possibilities for life, with emphasis on man's life and lifestyles.

## SOME ASPECTS OF THE EARTH AND ITS HISTORY

The mass of the earth is just under $6 \times 10^{27*}$ grams, and its mean density is about five and one-half times that of water. It circles the sun at an

---

*It is convenient, when dealing with very large or very small numbers, to express them as powers of ten. One convention is to write the actual digits of the number with one digit to the left of the decimal point and the remaining digits to the right. This number is then multiplied by a power of ten to show its actual magnitude. To write out the number in the usual way, move the decimal point to the right as many places as indicated by a positive exponent, or as many places to the left as indicated by a negative one. For example:

$$
\begin{aligned}
2.3 \times 10^{-10} &= 0.00000000023 \\
2.3 \times 10^{-3} &= 0.0023 \\
2.3 \times 10^{-1} &= 0.23 \\
2.3 \times 10^{0} = 2.3 \times 1 &= 2.3 \\
2.3 \times 10^{1} &= 23 \\
2.3 \times 10^{3} &= 2300
\end{aligned}
$$

8

average distance of 1.5 × 10¹³ centimeters, slightly less than 93 million miles. These characteristics of earth determine many important things, including the amount and intensity of solar radiation it receives, its physical dimensions, and the magnitude of its gravitational attraction.

*GRAVITY AND PHYSICAL LIMITS ON SIZE.*   The acceleration due to gravity, which is related to the mutual attraction between two bodies, is about 980 centimeters per second per second at the surface of the earth — slightly less at the equator and more at the poles. Gravity determines the weight of an object, which is related to its mass but is not identical with it. Because much of the work done by organisms on the surface of the earth is accomplished in opposition to the force of gravity, gravity places maximum limits on the size that organisms can attain. The largest animals that have ever existed, whales and the giant dinosaurs, could develop to such enormous size only in an aquatic or semiaquatic habitat. They could not support their weight on land. Gravity also decrees that no animal can be much taller than a giraffe because of limitations of the circulatory system. (As it is, a giraffe spends most of his time with his neck more nearly horizontal than vertical.) Trees do not have the same problems with locomotion and circulation that animals have, but they must draw water through their roots and to their topmost branches; and although the cohesive strength of a very thin column of water provides a simple mechanism for such transport, the height to which the water can rise is ultimately limited by gravity.

At the small end of the scale, a minimum volume is required to house the information and materials for conducting the activities characteristic of life. A typical coccus-type bacterium, a sphere about half a micron in diameter, seems to represent this minimum volume, although a few smaller organisms are known. Viruses are an **order of magnitude** smaller than bacteria in linear dimensions and many times smaller in volume, and are too small to carry on all life functions for themselves. They consist only of genetic information and a coat of protein that determines what their host will be. To manifest any characteristics of life — to survive and reproduce, rather than just to endure like a rock — they must parasitize living cells. Thus there is a lower limit on the size of the cell, which is the functional unit of life, and an upper limit on the size that agglomerations of cells can reach. It is certainly no accident that living things exhibit the range of sizes that they do.

*THE ATMOSPHERE AND LIFE.*   The gravitational field of the earth is strong enough to hold all but the lightest gases. Today, only hydrogen and helium are lost in any significant amounts. Yet Earth is deficient by from six to ten orders of magnitude in the noble gases (helium, neon, argon, and krypton) that are common elsewhere in the universe. Methane and ammonia, common molecules in the solar system, are also essentially missing;

yet water, comparable in weight, is abundant. Scientists have been trying for many years to explain this mystery.

Astronomers now believe that the "terrestrial" planets, Mercury, Venus, Earth, and Mars, lost their gases at a very early stage in their development, before they had become single, solid bodies. The gases may have been driven away by the pressure of radiation from the sun, much as the tail of a comet is formed as the comet approaches the sun. Thus the earth originally had very little, if any, atmosphere. Because the earth was not molten during its agglomeration from smaller particles, water was probably retained in liquid form; and, along with other chemically reactive gases, was chemically bound in various ways. The abundance of water on earth and its scarcity on Venus can be explained by the difference in their distances from the sun: Venus, in the nearer orbit, would have lost her water as vapor along with the other gases.

In any case, the solid earth is large enough to prevent escape of the envelope of gas that now surrounds it, and the chemical composition of this envelope has been determined by physical, chemical, and biological events on earth. The present atmosphere is believed to have originated from out-gassing of the earth, largely through volcanic activity. The chemical composition of volcanic gases today probably resembles that of several billion years ago, consisting largely of water vapor and nitrogen, with smaller amounts of carbon dioxide, carbon monoxide, sulfur oxides and sulfur, chlorine, hydrogen chloride, hydrogen, helium, and traces of a few others. Free oxygen is conspicuously missing. On the primitive earth huge volumes of water vapor condensed and fell as rain, accumulating in the growing oceans. Gases containing sulfur and chlorine reacted with materials in the crust of the earth, leaving an atmosphere of carbon monoxide, carbon dioxide, nitrogen, and hydrogen. When radiation interacts with such a mixture, hydrogen cyanide is formed. Ultraviolet radiation of solutions of hydrogen cyanide produces amino acids and other biologically important molecules — the raw materials of life.

**Photosynthesis** is given credit for introducing free oxygen into the atmosphere (Figure 2.1). The first photosynthetic organisms probably lived at the bottom of shallow lakes and seas and in warm pools associated with volcanoes. There they were protected from the harmful rays of the sun, but received light in the visible range for photosynthesis. At first the oxygen they produced was used immediately in **oxidation** of iron and other materials in solution or in the earth's crust. As oxidation of surface materials neared completion, the concentration of oxygen in the atmosphere began to rise. At first, because of the intensity of solar radiation, much of the ordinary molecular oxygen ($O_2$) was changed into ozone ($O_3$), which absorbs lethal ultraviolet rays. When the concentration of oxygen in the atmosphere reached about 1 percent of its present level, only the top few centimeters of water would be exposed to harmful radiation, opening surface waters and

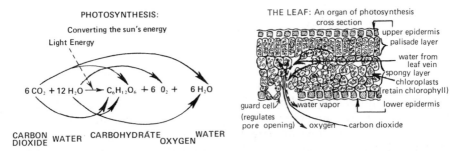

**Figure 2-1** In photosynthesis, light energy is used to split water, providing hydrogen for the reduction of $CO_2$. The diagram shows the overall chemical reaction and the fate of the atoms entering it. Synthesis of glucose ($C_6H_{12}O_6$) occurs through the multi-step Calvin cycle. Photosynthesis is mediated by the green pigment chlorophyll, which traps light making it available for splitting water. The chlorophyll is efficiently packaged in structures called chloroplasts, which contain all the materials required for glucose synthesis. The leaf (diagram at right) is marvelously adapted to its role as sugar factory. (Adapted from *Hammond Medallion Atlas*, Hammond, Inc., Maplewood, N.J., p. E-24.)

the oceans to life. Once this happened, life could spread quickly. Geology tells us that there was an evolutionary explosion during the Cambrian period, beginning more than 600 million years ago, which can be explained in this way. It was accompanied by the appearance of an advanced type of respiration depending on free oxygen.

As the oxygen level rose to 10 percent of its present concentration, dry land became shielded from lethal radiation, permitting life to spread ashore. The geologic record shows another evolutionary explosion beginning about 420 million years ago, when plants, followed by animals, invaded the land. There is much speculation on the changes in the atmosphere and related changes in climate during the years that followed, but whatever the details may be, the dry earth had at last become hospitable to the predecessors of man.

*SOLAR RADIATION.*    Except for relatively minor amounts of energy from interactions between the earth and moon, from decay of radioactive elements in the earth, and from chemical events in the earth and earth's own gravity and rotation, all of our energy comes from the sun. The distance of the earth from the sun determines the intensity of solar radiation that impinges on the outer atmosphere. The energy, per unit time, falling perpendicularly on a surface at the limits of the atmosphere averages 1.94 calories per square centimeter per minute. This number is known as the *solar constant*. At any given time, about half of the earth is receiving no radiation at all. The amount of energy falling on the illuminated half is determined by the solar constant and also by the angle at which the energy strikes.

The sun emits a broad spectrum of electromagnetic rays, ranging from high-energy gamma rays of very short wavelength through X-rays, ultraviolet, visible light, infrared, microwaves, and radiowaves. Radiation of different wavelengths is selectively absorbed, reflected, or passed unchanged by various components of the atmosphere, so that not only is the amount of radiation that actually reaches the earth reduced by up to 50 percent or more, depending on the weather, but the distribution of wavelengths is no longer typical of the solar spectrum. In particular, the life-damaging shorter rays are largely absorbed in the atmosphere, although some get through to react with biologic molecules and influence the rate of evolution. Within limits imposed by our distance from the sun, the composition of the atmosphere determines how much and what kind of radiation reaches the surface of the earth, and thus determines temperature and climate. The contrast between conditions on the earth and on the moon clearly shows how important this is.

*CLIMATE AND WEATHER.*   Moment-to-moment weather is *real*. It may be dry, clear, hot, and still, or cold, windy, cloudy, and snowing. Climate is an *abstraction* derived from average weather conditions over long periods of time. Climate is part of our environment. It governs the flora of a region and, directly and indirectly, the fauna as well.

The basic ingredients of both instantaneous weather and long-term climate are temperature, atmospheric pressure, precipitation, humidity, wind direction and velocity, and cloudiness. These are controlled by complex patterns of circulation of air and water as well as by the amount of solar radiation received.

The solid earth itself heats and cools quickly and conducts heat poorly. It is affected by annual temperature cycles to, at most, a depth of a few feet. Transfer of energy from one part of the earth to another is mediated by the highly mobile atmosphere and oceans, which are set into motion by small imbalances in temperature. Bodies of water absorb and store large quantities of heat during the summer, which they slowly release to the air during the winter. Because they heat and cool slowly, oceans provide relatively cool surfaces in the summer and warm ones in the winter. This has important consequences for general circulation and overall climate. There are also local, short-term changes in the ocean, analogous to weather. Although we tend to take the constancy of oceanic "weather" for granted, in contrast to the vagaries of the atmosphere, oceanographers find short-term fluctuations in oceanic circulation that resemble changes in the atmosphere. The reliable Gulf Stream, for example, may at times be 100 miles off course.

Topographic features of the land and the distribution of land and water also influence climate. The effects of mountains on temperature and precipitation are well known. Climates vary on small geographic scales as well as grand; the climate of a city is different from that of surrounding areas, as is the climate of a sheltered valley. Climate and vegetation mutually affect one another, and if the vegetation is altered, as by the intervention of man, climatic changes follow. Many climatologists believe that the Sahara Desert is largely the handiwork of man, as overgrazing by his flocks destroyed the vegetative cover. Similarly, conversion of forests to agricultural land can also have climatic repercussions through changes in the balance between evaporation and precipitation and changes in the reflectivity of the surface.

We commonly speak of five climatic zones, based on temperature: Arctic, North Temperate, Tropical, South Temperate, and Antarctic (Figure 2.2). In the tropics the mean temperature of the coldest month is above 64° F, and freezing temperatures practically never occur. The subtropics extend from the boundaries of this region to a line representing a mean temperature of 32° F for the coldest month. The temperate latitudes, characterized by cold winters and warm summers, extend from the border of the subtropics to a line representing a mean temperature of 50° F for the warmest month. This corresponds to the timber line, or limit of tree growth. Beyond this are the climates of the Arctic and Antarctic, the less severe being classified as tundra (characterized by herbaceous plants but no trees), and the more severe as the polar regions of eternal frost.

The standard method of climate classification is based on vegetation zones, which are determined jointly by all the climatic variables. This classification establishes five major categories, which are further subdivided. The major categories are: *tropical rainy climates*, hot at all seasons, such as occur in central Africa or Brazil; *dry climates*, divided into **steppe**, as in east central Russia, and desert; *warm, temperate, rainy climates* with mild winters, as in Alabama and Kentucky; *cold, humid forest climates* with severe winters, as in southern Canada; and *polar climates*, divided into tundra and eternal frost.

Climate has had a profound influence on human culture, because it determines what man must do to survive. Most basically, it determines how he will obtain his food and what that food will be. As climate has influenced man, man is now beginning to influence climate.

*SOIL.* Soils form a thin layer over much of the land surface of the earth. They are formed by the combined action of water, wind, chemical activity, and living organisms on the parent rock. Although the nature of the parent rock determines the basic composition of the soil, climate, topography, time, and life determine its character. Simple plants — algae, lichens, and mosses, growing on the surface of rocks — prepare the way for other types of life; soil-dwelling microorganisms, largely fungi and bacteria, play a major role in making nutrients available to other forms of life; small animals — worms, insects, and crustaceans — eat the microorganisms and each other and further condition the soil; higher plants and burrowing vertebrate animals exert their influence; and finally, man himself has a profound effect.

Mountain-building, erosion, **sedimentation**, and other geomorphologi-

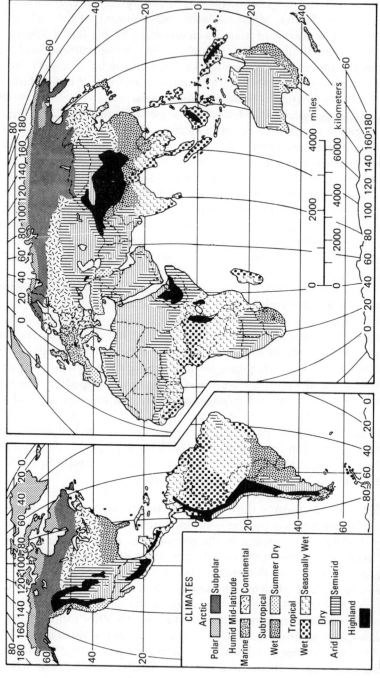

**Figure 2–2** World climate zones. (Adapted from Broek and Webb, *A Geography of Mankind*, 2nd ed., McGraw-Hill Book Co., New York, 1973, p. 44.)

cal processes have created a great variety of rocks and a corresponding variety in the soils derived from them. It became obvious to farmers and amateur geologists in the eighteenth century that chalky soils occur above chalk, sandy soils above sandstone, clayey soils on **shales**, and rich organic soils on **peat**. Not until later did it become apparent that soils of similar character extended across boundaries of rock type, forming the great soil belts that cross large portions of continents. Thus climate and vegetation could be as important as parent material in determining the ultimate nature of soil. In fact, the first soil scientists were so impressed with the apparent correlation between soil type and climate that they devised a zonal classification of soils which has persisted until today (Figure 2.3). It is generally useful, although it suffers from the same weaknesses as any classification based on one or two of a number of interacting variables.

A vivid demonstration of the development of soil in response to physical factors and the activities of a succession of organisms has been seen during the last century in the reforestation of the island of Krakatau, in Sunda Strait, between Java and Sumatra. In 1883 a violent volcanic explosion destroyed part of the island and buried the rest under many feet of white-hot volcanic ash. First the blue-green algae returned, able to grow on the most formidable inorganic surface as long as the climate was moist. Soon grasses began to invade, rapidly forming a closed ground cover. As the soil deepened, became richer in organic material and better able to retain water, a community of shrubs and trees began to emerge. Today, the original tropical rain forest has returned — not in all its former richness of species, because time for complete recolonization has been too short, but it is a tropical rain forest, nevertheless.

Soil is a mixture of inorganic and organic constituents. The inorganic constituents can be designated as sand, silt, and clay. The relative amounts of these determine the texture of the soil and its ability to hold moisture and mineral nutrients. Organic matter, consisting of decomposing tissues of plants and animals, makes up between 2 and 5 percent of the surface layer. It modifies the physico-chemical properties of the inorganic components of the soil and is a source of nutrients for microorganisms and higher plants.

The **interstices** between solid soil particles are filled with liquid and gases. The liquid, which usually comprises 10 to 35 percent of the soil volume, is a complex aqueous solution of many substances. It is the medium through which nutrients reach microorganisms and higher plants. Its **ions** are in **dynamic equilibrium** with those on the surface of soil particles.

The gaseous phase of the soil is essentially air. It is normally saturated with water vapor and contains ten to one hundred times as much carbon dioxide as air in the atmosphere, and a little less oxygen. If soil becomes waterlogged, it cannot exchange gases with the atmosphere, its oxygen is used up, and growth of plant roots and other aerobic forms of life is inhibited. Under

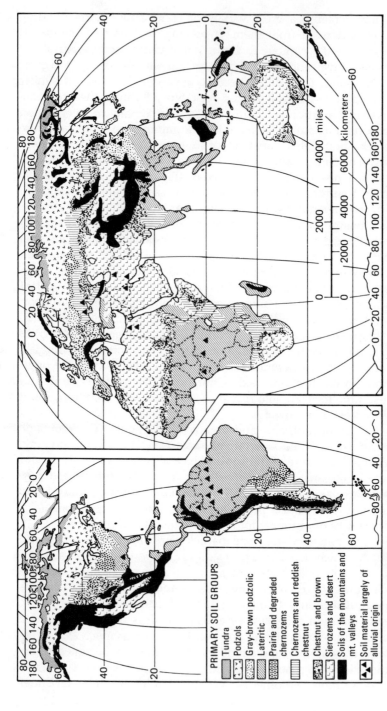

**Figure 2-3** World distribution of major soil types. Nations with low agricultural productivity have been described as poor pieces of real estate, as this map suggests. The richest soils are alluvial and prairie soils and chernozems. The other soils are relatively infertile or offer other problems to agriculture. (Adapted from Earl B. Shaw, *Fundamentals of Geography*, John Wiley and Sons, New York, 1965, p. 171.)

PRIMARY SOIL GROUPS

Tundra
Podzols
Gray-brown podzolic
Lateritic
Prairie and degraded chernozems
Chernozems and reddish chestnut
Chestnut and brown
Sierozems and desert
Soils of the mountains and mt. valleys
Soil material largely of alluvial origin

persistently waterlogged conditions, the types of plant and animal communities that can survive are affected.

Through their relationship with climate and vegetation, soils have a marked effect on the type of human civilization that can develop. The thin, nutrient-poor soils of the tropics cannot grow as much food and hence cannot support as dense a human population as the rich **alluvial soils** of the great river deltas. In fact, many tropical soils cannot support agriculture to any appreciable extent. To a large degree the underdeveloped nations are not favored by climate and soils, and no amount of tractors, fertilizer, and hybrid seed will help them very much.

The limits to the productivity of the earth's soils are becoming increasingly important in forecasting the future of man. Out of approximately 32 billion acres of land, about 10 percent is under cultivation, 18 percent is used for pasture and grazing, 28 percent is forest, and the rest is desert, tundra, mountains, and wastelands, or is covered with ice. (Although they are concentrated in certain regions, urban areas and roads constitute a negligible fraction — less than 1 percent.) About half of the potentially cultivable land is under cultivation and more than half of the potential grazing land is being used. The potential of what remains may be more theoretical than real, because the *best* land is already being used; and what remains has various limitations which will probably render it only marginally productive under any likely circumstances. Various attempts to open up virgin lands in Russia and Latin America have been disastrous failures, usually because of unanticipated problems in maintaining the structure and fertility of the soil.

By continent or region, the percentages of potentially cultivable land now under cultivation are shown in Table 2.1. There is little land left in Asia

**TABLE 2.1**
**Percentage of Potentially Arable Land Now Cultivated, and Amount Cultivated Per Person on Different Continents**

| Continent | Percent Cultivated | Acres Cultivated Per Person |
|---|---|---|
| Asia | 83 | 0.7 |
| Europe | 88 | 0.9 |
| South America | 11[a] | 1.0 |
| Africa | 22[b] | 1.3 |
| North America | 51 | 2.3 |
| USSR (Europe-Asia) | 64 | 2.4 |
| Australasia | 2[c] | 2.9 |

[a]Tropical limitation.    [b]Desert and tropical limitations.    [c]Desert limitation.
Based on Hendricks, S. B. 1969. Food from the land. Chap. 4 *In* Committee on Resources and Man, National Academy of Sciences-National Research Council. Resources and Man. Washington, D.C. pp. 65–85.

and Europe for cultivation, and much of what remains in South America, Africa, and Australia suffers from special defects that must be corrected before it can be used. The Sahara Desert and much of Africa could produce quite well if water were supplied. The same is true of many of the western states of the United States. Much of the cultivable land in South America and Africa is in the moist tropics, where the soil has been badly leached and requires heavy fertilization. Furthermore, much of it has undesirable physical and chemical properties, including a high content of iron and the tendency to become brick-like when water is removed.

Through natural variations in concentrations of various elements, soils subtly affect the health of organisms — especially of man and his crops and domesticated animals. Although plants are, to a limited extent, selective in their uptake of mineral nutrients, they cannot select what is not there. Similarly, an imbalance in soil nutrients is likely to be reflected by some kind of imbalance within the plant, although the relationships among intake of various nutrients are not simple. In general, plant growth is limited by the nutrient in shortest supply. Plants respond to an excess of a nutrient by decreased growth, concentration of the nutrient within their tissues, or both.

All this is relevant to the health of animals and man because they ultimately derive their food from plants. Cattle have been poisoned in several western states from forage growing in soil with a high content of selenium. At the same time, in several eastern states, a deficiency of selenium in the soil has led to "white muscle disease" of cattle. The well-known "goiter belt" corresponds to a zone of soils deficient in iodine. Prevalence of mottled teeth is related to a high concentration of fluorine in the soil, although a small amount of fluorine is necessary to prevent tooth decay. Finally, soils naturally contain varying amounts of radioactive elements. It is not known whether variations in levels of natural radiation are related to the incidence of disorders caused, at least in part, by exposure to radiation or radioactive materials.

## PERIODICITY

The term *periodicity* refers to recurrence of a phenomenon at more or less equal intervals. The earth's rotation imposes a periodicity on the alternation of light and dark, warming and cooling, the ebb and flow of tides, and other natural processes. Many biological rhythms are associated with these daily, or diurnal, periodicities. In the eighteenth century the systematic biologist Linnaeus developed a flower clock based on the facts that flowers of different species open and close at different times of day. Since then more than fifty rhythmic processes have been identified in **vascular plants**, including photosynthesis, leaf movements, and cell division. Animals, too, exhibit daily cycles, some of which are as obvious as alternating periods of activity and rest, but many more of which are subtle physiological changes, such as production of blood cells, body temperature, storage of glycogen and bile in the liver, hormone production, and secretion of urine. Related to these and other cycles are changes in emotional states, ability to learn and perform various tasks, susceptibility to disease, pain threshold, sleep and wakefulness, and probability of birth and death. People are becoming aware of the rhythms in themselves as they commute by jet halfway around the world and find that it takes more than a good night's sleep to get them back into shape again.

Biological rhythms may be either *endogenous* or *exogenous*, that is, determined by either internal or external factors. Among endogenous rhythms are those of the heartbeat, contractions of the intestine, movements of cilia (tiny hairlike appendages on some cells), and gait or walking rhythms. The inborn nature of walking rhythm, for example, is evident to anyone who works with horses. Exogenous rhythms may be related to any of a multitude of external cues and may follow daily, monthly, or annual cycles.

Perhaps most biological rhythms are controlled partly by internal, partly by external factors. Thus certain behaviors may be triggered by the arrival of cooler temperatures in the fall, but a cold snap in July would not evoke the same behavior because it would be out of phase with the internal cycle. The so-called **circadian rhythms** have periods of about a day, but if an organism is kept in an environment where conditions are constant, the period may vary from 24 hours — perhaps even in cyclical fashion. This phenomenon has been noted in people who volunteer to live in caves, out of contact with above-ground cycles of day and night and changing temperatures. It has also been studied in astronauts. Alternatively, circadian rhythms can be experimentally adjusted by exposing a plant, animal, or person to "days" of different lengths, of perhaps 20 hours, or 28, instead of 24. Most circadian rhythms seem to be basically endogenous cycles which adjust, within limits, to external conditions when appropriate stimuli are available. Otherwise, they set their own pace.

Annual cycles of migration, hibernation, and sexual activity are common in animals, and may be triggered by temperature, day length or changes in the daily path of the sun across the sky, or perhaps by combinations of conditions, including the availability of food and cosmic and geomagnetic phenomena. Cyclic change in coat color of mammals is a protective adaptation, while change of plumage in birds is related to the sexual cycle. People, too, exhibit annual rhythms in physiology, mood, and susceptibility to disease. A peak number of suicides occurs in May, while deaths from arteriosclerosis reach a peak in January.

Monthly rhythms are common in lower animals. The swarming of mayflies some days after the full moon, the sexual activities of herrings with their peak shortly after the full moon, and the mass production of sperm and eggs by the marine palolo worm during the last quarter of the moon in October and November are examples. Not surprisingly, organisms that live in the intertidal zone, the region between the highest high tide and the lowest low tide, tend to show cycles related to the moon.

Lunar cycles also occur in man, although for the most part they have been detected only as isolated instances in particular individuals. The most obvious cycle with an average period of 29.5 days is the female menstrual cycle. It seems unlikely that the length of this cycle is coincidental, especially since it has been shown that the time of ovulation can be regulated by light.

Living organisms constantly receive rhythmic stimuli from their environment. It is not surprising that their lives should be intricately adjusted to these stimuli. Structure in time seems to be as important for life as structure in space.

## NON-PERIODIC CYCLES

Rhythms are a type of cycle which runs its course and returns to the starting point after a regular period of time. Not all cycles, however, are rhythmic. Notable among these are the hydrologic cycle and the biogeochemical cycles of chemical elements and compounds. Some of these cycles, or parts of them, occur so slowly as to be of only theoretical interest in the affairs of men. For example, phosphorus, as phosphate, is constantly being carried to the sea, where it precipitates, and where it remains until geomorphological processes like mountain-building bring it to the surface again. Parts of the phosphorus cycle, however, and many other cycles, occur very rapidly, as earth's elements pass from inorganic to organic and back to inorganic form. These cycles have both biologic and geologic components and are the ones of most interest to us. They are important because human activity is having an impact on many of them, and because the efficient cycling of materials is necessary for the balance of nature and for the maintenance of life.

*WATER AND THE HYDROLOGIC CYCLE.* No matter how far we stretch our imaginations, it is difficult to imagine anything resembling life occurring in the absence of water. Life originated in the water, and all metabolic reactions occur in complex aqueous solutions. When a cell dries up, metabolism comes virtually to a halt. Most cells die under these conditions. Some, however, are able to survive for a very long time when dry, and this is an important adaptive mechanism. Familiar examples of survival in a dry state at a greatly reduced level of metabolism are seeds, the spores of algae and bacteria, and the baker's yeast you buy in the store.

Water has many remarkable properties. The structure of the water molecule is **asymmetric**, resulting in an asymmetric distribution of electric charge within it. Thus the positive and negative portions of the molecule not only attract ions and charged parts of other molecules, bringing them into solution, but they attract the negative and positive parts of other water molecules. In liquid water, many molecules are linked together in this way through hydrogen bonds, the strength of which makes water a liquid at temperatures at which molecules of comparable weight (methane and ammonia, for example) are gases. Another unusual property of water is that the solid phase is less dense than the liquid phase. In other words, ice floats.

All forms of water play key roles in the earth's energy budget. Ice, snow, and clouds reflect incoming radiation back into space. Clouds also retard the earth's back radiation of heat into space by re-reflecting it to the surface. Atmospheric water vapor strongly absorbs energy in the infrared region of the spectrum. In fact, water vapor is the chief insulating ingredient of the atmosphere, preventing the extremes of daytime and nighttime temperature that occur on the moon.

Relative to most other substances, a great deal of heat is required to melt, boil, or raise the temperature of water (Table 2.2). To evaporate the annual rainfall at an average rate of more than a billion gallons per second requires $2.2 \times 10^{23}$ calories, roughly one third of the solar energy that reaches the surface of the earth. About 85 percent of the evaporation takes place over the sea. Of the 15 percent occurring over land, half is transpired into the atmosphere by plants. Figure 2.4 shows the basic features of the water cycle and the distribution of water on earth.

Although all the water that evaporates falls again as precipitation, evaporation does not necessarily balance precipitation in a given region.

**TABLE 2.2**
**Thermal Properties of Water and Some Other Common Substances**

| Substance | Specific Heat at O°C (cal/g/°C) | Heat of Fusion (cal/g at freezing point) | Heat of Vaporization (cal/g at boiling point) |
|---|---|---|---|
| Water | 1.00 | 79.7 | 539.6* |
| Mercury | 0.03 | 2.8 | 70.6 |
| Lead | 0.03 | 5.9 | — |
| Ethyl alcohol | 0.54 | 24.9 | 204. |
| Oxygen | 0.22 | 3.3 | 50.9 |
| Carbon monoxide | 0.26 | 8.0 | 50.4 |

* At 20° C the heat of vaporization of water is 585 cal/g.
Specific heat is defined as the amount of energy needed to raise the temperature of one gram of a substance 1°C. Because this varies with temperature, the temperature is usually specified when the specific heat is given. The heat of fusion is the amount of energy required to melt one gram of a substance at the melting (freezing) point, without changing its temperature. The heat of vaporization is the amount of energy required to convert one gram of liquid to vapor without changing its temperature. The heat of vaporization is usually given at the boiling point of the substance, although liquid and gaseous phases are in equilibrium at lower temperatures.

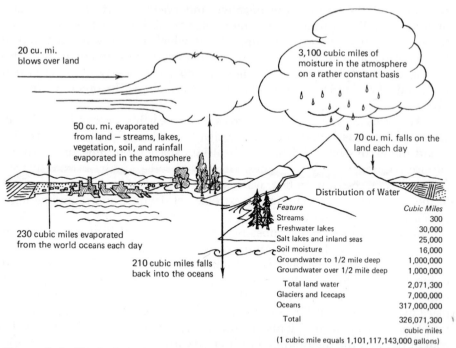

**Figure 2–4** The hydrologic cycle. Powered by the sun, the hydrologic cycle operates on an enormous scale involving land, air, oceans, and living organisms. More than 99 percent of earth's water is salty or unavailable. The rest, still a large amount, is unevenly distributed, so that there are critical water shortages on a planet largely covered by and soaking in water. (Adapted from Greenwood and Edwards, *Human Environments and Natural Systems*, Duxbury Press, North Scituate, Mass., 1973, p. 57.)

More than a third of the rain falling on land, $9.8 \times 10^{15}$ gallons per year, originates in the sea. This represents a gigantic worldwide desalination process — 7,500 gallons per day for every living person.

In many places the activities of man have changed the balance between evaporation and precipitation. By irrigating his crops, man increases evaporation and transpiration without affecting local precipitation. Deforestation also affects patterns of evaporation and rainfall in complex ways, by changing the local energy balance, increasing runoff, and decreasing the water-holding capacity of the soil. More evaporation will take place from the lake behind the Aswan Dam than took place from the river, and because of the dryness of the atmosphere and the nature of the prevailing winds, this water will not fall back on Egypt.

*THE CARBON CYCLE.* Life today depends on the capture of radiant energy by green plants and its conversion to the chemical energy of the carbon bond. By the process of photosynthesis, atmospheric carbon dioxide is fixed into carbohydrates which then undergo a vast number of chemical transformations. The energy stored in carbohydrates and their derivatives is passed from molecule to molecule and organism to organism until it is dissipated, and the carbon returns to the atmosphere once again as carbon dioxide.

Components of the carbon cycle as it occurs on land are shown in Figure 2.5. A similar cycle occurs in the sea. Between one quarter and one third of the carbohydrate made by plants is used in their own energy-yielding respiration. The rest is stored or converted into other types of compounds required by the plant. Living and dead plants provide organic compounds that are needed by other organisms.

The amount of carbon dioxide removed from the air by photosynthesis is approximately balanced by the amount returned through respiration. However, decomposition of organic matter is not always complete. Under

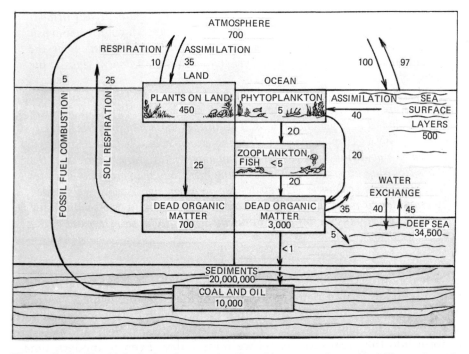

**Figure 2–5** The biological carbon cycle. Quantities are estimated in billions of metric tons. The natural cycle is approximately in balance, with equivalent amounts of carbon constantly added to and removed from atmosphere, soil, and ocean; but man's burning of fossil fuels is able to upset the balance. Besides the biological cycle there is a geological cycle involving vastly greater amounts of carbon and slowly moving on a time scale of millions of years. (Adapted from *Scientific American*, Sept. 1970, p. 130.)

## UNFORESEEN IMPACT OF THE ASWAN HIGH DAM

*Towering thirty-six stories above the river bed, the concrete wall reaches from bank to bank, forming a 2-mile-wide barrier. The waters imprisoned behind it create a shimmering lake that extends out of sight. Through sluices the pent-up waters gush forth from the wall, flowing fast and clear 600 miles to the sea. The Aswan High Dam is Egypt's proudest achievement and one of the most remarkable engineering feats of the century. Completed in 1967, the dam was to accomplish four major goals: (1) to prevent the severe floods of the Nile; (2) to increase Egypt's arable land through irrigation; (3) to store water in its 300-mile-long reservoir, Lake Nasser; and (4) to generate 10 billion kilowatt hours of electricity a year. These expectations have been partially fulfilled. Largely unexpected, however, were the disastrous side effects that have now become apparent.*

*Disrupting the normal interaction between river and valley, the dam has destroyed the delicate balance of nature. Annual floods used to deposit rich silt in the valley, fertilizing the soil, washing away salts, carrying nutrients to fish and shellfish, and replenishing land that the currents had eroded. Now the floodwaters are trapped in the reservoir, and most of the sediment sinks to the bottom of Lake Nasser.*

*Deprived of the Nile's silt, the land has lost its former fertility. To restore what nature had so generously bestowed, 1.5 million tons of artificial fertilizer must be applied to the land each year. The nitrates that drain from the fertilizer into the Nile end up in people's drinking water—a health hazard that will worsen as amounts of the chemical accumulate over the years. Deprived of the Nile's cleansing waters, the soil is absorbing more salts than crops can tolerate. New irrigation channels aggravate the problem by raising salt-loaded groundwater to plant-root level. To correct the salinity, a $460-million tile drainage system must be installed throughout irrigated areas. Deprived of the*

certain conditions, over the course of hundreds of millions of years, this matter becomes coal or petroleum, the fossil fuels. In the lush coal swamps and forests of the Carboniferous period, plant growth greatly exceeded both animal predation and decay, providing material for time, heat, and pressure to form into the great coal seams we mine today. Even in modern times, however, the early stages in the formation of coal and petroleum are still occurring.

Some aquatic animals make skeletons or shells out of calcium carbonate. The carbon dioxide fixed in this form is, like the fossil fuels, removed from participation in the carbon cycle of the **biosphere** for long periods of

*Nile's nutrients, fishing grounds in the delta and eastern Mediterranean are rapidly depleting: the Egyptian sardine catch alone dropped from 18,000 tons in 1965 to 500 tons in 1968. Deprived of the Nile's soil-building sediment, abrasive currents are left unchecked to erode river banks and delta. The delta coastline is receding several yards a year, and 3 old barrages and 550 bridges are in danger of being destroyed by the clear, fast-flowing river. To save these structures, 10 more barrages must be built at a cost of $250 million. The future of the delta is less secure.*

*Still more problems afflict the country as a result of the dam. In particular there has been a notable increase in the spread of schistosomiasis, a parasitic disease common to Egypt that causes severe stomach cramps and chronic inflammation of the bladder, and damages heart, lungs, and liver. The microscopic larvae are carried by snails that flourish in the quiet waters of irrigation channels. Before the Aswan project, channels dried out periodically and the snails perished. Now that the channels are constantly filled, the snails multiply freely, and the disease is readily picked up and transmitted when people bathe or use the channels as an open sewage system. The infection rate in the delta has risen from 6 percent to 80 or 100 percent. Another even more serious threat looms in the possibility that deadly malaria-bearing mosquitoes from the Sudan, fifty miles from Lake Nasser, may find a home in the impounded waters of the reservoir.*

*On balance, the costs of the Aswan High Dam seem to outweigh its benefits. Several smaller scale projects might have proved far more valuable in the long run. Now, however, the new problems caused by the dam may be worse than those it was expected to solve.*

*Sources: Claire Sterling, "The Aswan Disaster,"* National Parks and Conservation Magazine, *August 1971, pp. 10–13. Reid A. Bryson and Sarah Jenkins, "The Environmental Impact of the Aswan High Dam," publication of the Institute for Environmental Studies, University of Wisconsin, May 1972.*

time. Coral reefs and islands, limestone, and chalk beds are memorials to countless tiny creatures whose remains created them.

The cycling of carbon in the biosphere represents but a tiny part of the total carbon cycle. Table 2.3 shows the distribution of carbon in the earth. The amount tied up in living organisms and undecayed organic matter is a miniscule 0.02 percent of earth's total carbon reservoir, and the amount of carbon in the atmosphere is an order of magnitude smaller even than that. But the turnover of carbon between the atmosphere and the biosphere is extremely rapid. About one seventh of the carbon in the atmosphere is cycled through the biosphere each year.

**TABLE 2.3**
**Distribution of Carbon in the Earth**

| Site | $10^{14}$ kg Carbon |
|---|---|
| Atmosphere | 7 |
| Hydrosphere (oceans, fresh water) | 390 |
| Biosphere (living organisms and undecayed organic matter) | 44 |
| Lithosphere total (rocks, fossil fuels, and interstitial water) | 276,000 |
|     Fossil fuels | (81) |
|     All other lithosphere | (275,919) |
| Total carbon | 276,441 |

Adapted from W. Rubey, 1964, Geologic History of Sea Water. In P. Brancazio and A. Cameron, eds., *The Origin and Evolution of Atmospheres and Oceans.* John Wiley and Sons, Inc. New York. P. 24. The numbers given are rough approximations because of the difficulties in obtaining either accurate or precise global data of this nature.

Other parts of the carbon cycle proceed on a slower but larger scale. Carbon dioxide is removed from the atmosphere in the initial step in the weathering of limestone and other carbonate rocks. For every molecule of carbon dioxide that enters the reaction, however, there are formed two bicarbonate ions, each of which is potentially able to return a molecule of carbon dioxide to the atmosphere. Carbon dioxide is released to the atmosphere by escape from large bodies of water when their temperatures rise, by burning fossil fuels, and by outgassing of the earth through volcanic activity.

The **hydrosphere** accounts for about 0.1 percent of earth's carbon. Most of this is in the form of carbonate or bicarbonate ions, but about 1 percent of it occurs as dissolved carbon dioxide. The oceans may appear to be an almost limitless sink for excess carbon dioxide, but in fact they are not. Only the surface layer of seawater, no more than the first 500 meters, is in dynamic equilibrium with the atmosphere. The effective ocean reservoir contains only three to eight times the amount of carbon dioxide found in the atmosphere. Overturning of deeper waters is exceedingly slow. Exchange of surface water with water below 1 kilometer requires 500 to 1,000 years or more. One consequence of this is that about half of the carbon dioxide we have added to the atmosphere by burning fossil fuels is still where we put it — in the atmosphere.

Most of the action involves the 0.1 percent of carbon that cycles through the **atmosphere**, hydrosphere, and biosphere. The rest of it, 99.9 percent, sits sluggishly in the **lithosphere** where time is reckoned in eons, not in seasons. An amount of carbon roughly equal to that in the biosphere, or perhaps up to twice as great, is tied up in the fossil fuels and shales rich in organic matter. The rest occurs as rocks, chiefly limestone, or dissolved in the interstitial water of the rocks. New fossil fuel is constantly being formed, rocks weather, and new sedimentary rocks are deposited; but these processes are glacially slow, compared to the rhythmic "breathing" of the biosphere and the exchange between atmosphere and surface waters.

*THE NITROGEN CYCLE.* Nitrogen cycles so rapidly through the atmosphere and biosphere that the geologic nitrogen cycle is trivial by comparison. The nitrogen that makes up 78 percent of our atmosphere today came originally from outgassing of the earth through volcanic activity. Molecular nitrogen, $N_2$, is not very reactive chemically. Its combination with other elements, called fixation, requires energy, whether it is accomplished by lightning, by microorganisms, by a photochemical reaction, or by an industrial process. The activities of man have roughly doubled the rate of nitrogen fixation, and another doubling is expected by the end of this century. This will not cause a detectable change in the amount of atmospheric nitrogen, but it may affect other parts of the nitrogen cycle. For example, application of nitrate fertilizer to agricultural land has increased the amount of nitrate in groundwater and bodies of fresh water, as well as the runoff of nitrates to the sea.

The basic features of the nitrogen cycle are shown in Figure 2.6. Higher

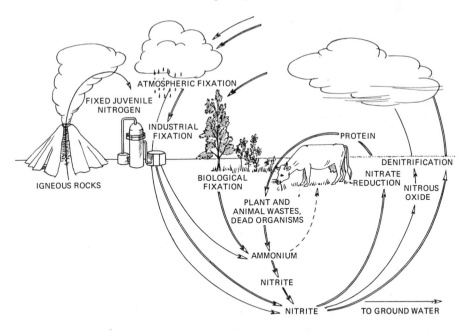

**Figure 2–6** The nitrogen cycle. Like the water and carbon cycles, this one involves soil, water, atmosphere, and living organisms. Microorganisms combine atmospheric nitrogen with hydrogen or oxygen, making it available to higher plants which, in turn, incorporate it into the organic compounds required by animals. As in the carbon cycle, the natural cycle is roughly in balance, while the activities of man—in this case industrial fixation—threaten to unbalance the cycle. (Adapted from *Scientific American*, Sept. 1970, pp. 138–139.)

plants require most of their nitrogen in the form of nitrate, although part of that requirement can be satisfied by ammonia. This inorganic nitrogen is incorporated into amino acids, protein, and other organic compounds which are subsequently utilized by animals and many microorganisms. The nitrates used by plants are supplied in many ways: by lightning and photochemical reactions, inorganic sources in soil and soil water, nitrogen fertilizers applied by man, fixation of molecular nitrogen by free-living or **symbiotic microorganisms**, the activities of decomposer organisms, and man-made nitrogen oxides dissolved and washed from the sky in rain. Nitrate released by decomposers forms a special loop of the nitrogen cycle that bypasses the atmosphere.

Everyone learns that the fixation of carbon by green plants is the key to life. This is only a half truth. Higher plants are unable to fix nitrogen, and for this fundamental process they depend largely on microorganisms. If biological nitrogen fixation were to stop, life would be decimated.

*THE SULFUR CYCLE.*    In addition to the fixation of carbon and nitrogen, which are incorporated in reduced form into organic compounds, there is a third critical step in the formation of life-stuff — also a biological reduction. It is the reduction of sulfate. Plants and microorganisms can reduce sulfate for use in organic compounds, but animals depend on their food for sulfur in organic form. When plants die, their decay returns sulfur to the environment in reduced form, useless to both higher plants and animals. The activity of the unsung sulfur oxidizing bacteria is thus essential to the maintenance of the sulfur cycle and of life. The sulfur cycle in the biosphere is shown in Figure 2.7.

There was very little sulfur in the atmosphere until the activities of man began to overwhelm nature's mechanisms for removing it. Now sulfur oxides are infamous components of air pollution. Even so, their residence time in the atmosphere is short and they accumulate only locally. The great reservoir of sulfur, as sulfate, is in the sea.

*THE OXYGEN CYCLE.*    Oxygen cycles as part of the cycles of water, carbon, nitrogen, and sulfur; in addition it takes part as free molecular oxygen, atomic oxygen, and ozone in many biological and chemical processes. It is rapidly exchanged between atmosphere, biosphere, and hydrosphere in a complex cycle which is really a system of interrelated cycles. It also takes part in the oxidative weathering of rocks and occurs in the lithosphere in sulfates, silicates, phosphates, nitrates, carbonates, and oxides of various metals, most notably iron.

There is a paradox in the relationship between oxygen and life. We have seen that there was no free oxygen in the atmosphere under which life began. The first living organisms depended on preformed organic molecules created by chemical processes in the environment. If photosynthesis, or

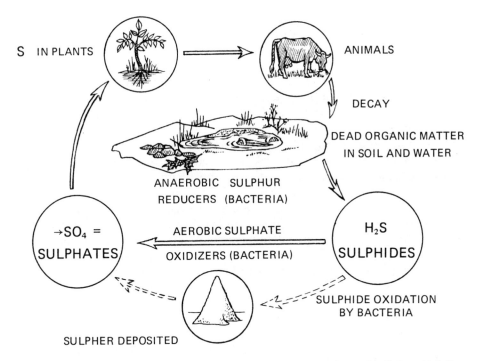

**Figure 2–7** The sulfur cycle. Plants utilize sulfur only in the form of sulfate, which they incorporate into the sulfur-containing compounds required by animals. Decay of organic matter releases sulfides to soil and water, where they must be oxidized to sulfates by sulfur oxidizing bacteria, unsung heroes of the cycle, in order to make sulfur available once again to plants and to keep the cycle going. (Adapted from Keith Reid, *Nature's Network*, The Natural History Press, Garden City, New York, 1970, p. 89.)

something like it, had not arisen, primitive life might have used up all the available food and that would have been the end of the story. Or perhaps the process might have been repeated again and again in a cycle leading nowhere, as life first arose and then ate itself back into oblivion. But photosynthesis did arise, and the by-product, oxygen, of this lifesaving process was deadly to cells of that time. The presence of free oxygen and an oxidizing atmosphere not only assured that the molecules that gave rise to life could no longer form spontaneously and persist, but it threatened life itself. When free oxygen appeared, cells had to devise means for protecting themselves from it, for the complex molecules in living organisms are easily destroyed by oxidation. It is likely that primitive cells coped with oxygen by combining it with hydrogen that was a by-product of metabolic reactions. The energy potentially available from this process was lost, however, because it was not coupled to other reactions in the cell. Later this coupling did take place, and aerobic respiration, the process by which energy is obtained from the oxidation of carbohydrate to carbon dioxide and water, evolved. Thus oxygen arose from life, is essential to higher forms of life, and protects life from destruction by the rays of the sun. It is also inimical to many forms of life, even today.

*THE CYCLES OF PHOSPHORUS AND MINERAL NUTRIENTS.*    The major reservoir of phosphorus is in rocks, which makes its natural movement very slow. In soil, rocks, and living matter it occurs almost exclusively as phosphates. The phosphorus cycle is thus quite simple, chemically. Phosphate is absorbed by plants, converted into organic phosphate compounds which are eaten by animals, and returned to the soil in inorganic form when plants and animals decay. Phosphate which is dissolved or eroded from the land finds its way to streams and lakes and eventually to the sea. Here some of it is used by marine organisms, but most of it is precipitated at the sea floor. In this form it is lost to the biosphere until the geologic processes that imperceptibly remold continents and oceans lift up new areas of dry land. The only significant return of phosphate from sea to land is in the excrement of sea birds and in food harvested from the sea.

Mining activities of man have greatly accelerated the movement of phosphates to the sea. Large amounts of low grade phosphate ore are left exposed to erosion by wind and water during the process of mining higher grade deposits. As much as half of what is recovered may be lost in washing and concentrating the ore. Worldwide, between 80 and 90 percent of the phosphate mined is destined for use as fertilizer, much of which also ends up in the sea as runoff from agricultural land. Ironically, we are running out of phosphate at the same time we are flooding the environment with it.

Other mineral nutrients are dissolved in soil water, absorbed and used by plants and microorganisms, eaten in food and excreted by animals, and thus returned to the soil. Again, man has complicated these very simple cycles by mining minerals in one location and applying them to the soil as fertilizer in another. He also removes nutrients in the form of food and transports them to centers of human population. Unwise exploitation of soil and forest resources has resulted in widespread loss of nutrients through erosion and leaching.

## RESOURCES

The resources man has at his disposal are, in the last analysis, matter and energy. Whether a particular form of matter or energy is of value in any given time or place depends on man's technology and needs. If this definition of resources seems too broad to be of use, we will see in the discussion of individual resources that follows that it can hardly be made narrower. Resources are often classified as depletable and nondepletable, or renewable and nonrenewable, but this distinction, too, is related to time, economics, and the scale of demand.

*AIR AND WATER.* Global resources of air and water are inexhaustible in quantity, but the activities of man can seriously impair their quality. The rapid cycling of materials through the atmosphere and hydrosphere used to insure safe dispersion and natural degradation of waste, but now it insures nothing but global dissemination of pollution. The next breath of air you inhale will contain atoms exhaled by Jesus in Gethsemane, Hitler in Munich, and the smokestacks of the world. There is DDT in the ice of Antarctica.

Man is engaged in wholesale modification, both deliberate and accidental, of the distribution of water resources. By "mining" groundwater, he lowers the water table, which means that he causes water to be returned to the sea faster than evaporation and rainfall bring it to the land. Irrigation and the building of dams to divert water for use in dry areas can have a similar effect. So although there is no shortage of water on this planet, clean, fresh water is in critically short supply in many places. Knowing that there is water in the ocean or the polar ice caps brings small consolation to the drought-stricken farmer in the western United States. The problems of our air and water resources are problems of quality, which will be discussed in Chapter 5, and also, in the case of water, problems of distribution.

*RESOURCES FROM LIVING ORGANISMS.* Food is a renewable resource, but it is not unlimited. We have already hinted at the limits imposed on production of food by the limitations of world climate and soils. Chapter 13 will discuss the limits of food production in detail. The inequitable distribution of food among the world's people is the most serious problem we face today, but if population growth continues, there will be no solution to the problem of hunger.

Until late in the nineteenth century in the United States, wood was the primary fuel for industrial and domestic use. It was replaced by fossil fuels partly because of the development of coal and petroleum technology, but it was the dwindling supply of fuel wood that stimulated this technology. The forests of Europe were depleted earlier still. In most parts of the world, wood has become too valuable to burn. It is instead a raw material for paper and construction. Even the forests are farmed by man. Not only does he plant and selectively harvest the forest crop, but he is engaged in intensive study of the genetics and breeding of forest trees.

Plants are an important source of fibers. Biologist Barry Commoner, among others, has suggested that we return to the use of natural products wherever possible, as a step in reducing our use of energy and dependence on energy-intensive technologies. This would mean abandoning nylon, dacron, and other synthetic fibers in favor of cotton and linen. If we were to do this, however, more agricultural land would be devoted to production of cotton and flax at a time when there is an increasing need for food in a hungry world.

Other plant products which are highly valued in some cultures and scornfully considered nonessential by others are coffee, tea, tobacco, and various drugs. Until recently, higher plants and microorganisms were our only source of medicinal drugs and poisons, including opium, cocaine, quinine, curare, strychnine, castor oil, antibiotics, and pesticides. The grapes and grain that are converted to ethyl alcohol would feed many people. Drug-producing plant resources, like food, wood, and fiber, are renewable but limited.

*MINERAL RESOURCES.*    Primitive man hammered various objects out of chunks of native metal and meteoritic iron. Then, between 5 and 6 thousand years ago, he discovered that he could melt metals from rocks, and that this metal was easier to work than that used in its original form. The most significant discovery of all was that certain uninteresting-looking rocks, when heated with charred wood, mysteriously yielded a supply of pure molten metal. This was the beginning of mining and metallurgy.

Mining has never been a pretty business. Here is a searing indictment written early in the sixteenth century by a physician and Renaissance man who called himself Agricola: ". . . mining is a perilous occupation to pursue because the miners are sometimes killed by the pestilential air which they breathe; sometimes their lungs rot away; sometimes the men perish by being crushed in masses of rock; sometimes falling from ladders into the shafts, they break their arms, legs, or necks. . . . Besides this the strongest argument of the detractors is that the fields are devastated by mining operations, for which reason formerly Italians were warned by law that no one should dig the earth for metals and so injure their very fertile fields, their vineyards, and their olive groves. Also they argue that the woods and groves are cut down, for there is need of endless amount of wood for timbers, machines, and the smelting of metals. And when the woods and groves are felled, there are exterminate the beasts and birds. . . . Further, when the ores are washed, the water which has been used poisons the brooks and streams, and either destroys the fish or drives them away." There is little to be added to this today. Metals must be very important for men and nations to suffer so much to obtain them. Indeed, the fortunes of many nations have been linked to their supplies of crucial metals.

Events in earth history have produced local concentrations of minerals which may exceed their average crustal abundance by thousands of times. These are the mineral resources that provide the metals indispensible to any but the simplest culture. Some parts of the earth are rich in mineral resources. Some are poor. *No* part of the world, not even an entire continent, is endowed with adequate resources of all important metals. North America is poor in tin, tungsten, and manganese. Asia has these metals but lacks molybdenum — which in North America is as abundant as it is anywhere. South Africa, home of most of the world's gold and much of its platinum, has little silver. The power of the British Empire in the nineteenth century was due in no small part to its control of world production of lead, copper, tin, iron, and coal.

The supply of mineral resources is nonrenewable and depletable in the sense that we mine the richest deposits and then spread the metals around until they are so widely dispersed that it is no longer economical or technically feasible to reclaim them. This situation illustrates the first two laws of **thermodynamics** which say that mass-energy can be neither created nor destroyed (we cannot change the amount of iron on earth unless we shoot it into space or transmute it into something else in a high energy accelerator), and that order naturally tends toward disorder unless it is maintained by an input of energy. But as far as their availability and usefulness goes, we are running out of mineral resources. Our most readily accessible and concentrated ores are already gone, and although continued exploration is likely to reveal additional rich deposits, common sense says that this process cannot go on forever. Meanwhile, our use of minerals usually leaves them in a form in which it is economically more feasible to mine a fresh supply than to reclaim what we have used. This, too, cannot go on forever. Civilizations of the future must be based on a philosophy, economy, and technology of recycling, or there will be no civilization.

The idea that, if economic and technical barriers can be overcome and we have abundant energy from nuclear fuel, we will be able to mine all the metals we need from ores of increasingly lower grade is attractive but not convincing. In the first place, it is not clear how nuclear energy will help much in concentrating metals from their vanishingly small concentrations in "ordinary rock." Fracturing the rock with nuclear blasts and selectively dissolving the desired material in the ground with chemical solvents has been suggested. It is an interesting idea. It promises many problems. There is also the question of whose ordinary rock we will dig up, if we come to that point. Not ours, says California. Nor ours, says Ohio. Whose, then? Social costs must be reckoned with pecuniary ones.

The idea that we will pay the price for something needed badly enough also has limits. In the foreseeable future it is likely, for example, that the fossil fuels will become too valuable to burn, although they will still furnish vital raw materials for the petrochemical industry. Another aspect of the economic problem is related to fallacious assumptions about the distribution of elements in the earth. Each metal has its characteristic pattern of distribution. Lithium, for example, does not accumulate to a very great extent in any ore, but is widely dispersed in low concentrations throughout the hydrosphere and lithosphere. Iron, in contrast, has been found in the form of almost pure iron oxide. A few metals occur in a continuous range of concentrations from very high to the average crustal abundance or less, and the amounts of ore existing increase as the concentration of metal decreases. These metals are the exceptions that have given rise to the widespread notion that all we have to do is solve the economic problems of mining lower and lower grade ore, and there will be plenty of whatever it is we want.

The sea is commonly touted as an inexhaustible source of minerals, but the cost of concentrating and retrieving most of them is prohibitive. Furthermore, if we mine the sea, we are less likely to be able to farm it (see Chapter 13). The biological productivity of coastal waters has already been affected by pollution from a wide range of human activities. The polar regions are another potential source of riches, but exploiting them has its special problems. One is the fragility of the polar ecosystem, brought dramatically to public attention in the controversy over trans-Alaskan and trans-Canadian pipelines for oil. Another is the problem and expense of producing materials far from the population centers where they will be used.

Ordinary rock and clay are also mineral resources, used for construction. Although we are in no danger of running out of these, they are not always available where they are needed. In the time frame of human affairs, they cannot be recycled. Once used, it is unlikely that they will be used again.

Unequal distribution of resources in the past has stimulated trade and influenced international economics and politics. It has also been a major cause of wars. It will take a strong international order in the future to prevent scarcity of resources from creating unbearable conflict. In 1969 the mineralogist Lovering said: "During the next century adequate supplies and equitable distribution will not be achieved merely by recycling scrap metal nor by processing dozens of cubic kilometers of common rock to supply the metal needs of each major industrial nation. When the time comes for living in a society dependent on scrap for high grade metal and on common rocks for commercial ore, the affluent society will be much overworked to maintain a standard of living equal to that of a century ago. Only our best efforts in all phases of resource management and population control can defer that day." Defer it, but not prevent it. The effects on human ecology of resource exhaustion are obvious.

*ENERGY.* Energy is defined as the capacity to do work, without which nothing happens in the universe. Energy can be recognized when it changes form or when it is transferred from something to something else. By directing and controlling the conversion or transfer of energy, man accomplishes his own ends.

Like matter, the total amount of energy in the universe remains constant — or rather, because of their equivalence, the amount of matter and energy combined is unchanging. Unlike matter, however, energy cannot be recycled. In doing work it is inevitably degraded to less and less concentrated form, until it ultimately is lost as useless heat at the temperature of the **environmental heat sink**. The cycles of nature are cycles of material only. They depend on a constant source of energy, most of which is supplied by the sun.

The history of man can be told in terms of the nature and amount of energy available to him at various stages of his cultural evolution. The first men had only the power of their own muscles, derived from the chemical energy of the food they ate. This corresponded to a power output of about 100 watts, that of an ordinary 100 watt lightbulb. At this level men had hardly more effect on their environment than any other animal. The taming of fire permitted them to cook their food and survive in colder climates, but it did not increase the energy at their disposal very much. Domestication of the wolf made hunting more efficient, but, except in transportation, did not provide much energy either. The invention of agriculture was a break-through in the utilization of energy. By hunting and gathering, man could obtain about 6 to 10 calories of food for every calorie of energy he expended. Simple agriculture increased this yield by a factor of about five. Even agriculture, however, did not place more energy at man's disposal. It merely meant that he had to devote less of his energy to feeding himself. With the domestication of draft animals and the invention of the yoke and harness, man's rate of energy use rose slowly to about 500 watts per person. One by one, water power, wind power, and coal were exploited. Energy use continued to rise relentlessly. During this time man also domesticated another animal: himself. Slaves built the pyramids and slaves kept Greek civilization running while philosophers issued profundities about democracy.

The early Industrial Revolution was powered by waterwheels and windmills. There was plenty of energy for burgeoning new industries. Steam engines caught on slowly, being designed and used principally for pumping water at the mines. In the nineteenth century, however, the noisy, dirty steam engine was king of industry and transportation, and the number of man's "energy slaves" continued to rise. Table 2.4 documents this rise by showing the power output of some of man's basic machines.

Only a few decades ago the curve showing rate of energy use turned almost vertically upward and is still rising. The present rate of energy use in the United States is about 10,000 watts per person, and this astonishing rate will double in the next 20 or 30 years. Even agriculture, which used to contribute net energy to man, now uses 6 to 10 calories for every calorie it produces.

While industrialized societies use dozens of times as much energy as is required to meet the nutritional needs of their people, much of the world still subsists near the 100 watt level. Its people are starving. With 6 percent of the world's population, the United States uses about a third of the energy that is used. But the gap is closing. The rate of energy use is increasing even faster in the world as a whole than it is in the United States. The implications of this growth are profound, both in terms of finding sources to supply the demand and of what the effects of this level of energy use will be. Nothing happens without the transfer or transformation of energy; and conversely, every transfer or transformation of energy brings about some change. In our energy transactions we are able to harness only a fraction,

**TABLE 2.4**
**Power Output of Some Basic Machines**

| Prime Movers* | Kilowatts |
|---|---|
| Man | 0.1 |
| Ox | 0.2 |
| Horse | 0.5 |
| Windmill | 15 |
| Waterwheel | 300 |
| Steam engine | 2,000 |
| Internal combustion engine | 10,000 |
| Gas turbine | 80,000 |
| Water turbine | 100,000 |
| Steam turbine | 1,000,000 |
| Liquid fuel rocket | 16,000,000 |

*A machine does not produce energy, but merely transforms or redirects it. If the machine converts *food, fuel,* or *force* to *work* or *power* it is a "prime mover." An electric motor is not a prime mover because it does not convert food, fuel, or force; and your home furnace is not a prime mover because it produces only heat, not work or power.

and sometimes a very small fraction, of the total energy involved. The rest eludes us, to do its work elsewhere. The scale of man's manipulation of energy is reshaping all aspects of the planet on which he lives. Although he tries to use energy to achieve his goals, many of the side effects are not consonant with his values.

The earth's supply of coal and petroleum — the fossil fuels, derived from solar energy stored over periods of hundreds of millions of years — is rapidly being consumed and will not be replenished in the lifetime of our species. Worldwide, men are nervously engaged in an inventory of alternative energy sources for the future. Many would like to plan for a future as long as our past, rather than for the pinch of the next few years or generations. Wind and water power (also derived from solar energy), the tides, and concentrated reservoirs of the earth's own heat can supply energy locally at modest levels and can raise large segments of the world's population to a more comfortable level of existence. A windmill of moderate size, producing between 20 and 50 kilowatts of power, can pump water for a small community and supply electricity for lighting, refrigeration, and the operation of radios. These communities do not want and could not even use a 3,000 megawatt nuclear power plant.

If highly industrialized societies are to survive, however, they will need new sources of concentrated energy on a very large scale. For the long term there appear to be but three options: nuclear fission, as accomplished in a breeder reactor, nuclear fusion, and the sun. Several small breeder reactors are in operation, but problems, particularly with regard to safety, remain in the design of a large breeder. In addition, the major fuel of a breeder is plutonium — one of the deadliest radioactive elements known. Added to the biological hazard of handling large amounts of this element is a political hazard: anyone with a chunk of plutonium can build an atomic bomb. As for fusion, it is not at all certain that net useful energy will ever be produced in sufficient amounts from the fusion of small nuclei, although if the technology can be mastered, it would provide a nearly ideal source of energy. (At least it appears so from our present perspective. The same was said for coal a century and a half ago, and for nuclear fission in the 1950s.) The main problem is that nuclear fusion takes place only in the stars or under simulated stellar conditions — conditions which are very difficult to maintain for a long time or on a large scale here on earth. Technology for solar energy is in a more advanced state. On small scale, for domestic water and space heating and a few other applications, solar energy has already proven feasible. What needs to be done is to apply our knowledge to determine if it is also feasible on a large scale for generation of electric power or bulk supplies of hydrogen for fuel. Unfortunately, the strong political lobbies of the Atomic Energy Commission and the traditional energy industries are not very interested in promoting solar technology.

The United States and other industrialized nations seem already to have opted for nuclear fission and the breeder reactor, although there are many unsolved problems in this technology and many people believe the choice is a mistake. In any case, once the commitment is made there can be no turning back. The situation has been compared, in the magnitude of its social implications, with the other commitment made thousands of years ago to an agricultural way of life.

## REFERENCES

BRANCAZIO, P., AND A. CAMERON, EDS. 1964. *The Origin and Evolution of Atmospheres and Oceans.* New York: John Wiley & Sons.

CLOUD, P., ED. 1970. *Adventures in Earth History.* San Francisco: W. H. Freeman and Co.

CLOUDSLEY-THOMPSON, J. 1961. *Rhythmic Activity in Animal Physiology and Behavior.* New York: Academic Press.

EHRLICH, P., AND A. EHRLICH. 1970. *Population, Resources, Environment: Issues in Human Ecology,* San Francisco: W. H. Freeman and Co.

FEDERAL POWER COMMISSION. 1971. *The 1970 National Power Survey.* Parts I-IV. Washington, D.C.: U.S. Govt. Printing Office.

HILDEBRANDT, A., G. HAAS, W. JENKINGS, AND J. COLACO. 1972. Large-scale concentration and conversion of solar energy. *Eos: Transactions of the American Geophysical Union.* Vol. 53 No. 7. Pp. 684–692.

KLAGES, K. 1942. *Ecological Crop Geography.* New York: Macmillan.

LOWRY, W. 1967. *Weather and Life: An Introduction to Biometeorology.* New York: Academic Press.

LUCE, G. 1970. *Biological Rhythms in Psychiatry and Medicine.* Public Health Service Publication No. 2088. Washington, D.C.: U.S. Govt. Printing Office.

MCKENZIE, G., AND R. UTGARD, EDS. 1972. *Man and His Physical Environment*. Minneapolis: Burgess Publishing Co.

NATIONAL ACADEMY OF SCIENCES-NATIONAL RESEARCH COUNCIL. 1969. *Resources and Man*. San Francisco: W. H. Freeman and Co.

ODUM, H. 1971. *Environment, Power, and Society*. New York: John Wiley & Sons.

SCIENTIFIC AMERICAN. 1970. *The Biosphere*. San Francisco: W. H. Freeman and Co.

SCIENTIFIC AMERICAN. 1971. *Man and the Ecosphere*. San Francisco: W. H. Freeman and Co.

SOLLBERGER, A. 1965. *Biological Rhythm Research*. New York: Elsevier.

STEINHART, C., AND J. STEINHART. 1974. *Energy: Sources, Use, and Role in Human Affairs*. North Scituate, Mass.: Duxbury Press.

TAYLOR, J., ED. 1967. *Weather and Agriculture*. New York: Pergamon Press.

TREWARTHA, G., A. ROBINSON, AND R. SALE. 1967. *Physical Elements of Geography*. 5th ed. New York: McGraw-Hill.

UNITED NATIONS. 1964. *Geothermal Energy*. Proceedings of the United Nations Conference on New Sources of Energy, vol 2 and 3. New York: United Nations.

UNITED NATIONS. 1964. *Solar Energy*. Proceedings of the United Nations Conference on New Sources of Energy, vol. 4, 5, and 6. New York: United Nations.

UNITED NATIONS. 1964. *Wind Power*. Proceedings of the United Nations Conference on New Sources of Energy, vol. 7. New York: United Nations.

U.S. DEPARTMENT OF AGRICULTURE. 1957. Soil. *The Yearbook of Agriculture*. Washington, D.C.: U.S. Govt. Printing Office.

WORLD HEALTH ORGANIZATION. 1964. Water. *World Health*. July-August 1964.

# · 3 ·

S. CHARLES KENDEIGH

# Man's Biological Environment

We are receiving disturbing messages from the biological world. The cleverest schemes to make life safer and more pleasant have unpleasant repercussions far beyond our expectations. We cannot divorce ourselves from interrelationships with other organisms and the physical environment. Most problems of today stem from misunderstanding or underestimating the depth and complexity of these interrelationships. We know that life depends on the sunlight on the leaf, but that is only the beginning.

Millions of living things share the skin of this small planet, each contributing to its maintenance as well as drawing sustenance from it. Chauvinistic man used to ask of a dandelion or a mosquito, "What good is it?" Meaning, of course, "What good is it to *me*?" In our greater sophistication we now ask, "What does it do, where is its place?" And when these questions have been answered, the first has been answered, too. This chapter considers the principles governing the bewildering variety of interactions among organisms with each other and their physical environment. Even when it seems to be talking about the life in a tiny pond, it is talking about the life of all of us.

## ADAPTATION

Organisms are adapted to their environment structurally and physiologically and, in the case of animals, behaviorally and socially as well. Chapter 4 will consider how these adaptations come about. For now we will just accept their existence.

*STRUCTURAL ADAPTATIONS.* Structural adaptations are the most obvious characteristics which enable a species to live where and how it does. Actual or potential structural adaptations are always inherited, furnishing the first basis for segregating species into different habitats and communities. For example, whales, seals, and beavers are adapted for swimming, moles and shrews for burrowing, bats for flying, and man for walking. Sometimes expression of the adaptation is evoked by environmental conditions, as illustrated by the contrasting forms of the spreading oak grown in the open and the slender, forest-grown tree.

Structural adaptations for feeding also segregate species and determine how they will live. Grazing mammals have flat molar-type teeth for grinding rough grasses. Carnivorous mammals have pointed canine-like teeth for tearing flesh. Birds have various shapes and sizes of bills for feeding on seeds, insects, fish, or rodents. Man, a rather unspecialized animal, has teeth suitable for chewing both plant and animal foods. (As in many other situations, however, man's culture has extended his structural capacities — in this case, through the means of cooking.)

Mode of defense is another structural adaptation. It may take the form of concealing coloration or simulation of certain parts of the surroundings — a device used by the walking stick and common in other insects, also. Teeth and claws of carnivores are their protection as well as their means of livelihood. The skunk has its odor, the porcupine its quills, and the turtle its shell.

Methods and structures for reproduction are suited to the organism's way of life. Most lower **invertebrates** and many fish expel their sperm and eggs into the water, where fertilization and development take place. This method would not be very successful on land. As a result, snails, insects, reptiles, birds, mammals, and other land forms have become adapted for internal fertilization. In this situation the embryo still develops in an aqueous environment, but it is inside an egg or inside the mother. The development of the "land egg" was a major evolutionary achievement that enabled animals to escape from their watery habitat.

Animals have also adapted in size. Large animals have a smaller ratio of surface area to body mass than small ones, which means that they lose heat less rapidly and can carry thicker, heavier fur or plumage for insulation. This is of obvious advantage in cold climates. In fact, birds and mammals do show a tendency toward increased size in cold climates *(Bergmann's Rule)*. Appendages (from which heat is lost rapidly) also tend to be smaller in cold climates *(Allen's Rule)*, as illustrated by the small ears of the arctic fox contrasted with the large ears of his African relative, the fennec (Figure 3.1), and the short limbs and stubby fingers of Eskimos. It has been suggested that the Pygmies are adapted to their environment by their small size, and even the giant Watusi, in a similar climate, are rangy in build and thus have a relatively large surface to mass ratio. However, this sort of speculation must be made with extreme caution because many other factors may also be involved.

**Figure 3–1a** The fennec, an African relative of the arctic fox. His large ears, from which heat is lost rapidly, are a structural adaptation to his warm environment. (Photograph courtesy of the San Diego Zoo.)

**Figure 3–1b** The arctic fox. His small ears are a structural adaptation for the conservation of body heat necessary in a cold climate. (Photograph by Gordon S. Smith, from National Audubon Society.)

*PHYSIOLOGICAL ADJUSTMENTS.*     Physiological adjustments to the environment determine the degree of environmental change that can be tolerated. They include the inherited capacity of an organism to respond to changes in its environment. The response to air temperature is an example of physiological adjustment. Birds and mammals, the "warm-blooded" animals, are able to regulate their body temperatures so that they remain almost constant within whatever range of external temperatures the animal can tolerate. The mechanisms for maintaining a constant temperature involve, among many other things, an increase in the rate of metabolism as external temperature decreases. This is effective only within limits, however. Naked man cannot long tolerate air temperatures approaching freezing, and he becomes distinctly uncomfortable at temperatures much above that of his own body. Body temperature and the rate of metabolism in cold-blooded animals, in contrast, decrease with a drop in temperature of the surrounding medium (air or water). Activity is also reduced under these conditions. The way animals are physiologically adapted to live in certain environments and not others controls both their numbers and their distribution over the face of the earth.

Organisms are not usually affected by only one aspect of the environment in isolation from the rest. Several factors, for example, influence an animal's tolerance of temperature. Relative humidity affects the rate at which evaporation occurs from the body. In man, evaporation (perspiration) is an adaptive mechanism which permits the body to cool itself when simple radiation becomes ineffective at high temperatures. Thus, with adequate water man can withstand hotter temperatures at low humidity than at high. Most **amphibians**, in contrast, cannot bear dry heat because of the intolerable water loss they suffer. Other factors related to the ability of an organism to endure heat are the availability of water, stillness or motion of the air, availability of shelter from direct rays of the sun or other radiating surfaces, and the amount of activity an animal must engage in.

Similarly, many factors influence the growth and functioning of an organism — which are also, in part, physiological responses to the environment. The rate of photosynthesis in a plant is related jointly to the amount of chlorophyll it possesses (which depends on genetic factors, the nutritional status of the plant, and the available light), the intensity of light, the carbon dioxide content of the air, the availability of moisture, and the temperature. If any of these factors is in short supply (or in some cases, present in excess), the rate of photosynthesis is limited by that factor, even if all others are favorable. This illustrates Liebig's *Law of the Minimum*, which states that the functioning or even survival of an organism is limited by the essential factor or combination of factors present to the least favorable extent. It is important to identify these *limiting factors* as a first step in any strategy to control natural processes. In agriculture, for example, fertilizers should supply nutrients that are deficient in the soil, and should supply them so that a correct balance of nutrients is available to the crop plants. Knowledge of limiting factors is also essential in meeting the nutritional needs of man. No amount of vitamin C will help you if you are not getting enough iron.

BEHAVIORAL RESPONSES. Every animal must use its structural and physiological adaptations to choose conditions that provoke the least stress to its system and to compensate for unfavorable situations. It makes no sense for a dog with teeth adapted for tearing flesh to consume grass like a cow, which has grinding teeth and special stomachs for its digestion. In some cases behavioral adaptations can compensate for lack of other types of adaptation. Reptiles, lacking a physiological mechanism for temperature regulation, can maintain a remarkably constant body temperature by behavior which seeks out favorable temperatures. They may bask in the sun, hide in the shade, take a swim, or burrow into the ground.

Choice of environmental conditions involves seeking and selection. This activity can be demonstrated by placing an animal in a **gradient** of temperature, light, moisture, or a combination of factors. The animal explores the gradient, selecting the site with the most favorable conditions. If the exper-

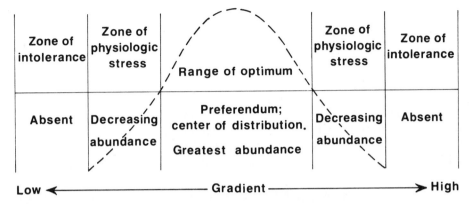

| Zone of intolerance | Zone of physiologic stress | Range of optimum | Zone of physiologic stress | Zone of intolerance |
|---|---|---|---|---|
| Absent | Decreasing abundance | Preferendum; center of distribution. Greatest abundance | Decreasing abundance | Absent |

Low ◄——————— Gradient ———————► High

**Figure 3-2** Relationship between suitability of the environment and number of choices made by an animal for that environment. No individuals will be found in the extreme zones which cannot support their life. Increasingly more individuals select conditions in the intermediate zones as they approach the optimum. By far the greatest number will choose conditions in the optimum range. The shape of this curve may vary from a narrow range of tolerance to a broad one, and in some cases it may be skewed in one direction or the other so it is not symmetrical. When two or more conditions are varied simultaneously, the same sort of results are obtained, but their graphical representation becomes more complex.

iment is repeated many times or with many animals, *optimum* conditions will be chosen most often, with progressively fewer choices in favor of more extreme conditions. If the number of choices for each point in the gradient is plotted on a graph, the resulting curve will show a normal, or Gaussian, distribution of choices (Figure 3.2).

Behavioral responses often permit a species to live in unexpected places. The house sparrow is common over much of North America, until it becomes limited by low temperatures in southern Canada. There is a colony of these sparrows, however, several hundred kilometers north of their normal limit at the shipping port of Churchill, on the Hudson Bay. Here they live in the large grain elevators, where they receive abundant food and protection from the cold. Man, too, lives in areas to which he is not adapted in structure of physiology. Basically a tropical animal, he survives outside his natural habitat only with the artificial shelter, heat, sources of food, and other conveniences that he has learned to provide for himself.

*COMMUNITY INTERRELATIONS.* When different organisms aggregate in the same habitat, interrelations are established. Aggregations of species including both plants and animals form *biotic communities.* A community is simply a distinctive aggregation of species found in a particular habitat. It may be of any size. The fungi, insects, millipedes, centipedes, sowbugs, and snails that live in a decaying log in a forest form one community and the forest itself forms another. The *environment* refers to both the physical and biotic conditions that surround and affect organisms. It includes the climate, the soil, as well as other animals and plants. The *habitat* is a subdivision of the environment that refers to a specific set of factors, usually physical, such as soil, water, temperature, light and oxygen supply that characterize a particular kind of stream, pond, prairie, or forest. The term *ecosystem* is used for a particular community in its special habitat and is especially useful when considering both functional interrelations between organisms and between organisms and their habitat. Much of the rest of this chapter deals with the relationships among organisms in their communities.

DOMINANCE.    In every habitat certain species largely control the composition and structure of the community. These species are said to be dominant. The larger plants generally dominate terrestrial communities because they receive the full impact of the prevailing climate (the macroclimate), and they modify the effects of sun, wind, and rain to create the particular conditions of the microclimate in which other members of the community live.

A distinct type of dominant vegetation characterizes each major climatic region, because the component plant species have specific demands for heat, moisture, and **photoperiod.** Each type of vegetation modifies the microclimate within its borders in a different manner and offers various kinds of food and shelter to the animals associated with it. Hence each type of dominant vegetation has associated with it a plant and animal community composed of a unique combination of species.

Trees are dominant in a forest community. They decrease light intensity, wind velocity, and rate of evaporation. They increase relative humidity and moderate the extremes in the daily rhythm of temperature.

Grasses are the dominant species in a prairie community. In the tall grass prairie, microclimates near the ground resemble those found in the forest, although the macroclimate is very different. Because of the similarity of microclimates, some species of small ground animals occur both in the tall grass prairie and in the forest. Larger animals, like the bison and pronghorn in North America, are not protected by the cover of prairie grass and may themselves receive the full impact of the physical environment. At the same time their grazing may reduce the abundance of more palatable plant species and allow the less palatable ones with their associated animals to invade. Animals, as well as plants, may thus become dominant in some communities.

Primitive man was not a dominant. He probably lived at the edge of the forest in the mixture of forest and grassland called *savanna,* subsisting on fruits and edible plants and whatever animals he could kill. His shelter was simple, often a cave or a crude erection of branches, leaves, grasses, and mud. With few tools he had little effect on the vegetation, and his survival depended on his not taking more of an animal species than could be replaced in a breeding season. His numbers were limited to what the natural environment could support.

With the evolution of his mind, culture, and technology, however, man made increasingly more extensive use of his natural resources and began to change the community to meet his needs. This ability to progress distinguished him from all other animals. He cut down forests for lumber, fuel, and pulp, plowed the prairie for cropland, and replaced wild animals with those that produced beef, milk, and mutton. With increased food and other resources his population increased, and his status changed from that of an ordinary member of the community to a dominant one. Now all other populations must adjust to the changes resulting from the activities of man.

STRATIFICATION. Each terrestrial community can be divided into layers or *strata*. In the forest, these strata are subterranean, ground, herb, shrub, and tree. Different species occur in each stratum, forming *stratal societies*, with the dominant plant species making up the top stratum. The strata, although clearly recognizable in a mature community, are not always distinct. A tree germinates from a seed in the ground, and in its growth it passes through each stratum until at maturity its foliage is largely confined to the canopy in the top stratum. Poison ivy will climb a tree, but it grows equally well along the ground. The stratal distribution of animals is even more diffuse than that of plants. Only a few animals are closely limited to a particular layer.

In terms of numbers, the *subterranean and ground societies*, teeming with bacteria, fungi, and tiny invertebrate animals, have larger populations than the *foliage society* found in the herb, shrub, and tree strata. During the winter in temperate climates, the difference in numbers is even more pronounced. The above-ground parts of **herbaceous** plants die, most invertebrates leave the upper strata to hibernate in the ground, some birds migrate, and mammals become less active.

PERIODICITY. Chapter 2 spoke of the many rhythmic patterns in living things that correspond to periodic cycles in the physical world. Animals are classified as *diurnal* (daytime), *nocturnal* (nighttime), or *crepuscular* (intermediate periods of dawn and dusk) according to the part of the day in which they are most active. The biotic community is different at night than in the daytime, not because of any change in the species present, but because of changes in their activities. Animals living in constant subterranean environments, in decaying logs and stumps, or in caves may show random periods of activity and rest and are said to be *arhythmic*.

Primitive man was diurnal. The eyes of man, possessing abundant color-sensitive cones, function effectively only at high light intensities. The retina of man's eye also has structures called rods, which respond to low intensities of light but do not discriminate among colors. Truly nocturnal species, however, have many more rods than man.

Primitive man had to hide from large nocturnal predators. Modern man does not face this danger. He has made night almost as bright as day with artificial lighting. It is not as easy as a flick of the electric light switch, however, to undo millions of years of evolution. Most people still set aside regular daily periods for activity and rest, which usually correspond roughly to day and night.

Seasonal changes in the physical habitat are revealed by cyclical changes of temperature and length of the daily photoperiod in temperate and polar regions. We recognize four convenient reference points in the celestial calendar: the spring and autumnal equinoxes, and the summer and winter solstices. In the biotic community the seasons do not necessarily agree with the celestial calendar, but are associated with changes in activity, particularly reproductive activity, of plants and animals. Animals make adjustments in their metabolism, time of breeding, feeding, migration, and hibernation that are correlated with seasonal climatic changes.

The tropical rain forest presents a monotonous uniformity of climate. Changes in conditions between day and night are sometimes more extreme than changes in mean monthly climate throughout the year. Other tropical habitats are more variable, however. Primitive man was at home in the tropical savanna, where he was exposed to rainy and dry seasons. He must have changed his diet with the seasons and may have been under more stress to find food during the dry season than when the rains came. The temperature varied little between rainy and dry seasons, and the daily photoperiod varied only by minutes throughout the year.

In 1918 W. W. Garner and H. A. Allard of the U.S. Department of Agriculture showed that the length of the photoperiod regulates the blooming of many plants. Flowering of some plants is triggered by the short days and long nights of early spring and autumn; others bloom in response to the long days and short nights of summer; and still others are not regulated primarily by photoperiod.

A few years later William Rowan of the University of Alberta showed that the nesting time of birds is controlled by the response of their **gonads** to the lengthening days of spring. Now we know that reproductive activity not only of birds but also of many animals from invertebrates to mammals is regulated by the response of their gonads to changing length of day and night.

Since the photoperiod in the tropics is an almost constant 12 hours of daylight each day, many tropical species, including man, are capable of reproduction at any season, although the actual time of reproduction may be influenced by other factors. Man's dispersal out of the tropics has been so recent and his daily activities so modified by artificial lighting and other modifications of his natural environment, that he still retains the year-round capacity for reproduction typical of tropical species.

DIVISION OF LABOR.  Activities of different species of the biotic community are integrated into a functional unit. This does not mean a *closed* unit: many animals move freely from one plant community to another. Nor does it mean that every role is necessary, nor that every conceivable role is filled. (No predator but man preys on wolves.) However, this division of labor among species culminates the evolutionary process of specialization that began with the first life forms. At first it must have been every cell (or whatever corresponded to a unit of life) for itself; and if this entity, whatever it was, could not do everything for itself, it did not survive or perpetuate itself. When clumps of cells began to remain together, as in the tumbling little colonial creature we call *Volvox*, certain cells could become specialized for reproduction while others maintained only the functions for moment-to-moment life. In somewhat more complex animals like the tiny *Hydra*, body cells differentiate into tissues for performance of special functions like digestion, contraction, and transmission of nerve impulses. In worms, tissues are coordinated into organs and organ systems which perform particular roles in the function of an organism. Bees, termites, and ants, the social insects, show the next step in organization — that of closely integrated societies of many members, in which different individuals are structurally, physiologically, and behaviorally specialized to carry out particular duties. In human society each role is controlled by a trade or profession to which individuals become behaviorally trained. Physiological and structural adaptations are of less importance, although they may influence a person's choice of role or his success in it.

In the larger and more complex biotic community, each species has its role. Green plants convert light energy into the chemical energy required by all living things. Vegetation also modifies the effects of climate and provides protection and reproductive sites for animals. Herbivores transfer energy from the plants that produce it to higher levels in the food chain. Predators help to regulate population size. Bacteria and fungi decompose dead organisms and excreta, maintaining the cycles of nutrients.

## THE CONTINUITY AND CHANGE OF LIFE IN SPACE AND TIME

Life occurs as discrete bundles which we recognize as individuals, but life is also continuous in space and time. Its continuity in space has given rise to the concept of the biosphere, the living skin of this planet. Individuals reproduce themselves, but not exactly. The difference is not great in one generation, but it can become great with the added ingredient of time, and we call this *evolution*. Plant and animal communities also change, until the original community has been replaced by another community. We call this process of change *succession*. Several different forces may collectively bring about this change.

*SUCCESSION.* The history in the rocks shows that in various periods since life began different organisms have predominated on the earth. At first there were only very simple organisms (whether "single-celled" or "acellular" is still debated among biologists), and they were confined to shallow seas. Then more complex types of invertebrate animals appeared and all the waters of the earth were colonized. Plants moved ashore in advance of animals and reached their peak in the lush forests and swamps of the Carboniferous period. Here were towering ferns and horsetails and other plants with strange names that have left only inconspicuous descendants. Plants were followed by insects and amphibians. Later still, reptiles ruled the earth. The whole process took about 3 billion years. Man did not enter the succession until about 2 million years ago. In the next million or billion years many new types of animals will appear, and man as he is today may either become extinct or greatly reduced in character and importance. Perhaps, like the plants of the Carboniferous coal forests, he will leave descendants only remotely resembling himself; perhaps as has been the fate of most animals, he will leave none. Geological succession results from the evolution of new types, their dispersal over the world, and the extinction of older types that can no longer compete in the struggle for existence. This process has been going on since life first began and can be expected to continue indefinitely into the future.

Succession also occurs in response to geomorphological processes that shape the face of the earth. Mountains rise up only to be eroded into plains. Coastal areas rise and sink and rise again. These changes are usually slow, as slow as evolution, although a volcanic island may be born or blast itself into nothingness in a day. Succession related to physiographic changes in the surface of the earth does not necessarily involve the evolution or destruction of communities, but rather the movement of communities up or down a mountainside or back and forth along the water's edge. The stages in this succession may be present simultaneously on a mountain slope or in a progression from deep water onto land.

Changes in climate cause changes in the location of particular communities. The earth has witnessed a number of drastic climatic changes since life began. These changes are associated with the disappearance of many kinds of plants and animals, the emergence of new kinds, and with the redistribution of the species that survived the change. The intermittent periods of glaciation which began about 2 million years ago produced geographic shifting of biotic communities in the north and, to a smaller extent, in the subtropics. Several animals that made their appearance during this time belonged to the genus *Homo*, man.

The changes in climate, vegetation, and animal life that have occurred in response to the advance and retreat of the glaciers, particularly those within the last 15,000 years (see Chapter 5, Table 5.2), influenced the dispersal of man and the development of civilizations. Even within historic time, smaller and shorter fluctuations in climate have been recorded in the growth rings of trees, shifting levels of lakes, and records of past civilizations. Much of history — the rise and fall of civilizations, the massive movements of population, and the greater advancement of culture in some regions than in others — may be related to climatic changes.

Succession may also result from changes in the habitat caused by the organisms themselves. Many simple plants can grow in relatively infertile soil or on bare rock, and they can tolerate (or perhaps they need) full exposure to the rays of the sun. When in the course of time their growth has enriched the soil and produced shade, other plant species can colonize the area. Conditions created by growth of the new plants may then be unfavorable for the survival of the pioneers. Plants may even make conditions unsuitable for further generations of themselves. Seedlings of some oak trees require a great deal of sunlight and frequently cannot develop in the shade of the older trees. Maple seedlings, however, are more tolerant of shade, and the oak forest may be replaced by a maple forest. Succession may continue over periods of decades or centuries until a *climax community* that is relatively stable in the prevailing climate is reached (see Figure 3.13)

The intervention of man has affected the normal course and rate of succession. Indians of North America burned the prairies to improve the habitat for game, thus retarding the spread of oak forests. Today we inadvertently fertilize lakes, rivers, and the sea through nutrient-rich runoff from agricultural lands, and by phosphate detergents, hastening the rate of plant succession in aquatic habitats. We also try, with varying success, to thwart the forces of plant succession by weeding our lawns and gardens.

*THE NATURE OF SPECIES.* The great diversity in form, function, and the roles of species within a community has come about as the result of a few principles which Darwin stated with clarity and precision (see Chapter 4). In each community various roles are filled by organisms that through time have become structurally and functionally adapted to fill them.

SEGREGATION INTO NICHES. Each species occupies a unique *niche* in its community. The niche occupied by a species is determined by the *microhabitat* in which it lives and by its role in the division of labor among species. The microhabitat is defined by the limits of tolerance to physical factors of the environment and especially by the area in which the species finds optimum conditions. The *role* of the species is defined by the type of vegetation or cover it requires, the stratum where it spends most of its time, its feeding habits, and the time of day and season of the year in which it is active. A species occupies a particular niche because it is better adapted to it structurally, physiologically, and behaviorally than any other species in the area. The segregation of species into niches gives organization to the community, reduces competition between species, and allows more complete utilization of the resources of the community.

Segregation into niches has come about through *competition,* the active demand by two or more organisms for material or space in limited supply. It is a potent force in the organization and regulation of the biotic community. Because competition inevitably develops, a niche cannot be occupied simultaneously by stable populations of two or more species. According to the *competitive exclusion principle,* the species which is better adapted will drive out another, either directly by interference or combat, or indirectly by exploitation of the niche through rapid population increase (Figure 3.3). Very slight differences in structure, function, or behavior may permit two species to occur in the same community or in adjacent niches. The fact that robins nest in the open rather than in boxes and feed on earthworms rather than on insects permits both robins and wrens to live peacefully in the same community.

Primitive man had to compete for his niche just as other animals did. His competitive success has meant that modern man has largely overcome competition of this sort, at least in terrestrial habitats. Today man is so powerful that he constructs his own niche by modifying whatever community and habitat he enters to make it conform to his own needs.

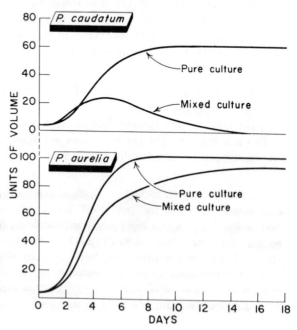

**Figure 3–3** Illustration of the competitive exclusion principle. Two similar organisms, *Paramecium caudatum* and *P. aurelia,* show different growth rates when grown separately. When grown together, the more rapidly reproducing *P. aurelia* is able eventually to eliminate its slower growing competitor. (From G. F. Gause, *The Struggle for Existence,* Hafner Pub. Co., New York, 1965.)

SPECIATION. Segregation of species into niches is related to the process of evolution and the formation of species. A useful working definition of species is that it is a population which will not interbreed with another population even if the ranges of the two overlap. Four principal kinds of mechanisms can prevent this interbreeding. The first is *ecologic,* when two populations live in different communities or are active at different seasons and have infrequent contact with one another. The second is *ethologic,* when patterns of behavior related to courtship and mating are so different that the sexes are not attracted to each other. The third is *physical,* when the size or structure of the copulatory organs of the opposite sexes of the two populations precludes successful mating. The fourth is *genetic,* when incompatibility in the hereditary material prevents normal development of offspring or results in infertile adults. The distinction between species is rather tenuous when the only isolating mechanisms are ecologic or ethologic, but it is firmly established when they are physical or genetic.

Speciation may occur when two portions of a population become geographically isolated from each other. One way in which this may happen is that a portion of land becomes separated from another by a water barrier. Islands off the coast of California, once connected with the mainland, were separated in this manner. Mountains may be uplifted between the populations, or unfavorable climate may intervene. In any case, new characteristics that arise in one population cannot spread to the other because interbreeding is no longer possible. If the two environments also change, natural selection will cause the two populations to diverge even more rapidly (see Chapter 4). Eventually, a new species will evolve, or perhaps two species will evolve from the parent one.

If the two now distinct species should come into contact with one another again and if the niches that they require are still similar, they will compete until one species displaces the other in the region. If, however, evolution has brought new requirements or adaptations to one or both species, the two may coexist by occupying different niches in the same community or equivalent niches in adjacent communities.

Speciation of early man centered in tropical Africa, where increasing aridity caused the tropical forest to split into scattered groves of trees in the midst of grassland, permitting the early man-like apes to occupy more open country (see Chapter 5). Dispersal into other parts of the Old World tropics brought differentiation into *Australoids, Mongoloids, Caucasoids, Negroids,* and their allies. They evolved as a consequence of geographic isolation, becoming adapted to different climates and vegetation. Differences in behavior and customs, including courtship rituals, also evolved. Speciation, however, had not developed far enough to prevent interbreeding when trade, exploration, and migration broke down geographic isolation. The only species of the genus *Homo* alive today is *Homo sapiens sapiens.*

Man is not the only extremely variable organism. Consider the domestic dog, whether it come in Chihuahua version or shaggy Saint Bernard, dachshund or bulldog. It has been undergoing vigorous selection and evolution for 30,000 years. Or take the many horticultural varieties of plants that man has developed: cabbage, Brussels sprouts, and broccoli, for example, are all the same species.

CENTERS OF ORIGIN AND DISPERSAL.　Conjecture about where a particular group of organisms first evolved is based partly on where the greatest variety of existing forms is found. The longer a group has been in an area, the more time there has been for its evolutionary diversification. The presence of fossil remains of primitive types along with the living forms adds to the evidence. Since there is a tendency for organisms to disperse in all directions through favorable habitats and to differentiate into new varieties as they become isolated in distant areas, the center of origin is often the hub of these dispersal routes.

Most groups of vertebrates probably originated in the Old World tropics and dispersed in various directions until they met impassable barriers (Figure 3.4). In moving from the tropics into the temperate zones and then into the arctics, organisms had to adapt to colder climates and wide seasonal fluctuations in photoperiod and food supply. Not all groups succeeded, hence the progressively smaller number of species from the tropics to the arctics.

Long ago there was a bridge of land extending from Southeast Asia through what is now the East Indies and into Australia. Across this bridge, from their Asiatic origin, two primitive orders of mammals migrated into what is now Australia and New Zealand. These were the monotremes or egg-laying mammals, represented today by the platypus and the spiny anteater, and the marsupials, which bear their young alive but in an embryonic stage of development. Then, before the evolution of placental animals some 100 million years ago, this land bridge disappeared. Placental mammals never evolved in Australia, but the marsupials developed to fill the niches which on other continents were occupied by placentals. There is a marsupial "rat" and a marsupial "dog", "bear" and "woodchuck." When man entered Australia, bringing with him many alien animals, the balance of many native communities was greatly changed. If placental man had not colonized Australia, would a marsupial man have evolved?

At several times during the past, what is now Central America was only a chain of islands. Between 60 and 70 million years ago, however, the northern and southern American continents were connected, and there was another land bridge across the Bering Strait between Asia and North America. At this time the climate was mild and the vegetation uniform over most of the Northern Hemisphere, permitting dispersal of many ancestral types of animals into far northern regions. They moved into northern Asia,

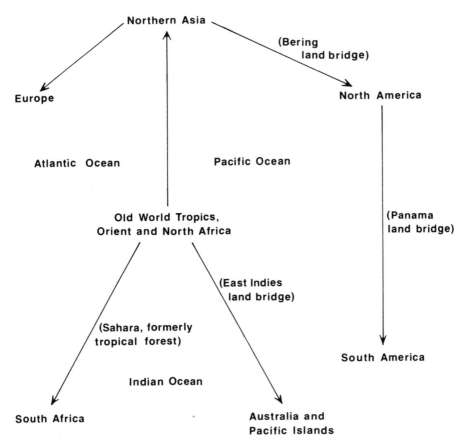

**Figure 3–4** Probable routes of migration of vertebrates out of the Old World Tropics. These migrations occurred more than once, in conjunction with changes in climatic and geological conditions.

across the Bering land bridge into North America, and on into South America. Then the land bridges were submerged, to be reestablished and lost again several times in the ages that followed. Many years after the original migration of mammals, a Mongoloid race of men entered the New World by the same routes. The Panama land bridge over which man may have reached South America still exists, but the northern bridge is marked only by a chain of islands.

At the time of rapid dispersal of mammals 60 or 70 million years ago, rich, tropical vegetation stretched continuously across what is now northern Africa, Arabia, and India. Availability of food and favorable habitats permitted free passage of animals throughout these areas. Later, the Sahara and

Arabian deserts came to separate the animal communities of India from those of central Africa. Thus a climatic and vegetative barrier blocked further exchange between these regions. This isolation, plus the actual physical isolation of continents, has led to the evolution of distinctive **faunas** in various zoological regions. An understanding of evolution and geologic history helps to explain present-day distribution of organisms.

## THE FLOW OF ENERGY AND THE CYCLING OF NUTRIENTS IN ECOSYSTEMS

The processes of life depend on a constant flow of chemical energy from molecule to molecule and from organism to organism. As energy flows through the biosphere on its inevitable course toward dissipation as heat, it mediates the cycling of nutrients which are as essential to life as energy itself. The basic role of energy and the cycles of several nutrients were discussed in Chapter 2. Here we will look in more detail at the flow of energy through the biotic community and the habitat (jointly called the ecosystem) and at how the cycling of nutrients is accomplished.

*FOOD CHAINS AND THE WEB OF LIFE.* All organisms can be classified as either producers or consumers, which divides the living world roughly into green plants and everything else. Although we tend to think of the producers as self-sufficient, no organism lives alone in the real world and it is doubtful if any could do so. Green plants depend on microorganisms for sources of nitrogen, sulfur, and other elements in appropriate forms. Autotrophic bacteria, which obtain their energy from inorganic sources, may depend on other organisms for certain preformed compounds.

Animals are commonly called *herbivores* if they feed predominantly on plants, *carnivores* if they feed on other animals, *omnivores* if their diet consists of both plants and animals, and *saprovores* if they consume excreta or decaying organic matter. We sometimes also define a group of *parasites*, although the concept of parasitism becomes fuzzy when we try to make it exact. Parasites do not necessarily kill or consume their hosts, although carnivores and herbivores consume their prey. The relationship between a parasite and its host is a relatively long-term one, while the attack of a carnivore or herbivore is swift and decisive. The aphid may be considered parasitic on plants, while the grasshopper is an herbivore. Bacteria and fungi are either parasites, feeding on living organisms, or saprophytes, feeding on non-living organic matter. A few higher plants have lost their chlorophyll and lead parasitic or saprophytic lives. The Indian pipe is a familiar example.

The best-known *food chains* begin with green plants. Green plants are eaten by herbivores, which are eaten by carnivores, which may be eaten by

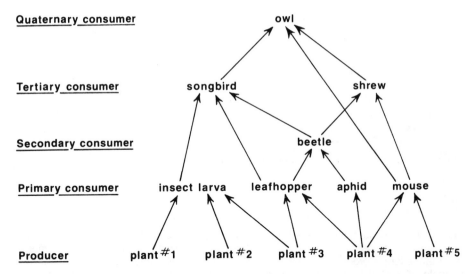

**Figure 3–5** A food web, showing some interconnected food chains. Food webs represent energy flow through an ecosystem. They begin with the solar energy captured and fixed into food energy by green plants, the *producers*. Producers are eaten by animals which are eaten by other animals, generating a set of relationships such as that diagrammed above.

still other carnivores. For reasons we will discuss shortly, there are seldom more than five links to the chain, although dozens of food chains may occur in the same community. These chains may interweave to form a *food web*, sometimes called the web of life (Figure 3.5).

Other food chains begin with detritus, the accumulation of decaying animal and vegetable matter. For example, there is the food chain of detritus-earthworm-robin-cat. It should be evident, however, that this kind of food chain could not exist without the others.

*PYRAMID OF NUMBERS AND BIOMASSES.* The complexities of the food web may be simplified by grouping all species with similar feeding relations into the same *trophic level*. Green plants are producers, since they use the energy of the sun to manufacture energy-rich organic compounds from raw materials in the soil and air. Herbivores are primary consumers, living directly off the producers. Carnivores are secondary, tertiary, or quaternary consumers. Saprovores, especially the small, abundant soil organisms, are decomposers.

There is a larger number of animal species in the lower consumer levels than in the higher ones. These species are generally characterized by their larger populations, smaller size, and faster reproductive rates than species belonging to the higher levels, although it is easy to think of notable exceptions, like **plankton**-eating whales. Because their ranks are constantly depleted by predators, these characteristics are adaptive. Predators must usu-

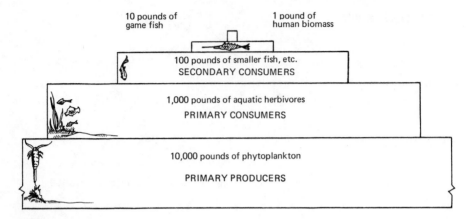

**Figure 3–6** A biomass pyramid. On the basis of a 10 to 1 ratio of mass between trophic levels, phytoplankton in the sea must produce 10,000 pounds of organic matter that man, a fourth-order consumer, may gain 1 pound in weight. This figure is not drawn to scale. (Adapted from Greenwood and Edwards, *Human Environments and Natural Systems*, Duxbury Press, North Scituate, Mass., 1973, p. 56.)

ally be larger than their prey, but again there are exceptions, such as wolves that sometimes hunt in packs. Although larger than their prey, predators cannot be more numerous or they would run out of food. The relationship between the size of an animal and the number of individuals in each size class is so striking that it appropriately has been called a *pyramid of numbers*.

A more accurate picture of the interrelationships between trophic levels is derived from the total weight, or *biomass*, of all the species in each trophic level. This expresses the contribution of both size and numbers in a single figure. For example, fifteen mice each weighing 20 grams have the same biomass as 1,500 grasshoppers each weighing 0.2 grams. For reasons which will become clear in the section on the flow of energy, the ratio of biomass from one trophic level to the next higher one is usually between 10 to 1 and 5 to 1 (Figure 3.6).

*NUTRIENT CYCLES.* Plants use water from the soil, carbon dioxide from the air, and sunlight to synthesize carbohydrates. From these carbohydrates and inorganic nutrients from the soil, they manufacture the fantastic array of chemical compounds found in living things. These include not only the abundant fats, proteins, and nucleic acids, but smaller amounts of vitamins, hormones, pigments, alkaloids, antibiotics, and other materials. When herbivores eat plants, their digestion breaks down plant proteins into their constituent amino acids, which are then recombined into animal proteins. Oxidation of carbohydrates and fats provides energy for this process. Vitamins are utilized directly.

When plants and animals die, small and large saprovores liberate the nitrogen from complex compounds in the form of ammonia. Certain groups of bacteria in the soil convert this ammonia to nitrites and nitrates, which are then available for reabsorption by higher plants. Nitrogen, carbon, and other nutrients may cycle repeatedly through air, plants, animals, microorganisms, soil, and back to the air again without leaving the system.

Two other types of bacteria are often abundant in the soil. One of these, the denitrifying bacteria, removes nitrogen from ammonia and releases it in gaseous form into the atmosphere. The other, the nitrogen-fixing bacteria, takes nitrogen from the atmosphere and fixes it into nitrites and nitrates that plants can use. Some nitrogen-fixing bacteria live freely in the soil. Others live symbiotically (in a mutually beneficial way) in nodules on the roots of leguminous plants. In mature systems the processes of nitrogen fixation and denitrification may balance, but in the early states of succession, nitrogen fixation exceeds denitrification as the soil increases in fertility. Certain blue-green algae can also fix nitrogen. They are probably responsible for this process as it occurs in aquatic habitats, but we still have much to learn about the cycle of nitrogen in the sea.

When man harvests a crop of plants or animals, he removes a significant amount of nutrients, a process which quickly decreases the fertility of the soil. In agriculture man removes nutrients from the system as food and replaces them as fertilizer.

Dead plants and animals and their excreta tend to recycle quickly and, in balanced, mature systems, completely. In some situations organic matter may accumulate faster than it is used, but the resulting increase in fertility of the soil permits more advanced successional stages to come in, leading toward greater stability of the system. Man, however, generates such enormous amounts of organic wastes — agricultural, industrial, and municipal — that they cannot be handled by natural recycling processes. Much of the inorganic waste is not degradable by natural processes at all. And many substances, organic and inorganic, are harmful to living things. The environmental deterioration that results from man's garbage poses a monumental problem today.

THE FLOW OF ENERGY.    Without energy the cycling of nutrients would stop and life would be impossible. While various forms of physical, nuclear, and gravitational energy are most important in the non-living world, the energy of life is the energy of the sun transformed into the chemical energy of the carbon bond. The reaction by which this process occurs in green plants can be summarized as:

$$6CO_2 + 6H_2O + energy \rightarrow 6O_2 + C_6H_{12}O_6.$$

carbon dioxide + water + energy $\rightarrow$ oxygen + carboyhydrate

The total energy captured by plants in carbon bonds represents the gross primary productivity of the system. Between one quarter and one third of this energy is used for the individual life processes of the plants that produced it. What remains is the net primary productivity available for all the consumers in the system. The efficiency of the producers in converting solar energy to chemical energy is low, usually less than 1 percent, although it can be increased in cultivated systems to about 2.5 percent. Net primary productivity is lowest in the desert and becomes increasingly higher in communities with denser vegetation. It is highest in certain aquatic systems, particularly **estuaries** and **reefs.**

Energy is transferred from one trophic level to another by predation (Figures 3.7), accompanied by considerable losses. Energy is diverted in excrement, in animals and plants dying from causes other than predation, in wastage from kills, and in respiration through the loss of body heat. The energy in excrement, dead organisms, and wastage is available to decomposers, and part of it may again be taken up by members of higher trophic levels feeding on bacteria and detritus.

Energy becomes available to an organism when a food is oxidized. Part of this energy is converted into the chemical or mechanical work of the cell and part is lost as heat. The general chemical reaction which makes energy available is similar to photosynthesis in reverse, and may be symbolized as:

$$C_6H_{12}O_6 + 6O_2 \rightarrow 6CO_2 + 6H_2O + \text{energy}$$

$$\text{carbohydrate} + \text{oxygen} \rightarrow \text{carbon dioxide} + \text{water} + \text{energy}$$

In a balanced system the total energy gained through photosynthesis equals the total energy lost through respiration. Energy does not cycle as nutrients do. Life could not continue unless photosynthesis continuously replaced lost energy.

Since the atmosphere reached approximately its present composition many thousands of years ago, the balance between photosynthesis (reduction) and respiration (oxidation) has been fairly constant. Within the last century, however, man has threatened to upset this balance by large-scale burning of fossil fuels. It is extremely unlikely that the activities of man will have any significant effect on the enormous amount of oxygen in the atmosphere (unless photosynthesis stops, in which case we will starve long before we are asphyxiated); but carbon dioxide occurs in only trace amounts, and its concentration has increased measurably (see Chapter 2). Carbon dioxide plays a major role in the heat balance of the earth, but it is unsafe to jump to conclusions about the potential effects of increased carbon dioxide because the situation is complex and many opposing forces are involved.

YIELD. Game or fur animals, timber, and food harvested by man are crops. Since man is an omnivorous consumer, he may take a yield from any

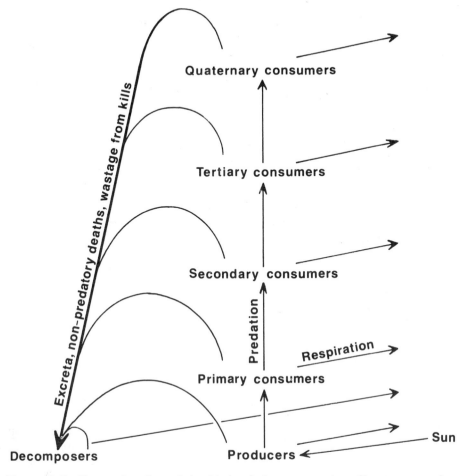

**Figure 3–7** Energy flow through trophic levels in an ecosystem. Energy conversion from one level to the next is a relatively inefficient process owing to losses from respiration, death due to causes other than predation, incomplete consumption of killed animals, and excretion of unutilized organic matter.

consumer level or from the plant producers. Because energy is lost at each trophic level, the potential yield is higher the lower the trophic level from which it is taken. A pond will yield more energy and nutrients in the form of carp than of bass; a marsh will yield more muskrat fur than mink; a farm will yield more corn than pigs. The earth will support larger human populations if they eat wheat instead of meat.

The relative productivity between trophic levels is variable, but 10 to 1 is an average value. At 10 to 1, 100 calories available at the producer level becomes 10, 1, 0.1, and 0.01 calories at progressively higher consumer levels.

For this reason there are seldom more than five links to the food chain, and usually fewer.

If man could learn to use sunlight to produce food as plants do, he would become a primary producer, a photosynthesizer, and the world could feed much larger populations than it can feed through agriculture. However, factors other than energy (including the energy that is food) may limit the ultimate size of human populations.

## REGULATION OF POPULATIONS

The ratio of biomasses between trophic levels is maintained under natural conditions so that there is a *balance of nature*. Maintenance of this ratio involves regulation of the number of individuals in each species. During a drought, plant growth is reduced and less food is available for primary consumers. The number of primary consumers is reduced, providing less food for their predators, and so on through successively higher trophic levels. Destruction of predators at the top of the pyramid results in increased survival of individuals in lower consumer levels, until the balance is restored when overgrazing by the increased number of herbivores reduces food supply for all.

*BIOTIC POTENTIAL AND ENVIRONMENTAL RESISTANCE.* If a mated pair of animals were introduced into an ideal environment with optimum climate, unlimited food and space, and freedom from predation and disease, all their offspring would survive — and their offsprings' offspring, and the offspring of those. Death would come only with old age. Such a population would increase in size at an exponential rate, which means it would double in a fixed period of time — which might be 25 minutes for a bacterium or 25 years for an elephant. The exact rate of growth and size of population depends on birth rate, length of life, and time of sexual maturity. Reproduction under these ideal (but unreal) conditions represents the *intrinsic growth rate* or *biotic potential* of the species (Figure 3.8).

The biotic potential is never completely realized in nature because the inherent ability to reproduce at a given rate is always opposed sooner or later by factors that act to limit population. Populations may increase exponentially for a time while recovering from a catastrophe or when invading a new niche, but eventually inhibiting factors reduce the success of reproduction or increase mortality until expansion is stopped. These inhibiting factors are often called the *environmental resistance*, a misleading phrase since much of the "resistance" is within the population as well as within the environment. The actual growth rate, resulting from the interplay between biotic potential and environmental resistance, is best represented by a **sigmoid growth curve.**

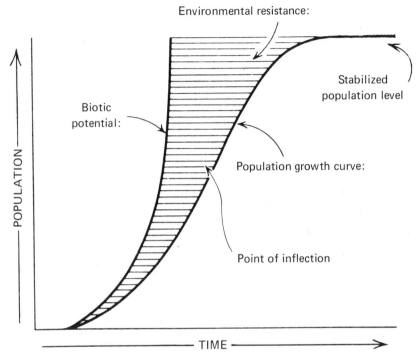

**Figure 3–8** Relationship between exponential growth curve and actual growth curve as modified by environmental resistance. In the curve representing the biotic potential, the doubling time of the population is constant. An actual population cannot sustain exponential growth. The rate of increase in the growth rate becomes zero at the inflection point, and the growth rate itself becomes zero when a steady state population level is reached.

The sigmoid growth curve is fundamental because it applies equally to growth of individual cells, complete organisms, and populations. It even applies to the establishment of biotic communities involving many species. Figure 3.8 shows a typical sigmoid curve. In the lower half of the curve for population growth, accelerating forces cause faster and faster production of offspring. In the upper half, inhibiting factors produce higher and higher mortalities, although the number of births per unit of time continues to exceed the number of deaths. Eventually a level is reached where deaths balance births, and the population becomes stabilized. The point on the curve where acceleration gives way to deceleration is the point of inflection.

*FACTORS THAT INFLUENCE POPULATION DENSITY.* The factors that deflect the growth curve from the curve representing reproductive potential to one of sigmoid form include competition, predation, disease, changes in

# UPSETTING NATURE'S BALANCE

In the barren lands of the Canadian north there is little to support human life. Traditionally, huge herds of big game such as caribou have been a main source of food for the few men who lived in the arctic regions. Large numbers of arctic wolves also preyed on the caribou, but a relationship existed between the wolves and the caribou which allowed them both to survive. However, when European emigrants began to settle the area, they failed to understand this relationship. By attempting to maximize the main resource they discovered, the caribou, they succeeded in jeopardizing the survival of the wolf, the caribou, and man.

In the Canadian north, the caribou are the largest herbivores. They roam in large herds, migrating with the seasons to feed on the moss and other small green plants of the tundra. On the other hand, the arctic wolf is a predator. Primarily a hunter of big game, such as elk, moose, caribou, and deer, it does not kill for sport. That the caribou have been prey for the wolves for a long time tells us that the two animals are evenly matched; that is, wolves cannot kill caribou at will, nor can the caribou always escape.

Wolves are fast runners and have great endurance, but a healthy caribou, even at three weeks of age, can outrun a healthy wolf. The wolves' most common method of hunting is to put a group of caribou to flight. If all the animals are healthy, the wolves will be unable to catch any of them and will quickly abandon the chase. The wolves will continue putting groups of caribou to flight until they discover a victim who cannot keep up with the group. Thus the wolves live by preying on the very young or on those slowed by infirmity or old age.

This relationship not only allows both species to survive, it ensures that the caribou will be continually strengthened by a test of fitness which eliminates the animals too weak to evade the hunters. In many cases the weak

birth rate, and emigration. The intensity of these forces varies in direct proportion to the density of the population; therefore, they are *density-dependent* factors. Competition disappears when the population is so small that there are more than enough resources to go around, but it increases rapidly when each individual has to fight for what it needs. Predation may or may not act in the same manner, exerting a regulating effect on population growth when the percentage of the population taken increases along with the population. Disease becomes epidemic only when populations become crowded. With overpopulation the birth rate declines and emigration occurs.

The density at which different populations become stabilized varies *caribou are killed when they are calves. Because they do not live long enough to reproduce, they cannot pass on their weakness to future generations. Even the killing of the old and sick, who may have no genetic defects, enhances the survival prospects of the caribou as a species by providing better grazing for the animals who remain. These caribou, who will be reproducing the species, have a better chance to prosper without competition from the inferior members of the herds.*

*For hundreds of years, the vast arctic regions have been inhabited by relatively small numbers of Eskimos. The Eskimos have been unable to kill enough caribou or wolves to change drastically the ecologic balance between the two species. But by the middle of the twentieth century, European emigrants had settled in the barren lands of Canada and begun to decimate the herds with technologically advanced weapons. When they saw the herds diminishing, the European Canadians blamed the only other "enemy" of the caribou, the wolf, and began attempts to exterminate it.*

*With men instead of wolves as hunters, the survival factors for the caribou were altered. The men had no desire to kill the weak and sick—when they discriminated at all, they chose the largest, healthiest animals as victims. And even now, where the laws strictly limiting the killing of caribou are success-fully enforced, hunters still destroy wolves on sight. To feed the weak animals who would have fallen prey to the wolves, the caribou have been forced to overgraze the scarce tundra vegetation.*

*The critical situation confronting the wolves and the caribou today is an example of how men have upset a very delicate ecologic balance. The relation-ship between the Eskimos, the wolves, the caribou, and the arctic flora was a time-tested one that allowed all of them to survive. It will probably never be restored. By harvesting the caribou too fast and then attempting to protect them from a perceived enemy, the wolves, man has greatly diminished a valuable source of food in a region where food is needed badly.*

with climatic conditions and the species' requirements for food and space. Limitations set by these factors are *density-independent*. The climate is the way it is. The ultimate food supply is related to climate and the fertility of the soil. The amount of space that can be used by the species is determined by features of the land and vegetation. It is when these factors start to become limiting that the active, density-dependent forces come into play.

Some species, including many rodents, are often not primarily control-led by competition or predation. These may continue to increase in numbers until an epidemic occurs and their numbers crash. Other species, including most songbirds, have such large territorial demands that competition main-tains population at a relatively low density. Certain species of insects never attain stabilized populations. They continue to expand until they eat themselves out of food and shelter or are reduced by severe weather. When rigorous winters cause population catastrophes, most controlling factors are in temporary abeyance until normal population levels are reached once again. In the end, all populations are controlled by either one or more density-dependent forces or density-independent limiting factors. No population can expand indefinitely.

A species becomes a pest when its activities affect man's interests adversely. Species seldom reach pest proportions under natural conditions when controlling factors are fully effective. However, when man disturbs this balance by removing predators or by cultivating plants or animals in extensive **monoculture,** species normally held in check explode in population and cause great damage. Pest control then becomes necessary. Man resorts to chemical sprays and other measures which often have undesirable side effects. The problem of pest control has become a major one in human health and economy. Some aspects of it will be discussed in Chapter 15.

*MAXIMUM SUSTAINED YIELD.* The cumulative growth curve is rising most rapidly at its inflection point (Figure 3.8). Here, the rate at which new individuals appear reaches its peak. Below the inflection point the population is not reproducing at its maximum potential; above it, through the action of density-dependent factors, the death rate increases faster than the birth rate. It is desirable to obtain the maximum sustained yield from any species of economic importance. To do this, **cropping** should be regulated to maintain the population at the point of maximum growth rate — a task which requires self control as well as skill and knowledge. We know today that we are hunting the great whales to extinction, yet political factors and short-sightedness prevent nations from cooperating to save them.

*POPULATION "EXPLOSION" OF MAN.* Populations of primitive man appear to have been stabilized at a rather low level. They were restricted by the usual factors of food, predation, and weather. Before he learned to exploit sources of energy other than food, there was little man could do to appropriate a large proportion of the resources of his environment for himself. Culture changed that, however, removing many regulating factors and accelerating expansion.

Through time man has escaped the threat of predation. Emigration relieved local congestion, but it has now brought about colonization of all suitable areas of this world, and those who talk about solving the population problem by emigrating to other worlds are deluding themselves. Clearly, population growth cannot continue indefinitely. Space is finite, even if we learn to live on or in the ocean as we now live on land. Competition remains an important force socially, economically, and politically. If man is to continue to escape the brutal controls imposed by nature, he must control his numbers through his own actions. The development of adequate birth control methods is one of the greatest challenges facing modern civilization.

## BIOTIC STRUCTURE

To even the most unsophisticated observer, the biosphere reveals great diversity. The preceding sections have discussed some of the factors that create and maintain this diversity. Now we will look at some of the actual habitats and communities, first on a local level and then on a grander geographic scale. Classification of these communities is merely a way to facilitate talking about them, because we have seen that life varies continuously without respect for boundaries or definitions. Nevertheless, if you do not try to define it too exactly, there is an obvious difference between a pond and a forest — although the precise point at which the edge of the forest yields to the edge of the pond may defy anyone's identification.

We will not consider estuarine, coastal, and open marine environments or the polar seas — not because they are not of great and growing interest and importance to man, but because an exhaustive survey of the many environments of earth is beyond the scope of this book.

*LOCAL HABITATS AND COMMUNITIES.*    Inland ecosystems are aquatic or terrestrial, with a continuous gradation between. Many forms of life are at home on land or water, and many aquatic animals, chiefly insects, are terrestrial creatures that have adapted to fresh water habitats for part or all of their life cycle.

STREAMS.    All streams go through an evolutionary cycle which begins when the area is geologically uplifted, often in association with mountain building, and ends when it becomes eroded flat. Stages in this physiographic succession may be seen successively in the swift-flowing water, the rapids and waterfalls interspersed with lakes near the stream's source in the mountains; the alternating rocky **riffles** and sand bottom pools of the middle-aged portion of the stream; and the mud-bottomed, marshy-margined, quiet waters near its mouth, commonly in flat terrain (Figure 3.9).

To live in a stream, organisms must come to terms with the current or be swept away before they can establish stable breeding populations. If they can do this, the conditions in a stream are generally quite favorable for life. Animals adjust to the current by avoiding it, by employing some sort of clinging mechanism, by exploiting strong swimming powers, or by burrowing into the banks or bottom of the stream. Algae and other plants are firmly anchored to rocks or other objects. A typical stream community is represented by insects, mostly in larval stages, snails, clams, crayfish, darters, minnows, and some larger fish.

**Figure 3–9** A typical stream community in the Mantahala National Forest, North Carolina. The constant flow of water carries food to the stream inhabitants. The stream current also transports organic food from material which falls from the overhanging shore. (Photograph courtesy of the U.S. Forest Service.)

The water of a stream is generally well aerated because of its constant agitation. In addition to the primary productivity of algae and other resident plants, organic food is added from material that falls, washes, or is blown in from the shore. The flow of energy in a stream may be more complex than in terrestrial systems because energy is constantly being imported from elsewhere and lost to a given area as the stream flows on.

Streams have always been important to man as sources of food, water, and pleasure. In colonial America the local mill was often established first, by the side of a stream; and with power for grinding grain assured, a town could then spring up around the mill. Streams have also been important for navigation and recreation. Man is now faced with the need to preserve traditional values of streams by controlling pollution caused by industrial, municipal, and agricultural wastes, erosion and silting, and thermal discharges from electric power plants. The old waterwheel did little harm to the environment. Its successor, the hydroelectric plant, causes major modifications.

LAKES.   Individual streams and rivers evolve, change their courses, appear and disappear; but the great river systems of the world are geologically quite old. The drainage web of the continents is an integral part of the world hydrologic cycle (see Chapter 2). Most lakes, however, are relatively young. The many lakes of Canada and the northern United States were gouged out of the face of the continent by the last glacier, only a few tens of thousands of years ago. Their lives will be short in terms of the earth's history; many of them have already disappeared. An exception is Lake Baikal in eastern Siberia, formed about 25 million years ago. Most of the organisms in this lake are unique, having had abundant time to evolve their special adaptations.

The life forms in most lakes are different from those in streams, but not dramatically so. The time for evolution has been too short for that. The major difference between life in lakes and streams is related to the fact that water in lakes is relatively still. Lake-dwelling animals must generally swim about in search of food instead of hanging on and letting the food flow past them. Small, weakly-swimming or free-floating plankton often abound. These organisms are both plant and animal: algae, bacteria, fungi, tiny crustaceans, and larval forms of insects are common. **Diatoms** and other algae or detritus form the first links of the food chains. Aquatic insects displaying a great variety of adaptations are abundant. The mineral content of lakes is extremely variable, particularly with respect to calcium. Mollusks are rare in "soft water" lakes because there is not enough calcium for them to build their shells.

In temperate regions lakes tend to become thermally stratified during summer and winter in response to seasonal changes in temperature. The density of water increases as its temperature decreases, until it reaches its greatest density at 4° C. In summer the upper layer of water is warmed by the sun; the colder water forms a layer at the bottom. The upper zone of warm water, which may be several meters deep, is called the *epilimnion;* the cold region extending to the bottom is the *hypolimnion;* and the zone of rapid temperature change between is the *metalimnion* (also called the *thermocline).* As temperatures drop in the fall, the surface waters cool until the temperature of the lake is uniform at 4° C. Light winds then mix the water to all depths in the autumn *overturn.* Further cooling below 4° C results in a layer of ice or very cold water at the top, with the densest water at a temperature of 4° at the bottom. After the ice melts in the spring and surface waters begin to warm, the lake "turns over" once more, becoming the same temperature throughout. As warming continues, stratification begins again.

This temperature cycle has great significance for aquatic ecosystems. Turning over of the waters brings nutrients to the top layers and oxygen to the bottom. The algal blooms and plankton pulses of spring and fall are related to the replenishment of nutrients in the epilimnion.

The productivity of lakes depends on the availability of nutrients. *Oligotrophic* lakes are relatively infertile. Their productivity is limited by lack of nutrients. Oligotrophic lakes are characterized by rocky shorelines and virtual absence of aquatic weeds. The hypolimnion is usually oxygenated the year around, although the oxygen supply diminishes during stratification and must be renewed when the waters turn over. Excellent game fish such as smallmouth bass, wall-eyed pike, pickerel, and cisco inhabit oligotrophic lakes.

During the later stages of their lives, most lakes become *eutrophic.* A eutrophic lake is, literally, a "well-nourished" (fertile) lake. Bog lakes, such as occur in the north, are exceptions. Man hastens this natural aging process by adding nutrients to the lake. Addition of waste heat from power plants sometimes enhances the effects of fertilization and may interfere with the thermal structure of the lake.

Eutrophic lakes have marshy shorelines and abundant growth of aquatic plants in shallow water. The death of these plants and their decomposition in the hypolimnion deplete the supply of oxygen below the thermocline. Thus most aerobic organisms are restricted to the waters of the epilimnion, although **anaerobes** flourish in the waters below. Food fish common in eutrophic lakes include perch, largemouth bass, white bass, and rock bass. As eutrophication proceeds, however, these disappear, to be replaced by other species of less value to man.

PONDS, MARSHES, AND BOGS.    Ponds are shallower and generally smaller in area than lakes, and their life-span ranges from a few weeks or months to several centuries. Conditions in an entire pond are often similar to those found in the margins of a eutrophic lake. Abundant vegetation occurs over the entire muddy bottom and around the margins in the form of a marsh.

Ponds and marshes often dry up during some seasons, or their water becomes stagnant. Animals living in these precarious circumstances must either adapt to variations in water level, temperature, and oxygen supply and survive dry periods in a dormant state, or be able to migrate to where conditions are more favorable. In spite of the hazards of pond and marsh life, animals are more varied and abundant here than in either lakes or streams. The plankton contains more **protozoa** and **rotifers** than that in lakes, the bottom-dwelling creatures are more varied and abundant, and the free-swimming animals include the less-desirable food fish such as suckers, bullheads, buffalo, and carp. There are many turtles, water snakes, and amphibians. Many species of sunfish typically occur in ponds, although they are also found in lakes and streams. Dabbler ducks, grebes, herons, marsh birds, and blackbirds may be very common, and the marsh around the margin provides a home for the muskrat and its predator, the mink.

Bogs are similar to ponds and marshes but are limited to colder climates. They are deficient in oxygen both above and below the thermocline and are deficient in nitrogen because decomposition of organic matter proceeds slowly and incompletely. Their highly acid waters largely restrict animal life to insects. The luxuriant vegetation, when it dies, becomes compressed into peat, which has been an important fuel for man through the ages.

Biotic succession is well illustrated by the sequence of plants and animals that occurs in ponds (Figure 3.10). In the newly formed pond there is considerable open water and the bottom is bare. After the phytoplankton, the first established plant community that invades is made up of pondweeds, milfoil, hornwort, and other species whose vegetative growth is completely submerged, although the flower stalks of some may rise to the surface. This submerged vegetation obstructs the flow of silt being washed in from the **watershed.** When it dies, its remains are added to material accumulating at the bottom.

Eventually, this process decreases the depth of water so that water lilies and pond lilies come in, their stems rooting in the bottom and their leaves floating on the surface. The leaves of these plants cast enough shade so that the submerged plants beneath them die from lack of light for photosynthesis. The emergent vegetation that follows is also rooted in the bottom, but in shallower water, and its stems and leaves project well above the surface. This vegetation forms the marsh. It consists of cattails, reeds, swamp loosestrife, wild rice, sawgrass, sedges, and rushes.

After the substratum of accumulated organic material builds up to the point where the water table is below the ground surface during most of the year, swamp shrubs, particularly buttonbush, alders, dogwoods, swamp rose, willows, and cottonwoods, come in. In the eastern United States, these shrubs are followed first by a swamp forest of red and silver maples, elm, ash, swamp white oak, and pin oak. Finally, the stable, or climax, forest typical of the climatic area may follow. In cold northern climates the

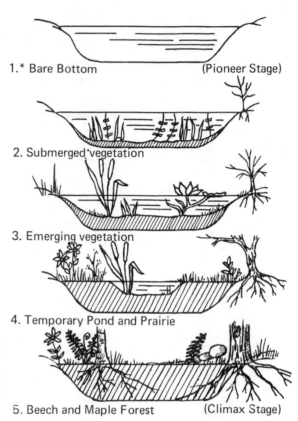

1.* Bare Bottom            (Pioneer Stage)

2. Submerged vegetation

3. Emerging vegetation

4. Temporary Pond and Prairie

**Figure 3–10** Typical stages in plant succession as a pond becomes a forest. This particular sequence of events occurred in a pond at the south end of Lake Michigan.

5. Beech and Maple Forest       (Climax Stage)

early stages of this succession are abbreviated or missing, the swamp shrub and forest are replaced by bog forest, and both it and the climax forest are **coniferous** rather than **deciduous.** In grassland and desert climates, the pond succession occurs less frequently, and the shrub and tree stages are confined to a narrow fringe around the water, if they are present at all.

The animal succession contains fewer stages. Fish, turtles, ducks and other marsh birds, muskrats, frogs and salamanders, insects, and snails move freely between the submerged, floating, and emergent plant stages — sometimes feeding in one plant stage and nesting or reproducing in a different one. The three plant stages furnish a variety of microhabitats or niches, and together with the animals they compose one biotic community. With invasion of shrubs, and later of several tree stages, the pond-marsh community is succeeded by the forest-edge community and finally by the forest community itself.

GRASSLANDS. Succession occurs whenever a bare area of land is exposed. In moist climates, grassy fields usually form an intermediate stage, leading to shrubs and then to forest. In semi-arid regions the succession does not proceed as far as forest. In fact, it may stop with the formation of grasslands. Many herbivores are adapted for feeding on grasses, and the grasses are adapted for grazing since their leaves grow from their base, permitting a considerable amount of cropping without harm to the plant. The grassland habitat is excellent not only for grazing animals but also for insects, rodents, and a variety of birds.

Before its agricultural and urban development, central North America was predominantly grasslands — the tall grass prairie to the east and the short grass prairie westward. The grass-buffalo-man food chain was the equivalent of the grass-cow-man food chain that replaced it.

FORESTS. Early stages in succession are characterized by plants which require high intensities of light but can flourish in infertile soil with poor moisture conditions. Many of these species have a very high growth rate and consequently a high net productivity. Each stage in the early succession improves the fertility and physical properties of the soil. When conditions are finally suitable for forest trees to move in, there is no form of vegetation that can follow, largely because of the shade that the trees cast. The several types of forests will be discussed in later sections.

CONTROLLING SUCCESSION. An understanding of succession is important to man so he can use natural resources without destroying them. A pond must not be excessively cropped for fish because inevitably it will become choked with vegetation and the open water will disappear. The productivity of a marsh for muskrat can be enhanced by maintaining the proper stage of vegetation and water level. The prairie was maintained by periodic burning — sometimes through fires started by lightning and sometimes by Indians. Game species such as the cottontail, fox squirrel, deer, bobwhite, pheasant, and dove, can be increased in numbers by control of plant succession in the mixed grassland, shrub, and scattered-tree or open-forest stage. With succession to dense forest, these species give way to gray squirrel, bear, moose, ruffed grouse, and turkey. The management of wildlife depends more on the proper management of the habitat and vegetation than on management of the animals.

It is important also to protect natural areas of virgin forest, prairie, and local communities of all kinds as a record of their primitive condition and as a sample of what other areas will revert to if left alone. These nature preserves provide a control against which man can evaluate the effectiveness of forestry, agricultural, and wildlife practices. At the same time, these preserves save from extinction native species which some day may be found valuable for food, medicine, biotic pest control, or domestication. Large natural areas in the form of national parks, national monuments, and state parks are of obvious esthetic and recreational value.

GEOGRAPHICAL COMMUNITIES.    Biomes are large biotic communities identified by the vegetation type of their climax stages — stages ultimately reached through succession. The final stage in this succession is determined by the prevailing climate (Table 3.1) In addition, each biome contains distinct populations of animals. The classification and distribution of the major terrestrial biomes are shown in Figure 3.11.

### TABLE 3.1
### Principal Biomes with Their Dominant Growth Forms
### and Some Representative Species

| Biome | Dominant Growth Form | Representative Plants (mostly Northern Hemisphere) |
|---|---|---|
| **Aquatic Systems** | | |
| Open oceans | Plankton, floating algae | Diatoms, plankton (dinoflagellates, etc.) |
| Estuaries and shores | Multicellular algae, grasses | Seaweeds, eelgrass, marsh grass |
| Lakes and streams | Algae, mosses, higher plants | Plankton algae, filamentous algae, duck weed, water lilies, pondweed, water hyacinth |
| Swamps, marshes, bogs | Algae, rushes, etc. | Cattails, water plantains, pipeworts, rushes, sedges, sphagnum moss, tamarack, baldcypress, mangrove |
| **Forests** | | |
| Tropical rain forests | Trees, broadleaved evergreen | Many species of evergreen, broadleaved trees (unfamiliar to us), vines, epiphytes (orchids, bromeliads, ferns) |
| Tropical seasonal forests | Trees, both evergreen and deciduous | Mahogany, rubber tree, papaya, coconut palm |
| Temperate rain forests | Trees, evergreen | Large coniferous species (Douglas fir, Sitka spruce, coast redwood, western hemlock, white cedar) |
| Temperate deciduous | Trees, broadleaved deciduous | Maples, beech, oak, hickory, basswood chestnut, elm, sycamore, ash |
| Temperate evergreen | Trees, needleleaved | Pines, Douglas fir, spruce, fir |
| Boreal coniferous (taiga) | Trees, needleleaved | Evergreen conifers (spruce, fir, pine), blueberry, oxalis |

| Reduced Forests— Scrubland | | |
|---|---|---|
| Chaparral, | Shrubs, sclerophyll evergreen | Live oak, deerbrush, manzanita, buckbrush, chamise |
| Thorn woodlands | Spinose trees and large shrubs | Acacia, large shrubs |
| Temperate woodlands | Small evergreen or deciduous trees, grass or shrubs | Pinyon pine, juniper, evergreen oak |
| Grasslands | | |
| Tropical savanna | Grass (and trees) | Tall grasses, thorny trees, sedges |
| Temperate grasslands | Grass | Bluestem, Indian grass, grama grass, buffalo grass, bluebunch wheat grass |
| Tundras | | |
| Arctic | Diverse small plants | Lichens, mosses, dwarf shrubs, grass, sedges, forbs |
| Alpine | Small herbs (grasslike) | Sedges, grasses, forbs, lichens |
| Deserts | | |
| Tropical warm | Shrubs, succulents | Spinose shrubs, tall cacti, euphorbias |
| Temperate warm | Shrubs, succulents | Creosote bush, ocotillo, cacti, Joshua tree, century plant, bur sage (in USA) |
| Temperate cold | Shrubs | Sagebrush, saltbush, shadscale, winterfat, greasewood (in USA) |

From Jensen and Salsbury, *Botany* p. 703

Primitive man had to make a number of adjustments in order to live in the various biomes, adjustments both to climate and in his use of available resources. Where these adjustments were easy to make, he attained his highest population densities and cultural development.

TEMPERATE DECIDUOUS FOREST. Temperate deciduous forest, dominated by trees that shed their leaves during the winter, presently occurs extensively in eastern North America, eastern Asia, and western Europe. When the world was much warmer, between 60 and 70 million years ago, these scattered portions of the temperate deciduous forest were interconnected from southeastern United States across Canada and the Bering land bridge,

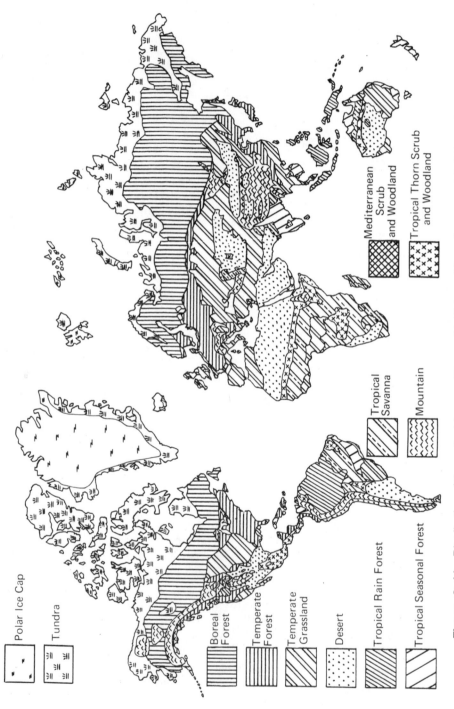

**Figure 3–11** Distribution of the major biomes of the world. (Adapted from Jensen and Salisbury, *Botany: An Ecological Approach*, Wadsworth Pub. Co., Belmont, California, 1972, p. 702.)

south into China and west into Europe. Animals passed back and forth freely, creating nearly worldwide uniformity within the biome. About 25 million years ago, cooling and drying of the climates over the Northern Hemisphere and disappearance of the Bering land bridge forced the three sections of the biome to separate and retreat southward.

The similarity seen in many species and genera of the plants and animals found in these temperate deciduous areas today can be explained by the continuity and uniformity of vegetation and climate that existed in these regions long ago. The differences that occur resulted from speciation after the areas became isolated. Man had not yet evolved when these movements were taking place. However, the Bering land bridge existed at intervals during the last glacial period when man was evolving, and the Indian and Eskimo probably crossed over from Asia at that time.

The conditions in the temperate deciduous forest are responsible for many characteristics common among its inhabitants. Animals living here are adapted to living in and under trees and are dependent on the shade and protection of the forest. Other animals are adapted to life on and in the soil and are aided by the rich humus that develops from fallen leaves. Since vision in these forests is restricted, the voice and hearing of birds, mammals, frogs and insects are often highly developed in compensation. Broad seasonal changes in photoperiod and temperature cause reproductive activities to be greatest in the spring. Severe winters force adaptations in the form of increased physiological tolerance, hibernation, or migration. Many herbaceous plants flower in response to the short days of spring, before the leafing out of the tree canopy (Figure 3.12).

Man finds the deciduous forest and its climate most favorable for good health, a high level of activity, high population densities, and high development of civilization. When white man first invaded the prairies of North America, he built his home in the strips of forest along the streams, using the trees for shade and protection from the weather and as a source of lumber and fuel. He preferred to clear the forest for agriculture, and only as settlement increased and he was crowded out of the forest into the open grassland did he learn to use the rich prairie soil for farming. Even then, he planted trees around his home.

CONIFEROUS FOREST.    Coniferous forests are characterized by trees that retain their foliage throughout the year. They are confined to the northern portions of both the Eastern and Western Hemispheres and to the higher mountains southward, where winters are long and cold and growing seasons short. When the needle-shaped leaves drop from the trees, they do not decompose as readily as the broad leaves of deciduous trees. Consequently, the soil in the coniferous forest is less fertile. The spruces, firs, and pines and the mammals and birds of the coniferous forest in North America and Eurasia are even more closely related than are the flora and fauna of the

**Figure 3–12** A typical temperate deciduous forest. The large trees are tulip poplars. (Photograph taken in Indiana Pioneer Mother's Memorial Forest by P. F. Heim, courtesy of the U.S. Forest Service.)

deciduous forests, because the parts of the biome have been in longer and more frequent contact (Figure 3.13).

Significant numbers of people occur only in the lower, warmer areas of the coniferous forest where logging and mining industries have been established and where some agriculture is possible. The more rugged, colder regions are sparsely populated by hunters and fur trappers.

**Figure 3–13** A typical coniferous forest, where plant and animal communities are adapted to high altitudes or latitudes and short growing seasons. This photograph was taken near Crescent City, Calif. (Photograph courtesy of the U.S. Dept. of Agriculture.)

Transition areas between the coniferous forest and grassland or desert contain broad-leaved evergreen and deciduous trees and shrubs, in addition to needle-bearing conifers. The woodland and **chapparal** of western North America are examples of these transition areas. Similar vegetation occurs around the Mediterranean Sea. Large portions of both regions are characterized by winter rains and dry summers.

TUNDRA. The tundra is the area between the tree line and perpetual snow and ice. It occurs both in the far north (arctic tundra) and on high mountains (alpine tundra). Vegetation consists of lichens, mosses, dwarfed heath-like bushes, sedges, and grasses. Trees could not grow in the arctic tundra even if they could withstand the rigorous climate, for the soil is always frozen a few inches below the surface. The plants that do grow in the tundra are those that can exploit the growing season of only a few weeks and can survive in the poorly-drained, mushy layer of topsoil that thaws during this season. Most reproduction is vegetative because there is not time for plants to grow from seed and set seed in their turn. The integrity of the vegetative cover is vital for maintenance of the soil, marginal as its quality is. One of the dangers of constructing oil and gas pipelines through the tundra is that, when vegetation is disturbed or permafrost is thawed, erosion is rapid and severe (Figure 3.14).

Animal species are few in number, but their populations are large. Many of the populations oscillate in 3 to 4 or 9 to 10-year cycles. Sometimes populations of predators and prey oscillate with a similar period but slightly out of phase with one another, as in the case of the lemming, a mouse-like creature, and the snowy owl. Since the lemming is the main food of the owl, it is tempting to postulate a causal relationship in this pattern, but such a

**Figure 3–14** The tundra, where plants are adapted to survive long, harsh winters, generally infertile soil, and growing seasons of only a few weeks. This photograph was taken in the Cape Dorset area, Northwest Territory. (Photograph by J. Feeney, courtesy of Information Canada Phototheque.)

relationship is difficult to prove. In environments where there are many microhabitats and many niches occupied by a great diversity of species, control mechanisms may exert a more steady and direct influence on populations than they do where the biotic community is less complex. Long-term stability of ecosystems in the tundra may be achieved through shorter-term oscillations in populations.

Most animal species in the far north are circumpolar in distribution. Birds take advantage of the summertime burst of vegetation which is accompanied by an explosion of blackflies, deerflies, and mosquitoes. Birds and the larger mammals migrate to avoid the winter cold and lack of food, some to the edge of the coniferous forest and some to havens farther south. Many small animals survive by burrowing under the insulating snow.

Man does not find the tundra an easy place in which to live. The hardy people who do make their homes here must make prudent use of the limited plant and animal life. In North America the Eskimo is largely confined to the coast, where he gets much of his living from the sea. Summers take him farther inland, where he hunts the caribou. Since most agriculture is impossible, fur-trapping is the chief source of income. In Eurasia the Lapp uses the reindeer for meat and milk and for pulling his sled. He, too, relies on fishing but attempts some agriculture below the tree line. The principal

**Figure 3–15** A prairie, such as the ones that covered much of the United States. This photograph was taken in Pottawatomie County, Kansas, site of the proposed Prairie National Park. (Photograph courtesy of the U.S. Dept. of the Interior, National Park Service.)

contributions that modern civilization has made to the people of the far north are overheated houses, respiratory infections, and a disorganized social order.

The alpine tundra is somewhat different from the arctic tundra. It is more fragmented in its distribution, it lacks permafrost, and its photoperiods are like those in the surrounding lowlands. Mammals, including man, must make physiological adjustments to low barometric pressure in order to live in the alpine tundra. Various aspects of this adjustment take place over the course of days or years. There is some indication that evolutionary adaptations have also taken place in populations that have long lived at high altitudes. On the Tibetan Plateau of Asia, a Mongolian culture has learned to practice limited agriculture in the sheltered valleys and uses the yak for power, clothing, and meat. Another culture has developed in the High Plateau of the Andes.

The tundra biome is commonly described as "fragile." Its fragility rests on the severity of its climate, on the shallowness and infertility of its soil, on the shortness of its growing season and on the relatively small number of species — a few hundred kinds of plants, compared to thousands in the tropics, a few dozen species of higher animals, some insects, soil invertebrates and microorganisms. Most food chains are simple and direct, such as lichens-caribou-man. If some part of the flow of energy and cycling of nutrients is disturbed, the system can take few, if any, alternative paths.

GRASSLAND.    Grasslands are widely dispersed over the world, both in temperate and tropical climates, where precipitation is too low and erratic and evaporation too high to favor growth of forests, and fires are frequent as a result of aridity. On the leeward side of the coastal ranges, the Sierra Nevada and Cascades, and the Rocky Mountains, the climate is very dry, as winds blowing in from the sea drop much of their moisture on the windward side, and evaporation over the adjacent plains is greatly in excess of precipitation. The vegetation is dominated by buffalo grass and other grasses only a few inches high. Winds bringing moisture from the Gulf of Mexico gradually increase the rainfall as you move eastward across the continent and the tall grass prairie begins. Species of bluestem reach heights of up to six feet. There is also a rich variety of flowering herbs. The soils of the tall grass prairie are among the richest in the world, because the amount of precipitation nearly equals the amount of evaporation, preventing large-scale leaching of nutrients from the soil (Figure 3.15).

It is in the grasslands that hoofed mammals and rodents reach their greatest abundance. Animals adjust to dry and cold seasons by becoming inactive or dormant or by migrating. In northern regions animal life above ground is scarce during the winter. Many species of animals are concentrated near small ponds, springs, and rivers; larger animals sometimes travel long distances daily to secure drinking water. The drying up of a waterhole is disastrous for the animals that depend on it.

The grassland was not extensively occupied by primitive man, although tribes of Eurasian nomads lived there with their herds of grazing animals. In Africa, overgrazing is thought to have destroyed the vegetative cover, reducing the ability of the soil to hold moisture and leading to expansion of the Sahara Desert. Indians in North America did not begin to use the grasslands on a large scale until they acquired horses that had escaped from the early Spanish explorers. Now, however, the prairie is the most productive agricultural land in the world, and the plains are widely used for grazing domestic animals.

DESERT.    Deserts are arid regions where the infrequent precipitation tends to occur in heavy downpours that result in most of the water running off before it can soak into the ground. Months or even years may go by with little or no rain; then suddenly, after a series of showers, the desert may burst into bloom. Small animals emerge from their dormancy, animals previously aggregated around waterholes scatter widely, and reproduction reaches a peak. When the ground dries out again, populations contract sharply and many species become dormant once more, to wait for the next wet period.

The vegetation is generally composed of short, widely-spaced bushes and shrubs, often leafless and thorny, and in the Western Hemisphere there is a rich variety of succulent cacti. Small rodents, lizards and snakes, and birds are the predominant animals (Figure 3.16).

**Figure 3–16** A desert biome, where arid conditions have led to ingenious adaptations in plants and animals for withstanding drought and making the most of rain when it comes. (Photograph courtesy of the U.S. Dept. of the Interior.)

Desert animals adapt to the hot, arid conditions in several ways. Many of them obtain their water entirely from morning dew, succulent food, or the oxidation of carbohydrates and fats in their diet. (The oxidation products of carbohydrates and fats are carbon dioxide and water. It is this "metabolic water" that sustains some organisms.) Desert animals have only slightly greater physiologic tolerance of the intense midday heat than animals from other biomes. They generally avoid the heat by becoming nocturnal or, at least, by becoming inactive at midday. Many occupy subterranean burrows or find other cover.

The desert is a difficult place for man to live in without an artificial source of water. When irrigated, the soil is often very productive. Irrigation brings its own problems, however, of accumulating salts and in some areas, such as the valley of the Nile River, of epidemic outbreaks of diseases carried by snails that live in the irrigation ditches. Plans have been made for large "nuclear-agro-industrial" complexes to be established in coastal deserts, with power from nuclear power plants used to desalinate seawater and provide energy for manufacture of fertilizer and other industries. These farms and related industries would support populations of several million people, although none of them has yet been developed. Even if successful, they could never be developed fast enough or on a scale to solve the food and population problems of the developing countries.

TROPICAL FOREST.    The tropical rain forest is a luxuriant broad-leaved evergreen forest which biologist Marston Bates compares to a cathedral, although he concedes that to many others it is a humid hell. The tropical rain forest grades into the tropical deciduous forest, the latter being characterized by having one or more months when rainfall drops below 10 centimeters and the leaves fall simultaneously from many of the trees. In general, the climate of the tropical forest provides copious precipitation during most months, high humidity, consistently high (but not excessive) temperatures, and a nearly constant photoperiod. While tropical forests occur on all continents, their flora and fauna differ. Among the primates, for example, lemurs, baboons, chimpanzees, and gorillas are found in Africa, the orangutan in Borneo and Sumatra, the macaques in northern Africa and the Orient, and the prehensile-tailed monkeys in South and Central America.

In contrast to the tundra, the tropical forest contains small populations of an incredible variety of species. There is nothing equivalent to an oak-hickory woods; if you come across a tree of one species, the next member of the same species may be half a mile away. Many families of plants that are represented only by herbaceous species in temperate climates grow as trees in the tropics. Ferns and grasses are not to be outdone: they occur as tree ferns and bamboo (Figure 3.17).

Everywhere are woody vines, or lianas, and epiphytes — the plants that grow on branches and trunks of trees. Among the epiphytes are ferns,

**Figure 3–17** A tropical forest, characterized by small populations of a very large number of species. Many plants and animals are specialized for life in the trees, never touching the ground. This photograph was taken at the Loquille Experimental Forest in Puerto Rico. (Photograph courtesy of the U.S. Forest Service.)

orchids, cactuses, and the strange plants called bromeliads, to which pineapple is related. Because they are not rooted in the ground, epiphytes must have adaptations for obtaining water and mineral nutrients. Many epiphytes trap pools of water in their leaves or flowers. These airborne pools are miniature ecosystems, harboring innumerable insects and other invertebrate animals and even tiny frogs.

Although populations of most animals are small, ants and termites are numerous. Cold-blooded species reach their maximum size, diversity, and vigor in the tropical forest. Mammals, on the other hand, tend to be smaller than their temperate relatives as well as sluggish and depressed metabolically. Most of the activity in the tropical forest occurs high in the trees.

Man has never found the dense tropical forest a favorable place to live. He moved into the forest in small numbers several thousands of years after he had dispersed into other biomes. Wherever man does inhabit the forest, he opens up the canopy and creates a forest-edge habitat in semblance of his more comfortable home on the savanna.

Where agriculture is practiced in the tropical forest, it is commonly of the slash-and-burn type. Portions of the forest are cleared and a variety of crops is planted. After 2 to 5 years the soil becomes depleted in nutrients, and it becomes increasingly difficult to hold back the regrowth of the forest. Plots are then abandoned and another area is cleared. This type of agriculture can be successful only where population pressure does not force extended periods of cultivation and decreased fallow periods. It is impossible to generalize about tropical agriculture because the quality of the soil varies so enormously. One secret seems to be a diversity of crops to prevent epidemics of pests and disease and to take advantage of different growth habits to exploit light, space, and nutrients. Attempts at intensive monoculture of cash crops are very often dismal failures.

TROPICAL SAVANNA.     In arid tropical climates trees occur in scattered groves, and grass forms a more or less continuous covering over the ground. The soil both here and in the tropical forest is easily depleted of nutrients and humus because of rapid decomposition, rapid reabsorption of nutrients by the vegetation, and extensive run-off and leaching. Conse-

**Figure 3–18**  Watering place at Ambaseli, an example of the tropical savanna biome. The typically African animals in view include plains zebras, yellow baboons, and a single bustard. Photograph by Irven and Nancy DeVore.

quently, the agricultural methods of temperate regions are not appropriate for the tropics, and the vast tropical lands will not become highly productive of food unless new agricultural procedures are developed.

The best formed and most extensive tropical savanna is in Africa. Here the prevalence of grass forage, the shelter of trees, and the presence of rivers and swamps provide habitats for the wildebeest, zebra, gazelle, antelope, elephant, hippopotamus, rhinoceros, giraffe, warthog, and African buffalo, and for their predators, notably the lion. The savanna is also home of the tsetse fly, parasitic scourge to man and domestic animals (Figure 3.18).

The tropical savanna is implicated as the ancestral home of man by his structural, physiological, and behavioral adaptations, fossil remains, cultural relics, and the proximity of related anthropoid primates. Many present-day inhabitants of the tropics, mostly Negroid races, are nomads with herds of cattle and goats. Others are hunters and fishermen. Still others, further advanced, are agriculturists. These cultures are all primitive in nature, lagging behind the highly developed industrial, agricultural, and economic exploits that man has achieved in regions more favored by climate and soil. Efforts of people in the tropical regions to improve their lives will sorely tax the resources of the earth and the patience, good will, and understanding of the already overdeveloped industrialized nations.

## MAN'S DOMINANCE OF THE BIOSPHERE

Man has escaped the dominance of other organisms to become a dominant himself. He has cleverly manipulated all aspects of his environment to fit his wants and needs. He has interrupted the progress of his own speciation by travel and cultural exchange and interbreeding. He has invaded unfavorable climates and biomes by controlling the microclimate around his person; he can even survive briefly on the moon. Through agriculture and the harnessing of many sources of energy he has appropriated an ever-increasing proportion of the earth's resources for himself. He has the potential to regulate his own population at the most suitable level.

Modern man is by no means near the end of this capacity for dominance. He may soon be able to solve the world health problem of infectious disease. He may emancipate himself from dependence on plants by industrial food production. He may produce a bioclimate independent of nature by air-conditioning entire cities or by controlling the climate itself. He may free himself from dependence on fossil fuels by harnessing either the sun or the atomic nucleus. He may go further than he has already gone in creating plants and animals according to his own design, through "genetic engineering." He may even apply these methods to himself.

This awesome ability for evolving an anthrosphere (man-world) or a noosphere (mind-world) brings equally awesome hazards. By creating a new set of conditions, dominance frequently brings about its own destruction. Dominant man must therefore understand the role he plays, acknowledge his limitations, and be prudent in exercising his powers. He may be able to anticipate and defend himself against the effects of natural laws, but he cannot ignore them with impunity.

## REFERENCES

BATES, M. 1960. *The Forest and the Sea.* New York: Time Inc.

BOUGHEY, A. 1971. *Man and the Environment: An Introduction to Human Ecology and Evolution.* New York: Macmillan.

COLINVAUX, P. 1973. *Introduction to Ecology.* New York: John Wiley & Sons.

DARLINGTON, P., JR. 1957. *Zoogeography.* New York: John Wiley & Sons.

HUNTINGTON, E. 1924. *Civilization and Climate.* New Haven: Yale Univ. Press.

KENDEIGH, S. 1974. *Ecology, with Special Reference to Animals and Man.* Englewood Cliffs, N.J.: Prentice-Hall.

KORMONDY, E. 1969. *Concepts of Ecology.* Englewood Cliffs, N.J.: Prentice-Hall.

PLATT, R., AND J. WOLFE. 1964. Ecology: Introduction. *BioScience.* 14(7): 9–10.

SOUTHWICK, C. 1972. *Ecology and the Quality of Our Environment.* New York: Van Nostrand Reinhold Co.

TIGER, L., AND R. FOX. 1971. *The Imperial Animal.* New York: Holt, Reinhart, and Winston.

# PART TWO

# Man's Physical Evolution

# · 4 ·

LAWRENCE I. O'KELLY

# The Basis of Human
# Evolution and Adaptation

Modern biology may be said to have begun when a substantial number of scientists rejected the hypothesis that life came about by a special act of creation. The creationist theory, explicit in Western theology, had long impeded man's insight. If all species owed their existence to a creator, there was little possibility of discovering the principles underlying their diversity, unless these principles were announced from on high, like the Ten Commandments, or could be inferred from examination of the created products. Religious literature was generally uncommunicative on the subject, but man's restless curiosity did give rise to attempts at inference.

In the early decades of the nineteenth century, many biologists agreed with the clergyman William Paley that "There cannot be design without a designer; contrivance without a contriver; order without choice; arrangement without anything capable of arranging; subservience and relation to a purpose, without that which could intend a purpose, means suitable to an end, and executing their office in accomplishing that end, without that end ever having been contemplated, or the means accommodated to it." If a man found a watch on a beach, he would not assume, said Paley, that the admirable arrangement of gears and cogs, of springs and hands, had happened by chance.

Along with others of his time, Paley also assumed the "fixity of species," based on the Biblical story of creation. It was logical enough to have a "watch . . . produce another watch, similar to itself," but it was inconceivable that a watch might produce another watch dissimilar to itself and perhaps more complex, without the intervention of a creator.

A few voices had now and then suggested another possibility, but they were ignored in the general contentment with the creationist theory. As early as the sixth century B.C., evolutionary thinking influenced Greek philosophy. In the latter part of the eighteenth century, Erasmus Darwin, grandfather of Charles, had boldly suggested that all animals were descended from one "living filament." About the same time, Jean-Baptiste Lamarck, calmly classifying invertebrates while the French Revolution raged in the streets outside, was impressed by the orderly progression from simple forms to complex. It seemed reasonable to him that animals adapted to environmental conditions by using certain of their parts and abilities and neglecting other, less-suitable ones. Use led to special development, while disuse led to atrophy, and the modifications acquired by an individual in its lifetime were passed on to its offspring. Thus the giraffe got its long neck and the elephant its trunk. (It would be amusingly possible, to a Lamarckian, that the remarkable elephant's trunk *did* originate in a chance tug-of-war between an overly curious elephant's child and a crocodile, as told by Kipling in his delightful story — so long as the stretched-out proboscis was as advantageous as it seemed to be.)

During the nineteenth century the study of fossils was accelerating, and discerning scientists were becoming increasingly dissatisfied with resorting to catastrophes like the Great Flood in order to explain them. Lamarck, for example, was aware that lower, and presumably older, strata of rocks contained less complex fossils than higher, younger strata. In the 1820s Charles Lyell began to publish his classical volumes in geology which, although in the beginning had nothing explicit to say about life of the past, were to have great influence on evolutionary and biological thought.

## CHARLES DARWIN AND THE PRINCIPLES OF EVOLUTION

Like many other naturalists before him, Charles Darwin was impressed by the variability and adaptedness of living things as well as by striking similarities among them. Unlike his predecessors, however, he became unable to credit these things to the virtuosity of a creator. Young Darwin was studying for the clergy when he got the opportunity to become the unpaid naturalist aboard the research vessel *Beagle*. He did not intend to rock the world with any new theories; he was merely eager to go to strange places, see new living things, and add modestly to the knowledge of natural history. Although interested in the ideas of his grandfather, and an enthusiastic collector of beetles, he had no quarrel with the religious dogma of his day.

His own observations and study of the work of others soon led him to dissatisfaction with the creationist theory, although he was at a loss for an alternative explanation. Writings of Charles Lyell and Thomas Malthus finally gave him the keys he needed. From Lyell he got the geological time scale with which to work, as opposed to the mere 6,000 years since Biblical creation supposedly occurred. Malthus gave him a selective force. Of the influence of Malthus on his thinking, Darwin wrote: "In October, 1838, that is, fifteen months after I had begun my systematic inquiry, I happened to read for amusement Malthus on *Population,* and being well prepared to appreciate the struggle for existence which everywhere goes on from long-continued obser-vation of the habits of animals and plants, it at once struck me that under these circumstances favourable variations would tend to be preserved, and un-favourable ones to be destroyed. The result of this would be the formation of new species. I had at last got a theory by which to work." This theory has five main steps in its argument:

1. *Each generation of reproducing adults yields offspring in excess of the number that survive to reproductive maturity.* If all, or even most, of the offspring did survive, there would be a population "explosion" of that species (such as we are witnessing in the human population today). As an extreme example Darwin quotes the elephant, "reckoned the slowest breeder of all known animals . . . it will be safest to assume that it begins breeding when thirty years old, and goes on breeding till ninety years old, bringing forth six young in the interval and surviving till one hundred years old; if this be so, after a period of from 740–750 years there would be nearly nineteen million elephants alive, descended from the first pair."

2. *The progeny show a range of variability in their individual traits.* This variability gives natural selection the material on which to work. Without it the ecologic influences discussed in Chapter 3 would have no effect on species at all — except perhaps to bring about their extinction, if conditions became intolerable.

3. *The excess population leads to the competitive struggle for survival.* As Darwin's theory became widely known, this proposition achieved a certain notoriety as an implicit (or sometimes quite explicit) part of various exploita-tive economic and social philosophies which argued that "struggle for survival" and "might makes right" were inseparable and inescapable laws of nature. These phrases bring to mind the image of general civil strife in the organic kingdom, with brother pitted against brother and all nature "red in tooth and claw," as Tennyson expressed it. But direct physical combat is only a small portion of the meaning Darwin gave to the struggle for surviv-al. In fact, the function of many behavioral adaptations — displays and bluffs of various sorts — is precisely to avoid the necessity for physical combat. The bird that sings loudly from his perch rarely actually needs to defend his territory. Darwin gave many examples of the "struggle." A plant on the edge of a desert struggles for life against an insufficiency of moisture; a plant which produces a thousand seeds of which only one will come to maturity struggles with other plants of its kind and of other kinds for a place in posterity; the mistletoe struggles with other plants in tempting birds to eat and thus disseminate its seeds.

4. *Competition leads to survival of the fittest and death of the least fit.* It is

important to remember that populations evolve, not individuals. We will say more about this in later sections. No matter what remarkable traits an individual may possess, they are of no consequence to the evolution of the species unless they become fixed in the population and eventually occur in a large number of individuals. This means that individual survival and adaptive excellence must be coupled with superior performance in reproduction — a situation which usually, but not always, prevails. "Fitness," in terms of evolution, means only reproductive success. The proof of fitness is survival into succeeding generations, regardless of whatever other strengths or weaknesses an individual might have. Beethoven, da Vinci, Washington, Lenin, and Schweitzer left no offspring. Their Darwinian fitness was zero.

5. *Progeny of those who survive to reproduce will inherit their parents' characteristics.* The problem that plagued Darwin throughout his studies was that, although he recognized the central role of heredity in evolution, he had no idea what the mechanism of heredity might be. The most widely held theory of the nineteenth century was that of blending inheritance, in which qualities of the two parents flowed together and blended much as blue ink mixes with red to give purple. Darwin was never able to reconcile this theory with his observations, for the blending theory would lead rather rapidly to a monotonous sameness of individuals in a population, and would resist any change thereafter. It was easier to accept Lamarck's ideas about the inheritance of acquired characteristics.

Despite problems with theory, however, Darwin had before him the obvious results of selection as practiced by man, and he eloquently compared these with what Nature with all of time and all possible characters and environments at her disposal could do: "Man selects only for his own good: Nature only for that of the being which she tends. . . . Man keeps the natives of many climates in the same country; he seldom exercises each selected character in some peculiar and fitting manner; he feeds a longer and a shorter beaked pigeon on the same food; . . . he exposes sheep with long and short wool to the same climate. He does not allow the most vigorous males to struggle for the females. He does not rigidly destroy all inferior animals, but protects during each varying season, as far as lies in his power, all his productions. He often begins his selection by some half-monstrous form; or at least by some modification prominent enough to catch the eye or to be plainly useful to him. Under nature, the slightest difference of structure or constitution may well turn the nicely balanced scale in the struggle for life, and so be preserved. How fleeting are the wishes and efforts of man! how short his time! and consequently how poor will be his results, compared with those accumulated by Nature during whole geological periods! Can we wonder, then, that Nature's productions should be far 'truer' in character than man's productions; that they should be infinitely better adapted to the most complex conditions of life, and should plainly bear the stamp of far higher workmanship?"

If the strains of plants and animals that man has "improved" are considered in this light, some problems associated with modern agriculture are explained. While nature selects for the overall balance of the organism with respect to its environment, man selects for meat, milk, egg, or wool production or for large and beautiful fruit. When he tries to select, in addition, for resistance to drought or disease, he must often compromise something else. High yield in grains is usually associated with relatively lower protein content. Most of man's creations could not survive without man to feed and shelter them, protect them from predators, parasites, and disease, and even help them to breed, bear, and raise their young. Corn would vanish in a season or two: it can no longer shed its seed.

In natural selection, as opposed to selection practiced by man, characteristics of each generation are largely determined by differential rates of reproduction among individuals with different hereditary endowments. The actual hereditary material of the individual is its *genotype,* which constitutes the information that the individual can pass on to its offspring. The genotype is expressed in the *phenotype,* which represents the characteristics we observe and on which natural selection operates.

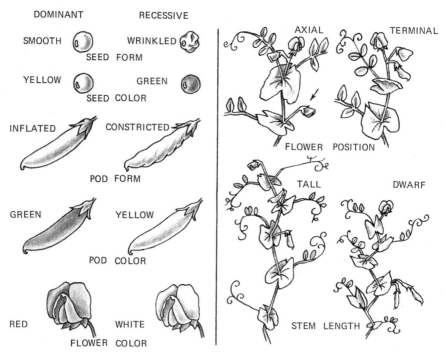

**Figure 4–1** The seven pairs of characters selected by Mendel for his genetic experiments with peas. By making many experimental crosses of plants with these characters, he was able to formulate his laws of genetics which are still basically valid. (Adapted from W. A. Jensen and F. B. Salisbury, *Botany: An Ecological Approach*, Wadsworth Pub. Co., Belmont, California, 1972, p. 176.)

## PHYSICAL BASIS OF INHERITANCE

While Darwin explained how natural selection acts, he could not explain the mechanisms of heredity and variation. This was begun by an Austrian monk named Gregor Mendel, who was working on his definitive experiments at the very time when Darwin was struggling to find a theory of inheritance compatible with his theory of evolution. The explanation was completed, in principle, more than a century later with the cracking of the genetic code.

*MENDEL'S EXPERIMENTS.*    Like Darwin, Mendel had no idea of the physical and chemical basis of heredity, but through careful experimentation he showed that inheritance was not a blending of characteristics as had been thought. He worked with pea plants, selecting for study seven characteristics that were clearly defined and remained defined through successive generations (Figure 4.1). Some results of his experiments are shown in Table 4.1. From data of this type he formulated his famous "laws" of genetics. These laws are now known to be greatly oversimplified, as a result of the way in which Mendel selected the traits he studied. However, they describe approximately how a great many traits are inherited, and they provided a

**TABLE 4.1**
**Mendel's Experiment**

When Mendel crossed plants having contrasting traits, he found that the offspring in the first generation uniformly resembled one parent or the other. The trait that appeared was dominant; the one that was masked was recessive. The results of seven types of crosses are shown below. Smooth × Wrinkled means smooth crossed with wrinkled.

| | |
|---|---|
| Seed form: | Smooth × Wrinkled = Smooth (∴ smooth is dominant) |
| Seed color: | Yellow × Green = Yellow |
| Flower position: | Axial × Terminal = Axial |
| Flower color: | Red × White = Red |
| Pod form: | Inflated × Constricted = Inflated |
| Pod color: | Green × Yellow = Green |
| Stem length: | Tall × Short = Tall |

When plants from each of these crosses were crossed with each other, the masked traits reappeared in the numbers shown below.

| Trait | Dominant | Recessive | Ratio, D:R |
|---|---|---|---|
| Seed form | 5474 smooth | 1850 wrinkled | 2.96:1 |
| Seed color | 6022 yellow | 2001 green | 3.00:1 |
| Flower position | 651 terminal | 207 axial | 3.14:1 |
| Flower color | 705 red | 224 white | 3.15:1 |
| Pod form | 882 inflated | 229 constricted | 2.95:1 |
| Pod color | 428 green | 152 yellow | 2.82:1 |
| Stem length | 787 tall | 277 short | 2.84:1 |

theoretical basis for the fruitful research of the first decades of the twentieth century.

To explain his data, Mendel postulated that hereditary traits were determined by discrete factors or "elemente," which later came to be called *genes*. They occurred in pairs, one of the pair coming from each parent. If both members of the pair are the same, the organisms will breed true from generation to generation. If they are different, one of them, the *recessive*, will be masked in the first generation and the other, the *dominant*, will be fully expressed. When *gametes* (male and female reproductive cells, typically sperm and eggs) form, the elemente are passed on to them, but only one member of each pair occurs in each gamete. This is the *principle of segregation*, Mendel's first law.

Mendel's second law, the *principle of independent assortment*, states that each trait is inherited independently of the rest. In the case of Mendel's peas, this means that if a plant has red flowers, the fact that the flowers are red has no relationship to whether the plant is tall or short or the pods are green or yellow.

THE DISCOVERY OF CHROMOSOMES AND THEIR BEHAVIOR. When Mendel first reported his work in 1865, cytology, the study of the cell, was in its infancy and chromosomes had not yet been discovered. When chromosomes were described in the 1870s, many scientists branded them artifacts of the staining procedures. By the 1880s, however, cytologists had followed the chromosomes through all stages of nuclear division. They observed that the number of chromosomes in the body cells of any species is constant, and that when the nucleus divides during *mitosis*, the chromosomes are always distributed between the two daughter cells so that each receives a full complement (Figure 4.2). They also observed that the gametes contain only half as many chromosomes as the body cells. But Mendel's papers lay forgotten, and the relationship between these discoveries and Mendel's work was not appreciated.

Cytology and genetics were united through the work of Walter Sutton in 1902. Sutton was studying the process of *meiosis*, which results in the formation of gametes, as shown in Figure 4.3. He saw that the chromosomes came together in pairs and that the members of the pairs resembled each other. Some pairs were long, some short, some joined at their ends, some in their middles, and so on. Chromosomes evidently occurred in **homologous** pairs, which remained independent during ordinary nuclear division but came together for the production of gametes. When meiosis was complete, each sperm and each egg had half the number of chromosomes that characterized the body cells. This **haploid** complement consisted of one member of each homologous pair. At fertilization the **diploid** number was restored in the new individual. It occurred to Sutton that the chromosomes behaved like the elements postulated by Mendel. They came in pairs, they main-

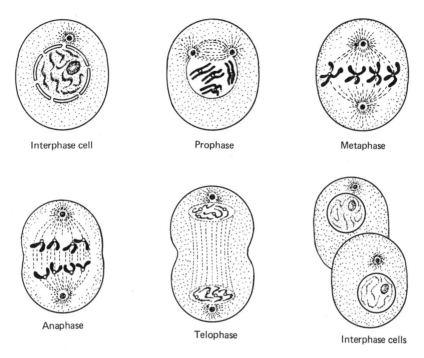

Interphase cell   Prophase   Metaphase

Anaphase   Telophase   Interphase cells

**Figure 4–2**   Phases of nuclear and cell division in an animal cell. When prophase begins, chromosomes have doubled; and in the events that follow first the chromosomes and then the cell divide. Each new cell contains the same complement of chromosomes as the original cell. (Adapted from Karl F. Guthe, *The Physiology of Cells*, Macmillan Co., New York, 1968, p. 34.)

tained their identity throughout successive generations, and they assorted independently of one another at meiosis, coming together in new combinations in each generation. (Now it is clear that Mendel's experiments worked out so nicely because each of the seven traits he selected for study was governed by a different one of the pea plant's seven pairs of chromosomes. If two of the traits had been controlled by the same chromosome, they would not have assorted independently. In genetic language, they would have been "linked.")

There are many genes on each chromosome. We would expect them to be passed on in a group, but this is not always the case. In most organisms the homologous chromosomes tend to exchange segments with each other during meiosis. This phenomenon has great significance. It permits new combinations of genes within linkage groups. Suppose that a gene for a new and favorable characteristic arose on a chromosome that contained other genes not very favorable for survival. If the new gene were hopelessly linked with the detrimental ones, it would have little chance of establishing itself in the population, unless its advantages outweighed the disadvantages

**Figure 4–3** Stages of meiosis. Two meiotic divisions typically result in formation of four nuclei, each containing half the number of chromosomes as the original cell. In the first meiotic division homologous chromosomes come together and form pairs. Crossing over (see text) occurs at the end of the first prophase, as shown in the diagram . The homologous chromosomes then separate, one member of the pair going to each new nucleus. This first division differs from mitosis in two ways: the daughter nuclei contain only half as many chromosomes as the parent, and the chromosomes themselves contain a different set of genes, having exchanged parts with their homologues. The second meiotic division resembles mitosis, as the chromosomes, which are double structures, divide 'and one set passes to each new nucleus. (Adapted from W. A. Jensen and F. B. Salisbury, *Botany: An Ecological Approach*, Wadsworth Pub., Co., Belmont, California, 1972, p. 144.)

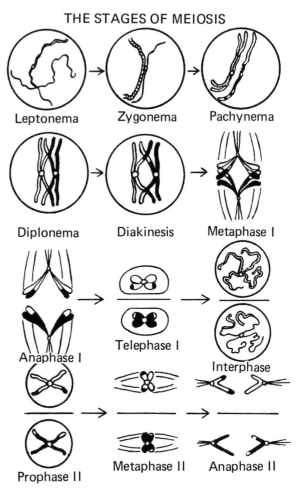

THE STAGES OF MEIOSIS

Leptonema  Zygonema  Pachynema

Diplonema  Diakinesis  Metaphase I

Anaphase I  Telephase I  Interphase

Prophase II  Metaphase II  Anaphase II

of its partners. If, however, it could become associated with the homologous chromosome and linked with more favorable genes, natural selection could enable its rapid spread throughout the population.

Many traits are not inherited in the simple way described by Mendel. These include traits like height and skin color — characteristics that span a range of values rather than occurring discretely like blue eyes or brown. They result from interaction or joint contribution of two or more pairs of genes, rather than a single pair. Other genes may express themselves incompletely or not at all in some genotypes — in the presence of certain other genes. For example, women carry the dominant gene for baldness as frequently as men, but they are not phenotypically bald because the gene cannot express itself.

MUTATION.    Natural selection explains the directing force behind evolution, and segregation and independent assortment of chromosomes explain the vast numbers of combinations of traits that are possible; but neither of these explains the source of the variation in genes. Without a mechanism for changing the genetic information, genetic recombination would lead only to randomness in the characteristics of a population, but not to any kind of sustained change, and natural selection could, at most, bring about increased frequency of certain combinations of genes under particular environmental conditions. In 1900 the botanist Hugo DeVries suggested that, although genetic instructions are usually passed from one generation to the next with amazing fidelity, there are sometimes mistakes or changes. A sudden and relatively permanent change in the hereditary material is called a *mutation*. Mutations are the source of the variation on which natural selection works.

We now recognize four major kinds of mutations. The first is a change, usually a chemical substitution of one molecule for another within a single gene. The second is a change in a group of genes on a chromosome. This change may take the form of deletion of a segment of chromosome, duplication, or inversion. If the normal order of genes is represented by A B C D E F G, then A B F G would represent a deletion, A B C D E C D E F G a duplication, and A B E D C F G an inversion. The third kind of change involves an entire chromosome. A chromosome may be lost during the process of mitosis or meiosis, or a cell may receive an extra one. Sometimes a piece becomes broken from one chromosome and reattached to the end of another, a type of mutation which is called a translocation. Finally, the entire complement of chromosomes may be duplicated one or more times, giving rise to an organism that is triploid, tetraploid, or characterized by an even higher level of ploidy. Mutations involving major chromosomal changes are usually lethal or severely incapacitating to animals, but among plants they contribute significantly to formation of new species.

The known causes of mutation are radiation and various chemicals. There are also "mutator genes," which increase rates of mutation in their carriers; and it is possible that some mutations "just happen," without any identifiable cause.

Living things have always been exposed to a certain amount of background radiation, arising from cosmic rays, solar radiation, and decay of radioactive elements in the earth. The activities of man promise to increase this exposure by a factor of two or more, through use of X-rays and radioactive elements in medical diagnosis and therapy, and use of nuclear energy. What radiation actually does is to impart energy to atoms and molecules in the cell, causing their **ionization** and leading to broken chemical bonds and chemical changes.

A chemical that causes mutation is called a *mutagen*. Mutagens are

## CHEMICAL MUTAGENS

*The slogan "Better living through chemistry" heralds the chemical industry's role as benefactor of mankind. To be sure, chemical products serve people in many ways—preservatives keep food from spoiling, pesticides shield crops from the ravages of insects, and miracle drugs save countless lives. Yet behind the promise of well-being and abundance lurks a serious threat to human life, namely, genetic mutation.*

*Evidence of birth defects due to chemical agents was dramatically revealed in 1962 during the thalidomide disaster, when severe deformities in infants were traced to their mothers' use of the drug thalidomide during pregnancy. Although most chemical compounds are not likely to produce such tragic consequences, the gene mutations and chromosome breaks caused by prolonged exposure to certain chemicals are clearly cause for concern.*

*Since the middle of the last century there has been an explosive increase in the number of chemical compounds in our environment, primarily as a result of developments in synthetic organic chemistry and the related pharmaceutical industry. Human contact with potential mutagens has intensified through the widespread use of insecticides for fruits and crops; the addition of compounds for buffering medicine, coloring food, and preserving meat and poultry; the injection of hormones for fattening; and so forth. Thus man is regularly exposed to many compounds that did not even exist a short time ago and whose mutagenic potential is unknown. The number and variety of these chemicals and the extent of exposure continue to escalate.*

*Some scientists think that chemical agents may account for more genetic damage and birth defects than do all sources of radiation combined, including cosmic rays, natural radioactivity in the earth's background, fallout, and the*

naturally present in low concentrations in many foods we eat. Exposure to small amounts of them is unavoidable, just as exposure to the background radiation around and in us is unavoidable. However, many drugs, poisons, and other substances that we use with increasing frequency are also mutagens, and use of these materials requires understanding and caution.

## CHEMICAL BASIS OF INHERITANCE

In the first half of the twentieth century, scientists studied the inheritance of many characteristics and related their observations to the structure and behavior of chromosomes. They even "saw" genes in the giant chromosomes in salivary glands of certain insects (Figure 4.4) and were able to correlate various abnormalities in the insect with deviations from the usual *effects of natural radioactivity in the human body. Chemically, there are several ways mutagenesis can take place. Mutagens can directly modify the DNA molecules of chromosomes or, in the case of most drugs, they can intervene in the normal process of chromosome division. Rather than producing obvious physical deformities, genetic mutation is often expressed as a shorter life span, lower resistance to disease, infertility, and general physical weakness; moreover, many mutagens are known to cause cancer.*

*How can human populations be protected from these dangers? At least two safeguards might be considered. First, a standard testing technique should be devised to detect mutagenicity in new chemical compounds. As yet the testing of compounds for genetic activity is highly complex: mutations range from drastic lethal changes to changes so subtle that detection presents difficult technical problems. Financial support for research to develop an efficient testing technique must be encouraged.*

*In addition, some scientists recommend that a program of population monitoring be instituted to warn public health officials of a possibly dangerous rise in the rate of mutation. A sample of the population could be selected and their blood analyzed to check for protein loss or abnormality, a sign of mutation. If the rate of protein damage were to exceed an acceptable level, exposure to mutagenic agents could be assumed and further tests performed to identify the agents. Although implementing such measures may pose difficulties, we cannot afford to ignore the menace of chemical mutagens in our environment. The health and vitality of tomorrow's children may depend on the precautions we take today.*

*Source: Maureen Harris, "Mutagenicity of Chemicals and Drugs," Science 171(1971):51–52.*

pattern of bands in the chromosomes. Biochemists found that some mutations led to lack or non-function of specific enzymes, the proteins which mediate chemical reactions within a cell. This condition came to be called an "inborn error of metabolism." The idea that each gene was responsible for production of a particular protein (or enzyme) followed naturally. Still, no one knew what a gene actually was or how it worked.

As frequently happens in science, clues had been around for a long time. In 1869 a German chemist named Friedrich Miescher had extracted a new substance from the **nuclei** of cells. He called it nucleic acid. It later became known more precisely as deoxyribonucleic acid, or DNA, and a related molecule, ribonucleic acid (RNA) was also discovered. In 1914 another German, Robert Feulgen, found that DNA had a striking affinity for the dye fuchsin. The Feulgen staining method was eventually refined to the point where it gave a semi-quantitative estimate of the amount of DNA in a

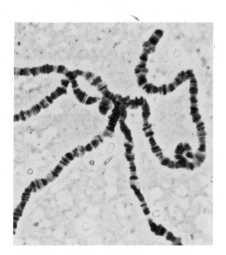

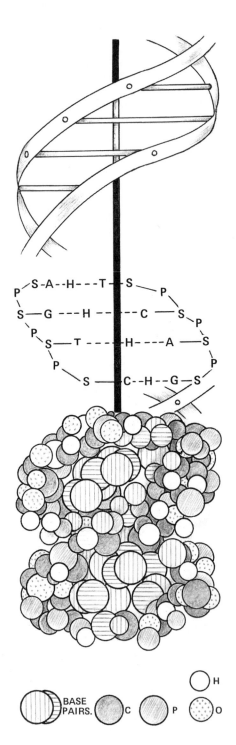

**Figure 4–4** Photomicrograph of giant chromosomes in the salivary gland of a *Drosophila* larva. The pattern of light and dark bands corresponds closely with the arrangement of genes on chromosome maps developed from analysis of experimental breedings. For example, deletions or duplications of chromosome segments could be identified microscopically and their effects seen as specific abnormalities in the affected flies. (Photograph courtesy of Juan Valencia, Dept. of Genetics, University of Wisconsin.)

**Figure 4–5** The double helix of DNA. At the bottom of the diagram is a molecular model of DNA, with different-sized circles representing different atoms or atomic groupings. Experiments with models such as this to see which structure best fit experimental data led Watson and Crick to their discovery of the structure of DNA. The center of the diagram shows schematically the arrangement of nucleotide building blocks and their component parts, with the base pairs held together in the center of the helix by hydrogen bonds. The top part of the diagram shows very simply the double sugar-phosphate backbone of the molecule, with the base pairs in the middle like rungs in a twisting ladder.

cell; but in 1914 even the discoverer of this remarkable technique did not think it very important.

Chemical analysis showed DNA to consist of a sugar, a phosphate group, and four nitrogen-containing bases, in proportions suggesting that DNA was composed of a series of units containing a sugar, a phosphate, and one of the bases. Such a unit was called a *nucleotide*. Because it appeared at first that the four bases were present in approximately equal amounts, scientists assumed that the nucleotides were grouped in clusters of four, and that DNA was built from these probably identical tetranucleotide building blocks. In this case the molecule was repetitiously dull and could never store the information necessary to tell an organism how to become a man — or even a jellyfish.

Interest in DNA began to revive when the biochemist Avery showed that DNA was the agent from dead bacterial cells that could impart new genetic information to related strains of living cells. More clues came from studies of viruses that infect bacteria. It was known that viruses consist only of protein and nucleic acid, one of which must contain the information needed for the production of more viruses. Then it was shown that the protein remains outside the bacterial cell, and only the nucleic acid enters to participate in synthesis of new viruses. After James Watson, Francis Crick, and Maurice Wilkins elucidated the structure of DNA in 1953, there was no longer any doubt that this molecule had all the properties necessary for the coding and precise transmission of genetic information generation after generation.

Watson and Crick described the now-famous *double helix,* a structure like a twisted ladder with the side pieces built from alternating molecules of sugar (deoxyribose) and phosphate and the rungs represented by pairs of nitrogen bases weakly held together by hydrogen bonds (Figure 4.5). Geometrical and chemical restrictions make it possible for these bases to pair in only one way: the purine adenine with the pyrimidine thymine, and the purine guanine with the pyrimidine cytosine. The pairs can occur in any order, however, and in this order information is stored. Since there is an essentially infinite number of arrangements of the four "letters" of the "code," an essentially infinite number of genetic messages can be coded. At last, too, it became clear in principle how the genetic information is duplicated. The hydrogen bonds between base pairs are broken, separating the strands of the helix, and each half of the helix reconstructs its partner from molecules present in the nucleus.

*THE NATURE OF A GENE.*    The concept of the gene has undergone consistent revision and refinement since the time when one gene was thought to control one "trait" — which might be anything from a bad temper to curly hair. Many of the traits we observe are controlled by a number of genes, and, conversely, the effects of one gene may be widespread and manifest in a number of traits. For example, substitution of a single base in the DNA sequence that codes for one of the amino acid chains in hemoglobin results in substitution of valine for glutamic acid in a critical position. This abnormal hemoglobin causes "sickling" of red blood cells, which shortens their life and leads to circulatory disturbances and accumulation of sickle cells in the spleen. Because the red cells are rapidly destroyed, there is a tendency to anemia, physical weakness, and impaired mental function. Circulatory problems lead to heart failure, brain damage and paralysis, and damage to other organs, especially the kidneys. Accumulation of sickle cells in the spleen may also cause irreversible damage to this organ.

The "one gene-one enzyme" hypothesis was a step in the right direction, but even that is only an approximation. Today the definition of a gene is much more complex. It can be defined as a sequence of nucleotides in DNA which codes for the synthesis of one chain of amino acids. Many enzymes are made up of a number of chains, each of which is formed through the action of a separate gene.

During the course of evolution, genes for the individual parts of an enzyme and for the several enzymes involved in one sequence of biochemical reactions (as, for example, the synthesis of an amino acid) have often come to occupy adjacent locations on a chromosome. Along with this clustering of genes has evolved a system for controlling their action as a group. We now recognize a class of "operator" genes which are a sort of master switch turning on or off whole blocks of "structural" genes that code for amino acid sequences. In addition, there are "regulator" genes which produce a product that controls the master switch itself. One of the nagging problems in biology has been to understand the diversity in form and function of cells in an organism if each cell contains, as we believe it does, the same genetic information as all the rest. Clearly, not all the information in each cell is utilized, at least not at all times, but this is more an observation than an explanation. Understanding of the function of regulator and operator genes may go far toward explaining the complex web of events in the development of an organism (see Chapter 7). It has been suggested that the number of structural genes may not differ widely between simple organisms and complex ones, but that complex organisms require extensive regulatory systems to integrate activity of structural genes. This may account for the larger quantities of DNA per cell in complex organisms. Perhaps, too, the regulatory functions reside in the highly redundant DNA sequences, which, again, would explain why greatest levels of redundancy occur in higher life-forms. Certainly the coded developmental program for a fish, an insect, or a tree is much more complex than that for a bacterial cell or blue-green alga — which divides and is done with it.

## GENETICS OF POPULATIONS

A population is any group of interbreeding individuals. The total of all genes in the population is the *gene pool*. If breeding within a population is random (that is, there is no bias that makes one type of individual favor or discriminate against another as a mate), and if no gene is being selected for or against, then each gene will have a probability of being sampled that corresponds to its frequency in the population, the gene pool will stay constant, and the average genotype will show little change from generation to generation. This situation is at best only approximated in real life. Even so, in a population that is well adapted to its environment, heredity is a conservative force, resisting change.

Genetic variability arises through mutations and is maintained in a variety of complex, often subtle, ways. The different forms of a gene are called *alleles*. If an organism carries the same allele on both members of a pair of chromosomes, it is *homozygous*. If the alleles are different, it is *heterozygous*. Frequencies of alleles in a population are determined by the rate at which they arise by mutation, by the rate at which they are lost by further mutation (including mutation back to the original form), by migration into and out of the population, and by differential rates of reproduction of various genotypes.

Because few mutations are truly neutral — that is, have no selective advantage or disadvantage — geneticists have tried to learn how different forms of a gene can coexist in equilibrium in a population. Very harmful dominant mutations tend to be eliminated about as fast as they arise, but harmful recessives are another matter. A recessive mutant can spread under cover for many generations before a chance mating brings two mutant genes together and the trait is expressed. One surprising revelation of population genetics is that, no matter how rare a homozygous recessive trait may be, the number of heterozygotes for that trait is surprisingly large. Let us look, for example, at the frequencies of several disorders that are inherited as recessive genes in man.

| Disorder | Percent of Population Affected | Percent of Heterozygous Carriers in Population |
|---|---|---|
| Diabetus mellitus (Where inheritance is clear) | 0.5 | 13 |
| Albinism | 0.005 | 1.4 |
| Phenylketonuria | 0.004 | 1.2 |
| Amaurotic family idiocy | 0.0025 | 1.0 |
| Alkaptonuria | 0.0001 | 0.2 |

These genes, harmful in varying degrees, are maintained in the population partly through recurrent mutation and partly because the rate of elimination of a deleterious recessive gene becomes progressively slower as its frequency decreases. In the case of phenylketonuria, heterozygous carriers outnumber those actually afflicted with the disorder by about 300 to 1. Even if new mutations never occurred and the recessive homozygotes never reproduced, it would take almost 100 generations — some 2,000 to 2,500 years — to halve the frequency of the gene in the population and decrease the frequency of the disorder by a factor of four. In fact, a state of equilibrium is reached at which the rate of gene loss through failure of homozygotes to reproduce is balanced by the rate of addition of new genes through mutation. For this reason, as well as on moral grounds, it is folly to advocate programs to prevent the reproduction of individuals homozygous for a rare trait in an attempt to eradicate the gene from the population. (Genetic counseling, on the other hand, provides an opportunity to prevent personal suffering.) To really eliminate a gene, heterozygotes, as well as homozygotes, would have to be prevented from reproducing. But since each one of us is heterozygous for a number of undesirable genes, such a program would eliminate people at the same time it eliminated particular genes.

Other factors act to maintain relatively high frequencies of genes that are deleterious in the homozygous state. Some genes may be harmful under certain conditions or in certain genotypes and beneficial in others. In races of fruit flies heterozygous for chromosomal inversions, the frequency of various homozygotes and heterozygotes changes with altitude, temperature, and food supply, and thus exhibits seasonal changes. Some populations of frogs have seasonal fluctuations in frequency of a gene for color pattern, as one phenotype shows increased survival over the winter but declines during the summer. In peripheral and suboptimal parts of its range, a species may exhibit little variability because environmental restrictions are so stringent that many phenotypes are selected against; but in the central, or optimal, part of the range, the entire spectrum of genes may be present.

It is not uncommon for the heterozygote to be better adapted than either homozygote. The classic example of this is the gene which, when homozygous, causes sickle-cell anemia. In regions where one type of malaria is prevalent, a large proportion of homozygous "normals" perish from this disease, while individuals homozygous for the sickle-cell trait succumb to anemia and its consequences. The hetrozygotes, however, are both relatively resistant to malaria and free from sickle-cell disease. Another situation that favors heterozygotes is that in which different alleles have adaptive advantages at different stages of the life cycle, as for example, larval and mature stages of an insect or prenatal and postnatal human life.

Each gene mutates with a characteristic frequency, and the same mutations tend to recur. Estimates of mutation rates and overall heterozygosity of populations are fraught with uncertainties. The rates at which dominant mutations arise are determined easily enough: they vary from less than one mutation per million gametes to about 100 per million in the known genetic disorders of man. Recessive mutations, however, may be difficult or impossible to detect, and there is no agreement on their rates. As for overall heterozygosity in populations, an altered protein is *a priori* evidence for an altered gene. Studies of proteins in fruit flies, with methods that detect slight changes in electric charge, suggest that the flies analyzed were heterozygous for a minimum of 12 percent of their genes. Many amino acid substitutions, however, cause no change in distribution of charge; and about one quarter of the base substitutions in DNA do not lead to amino acid substitutions. Thus only a fraction of the variants can be detected by the method used. For the human species, using the most conservative estimates for overall mutation rates and numbers of genes, the American geneticist Dobzhansky has concluded that there is more than one allele for at least 6,000 genes and each individual is heterozygous for 3,200 genes.

It is not an unmitigated curse that the same mutants occur again and again and persist even though they are harmful. A gene that is harmful in one time and place and genotype may be beneficial in another, and it may pay for a gene to try again. Genes not only act but interact — with other genes and with the environment. As the English biologist Julian Huxley expressed it, ". . . the offer made by a mutation to the species is not necessarily a final offer. It may be merely a preliminary proposal, subject to negotiation. Biologically this negotiation is effected in the first instance by recombination and secondarily by mutation in the residual gene-complex. It can lead to a marked alteration in the effects of the mutation, which may make the proposal acceptable to the organism." *(Evolution in Action.)* From the moment of its conception each individual must develop the right structures and functions at the right time. It must withstand infection and all the vicissitudes of the environment. It must compete within its species and without, and finally, it must obtain a mate and engage in a fertile mating. In this long and exacting process the unmitigated effect of a single gene acting alone is seldom the sole cause for success or failure.

*EFFECTS OF NATURAL SELECTION ON POPULATION GENETICS.* Large populations that are well adapted to their environments often remain remarkably stable over long periods of time. (The species of crustacean *Triops cancriformes* is about 170 million years old.) It is only when a population is placed under environmental stress or artificial selection imposed by man that the extent of its latent variability becomes evident. When the environment changes, organisms must change or become extinct. The fossil record is rich with both kinds of examples.

Variability in a population is a defense against environmental change. Organisms that reproduce prolifically, maintain a high degree of variability, or have high rates of mutation are well prepared to meet almost any environmental contingency. Bacteria, insects, and rodents are notorious for their ability to adapt to almost any conditions man or nature can devise.

Chapter 3 stressed the adaptation of an organism to its environment. Now we see that it is not the individual organism but the population that adapts. When environmental conditions change, natural selection favors the differential survival and reproduction of certain phenotypes, thus changing the composition of the gene pool. This is evolution.

Sexual selection is a special case of natural selection. The distinctiveness of the sexes, not only in the actual reproductive structures but in all the secondary sex characteristics, led Darwin to ponder the possible value of the prominent plumage of male birds, the antler growth of male deer, and the striking differences in vocalizations of the males of many species. Traits possessed by only one sex are less likely to have survival value for the individual than to influence its success in attracting a mate. Thus structural and behavioral characteristics related to sexual activity and reproduction are added to the traits that determine the gene pool of future generations.

SPECIES MODIFICATION.     Ecologic influences on species modification discussed in Chapter 3 can now be seen in the light of what we have said about population genetics. The American geneticist Sewall Wright has classified the mechanisms by which gene frequencies change, although it is important to remember that any one of these processes is rarely, if ever, the sole cause of change. There are directed processes, random processes, and unique events. Directed processes include recurrent mutations, recurrent migration and crossbreeding, and selection. Random processes are best illustrated by accidents of sampling of the gene pool. A unique event may be a favorable *new* mutation, a unique **hybridization,** a unique selective incident, or a unique and catastrophic reduction in numbers.

One of the most effective mechanisms of speciation is isolation. When a population is divided, the gene pool is also divided, so that changes brought about by mutation, selection, or chance in one subpopulation cannot influence the course of events in the other. Most isolation has come about through formation of climatic or geologic barriers. The effect of the barrier is not only to divide the gene pool, but to present different environments and different selective criteria for the subgroups.

Another evolutionary mechanism is dispersal, or migration. Animals tend to move out of regions in which they are under stress. In dispersing, the group may move into habitats posing different challenges and therefore altering the criteria for survival. Genetic effects of dispersal into multiple new habitats may be compounded if each habitat is preferentially colonized by individuals with particular phenotypes, as would be expected if each phenotype sought the environment to which it was best adapted. Some of the great migrations of geological history took place during periods of widespread climatic and geological change. Some of the species involved found new habitats similar to their old ones, where they could continue much as before. Others were unable to adapt fast enough to new or changing conditions and became extinct. Sometimes one or more subgroups of the species found conditions under which they could survive, and the parent species gave rise to one or more new species while it, itself, became extinct. The vast majority of extinct forms have no living descendants. Conversely, the 2 million or more living species arose from a handful of species from the remote past.

Some cases of species modification may be explained on purely statistical grounds. Evolution is controlled by an interplay of the forces of mutation, selection, and chance. In small populations, chance may be the strongest of these, as laboratory experiments have illustrated. If several small samples of fruit flies are taken at random from a wild population and the members of each sample are allowed to breed among themselves for many generations, the resulting populations will become distinctive even though they are maintained under identical conditions. Or if populations are derived from only a few breeding pairs, with breeding pairs for successive generations selected at random, unfavorable genes may become fixed and favorable genes lost, even though the initial frequencies of the alleles were the same.

When man practices rigorous selection for a particular trait, he can bring about remarkable change in relatively few generations, but usually at the cost of overall vigor or reproductive success. For example, if breeders of egg-laying chickens select only for the rate of egg-laying, problems of fertility, hatchability, malformation of chicks, egg quality, and various aspects of development arise. It is as if man selects for one trait so fast that the rest of the genotype cannot keep up, and the organism becomes unbalanced. Nature does not do this. She selects entire organisms, not traits. Two other results have been observed in experiments on artificial selection. First, a plateau is usually reached beyond which change no longer occurs. Second, if selection is relaxed, the population reverts to a less extreme value of the trait selected for, although the new average value may be higher than the initial one.

## TIME SCALE OF EVOLUTION

After intensive study of Biblical records, James Usher, Archbishop of Armagh in Ireland in the 1600s, concluded that the earth was created in 4004 B.C., with the creation of Adam taking place on October 23 at approximately 9 a.m. Two centuries later, when calculations of the earth's age became based on rates of deposition of sedimentary rocks rather than counts of the generations since Adam, a vastly different time scale began to emerge. Darwin had a clear understanding of the processes of erosion and sedimentation and the awesome temporal scale on which organic evolution was projected, remarking that "consideration of these various facts impresses the mind almost in the same manner as does the vain endeavour to grapple with the idea of eternity." *(Origin of Species.)*

Modern estimates based on radiometric dating, added to a century of accumulated knowledge from geological mapping, place the age of our planet somewhere between 4 and 5 billion years. Determination of ratios of the **isotopes** of lead (one of which is "normal" and the rest derived from decay of radioactive elements) place the age of the oldest **meteorites** and the earth at 4.7 billion years. Table 4.2 suggests the relative scales of time in earth history, the evolution of life, and the affairs of men. Some of these dates are known with much more certainty than others — or at least there is more widespread agreement on them. For the earliest events there is some disagreement or lack of communication between geologists and biologists. Some of the conditions on the primitive earth that were involved in early chemical and biological evolution were discussed in Chapter 2.

Chemical evolution began some 3.5 billion years ago with the synthesis of amino acids and other nitrogen-containing compounds in the primordial seas. The step from nonlife to life may have been taken tentatively and many times. Recent probes into space in search of clues to extraterrestrial life have changed the question "would we recognize a primitive form of life if we saw it" from one of only theoretical interest to one of practical importance. We do know there would have to be self-reproducing molecules: "There are several reasons why the self-reproduction of particles is stressed as the essential step with which life commenced. Self-reproduction of neces-

**TABLE 4.2**
**How Long Ago?**

| | |
|---|---|
| Origin of the earth | 4,700,000,000 years ago |
| Chemical evolution | 3,600,000,000 years ago |
| First life forms | 3,000,000,000 years ago |
| Origin of photosynthesis | 2,000,000,000 years ago |
| First nucleated cells | 1,800,000,000 years ago |
| First multicellular organisms | 700,000,000 years ago |
| First vertebrate animals | 500,000,000 years ago |
| First land plants | 400,000,000 years ago |
| First mammals | 200,000,000 years ago |
| First primates | 70,000,000 years ago |
| First hominoids | 30,000,000 years ago |
| First hominids? | 15,000,000 years ago |
| First certain hominids | 5,000,000 years ago |
| First of genus *Homo* | 750,000 years ago |
| First *Homo sapiens* | 250,000 years ago |
| First art | 45,000 years ago |
| First agriculture | 10,000 years ago |
| First writing | 6,000 years ago |

sity implies growth through assimilation, maintenance of definite organization, and transmission of heredity . . . Self-reproduction and heredity may lead, through action of natural selection, to adaptation of the environment and to progressive evolution. Formation of the first self-reproducing particle, whatever might have been its precise chemical makeup, was at least potentially, the dawn of organic evolution. Although at present self-reproduction is not known to occur except in nucleoproteins, self-reproducing units of other composition might have occurred on earth or in other parts of the cosmos." (Theodosius Dobzhansky, *Evolution, Genetics, and Man.*)

In any case, after half a billion years of chemical evolution, primitive, self-reproducing life arose. Remains of these forms are not neatly preserved hard parts, as later fossils are, but organic substances chemically changed to varying degrees, or soft parts preserved as casts or impressions, or sedimentary materials formed by life activities of the organisms. Nevertheless, the origin of photosynthesis has been set at more than 2 billion years ago (well before free oxygen began to accumulate in the atmosphere) at a time when layers of oxidized rocks suddenly began to appear in the geologic record.

It took more than another billion years for the first multicellular animals to appear, but then change began to occur more rapidly. Ehrensvärd puts the ever-accelerating rate of change into perspective in his famous calendar analogy: ". . . we have gradually become conscious of the fact that our own evolution — to *Homo sapiens* from advanced primate — represents a minimal fraction of the time that has passed since the formation of the earth from cosmic dust. If we let this span of time symbolize one year, we find that from January 1 to December 1 there is little to be noted concerning organisms as we define them. By the middle of December, however, we can ascertain that life exists in the form of quite advanced organisms in the Cambrian seas. The latter part of the last week of the year finds dinosaurs in full activity and the prehistoric bird, *Archaeopteryx*, flying with difficulty between primitive pine trees. During the last two days of the year some newcomers appear on the scene, some mammals, the saber-tooth tiger representing their uninhibited vitality. During the last day, at 2300 hours the first man-like creatures appear: *Sinanthropus, Pithecanthropus*, and their African colleagues. The last minutes show the drawings in the Altamira cavern and the last glacial epoch. The last second of the year contains all the latest news: the fall of the Bastille, the battle of Trafalgar, Darwin's *Origin of Species*, two world wars, and the development of the vacuum cleaner. In the last tenth of a second come the utilization of atomic energy and fumbling attempts to reconstruct the origin of life." (*Life Origin and Development.*)

Perhaps we now glimpse the staggering truth that all of us, and all of the organisms sharing our contemporary scene, are alive because our ancestors, back through unbroken generations for more than 2 billion years, were well adapted and fortunate enough to survive and to reproduce.

## REFERENCES

DARWIN, C. 1896. *The Origin of Species.* New York: D. Appleton and Co.

DOBZHANSKY, T. 1970. *Genetics of the Evolutionary Process.* New York: Columbia Univ. Press.

FORD, E. 1964. *Ecological Genetics.* New York: John Wiley & Sons.

LERNER, I. 1968. *Heredity, Evolution, and Society.* San Francisco: W. H. Freeman and Co.

MANWELL, C., AND C. BAKER. 1970. *Molecular Biology and the Origin of Species.* Seattle: Univ. of Washington Press.

MAYR, E. 1963. *Animal Species and Evolution.* Cambridge: Harvard Univ. Press.

SIMPSON, G. 1967. *The Meaning of Evolution.* New Haven: Yale Univ. Press.

SRB, A., R. OWEN, AND R. EDGAR, EDS. 1970. *Facets of Genetics: Readings from Scientific American.* San Francisco: W. H. Freeman and Co.

WATSON, J. 1970. *Molecular Biology of the Gene.* New York: W. A. Benjamin Inc.

# · 5 ·

NORMAN D. LEVINE

# The Appearance of Man

Darwin was reluctant to trigger the uproar he knew was inevitable if he discussed the evolution of man. It was illogically possible for many people in the nineteenth and early twentieth centuries to accept the idea that other organisms had evolved, but not they themselves. Therefore, Darwin only alluded to man's origins in his first great book, *On The Origin of Species*, saving his theories on man for *The Descent of Man*, published twelve years later. If it was remarkable that Darwin could deduce the principles of evolution without any idea of the genetic mechanisms involved, it is even more remarkable that he had such keen insights into man's evolution with but one fossil ape and a few pieces of a Neanderthal man as evidence. He even postulated the African origin of man, a theory that enjoys wide acceptance today.

Both evolutionary and current taxonomic relationships among organisms are commonly illustrated by analogy to a tree. In the taxonomy of living forms, the twigs represent *species* (or perhaps subspecies or races, if the division is carried that far). Similar species are grouped into *genera*, which are the smallest branches. Genera are further grouped into *families*, families into *orders*, orders into *classes*, classes into *phyla*, and phyla into *kingdoms* — which are the main limbs branching from the tree of life. Except at the level of species, which is a clearly defined concept, these divisions are arbitrary; they merely provide a way to discuss various degrees of resemblance among organisms. Although the rules for assigning to each organism a genus and a species name have been generally accepted since Linnaeus developed the **binomial system of nomenclature** in the eighteenth century, the detailed classification of organisms has undergone constant revision, and there is no single classification accepted by all taxonomists. (Onions, for example, have been switched back and forth between the lily family and the narcissus family several times.) Classifying fossils is much more difficult than classifying living species because there is less information to go on; and disagreements among scientists in this field are correspondingly more frequent and spirited.

Modern methods of numerical analysis are influencing the traditional, intuitive approach to taxonomy by suggesting a degree of statistical correlation as a criterion for membership in each level of the taxonomic hierarchy. There is no ideal type, in the Platonic sense, against which each individual can be measured. There are only populations of variable individuals. Each taxonomic level is described by a constellation of features shared by its members in various degrees and combinations. Mammals, for example, are warm-blooded animals that nurse their young. *Most* of them are covered with fur or hair, *most* of them live on land, and *most* of them walk on four legs.

Because the taxonomic tree has no time sense, it can tell you that your house cat is related to the ocelot in the zoo, without giving any clue about just which ancestor they have in common. In the same sense, you are related to the gorilla in the zoo, but he clearly cannot be your ancestor because he is your contemporary. The evolutionary tree attempts to show ancestral relationships—the oldest and most basic modifications appearing near the trunk, with progressively more recent and more minor ones occurring in progressively smaller branches. As in the taxonomic tree, the twigs are species, but they include forms both living and extinct.

"Common ancestors" are located at branch points. The search for ancestral forms (popularly called "missing links," a term coined by P. T. Barnum for some of his side show attractions) is the search for organisms showing a tendency toward one or more basic traits of the group but with no marked degree of specialization. The reasoning behind this is that once specialization occurs, evolution has not been known to reverse itself and produce less-specialized forms again. It is unlikely, for example, that man will return to walking on all fours or laying eggs.

Basic modifications are recognizable only in hindsight. Again, the element of time is involved. The changes that eventually enabled certain ancient fish to struggle overland for short distances would have been minor at first, only at the twig level. But an entire new class of vertebrates, the amphibians, arose from those creatures and invaded the land. Are comparable changes going on today? It is hard to tell. Some people consider man's achievement of culture a basic evolutionary modification, but we can only guess at its implications for further evolution. If man leaves no descendants, culture and his brain will have proved to be only a remarkable specialization and an evolutionary dead end.

A minor modification becomes major when it enables the diversification of the new type into many species that can either fill newly available environmental niches or displace older species in the existing ones. This process is called *adaptive radiation*. Adaptive radiation can take place very rapidly, geologically speaking. An "explosion" of new types occurred after the development of aerobic respiration, when metabolism became much more efficient and organisms no longer had to be protected from exposure to oxygen. When the early models of bony fish with jaws became perfected, they were highly mobile and successful predators which could spread through all the waters of the earth, adapting to different modes of life. The first amphibians shared the land only with plants and insects, on which they fed, and they enjoyed a period of rapid diversification and large populations until they were eclipsed by the more successful reptiles. Similarly, the mammals, which were inconspicuous little creatures during the age of reptiles, were able to expand rapidly when environmental conditions grew unfavorable for their cold-blooded predecessors.

The taxonomic classification of man is shown in Table 5.1, and his relationship to other living primates is in Figure 5.1. How he developed to his present form is the subject of the rest of this chapter.

### TABLE 5.1
### The Classification of Man

| | |
|---|---|
| Kingdom | Animal. Usually **motile** organisms that ingest their food. |
| Phylum | Chordates. Bilaterally symmetrical animals with internal supporting structure, either **notochord** or skeleton. Nervous system in a **dorsal** position. |
| Subphylum | Vertebrates. Animals with an internal bony or cartilaginous skeleton, and a spinal cord with a brain at the head end. |
| Class | Mammals. Warm-blooded animals with fur or hair, that nurse their young. |
| Subclass | Placental mammals. Developing embryos connected with the body of the mother by a structure called the placenta. |
| Order | Primates. Mostly **arboreal** animals that grasp by opposing their thumb and fingers. Have nails instead of claws on one or more of their digits. |
| Suborder | Anthropoids. "Higher" primates, with fine control of digits and great ability to learn. Characteristic dental structure. |
| Superfamily | Hominoids. Tailless primates with great freedom of arm movement. |
| Family | Hominids. Bipedal, tool-making primates. Terrestrial. |
| Genus | *Homo*. Modern man and his immediate ancestors. |
| Species | *Homo sapiens*. All postglacial and some earlier populations of man. |
| Subspecies | *Homo sapiens sapiens*. Modern man. |

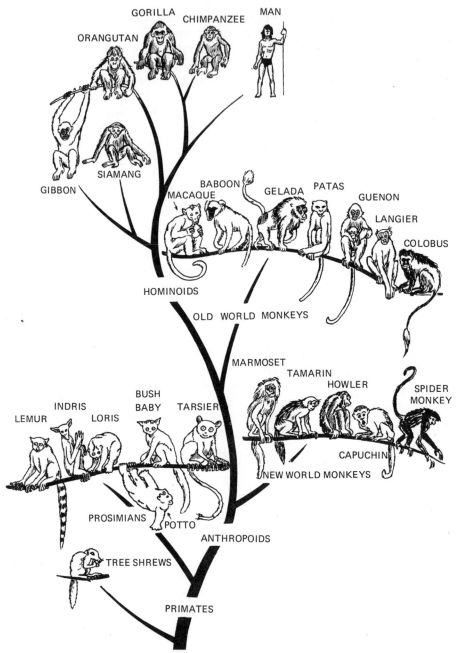

**Figure 5–1** The family tree of primates. Although there is an element of time represented in this grouping in that the tree shrews, for example, are at the bottom of the tree and represent the oldest and most primitive type of primate, it is important to remember that none of the animals illustrated is "our ancestor" because they are all our contemporaries.

## EVOLUTION OF THE PRIMATES

Although the ancestry of man theoretically could be traced through unbroken generations back to some self-replicating structure scavenging nutrients from the primitive sea, we will begin our genealogy with the origin of mammals. Table 5.2 shows the geologic timetable for the last 230 million years, with major climatic patterns and predominant forms of life, and the origins of major groups of animals.

Toward the end of the Triassic period, almost 200 million years ago, certain reptiles were beginning to show mammalian characteristics. There were subtle changes in their palates and lower jaws, and their teeth were differentiating into the various types characteristic of mammals, in contrast to the single type of reptilian tooth. In addition, the structure of their hip and shoulder girdles and the position of their legs were gradually changing, so that they could walk with their bodies raised from the ground instead of shoveling along, legs out sideways. It is impossible to know from their bones, however, whether they had taken the first steps toward maintaining a constant body temperature.

In the Jurassic period, lasting some 45 million years, reptiles of all kinds — but especially dinosaurs — flourished in the semitropical climates of widespread swampy lowlands. Other reptiles returned to the sea or took to the air. By now mammals, although small, inconspicuous, and rather rodent-like, had unquestionably arrived. They were working out a new system of reproduction and infant care. Instead of laying dozens or even thousands of eggs and leaving them to their fate, egg-laying mammals laid only a few. When they hatched, the mother cared for her infants and nursed them on a liquid she produced in her body. The duckbilled platypus is a descendant of these primitive egg-laying mammals. The rest of the new mammals bore their young alive but in embryonic form. The mothers nursed and protected them throughout the rest of their fetal and infant development in an abdominal pouch. These were the *marsupials,* of which the opossum is both a contemporary and a relatively ancient example.

The Cretaceous period witnessed several momentous events in evolution. The first flowering plants appeared. As with most evolutionary beginnings, there was little sign in these first forms that they would diversify rapidly to become the dominant plants over most of the earth. Another event, an ending, has captured the imaginations of perhaps more people than any other story in the book of evolution: the mighty dinosaurs met extinction. The obvious and accepted explanation is that the environment changed and they were unable to change adaptively along with it. Still, we would like to know exactly what happened. The climate became cooler, mountains rose up, and much of the swampland and lush swamp vegetation vanished. But were *all* the habitats of the great reptiles destroyed? Perhaps the dinosaurs could not compete with the newer animals that could, by keeping a constant body temperature, remain active when the

**TABLE 5.2**
**Geological and Biological Events in the Mesozoic and Cenozoic Eras**

| Era | Period | Epoch | Millions of Years Ago | Predominant and Emerging Forms of Life: Other Biological Events | Climate and Geological Events |
|---|---|---|---|---|---|
| Cenozoic | Quaternary | Recent | 0–0.011 | Modern man | Retreat of last glacier; emergence of middle latitude temperate forest |
| | | Pleistocene | 0.011–3 | Early man; extinction of many large mammals; spread of man throughout the world | Periods of glaciation alternating with climate similar to that of today; intermittent land bridge across Bering Strait; emergence of the tundra |
| | Tertiary | Pliocene | 3–10 | Modern genera of mammals; large carnivores and elephants widespread | Mountain building (Alps and Himalayas) and cooler, drier climate |
| | | Miocene | 10–25 | Full development of flowering plants; ancestral dogs and bears; abundant grazing mammals; ancestral gibbons and perhaps ancestral man | Spread of grassy plains; submergence of Bering land bridge; cooling |
| | | Oligocene | 25–40 | Modern families of mammals; ancestral apes and monkeys; large running mammals and first pigs | Warm climate, but arctic becoming colder; continents largely free of seas |
| | | Eocene | 40–52 | Modern orders of mammals; first cattle, horses, and elephants; migrations of prosimians over Bering land bridge | Warm climate; broad plains connecting North America and Asia across Bering Strait |

|  |  | Paleocene | 52–62 | Expansion of mammals and prosimian primates; dominance of archaic mammals; migrations of prosimians | Warm climate, widespread tropical forests |
|---|---|---|---|---|---|
| Mesozic | Cretaceous | — | 62–135 | First placental mammals, including first primates; first flowering plants; extinction of dinosaurs | Extensive swamps, followed by mountain building (Alps and Rocky Mountains) and cooler climates |
| | Jurassic | — | 135–180 | Age of reptiles, dinosaurs abundant; first birds; first egg-laying and marsupial mammals | Widespread swampy lowlands, warm climates |
| | Triassic | — | 180–230 | First dinosaurs and flying reptiles; modern corals; abundant coniferous trees; reptiles with some mammalian characters | Desert conditions over much of continents |

external temperature fell. It has been suggested, semifacetiously, that the upstart mammals hastened the departure of dinosaurs by eating their eggs. Perhaps the competition was real, if less flagrant. In any case, the dinosaurs are gone and the mammals are here, and the death of species is as necessary for evolution as the death of individuals.

During the Cretaceous the mammals were trying still another experiment in reproduction. The embryo developing inside the mother's body attached itself to the uterine wall by means of a structure called the *placenta*, through which the embryo obtained nourishment and excreted waste products. After it was born, its mother continued to nurse and care for it as other mammalian mothers cared for their young. By the end of the Cretaceous, three orders of placental mammals had begun to branch from the primitive stock: insect eaters or *insectivores*, represented by modern moles and shrews; *rodents*, with their continuously growing front teeth; and *primates*.

The earliest known primates appeared about 70 million years ago. They were small, primarily insectivorous creatures. Their surviving relative, *Tupaia*, looks something like a long-nosed rat (Figure 5.2). Not much

**Figure 5–2** The tiny tree shrew, *Tupaia*. Although these Southeast Asian animals have some primate characteristics, they are a far cry from even the most primitive prosimian. Their special interest lies in the fact that they are thought to straddle the fence between insectivores (among which they were formerly classified) and primates. Their ancestors took to the trees during the end of the Cretaceous, founding the order to which we belong, the primates. (Photograph courtesy of the San Diego Zoo.)

seemed to happen in primate evolution for the next 20 million years. The animals remained small, scurrying about on all fours on the ground and in the trees. Perhaps they were at an adaptive disadvantage to rodents on the ground, because they took to the trees completely about 50 million years ago and did not come down again to stay until they were almost men.

Mild climates and extensive forests during the next 10 million years encouraged diversification and global expansion of tree-dwelling **prosimians.** By now these animals had relatively large brains. Their snouts had become shorter and their eyes larger, reflecting the decreased value of smell and increased value of sight as a way of obtaining information about the arboreal environment. At the same time, their eyes were situated well forward in their heads, giving them a partially overlapping field of vision and making them the first animals to perceive a three-dimensional world.

Prosimians, like the earlier primates, climbed by grasping instead of by digging their claws into the trees. For this their thumb and great toe were set apart from the other digits, and nails replaced claws. Later, more intelligent higher primates would develop the prosimian hand still further for the precise manipulation of objects. These higher primates would replace prosimians as masters of the trees. Today only a few kinds of nocturnal prosimians survive in Asia and Africa, and some twenty species thrive on the island of Madagascar, where there are few rodents and no higher primates except man.

The higher primates evolved from prosimians between 45 and 35 million years ago. The newcomers, monkeys, were bigger, stronger, better coordinated, and, above all, more intelligent than their prosimian ancestors and cousins. The areas of their brain associated with vision, memory, learning, and manipulative ability were more highly developed, and their sense of smell was further reduced.

Since monkeys of the New World were geographically isolated from the scene of man's evolution, they are not considered to be in his ancestral line. Much of our information about the early development of the Old World monkeys and apes comes from one geological formation near Cairo, Egypt, where a variety of fossils foreshadowing the emergence of a number of later types has been found. Among them is a skull of the earliest known type of ape, dating to about 29 million years ago. This genus became widespread, extending from western Europe to China and throughout much of Africa. It is thought to be close to the common ancestry of the great apes (gorilla, chimpanzee, and orangutan) and man. Parts of another skull with gibbon-like characteristics suggest that the ancestral line of these apes had already begun to diverge.

Fossils of the earliest plausible ancestor of man *(Ramapithecus)* have been found in India, East Africa, China, and Europe, indicating that *Ramapithecus* was a widespread fellow. The oldest remains date to 15 million years ago. Specimens consist only of portions of jaws and teeth, however, and until other bones are found the relationship of *Ramapithecus* to man will remain controversial.

There is a gap in the primate record during the last 5 or 10 million years of the Tertiary period. When the record resumes, there are widespread remains of *Australopithecus,* earliest undisputed member of the family of man.

## THE DEVELOPMENT OF MODERN MAN

The study of the evolution of man has been marked by deductions that would make Sherlock Holmes proud, by mistakes and controversy, and even by a classic fraud — the Piltdown Man, cleverly fabricated from the skull of a man and the jaw of an ape. It has also been hampered by preconceived notions about what man's ancestors should look like. They were supposed to be hunched-over creatures with big brains and ape-like teeth and jaws. So it came as some surprise that *Australopithecus* was upright, with a small brain and man-like teeth and jaws. Early workers created a multiplicity of species and genus names, obscuring similarities of fossils found in different places or dating from different times and sometimes assigning different names to several parts of the same fossil. There is still controversy, which is healthy for science. But a picture of the physical evolution of man is coming into focus, and each new bit of evidence tends to sharpen the focus, to increase the detail, and to add to our confidence in the general picture.

Australopithecus means southern ape. It was the name that anatomist Raymond Dart gave to the skull of a child recovered from a South African quarry in 1924. Since then a large number of similar fossils have been found

# FOSSILS: SURVIVORS OF PREHISTORY

*Fossils have provided scientists with all the concrete information they have about extinct organisms. Using such advanced techniques as carbon dating, paleontologists can pinpoint the ages of fossils millions or even billions of years old and fit them into an evolutionary scheme. They can study not just the remains of trees and mammoths but also the records that man himself has left behind. The bones of a hand with a thumb, or a prehuman skull ascertained to be four million years old, can tell us a great deal about our ancestors and our history.*

*A fossil is a naturally preserved piece of evidence describing the existence of an organism which lived in the past. It may be the remains of the organism, but it may also be the traces of the direct effect the organism or its remains had on its environment.*

*One of the characteristics of living things is that they can protect their physical integrity from the world around them. After death an organism can begin to decay. Its component parts begin to recombine with its environment if the environment is suitable.*

*In extremely rare cases an extraordinary environment may preserve an organism* in toto *instead of reacting with it. In Siberia the climate is cold enough to freeze large organisms quickly and to make life very difficult for bacteria. Frozen mammoths, extinct for thousands of years, have been found in Russia and Alaska, preserved so perfectly that their flesh can still be eaten. An unexplained mystery is the fact that the partially digested food preserved in their stomachs appears in some cases to be the leaves of tropical plants.*

*An unusually dry climate may also preserve a good record of a dead organism. Rapid dehydration occurs after death, leaving a natural mummy of the organism.*

*If an organism has hard parts that are stable chemically (such as shells or bones composed of some calcium compounds), those hard parts may survive*

in southern and eastern Africa and in Asia. It is not clear whether there was one highly variable species of *Australopithecus* or several, but whether glorified by separate species names or not, there was more than one type of early man. What is clear is the surprising antiquity of the genus, which dates back more than 4 million years, and the advanced features of the populations it represents. *Australopithecus's* bones clearly show him to be erect and bipedal, his jaws and teeth have a definitely human look, and he made and used a variety of stone tools. Only his brain is unexpectedly small — more like the brain of a chimpanzee than a modern man (Figure 5.3).

*through centuries if they are buried quickly in a protective medium. In rare cases they may survive intact. More often, however, they are altered in one of a few ways.*

*They may be carbonized; that is, the more volatile elements (such as oxygen, hydrogen, and nitrogen) may recombine with the environment, leaving a carbonaceous record of the organism. Fossils may also be permineralized, a process that can occur when ground waters deposit minerals such as silica and calcium carbonate throughout the pores, "filling" the organism. In this case the fossil will be heavier and somewhat larger than the organism whose past it records. When complete mineralization occurs, the minerals entirely take the place of the organic material, although the structure may remain nearly the same. The petrified wood common in the American Southwest is an example of fossils which have been mineralized.*

*If an organic structure, particularly a hard one, is pressed into a soft substance, it makes an imprint. If this imprint is protected from erosive forces, a mold of the organism's surface may survive even when the organism has decayed. From this mold, paleontologists can produce a cast which replicates, at least on one side, the structure which made the imprint.*

*Modern techniques make the study of fossils more productive than ever before. New fossil discoveries and better means of analysis can be expected to continue to enlarge our picture of the history of man and the history of his environment.*

## REFERENCES

ROBERT SHROCK AND WILLIAM TWENHOFEL, *Principles of Invertebrate Paleontology.* New York: McGraw-Hill, 1953.

RAYMOND C. MOORE, CECIL G. LALICKER, AND ALFRED G. FISCHER, *Invertebrate Fossils.* New York: McGraw-Hill, 1952.

WILLIAM H. MATTHEWS III, *Fossils.* New York: Barnes and Noble, 1962.

There is general (although not unanimous) agreement that there may have been two contemporaneous species of *Australopithecus*. The smaller, *Australopithecus africanus*, stood about 4 feet tall and weighed only 60 or 70 pounds. He probably had omnivorous feeding habits and was the user and maker of tools. Although there is a break in the fossil record between *Australopithecus africanus* and more modern forms, anthropologists believe that he or one of his ancestors eventually evolved into *Homo erectus*, the immediate predecessor of *Homo sapiens*. The larger type, *Australopithecus robustus*, stood 5 feet tall and weighed about 120 pounds. He does not appear to have made tools, although it is possible that he used sticks and stones without altering their form. He was probably a vegetarian, although he may have supplemented his diet with eggs, small lizards, and an occasional small or baby mammal, just as chimpanzees do today. *Australopithecus robustus* survived for about 3 million years, but he never spread beyond Africa. He shows no signs of evolving; the most recent specimens of him are just as primitive as the oldest. Eventually he became extinct, apparently without leaving any descendants.

The fate of *robustus* has intrigued many people. Why did he fail? Some scholars postulate that he became extinct because he did not evolve, and, not evolving, could not compete with *africanus*, who did. One reason he did not evolve (and this is the critical part of the argument) is that he did not make tools. The significance of toolmaking in human evolution will be discussed in Chapter 10. Here we will merely note that without tools man is inferior in physical abilities to his primate relatives and to most animals of his size. He is less agile than the monkeys and has less strength than the great apes. He cannot climb and move freely in the trees to escape from predators. He has no hoofs or horns to fight with, and no fangs for offense or defense. Perhaps it is no wonder after all that *Australopithecus robustus* became extinct.

Generation by generation *Australopithecus* evolved toward *Homo*. We can draw the line between them, saying "This is *Homo*, this is not," only because the fossil record is incomplete, and the line is drawn in one of the gaps. The problem is different from dividing contemporaneous organisms into species because organisms existing at the same time are adapted for particular environmental niches. Although their populations are variable, they cluster in "adaptive peaks" surrounded by "adaptive valleys" (see Chapters 3 and 4). In contrast, every organism alive at any moment can trace its genealogy through unbroken generations back to the beginnings of life. Let him who dares draw a species line between parents and offspring.

By at least 1 million years ago, and perhaps by 1.5 million, our ancestors had achieved the status of the genus *Homo*. On the basis of anatomical and geographical differences, a number of species names have been assigned to early representatives of *Homo*, but the recent trend has been to consider most (if not all) of them as belonging to the single species *Homo erectus*, our ancestor. Although there are differences between *Homo erectus* and modern man, the range of variation of most features of the early form overlaps that of human populations today. The most significant difference between the two species is in the size and complexity of the brain (Figure 5.3).

*Homo erectus* was widely distributed throughout Asia and Africa and parts of Europe. He displayed a high degree of variability within as well as between populations. This variability is the reason for using caution in splitting him into a number of species. By perhaps 500,000 years ago, but certainly by 250,000, *Homo erectus* had evolved into the equally variable *Homo*

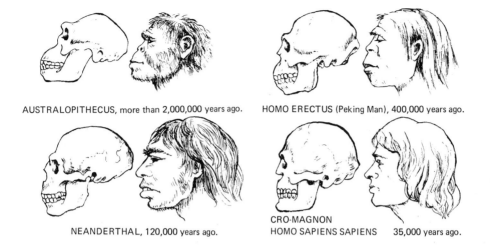

AUSTRALOPITHECUS, more than 2,000,000 years ago.

HOMO ERECTUS (Peking Man), 400,000 years ago.

NEANDERTHAL, 120,000 years ago.

CRO-MAGNON
HOMO SAPIENS SAPIENS    35,000 years ago.

**Figure 5–3**  Skulls of our ancestors show a progressive increase in brain size through-out the course of evolution.

*sapiens*, which includes the famous Neanderthal man of western Europe and others like him on other continents (Figure 5.3). In western Europe, where their story is known best, the Neanderthal men met extinction about 35,000 years ago, giving way to *Homo sapiens sapiens*, our own subspecies (Figure 5.3). Their fate is puzzling. They seem to have developed more primitive features toward the end of their existence, for some of the youngest specimens known appear less modern than older ones. They vanished abruptly (but remember that "abruptly" can mean thousands of years when you are reading rocks of this age). Perhaps, like *Australopithecus robustus*, they failed because they did not evolve, although *why* they did not evolve is another question. Perhaps they were unable to adapt to milder conditions in the interglacial period. When more advanced populations moved into their homeland, probably from the southeast, they may have been annihilated, assimilated, or merely crowded out of the places in which they knew how to live. Native populations have met these fates singly or in combination many times in more recent history.

## THE SPECIAL FEATURES OF MAN

The most obvious and significant difference between man and the apes is the size and complexity of man's brain. This brain, however, did not evolve by itself. Its evolution was accompanied by many other changes which contributed jointly to the success and nature of emerging man. The switch to upright stance and bipedal locomotion had profound significance for man's way of life as well as for his skeleton. He paid for total freedom of his hands and greater visual range by forfeiting the safety of the trees.

Among the most important changes for the men who study the evolution of man are those that took place in man's teeth and jaws and parts of the skull related to support of chewing muscles. These parts are frequently found as fossils. Together with other evidence and some informed guesswork, they document changes in diet and methods of offense, defense, and the procurement of food.

Another modification has to do with man's big brain and is related to birth. In the process of evolving a bigger and bigger head, man had to strike a compromise between size of head and size of pelvic opening through which the head must pass at birth. He seems to have done this to a degree by being born at an earlier stage of development than his primate relatives. Large brains had an obvious advantage, but brains *too* large were selected against at birth. Earlier birth meant birth at a smaller size, but *too* early a birth meant death. A large pelvic opening meant successful birth of large-headed infants, but *too* extensive a change in the pelvis may have exacted its toll in other ways. The situation is much more complex than has been indicated here. It involves other factors, including the overall size of the mother and the infant's rate of prenatal development. It illustrates, however, that the entire organism evolves, not isolated parts of it.

There is a trend in all primates toward a flexible estrous cycle, which depends in large part on the conditions in which the animal finds itself. Some rhesus monkeys in captivity have gone the way of man, abandoning the usual cycle in favor of year-round sexual activity. Although this behavior in the monkey is considered abnormal by some, because the animal is not in its natural environment, it shows that the potential for continuous sexual receptivity in the female exists in primates other than *Homo sapiens*. *Homo sapiens* is unusual, however, in that it is the norm for females to be sexually receptive at all times. This phenomenon is thought to be related to the development of permanent male-female pairs and the family. Although some mammals mate for life, no other primates do. And although most primates from prosimians to man are organized into relatively stable social groups, none except man is organized into nuclear families. Female chimpanzees and their children from infancy through adolescence remain together, but the father plays no part in this group. Indeed, the father is unknown, for a chimpanzee in estrus may mate successively with every male in the troop. Thus the permanent family is a uniquely human invention.

*EVOLUTION OF THE BRAIN.* The part of the brain which has played the main role in mammalian evolution is the **cerebral cortex** — the celebrated "gray matter." The cortex first appeared as a patch of cells on the olfactory bulbs of the reptiles. In prosimians this patch expanded into a thin sheet of millions of cells, covering the surface of the brain. It dealt with the translation of experience intơ action. A large part of it, the older part, was still related to the sense of smell. The newer part at the back of the brain was the visual cortex, which dealt with the tremendous amounts of visual information received and acted on by a successful tree dweller. Other parts had to do with muscle coordination and voluntary movement. An animal that fell from a tree to be broken or eaten by a predator did not pass on its inferior abilities to many offspring.

In monkeys the cortex expanded much further. Although in large part this resulted from the still increasing dominance of sight over smell, other functions were also involved. These included control of finger action. Prosimian fingers operated together in a grasping movement. Monkey fingers moved freely and independently, their precise manipulative ability complementing the increased curiosity and intelligence of their owners. For the larger cortex of the monkey's brain also contained centers which analyzed and integrated information flowing from all the sensory organs, and which learned, and remembered, and made choices.

Apes ventured out of the trees more frequently than monkeys and encountered new and varied environments. They owed their success in coping with new situations to two evolutionary developments. One was increased freedom of movement — due jointly to skeletal changes and to further development of cortical regions that coordinated voluntary movements. The other was increased intelligence, a rudimentary ability to think and solve problems by hypothesis testing rather than by trial and error.

The cerebral cortex of modern man is large and complexly convoluted. From a few hundred cells in the pre-mammalian past it has increased to billions. It constantly exchanges messages with more primitive parts of the brain, many of whose functions it has preempted. To the cortical functions of the ape, man has added one more — a center for speech and language, which has increased his potential for learning, abstract thinking, and pur-

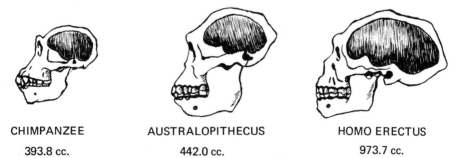

| CHIMPANZEE | AUSTRALOPITHECUS | HOMO ERECTUS |
| 393.8 cc. | 442.0 cc. | 973.7 cc. |

**Figure 5–4** The brain of *Australopithecus* was not much larger than that of a modern chimpanzee. It evolved rapidly in size and complexity, more than doubling by the time *Homo erectus* appeared. (Adapted from John E. Pfeiffer, *The Emergence of Man*, Rev. ed., Harper and Row, New York, 1972, p. 119)

poseful action. In man, too, coordination of fine finger movements reaches its highest development. Only man can play exquisite music on a violin or perform delicate surgery on the brain. Figure 5.4 illustrates the development of the organ that is the seat of intelligence, creativity, and all that is human.

EVOLUTION OF STRUCTURES ASSOCIATED WITH LOCOMOTION. Every part of man's skeleton has responded to his erect stance and bipedal locomotion. The hole in the base of the skull through which the spinal cord enters the brain is located farther forward than in quadrupeds, and the angle at which the head is carried is rotated downward about 90 degrees. (If it were not, man would be gazing into the sky in his upright position.) The spine has a series of curves related to balance and movement. The rib cage is broad rather than deep as in the quadrupeds, affording easier balance. The pelvis is broad, shallow, and bowl-shaped, adapted for

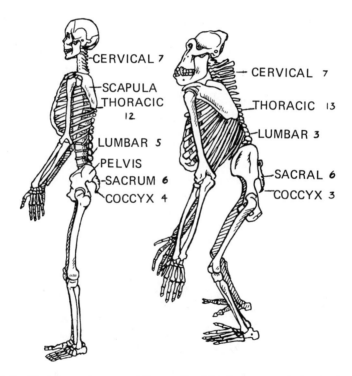

**Figure 5–5** Skeletons of man and the gorilla. Man has many skeletal adaptations for his upright stance and bipedal gait (see text). There are corresponding adaptations in the musculature, as the muscles move the skeleton and are attached to it. Note the difference in structure and position of the scapula (shoulder blade) and pelvis, and differences in the number of vertebrae in the various regions of the spine. (Adapted from Mischa Titiev, *The Science of Man*, Rev. ed., Holt, Rinehart and Winston, New York, 1963, p. 89.)

support of the abdominal organs. It also shows adaptations for attachment of abdominal muscles and muscles that control posture and leg movements. The thigh bones are not straight and parallel as in the apes, but are set at an angle so that weight does not shift from side to side in walking. The foot, marvelously adapted for walking, transmits weight smoothly from heel to toe at each step. A comparison of the bony structures of man and gorilla is shown in Figure 5.5.

*EVOLUTION OF THE HAND.*    The earliest mammals had five separate digits on each of their four feet. While many later mammals developed hooves or paws, primates retained the primitive pattern (Figure 5.6). Clearly, they needed digits for the grasping way of life in the trees. They were also preadapted for the manipulation of objects, but this use had to wait for the brain to catch up. Long-snouted mammals dependent on smell used their eyes to corroborate and embellish what their noses told them. Short-snouted higher primates got information about their world by use of eyes and hands together. Figure 5.7 shows that the hand of man has changed little in tens of millions of years. The changes of note have been in his head.

*EVOLUTION OF TEETH AND JAWS.*    The anthropologist's traditional reliance on teeth has been a source of amusement for many. But as teeth often are the only fossil material he has to work with, it is fortunate that they tell a story of relationships among animals. Typical reptilian teeth were built on only one pattern. Mammals, however, have characteristic arrays of sharp incisors for cutting or gnawing, large pointed canines for defense or tearing of flesh, and flattened molars for grinding food. The first placental mammals probably had forty-four teeth, a number that has been reduced to thirty-two in all higher primates. The pattern is typical: four incisors fol-

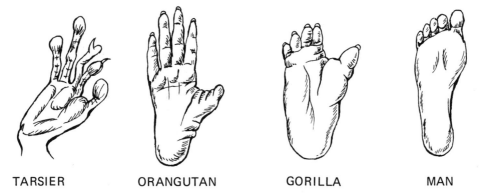

TARSIER          ORANGUTAN          GORILLA          MAN

**Figure 5–6**  Variations in the primate foot. The human foot has become adapted for walking, while the feet of other primates retain adaptations for climbing and grasping. All primates, however, have the basic mammalian pattern of five digits. (Adapted from Helena Curtis, *Biology*, Worth Pub., New York, New York, 1968, p. 797.)

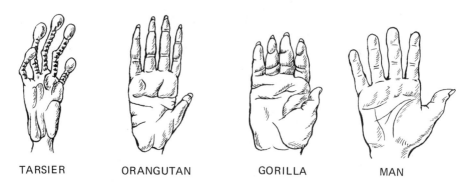

**Figure 5–7** Variations in the primate hand. Primate evolution has been accompanied by increasing skill in grasping and manipulating objects, although most primates also use their hands for climbing, walking, or swinging from branches. The human hand is most skillful at manipulation, but its structure has changed very little from the basic vertebrate pattern. (Adapted from Helena Curtis, *Biology*, Worth Pub., New York, 1968, p. 797.)

lowed on each side of each jaw by a canine, two premolars, and three molars. The details of size and structure, however, are variable among species and show evolutionary trends. Much can be inferred about an animal from a sample of its teeth. Although in the past we have sometimes inferred too much, much that seems valid remains.

Man's dentition reflects changes in his behavior that go back to *Australopithecus* and beyond. Increased reliance on hands and tools and decreased use of teeth for obtaining food can be read in the decreasing size of jaws and teeth, especially canines. Perhaps, in this case, it is not so much a matter of natural selection favoring the human type as of the relaxation of

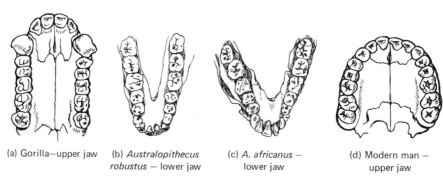

(a) Gorilla—upper jaw

(b) *Australopithecus robustus* — lower jaw

(c) *A. africanus* — lower jaw

(d) Modern man — upper jaw

**Figure 5–8** Apes have relatively larger canines than man and his ancestors, and two parallel rows of teeth that give the jaws the shape of a croquet wicket. Jaws of *Ramapithecus* (not shown), *Australopithecus,* and *Homo* have a parabolic shape. Canines are reduced in size and there is no gap to accommodate the interlocking canines of the other jaw. The size of the molars is reduced from *A. robustus* (basically a vegetarian) to *A. africanus* (omnivorous, highly dependent on tools) to the genus *Homo* and modern man.

selection for the ape type. It is hard to imagine how we would function less well in our present lives with the teeth and jaws of an ape, although an ape would probably do poorly with ours. The invention of cooking probably permitted further reduction in size of teeth.

Many male primates have retained relatively enormous canine teeth, while those of females are small. This seems to be a clear case of sexual selection, having little to do with feeding behavior (although perhaps it is related to defense). It may be related to the way in which males achieve and display dominance within their group. The dominant males may be the ones that can bare the biggest set of canines and look the fiercest. These are the ones that will leave the most offspring to have teeth like their own. However, leadership in human society has long depended on more than a show of teeth. Patterns in the evolution of human teeth and jaws are shown in Figure 5.8.

## THE WILDNESS THAT REMAINS

A threat or an insult to one of our primitive ancestors would have resulted in a set of physiological and behavioral responses that triggered an aggressive display, brought a rapid resolution to the crisis, and restored the body to its normal state. In the more recent days of chivalry a gentleman similarly affronted regained his honor in a duel. In the board of a large corporation the same set of physiological responses may be triggered in a man, but then — nothing happens. He cannot fight. Results of suppression of the ancient behavioral response are seen in the increased incidence of heart attacks, circulatory disorders, and emotional disturbances, the well-known ills of modern society. We were wild animals for millions of years and have been approaching a civilized state for only a few thousand. This is not long enough for genetic change to adapt us for the way of life we now impose on ourselves. We are still hunters in a society where we can no longer hunt, adapted to run or attack in a society where neither response is any longer appropriate.

The more we learn about the behavior of other primates, the more we see ourselves reflected in the most humble of our relatives. The small-brained lemurs, showing no higher mental functions, exhibit social behavior in many ways reminiscent of our own. Origins of incest taboos are foreshadowed in the sexual behavior of the chimpanzees, among whom males seldom mate with their mothers or sisters. We have superimposed language on more primitive forms of communication, but the latter remain and sometimes they belie our words. Facial expressions, bodily attitudes, scratching our heads in perplexity — all are typically ancient responses. We still use our voice in the mode of the chimpanzee to communicate news of our emotional states rather than precise information. Laughter and crying. Ouch! Ooh. Oh! In language these are translated into I burned myself. That is nice. I am surprised. But we do not need language for this; the primitive response conveys our message equally well. A pantomimed display of human aggression is uncomfortably similar to a similar display by an ape.

Man's brain evolved in a time of great physical danger and little social change. It must now cope with the reverse — little physical and great social change. How close we are to our primordial ancestors can be seen in our devotion to blood-and-guts fiction, our glorification of the physical over the mental, and our continuing tolerance of violence and warfare. Appreciation of this aspect of man's psychoneurologic makeup is fundamental to understanding how man, the "thinking animal," can so frequently involve himself and other species in the kinds of dilemmas which are the motivating force for this book.

## REFERENCES

BORDES, F. 1968. *The Old Stone Age*. New York: McGraw-Hill.

BOUGHEY, A. S. 1971. *Man and the Environment*. New York: McGraw-Hill.

BRAIDWOOD, R. J. 1967. *Prehistoric Men*. 7th ed. Glenview, Ill.: Scott, Foresman.

BROOKS, C. E. E. 1926. *Climate Through the Ages*. New York: Coleman.

CAMPBELL, B. G. 1966. *Human Evolution*. Chicago: Aldine Publishing Co.

DART, R. A. 1961. *Adventures with the Missing Link*. New York: Viking Press.

DOBZHANSKY, T. 1962. *Mankind Evolving*. New Haven: Yale Univ. Press.

LASKER, G. 1973. *Physical Anthropology*. New York: Holt, Reinhart, and Winston.

LEAKEY, L. S. B. 1960. *Adam's Ancestors*. New York: Harper & Row.

OAKLEY, K. P. 1961. *Man the Tool-Maker*. 5th ed. Chicago: Univ. of Chicago.

PFEIFFER, J. E. 1969. *The Emergence of Man*. New York: Harper & Row.

PILBEAM, D. 1972. *The Descent of Man*. New York: Macmillan.

SIMPSON, G. G. 1949. *The Meaning of Evolution*. New Haven: Yale Univ. Press.

WELLS, H. G. 1971. *The Outline of History*. Revised ed. by H. G. Wells, R. Postgate, and G. P. Wells. New York: Doubleday.

WILLIAMS, B. 1973. *Evolution and Human Origins*. New York: Harper & Row.

# · 6 ·

NORMAN D. LEVINE

# Human Variation
# and Individuality

We have defined ecology as the study of the relationships between an organism and its environment. We have also seen that each organism is the product of interactions between its genes and its environment, and that the environment determines which organisms will survive. But environments change, and survival in the face of change requires either a capacity of the individual to adapt to new conditions or a reservoir of genetic variability in the species that will allow at least some members to survive. The potential for adaptation to certain conditions must exist before the conditions arise, because there is not time to wait for favorable new mutations after the challenge has been presented. It is too late for a fly to become resistant to an insecticide after it has been sprayed.

The range of phenotypic variation exhibited by individuals results from integrated activity of the almost endless number of possible gene combinations, interacting with the environment. All evidence indicates that man has always been a highly variable species, and that this variability probably extended to his ancestors who were not yet fully men. The variability of man is the subject of this chapter. Its documentation is fascinating in its own right. Explaining it is another matter, equally fascinating, but subject to much more speculation and uncertainty. Two questions related to human variability and to each other arise. The first: does natural selection still operate on our species? And the second: why, as far as we know, has there never been more than one species in our genus at any one time? (There is general, though not unanimous, agreement on this.) The answer to the first question is almost certainly yes, natural selection still works on us, although not as starkly as on other species because culture has mitigated its effects in many ways. Dobzhansky estimates that nearly half of all

131

fertilized eggs do not reproduce. Some 15 percent are lost before birth, 3 percent are stillborn, 2 percent die soon after birth, 3 percent die before maturity, and 25 percent never have children. There is plenty of opportunity for natural selection. The answer to the second question is more tentative. Perhaps our ancestors were able to adapt to such a wide variety of conditions while maintaining an open gene pool that there was no niche left for another similar primate and no chance for one to evolve. The evolution of man is very unusual in this respect. It proceeded linearly, without the extensive branching that gave rise to the many species of prosimians and monkeys. Perhaps it is because he has always been such a variable, resourceful, and adaptable animal that he has no close relatives.

## THE EXTENT OF VARIABILITY IN MAN

If a person is heterozygous for one pair of genes he can produce two kinds of gametes, because some gametes will contain one form of the gene and some the other. If he is heterozygous for two pairs of genes he can produce four types of gametes. In general, a person heterozygous for a number of genes, N, can produce $2^N$ kinds of gametes, each carrying a different combination of genes. Dobzhansky estimates that there are two or more gene variants at a minimum of 6,000 chromosomal loci in man, and that each person is heterozygous for an average of at least 3,200 genes. There would be $2^{3200}$ possible arrays of genes in the gametes of such a person — more than $10^{960}$, an unimaginably large number, many times greater than the total number of people that will exist in the entire history of our species. Clearly, only a small fraction of the possible genotypes can ever be realized, and the chances of any two individuals (except for identical twins) bearing the same genotype are vanishingly small. Even if this estimate of the number of variant genes is wrong by a factor of ten, the number of possible combinations is still so large (or so much larger) that the genetic uniqueness of each person is virtually guaranteed.

Because we cannot determine the sequences of nitrogen bases in all the DNA of human chromosomes, we cannot measure genetic variability directly. An altered sequence of amino acids in a protein, however, is evidence of an altered sequence of bases in DNA, and to the extent that we can determine variant proteins we can determine variant genes. When we begin to talk about "traits," the connection with individual genes becomes very tenuous. A person has a definite (although unknown) number of genes; but he has as many traits as you care to define. Many of these traits are determined by the action and interaction of a number of genes, and, conversely, many genes exert an influence on a number of traits. In addition, the influence of genes on traits varies from 100 percent (as in the inheritance of blood type) to 0 percent (as in the language a person speaks). It is therefore important to remember the difference between genotype and phenotype. We say, inaccurately, that someone has a gene for brown eyes, when what he really has is a gene containing coded information for making a protein that can, under appropriate conditions, take part in the synthesis of a particular pigment in certain cells. In general, measurements of human variability are measurements of phenotypic variability, which is related to, but is not the same as, genotypic variability.

MEASURING HUMAN VARIATION. Determinations of many measurable traits exhibit a so-called normal distribution, which means that if the results of a large number of measurements are plotted on a graph, the values cluster symmetrically about a central value as shown in the familiar bell-shaped curves of Figure 6.1. Traits whose measured values show this type of distribution include height, weight, intelligence, metabolic rate, blood pressure, levels of blood sugar, and a host of others. Whether the bell-shaped curve is broad or narrow depends on the variability of the measurements, which is commonly expressed as the *standard deviation from the mean*. (For an explanation of this, see the caption to Figure 6.1(a)). The dashed curve in Figure 6.1(b) represents a less variable set of measurements than the curve in 6.1(a), and the solid curve a more variable set. The same statistical treatment, however, is valid for all three curves.

For any trait whose values are normally distributed in a population, two-

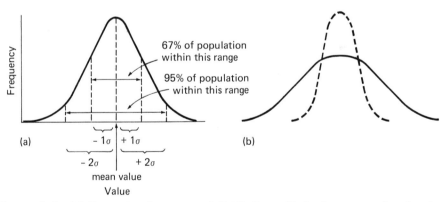

**Figure 6–1** (a) Curve showing a normal distribution, with the frequency of each value plotted against the value. A measure of the scatter of points around the central value is given by the standard deviation, which is defined as the square root of the sum of the squared deviations from the mean, divided by the number of measurements minus 1 Note that a normal distribution curve is symmetrical, and 95 percent of a population will fall within plus or minus two standard deviations from the mean. (b) Normal curves showing more (solid) and less (dashed) variation than the curve in (a). The standard deviation will be larger for the solid curve and smaller for the dashed one.

thirds of the individuals in the population will fall within one standard deviation above and below the mean and about 95 percent will fall within two standard deviations. For most purposes the range of values exhibited by 95 percent of the population is considered "normal," and anything outside this range is "abnormal." If values within three standard deviations of the mean are taken as normal, more than 99 percent of the population will be included.

The average man is a statistical invention, as was first pointed out by the anthropologist Franz Boaz at the turn of the century. No such person exists in real life. While it is possible to establish ranges of normal values for particular factors or measurements in a population, the number of people who fall within the normal range for all factors decreases rapidly as the number of factors increases.

Values for some measurements may be independent of each other, as, for example, your height and the range of sound frequencies you can hear. Other traits are not completely independent of each other but are correlated to various degrees, as, for example, your height and weight, or your height and the length of your legs. Assuming that the traits are independent of each other, Table 6.1 shows how the number of normal individuals decreases as the number of measured traits increases. If normal is defined as the range of values characteristic of the middle 50 percent of the population, then half the individuals will be normal for one trait, half of that half (or one quarter) for two traits, half of the quarter (one eighth) for three traits, and so on. If the middle 95 percent of the population is normal for *each* of N traits,

**TABLE 6.1**
**Relationship Between Percentage of a Population Considered Normal for a Factor, Number of Factors, and Percentage of Population Normal for All Factors**

| Number of Factors | Size of Medial ("normal") Group–Percent of Population | | |
|:---:|:---:|:---:|:---:|
| | *50* | *95* | *99.8* |
| 1 | 50 | 95 | 99.8 |
| 5 | 3 | 77 | 99 |
| 10 | 0.1 | 60 | 98 |
| 15 | 0.003 | 47 | 97 |
| 100 | $10^{-28}$ | 0.6 | 82 |

Numbers in the boxes show the percentage of a population normal for the number of factors indicated, with the middle 50%, 95%, and 99.8% of the population considered normal for each factor. Taking the middle 50% as normal, the table shows that a world population of several hundred billion billion times the present size would be required before we would expect, statistically, to find one person normal for 100 factors. The way in which these numbers decrease can be thought of as exponential shrinking, by analogy with the reverse process, exponential growth.

then $0.95^N$ of the population will be normal for *all* N traits. After a large number of traits are measured, the completely normal person would be the most unusual person of all!

One area in which the figment of the normal person has important implications is nutrition. The United States Food and Drug Administration has set up recommended daily allowances and minimum daily requirements for twelve human nutritional items. If a diet contained these twelve items each in an amount satisfactory for 90 percent of the population, then the total diet would satisfy the needs of only $0.90^{12}$, or 28 percent of the population. This assumes that the need for each item is independent of the need for the others, a situation that does not hold strictly in real life. Because there is a tendency for the same individuals to fall in the middle 90 percent of the range of requirements for a number of items, the diet will be adequate for somewhat more than the calculated 28 percent. For how much more we do not know. Many people on learning of this situation will be tempted to swallow many times the recommended minimum amount of each nutrient to insure that their own peculiar needs will be met. This is an unwise step, because in some cases the balance among nutrients is important, and in others overdoses are as harmful as deficiencies.

Data collected from various sources by Roger Williams confirm the principle illustrated by the nutrition example. A group of characteristics of the **lipids** in blood **plasma** of sixty-five men was measured: total carbon in the lipid fraction, total phosphorus, total nitrogen, nitrogen contained in amino ($NH_2$) groups, total **cholesterol,** free cholesterol, and esterified cholesterol (cholesterol chemically combined with an organic acid). His results are shown in Table 6.2, along with the results that would have been expected if the measured items varied independently of one another. Taking the middle 50 percent as standard, it was found that only two out of the sixty-five men were standard for all seven items. The observed values are consistently higher than the expected, indicating that the measured traits are not independent of each other. Still, the percentage of individuals standard even for a group of factors that might be expected to be closely related dropped off rapidly as the number of factors increased.

**TABLE 6.2**
**Numbers of Men in Medial 50% Group after Successive**
**Measurements of Plasma Lipid Components**

| *Number of Individuals in Medial Group* | *Number of Measurements* | | | | | | |
|---|---|---|---|---|---|---|---|
| | *1* | *2* | *3* | *4* | *5* | *6* | *7* |
| Actual | 33 | 21 | 14 | 10 | 8 | 3 | 2 |
| Theoretical (Assuming Independent Variation of Measurements) | 33 | 16 | 8 | 4 | 2 | 1 | 0.5 |

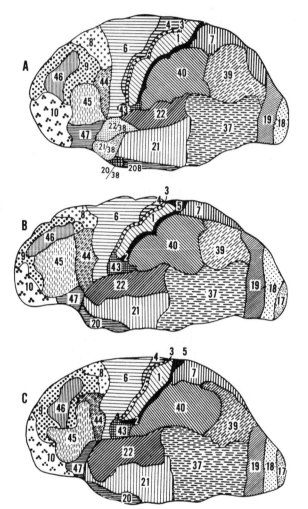

**Figure 6–2** Cytoarchitecture of the side surfaces of three typical human brains studied at the Brain Institute in Moscow. Cell structure varies from area to area in the brain, and it is possible to map the surface of the brain according to cell type. The three brains diagrammed here are qualitatively similar in their types of cells and general position of specific areas, but there are many quantitative (as well as a few qualitative) differences. As cell structure and function are intimately related, it is reasonable to assume that these brains also have functional differences. (From S. A. Sarkisov, *The Structure and Function of the Brain*, Indiana Univ. Press, 1966.)

For those who are interested in the anatomical and physiological variability of man, the book by Williams cited at the end of this chapter contains a great deal of information. The data, although not recent, are still valid. Among other examples of variation cited by Williams is variation in the cellular structure of the surface of the brain. Cellular "maps" of three normal brains are shown in Figure 6.2. All three brains had areas containing the same types of cells, but the sizes, shapes, and locations of these areas varied widely. It is inconceivable that differences in function would not result from these differences in structure.

As another example, Williams felt that alcoholism, insofar as a disposition toward it is genetically determined, was related to nutritional deficiencies or unusually high requirements for particular nutrients, notably some of the B vitamins. Studies with rats maintained on a standard laboratory diet with free access to both water and alcohol showed that some rats shunned alcohol altogether, some imbibed copiously, and others drank intermediate amounts. Under these conditions, some rats were alcoholics and some were not. As the diet was made progressively more deficient in various nutrients, all rats began to drink alcohol, and the less adequate the diet, the more they drank. When the diet was heavily fortified with nutrient supplements, the rats drank less, and some "alcoholics" were "cured." Thus, in rats, the tendency to drink alcohol seems to be related to individual differences in nutritional requirements and the degree to which these requirements are met. It is risky to apply these findings to man, but tentative analogies may be drawn. The diet of a heavy drinker usually leaves much to be desired, and if the degree to which this diet satisfies the individual's nutritional needs is related to the degree of his alcoholism, the situation may in fact be similar to that observed in laboratory rats. Unfortunately, massive nutritional supplements do not cure many alcoholics. This does not disprove Williams's thesis, however. For one thing, *some* alcoholics have benefitted from this treatment, and one could argue that this is exactly what would be expected if multiple factors were involved and the treatment were appropriate for only certain individuals with certain combinations of requirements. For another, the mere presence of a substance in the diet does not insure that the body can use it. The problem may lie elsewhere than in the supply of the nutrient.

Sargent and Weinman (1964, 1966) measured several traits in a group of twenty-three healthy male college students kept under a "regulated metabolic regimen," meaning that they ate exactly the same kinds and relative amounts of foods. These men differed strikingly in measurements for individual traits and in overall patterns of measurements for the traits. Sargent and Weinman also measured the reactions of healthy young men to the stress of physical exertion at various temperatures. Again, the subjects were quite variable, not only in their metabolic rates under the experimental conditions but in all other traits as well. Sargent and Weinman thought that the configurations of the traits they measured were inherited. Other evidence supports their view. Williams, for example, determined the urinary excretion of a number of chemicals in a group of men, including two who were identical twins. The results for the twins were strikingly similar, but all other patterns were distinctly different from each other. This is not to say that environment has no effect on physiological traits, but it indicates that the genetic influence on some of these traits is very high.

Williams suggested that if some biological trait in an individual were farther than three standard deviations from the population average, it should be called a disconformity. Three standard deviations is a large divergence (Figure 6.1), yet among the twenty-three apparently normal, healthy young men in Sargent and Weinman's study there were three who were *multiple* disconformers for several biochemical traits and four who were multiple disconformers for several traits related to functioning of organs and organ systems. Even a normal, healthy person becomes sick periodically, however, and eventually dies from one cause or another. It is important to note that these very differences in normal, healthy people may explain why certain people develop certain health problems or diseases and others do not. The implications of Sargent and Weinman's work and similar studies for medicine are profound. The problem of selecting normal individuals to serve as comparisons or "controls" for medical research has plagued scientists consistently, because the ranges of measurements of interest so often overlap between the control group and the patients. Yet one person is presumably suffering from his abnormality and the other is not.

*BLOOD GROUPS.* The best-known and most-studied characteristic of man that is determined by a series of genes (alleles) at a single locus is the ABO blood type. These blood groups were discovered in 1900 by Karl Landsteiner, who found that samples of blood from different people sometimes reacted strangely when mixed together. Experiments showed that there were four major blood groups, inherited according to simple Mendelian principles. Subsequently, other blood groups, determined by groups of alleles at other loci, were identified and there is no reason to suppose that even now we have found them all. Knowledge of the nature and inheritance of blood types has contributed importantly to the fields of medicine, genetics, evolution, anthropology — and even law, in settling disputes over paternity and "mixed-up babies."

Normally, the body of an animal can distinguish the proteins and other large molecules characteristic of itself from those of other organisms. It reacts to foreign *antigens* (usually proteins or polysaccharides, large sugar-like molecules) by producing specific protein *antibodies*, which combine with the foreign antigens to inactivate them. This is the first step in the body's fight against infectious disease: it produces antibodies which react with antigens on the invading microorganisms, rendering the invaders more susceptible to destruction by other disease-fighting elements in the body.

A person's blood type depends on certain substances present in the walls of his red blood cells, each of which appears to be related to a particular gene. In addition to being structural components of the cell wall, these blood group substances also act as antigens. An individual with type A blood has antigen A on his red cells; one with type B blood has antigen B; one with type AB blood has both; and one with type O blood has neither. The ABO system is a bit unusual in that antibodies to A and B antigens exist in people who do not have the antigens, even though they have not previously been exposed to foreign blood cells. Thus individuals with type A blood carry antibodies to the B antigen in their blood serum; those with type

B blood carry antibodies to A; those with type AB blood have neither anti-body; and those with type O have both. When a foreign blood antigen is introduced into an animal, the animal's body reacts as it would to any substance perceived as "not-self." Antibody reacts with antigen, and the invading cells are destroyed. Thus, in selecting a donor for a blood transfusion, care must be taken that no foreign antigens are introduced into the body of the recipient. Incompatibilities between the blood of a pregnant woman and her unborn child, resulting in abortion, may be more common than was once thought. It is estimated that up to 35 percent of the abortions in women carrying fetuses with a foreign antigen in their blood may be due to incompatibility in the ABO system, with antibodies from the mother destroying blood cells of the child. It has also been found that the major blood group antigens are related to certain antigens in other tissues, so that the potential success of a tissue or organ transplant can be estimated from knowledge of the blood types of donor and recipient.

In addition to the ABO system, there are at least a dozen other major blood systems in man. The best known of these are the MN and the Rhesus. As in the ABO system, incompatibility in the Rhesus (Rh) system may cause problems in blood transfusion or pregnancy. Problems with the other major systems are uncommon, although when large or repeated blood transfusions are to be given, as in heart surgery, blood of donors and recipients may be matched for as many factors as possible. There are about eighty known red blood cell antigens altogether, however. Recalling the discussion earlier in this chapter, you will see that you are not likely to meet many people in your lifetime who have exactly the same genes for blood type as you.

There are still other red cell antigens of very minor importance. These are either essentially universal in man, or are known only in isolated individuals or families. Antigens common to all men may be of interest in comparative studies of blood groups in primates. While apes share some blood groups with men, they also have some specific blood group systems of their own or shared with primates other than man.

Aside from their practical interest in modern medicine, blood groups hold out some tantalizing clues to puzzles in the history of man. Why are they present in the observed proportions? Why do they vary in frequency from population to population? Some answers have been suggested, but they are difficult to prove or disprove. Some of the ideas about the relationship between human blood groups and human adaptation to the environment — human ecology — will be reviewed in the following paragraphs.

There are disadvantages to having multiple blood type alleles within a population. Clearly, the problems caused by blood transfusion and tissue transplantation are too recent to have had any effect on human evolution, but loss of up to 10 percent of the fetuses resulting from mating of people

## THE Rh FACTOR AND PREGNANCY

*In hospitals throughout the world the tragedy was repeated over and over again: mothers, immunized against their own offspring, gave birth to stillborn infants or to infants so severely anemic, jaundiced, or brain-damaged that many of them died soon after birth. These deaths and illnesses had puzzled doctors for years. In most cases the mothers' first and second pregnancies had been normal and the babies were healthy. Why the sudden change?*

*Then in 1940 scientists discovered a substance in the blood of rhesus monkeys which proved to have an important bearing on the mystery. This crucial substance was a protein antigen on the surface of red blood cells, called the Rh factor after the monkeys. Rh factor is found in the blood of most human beings, who are thus said to be Rh-positive; those who lack the antigens are Rh-negative. It is when the child of an Rh-positive man and an Rh-negative woman inherits his father's antigens by genetic chance that problems may occur.*

*The difference between the blood of the Rh-negative mother and the Rh-positive fetus usually has no ill effect in the first or second pregnancy. But if the blood of the fetus passes into the mother's bloodstream through the placenta or because of a hemorrhage during delivery, subsequent offspring may be endangered. The antigens of the fetus's red blood cells sensitize the mother's Rh-negative cells, which will produce antibodies if combined with the Rh-positive cells of a fetus in the second or third pregnancy. The mother's antibodies, returning to the circulation of the fetus, attack his red blood cells and destroy them through clumping (agglutination). The blood-producing organs*

with incompatible blood types would seem to be a significant factor in natural selection. Every time a heterozygous genotype is lost from the population, the effect is relatively larger on the rarer of the two alleles; and if heterozygotes are continually selected against, other things being equal, the rarer gene should eventually be lost from the population. This does not seem to be happening in the blood groups, although there is some difference of opinion on the subject (see reference to Race and Sanger). Clearly, "other things" are *not* equal; other factors are operating to preserve the gene frequencies in what is known as a *balanced polymorphism*.

The Rh factor is a mystery. There is no known advantage to the heterozygote, and a distinct disadvantage to a heterozygous fetus in an Rh negative mother. There may be a slight selective advantage to the MN heterozygote, as indicated by the excess of heterozygotes over what theory predicts from the frequency of M and N alleles. It has been suggested that the MN genotype confers relative immunity to malaria, but the data are in dispute.

*of the fetus then labor to make up for the destroyed cells. The fetus's bone marrow increases its manufacture of red blood cells and pushes them into his bloodstream before they are fully mature. Because these immature cells cannot function properly, wastes accumulate and poison the fetus's system. His over-burdened organs may swell and eventually cause congestive heart failure.*

*Each year in the United States nearly 26,000 newborns are subject to Rh disease, or* erythroblastosis fetalis. *Until recently, the only remedy was to give the afflicted infant a complete blood transfusion before or shortly after birth. In the early 1960s, however, a more effective treatment was developed simultaneously in the United States and England: by injecting the Rh-negative mother with a serum from human blood, Rh immune globulin, the production of antibodies can be curtailed. The globulin, which acts as a vaccine, must be applied to the mother immediately after the birth of her first Rh-positive child; otherwise she may develop an immunity to the Rh factor, after which injection with the serum would be useless. Besides saving the lives of future infants, Rh immune globulin protects the mother against danger within her own bloodstream should she accidentally be given transfusions of Rh-positive blood.*

*There is also hope for the unfortunate infant whose body has been invaded by large numbers of antibodies from the mother's bloodstream. Modern techniques enable doctors to determine whether a fetus is ill while still in utero; if antibodies are present they can be destroyed by treatment with ultraviolet light, or the blood of the fetus can be replaced through intrauterine techniques before birth or immediately after delivery. Thanks to these medical breakthroughs, the deadly biological conflict between a mother and her unborn child has successfully been resolved.*

More is known about the possible adaptive significance of the ABO blood groups. Some microorganisms have antigens very similar to human blood antigens. It has been suggested, in fact, that the reason antibodies to the A and B antigens exist in people who have never been exposed to them, when in general antibodies are not formed until after exposure to the antigen, is that the antibodies were formed early in life in response to bacterial infection. If a bacterial or viral antigen is similar to a human one, then a person having this antigen should be susceptible to bacterial infection because he would not recognize the bacterial antigen as foreign. The smallpox virus has an antigen similar to human antigen A. Therefore individuals with type B and O blood, having antibody to A in their blood serum, should be relatively resistant to smallpox; while those with type A or AB blood, and no antibody to A, should be relatively susceptible. It is a nice theory, but evidence is inconclusive. It is at least possible, however, that the present frequencies and distribution of ABO blood types are related to great epidemics of infectious disease in the past.

The incidence of other disorders is known to be correlated with blood type. Stomach cancer and pernicious anemia are most common in people with blood group A. Stomach ulcers are most common in people of group O. These disorders are unlikely to have much effect on gene frequencies, however, because they usually occur after the period of reproduction is past. Of possible significance for the future is the fact that women of blood group A are most likely to have clotting problems from birth-control pills.

It is possible, but difficult to prove, that certain blood types are more advantageous in some genotypes. Since natural selection works on phenotypes, and thus on entire genotypes rather than on individual genes, a variety of genes for blood type would tend to be maintained. In this case, correlations of other traits with blood type may be spurious; the real relationship may be with other genes in the genotypes where a particular blood type tends to occur most often. Finally, there is growing evidence that the primary significance of the blood antigens may not lie in their antigenic properties at all, but rather in their effect on the overall properties of the cell membranes where they occur.

## RACE AND THE VARIABILITY OF POPULATIONS

Although all human populations exhibit the same types of variability discussed in the first part of this chapter — variability in physical, physiological, and biochemical characteristics, it is a matter of observation that all human populations are not, on the average, the same. In the language of genetics, certain genes and groups of genes are commoner among some populations than others. In this respect *Homo sapiens* is no different from other species. A *species* is a genetically closed population or group of populations, throughout which breeding with the production of fertile offspring is possible; but such breeding is not normally possible between species. Within the species, however, genetically distinctive populations exist between which interbreeding can and does occur. According to the degree of distinctness and the inclinations of the taxonomist, these populations are called subspecies, races, or varieties. A *subspecies* is a breeding population that has been reproductively isolated from other populations in the species long enough to have become distinguishable from them. The most commonly accepted criterion for delimiting subspecies is that 75 percent of the individuals in one group can be unambiguously distinguished from all individuals of other groups. Many people consider racial differences to be still smaller than differences at the level of subspecies, but there is not unanimous agreement on this point. In any event, although there are no unresolvable disputes about the species to which an individual belongs, by the very definition of subspecies or race a large number of cases must remain in doubt. These taxonomic difficulties do not make the differences between populations less real. Subspecies and race are valid and respectable biological concepts — indeed, they are biological facts. Race has become an ugly word, with its present social and political connotations, because people have misunderstood and distorted the meaning of it.

*ORIGIN AND CLASSIFICATION OF RACES.* The same processes that produce species also produce races, namely mutation, selection, and chance, coupled with isolation imposed by climatic or geographic barriers or sheer distance between breeding populations. Formation of races is probably the first step in the formation of species, although it does not necessarily lead to speciation. The point to remember is that races are genetically open systems. Interbreeding can and does occur between them. There are not now and there never have been any "pure" races; for although a Norwegian may never interbreed with a Bushman, there are genetic links between them from interbreeding of neighboring populations all along the way. Races form and recombine and disappear. The major races today are the Caucasoid, the Mongoloid, and the Negroid. However, at the height of the last glaciation, there were relatively few scattered bands of ancestral Europeans struggling in the shadow of the ice, while the forebears of today's Bushmen were a widespread and numerous race in Africa. Today, Europeans have spread throughout Europe and the New World, but Bushmen are near extinction. They are largely confined to the inhospitable Kalahari Desert, where they are not native, but were pushed by migrations of other races. The American Indians are probably descended from ancient Mongoloids who crossed the Bering land bridge, but today they are racially distinct. Classical Neanderthalers represent a race that died out (although probably not without leaving some of its genes in the gene pool of its successors). The American Negro race is one of several that have appeared within historical times. The important thing is that we are all descended from one ancestral species of *Australopithecus;* we can be certain of this because we are only one species now. It is probable, however, that today's races have different mixtures of genes from various ancient races of *Homo erectus,* resulting from isolation, migrations, and interbreeding in the past (Figure 6.3).

While racial differences are an observed fact, the number of races we recognize is a matter of choice. Most of the world's people fall into the three races already named: Caucasoid, Mongoloid, and Negroid. Another classification recognizes five races, corresponding to five major continental regions: the American Indians of the New World, the Caucasoids of Europe, the Negroids of Africa, the Mongoloids of Asia, and the Australian Aborigines. Other classifications identify still other races intermediate between these — and races intermediate between the intermediate ones, and so on until one classification lists more than 200 races of man. The harder one tries to fit every individual or every population into a neatly defined race, the fuzzier the distinctions become. This should come as no surprise, consider-

**Figure 6–3** Examples showing facial characteristics of the human races. Upper left: (African Negroid. Photograph courtesy of The American Museum of Natural History.) Upper right: Australian aborigine. (Photograph courtesy of The American Museum of Natural History.) Middle left: European caucasoid. Middle right: American Indian. (Photograph courtesy of the Peabody Museum, Harvard University.) Lower left: Asian mongoloid. (Photograph courtesy of The American Musuem of Natural History.)

ing the nature and origin and the very definition of race. The classification of people becomes a useless and meaningless exercise unless it is done to clarify our history or improve our prospects for the future, and unless it is based on what is now known about genetics and evolution.

How did the races of man originate? In the not so distant past, man was a rather rare animal, living in small groups that met and interbred with other groups only occasionally. Each of these groups contained but a fraction of the total variability of the human gene pool. In addition, they lived in a variety of climates and physical habitats, had different diets and ways of obtaining their food, and were exposed to different predators, pests, and diseases. In those days it would take many generations for a mutation arising in the southern tip of Africa to reach China. Its rate of progress was limited by the rate at which man traveled on foot, the distances he was accustomed to travel, and the presence or absence of motivation for him to travel at all. Thus mutation *could* have contributed to the formation of races. It cannot be a major cause of racial differences, however, because as far as we know the same types of mutations occur in all populations at about the same rate. It is the fate of the mutation that is significant.

The fate of a mutation is determined by chance and by natural selection, as described in Chapter 4. Chance must have been a significant factor, operating on small numbers of individuals in whom the occurrence and frequency of genes was not representative of the species as a whole; but even so, natural selection has the last word on the cards dealt by chance. Results of the experiment with fruit flies described in Chapter 4 illustrate how chance and natural selection might interact to produce racial differences. Remember that small groups of flies were selected at random from a large population and allowed to breed for many generations. At the end of the experiment, the descendants of the original groups of flies had become genetically distinct from each other. "Races" had been formed, even though environmental conditions had been held constant. The statistics of small samples show that at least part of this change could have been due to chance — to chance differences in the original groups, to chance loss of some genes originally present, to chance fixation of new mutations. However, another interpretation is that, given different arrays of genotypes to begin with, natural selection did what it could with the material it had. Many gene complexes can lead to adapted phenotypes. In the experiment, natural selection selected combinations of characters that were adapted not only to the environment (the experimental conditions) but *to each other*. Thus we may look in vain for the "adaptive value" of certain racial characteristics, because their adaptive value is only that they lead to well-balanced phenotypes.

*ADAPTIVE VALUE OF RACIAL AND POPULATION DIFFERENCES.* Although we can be confident that natural selection has played a major role in differentiation of the races, we are much less confident about what, if any, adaptive value specific racial differences have. Speculation is abundant; evidence is very scarce, and is for the most part restricted to very simple traits whose genetic nature is known and whose connection with environmental factors is direct, as the gene for sickle-cell anemia which confers some resistance to malaria. In most cases, the extent to which the trait is under genetic control is in doubt, or the adaptive value of the trait is equivocal. Because of cultural changes and historical events, many people today are living successfully under conditions quite different from those in which their ancestors evolved.

One of the most obvious ways in which the races of man differ is in the color of their skin, which is primarily due to the amount and distribution of the pigment melanin. In general, the darkest-skinned people live near the equator and skin becomes progressively lighter in populations living farther north or south. The conclusion that skin color is in some way related to the amount and intensity of sunlight is inescapable. The obvious becomes less and less obvious, however, as the evidence is considered. Dark skin absorbs more sunlight than light skin, converting it to heat and adding it to the heat load that the body must dissipate. On this basis dark skin would be a liability in hot climates and an asset in cold. (This factor becomes insignificant as soon as clothes are worn.) Other possible effects of melanin are related to protection from excessive exposure to the ultraviolet portion of the sun's rays. Ultraviolet light is known to cause sunburn and skin cancer, and to participate in photochemical reactions in the skin that convert precursors of vitamin D to vitamin D. But light skin usually becomes resistant to sunburn with only a few exposures to the sun, and an increase in thickness of the outer layer of skin contributes to this resistance at least as much as does the formation of melanin in the process we call "suntanning." The outer layer of skin in Negroids and Mongoloids is normally much thicker than in Caucasoids, and it is this layer that provides the first line of defense against the ultraviolet rays of the sun. Skin cancer induced by sunlight is a slow-growing malignancy that usually strikes its victims after the age of reproduction. Neither skin cancer nor sunburn would seem to affect the reproductive fitness of a population, and it is difficult to see how either of these effects could have been important in evolution. The question of vitamin D synthesis is complicated by the fact that this vitamin is also available in the diet, and both diet and nutritional requirements vary widely among people. The argument goes, however, that melanin protects against excessive synthesis of vitamin D under conditions of year-long exposure to intense sunlight; while reversible melanization in light-skinned people of temperate climates permits maximum synthesis in winter. Finally, it has been suggested that melanin provided protective coloration for early hunters of the African forests and savannas. In balance, it is probable that "black," "white," "red," or "yellow" skin was advantageous to the populations in which it evolved, but the nature of the advantage is neither simple nor obvious at the present time.

In Chapter 3 we mentioned that animals tend to be larger and more compact in cold climates, smaller and slimmer in hot ones. This generalization seems to hold for people, despite the invention of clothing and the use of fire, which must have preceded migration into cold regions. Ratios of height to weight are significantly correlated with latitude, and play an important role in the conservation or dissipation of body heat. Residents of cold climates show other adaptations to the cold, but it is difficult to determine to what extent these are genetically controlled. A Pygmy raised from infancy by Eskimos might (or might not) possess a degree of cold-adaptedness similar to that of the Eskimos, or greater than that developed by an adult Pygmy immigrant to Alaska. One suspects that the adaptation of such an infant would be intermediate between that of the natives and the adult immigrant, but this is the kind of human experiment that can rarely, if ever, be performed. A similar situation holds for the adaptations to altitude present in natives of the High Plateau of the Andes.

Evidence is beginning to accumulate that populations, just as individuals, vary in their nutritional tolerances and requirements. Well-nourished populations exist on a wide range of diets, from the almost totally carnivorous fare of the Eskimos to almost completely vegetable diets of many descriptions. Since selection would favor individuals for whom the diet is adequate, and since levels of various nutrients differ among diets, it is likely that populations differ, on the average, in their requirements. The best known example is the inability of most adult Africans and Chinese to digest the sugar lactose, which occurs in milk. This is due to a lack of the adult form of the intestinal enzyme lactase. (Of course, normal infants of all races can tolerate milk. Mammals whose babies could not drink milk would certainly represent a new evolutionary step!) Populations where lactase deficiency is common either do not practice dairying or use fermented milk products, letting microorganisms do the job they cannot do for themselves. An interesting chicken-and-egg type question is related to the lack of dairying in much of Asia and Africa. Was it not practiced because adults could not tolerate milk? Or was the gene for lactase deficiency able to become common because dairying was not practiced for other reasons, like the prevalence of cattle diseases?

INTELLIGENCE.    The races of man differ in frequencies of certain genes and combinations of genes. These differences lead to average differences in surface features like skin color, eye color, and the color, form, and distribution of body and facial hair. They also lead to average differences in skeletal features, average differences in blood types, and average differences in the occurrence of genetic and genetically influenced disorders and diseases. Some of these differences have been advantageous to people living in different environments. However, one "trait" that seems to be common to all mankind is a high degree of intelligence. This is not surprising when you think about it. The story of the evolution of mammals and particularly of primates is the story of evolution of increasingly flexible behavioral responses to the environment. These responses depend on learning and intelligence. Most animals cannot devise novel solutions to novel problems. They react automatically, and their reaction is one of a limited number in their repertoire of possible reactions. But man has an unprecedented capacity to learn and to modify his behavior according to what he has learned. This is the secret of his success as a species, and no race or population has a monopoly on it. Survival has never been easy. The biggest asset man has is his brain, and natural selection has consistently favored big ones.

Psychologists have long tried to define, identify, and measure both "general intelligence" and "specific abilities." Their success in these endeavors has not been outstanding. For the most part they have merely identified problems in method and interpretation of results. One colossal and apparently negative experiment in breeding people with specific characteristics or abilities, perhaps analogous to the breeds of dogs, horses, and other domestic animals, was the Indian caste system. The system was much more complex than will be described here. Essentially, it divided all inhabitants of India into groups, each of which traditionally performed a certain function. People were permitted to marry only within their group. The oldest of these groups or castes date back at least 3,500 years; others are much more recent. Some genetic observations have been made on these groups, and as might be expected, the groups have tended to become genetically distinct. The significant point is that, whatever the frequencies of blood types may be, there is no sign that generations of restriction to a particular occupation has produced individuals uniquely adapted to weaving or bookkeeping or herding, or in any way unable to learn a new trade when the opportunity arises.

Still, individuals vary — at least in their motivation and ability to perform well on aptitude and intelligence tests! This variation, like most, is determined partly by genetic and partly by cultural and environmental factors. Instead of fretting about the genetic component of intelligence, which we can do very little about, it would seem more sensible to do as much as we can to create a favorable environment for intelligence to express itself. One of the startling realizations to emerge from studies of human intelligence and capacity to learn is that none of us achieves more than a fraction of his total potential for learning and living. The genetic component is there; our environment limits its expression. With this vast unrealized potential in each of us, how absurd it is to quibble over what may or may not be a statistically significant difference in an intelligence test score.

As an individual you are an incredibly improbable phenomenon. Only one chance for you in $2^{3200}$ or $4^{3200}$, yet despite the odds against you, *you are.* You are "normal" or "average" only in being abnormal and not average in a great many ways, and yet, overall, in being fairly well attuned to your environment. You could learn another language if you had to, and adopt another culture with at least a modicum of success. Your body could adjust within limits to a different altitude or to a warmer climate or a colder one — but this is the subject of Chapter 8. Your name may be "Ole Svenson," which brings to mind a blue-eyed, blond man, and yet you may not look like that at all. Certainly one cannot decide from your name what your other characteristics are. You may be able to run a mile in 4 minutes or it might take you 10, or you might break down and pass out before getting 100 yards down the track. Your genes and your personal history have combined to make you what you are; and although it would be unwise for you to try to become a basketball player if you are 4 feet tall or a concert violinist if you are tone deaf, you are flexible enough to fill any of a large number of the niches our cultural and physical environment provides.

## REFERENCES

BROZEK, J., ED. 1966. *The Biology of Human Variation.* Ann. N.Y. Acad. Sci. 497–1068.

BUETTNER-JANUSCH, J. 1966. *Origins of Man: Physical Anthropology.* New York: John Wiley & Sons.

CAVALLI-SFORZA, L. L., AND W. F. BODMER. 1971. *The Genetics of Human Populations.* San Francisco: W. H. Freeman and Co.

HIRSCH, J., ED. 1967. *Behavior-Genetic Analysis.* New York: McGraw-Hill.

LIVINGSTONE, F. B. 1967. *Abnormal Hemoglobins in Human Populations.* Chicago: Aldine.

MATHER, K. 1964. *Human Diversity: The Nature and Significance of Differences Among Men.* Edinburgh: Oliver & Boyd.

MEDAWAR, P. B. 1956. *The Uniqueness of the Individual.* London: Methuen.

OSBORNE, R., ED. 1971. *The Biological and Social Meaning of Race.* San Francisco: W. H. Freeman and Co.

RACE, R., AND R. SANGER. 1962. *Blood Groups in Man.* 4th ed. Oxford: Blackwell Scientific Publications.

SARGENT, F. II, AND K. P. WEINMAN. 1966. *Physiological Individuality.* Ann. N.Y. Acad. Sci. 134: 696–719.

WECHSLER, D. 1935. *The Range of Human Capabilities.* Baltimore: Williams & Wilkins.

WILLIAMS, R. J. 1956. *Biochemical Individuality: The Basis of the Genetotropic Concept.* New York: John Wiley & Sons.

WILLIAMS, R. J. 1957. Normal young men. *Persp. Biol. Med.* 1:97–104.

WILLIAMS, R. J. 1969. Heredity, human understanding, and civilization. *American Scientist.* 57:237–243.

# · 7 ·

JOHN J. B. ANDERSON

# The Human Life Cycle

It has been said that we begin to die as soon as we are born. Actually, we begin to die as soon as we are conceived, as soon as the ovum is fertilized by a sperm. Cellular death plays an important role in the development of an embryo. Death of individuals and species plays an equally important role in the development of new forms of life. Without death, life would never have progressed beyond the first few generations of primitive organisms that lived more than 2 billion years ago. Without it there would have been no complex life forms, no evolution, and no man.

This chapter discusses human development from conception through old age to death. The life cycles of organisms are usually pictured as the succession of stages they pass through from their origin in the union of two sex cells until they produce more of the kinds of cells from which they originated, and a new generation is born. Although the process is called a cycle, it really is a spiral. It does not go back to exactly where it started. Each generation is followed by another which traverses approximately the same path but in a slightly different place and time. Furthermore, only a part of the life of an individual is involved in the spiral — only that part from one conception to the next. After the individual can no longer reproduce, he is dead as far as physical evolutuion is concerned. An aging person, however, can still contribute to cultural evolution. Our species is unique in this respect.

## CONCEPTS BASIC TO UNDERSTANDING THE LIFE CYCLE

The stages in the human life cycle are programmed in the DNA of the fertilized egg, but successful execution of the program involves the way in which cells of the developing person interact with their neighbors and with

150

their environment. Throughout life there is an interplay of building up and breaking down of complex molecules, cellular structures, and cells. At first the constructive processes predominate as we grow and mature; later, the breaking-down processes supersede, and we senesce and finally die. Before examining the major events in the stages of the human life cycle, we will review some basic terms and concepts.

*CELLS.* Cells are the basic units of life. Their development and diversification in form and function are involved in the development of each person as a whole organism. Three processes in cellular development can be recognized conceptually, although they are not separable in the normal life of a cell. *Growth* is the irreversible increase in size or number of cells. Increase in cell size is called *hypertrophy*; increase in cell number is called *hyperplasia*. *Determination* is the process by which a cell becomes limited in its possible developmental paths; for example, at some point early in the life of an embryo, certain cells become destined to form muscle cells, and muscle cells they will be despite any experimental attempts to change them. Similarly, regions of the embryo become determined to form eyes, limbs, or other structures before cells of these regions can be distinguished structurally or functionally from their neighbors. *Differentiation* is the actual appearance of new biochemical or structural properties in a cell. Integrated development of cells leads to formation of tissues and organs — to *morphogenesis*, or the generation of form.

Reference is often made to an "unspecialized" — a sort of average — cell. But the average, unspecialized cell is as illusory as the average person. Even an unfertilized egg, or a fertilized egg, a *zygote*, is highly specialized. It is specialized for development, and for this it contains an enormous amount of food and the kinds of RNA that will launch the new individual on its developmental course. Figure 7.1 shows some of the kinds of cells that make up the human body.

Some kinds of cells are renewed continuously throughout life. These cells occur in the skin, the blood-forming organs, and the respiratory, digestive, genital, and urinary systems. Other cells normally experience little renewal, although some may show hypertrophy or hyperplasia, or both, in response to injury or to surgical removal of part of an organ. These cells occur in the liver, kidney, various glands, and connective tissue. Still other cells, such as those of the central nervous system, sense organs, the medulla of the adrenal glands, and muscle, are never or infrequently renewed. For the most part man and other mammals have lost the powers of regeneration common in some lower animals like the salamander, which can grow a new limb or tail if it loses the old one. Except for the few cases mentioned, we can *heal* but we do not *regenerate* a lost or damaged part. A skin wound may leave a permanent scar called a keloid, consisting of connective tissue which is not the same as the tissue that was destroyed.

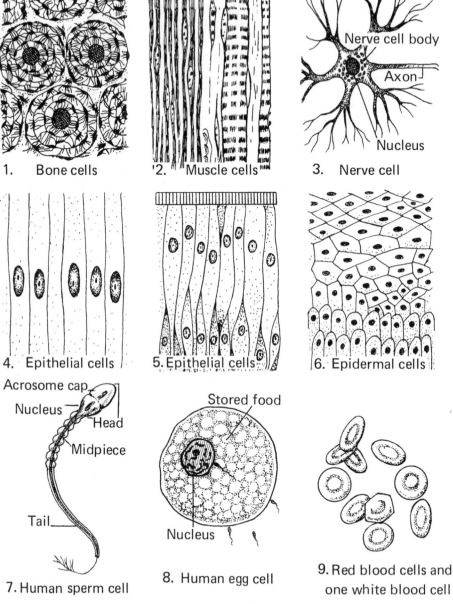

1. Bone cells
2. Muscle cells
3. Nerve cell

Nerve cell body
Axon
Nucleus

4. Epithelial cells
5. Epithelial cells
6. Epidermal cells

Acrosome cap
Nucleus
Head
Midpiece
Tail
7. Human sperm cell

Stored food
Nucleus
8. Human egg cell

9. Red blood cells and one white blood cell

**Figure 7–1** Some types of cells found in the human body. The function of each cell is related to its structural specialization. The nerve cell, for example, has many branches which communicate with other cells. The tail of the sperm confers motility necessary for reaching the egg. The egg stores food to nourish the embryo during early cell divisions. Red blood cells lose their nuclei during maturation and become flattened discs loaded with one important protein, hemoglobin, for the transport and exchange of gases. (From W. D. McElroy and C. P. Swanson, eds., *Modern Cell Biology*, Prentice-Hall, Englewood Cliffs, N. J., 1968.)

CHROMOSOMES AND MITOSIS.    We have seen that the hereditary material, DNA, resides largely in the chromosomes of the cell. Although the construction of a large molecule and the final form of an individual depend on many interactions beyond the gene, beyond the cell, and even beyond the individual in the external environment, fundamentally all development rests on the DNA in the genes. The genes set the limits and determine the range of possibilities within which development occurs.

Except during preparation for sexual reproduction, most nucleated cells in man have 46 chromosomes, 23 pairs, which reside in a structure called the *nucleus* (see Figure 7.1). Typical cell reproduction involves a definite series of steps. If you recall the structure of DNA described in Chapter 4, you will remember that DNA is a double helix, two paired, parallel, spiral strands consisting of specific sequences of **nucleotides.** Before cellular reproduction takes place, each of these strands produces an exact (barring mistakes!) copy of its partner. The next step is *mitosis*, the division of the chromosomes and cell nucleus (see Chapter 4, Figure 4.2). This process results in formation of two new nuclei, each containing a full complement of 46 chromosomes. The later stages of mitosis are usually accompanied by cell division, a process which is accomplished by the formation of a new membrane between the daughter cells or the "pinching off" of one cell from the other.

MEIOSIS.    The specialized cells which are destined to take part in formation of new individuals are the sex cells, also called germinal (germ) cells or *gametes:* sperm in the male and ova or eggs in the female. These cells have a remarkable story of their own. Early in the life of the *embryo*, about 24 days after fertilization, primordial germ cells are first distinguishable in the wall of the yolk sac. From there they migrate into the developing *gonads*, ovaries in the female and testes in the male. We will first consider the development of eggs, a process called *oogenesis*.

Once in the ovary, where they are now called *oogonia*, the germ cells divide many times by mitosis. At the end of this period of proliferation there is a phase of growth and differentiation as the oogonia develop into *oocytes*. Human females, and probably the females of all mammalian species, are born with all the oocytes they will have in their entire lifetime — some 400,000. (A single ejaculation of semen, in contrast, may contain hundreds of times this many sperm. A normal male will have about 100 million sperm per milliliter in an ejaculate of 2 to 4 milliliters.) When a woman becomes sexually mature, her oocytes develop, usually one each month, into *ova*. In this process they undergo two meiotic divisions (Figure 7.2), as a result of which the number of chromosomes is reduced from the diploid number of 46 in the oocyte to the haploid number of 23 in the ovum. Although two meiotic divisions result in formation of four haploid nuclei, only one of them survives in a functional ovum. As you can see from Figure 7.2, the products of meiotic division are very unequal in size. The significantly larger ovum

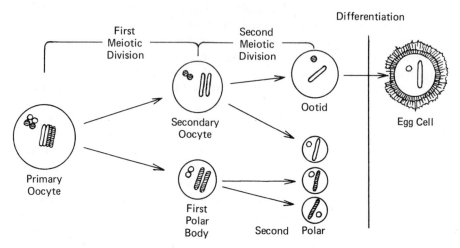

**Figure 7-2** The formation of an egg cell. Chromosomes in the primary oocyte are shown as already having doubled and come together in homologous pairs. The homologous pairs separate in the first meiotic division. The division is unequal, resulting in a large secondary oocyte and a small polar body. Note that these two cells do not contain identical sets of chromosomes. (How else could the chromosomes have been distributed?) Four cells result from the second meiotic division: a large ootid and three tiny polar bodies. The ootid develops into the egg. The polar bodies eventually disintegrate.

may result because of a need for nutrient stores and metabolic machinery for development of the embryo. About a month elapses before the developing embryo is able to derive all its food from its environment or to manufacture some of the molecules and structures necessary for its development; it must exist on what is provided by the egg.

Development of sperm is similar to development of eggs, but there are some important differences. Once they are located in the testis, primordial germ cells are called *spermatogonia*. Some spermatogonia, unlike oogonia, maintain their capacity to proliferate throughout the lifetime of the individual. Thus there is always a source of abundant *spermatocytes*, which, unlike oocytes, grow very little. Two meiotic divisions produce four spermatids, each of which can develop into a functional sperm (Figure 7.3). The egg is specialized to provide the early needs of the embryo; the sperm is specialized for motility so that it may reach and fertilize the egg within 24 hours after release. The process of meiosis is essential to sexual reproduction; if the number of chromosomes were not halved in the sex cells, each generation would have twice the number of chromosomes its parents had.

SEX CHROMOSOMES.    Of the 23 pairs of chromosomes, the members of 22 pairs are similar as seen under the microscope, but the members of the 23rd pair differ between the sexes (Figure 7.4). This pair is known as the *sex chromosomes*. In the female the two sex chromosomes are structurally

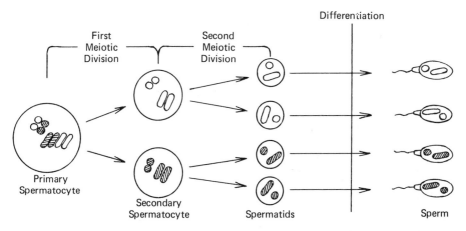

**Figure 7-3** The formation of sperm. Chromosomes shown in the primary spermatocyte have doubled and come together in homologous pairs, which separate in the first meiotic division. The second meiotic division yields four spermatids, which develop into mature sperm. It appears that there are two types of sperm, with respect to the chromosomes they contain; but if crossing over has occurred (as it almost invariably has), no two sperm will carry the same genetic information.

identical and are called X chromosomes, whereas in the male the two differ in size and shape. One of them is the same as the X chromosome of the female; the other is much smaller, bears a different complement of genes, and is called a Y chromosome. All body, or *somatic*, cells of the female contain two Xs and each ovum contains one X. All body cells of the male

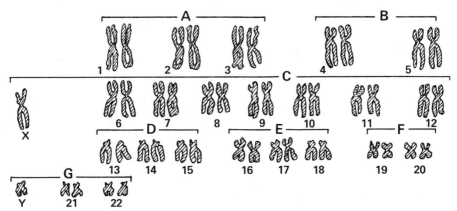

**Figure 7-4** The chromosomes of a human male. When white blood cells are grown in culture and treated in a certain way, the chromosomes can easily be counted and classified. Here, the homologous pairs are shown grouped according to structural similarities. The chromosomes are in the metaphase of mitosis, when they can be seen as double structures of various lengths joined at a place characteristic of each chromosome. Note the large X and the small Y, the sex chromosomes. (From Helena Curtis, *Biology*, Worth Pub., New York, 1968, p. 394.)

contain one X and one Y, and each sperm contains either an X or a Y. Not all genes on the sex chromosomes are related to sexual characteristics, however. Among the better known mutant genes on the X chromosome are those that cause **hemophilia** and color blindness. Because they are on the X chromosome, such genes are said to be sex-linked, although they have nothing to do with sex itself. And although a Y chromosome is essential for development of a normal male, for many years the only trait known to be determined by the Y chromosome was hairy ears! Genes related to sexual development are also found on chromosomes other than the sex chromosomes. Finally, many things can go wrong in the process of development to make a person with normal sex chromosomes abnormal in sexual characteristics. People with abnormal complements of sex chromosomes show sterility and other types of abnormality. Some of the combinations of sex chromosomes that have been observed, and their phenotypic results, are shown in Table 7.1.

*FECUNDITY AND FERTILITY.*    These two terms are often used interchangeably by those who do not understand their difference. *Fecundity* is the ability to produce offspring, and it is a characteristic of the species. *Fertility* is the actual production of offspring. A person may be fecund but

**TABLE 7.1**
**Variations in Number of Sex Chromosomes**

| Genetic Constitution | Phenotype |
|---|---|
| XY | Normal, fertile male |
| XYY | Fertile male; may be very tall |
| XXY | Sterile male, sexually undeveloped |
| XXYY | Sterile male |
| XXXY | Sterile male, sexually undeveloped |
| XXXXY | Sterile male, sexually undeveloped |
| XX | Normal, fertile female |
| XO (1 X chromosome; second sex chromosome missing) | Sterile female with webbed neck, short stature, and other abnormalities; many XO fetuses abort |
| XXX | Female, usually sterile |
| XXXX | Sterile female |
| XXXXX | Sterile female |

You may wonder how gross chromosomal abnormalities like these could result in a viable individual, when similar abnormalities involving other chromosomes are almost invariably incompatible with life. The explanation is probably related to the fact that very early in embryonic life, all X chromosomes but one become almost completely inactive, so that the effects of multiple X chromosomes, unlike the effects of excess chromosomes of the other 22 pairs, are minimal. That the inactive X is not *completely* inert is suggested by the fact that individuals with extra Xs are somewhat abnormal, and the XO female (who has only one sex chromosome) has multiple defects. The Y chromosome carries few genes, and none that are necessary for life. Extra Ys do not appear to create a drastic imbalance.

not fertile; that is, he or she may be capable of producing offspring but may never produce any. On the other hand, if a person is fertile, he or she must be fecund.

In women fecundity and fertility are related to the processes of ovulation, fertilization of the egg, implantation of the early embryo, and maintenance of pregnancy. In the male the formation, ejaculation, motility, and capacitation of sperm are key factors. Although it takes only one sperm to fertilize an egg, many sperm are necessary in order for a successful fertilization to occur. If the number of sperm in an ejaculate falls below 150 to 200 million, fertilization usually does not occur. Probably no more than 100 sperm ever reach the vicinity of the egg. It is thought that the additional sperm produce enzymes and other substances that make it possible for the one successful sperm to enter the egg.

*STERILITY.*     Sterility is the inability to produce offspring. It may be caused by structural or physiological defects of the reproductive system of either sex. In the female the oviducts or the uterus may be blocked, or the ovaries may not function properly because of the presence of fluid-filled cysts. In the male there may be structural defects in the ducts that collect and transport sperm and seminal fluids. Endocrine malfunctions and **infantilism** may occur in either sex. **Psychosomatic factors** may also play a role. Any abnormality in the number and type of sex chromosomes usually results in sterility. The range of sexual development that is observed is related to the fact that although genetic sex is determined at conception, sexual differentiation does not occur until the third month of **gestation** and it can be modified by many factors. The early embryo is potentially bisexual, containing all the structures necessary for development of either sex. The chromosomes merely give it a bias toward one sex or the other.

*METABOLISM.*     Metabolism is the total of all chemical reactions within a living cell or organism. It includes both synthetic, or anabolic, processes, and destructive, or catabolic, ones. Examples of *anabolism* are the fabrication of the complex molecules and structures of the cell, including DNA, RNA, proteins, and cell membranes. Examples of *catabolism* are cellular respiration and digestion. Metabolism as a concept represents the seething, ceaseless chemical activity of the molecules in a cell, and there is no way to measure it in its entirety. The basal metabolic rate, abbreviated BMR, can be measured, however, in terms of oxygen consumption and carbon dioxide release under controlled environmental conditions. The BMR represents the minimal rate at which energy is expended to maintain respiration, circulation, body temperature, glandular function, and the other activities of the body at rest. It is usually estimated in the morning in an individual who is at rest, after a night's fasting has eliminated the component of metabolism involved in digestion. The metabolic rate is high during periods of growth and lower when growth slows down or stops; it decreases steadily with age. Metabolic rate is also related to the total surface area of the body, being higher in smaller individuals. In a general way the hormone thyroxin regulates the BMR, but other hormones are also involved, especially during periods of rapid growth.

*HORMONES.* Hormones are biologically active molecules synthesized in minute amounts by specialized glands called *endocrines*, in response to internal or external environmental stimuli (Figure 7.5). The endocrine system has an integrating function and it operates at a nonconscious or automatic level. The hormones serve as chemical messengers which act on specific target organs, whose cells in turn respond in a variety of ways — in-

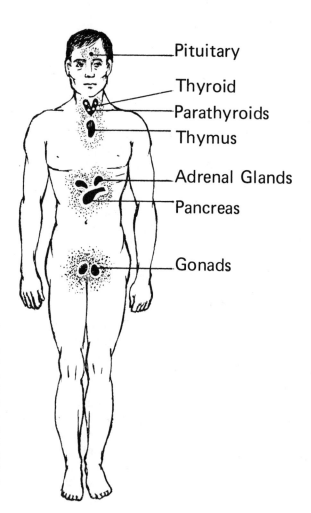

Pituitary

Thyroid

Parathyroids

Thymus

Adrenal Glands

Pancreas

Gonads

**Figure 7–5** The endocrine glands. These glands secrete tiny amounts of chemicals called hormones, which enter the bloodstream and act on target organs in various parts of the body. The endocrine glands in turn respond to messages received through the bloodstream or nerves, to either increase or decrease production of hormone. They are vital in regulating the function of the body.

cluding, sometimes, the release of another hormone. Some of the many hormones that exist in man will be discussed in this chapter and in Chapter 8. A partial list is given in Table 7.2.

Hormones are chemically diverse. The pituitary hormones are proteins, as is insulin. Thyroxin is an amino acid combined with four atoms of iodine. The sex hormones and those produced by the cortex of the adrenal glands are members of a biologically important group of compounds called steroids, which share a basic molecular ring structure. Some steroids are poisons; others are among the substances that cause cancer.

The *pituitary gland* has been called the master gland. This small body, about the size and shape of a kidney bean, is located at the base of the brain near the *hypothalamus,* in the center of the skull (Figure 7.5). Although its secretions control the activity of many other glands and organs, the pituitary itself takes many of its cues from the hypothalamus, some of whose cells have extensions which terminate in the posterior part of the gland. The hypothalamus is part of the "old brain," in terms of evolutionary development. Its role is to keep various vegetative functions of the body proceeding smoothly and without the intervention of conscious control. It communicates with the anterior pituitary by means of "release factors" (RFs). The two hormones secreted by the posterior lobe of the pituitary are actually synthesized in the hypothalamus and transmitted to the pituitary, where they are stored.

Among the hormones secreted by the anterior pituitary are several *tropic* hormones, hormones that act on other glands to regulate their activity. The tropic hormones act on the thyroid, the sex glands, and the adrenals (Table 7.2). Another important pituitary product is growth hormone, which stimulates the growth of many tissues, most notably bone and muscle. The long bones (bones of the arms and legs, hands and feet) consist of a shaft with a knobby *epiphysis* or growth center at each end. Throughout childhood the shaft is separated from its epiphyses at either end by a plate of dividing cells which lay down a **cartilage** model to be replaced subsequently by true mineralized bone. At the same time, the cartilage grows away from the shaft, pushing the epiphyses ahead of it, thus increasing the length of the bone. Normally, some time during adolescence, the shaft "catches up" with its epiphyses, mineral matter is deposited throughout the epiphyseal plate, and so-called *epiphyseal closure* results. Growth in length is no longer possible. If there is insufficient growth hormone during childhood, hardening of the shaft outruns growth of cartilage, epiphyseal division ceases, and a dwarf results. An excess of growth hormone keeps the cartilage ahead of the bone in the race, long after growth ordinarily stops. The product of this unfortunate condition is a giant. Sometimes there is a renewed output of growth hormone after epiphyseal closure has occurred and increase in length of long bones is no longer possible. In this case growth is induced in the few epiphyses remaining "open," such as the lower jaw and the ends of

**TABLE 7.2**
**Principal Hormones of Human Endocrine Glands**

| Gland | Hormone | Principal Action | Mechanism Regulating Secretion |
|---|---|---|---|
| Pituitary, anterior lobe | Thyrotropic hormone | Stimulates thyroid | Hypothalamus, RF*; thyroxin in blood |
| | Gonadotropic hormones: Follicle-stimulating hormone (FSH) | Stimulates ovarian follicles | Hypothalamus, RF; estrogen in blood |
| | Luteinizing hormone (LH) | Stimulates testes in male, corpus luteum in female | Hypothalamus, RF; progesterone or testosterone in blood |
| | Adrenocorticotropic hormone (ACTH) | Stimulates adrenal cortex | Hypothalamus; adrenal cortical hormone in blood |
| | Growth hormone | Stimulates growth of bone and muscle | |
| | Prolactin | Stimulates lactation | Fetal hormones in maternal blood; corpus luteum |
| Pituitary, posterior lobe | Oxytocin (synthesized in hypothalamus) | Stimulates uterine contractions and ejection of milk | Nervous system |
| | Vasopressin (synthesized in hypothalamus) | Controls excretion of water | Nervous system |
| Thyroid | Thyroxin | Regulates metabolism and some aspects of development | Thyrotropic hormone |
| | Calcitonin | Regulates calcium metabolism | Concentration of calcium in blood |
| Parathyroid | Parathyroid hormone | Regulates calcium metabolism | Concentration of calcium in blood |
| Pancreas | Insulin | Decreases blood sugar, increases storage of glycogen | Concentration of sugar in blood |
| | Glucagon | Stimulates release of glycogen from liver | Concentration of sugar in blood |
| Adrenal cortex | Cortisone, aldosterone, and related hormones | Regulate metabolism of carbohydrate and salt and water balance | ACTH |
| Adrenal medulla | Adrenalin (epinephrine) | Increases blood sugar, dilates blood vessels, increases heartbeat | Nervous system |
| Ovary (corpus luteum) | Progesterone | Stimulates growth of uterine tissue | LH |
| Ovarian follicle | Estrogens | Stimulate development and maintenance of female sex characteristics | FSH |
| Testis | Testosterone | Stimulates development and maintenance of male sex characteristics | FSH |

* Release factor

the limbs, resulting in grotesque enlargement of hands, feet, and jaw, a condition called acromegaly.

Thyroxin, product of the thyroid gland, affects growth through its control of metabolic rate. If thyroid function is impaired during infancy, a condition known as cretinism results. It is characterized by retarded physical growth and development and severe mental retardation.

The deficiencies in pituitary growth hormone and thyroxin described above are genetically controlled, in most cases. The symptoms can be treated or prevented by administration of the needed hormones, although the condition cannot be cured because mutant genes will still be passed on to offspring. This kind of treatment of genetic disorders is one of the more obvious examples of how the environment can act to modify the phenotype. Under certain environmental conditions (namely, an external supply of hormone), a normal phenotype can be produced from an abnormal genotype.

The pituitary gonadotropins are follicle-stimulating hormone (FSH) and luteinizing hormone (LH). FSH triggers the growth of ovarian **follicles** and their secretion of estrogens, a group of female hormones. The process culminates in the maturation of one follicle and its rupture with the release of an ovum. Under the influence of LH, the ruptured follicle persists for a time as the corpus luteum (yellow body) and secretes a hormone called progesterone. In females, synthesis and release of all these hormones follows a cyclic monthly pattern. In males, however, the action and production of hormones is continuous. The action of FSH and LH in the male is incompletely understood, but they are necessary for the production of sperm and the synthesis and release of male hormones.

## STAGES IN THE LIFE CYCLE

As the individual develops from the fertilized egg to the adult to death, he progresses through seven stages of life, which have been broadly classified as prenatal life, neonatal life, infancy, childhood, puberty and adolescence, adulthood, and senescence (Table 7.3). While these categories are neither sharply defined nor universally accepted, they are useful for our purposes.

*PRENATAL LIFE.* The human egg is the largest cell in the body, and one of the most sluggish, metabolically. It possesses a unique complement of genes, but these have not yet expressed themselves. The egg does not complete its meiotic divisions until after fertilization, a process that generally occurs in the upper end of the *oviduct* (Figure 7.6). As the fertilized egg, or zygote, travels down the oviduct it divides a number of times. These divisions are called *cleavages*. During cleavage, the overall size of the embryo remains constant or even decreases slightly, so that after 3 or 4 days of its journey the embryo consists of several dozen or perhaps 100 cells approximating the average size of cells in the adult body. The embryo's own genes have begun to function; it is synthesizing RNA and protein; and its metabolic rate has increased from the minimal level in the egg to the highest of any tissue in the adult. It is already an individual, capable of evoking an **antigen-antibody response** in the mother, but a mucoid coating protects it from this fate.

After about 3 days the embryo enters the **uterus,** which itself has undergone changes since ovulation. At the time of ovulation it presented an environment favorable to sperm but deadly to an embryo. During the

**TABLE 7.3**
**Classification of the Stages of Human Life**

| Stage | Approximate Age Span | Major Physical Characteristics |
|---|---|---|
| Prenatal Life | | |
|   Fertilized ovum | From fertilization to about 1 week | Free-living |
|   Embryo | About 1 to 8 weeks | Free-living, but implanted |
|   Fetus | About 8 to 40 weeks | Dependent on placenta for nutrition |
| Neonatal Life | First 2 post-natal weeks | |
| Infancy | From the 3rd postnatal week to about 1 year | Improved physical coordination until attainment of erect posture |
| Childhood | | |
|   Early | About 2 to 6 years | Milk teeth |
|   Middle | About 7 to 9 or 10 years | Permanent teeth |
|   Late | About 9-10 to 12-16 years | Prepuberty; longer period by about 2 years in males |
| Adolescence | About 12-13 to 16-18 in females About 14-16 to about 20 in males | Changes in body size and conformation |
| Adulthood | About age 20 to beyond age 65 | General decline in bodily function and conformation |
| Senescence | Sometime beyond age 65 | More rapid deterioration of bodily function and mind |

Adapted from L. B. Arey, 1965. *Developmental Anatomy*, 7th ed., Saunders, Philadelphia.

embryo's journey down the oviduct, the uterus changed to a favorable place for the receipt of the embryo and its implantation. After about 5 days of living free in the uterus, the embryo has differentiated into a *blastocyst*, consisting of an inner cell mass surrounded by the *trophoblast* — a tissue highly specialized for the critical process of implantation in the uterine wall. Now the embryo must become united with the mother if it is to survive. The trophoblast invades the wall of the uterus and engulfs the maternal blood vessels; the *placenta*, which will be the mediator between the mother and the developing child for the next 8 or 9 months, has begun to form. The placenta is a remarkable tissue, composed largely of cells from the embryo but richly supplied with maternal blood. Through it the embryo obtains oxygen and nutrients, and exchanges carbon dioxide and some waste products. It also provides an immunological barrier (but not a foolproof one) between mother and child.

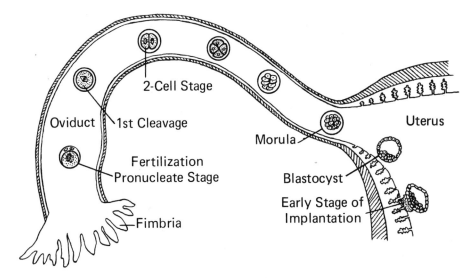

**Figure 7–6** Development of the human embryo from fertilization to the beginning of implantation in the uterine wall. The events diagrammed above take about 7 or 8 days time. It is thought that a very large number of embryos fail to become implanted, and abort without the pregnancy's being suspected.

The cozy picture of an unborn child developing safely and serenely in its watery home, remote from the outside world and the vicissitudes of environmental change, could not be farther from the truth. The chances of death are greater before birth than at any other time except for extreme old age. An educated guess puts the mortality of pre-implantation embryos at about 30 percent. In later pregnancy, losses occur as abortions; and these, together with stillbirths, claim about 20 percent of all conceptions. So about half of the fertilized eggs fail to produce surviving infants. Losses may be due to genetic defects, chromosomal errors during meiosis (like loss or duplication of one or more chromosomes), inadequacies in the maternal environment, or damaging agents — radiation, drugs and other chemicals, immune reactions of the mother against the child, or pathogenic organisms like those causing German measles and venereal disease. Even before birth man is at the mercy of his environment!

The unborn child is not simply a small and immature baby. In many ways it is a very different organism, with specialized needs, functions, and responses. Table 7.4 shows the approximate times at which various structures and functions develop. By 8 weeks of age the embryo already resembles a human being, and from this time until birth it is called a *fetus*.

The fetal digestive system is immature, but it need not function because nutrients are received through the placenta as simple molecules ready for use: glucose, amino acids, fatty acids, vitamins, and minerals. Respiratory

**TABLE 7.4**
**Timetable of Prenatal Development**

| Age | Length, mm (crown/rump length, where applicable) | Weight, gm | Developmental Events* | | |
|---|---|---|---|---|---|
| | | | Blood and Circulatory System | Nervous System | Skeleton and Muscles |
| 1 day 3 days | 0.15 | | | | |
| 7 days | 0.3 | | | | |
| 9 days | | | | | |
| 14 days | 1.3 | | First blood cells produced in yolk sac; heart primordia | First differentiation of nervous system, as neural plate | |
| 18 days 21 days | 2.5 | | Heart fused into single tube; pulsations of heart | Spinal canal closing | Spinal column forming (cartilage) |
| 26 days | | | Heart beating | Spinal canal closed | |
| 4 weeks | 4 | 0.02 | | Spinal & cranial nerves developing | Spinal column complete (cartilage) |
| 4½ weeks | 5 | | | | |
| 5 weeks | 7-8 | | Lymphatic system developing | | |
| 6 weeks | 12-13 | | First blood cells formed in liver; heart enclosed inside body | Five primary divisions of brain established | |
| 7 weeks | 17-20 | | Electrocardiogram shows wave patterns similar to adult; heart valves formed | | First bone cells formed, in arms |
| 8 weeks | 27-30 | 1.0 | Blood vascular system is complete | Optic nerve developing | Reflexes developing; muscle contraction on electrical stimulation; diaphragm developing |
| 9 weeks | 39-41 | | Abundant blood cells forming in liver | | Kicking; movement may be felt |
| 10 weeks | 50-55 | | First blood cells formed in bone marrow | | Sucking reflex developed |
| 3 months | 75-80 | 14-20 | | Respiratory center of brain functional | Swallowing; respiratory movements; Babinski reflex developed |
| 4 months | ca. 150 | 105-120 | Blood cells formed in spleen | | |
| 5 months | ca. 200 | 200-310 | | | |
| 6 months | ca. 240 | 635-650 | | | |
| 7 months | ca. 280 | 780-850 | | | |

[1]The sequence of events in normal development is inviolable, because each event depends on preceding events. There are some differences in the developmental timetable among sources because of the difficulty of pinpointing

| Endocrine System | Digestive System | Face and Head | Miscellaneous |
|---|---|---|---|
| | | | Fertilization in Fallopian tube<br>Clump of ca. 32 cells enters uterus<br>Embryo a two-layered disc with amniotic cavity; contacts uterine wall, implanatation begins<br>Embryo secreting chorionic gonadotropin hormone which prevents menstruation; implantation continuing |
| | | Beginning of head process | Sex chromatin may be detected; primitive streak forming |
| Thyroid primordia | Liver primordia; differentition of foregut, midgut, hindgut | Eye primordia and ear pits | Placental circulation developing; lung primordia; beginning of embryonic kidney |
| Pancreas primordia | Stomach forming | | Arm buds forming |
| Thymus primordia | Gall bladder primordia; esophagus and small intestine forming | Lens of eye forming | Leg buds; hands and finger primordia; paired lungs; placental circulation well established |
| | | Tongue primordia; pigment in retina | Trachea developing |
| | | Cornea forming; jaws and epiglottis developing; nasal pit and outer ears forming | Spleen primordia; genital ridges and ureters; membranes forming heart, lung, and abdominal cavities |
| Parathyroids differentiating | Salivary glands and large intestine developing | Inner and outer ears developing | Mammary glands beginning; undifferentiated gonads; first signs of fingerprints; heart enclosed within body wall |
| Pituitary developing; traces of thyroxin formed in thyroid | | Neck region becomes distinct from head | Differentiation of testes and ovaries; primordial germ cells present; permanent kidney developing |
| Testes secreting androgens; adrenals developing, may be secreting hormones | | Palate, taste buds, and eyelids developing | Embryo is now a fetus; external sex organs developing; larynx, rectum, urinary bladder forming |
| | Secretion of gastric juice | Lips and buds of baby teeth developing | Hair follicles, oil and sweat glands in skin; fingernails; genital sex determinable; permanent kidney excreting urea and uric acid |
| Islets of Langerhans developing in pancreas | Gall bladder secreting bile | | Skin completed |
| | | | Structure of placenta fully developed and functional |
| Pancreas secreting insulin | Digestive enzymes secreted by salivary glands, stomach, liver, and small intestine | Eyebrows and eyelashes growing | Tonsils developing |
| | | Buds of permanent teeth forming | Fat being deposited in body |
| Large amounts of thyroxin secreted | | Fetus opens and closes eyes, responds to sound | Body hair growing |
| | | | Excellent chance of survival if born |

the exact time at which a structure or function first appears and because of differences in criteria for identifying a structure or function. In general, we have taken the earliest times mentioned.

functions are also carried out through the placenta. Because gases must move to and from the fetus along a concentration gradient and through a placenta that requires a large amount of oxygen for its own metabolism, the concentration of oxygen in fetal blood is only about one third that in maternal blood and the concentration of carbon dioxide is somewhat higher. Clearly the fetus does not suffer from this. Its hemoglobin and heart function efficiently so that plenty of oxygen is available to fetal tissues even though the concentration is low. (In the same way, the concentration of glucose is higher in maternal blood than in fetal, because glucose must pass from mother to fetus through the placenta, which uses a large portion of it for its own respiration. Still, the fetus does not suffer from hypoglycemia.)

The fetal circulatory system is essentially like that of the child, except for an ingenious shunt that diverts blood from the lungs and into the umbilical cord and placenta. The shunt involves two openings, which must close at birth when umbilical circulation is cut off and the lungs begin to function. One of these is a muscular opening between the pulmonary artery (which, after birth, carries oxygen-poor blood to the lungs) and the aorta (which carries oxygenated blood from the heart). The other is a valve between the right and left upper chambers of the heart, which serves to equalize pressure in the two chambers. (Since the lungs are nonfunctional, there is little or no blood returning directly to the left chamber.)

The fetal endocrine system becomes functional some time during the third month of development, producing the same hormones that are produced in the adult, in response to the same stimuli. Fetal hormones, however, can profoundly influence the mother, while maternal hormones only indirectly affect the fetus. For example, a deficiency of insulin in the mother, leading to high concentrations of blood sugar, will cause an increase in secretion of insulin in the fetus. In response to increased levels of insulin, glucose in the fetal blood is converted at a high rate to glycogen and fat. For this reason the baby of a diabetic mother may be very large and fat at birth. As another example, adrenal steroid hormones administered to the mother may cross the placenta and enter the fetus, where they depress secretion of similar hormones by the fetal adrenal glands.

The fetal endocrine system has several specialized functions which it performs once and then never again. One of these is sex determination, which we have seen is sensitive to many influences, sex chromosomes notwithstanding. Another is the synthesis of huge quantities of estrogens which are secreted by the placenta into the maternal circulation, and which are involved in the initiation of **lactation** and labor.

While the fetus is immature in many ways at the time of birth, its survival depends on almost immediate adjustment to the new conditions in the outside world. Recent studies of fetal behavior indicate that the fetus has been "practicing" many of the behaviors on which its survival will depend.

Although the lungs do not function, unmistakable breathing movements occur before birth, especially during periods of sleep. The fetus also swallows large amounts of fluid from the sac in which it floats. And it is not uncommon for x-rays to show a fetus sucking its thumb! Finally, the fetus can, and does, respond to unusual levels of any sensory stimuli — temperature, light, sound, and tactile stimuli.

We have seen that the embryo and fetus are influenced by an interplay of genetic and environmental factors, just as is the person after birth. Genes and groups of genes are "turned on," function for a while, and then are "turned off," perhaps never to function again in the life of the cell or the man. Beginning with a common genetic heritage, cells fulfill their destiny through their location and the messages they exchange with their neighbors. Some cells are programmed to die, and in their death the shape of an arm and a hand emerges from shapelessness. At almost any step of the way the genetic plan can be sabotaged by maternal malnutrition or disease, by drugs or radiation, or by immune reaction of the mother against the foreign life in her body.

Scientists have long remarked at the resemblance between embryonic development of the individual (ontogenesis) and the stages of evolutionary development of the species (phylogenesis). The course of development seems strangely devious at times. What place have gill slits, for example, in an animal like a man? A clue comes from merging the insights of genetics, evolution, and development. Both evolution and development proceed step by step, with no shortcuts, each step being evoked by what went on before. Development reflects sequential expression of different parts of the genetic instructions, and the different genes can exert their influence only if conditions are right for them. Genes that prevent the hair from graying are not much use to a man who is bald at 30. Our genes have evolved from the genes of our ancestors, however far back you care to go. When natural selection selects phenotypes with advanced characteristics and adaptations, it selects genes not only for the new traits but also all the genes involved in early developmental events that prepared the way for expression of the new genes. Our eustachian tubes, tonsils, and several other structures evolved from parts that gave rise to gills in aquatic animals. Thus we must begin to make gills in order to have our complicated inner ears.

*NEONATAL LIFE.* This period encompasses the first two weeks after birth. Labor and delivery are critical times for both mother and child because of the many physiologic and anatomic adjustments necessary for success. Normally, once breathing begins, the opening between the pulmonary artery and the aorta closes in response to increased oxygen concentration, and the valve between the upper chambers of the heart closes in response to higher blood pressure. If either of these closures fails to occur, much blood

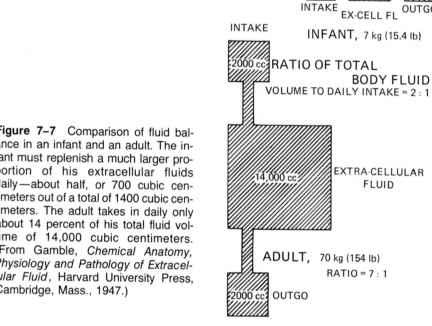

INTAKE  OUTGO

INTAKE  EX-CELL FL

INFANT, 7 kg (15.4 lb)

RATIO OF TOTAL
BODY FLUID
VOLUME TO DAILY INTAKE = 2 : 1

EXTRA-CELLULAR
FLUID

ADULT, 70 kg (154 lb)
RATIO = 7 : 1

OUTGO

**Figure 7–7** Comparison of fluid balance in an infant and an adult. The infant must replenish a much larger proportion of his extracellular fluids daily—about half, or 700 cubic centimeters out of a total of 1400 cubic centimeters. The adult takes in daily only about 14 percent of his total fluid volume of 14,000 cubic centimeters. (From Gamble, *Chemical Anatomy, Physiology and Pathology of Extracellular Fluid*, Harvard University Press, Cambridge, Mass., 1947.)

will continue to bypass the lung and the newborn will suffer from lack of oxygen. The digestive system must begin to break down complex molecules. The newborn is susceptible to a variety of problems stemming from his incomplete ability to regulate his own systems under the variable conditions of the outside world. Common problems involve temperature regulation nutrition, fluid imbalance, endocrine disorders, **jaundice,** liver dysfunction, and allergic and immunologic reactions.

Fluid balance is especially difficult for a newborn to maintain, particularly if he is suffering from fever or diarrhea, because of his small volume of total body water. Figure 7.7 compares the water balance in a 7 kilogram infant with that in a 70 kilogram adult. Note the infant's relatively large daily intake and outgo of water in comparison with the total volume of extracellular fluid. The body surface is proportionately large, and the basal metabolic rate per kilogram is concomitantly increased. Taking an infant's minimal fluid output as 300 milliliters per day, its extracellular fluid would be exhausted in 5 days if it were not replenished. In contrast, the extracellular fluid of an adult, taking his minimal output as 1,400 milliliters, would be exhausted in 10 days. Other things being equal, an infant's survival margin is about half that of an adult. Added to this, an infant is relatively imprecise in regulating his extracellular fluid volume.

The newborn's immune system is not fully developed. The mother's blood, which passes through the placenta, contains antibodies that help to defend the newborn against disease in his most vulnerable period. However, since the newborn is unable to produce his own antibodies (gamma globulins), his immunity is decreased as these molecules are degraded, until in the second month when he becomes able to synthesize his own antibodies.

It is difficult enough for an organism without gross defects to adjust to the new environment after birth. Many defective fetuses that were viable in their intrauterine world cannot make it outside. For example, living fetuses have been born lacking kidneys or almost completely lacking brains. These are doomed to die shortly after birth.

*INFANCY.*　　Infancy begins the third week after birth and continues until about the end of the first year. During this period all organ systems develop following a genetically determined pattern — which, again, can be modified by malnutrition, disease, and other environmental factors. Figure 7.8 shows how the proportions of the body change with age as the limbs grow more than the initially oversize trunk and absurdly large head. Table 7.5 shows the order and time of development of motor skills. Other activities requiring considerable coordination soon follow. No one has to teach a baby to do those things. He does them automatically as soon as he is able, just as a squirrel climbs and a bird flies.

Because growth requires constant remodeling, the skeleton changes enormously during the infant's first year. Bone has a very high metabolic

## GENERAL FEATURES OF DEVELOPMENT

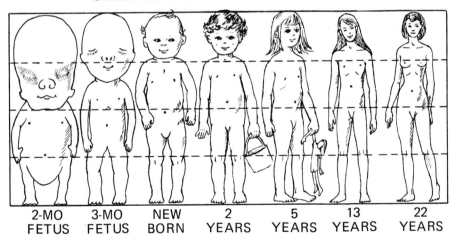

| 2-MO FETUS | 3-MO FETUS | NEW BORN | 2 YEARS | 5 YEARS | 13 YEARS | 22 YEARS |

**Figure 7–8** Changes in relative size of head, trunk, and limbs as a function of age. (Adapted from L. B. Arey, 1965. *Developmental Anatomy*, 7th ed., W. B. Saunders Co., Philadelphia, 1965.)

**TABLE 7.5**
**Behavioral Development of the Neonate**
**and Infant During the First Year**

| Behavior | Age in Months |
|----------|:---------------:|
| Suckles | 0 |
| Smiles | 1 |
| Vocalizes | 1-2 |
| Controls head | 2-3 |
| Controls hands | 3-4 |
| Rolls over | 4-5 |
| Sits briefly | 6-7 |
| Crawls | 7-8 |
| Grasps | 8-9 |
| Pulls up | 9 |
| Walks with support | 9-10 |
| Stands alone | 10-11 |
| Walks alone | 11-12 |

From A. C. Guyton. 1971. *Textbook of Medical Physiology*, 4th ed. Saunders, Philadelphia.

rate. There is almost a complete turnover, or renewal, of skeletal calcium. For this reason it is thought that infants might be less susceptible than adolescents to the effects of strontium-90, a long-lived radioisotope produced in large amounts in nuclear explosions, which may replace some of the calcium in bone.

Other notable changes take place during infancy. The major tracts of the central nervous system become covered by an insulating **lipid sheath,** which allows nerve impulses to travel faster. The gastrointestinal tract is able to handle an increasing variety of solid foods. There is improvement in neural and endocrine control of all body systems. By the end of the first year the infant has learned a good deal about his world, including some comprehension of that uniquely human achievement, language.

Infancy and old age are the two periods when susceptibility to infectious disease is greatest. Respiratory infections are frequent and often severe. In infancy, too, malnutrition can cause irreversible reduction in growth, sometimes accompanied by mental retardation. Malnourished babies are especially susceptible to diseases of all kinds.

CHILDHOOD.   This period follows infancy and lasts until puberty. It can be subdivided into three periods: early childhood, the milk tooth period, from years 2 through 6; middle childhood, the permanent tooth period, from 7 through 9 or 10; and late childhood, the prepuberal period, from 9 or 10 to 12–15 in girls and 13–16 in boys. In the Western nations, improved nutrition has been bringing earlier sexual development and shortening the prepuberal period, particularly in girls.

Skeletal growth and remodeling continue during childhood, accompanied by a high rate of metabolism. The full complement of 24 deciduous ("milk") teeth is present by about the sixth year; during the following year the permanent teeth begin to erupt (Figure 7.9). The importance of a well-orchestrated metabolism and good nutrition during childhood cannot be overemphasized.

Childhood is also characterized by certain diseases such as mumps, infectious hepatitis, poliomyelitis, diptheria, measles, scarlet fever, and whooping cough. Whereas the scourge of these "childhood diseases" in advanced nations has been largely eliminated within the last two decades by immunization and antibiotics, in less-developed countries when a malnourished child contracts measles, he may die as a result of depressed immunologic responses. However, older people who are not immunized or who did not contract the diseases as children may suffer severely from them. Two common childhood diseases of malnutrition seen in less-developed countries are kwashiorkor (mainly protein deficiency) and marasmus (protein-calorie malnutrition) which are illustrated in Figure 7.10.

Childhood or its counterpart in other mammals is the time of greatest behavioral flexibility and learning. Basic behavioral patterns in most animals become firmly established during this period. The process of play, whether in wolf cubs, chimpanzees, or human children, is serious business — a pre-

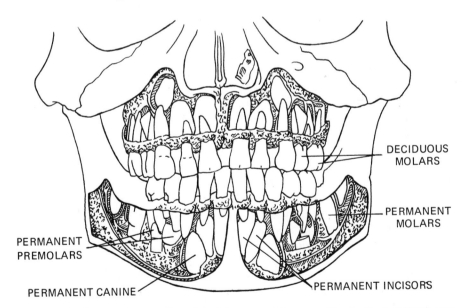

**Figure 7–9** The relative position of deciduous and permanent teeth. Buds for both sets of teeth develop during prenatal life and the permanent teeth are well formed by the time the complete set of deciduous teeth has erupted. (From L. B. Arey, *Developmental Anatomy*, 7th ed., W. B. Saunders Co., Philadelphia, 1965.)

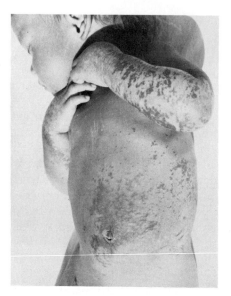

**Figure 7-10** (a) Photograph of a child with kwashiorkor, resulting from severe protein deficiency. Kwashiorkor frequently makes its appearance around the time of weaning. (b) Photograph of a child with marasmus, a disease caused by severe deficiency of both protein and calories. Treatment of these children is long and difficult, and many of them cannot be saved. (Both photos courtesy of Dr. Nevin S. Scrimshaw, Massachusetts Institute of Technology; Kwashiorkor is also reproduced with the permission of the publisher of P. B. Beeson and W. McDermott, editors, *Cecil-Loeb Textbook of Medicine*, 13th ed. W. B. Saunders Co., Philadelphia, 1971.)

paration for adult life. In social animals patterns of interacting with other individuals are developed. If they are prevented from developing at the proper stage, the deprived animal or person may be a social cripple for the rest of his life, perhaps even unable to mate or to bear and raise young. Studies by Harlow at the University of Wisconsin's Primate Center and others have vividly demonstrated this in rhesus monkeys. And it is a cliche in our society that a deprived child becomes a deprived adult and passes his problems on to his own children.

Because so much of human behavior is learned and because culture must be transmitted through learning to each new generation, the extended period of immaturity and dependence that characterizes our species is a necessary evolutionary companion of our big brain. It is possible to "teach an old dog new tricks," but more difficult than to teach a young one. Once we understand and accept our animal origins, it should come as no surprise that adults tend to become rigid in their behavior, with decreased ability to accept and adapt to new conditions.

*PUBERTY AND ADOLESCENCE.* Although sex is established *in utero*, it does not express itself fully until puberty, when an increased hormonal output fulfills the potential differences between the sexes. The sex hormones are involved in *feedback mechanisms* to the hypothalamus and the anterior pituitary gland. Feedback mechanisms will be discussed in detail in Chapter 8.

Adolescence is anticipated during the prepuberal period, when sex organs renew their development, sex hormones are synthesized in increasing amounts and released into the bloodstream, and secondary sex characteristics begin to emerge. These processes occur slightly earlier in girls than in boys. In girls, when the circulating hormone concentrations are high enough to initiate the first ovulation, puberty has been achieved. The exact time of puberty in boys is not easily defined, as we do not know exactly when the potential for ejaculation of semen is attained. Confusion over the onset of puberty may also occur because different authorities assign different definitions to the term. Nevertheless, it is agreed that adolescence immediately follows puberty.

The developmental processes involved in attaining reproductive capacity are called *maturation*. These processes take place throughout adolescence and their completion, although it is not sharply defined, marks the beginning of adulthood. The processes related to maturation were studied over a period of 5 years in a group of more than 1000 Dutch girls (Figure 7.11).

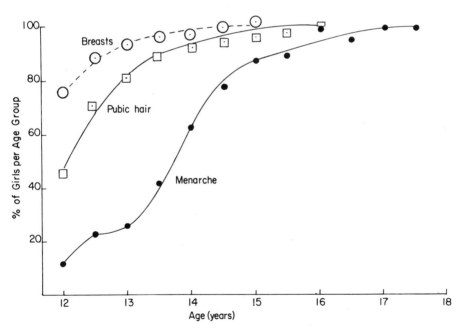

**Figure 7–11** Developmental pattern in adolescent girls. These results were obtained in a study of about 1000 girls over a period of five years. In general, breasts develop first, then pubic hair, and the onset of menstruation comes last. (From B. T. Donovan and J. J. Van der Werff Ten Bosch, *Physiology of Puberty*, Williams and Williams, Baltimore, 1965.)

## PUBERTY AT AN EARLY AGE

*Almost everyone knows that people are taller today than they used to be—a look at a suit of armor in a museum will tell you that. Not everyone knows that the age at which children become sexually mature has been steadily decreasing for the last 100 years.*

*If you were a typical American girl of the 1960s, you probably began menstruating before you were thirteen. But if you had been a typical American girl in 1900, you would not have reached menarche (first menstruation) until you were fourteen. Boys, too, reach puberty earlier now than they did in the last century, in all of the industrialized nations as well as in the United States. But in parts of the world where not much technological advance has taken place, the average age of puberty has not decreased. In societies which have enjoyed the greatest technological and social advantages, such as in Norway, England, and in the upper classes of the United States, this trend toward earlier puberty now appears to be leveling off.*

*What has caused this downward trend—and why has it happened only in industrial societies? The most obvious reason for the trend toward earlier puberty, and probably the most important one, is that people in industrial societies are better housed, better cared for as children, and especially better fed than they were 100 years ago. As you might expect, both growth and maturation are slowed by poor nutrition. For example, studies done in Europe during the war famine of the 1940s showed that undernourished children were smaller and less developed than well-nourished children of the same age. When their diets were supplemented, they grew and matured rapidly until they reached a stage of development normal for their ages.*

*However, many people—and many children—in the United States and other industrial countries are not only well-fed, but fat. And obesity is another factor which seems to influence age of puberty. Studies have found that overweight (although not grossly overweight) girls tend to reach menarche earlier than those of normal weight.*

Development proceeds along different lines at different rates. On the average, breast development is completed first, pubic hair appears next, and the onset of menstruation occurs last, about 2 years after the first signs of puberty. Other stages in the maturation of girls are given in Table 7.6.

In boys, puberty begins when pubic, axillary, or facial hair is first noticeable, and when the penis, testes, and prostate gland begin to enlarge. Seminal emmision marks the conclusion of puberty, or the attainment of maturation. The relationships of these developments to each other in time have not been as well studied in boys as in girls; so a more precise comparison cannot be made.

Maturation is also characterized by changes in the skeleton and teeth.

*Another possible cause of early maturation is the social stimulation of our modern city-dwelling society. It has been shown that children living in the same country reach puberty earlier if they grow up in a city than if they grow up on a farm. Of course, it is possible that city-dwelling children receive better nutrition than those on the farm, or that they exercise less, and therefore tend to be fatter.*

*However, recent experiments performed with mice tend to support the theory that* social *stimulation does affect rate of maturation. These experiments showed that the presence of a male mouse (or even his soiled bedding) was more effective than superior nutrition in lowering the age of first ovulation in female mice. But if social stimulation has a similar effect on young human females, the stimulation is not necessarily direct association with males. Girls who attend all-girl schools do not reach menarche any later than those who attend coeducational schools.*

*"The bigger, the better; the faster, the better"–these have been basic assumptions of Western technological society. But as we are starting to realize, these assumptions need some modification–bigger and faster cars, for instance, cause more air pollution. What, then, are some implications of the trend toward bigger and faster-maturing children? Obesity, one of the factors associated with earlier puberty, is obviously undesirable. But there may even be some disadvantages to the large amounts of protein and calcium in the modern diet. Studies conducted in the Caucasus, and in other parts of the world where old people tend to be healthy and vigorous, have linked a long and active life with slight undernourishment and* late *maturation.*

*A final consideration is that children who reach puberty earlier in our society have to endure a longer adolescence. At present in the United States, young people often do not become economically independent, or considered adults, until they are in their twenties. The earlier they become sexually mature, the longer that uncomfortable period between sexual maturity and independence. Unless our society adjusts to accommodate earlier maturation, we can expect increasing problems.*

Growth in height ceases, as nearly all skeletal epiphyseal plates close; and the full set of 32 permanent teeth is acquired. Growth decelerates in girls when menstruation begins, and stops completely a couple of years before it stops in boys. Some evidence suggests that estrogens hasten epiphyseal closure. There is a final growth spurt in both girls and boys, but it comes earlier in girls and lasts a shorter time, resulting in a shorter average height in women than in men. Growth curves for both sexes to the age of 20 are shown in Figure 7.12.

Variations in the time of puberty are linked to a variety of genetic and environmental conditions, many of which are not well understood. Among the environmental factors are climate, light, season of the year, nutrition,

**TABLE 7.6**
**Normal Progression of Puberty in Girls**

| Age in Years | Growth Characteristics |
|---|---|
| 9-10 | Growth of the bony pelvis; beginning female contour and fat deposition; nipple budding |
| 10-11 | Budding breasts; appearance of pubic hair (in 10% pubic hair is present before breast development) |
| 11-12 | Increased glycogen content and increased acidity of vaginal secretion; change in cell type of **vaginal epithelium** |
| 12-13 | Pigmentation of the nipples; growth of the breasts |
| 13-14 | Axillary hair appears; menstruation begins; pubic hair increases in amount; acne is present in 75% to 90%; cervical mucus appears |

From A. F. Goldfarb. 1969. Understanding physiologic change. Ped. Clinics of N. Am. 16:395.

and socio-economic factors. Nutritional and socio-economic factors, for example, are almost certainly related to the trend toward the earlier onset of puberty in Western nations. Western culture is thus influencing the biology of Western man. Conditions producing nervous and endocrine stress are also significant.

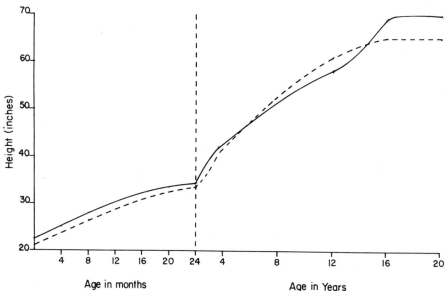

**Figure 7-12** Growth curves for girls and boys from birth until age 20. Solid line, boys; broken line, girls. In infancy, boys tend to somewhat taller than girls. The difference is made up during late childhood, and in early adolescence girls are on the average slightly taller than boys. The growth rate in girls decreases, however, when menstruation begins, and growth stops altogether several years earlier in girls than in boys. (From A. C. Guyton, *Textbook of Medical Physiology*, 4th ed., W. B. Saunders Co., Philadelphia, 1971.)

*ADULTHOOD.* Adulthood is imprecisely defined as beginning at about age 20. It is still more difficult to assign a time when adulthood ends and senescence begins, because individual variations are even more pronounced toward the end of life than in earlier stages. Many Western societies seem to have decided that adulthood ends around the age of 65, because this is when retirement often begins. Biologically, however, the line must be drawn on an individual basis, and variation among individuals is enormous.

Adulthood is characterized by a relatively steady state of physiologic processes. Building and degradative processes are fairly constant and equal. Between ages 20 and 40, total anabolism is equal to or only slightly less than total catabolism. Generally, at about age 40, catabolic processes begin to predominate, but the time at which deterioration begins varies for different organs and functions, and among individuals. Muscular strength generally begins to decrease after age 27, and motor reactions after age 34. The resorption rate of both the mineral and organic components of bone begins to exceed the rate at which these components are built up in the mid-20s, as illustrated in Figure 7.13. These data, obtained from cadaver specimens of both sexes, demonstrate the greater relative resorption rates beyond age 40.

Adulthood is the time when certain cells, such as those of the muscles and nervous system, begin to die and are not replaced. Wounds heal more

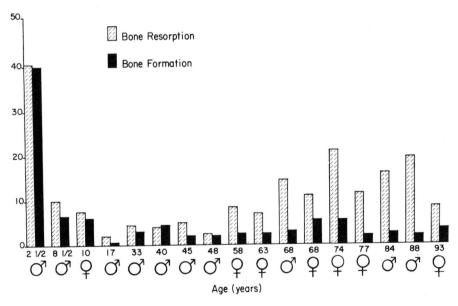

**Figure 7–13** Bone resorption and formation in the femoral cortex at various ages. Bone is metabolically active tissue; there is a constant turnover in its mineral and organic constituents. These data show that the excess of resorption over formation of bone increases sharply during the sixth decade of life. (From J. Jowsey, 1960, Clinical Orthopaedics, No. 17, 210.)

slowly than before, general damage from disease or stress is repaired more slowly, and sensory organs often decline in functional capacity. Decrease in overall physical fitness with age is due partly to the aging process, but its rate is also influenced by the type and amount of physical exercise an individual engages in.

Women undergo *menopause* during the late 40s or early 50s, a time extended by better nutrition in developed countries. This period is one of either a rather abrupt or a gradual lessening of reproductive capacity and secretion of sex hormones. Ovulation and menstruation stop or become sporadic, and depression, nervous tension, or even more serious emotional problems may occur. It takes months or sometimes years for the mind and body to adjust to the ending of a hormonal cycle that operated for more than three decades. There is no known explanation for the occurrence of menopause. It has no exact counterpart in the male or in females of other species.

In man as in other animals, adulthood is the period when the learned behaviors of youth are put to use. In other animals the types of learned behaviors are for the most part limited and stereotyped, characteristic of the species. Through culture, however, our species has created about as many cultural niches (by analogy with environmental niches) as there are people to fill them. Determined by the selected combination of job, leisure-time activity, and lifestyle, a person's role in society may be as unique as his genotype. Despite protestations to the contrary, we are not — or need not be — puppets or replaceable identical parts in the machinery of "the system."

There is always the opportunity for creativity, and adulthood is the period when creativity (in the sense of true innovation and original contribution to society) is usually expressed. Creativity is a concept as difficult to define as intelligence and perhaps more difficult to measure, and for most of the same reasons that a firm quantitative description of intelligence eludes us. But everyone has a "feeling" for what creativity is, and that will do for our present purposes.

Of the many aspects of a person's environment, background, and characteristics that have been studied in relation to his creative achievements, one which definitely is involved is his age. Data collected on creativity versus age for most fields, including science and medicine, literature and the arts, and even specialties like checkers, show that an individual is most likely to make his most outstanding contribution between ages 25 and 45. The sharpness of the peak may vary and the peak comes later in some fields than in others, but variations are minor: a mathematician's most creative years are 25 to 30; an inventor's, 30 to 35; an astronomer's, 30 to 40; a chemist's 25 to 35. The average age at which Nobel laureates do their award-winning work in physics, chemistry, and medicine is under 40.

Nobel laureates are not "average" people. But tests of large numbers of people from all backgrounds and occupations also show that the originality of ideas and associations decreases with age. Interpretation of these results is beset with difficulties, however, just as is interpretation of intelligence test scores. In addition, it is difficult to devise a test that is fair to all age groups.

Some people believe that the decline in creativity with age is caused by overall deterioration of the individual. Others believe that it is the feelings of inferiority and insecurity due to decline in physical vigor that are to blame, rather than the physical problems themselves. If higher mental processes, which presumably include the kind of integrative thinking required for creativity, do remain fairly constant in at least some people throughout adulthood and old age even though creativity declines, it might be fruitful to examine aspects of the environment which could be manipulated to favor creativity in older people.

*SENESCENCE.*    Senescence begins when physical and mental functions start deteriorating more rapidly than in adulthood. Its onset is indiscernible and there are no well-defined criteria for marking its beginning. All organ systems decrease substantially in capability, the most conspicuous failing in many individuals being the nervous system. Loss of memory and imperfect integration, perhaps related to poor sensory reception or to other psychologic factors, are common in senescent individuals. Table 7.7 shows the decline in function of several organ systems in aged persons.

Cardiac output decreases with increasing age so that by age 75 it is only about 70 percent of what it was at age 30. Atherosclerosis, the laying down of fatty deposits in the lining of the major blood vessels, causes greater vascular resistance and makes the heart work harder to supply oxygenated

**TABLE 7.7**
**Mean Percent Decrease of Several Physiologic Parameters**
**(Age 75 Compared to Age 30)**

| *Parameter* | *Percent Function Remaining (100%)* |
|---|---|
| Brain weight | 56 |
| Speed of return to equilibrium of blood acidity | 17 |
| Cardiac output at rest | 70 |
| **Glomerular filtration rate** | 69 |
| Renal blood flow | 50 |
| Number of taste buds | 36 |
| Maximum oxygen uptake during exercise | 40 |
| **Vital capacity** | 56 |
| Hand grip | 55 |
| Maximum work rate | 70 |
| Basal metabolic rate | 84 |
| Body water content | 82 |
| Body weight | 88 |

From N. W. Shock. 1962. The physiology of aging. Sci. Amer. 206:100.

blood to the tissues, particularly to the brain. Mineralization of these fatty deposits causes the condition known as arteriosclerosis. Decline in cardiovascular function causes serious debilities in the respiratory system: respiratory and vital capacities are decreased, and the maximal volume of gas exchange during exercises is reduced by 50 percent or more. Musculoskeletal coordination also degenerates. More than moderate exercise is thus a serious challenge to the aged body. Our sedentary way of life with its many stresses, rich diets, pollutants, and various habits detrimental to health further decrease the body's ability to withstand such challenges as age advances.

Thyroid function diminishes with age, and with it the BMR. And not only does the ability to convert food energy to heat decline, but the body's mechanisms to rid itself of excess heat also fail. Endocrine function in general decreases, one result being that the prevalence of diabetes mellitus increases with age. The feedback mechanisms that regulate our internal environment also change with age, some more than others. Overall, the efficiency of adjustment or response to stimuli declines. Resistance to microbial and viral infections decreases, and the chronic diseases commonly associated with aging increase — cancer, arteriosclerosis, heart disease, arthritis, bronchitis, and emphysema. Shrinkage in height becomes noticeable. It is caused by loss of mass in both the **intervertebral discs** and the **vertebrae** themselves. Loss of weight is related to cell death without replacement, and to a decrease in the density of bone through demineralization.

When the controlling nervous and endocrine systems are sufficiently affected, general disorientation and eventually death result. Chronic vascular or cardiovascular, respiratory, and renal disease cause many deaths. Death from old age, as superficially distinguished from death by disease, culminates the subnormal functioning and generalized decay of many organ systems. A transplanted heart here, a new kidney there, is not the answer, even if all the immunologic, economic, and moral problems of transplantation were solved. Our cultural achievements have tripled the average human life expectancy, but the maximum life span — slightly more than 100 years — has apparently remained about the same through the ages.

No explanation of aging is completely satisfactory, although many partial explanations have been invoked. There is some evidence that a lifetime's accumulation of mutations in the body or somatic cells is related to the aging process. But the rate of mutation is about the same in a man as in a fruit fly. Why then does a man live 70 years and a fly 70 days?

The comparison between a man and a fly is unfair. We should confine ourselves to mammals. The life span of a mammal is strongly correlated with its size, and both size and life span are correlated with BMR and rate of heartbeat. A shrew may live 1.5 years, a dog 18, a horse 40, and an elephant 70. A chimpanzee, smaller than man, is senile in his 30s; a gorilla, larger than man, may dotter on into his 40s. All these animals, if they escape accidents, disease, and predation, may expect to live about as long as it takes their hearts to beat a billion times — give or take a few hundred million. Man is an anomaly. The heart of Grandma Moses beat about 3.5 billion times before she died at 101. If we fit into the pattern that seems to apply to all other mammals, our maximum life span would be 35 or 40 years.

The aged animal is of no biological use to the species, and therefore there is no selective advantage to genes for longevity unless the same genes confer an advantage on some earlier stage of life. All mammals care for their young; only *Homo sapiens* cares for the old. Thus the occurrence of aged animals is largely restricted to our own species and the captive and domesticated animals to which we extend our care. Still, no matter how much care we lavish on our dog, he will not live past 20. The mystery remains. Noting that life span is related to size and BMR does not explain the phenomenon of aging, and though man is exceptional with respect to his life span, even he must die.

The answer, again, may lie in the genes. Cells contain structures called *lysosomes*, which have been dubbed "suicide bags" because in them are digestive enzymes which, if released, are capable of destroying the cell. During senescence many cells open their suicide bags. But what is their signal to self-destruct? It has been suggested that the genetic instructions include a program for senescence and death, and that these instructions are "read" by the cell and obeyed as part of the programmed developmental sequence that begins with the first division of the fertilized egg. Two indirect lines of evidence support this theory. First, we have seen that specific cells in the embryo are scheduled to die during the normal course of embryonic development; so much programming for death can and does occur. Second, most normal mammalian cells (normal in the sense of their having the diploid number of chromosomes and not being malignant) cannot be grown indefinitely in the laboratory, although they may be grown for a long time through many cell divisions. The second argument is vulnerable because the laboratory technique can always be held responsible for the results. It cannot be denied, however, that in the intact individual the deterioration of some organ systems with age results from death of cells and a decreased capability for division in the cells that remain. Particularly, the lessened capacity of the aged to make antibodies can be attributed in part to a decrease in the number of cells that can proliferate in response to challenge by antigens.

So perhaps death is the phenotypic expression of the last group of genes in the developmental sequence.

## PHYSIOLOGY AND HUMAN ECOLOGY

We have seen that the human life stages are intrinsic. They are the result of internal processes stemming from conditions in the internal environment. It is the task of the physiologic branch of human ecology to determine how the external environment affects them. Environmental physiologists try to uncover the origin or cause of adaptive variations, such as the responses to extreme temperature variations by Australian aborigines, and to understand how these evolutionary changes are (or are not) advantageous under conditions of life today. Environmental physiologists also attempt to identify factors in our surroundings that impinge on us and to understand how our bodies respond to them. These factors include climate, nutrition, psycho-social setting, pollution, drugs and a variety of toxic agents, and perhaps yet unknown factors all of which have in common that they stress the organism in one way or another. Even though we have become dominant in our ecologic setting, we must still contend with the natural elements and, increasingly, with our own perturbations of the environment.

## REFERENCES

ADOLPH, E. F. 1970. Physiological stages in the development of mammals. *Growth* 34:113.

AREY, L. B. 1965. *Developmental Anatomy*. 7th ed. Philadelphia: Saunders.

AUSTIN, C., AND R. SHORT. 1972. *Embryonic and Fetal Development*. Reproduction in Mammals, vol. 2. London: Cambridge Univ. Press.

CHEEK, D. B. 1968. *Human Growth*. Philadelphia: Lea and Febiger.

DAWES, G. S. 1968. *Foetal and Neonatal Physiology*. Chicago: Yearbook Medical Publishers.

DONOVAN, B. T., AND J. J. VAN DER WERFF TEN BOSCH. 1965. *Physiology of Puberty*. Baltimore: Williams and Wilkins.

EBERT, J., AND I. SUSSEX. 1970. *Interacting Systems in Development*. 2nd ed. New York: Holt, Rinehart, and Winston.

FOLK, G. E., JR. 1966. *Environmental Physiology*. Philadelphia: Lea and Febiger.

GUYTON, A. C. 1971. *Textbook of Medical Physiology*. 5th ed. Philadelphia: Saunders.

HAEFELE, J. 1962. *Creativity and Innovation*. New York: Reinhold Publishing Corp.

KILBOURNE, E. D., AND W. G. SMILLIE, EDS. 1969. *Human Ecology and Public Health*. 4th ed. New York: Macmillan.

LEE, D. H. K., AND D. MINARD, EDS. 1970. *Physiology, ·Environment, and Man*. New York: Academic Press.

LEHMAN, H. 1953. *Age and Achievement*. Princeton: Princeton Univ. Press.

MARSHALL, W. A., AND J. M. TANNER. 1968. Growth and physiological development during adolescence. *Ann. Rev. Med.* 19:283.

NALBANDOV, A. V. 1964. *Reproductive Physiology*. 2nd ed. San Francisco: W. H. Freeman and Co.

SCRIMSHAW, N. S. 1970. Synergism of malnutrition and infection. *Journal of the American Medical Assoc.* 212:1685.

STREHLER, B. L. 1967. Environmental factors in aging and mortality. *Environmental Research*. 1:46.

SHOCK, N. W. 1970. Physiologic aspects of aging. *Journal of the American Diet. Assoc.* 56:491.

SOCIETY FOR EXPERIMENTAL BIOLOGY. 1967. *Aspects of the Biology of Aging*. Symposium No. 21. New York: Academic Press.

TURNER, C. D., AND J. T. BAGNARA. 1971. *General Endocrinology*. 5th ed. Philadelphia: Saunders.

# · 8 ·

JOHN J. B. ANDERSON

# Homeostasis: Human Self-Regulation

When we speak of ecology and the human environment, the environment external to our bodies is the one that generally comes to mind. But a moment's thought will convince you that only the outer surface of our bodies and the lining of the uppermost portion of the respiratory and digestive tracts are actually in contact with this external environment. The outer layer of our skin is a protective coating. It is dead.

The cells inside our body, the ones that carry on the everyday functions of living, exist in a totally different environment from the one in which our body as a whole moves. It is warm, moist, dark, and above all, remarkably constant. To be sure, these cells receive messages from the outside world and act on them, but these actions are usually to preserve the constancy of the internal environment. There is a name for the tendency toward uniformity and stability of the internal environment. It is *homeostasis,* and it is the subject of this chapter. Homeostatic mechanisms reach their greatest level of complexity and precision in the mammals and birds, giving these animals the greatest degree of freedom from the vagaries of the external environment.

There is order, of course, in even the simplest and most primitive organisms, and that implies regulation. The opposite would be chaos, and would be incompatible with life. But lower animals tolerate much greater fluctuations in internal environmental conditions than more complex ones do. The process of evolution involved development of increasingly intricate mechanisms for controlling the internal environment. The controls exist as a hierarchy, at all levels of biological organization from a single biochemical pathway to a cell, to cells organized into tissues and tissues into organs and systems of organs, to entire organisms. The concept of homeostasis can be extended by analogy beyond the organism to populations, communities, ecosystems, and the biosphere as a whole.

The idea of an organism's self-regulation was introduced by Claude Bernard, a French physiologist and physician in the late nineteenth century. He summed up the observations of years of study and clinical practice in the often-quoted statement: "The constancy of the internal environment is the condition of free and independent life." It was a famous American physiologist, Walter B. Cannon, who actually coined the word homeostasis in the 1930s. The concept of homeostasis embraces all the built-in, automatic mechanisms by which the organism maintains its own inner medium in a steady state. One of the simplest mechanisms is at the biochemical level, whereby the end-product of a series of biochemical reactions inhibits the initial reaction in the series, thus regulating the amount of product synthesized. For example, cells of the human body can synthesize a number of amino acids, given the appropriate precursors of these compounds; but if adequate amounts of the amino acids are present in the diet, they may inhibit cellular synthetic pathways. Other control mechanisms require the integrated responses of many body systems. An example is the increase in rate of breathing, heartbeat, and metabolism that accompanies strenuous exercise in order to maintain the balance of gases in the blood.

Our homeostatic mechanisms have their origins far back in evolutionary history. Two great control systems in particular have emancipated us from the tyranny of the external environment. One is the excretory system, with its prime role in regulating blood chemistry both by ridding the body of toxic and excess metabolic products, including acid (hydrogen ions), and by manipulating fluid balance and the balance and concentration of salts. We regulate our chemical environment largely through the work of our kidneys. The other system, one that has permitted us to survive and to maintain a constant level of activity in all the climates of the earth, is temperature control.

Evolution itself may be considered a conservative or homeostatic force — which seems paradoxical when you first think of it. But natural selection has no foresight. The first land animals used lungs instead of gills to obtain oxygen from air instead of water. But lungs did not begin to evolve as an adaptation to life on land. Quite the contrary: the first lungs served as a means to permit a continuation of life in the water! They began as little air sacs off the **trachea,** in which the strange creatures called lungfish stored air that they had swallowed. This air enabled the lungfish to survive in stagnant water where ordinary fish would suffocate. It permitted them to move short distances through the mud from one drying pond to another. It even helped them to withstand long dormant periods sealed in a cocoon of mud, waiting for the rains to come again and fill their pools. The air sacs of the lungfish took two diverging paths in evolution. In modern fish they are represented by the swim bladder, an organ which receives its store of gases from the gills and is used to adjust buoyancy. In amphibians and other land verterbrates they became the lungs. (Modern frogs still fill their lungs by gulping air like the lungfish, instead of by proper breathing.) Thus an organ that first served a homeostatic function in an aquatic form of life only later became the means by which animals could forsake the water. It has been this way throughout evolution.

We are the evolutionary beneficiaries of many elaborate physiologic regulatory mechanisms, several examples of which will be examined in this chapter. We will also discuss genetic and social regulation, two other aspects of homeostasis. A significant feature of homeostatic mechanisms is that they are automatic and generally operate without our being aware of them. In fact, for the most part, they are beyond our conscious control. This is not to say that they have no effect on conscious behavior, because they sometimes do — as in stimulating us to eat or drink or to seek a more comfortable temperature. But where the brain is involved, it is with the part that evolved first with the function of nonconscious control and integration of body processes, not the more recent conscious, thinking part. And even though recent experiments have shown that we can learn to exercise a degree of control over many of our "automatic" processes, these processes have operated in us and in other animals for millions of years without conscious control, and they still do.

## PRINCIPLES OF HOMEOSTASIS

Our internal environment is regulated by feedback mechanisms, as briefly described in Chapter 7. The theory of feedback was worked out by engineers, who are traditionally interested in self-regulating systems. Physiologists have adopted much of this theory, including its vocabulary; so if you think the description which follows seems to be written in the language of engineering, you are correct. The nature of feedback control, whether in animals or machines, is such that the processes involved can be stated in mathematical equations which can be solved by a computer. Thus today, some physiologists perform their experiments on computers as well as on animals, changing the numerical values of experimental variables and introducing perturbations to see how the system will respond. In some cases computer simulations of actual experiments duplicate the observed experimental results quite closely. The value of these computer models is to show how complete our understanding of the system is, and to carry out simulations of experiments that might be difficult to conduct with living animals.

Regulatory mechanisms control dynamic processes by either correcting or accentuating the signals fed into them. They thus return the system to normal when it is out of adjustment (*negative feedback*) or allow it to go even further out of adjustment for a short time to meet a particular functional need *(positive feedback)*. Negative feedback is by far the more common system of biological control. Positive feedback is important in the development of behavioral patterns, but in a physiologic process uncontrolled positive feedback would lead to continuous amplification of a response until some biological limit was reached, with resultant discomfort, disability, disease, and finally, death — "the more you try, the worse it gets" kind of thing. Positive feedback mechanisms that actually do operate in man are generally controlled by a time-dependent factor, as in a diurnal rhythm, or there is a mechanism to turn them off before they go too far. A positive feedback mechanism may be part of a more complex regulatory system which is ultimately governed by negative feedback controls. The theoretical discussion and examples which follow all concern negative feedback control.

If the internal environment is to be held constant, there must be a *sensor* which responds to relevant aspects of the environment and an *effector* which can alter the environment. There must also be some kind of circuit connecting the sensor and the effector, and a shut-off device to control the effector. The basic components of a negative feedback system are illustrated in Figure 8.1. Each physiologic variable has a normal or reference level built into it. Disturbances that perturb the system have their input at the level of the effector (see diagram), and these in turn are fed back to the sensor. The sensor detects a deviation from normal (the error), which is the difference between the actual value (feedback signal) and the desired one (reference signal). The sensor is often associated anatomically with a regulatory center, the *control-signal transducer*. This center transforms the error signal from the sensor into a control signal and relays it to the effector, or *feedback-signal transducer*. The effector does its job in the external or internal environment

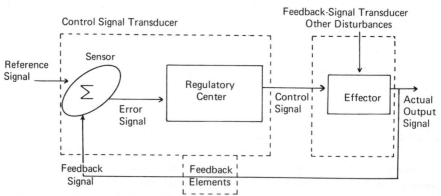

**Figure 8–1** Mechanism of negative feedback control. A sensor receives information on the actual value of some variable and compares it with the desired value. If there is disagreement, it sends out an error signal which is transformed by a regulatory center into a control signal. The control signal is received by an effector, which does something about the situation and sends a new signal back to the sensor.

and also sends the output signal back to the sensor via feedback elements, and by successive approximations the error is corrected. The sensor then reports on the resultant situation (really a summation of two signals or difference between two signals.) This process can be repeated many times, as long as an error or disturbance persists. If the system is operational, however, conditions will return to normal within a length of time that is characteristic of the system. In general, nervous regulation is much more rapid than endocrine control.

In living organisms the sensors are generally called *receptors.* The circuits may involve either nerves or hormones (or both) circulating in the blood. The parts of the system that detect the messages from nerves or hormones are *transducers* which means that they transmit the energy from one system to another, perhaps also translating it to a different form. Thus, a regulatory center in the brain may receive a chemical message and transmit an electrical one in response.

Many negative biological feedback mechanisms are of the simple proportional type, in which the magnitude of the response is directly proportional to the magnitude of the error. Some control mechanisms, however, depend on the rate of change of the error. Still others depend on the rate of change of the rate of change (in other words, the acceleration) of the error. These two time-dependent types of control increase the accuracy of regulation and decrease the likelihood of the system's drifting from the reference value, because they detect a change as soon as it begins, rather than after the error has built up. However, the complexity of biological feedback systems renders their mathematical description imprecise.

*HOMEOSTASIS OF BLOOD GASES.* Regulation of carbon dioxide and oxygen in the blood via the respiratory system is an example of the general principles of homeostasis. The concentrations of these gases are monitored by specialized sensors called *chemostats*, some of which are located in the major vessels of the circulatory system, and others in the brain. The chemostats send messages via nervous pathways to the respiratory center of the brain, which relays messages via nerves to the muscles involved in breathing. As a result, when carbon dioxide increases, the rate and depth of breathing increase. An illustration of the carbon dioxide chemostat is given in Figure 8.2. If you compare it with Figure 8.1, you will see that this example fits the general model well.

Strenuous exercise also causes an increase in the rate of heartbeat and in the capacity of the blood vessels supplying the muscles. But sometimes the muscles demand even more than the lungs, the heart, and the blood can give. Then they resort to **anaerobic respiration,** which releases energy without using free oxygen. In doing this they accumulate an "oxygen debt." That is why deep and rapid breathing, pounding of the heart, and a flushed

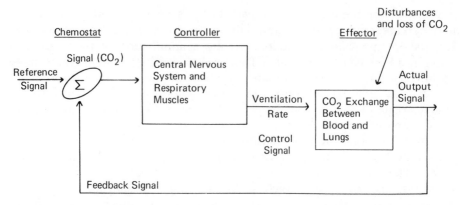

**Figure 8–2** Control of respiration through the carbon dioxide chemostat mechanism. $CO_2$ concentration in the blood is detected by the chemostat which relays the information to a control center. The control center sends a message which adjusts the rate of breathing to increase or decrease the $CO_2$ exchange between the blood and the lungs.

appearance persist for a time after exercise is finished. The body is working to pay off its oxygen debt. Products of anaerobic respiration are being either oxidized or converted back into the material from which they were derived. Under normal conditions, however, this regulatory system is so responsive that no oscillations occur in the levels of gases in the blood.

Chemostats in the circulatory system also detect changes in the acidity or alkalinity of the blood, as measured by the concentration of hydrogen ions, or pH. The blood is buffered, however, which means that it resists changes in pH through simple shifts in the degree of ionization of various components without resort to a more complicated regulatory system. In addition, the lungs and kidneys play an important role in maintaining the acid-base balance in the blood.

At high altitudes we must make adjustments beyond those made to exercise. There is an increase in **hemoglobin,** red blood cells, and total volume of blood. The heart and lungs of people native to high altitudes show structural adaptations to the decreased availability of oxygen, the most striking of which is their increase in size. A resident at sea level takes at least three months to adjust fully to conditions at an altitude of 14,000 feet. The time may be as long as a year or more, and some individuals never adjust. Even in fully adapted or acclimatized individuals, the pressure of oxygen in the major arteries is lower than it is at sea level. Studies of natives of the Peruvian Andes strongly suggest that natural selection has operated on populations living at high altitudes, but no one has been able to determine to what extent adaptation to altitude is genetic and to what extent it results from a lifetime of exposure to the conditions. As usual, both genetic and environmental influences are involved.

## ENDOCRINE CONTROL MECHANISMS

There are three types of physiologic homeostatic mechanisms: *endocrine, neural,* and *neuroendocrine.* One characteristic common to all three is the release of chemical substances within the feedback loop. In the case of endocrine mechanisms these substances are, by definition, hormones. In general, endocrine and neuroendocrine regulatory mechanisms are much slower in responding to deviations than are strictly neural mechanisms, because hormones traveling in the circulatory system take longer to reach target organs than do nerve impulses. The times required are on the order of a second or less for neural mechanisms and minutes to hours for endocrine mechanisms. In addition, correction of the error by neural regulation may be prompt and final, whereas endocrine adjustments may be gradual and may continue for hours or sometimes days.

Although it is not yet totally understood, the system regulating the concentration of calcium in the blood is perhaps the simplest of the endocrine control mechanisms. Calcium has two major functions in the body. It is the element that gives mechanical strength and hardness to teeth and bone, and, in solution, calcium ions affect neuromuscular activity, the permeability

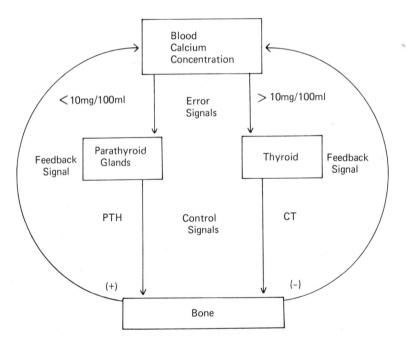

**Figure 8–3** Regulation of calcium concentration in the blood. PTH = parathyroid hormone; CT = calcitonin. The effector in this simplified illustration is bone.

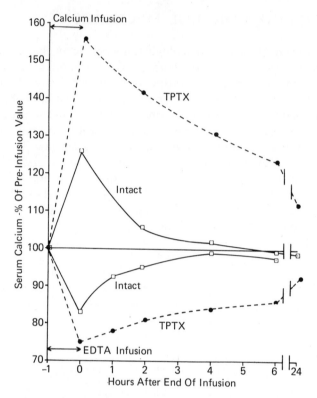

**Figure 8–4** Calcium homeostasis. TPTX (broken line) = dogs with thyroid and parathyroid glands removed; intact (solid line) = unoperated controls. Hypercalcemia was induced by an infusion of calcium. Hypocalcemia was induced by an infusion of EDTA, which combines with calcium to decrease its apparent concentration in the blood.

of cell membranes, coagulation of blood, and various enzymatic and secretory processes. About 1 percent of the total body calcium is in the circulation and soft tissues; the remaining 99 percent is in the skeleton.

The normal level of calcium in blood serum is about 10 mg/100 ml, and the normal range is between 9 and 11 mg/100 ml. A permanent level exceeding 11 mg/100 ml probably indicates that demineralization of bone is taking place, and it leads to deposition of calcium in soft tissues and excessive excretion of calcium in the urine. On the low side, as the level approaches 6 mg/100 ml, muscle spasms and convulsions occur, and sometimes coma and death.

Two hormones are primarily and directly involved with calcium homeostasis. They are parathyroid hormone, secreted by the parathyroid glands when calcium falls below the reference level, and calcitonin, secreted by a special group of cells in the thyroid when calcium exceeds the reference level. Of these, parathyroid hormone is generally more important in man because if calcium deviates from normal it is usually on the low side. Furthermore, if levels of calcitonin are elevated as they are when certain types of thyroid tumors occur, the concentration of calcium in the blood remains normal (perhaps through a compensating increase in parathyroid activity). The simplified system involving these hormones and calcium concentration is shown in Figure 8.3. The actions of both hormones are illustrated in Figure 8.4. This graph shows the results of an experiment in which both the thyroid and the parathyroid glands were removed from experimental animals, and the animals were then treated in one of two ways. Some received an injection of calcium into the bloodstream, and others received an injection of EDTA, a chemical which combines with calcium and thus decreases its ionic concentration. Note that the effect of added calcium or EDTA was smaller in the animals whose glands remained intact than in the animals whose thyroids and parathyroids had been removed. In addition, levels of calcium in the blood of the unoperated animals had returned to normal within about four hours after treatment, while levels in the operated animals were not yet back to normal after 24 hours.

The metabolism of calcium and inorganic phosphate are closely linked.

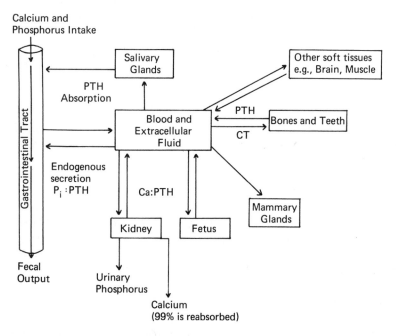

**Figure 8–5** Schematic illustration of the hormones and organs involved in regulation of calcium and phosphorus in the blood. PTH = parathyroid hormone; CT = calcitonin; $P_i$ = inorganic phosphate. Calcium and phosphate are lost from the body in the urine and feces; in a pregnant woman they are lost to the fetus; and in a lactating woman they are secreted in the milk.

For one thing, calcium is combined with phosphate in bone. Parathyroid hormone stimulates reabsorption of calcium by the kidney and excretion of phosphate into the urine; it also stimulates release of both calcium and phosphate from bone. If the parathyroids are removed, the level of calcium in the blood falls while phosphate rises. (This problem, like many hormonal deficiencies, can be treated by administration of parathyroid hormone.) Calcitonin, on the other hand, appears to stimulate removal of phosphate from the blood and to inhibit the breakdown of bone, so that its action results in lowered concentrations of both calcium and phosphorus in the blood. A schematic diagram showing these relationships is given in Figure 8.5.

Earlier we mentioned that about 99 percent of the body's calcium is in the bones and 1 percent in the circulation and soft tissues. This partitioning of a substance into various "compartments" in the body is called compartmentalization. Calcium exists in a number of compartments, including the blood, the mineral in bone crystals, and the fluid compartment of bone. There is some movement of calcium from one compartment to another according to the basic rules of chemical equilibria. Under the influence of hormonal stimuli, however, large amounts of calcium can be mobilized and transferred from one compartment to another. Thus, under the influence of parathyroid hormone, the calcium in the blood compartment is increased at the expense of that in the bone-fluid compartment and crystalline material of bone.

Other glands and their secretions are indirectly involved in the regulation of calcium. Some of these effects are summarized in Table 8.1. Vitamin D also plays a role. This vitamin is sometimes considered a hormone in the broadest sense because it is secreted by different tissues into the bloodstream. Dietary vitamin D is converted to the active form by an enzyme system in the liver, while a precursor of vitamin D in the skin is converted to the active compound by the action of ultraviolet light. After transformation in the liver and kidney, the active vitamin enters the nuclei of cells in the intestine and bone, where it stimulates production of RNA that codes for synthesis of enzymes or other proteins involved in calcium transport — the so-called calcium "pump." Without these molecules, active absorption (as opposed to simple chemical diffusion) of calcium cannot take place in the intestine, and parathyroid hormone cannot exert its effect of stimulating the pumping of calcium from the bone compartments to the blood.

There are many known disturbances of calcium metabolism. Tumors of the parathyroids may cause excessive secretion of parathyroid hormone, with consequent demineralization of bone. Excessive intake of vitamin A and D also causes decalcification of bone and calcification of soft tissues. Osteoporosis, the name given to chronic decalcification of bone, occurs in about half of all women over 50 years old. The most probable explanation of this lies in the effect of estrogens on calcium metabolism (Table 8.1). A high level of estrogens, such as is present in the blood of women during their

**TABLE 8.1**
**Effects of Various Hormones on Calcium (Ca)**
**and Inorganic Phosphorus (Pi) Metabolism**

| *Hormone* | *Plasma* | | *Urine* | | *Intestinal Absorbtion* | | *Bone Resorption* | |
|---|---|---|---|---|---|---|---|---|
| | *Ca* | *Pi* | *Ca* | *Pi* | *Ca* | *Pi* | *Ca* | *Pi* |
| Parathyroid hormone | + | − | − | + | NC | NC | + | + |
| Calcitonin | − | − | ? | − | NC | NC | − | − |
| Vitamin D* | + | + | − | − | + | + | + | + |
| Thyroxin | + | NC | + | − | − | ? | + | + |
| Cortisol | − | − | + | + | − | ? | − | − |
| Estrogen | − | − | − | + | + | ? | − | − |
| Growth hormone | + | + | + | − | ? | ? | + | + |

(+) increase   (−) decrease   (NC) no change   (?) unknown
* Vitamin D is considered a hormone because it is synthesized in the skin and released into the blood prior to its action on various tissues.

reproductive years, inhibits the resorption of bone, resulting in a small depression of blood calcium and release of parathyroid hormone. In postmenopausal women, however, bone resorption stimulated by parathyroid hormone may continue at its premenopausal rate, but estrogens are no longer present in any significant amount to exert an antagonistic effect.

An unusual mental disorder known as piblokto (hysteria), which occurs in the Thule Eskimos of Greenland, has been linked to deficiencies of calcium and possibly vitamin D. The diet of the Eskimo is largely meat and fish, which are notoriously low in calcium. Dietary sources of vitamin D may also be inadequate; very little ultraviolet radiation from the sun strikes the earth even in the long days of summer. Because the sun is low in the sky, most of the ultraviolet light is absorbed on its long path through the atmosphere. Thus piblokto can be considered an environmental disease. The people have been unable to adapt biologically to their deficient diets, but they have made cultural adaptations to the prevalence of the disease.

The first sign of an impending attack of piblokto, usually in early spring among older women, is a period of lassitude and social withdrawal. This stage of anxiety may actually precipitate the hysteria which follows. During the acute or attention-getting stage of piblokto-hysteria, the affected individual may race wildly about, behaving in a thoroughly irrational way, before lapsing into a state of generalized muscle spasms. The most prevalent spasms are in the wrists and ankles — classic signs of a low blood concentration of calcium. Such individuals need help, but a person may recover completely from such an attack, either immediately or after a period of sleep and return to his everyday life none the worse for the experience.

Not only do the Eskimos take this unavoidable ailment in stride, but

**Figure 8–6** The Eskimos of Greenland live where ultraviolet radiation from the sun is inadequate for their bodies to synthesize enough vitamin D; their carnivorous diet is low in calcium and possibly in vitamin D as well. These deficiencies manifest themselves in a strange behavioral disorder called piblokto. Some of the aberrant behavior patterns of this disease have been incorporated into the rites of shamans like those pictured at the right. (Photograph courtesy of the American Museum of Natural History.)

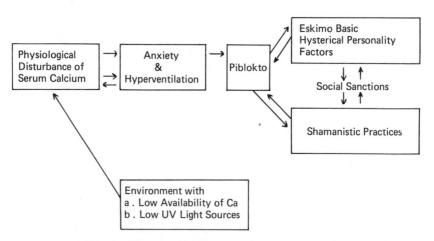

**Figure 8–7** Interrelationships among cultural, environmental, physiological, and behavioral factors related to the nervous disorder pibloktohysteria. (From the Am. J. Phys. Anthrop. 32:299–304, 1970.)

they incorporate many of its manifestations into their institutionalized rituals. Thus the rites of the **shaman** in times of social stress closely parallel the manifestations of piblokto (Figure 8.6). Where the body has been unable to adapt physiologically to environmental conditions, cultural adaptation has stepped in to fill the gap by accepting the aberrant behavior and even incorporating it into everyday social practices. The relationships between the environment, physiology, behavior, and culture of these people are shown in Figure 8.7.

*REGULATION OF BLOOD GLUCOSE.* A second example of an endocrine homeostatic mechanism is the regulation of the concentration of glucose, the basic source of energy, in the blood. What appears on the surface to be a relatively simple mechanism is in reality even more complex than the calcium regulatory system. Several hormones, including insulin, glucagon, adrenalin, thyroxin, growth hormone, and glucocorticoids, affect the concentration of glucose in the blood. (A glucocorticoid is a hormone secreted by the adrenal cortex which promotes the formation of glucose or other carbohydrates from proteins and fats.) In addition, activity of centers in the hypothalamus that control feeding and satiety and of other specific centers in the brain can modify the basic hormonal regulation. Thus both internal and external environmental influences have roles in controlling blood glucose, in addition to overt behavior. When the level of glucose in your blood falls, you become hungry and you eat.

Glucose can be used as an energy source for almost all cellular functions, and for some tissues, like the brain and the germinal epithelium of the gonads, it is essentially the only energy source. Glucose is carried to all cells of the body in the circulating blood. Of course, its ultimate source is the food we eat, but it is also converted to other substances and stored in the body. The most important form in which the energy of glucose is stored is glycogen ("animal starch"). Excessive carbohydrate intake results in fat storage as well. When blood glucose is low, these materials can be reconverted by hormonal actions to glucose.

A concentration of 90 mg of glucose per 100 ml of blood should be maintained during a normal fasting period. After a meal the concentration may rise to 140 mg/100 ml or even higher, but in a healthy person it returns to normal within a few hours. If the concentration remains high (hyperglycemia), the body fluids are lost and there is excess sugar in the urine. If it is too low (hypoglycemia), the brain and other tissues are not sufficiently nourished and cannot function properly. A major role of insulin, among its other effects on metabolism, is to reduce blood sugar to the reference value, especially after meals, by enhancing the transport of glucose into "peripheral" cells. It also stimulates the rate of glucose utilization by cells of the liver, where much of the glycogen is synthesized and stored. On the other hand, thyroxin, growth hormone, and glucocorticoids like cortisol increase the concentration of glucose in the blood under various non-

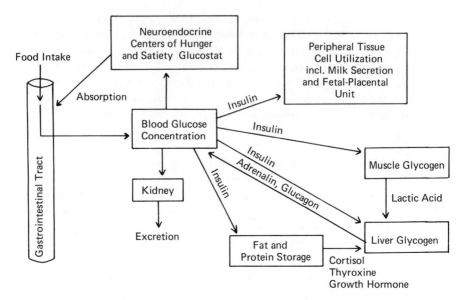

**Figure 8–8** Mechanism of blood glucose regulation. Several hormones act to increase the concentration of glucose in the blood, but only insulin can decrease it. Glucose is a major fuel for most cells and the only one for some; it is also a key compound in many metabolic pathways.

**TABLE 8.2**
**Influence of Hormones and the Brain on the Various Parameters of Blood Glucose Input and Output to Maintain Reference Value of 90 mg/100 ml**

| *Blood Glucose Input* | *Under Influence of Hormones and Brain* |
|---|---|
| Hunger, food intake activity, intestinal absorption | Hypothalamus |
| Storage in fat | Glucocorticoids (cortisol) thyroxin, growth hormone |
| Storage in protein | Glucocorticoids (cortisol) |
| Storage of glycogen & glucose in muscle | ? |
| Storage in tissue fluid | ? |
| Storage of glycogen in liver | Adrenalin, glucagon |
| *Blood Glucose Output* | |
| Renal excretion | ? |
| Metabolic use by cells (except brain and erythrocytes) | Insulin |
| Storage in fat | Insulin |
| Storage in protein | Insulin |
| Storage of glycogen & glucose in muscle | Insulin |
| Fluid storage in tissue | Insulin |
| Storage of glycogen in liver | Insulin |

emergency conditions. Under "fight-or-flight" conditions, glucagon and adrenalin mobilize glucose rapidly from the liver. The interlocking mechanisms regulating glucose metabolism are shown in Figure 8.8.

We have mentioned that the immediate inputs of glucose into the blood are food and stored reserves. However, the control system involves both input and output. Factors involved in control of blood glucose are shown as input-output parameters in Table 8.2. Note that there is a redundancy of factors opposing the action of insulin, affording the body a large margin of safety in case of depressed blood glucose. However, if the individual is deficient in insulin, as is the case if he suffers from diabetes mellitus, the fasting blood glucose concentration rises above 120 mg/100 ml and the body has no defense. Synthetic insulin-stimulating drugs, carefully regulated diet, and other forms of medical treatment will help to correct this deficiency, but the basic defect remains.

If there is too much insulin in the blood, as occurs in certain types of pancreatic tumors, the resulting hypoglycemia adversely affects the central nervous system. Temporary hypoglycemia caused by administration of too much insulin (insulin shock) can be corrected by intravenous administration of glucose or adrenalin. The long-term hypoglycemia caused by a pancreatic tumor may require surgical removal of the tumor.

## NEURAL CONTROL MECHANISMS

The second type of homeostatic mechanism is neural —regulation by the nervous system. Nerve cells, also called *neurons,* release chemicals at junctions (synapses) between nerves, between nerves and muscles, and between nerves and glands. These chemicals are known as *neurotransmitters.* Unlike hormonal transport, however, the rate of transfer of these neurotransmitters is very fast.

The nervous system is involved in a variety of regulatory mechanisms, both voluntary and involuntary. Stimuli are received by many different kinds of sensors which relay messages to the brain along *afferent* nerves. These messages go to specific centers in the brain, from which they are relayed via *efferent* nerves back to various muscles and glands. These effector organs make their characteristic responses to the stimuli.

*REGULATION OF ARTERIAL BLOOD PRESSURE.* A typical example of involuntary nervous control is control of blood pressure in the arteries that carry oxygenated blood to all parts of the body. If you think of your arteries as being analogous to a length of garden hose, there are two ways you can control the pressure inside. One is to regulate the rate at which fluid enters, and the other is to control its pressure as it leaves. In the garden hose you do this by manipulating the spigot at the inlet or the nozzle at the outlet. In the arteries these two controls are exerted by the force and rate of the heartbeat and by the dilation and constriction of the smaller branches of the arteries known as *arterioles*. But what mechanisms are at the controls?

In the large arteries are specialized sensors called pressoreceptors or baroreceptors because they respond to pressure. The *baroreceptors* send messages by way of nerve impulses to three specific centers in the brain. One of these centers relays signals to the muscles in the walls of the arterioles, which contract if blood pressure is too low, causing *vasoconstriction,* or relax if pressure is high, causing *vasodilation.* Very small changes in the size of these branches are effective in altering pressure, because the pressure varies inversely with the fourth power of the radius. Thus, if you double the radii of all the arterioles, you reduce the blood pressure by a factor of $2^4$ or 16!

A second brain center controls the force of the heartbeat (*contractility*) and a third controls its rate. Together these regulate the volume of blood ejected from the heart per unit of time. If the blood pressure has increased, heart rate and contractility decrease, and conversely. These feedback controls are illustrated in Figure 8.9. Particular demands are made on this regulatory system during exercise or changes of posture as from reclining to standing. In these cases the circulatory system must respond promptly to changes due to gravity or increased requirements for oxygenated blood. The value of this mechanism can be clearly seen in the event of loss of blood. If vasoconstriction is prevented, blood pressure falls below the value that can sustain life when only about 10 percent of the blood has been lost. Normally, however, the body can withstand loss of up to 40 percent of its circulating blood! The victim of massive hemorrhage is not pale from loss of blood so much as from constriction of blood vessels near the skin.

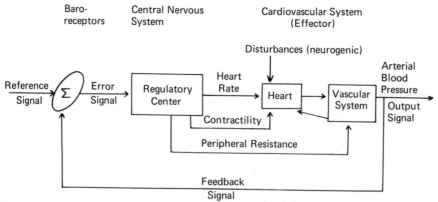

**Figure 8–9** Feedback mechanisms regulating arterial blood pressure, a system of nervous control. Pressure-sensitive receptors send error signals to the central nervous system, whose control signals affect heart rate, force of the heartbeat, and the diameter of small arteries. Through constriction of blood vessels near the skin when blood pressure falls, blood pressure deeper in the body is maintained and blood supply to vital organs conserved.

## NEUROENDOCRINE CONTROL MECHANISMS

Neuroendocrine control mechanisms involve both the central nervous system and the pituitary gland. The pituitary gland and the hypothalamus are closely linked both anatomically and functionally, as was described in Chapter 7. The posterior part of the pituitary is actually an extension of the hypothalamus which serves as the terminal for nerves from hypothalamic centers whose secretions are released into the blood. The anterior pituitary receives *hypothalamic release factors* (RFs) directly through a small blood portal system. The hypothalamus receives nervous input from various parts of the brain and chemical feedback through hormones in the circulating blood; it then communicates appropriate information to the pituitary gland, which responds by releasing its own hormones.

Although neuroendocrine responses are generally slower than strictly neural ones, the response of adrenalin to a "fight-or-flight" stress occurs in about a second. But even here the overall adjustment is slower than in neural control, because the effects of adrenalin and its high concentration in the blood linger for a much longer time than the effects of a neural response.

*REGULATION OF BODY TEMPERATURE.*   In the regulation of body temperature, which is accomplished through a neuroendocrine mechanism, the interplay between internal and external environment and purposeful behavior can be clearly appreciated. The rate of metabolic reactions depends on temperature just as does the rate of any other chemical reaction. Thus it was an evolutionary step of tremendous importance when animals developed the ability to maintain their body temperatures at a constant level, rather than being at the mercy of fluctuating environmental temperatures. Although a reptile can regulate its temperature to a degree by seeking either exposure to the sun or refuge from it, there is no way it can remain warm and active in the arctic, no matter what its other adaptations may be. Birds and mammals, in contrast, have become adapted to living in all climates where they can find food.

Nothing happens in the body or in the universe without the transfer of energy from one form to another or from one object to another. In each transformation, some of the energy is inevitably converted to heat. The source of our body's heat is waste energy from metabolic reactions. This heat must be dissipated to the environment — the problem of temperature regulation is as much a problem of keeping cool as of keeping warm. If our bodies are warmer than the surrounding air, we lose heat by *radiation* in the form of electromagnetic waves and by *conduction,* or the direct transfer of heat from the molecules at the surface of our bodies to the molecules of the air. We also lose heat through evaporation of water from our bodies. As the external temperature rises, we begin to sweat more and more profusely, and the evaporation of this sweat is a very effective cooling device. The evaporation of 1 gram of water from the surface of our bodies at 30° C (86°F) requires about 580 calories of heat energy, which is extracted from the body and the air immediately in contact with it. (This is 0.580 kilocalories, the "calorie" by which food energy is measured.) It is estimated that we use energy to evaporate water at about 15 percent of our basal metabolic rate, even when we are at rest in a comfortable external temperature.

Primates, including man, are basically tropical animals, and as such are much more adept at getting rid of heat than at conserving it. In particular, the great apes have lost most of their hairiness during the course of evolution, and an insulating coat of hair is a mammal's first line of defense against the cold. (It is interesting to note in this regard that elephants and rhinoceroses are also tropical animals and are also almost hairless, but their relatives who roamed the north during the time of the glaciers were the *woolly* mammoth and the *woolly* rhinoceros.) Natural selection has favored some physical and physiologic modifications among people in cold climates, but it is the cultural adaptations of wearing clothing, building shelters, and using fire that had the greatest impact on man's survival in these areas.

The normal body temperature is characteristic of each species and is no doubt genetically determined. By now you realize that genetic determination does not mean that there is "a gene for body temperature," but rather that all the genes that influence size and shape of the body, metabolic rate, endocrine activity, and perhaps many other characteristics as well have the combined result of determining the normal internal temperature of the body. In man the normal temperature is about 98.6° F, with a normal range of from 97° to 99° F.

The thyroid gland plays a major role in temperature homeostasis through its control of the BMR and thus of the amount of heat that is produced. Energy use above that required by the basal metabolism results in additional production of heat which also must be eliminated. Examples of the energy expended in several activities are given in Table 8.3. The burden of waste heat produced by strenuous exercise becomes greater as the external temperature rises, and at high temperatures the body's homeostatic mechanisms may be overwhelmed. When this happens, the body temperature may either drop below normal or soar above it, and it is important to determine which change has occurred before trying to help the victim! Salts and fluids lost through sweating must be replaced.

In the case of fever the control mechanism may still be functioning, but the "thermostat" is merely set at a higher temperature. In newborns and infants, however, the temperature-regulating mechanism is not yet well developed, and the temperature may rise high enough to permanently damage sensitive parts of the brain.

Individuals with particular genotypes may be better adapted than others to extremely hot or extremely cold climates, but everyone has the ability to adjust to temperature changes to a remarkable degree. The time required to adapt to a change from a high temperature to a lower one has

**TABLE 8.3**
**Energy Expenditure in Calories\* per Hour During Several Types of Activity by a 70 Kilogram Man**

| Activity | Calories per Hour |
|---|---|
| Sleeping | 65 |
| Sitting at rest | 100 |
| Light exercise | 170 |
| Walking at 2.6 mph | 200 |
| Active exercise | 290 |
| Severe exercise | 450 |
| Swimming | 500 |
| Running at 5.3 mph | 570 |
| Very severe exercise | 600 |
| Walking at 5.3 mph | 650 |
| Walking up stairs | 1100 |

\*Food calories, or kilocalories.
From A. C. Guyton. 1971. *Textbook of Medical Physiology.* Saunders, Philadelphia.

been found experimentally to be about 6 weeks. The reverse experiment has not been performed, but subjective reports suggest that it takes at least several weeks to adjust to the change from a cold temperature to a warm one.

Figure 8.10 presents a simplified scheme of the neuroendocrine temperature control mechanism. There are temperature-sensitive thermoreceptors in both the brain and the skin which relay messages to control centers in the brain. As the external temperature drops and the internal temperature also starts to fall, the hypothalamic temperature center initiates a series of reactions which increase the rate of heat production and decrease the rate of heat loss. Accelerated secretion of thyroxin brings about an increase in metabolic rate with consequent increase in rate of heat production. Constriction of the blood capillaries in the skin reduces circulation of blood and loss

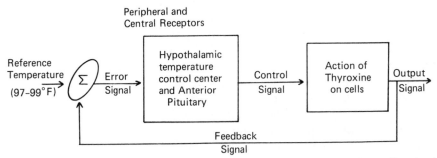

**Figure 8-10** Schematic illustration of the neuroendocrine system controlling body temperature.

of heat at the body's surface. Increased secretion of adrenalin enhances the effects of thyroxin, causing heightened muscular activity in the form of shivering and the contraction of tiny muscles at the base of each hair (giving you "goose pimples"). The brain also sends stimuli directly to muscles to initiate shivering. Through these mechanisms heat production can be increased to as much as five times the basal level.

As the temperature rises, secretion of thyroxin and adrenalin slows down and the surface capillaries become dilated, bringing more blood to the surface where it it is cooled by radiation and conduction. In addition, the sweat glands increase their activity enormously. All these processes, however, may not be enough to prevent a slight rise in heat production which does *not* result from the homeostatic mechanism, but rather from the general effect of temperature on the rate of chemical reactions.

THE MENSTRUAL CYCLE.   The menstrual cycle is also controlled by a neuroendocrine homeostatic mechanism, which involves the hypothalamus, the anterior pituitary, and the reproductive organs. It occurs only in primates and is related to, but is not the same as, the heat or **estrous cycle** of lower mammals. Disorders of the menstrual cycle commonly result in varying degrees of infertility. The reproductive system as a whole may be severely affected by malnutrition and other types of stress. For example, temporary infertility is common in people moving to high altitudes, and experimental animals have been rendered permanently sterile by these conditions.

Several possible feedback mechanisms between estrogen, progesterone, FSH (follicle-stimulating hormone), LH (luteinizing hormone), and the hypothalamus have been demonstrated experimentally. Of these, the stimulatory effect of estrogen on secretion of LH and the inhibitory effect of progesterone on LH are most important in regulating the menstrual cycle. Estrogen and progesterone have a feedback effect on both the hypothalamus and the pituitary. In addition, the pituitary gonadotropins appear to be self-inhibitory as well as to exert feedback inhibition on the hypothalamus. These interrelationships are shown in Figure 8.11.

At the beginning of the menstrual cycle, when levels of estrogen and progesterone in the blood are low, FSH is secreted by the pituitary in response to FSH-RF from the hypothalamus. Acting on the ovary, the FSH stimulates growth of a number of follicles, which begin to secrete estrogen into the bloodstream. The estrogen acts on the hypothalamus and the pituitary, stimulating the hypothalamus to produce LH-RF and, in the beginning, and just prior to ovulation additional FSH-RF. It increases the responsiveness of the pituitary to LH-RF and FSH-RF, causing it to secrete LH and FSH. As a result of the increased levels of gonadotropins, production of estrogen is further enhanced, especially within 24 hours of ovulation. (This is an example of positive feedback, the only one we will mention in this chapter.) Under the influence of the surge of LH, only one follicle matures

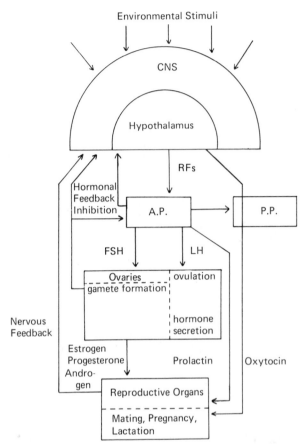

**Figure 8–11** Feedback mechanisms regulating ovulation and the menstrual cycle. CNA = central nervous sytem; RFs = release factors; AP = anterior pituitary; PP = posterior pituitary; LH = luteinizing hormone; FSH = follicle stimulating hormone. This is a complex system involving both nervous mechanisms and a number of hormones from several sources (see text).

and ruptures, releasing an egg. The other follicles stop developing and usually degenerate. After ovulation, still under the influence of LH, the old follicle is converted into a yellow mass of cells called the corpus luteum; and the corpus luteum begins to secrete progesterone. Levels of FSH and LH in the blood decline sharply after ovulation, while progesterone continues to rise. Thus, not only does secretion of progesterone not depend on the gonadotropic hormones, but it probably contributes through a feedback inhibition to their decline. If an embryo becomes implanted in the uterine wall, the corpus luteum continues to secrete progesterone throughout the first few months of pregnancy, stimulated by a placental gonadotropin. If no implantation occurs, the corpus luteum stops functioning after about 12 days, and the thickened lining of the uterus sloughs off. This is the

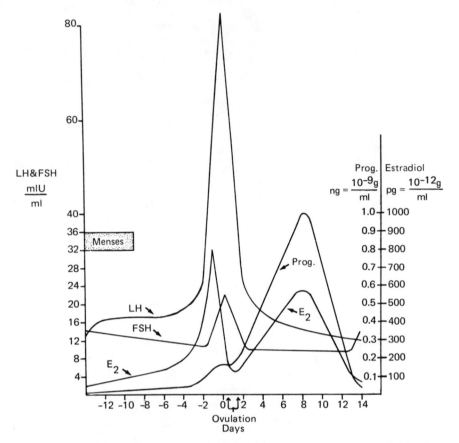

**Figure 8–12** Cycles of the gonadotropic and ovarian hormones. LH = luteinizing hormone; FSH = follicle stimulating hormone; E₂ = estradiol; Prog. = protesterone. (Adapted from L. Speroff and R. L. Vande Wiele, "Regulation of the human menstrual cycle," *Am. J. Obstet. Gynecol.*, 109:234–247, 1971.)

menstrual flow. Now the levels of estrogen, progesterone, and the gonadotropins in the blood are low, and the cycle begins again. The cyclic rise and fall of the tropic and ovarian hormones is illustrated in Figure 8.12.

Note that the positive feedback effect of estrogen does not lead to instability but to an oscillatory pattern. This is because a negative control is included in the system; and in addition, it appears that a timing mechanism or clock in the hypothalamus is involved as well. In hindsight, it is difficult or impossible to conceive of a steady-state mechanism that would allow periodic maturation and release of an egg; thus, the survival of the species requires that the system depart from "normal" in a controlled manner. Except for interruptions due to pregnancy, the menstrual cycle repeats itself on an average of once every 28 or 29 days throughout the 30 to 35 years of a woman's reproductive life.

Chapter 7 indicated that FSH and LH and the corresponding release factors also play a role in men, and that the phenomena of sex determination and sexual development cannot facilely be explained by a difference in sex chromosomes. There is not only "chromosomal sex," but the sex of the gonads, the sex of the hormones, and the apparent, or phenotypic sex — which may or may not agree with chromosomal sex and with each other. The term "brain sex" has also been used, to indicate that the hypothalamus acts in either a male or a female pattern. Evidence is accumulating for a hypothalamic clock, a biological rhythm, which lies at the source of the cyclic pattern of secretion of female reproductive hormones. At an early stage of development this innate clock can be overwhelmed by a surge of male hormones, which is what happens in the normal development of a male fetus. Endocrine abnormalities can induce the same effect in female fetuses, and it has been achieved experimentally in laboratory animals. The hypothalamus becomes imprinted with the male pattern, so that the cyclical pattern is obliterated and the synthesis and release of RFs continue steadily.

Some cases of infertility result from failure of the pituitary to produce gonadotropins. Women with this problem often respond to treatment with gonadotropins by ovulating normally and being able to produce children. Many of the much-publicized multiple births resulting from treatment for infertility probably are due to overdoses of FSH and LH, which lead to maturation of many follicles and the release of multiple eggs. Gonadotropin therapy must be tailored to the individual, because patients' needs and responses are known to vary over a 32-fold range.

While the tropic hormones are used to promote fertility, the ovarian hormones are used in contraception. The common combination pill mounts a double-barreled attack on the function of the ovary. The progesterone component of the pill abolishes the mid-cycle peak of LH by feedback inhibition of the hypothalamus and pituitary. It is the surge of LH midway in the normal cycle that induces ovulation. FSH secretion is inhibited by the estrogen in the contraceptives, leading to failure of follicular development. Most of the known dangers of oral contraception are due to the estrogen component, and for this reason a progesterone pill was developed. This pill does not suppress ovulation, but apparently acts by causing changes in the cervical mucus which prevent penetration of sperm. It possibly interferes with implantation in the uterus as well.

The preceding sections describe only a few of the many physiologic control mechanisms that operate in the human body. Many of the details were omitted. In addition, although the physiologist is fond of picking one feedback system out of the whole and scrutinizing it in isolation (as he must do, to unravel the pieces of the puzzle), there is no such pigeon-holing of processes in a living organism. In our internal environment as in our external one, when you try to isolate a phenomenon you are more than likely to find that "everything is attached to everything else."

## GENETIC HOMEOSTASIS

All physiologic homeostatic mechanisms are genetically derived and are a result of the genetic, adaptive, and developmental processes discussed in earlier chapters. But the concept of genetic homeostasis involves more than the kinds of physiologic regulation that have been described in this chapter. Heredity is a conservative or homeostatic force. By itself it permits endless recombination of genes but not sustained change — a constant reshuffling of the same old deck of cards. Children resemble their parents and their grandparents and their great great . . . grandparents. The way in which the frequency and distribution of genes is maintained in populations can be described by simple mathematical equations. This, in a sense, is also genetic homeostasis. The balance between genes for normal and abnormal hemoglobins is a pertinent example.

It is important to remember that many genotypes lead to well-balanced phenotypes and that a particular gene may be beneficial or harmful only in the context of the total genotype. Again, analogy to a deck of cards is helpful. Any card may have a positive value in one hand and negative in another. It is the entire hand that wins the round, not a card, and it is the genotype that manifests homeostasis, not a gene. Natural selection ruthlessly weeds out genotypes that are not well balanced, either by death of the individual or by failure to reproduce. Modern medicine and social institutions do not change this; they merely redefine the criteria for balance.

Almost all human genotypes insure the development of a clearly recognizeable human being, which means that they give rise to essentially the same phenotype. We take this so much for granted that it may seem surprising even to mention it, but this kind of genetic homeostasis has been discussed by many geneticists and given the name of *canalization* (see the reference to Dobzhansky at the end of Chapter 4).

Occasionally a single mutant gene can drastically upset physiologic homeostasis. These inborn errors of metabolism result when an altered gene leads to production of a nonfunctioning or malfunctioning enzyme that is required for some crucial biochemical pathway. Five different disorders of this kind are known to occur in various aspects of the metabolism of the amino acids, phenylalanine and tyrosine, which is derived from phenylalanine. One of them causes phenylketonuria, a disease which may result in extreme mental retardation. Another prevents the synthesis of the pigment melanin, resulting in albinism. A third leads to deficiency of the hormone thyroxin and the condition known as cretinism. A fourth produces tyrosinosis, a condition characterized by an accumulation of a breakdown product of tyrosine in the urine. Finally, there is the disease alkaptonuria, which is caused by faulty metabolism of tyrosine. Alkaptonuria is characterized by a blackening of the urine on exposure to air, by arthritis, and by pigmentation of cartilage. Phenylketonuria and alkaptonuria may be controlled, but not cured, through nutritional and medical management.

It is at least theoretically possible, now that the causes and sequences of events of genetic diseases are known, to influence some genetic disorders at the level of the gene or gene action at an early stage of embryonic development. Although these ideas are very far from practical application, they reopen questions of what life really is and to what extent man can and should tamper with it. Our answers today are not the same as they were a hundred years ago. What they will be in another hundred years is anyone's guess.

## SOCIAL HOMEOSTASIS

What has been said about homeostasis in the individual also applies to society. Institutions of all sorts — land tenure, inheritance, marriage, religion, primogeniture, and so on — are designed to resist change, to promote homeostasis. The Indian caste system, the medieval custom of binding serfs to the soil, the medieval guilds, and our recent traditions of family occupations — of sons following their fathers into the protection of the trade unions or the professions — all had, or have, the effect of preserving the status quo.

Homeostasis applies to populations as well as to institutions. Ironically, zero population growth was attained in primitive cultures long before the modern realization of its significance. Both positive and negative feedback were involved: on the positive side was a high birth rate, and on the negative were pestilence, starvation, and emigration — and, if these did not suffice, infanticide, abortion, and war were added.

The homeostatic mechanisms that govern society are not as well known as are those of the body. Their recognition, discovery, description, and control are necessary before we can hope to rationally guide the progress of society. In a complex system like our body, or such as society has become, there is an interlocking system of checks and balances which resists change. The resistance to change manifests itself in various forms. It causes no end of frustration because, no matter what your political persuasion, it seems to matter little who holds political office. For all the conflicting ideologies, the opposing sides *behave* like Tweedledum and Tweedledee. This is because homeostatic mechanisms cooperate to overcome any perturbation in the system and return it to "normal." We see this in the discouraging results of our piecemeal attack on poverty, discrimination, traffic jams, pollution, health care, and all the other problems of modern society: "Everything is attached to everything else."

Despite the power of homeostasis, however, it is clear that profound changes have occurred in society, and rapidly at that, just as biological evolution has occurred in spite of genetic homeostasis. Furthermore, social change is taking place more rapidly now than it did a century ago, and it was more rapid then than at the time of the Roman Empire. This is in the realm of cultural evolution, and it will be the subject of the next two chap-

# GENETIC PROGRAMMING

*Imagine, if you can, a baseball team boasting an outfield composed of two Mickey Mantles and a Babe Ruth; a catcher whose hand is as large as a baseball glove; a shortstop who has round ball-bearing-like feet, three infielders whose catching arms are long enough to hand the ball to each other rather than throw it; and a pitching staff who collectively bat .385 and boast the healthy pitching arms of Sandy Koufax, Bob Feller, Walter Johnson and Tom Seaver.*

*The above may sound like gross hyperbole, but current genetic research is transforming what was once sheer fantasy into experimental reality. With the discovery and understanding of DNA, man took a step in history that will probably someday be compared to the discovery of fire. Man will be the first animal who will have the knowledge and ability to shape his own future. Such power carries with it great possibilities as well as great hazards.*

*By understanding the genetic code which is written on long molecules of DNA, man will be able to reprogram genes. For example, a person who suffers from diabetes has a gene which for some reason is not telling the pancreas to produce insulin. A new gene which carries a "produce insulin" message would be introduced into the diabetic's body. This technique is called "gene therapy" and the science is called euphenics. This same person risks passing the wrong genetic information (non-reproduction of insulin) on to any offspring. Reprogramming genes in the developing embryo is a way of solving the problem of inheriting the wrong genetic information. Theoretically, this technique can be refined to such an extent that whatever is deemed "necessary" or "desirable" for society or an individual can be programmed right into the system of a developing child.*

*Selective breeding or eugenics is another way to improve man's gene pool. In other words, people who have "desirable" traits (physical, mental, or medical) would be combined to produce an even superior human being. In the event that these individuals do not wish to marry or do not wish to have the responsibility of a child, they could serve as the biological parents alone. Their sperm and egg would be united and placed in a "proxy" mother who would incubate a child. The legal parents would be that couple who wishes to raise the child. Sperm and egg banks could be established to aid in selective breeding. After an individual's life has ended, his worth would be assessed; if his strengths were such that society wanted a similar human being, his sperm or her egg would be retrieved from a bank and put to work building another human.*

ters. Clearly, however, we must seek to understand not only the mechanisms by which social homeostasis operates but the mechanisms by which it is overcome. We have some examples from experience. Sometimes a change does overwhelm the homeostatic mechanisms, and when this happens the results can be unanticipated and chaotic. You cannot change one aspect of an organized system without affecting everything else as well.

*This embryo might be implanted in a woman or it might be nurtured* in vitro *(test-tube) with medical science keeping a watchful machine on its every development.*

*Despite the predictability of gene combinations, selective breeding always carries with it the risk of a recessive gene appearing unexpectedly. "Cloning," which is reproduction without sperm and egg, eliminates the uncertainty of selective breeding. "Cloning" is similar to taking a cutting from a plant to produce an exact copy of the original plant. Human offspring would be reproduced from human tissue. Thus man could carbon copy anyone. The important difference between genetic engineering and cloning is that genetic engineering produces human beings with* similar *qualities. Cloning produces an* exact *copy of the original, and while the theory is applicable to man, the actual procedure is yet in the future. Successful cloning, however, has been accomplished with frogs.*

*Perhaps the final step in the process of genetic improvement is the man-machine or cyborg. Currently, plastic arteries replace real ones, steel pins are inserted into hips, and new organs are transplanted into those who need them. The day of the artificial man is fast approaching. Perhaps all organs and bodily parts will be serviced on a regular basis, with the option of replacement by manmade devices when necessary.*

*A scientific discussion of man's genetic potential cannot help but invoke visions of a Frankensteinian scientist smirking over a room full of human test-tube experiments. The fact is that genetics is making discoveries which will enable man to improve himself. Such knowledge confronts man with ethical and moral dilemmas. What if all known diseases could be erased from man's genetic computer? The effect on social homeostasis, population, food supplies, institutions, education, and so on would be staggering. In eliminating those genes which in combination are harmful, man risks eliminating the good that genes often do when they appear singly. Before man can tamper with the basis of life, he needs to explore the ramifications of such experimentation. The basic question of what is genetically desirable in a human being is complex and somewhat unanswerable. Perhaps by answering it man relinquishes a certain amount of his freedom and free will. Yet to refuse to accept and use the discoveries of genetics is to take an ostrich approach to life. Man needs to determine where his energies would best be utilized. Solving the problem of what is possible technologically and what is morally and ethically in mankind's best interest will be paramount in determining the fate of genetics.*

## HOMEOSTASIS AND HUMAN ECOLOGY

Man's rise to dominance in his ecosystem was accompanied by an increasing ability to modify the environment — to overcome the homeostatic mechanisms that, through a complexity of interrelationships and feedback controls, kept the balance of nature (see Chapter 3). The activities of man have continually forced adjustments in all other species. This can be seen perhaps most vividly in the results of modern agriculture. Where a single crop is cultivated in intensive monoculture, conditions become favorable for explosive spread of disease and insect pests. As a result of the large-scale clearance of land for the crop, habitats of natural enemies of these pests are destroyed. In addition, the poisons applied to kill the pests become decreasingly effective as they begin to have adverse effects on the predators and as the pests themselves acquire resistance. A natural homeostatic mechanism, the delicately balanced predator-prey relationship, has been upset.

The increase in organisms that we consider nuisances in polluted water is another example of a natural trend toward a new equilibrium when the old has been disturbed by man. As in society, human activities may seem to have little effect on the overall state of affairs — until they overwhelm a homeostatic control system. Then the consequences may be far-reaching and unexpected.

## REFERENCES

ADOLPH, E. F. 1968. *Origins of Physiological Regulations.* New York: Academic Press.

APTER, J. T. 1966. *Cybernetics and Development.* New York: Pergamon Press.

ASHBY, W. R. 1961. *An Introduction to Cybernetics.* London: Chapman & Hall.

BEKEY, G. A., AND M. W. WOLF. 1971. Control theory in biological systems. In *Biomedical Engineering.* J. H. U. Brown, J. E. Jacobs, and L. Stark, eds. Philadelphia: F. A. Davis Co.

BERNARD, C. 1957. *An Introduction to the Study of Experimental Medicine.* New York: Macmillan.

CANNON, W. B. 1932. *The Wisdom of the Body.* New York: Norton.

GRODINS, F. S. 1963. *Control Theory and Biological Systems.* New York: Columbia Univ. Press.

GUYTON, A. C. 1971. *Textbook of Medical Physiology.* 4th ed. Philadelphia: Saunders.

LANGLEY, L. L. 1965. *Homeostasis.* New York: Van Nostrand, Reinhold.

MESAROVIC, M. D., ED. 1968. *Systems Theory and Biology.* New York: Springer-Verlag.

MILHORN, H. T. 1966. *The Application of Control Theory to Physiological Systems.* Philadelphia: Saunders.

MILSUM, J. H. 1966. *Biological Control Systems Analysis.* New York: McGraw-Hill.

RIGGS, D. S. 1970. *Control Theory and Physiological Feedback Mechanisms.* Baltimore: Williams and Wilkins.

SUTTON, H. E. 1961. *Genes, Enzymes, and Inherited Diseases.* New York: Holt, Rinehart & Winston.

TURNER, C. D., AND J. T. BAGNARA. 1971. *General Endocrinology.* 5th ed. Philadelphia: Saunders.

VON BERTALANFFY, L. 1960. *Problems of Life.* New York: Harper.

WOLSTENHOLME, G. E. W., AND J. KNIGHT. 1969. *Homeostatic Regulators.* London: Churchill.

YAMAMOTO, W. S., AND J. R. BROBECK, EDS. 1965. *Physiological Controls and Regulations.* Philadelphia: Saunders.

# PART THREE

# *Man's Socio-Cultural Evolution*

# · 9 ·

NORMAN D. LEVINE

# Socio-Cultural Evolution

As animals go, man is one of the giants: he is in the upper 1 percent of species by weight. However, in his physical abilities he is extremely generalized. The eagle and the hawk see better, the dog and the shark have a keener sense of smell, the deer and the horse run faster, the gorilla and the lion are stronger, the fish and the seal swim better, the monkey and the squirrel climb better, the kangaroo and the kangaroo rat jump farther relative to their size, and, of course, man cannot fly at all. But except for flying, he can do all these things tolerably well, and most other animals cannot. This is one reason he dominates the earth.

As was noted in Chapter 5, the few physical specializations that man does have were important in his rise to dominance, although by themselves they do not tell the whole story. But combine stereoscopic vision, manipulative skill, and the ability to walk or run on two feet with a brain that can make choices, peer into both the past and the future, associate experiences in novel ways, think abstractly, and communicate precise information about facts, emotions, and ideas, and you have the truly formidable animal that is man.

Human evolution has physical, mental, and cultural aspects. For the last 20 or 30 thousand years or more, changes in physical characteristics and mental ability have been minimal, while the socio-cultural evolution that began with our Australopithecine ancestors has continued at an accelerating pace. Once socio-cultural evolution was initiated, the seed for continuing adaptation and change was sowed. Other species have the rudiments of culture, but only human culture evolves. Social and cultural change is the subject of this chapter.

The principle of adaptive change in culture is a basic one. Like a species of plant, animal, or microorganism, if a human culture does not adapt to changing circumstances, it does not survive. Indeed many cultures have

212

become extinct. But, in general, proofs of man's cultural adaptability are his increase in numbers and his penetration of practically every environment. The adoption of fire, the working of metals, the domestication of animals and plants — each change opened up a new and unending series of adaptive possibilities, and once any change was made, it was difficult or impossible to go back to an earlier condition. This is an important concept today, when many dreamers would, in effect, repeal the twentieth century and return to some Golden Age of long ago. There is no going back. The future must be built on the present.

## CULTURE AS THE UNIQUE ADAPTIVE MECHANISM OF MAN

One of the few things that can be said with certainty about "the nature of man" is that he is a social animal; and no animal society can function unless its members behave in sanctioned and predictable ways. Among other animals the range of possible behaviors is narrowly limited genetically. Within this circumscribed range, particular behaviors are learned by a young animal, and once learned, they endure throughout its lifetime. However, as man's mental powers increased during the course of evolution, so did his behavioral flexibility. His enormous range of possible responses gives him great adaptability but leaves his actions largely unregulated. Increasingly, as biological control of behavior diminished, the regulatory role fell to culture. Human success or failure to adapt to various environments became a measure of cultural, not of biological, success or failure. "Fitness" still meant reproductive success, but reproductive success was largely determined by cultural factors.

In discussing culture we will move back and forth between the abstract concept and specific examples. Culture is composed of the energy systems of a population and its methods of exploiting them, of the organization of social, political, and economic relations, of language, customs, beliefs, rules, and arts — of everything that is *learned* from other people or their works. Each human being is born with a generalized capacity to acquire a culture — any culture, according to the accident of the time and place of his birth. To be human means to exist within the framework of a culture, to be shaped, nurtured, and controlled by a *particular* culture from birth until death.

Because culture determines the relationships between human populations and their environment, its study is of fundamental importance to the study of human ecology. All cultures change in time — sometimes rapidly, sometimes imperceptibly slowly. They change both in response to changes in the habitat and to imbalances within the cultural institutions that maintain the relationship to the habitat. For a culture is like an organism in one important respect: all elements of it seem to be seeking balance and integration with respect to one another. A particular feature of a culture or an organism can be judged only in its relationship to the whole and to the environment. A woodpecker's bill is a useful tool only for a woodpecker; it would be an abomination for a goldfinch. The Mexican Indians knew about the wheel, but they had no practical use for it because they lacked domesticated animals that could be taught to pull wheeled vehicles.

The anthropologist Cohen distinguishes between cultural *adaptation* and cultural *adjustment* (see references). He considers an adaptation to be a major relationship of a society to its habitat, such as the energy systems it exploits and the political organization that controls the mode of exploitation (Figure 9.1). An adjustment is similar to a homeostatic change which restores satisfactory relationships between the population's technology and its social and political institutions, beliefs, and customary behaviors. Just as biological evolution tends to maintain a stable relationship between an organism and its environment, so, too, is cultural evolution basically conservative. It proceeds through a multitude of minor adjustments, consciously or unconsciously designed to keep things from changing. Major adaptive leaps have been few, and we speak of them with awe, as the "Agricultural Revolution," for example. It is not possible to draw a sharp distinction between adaptations and adjustments, but it seems intuitively clear that the energy systems employed by a population are more significant adaptively than the language it speaks or whether its women show their faces in public.

Figure 9.1 shows Cohen's concept of how various aspects of culture are related to one another. Technological and political institutions are shown as the most important means of adaptation, interacting most directly with the habitat. The importance of the political system lies in the degree of its organization and control of technology. The political organization, in turn, is related to kinship and mating systems, the organization and specialization of labor, and the degree to which society is stratified — the number of social, political, and economic roles that exist. The level of technology is related not only to political organization, but to social stratification, the way in which household affairs are organized, and the settlement pattern. What is possible for a population of moderate density, for example, is not possible for a population consisting of widely scattered families or small tribes. Laws and religion are directly related to the political organization of a population and its means of subsistence.

Perhaps because they are less directly involved with a population's adaptation to its habitat than the institutions just mentioned, the *adjustive institutions*, including language, the arts, and various behaviors and attitudes, show a rich variety among cultures, giving each culture its fascinating uniqueness. Traditional classifications of cultures, on the other hand, are usually based on the *adaptive institutions*, which are less variable and, because of the possibilities for homeostasis provided by adjustive institutions,

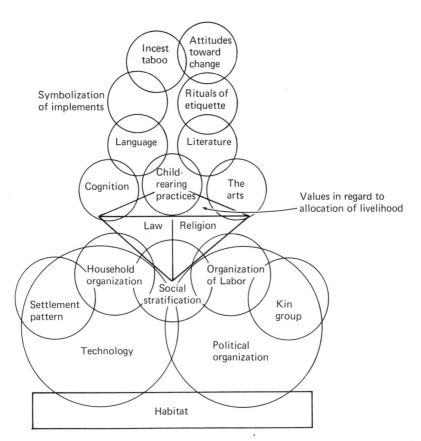

**Figure 9-1** Relationships between some institutions of cultural adaptation and adjustment. (Adapted from Y. Cohen, ed., *Man in Adaptation: The Cultural Present*, Aldine Pub. Co., Chicago, 1968, p. 58.)

slower to change. A technological innovation is generally acceptable only if it does not necessitate major changes in other institutions — a rare occurrence. A familiar classification based on technology includes cultures that subsist by foraging, pastoralism, simple agriculture, advanced agriculture, or industrialism. A classification based on political organization would include the family, tribe, and various kinds of multicommunity states.

Culture teaches us what we must do to survive in our particular habitat and social group. It tightly restricts our innate range of possible behaviors to that collection of behaviors which is adaptive in our circumstances. We can flee from one culture to another, but we cannot flee from culture. The vaunted human brain evolved through interaction with culture. Our intellect is of no use if there is nothing to learn, and we have few useful instincts. Without culture, the brain would be not the crowning human glory but the crowning human curse.

## THEORIES OF SOCIO-CULTURAL EVOLUTION AND CLASSIFICATION OF CULTURES

Socio-cultural evolution differs from biological evolution in at least one important way. Biological evolution proceeds through isolation and specialization until there can no longer be any exchange of genetic information between two once-similar populations. Hybridization is not common among animals, and most hybrids are sterile. In socio-culture evolution, however, there is continuous hybridization of behavioral codes and the assimilation of one code by another. When a chimpanzee meets a baboon, there is no way the two can exchange genetic information, a minimum of stereotyped communication is possible, and neither animal is much affected by the contact, unless the baboon happens to be a young one and gets eaten. When a Pygmy meets an American, however, he is likely to come away from the encounter with a transistor radio, and his life may be forever changed as a result. The present trend in socio-cultural evolution is toward a decrease in the number of distinct societies. A single world government, either the United Nations or its successor, might be the final outcome of this process.

Linear, "stage" theories of socio-cultural evolution have been pervasive in our thinking. Only recently have the fallacies in these theories — which masquerade in many forms — begun to be exposed. One idea was that cultural evolution took place through an inevitable succession of "Ages": the Old Stone Age, the New Stone Age, the Bronze Age, the Iron Age, to whatever term we choose to use for the modern age of industrialized Western civilization. But then it was found that there had been no Bronze Age in most of Africa — that man had skipped from the Stone Age to the Iron Age. Other stages commonly mentioned were foraging, pastoral nomadism, and sedentary agriculture. But it became clear that pastoralism and **horticulture** were cultural adaptations to specific habitats, and that, because of environmental limitations, neither was likely to give rise in evolution to the other.

Another idea, characteristic of nineteenth century evolutionists like Herbert Spencer and E. B. Tyler, was to use "index features," such as agriculture and writing, to classify cultures. The weakness of this system lies in the impossibility of choosing a single index feature that reflects the degree of "advancement" or "primitiveness" of a culture. The Mayas had a written language, but their administrative system was weak. The Incas had a highly developed administrative system, but no writing. The Mayas used a positional number system which included zero; the Roman number system, by comparison, was cumbersome and limited. In Chapter 13 we will see that systems of agriculture evolve in response to most intimate interactions with the habitat, and that it is absurd to say that wet rice culture is more or less advanced than tropical slash-and-burn. Both systems take maximum advantage of the habitat.

Still others have visualized a primitive society in which everything was commonly owned and in which primitive promiscuity prevailed. Later cultures developed from this state, again through an inviolable series of stages, to modern civilization. The problem here is that there is no regular correspondence between subsistence systems and socio-political systems. The American Plains Indians were "primitive" hunters, yet they had strict police systems, institutionalized warfare, and social grading. In the Philippines, advanced rice culture depended on elaborate systems of irrigated terraces, yet there was no strong central political authority. The Australian aborigines have a very primitive culture, but their kinship system is one of the most complex ones known.

Another weakness of the stage theory of cultural evolution is that the exploitation of a particular resource does not depend as much on the innate properties of the resource or the ability of the culture to exploit it as on man's *idea* of the resource and his perception of his own needs. In Western civilization, for example, cattle are used only for meat and dairy products. In the Orient they are used primarily as draft animals, although dead animals may be eaten and some use is made of other animal products. In India cattle are religious symbols, but working bullocks are important to the economy and cattle dung is a major fuel for domestic use. In Africa cattle are used for milk and blood, but not as draft animals.

It also became clear that a major cause of cultural change has always been *cultural diffusion* — the hybridization of cultures, or borrowing of technologies and ideas from other cultures. Finally, our chauvinistic attitudes toward Western civilization are being shaken with the realization that the values and achievements of the West are neither the highest and best nor those toward which all cultural evolution is inevitably tending. The conventions of Indian music are no longer considered inferior to those of Victorian hymns.

Another form of the stage approach to cultural evolution stems from Oswald Spengler (1880–1936), who argued that every civilization passes through the same ages as an individual man. It is born; it grows, matures, and flourishes for a period; and then it declines and dies. The historian Toynbee identified twenty-one distinct societies, each of which began as the response to environmental challenge of some sort, either physical or social, passed through a "time of troubles" during which it found an effective way of dealing with this challenge, went on to a "universal state" during which it dominated its territory, and then declined and died out. Some of the societies recognized by Toynbee are still with us, including such "fossil" ones as the Jewish and Parsee remnants of the Syriac Society. Some societies evolved into others; some became extinct. According to Toynbee, western civilization is now in the midst of its time of troubles.

A more fruitful approach to the evolution and classification of cultures recognizes the branching, or multi-linear pattern of evolution and the central role of the exploitation and management of energy systems. The anthropologist Shimkin has emphasized the process of industrialization. He defines elemental industrialization as a system of maximizing the output and efficiency of fabricating activities by the introduction of five practices: the breakdown of products and processes into parts and stages which can be handled separately; the standardization of these parts and stages so that they can be assembled to form similar units; a shift from self-sufficiency to specialization and systematic exchange; a change from custom work designed to satisfy needs as they arise to the production of goods in anticipation of demand; and a change from unit or irregular production to standardized batch production or even continuous flow output.

Even the most rudimentary industrialization requires property, labor and exchange, and political stability, organization, and motivation. No foraging peoples have the cultural prerequisites for industrialization. However, elemental industrialization is found in many agrarian societies. It originated long ago, and was well developed by 2000 B.C. in the Near East.

In Europe, Japan, and the United States, elemental industrialization has evolved into complex industrialization. The transformation took place along two distinct lines: market economics (private capitalism) and command economics (state capitalism). Both types of economy exist in every industrialized country. For example, in the United States private capitalism was represented by **entrepreneurism,** and state capitalism by land grants to railroad construction companies and by protective tariffs. In the USSR, both before and after the revolution, peasant entrepreneurism persisted. Even now it competes intensely with state or state-fostered activities in providing food and other consumer goods and services.

Complex industrialization is compounded of many interrelated changes. One is the development of impersonal, hierarchical, and self-perpetuating organizations for decision-making, administration of resources, and direction of production, both public and private. Another is systematic, institutionalized effort to expand resources and promote useful innovations, whether for individual gain or national power. Of most direct importance has been the harnessing of inanimate energy, chiefly the fossil fuels, and the mastery of a tremendous range of physico-chemical processes; these have provided entirely new classes of goods and services. Implicit in all this is the planned obsolescence of skills, natural resources, and equipment which result in new demands on the surplus of an economy, whether reflected in unused capacity and unemployment or in state subsidies and underemployment. Finally, complex industrialization involves the spread of industrialization from manufacturing to all other economic activities. Chapter 13 will discuss the implications of this for the most basic economic activity, the production of food.

According to the modern view, socio-cultural evolution has proceeded along several fronts, related to technology, population growth, social and spatial organization, and division of labor and behavior. No common evolutionary origin is uncritically assumed for various cultures. Nor is there any moral evaluation, except for the obvious conclusion that if a culture is successful it exemplifies a satisfactory adaptation of a population to its habitat.

Just as no living species is our biological ancestor, no living culture can be our cultural ancestor. Some may be closer than others to the original way of life, but all have changed through time. We will see in Chapter 10 that human culture had its beginning in our prehuman ancestors living where the African savanna merged with the forest. As our forebears spread into new habitats which presented new challenges and imposed relative isolation from other groups, there was an adaptive radiation of cultures analogous to the adaptive radiation of species invading new habitats. There were many cases of parallel evolution, just as in biological evolution, for example, there were parallels between the evolution of Australian marsupials and placental mammals of the other continents. In addition, of course, cultural diffusion has been ubiquitous. Both the "cultural gene pool" and the biological gene pool have remained open, keeping the human species one.

It is not necessary to become tangled in the myriad details that distinguish one culture from another, although the study of cultural individuality is fascinating. There are some generalizations that can be made to clarify the relationships between cultures and habitats. In his socio-political classification, Demitri Shimkin recognizes the following seven major categories.

*KINSHIP-BASED, SUBSISTENCE-DOMINATED SOCIETIES.* These societies were probably universal until fishing techniques were invented during the Middle Stone Age. Remnants of these societies remained until modern times among the South African Bushmen, the African and Southeast Asian Negritos, the Tasmanians, the Central Eskimo, the Great Basin Shoshoneans, and a number of South American tribes. These peoples had no control over their food resources, although they had extensive knowledge of what those resources were. For the most part, they had no way to preserve or to deal with surplus food. Even during times when food was abundant, they seldom took more than enough to meet their immediate needs. Their mobility was limited to distances they could travel on foot, and their travels were generally in pursuit of food. Because of the area required to meet the food requirements of each person, they seldom lived in groups of more than fifty persons; although when conditions were favorable, several groups might come together for a cooperative hunt. Each individual could trace his kinship to the others. The temporary alliances between groups during times of food surplus were customarily the times for acquiring wives and indulging in ceremonies. There was little organization of labor, except for the division of duties between men and women. Even the leader of an organized hunt was only an ad hoc leader. Priests or shamans were the sole specialists.

## KALAHARI BUSHMEN: SPECIALISTS IN DESERT SURVIVAL

*The Bushmen of the Kalahari live in a region considered by most of their fellow Africans to be an uninhabitable wasteland. Their lives are short and spent in continual exhausting effort to gain the bare essentials of life from an ungenerous land. Bushmen were not always condemned to such a hard existence; hunting and gathering peoples, including ancestors of present day Bushmen, once roamed freely over much of Africa, but they were no match for the new order of farmers and herdsmen who were equipped with iron tools and weapons, and superior political, social and military organization. The primitive economy gradually gave way to the more efficient agricultural one, and in Africa, as in the rest of the world, few hunters and gatherers have managed to survive into modern times. The Kalahari Bushmen are some of the few who have survived, escaping extinction by exiling themselves in a hot, dry land, unsuited for agriculture or animal husbandry and adjusting to the rigors of life.*

*Having become desert dwellers, the Bushmen immediately face the problem of satisfying their hunger and thirst in the Kalahari Desert where neither food nor water is plentiful. To do this, they have become desert specialists, expert at gathering together a sufficient diet of desert vegetables and occasional small amounts of meat. The important task of finding and collecting edible plants and roots is generally women's work, but both men and women know the location of all the patches of desert vegetables in their territory and, if need be, can even return to individual plants they may have noted months earlier. Thus, Bushmen do not waste effort wandering aimlessly in search of food when it runs short. The less favored the areas of the Kalahari, the more careful the observation and dietary ingenuity required of Bushmen living there. Even where there are no permanent waterholes, they are able to make do entirely on plant liquids during the dry season.*

*The harsh realities of undependable water supply and scarce food have had equally pervasive consequences for the political and social mores of the Kalahari Bushmen. They live a simple life, both in structure and content; desert survival requires it. They do not recognize any organizational unit beyond their small family bands. Within the band, there is no complicated system of social classes and no formal leadership. Because filling one's stomach must be a full-time undertaking, there is no place for an individual whose political or*

*EXPANDED PRIMARY SOCIETIES.*    These societies were associated with increases in food supply because of the nature of the habitat or technological advances. Such a society became possible, for example, with the advent of large-scale fishing, intensive gathering, and small-scale cultivation of crops. Its development required the motivation and means to amass surplus; large-scale fishing made no sense for people who did not know how to *religious duties interfere with his ability to feed himself. No Bushman "rugged individualist" accumulates more possessions than his companions; excess baggage of any kind only encumbers people who must move on whenever the food or water runs low. A hunter shares his kill as a matter of course and it is considered a right and not a privilege of every band member to benefit from one man's good fortune. The fortunate hunter gives willingly, for sharing is his insurance against the inevitable hard times when he too will have to depend on the generosity of his friends. The prestige gained from being able to share will often motivate a hungry man to eat only the least desirable parts of the animal he has killed and to give away the rest.*

*If there is any competition among band members, it is for this prestige. They almost never indulge in aggressive competition because it may lead to violence which, for good reason, is anathema to the Bushmen. Their only weapon, the poison arrow, is always fatal to its victim and he will usually leave behind him young children and old parents. The loss of a single member of a small band can dangerously upset the balance which exists between productive members and dependent members, a balance which is precarious enough to begin with.*

*In a less exacting environment, the well-watered Drakensberg Mountains, extensive cave paintings have been found which indicate that Bushmen were once skillful artists. The Kalahari Bushmen of today have no knowledge of this tradition of graphic art. If their pre-Kalahari ancestors ever were great painters, today's Bushmen have had to forsake that artistic proficiency to concentrate on survival skills.*

*The exigencies of desert survival have led the Bushmen to minimize strife and to emphasize sharing, co-operation and non-violence, values which, in a less precarious situation, might be dismissed as idealistic and impractical. The main battle has been for subsistence against the elements and not among themselves. But the cost of having to devote their talent and energy single-mindedly to feeding themselves has been great neglect of the arts and of material comforts. And so, well-tuned as they may be to the Kalahari, Bushmen who have seen the outside world and its material wonders will not need much encouragement to abandon their Stone Age way of life and leave the desert permanently. Their adjustment to new circumstances may be difficult, but certainly within the grasp of people who have coped with the harshest of human habitats.*

preserve fish, and they did not engage in it. In addition, a higher level of population density seems necessary for this type of society than for the type described first. Population density is related to the physical environment. When the population of a foraging group became too great, the group would split, if possible, and one or both of the resulting groups would move into new territory. If the nature of the territory was such that dispersal was impossible, then the group would be forced to remain together and develop new adaptations. Whatever the cause for the increase in population density, expanded primary societies could accommodate permanent groups of several hundred individuals, and temporary ones of 1,000 or more.

These societies had elementary political authorities (chiefs, shamans, priests, police) and an accompanying social differentiation according to status; but the leaders were often limited in power and had only a tenuous hold on their positions. Such societies distinguished themselves from other, similar groups by means of special names, cemeteries, war cries, rituals, and other customs, and they often fought with neighboring groups over territory and resources. It is thought that semisedentary cultures of this type probably arose in favored localities during the Stone Age, while mobile hunting cultures developed later as an adaptation to more hostile environments. Both types, semisedentary and mobile hunting, are exemplified by numerous tribes of North and South American Indians.

CEREMONIALLY CENTERED, MULTI-COMMUNITY, DIFFERENTI-ATED SOCIETIES.     These societies reflect still further population growth and economic diversification. They had generally achieved local specialization in the cultivation of crops, as well as in animal husbandry, mining, and some specialized technologies. Communication between neighboring villages was good, and regions were further solidified by common religious values. Ceremonial centers were tended by a priesthood that was often hereditary. This priesthood might also be responsible for teaching, welfare, and justice.

Evolutionary forces leading to this increased degree of cultural complexity are not fully understood. Conventional wisdom has it that once people had achieved control of their food supplies and increased their productivity, it was possible to channel surplus production into the maintenance of complex social institutions. This is not an explanation, but a description of what happened. Clearly, as long as the environment is severely limiting and thinly scattered, families can do no more than meet their individual energy requirements. If everyone must be a food producer, there is no surplus energy to support a diversified society and its institutions.

Until recent developments in Western agriculture, the production of food has been a labor-intensive process. But with increasing population density, an additional input of labor did not necessarily yield an equivalent output of food. Conventional wisdom says, again, that the "surplus" people were then freed for other pursuits. But why should some people continue to work hard producing food, while others did not engage in this activity at all? Why did not everyone simply work less? The answer is not clear in all instances. In our culture today, some people work only enough to satisfy their basic needs, while others are driven to amass as much wealth as possible. In cultural evolution the motivation to produce a surplus must have developed simultaneously with the practical ability to do so. It did in some cultures — but not in all.

It is thought that the great early agricultural civilizations in the Old World arose in relationship to the need for centralized control of water for irrigation. The individuals who had power to give or withhold water had ultimate control over the lives of the people. Water authority was the nucleus of political power and social stratification; once the initial step was taken toward complex political organization, later steps followed naturally. This is a nice theory, and it is probably true in many cases. We have seen that in the Philippines, however, central political authority is weak, even though life depends on careful control of irrigation. Nor was irrigated crop production invariably associated with political development.

However the first political leaders achieved their power, and for whatever reasons, they were able to motivate the food producers to produce an ever greater surplus, which, in turn, required new institutions for distribution and use. Wealth accumulated at ceremonial and political centers through support of outlying areas, and centralized markets developed. There was specialization in handicrafts. Products of craftsmen as well as food growers were exchanged at the markets. Societies of this type — complex, ceremonially centered, multi-community — developed in ancient Egypt, in Mesopotamia, among some groups of North and South American Indians, and among the Lobi of West Africa, to mention a few.

*STRATIFIED CONQUEST STATES.* This type of society is thought to have arisen from the type just described, as the result of even more increased concentration of wealth and power. It is probable that population growth progressed to the point of creating population pressure (see Chapter 11). A further influence was increased mobility, brought about through advances in transportation. Domesticated animals suitable for riding or drawing wheeled vehicles had been around for some time. Their efficient use, however, awaited the invention of the iron horseshoe, appropriate harnesses and related equipment, and advances in road-building technology.

A "stratified conquest state" must impose itself on adjacent societies. Its religion is the only right one; barbarians must be converted to it. The need to acquire new territory and resources is masked by the desire to save souls. Militarism arises; this, together with religious certainty, leads to **absolutism,** looting, human sacrifice, slavery, and **concubinage.** A warrior class is established. Division of labor increases further. There is greater separation of the rulers from the people, and a tendency to elaborate a glittering court life.

Each social stratum develops its own behavioral code, which engenders intense feelings of dignity and honor. Motivation to surplus production is further enhanced to meet the new demands of the material culture. Roads must be built, and fortifications. Arms must be produced. (An army has always been a wonderful thing for the economy. It consumes and consumes and consumes.) Increased levels of planning, management of labor, and mass production were also required to meet the new material demands. The state was usually a tyranny; and tyrannies promote constant unrest. Societies of this type occurred in Shang China and Assyria. The Scythic kingdoms, the Aztec confederacy, the Iroquois confederacy, and many Polynesian and African kingdoms were also examples.

*INTEGRATED, BUREAUCRATIC MONARCHIES.* In some cases, these states stemmed from the preceding. Personal rule was replaced in large part by a bureaucracy of officials stemming from the proliferation of procedures and records. Public works, both civil and military, grew prominent, supported by taxation, which replaced looting. With the introduction of currency and standard measures, commerce expanded, cities became open rather than walled, and wealth, with its concomitant of conspicuous consumption, increased. Although there was a *national* language and a *national* religion, there was also a hierarchical organization of local groups. This type of society was characteristic of the Near East after 2000 B.C., and of the Incas, Achaemenid Persia, Han China, the Mourya Empire of India, and the Roman Empire. Its pinnacle was the **totalitarian state.** Such states exist even now.

*LAW-BASED CORPORATE STATES.* Many of the integrated, bureaucratic monarchies developed into less-centralized, less-authoritarian systems. Sometimes the term "feudal" is applied to these systems. The concept of conditional land tenure or **fiefdom** arose. There was an increasing emphasis on personal choice and responsibility, including a sense of obligation for prayer, alms, ritual abstinences, and salvation in some other world. Slavery was considered reprehensible, although it still existed.

Social organization reached new levels of complexity, as people were organized into corporate bodies — guilds, religious groups, socio-economic groups like nobles and peasants. These bodies became the foci of social and regulatory activities. Public law dealt mainly with inter-group conflicts.

This type of society arose in association with still greater specialization of labor. There were specialists in various types of metallurgy, in masonry, cloth-making, and weapon-making, and in many crafts. Law-based, corporate states arose in western Europe in late Hellenistic times, and also in the Middle East, where they are still common. They never developed in aboriginal America.

*MOBILE, PERSUASION-CONTROLLED, HIGH-ENERGY SOCIETIES.* These societies are developing throughout the world today, based on law-based corporate systems. They are typified by highly productive industrialized agriculture, unparalleled urbanization, mass communications, general education, and individualized status. Because of their extraordinary complexity, they can be controlled only with the informational means of the machine age.

The process of cultural borrowing and hybridization is going on today on an unprecedented scale, as the less-developed nations attempt to adopt in a short time the practices and ideas which arose in the Western World over a period of centuries. In addition to the effects of mass communication in changing people's perceptions of the world and their own needs, many of the cultural changes are deemed necessary to solve economic and food production problems created by the introduction of Western medicine (see Chapter 11). We have seen that when one aspect of culture is changed, adjustments are usually required in many other aspects as well. Even in America we are experiencing widespread "future shock" as a result of the rate and magnitude of the social and cultural change we have witnessed within our own lifetimes. It remains to be seen whether, and to what extent, our "mobile, persuasion-controlled, high-energy" culture can be adopted by nations with far different traditions, without causing intolerable social conflict and upheaval.

## REFERENCES

ARENSBERG, C. M., AND A. H. NIEHOFF. 1964. *Introducing Social Change: A Manual for Americans Overseas.* Chicago: Aldine Publishing Co.

COHEN, Y., ED. 1968. *Man in Adaptation: The Cultural Present.* Chicago: Aldine Publishing Co.

MOORE, W. E. 1963. *Social Change.* Englewood Cliffs, N.J.: Prentice-Hall.

MOORE, W. E. 1965. *The Impact of Industry.* Englewood Cliffs, N.J.: Prentice-Hall.

MUMFORD, L. 1971. *Technics and Civilization.* New York: Harcourt Brace Jovanovich.

SAUER, C. O. 1969. *Agricultural Origins and Dispersions.* 2nd ed. Cambridge: M.I.T. Press.

SINGER, C., E. J. HOLMYARD, A. R. HALL, AND T. I. WILLIAMS, EDS. 1954–1958. *A History of Technology.* 5 vols. Oxford: Clarendon Press.

STEWARD, J. H. 1955. *Theory of Culture Change.* Urbana: Univ. of Illinois Press.

TOYNBEE, A. J. 1934–1961. *A Study of History.* 12 vols. Oxford: Oxford Univ. Press.

WHITE, L. 1949. *The Science of Culture.* New York: Grove Press.

# · 10 ·

CAROL E. STEINHART

# Antecedents and Forces of Socio-Cultural Evolution

Many details of cultural evolution will remain unknown forever, speculate on them as we will. The early stages of cultural evolution took place millions of years ago and there is no record of them. Primitive language left no fossil remains, nor did the origin of love and the family. About phenomena like these we can only guess.

But in piecing together the story of cultural evolution we have evidence from diverse fields. Coupling this evidence with informed inference and imagination, we can at least present a plausible theory of how the present array of cultural adaptations came about. Clues to cultural evolution come from living primates and other social animals, archeological remains, living creatures, the behavioral development of a human child, written history, and experiment — hypothesizing that our ancestors did something a certain way and then trying it to see if it works. All of these (including inference and imagination) have contributed to the ideas summarized in this chapter.

## ANIMAL ANTECEDENTS OF CULTURE

The paradox of human culture is that it is unique, yet all essential aspects of it had their origins in our prehuman past and are found in other species today. Four prerequisites for the development of culture are the ability to learn, social behavior, symbolic communication, and the use of tools.

226

*LEARNING.* Culture is neither useful nor possible without a high degree of intelligence and behavioral flexibility. A microorganism, plant, or lower animal is genetically programmed to respond in specific ways to specific stimuli. Although such responses may be called behavior, they are innate and automatic. Increasingly, as animal evolution progressed, natural selection favored creatures whose behavior was not wholly automatic but could be modified by experience. It favored the ability to learn. There are reports that even one-celled organisms can be conditioned to respond in certain ways to stimuli, and simple animals like flatworms learn to select the "correct" path in a T-maze. Birds and lower mammals show considerable learning ability. But despite their latent ability, most animals function most of the time according to genetically programmed behavior patterns.

Behavioral flexibility and intelligence reach their pinnacle in the primates. In fact, with much behavior no longer automatic, learning becomes a necessity. If culture is defined as learned behavior that is socially transmitted, the higher subhuman primates certainly exhibit the rudiments of culture. Although true culture is more than the acquisition of new habits or skills and their transmission to other members of the group, patterns of social transmission of learned behavior in other animals make it difficult to define precisely what makes human culture unique. One important difference between man and other animals is that while other animals learn through imitation, they do not consciously teach. Only man chooses what behaviors will be transmitted.

*SOCIAL ORGANIZATION.* Many vertebrate and some invertebrate animals show social behavior in the development of hierarchies, flocks or herds, territorial systems, and the division of labor. Social animals have added a new dimension to adaptation: natural selection acts on the group as a whole, as well as on individuals.

All social groups must develop adaptive mechanisms in the organization of their social relations to achieve order and predictability in their patterns of competition and cooperation (Figure 10.1). Hierarchies establish the place of individuals or groups in the social structure, minimizing conflict over food, mates, and territory. Territoriality is a means of ordering and dispersing the total population spatially.

By definition, all forms of cultural adaptation are based on social interaction. Cultural adaptation through social action is a mode of behavior deeply rooted in our prehuman past, for social action is characteristic of all higher primates and many prosimians as well. Among primates, social behavior must be learned; but this learning is almost inevitable, just as our learning to talk is inevitable except under most unusual circumstances. All ape and monkey babies live within a social group. The mother-infant relationship is imbedded in a matrix of social interaction, and the group is the

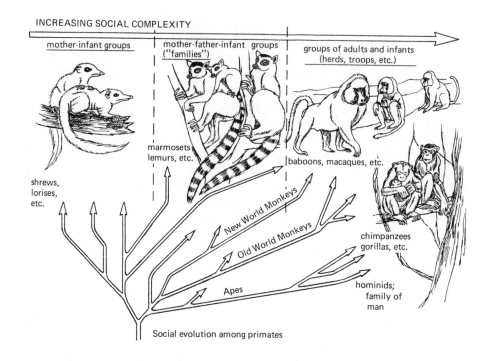

INCREASING SOCIAL COMPLEXITY

mother-infant groups

mother-father-infant groups ("families")

groups of adults and infants (herds, troops, etc.)

marmosets, lemurs, etc.

baboons, macaques, etc.

shrews, lorises, etc.

New World Monkeys

Old World Monkeys

chimpanzees gorillas, etc.

Apes

hominids; family of man

Social evolution among primates

**Figure 10–1** Social evolution among primates. Social complexity is related both to the position on the primate family tree and to environmental conditions. (Adapted from J. Pfeiffer, *The Emergence of Man*, Harper and Row, New York, 1969, p. 252.)

fundamental adaptive unit. Infants and young receive intense attention from adults of both sexes from birth to maturity. Juveniles and adolescents, especially females, are eager to touch and hold infants. An animal deprived of experience with infants may fail to care for her own first baby, although she may do better with subsequent ones.

Males are generally dominant over females and there is a hierarchy among the males themselves. Establishment of rank order reduces aggression and determines the priorities and behavior of the group. Although often present among females, the hierarchy tends to be weaker because a female's status is influenced by the status of her male companions and whether she is in estrus or has an infant.

The social organization of baboons is of special interest because these monkeys occupy the same habitat as pre-men and primitive men — the savanna and the forest edge. Baboons face problems that are probably similar to those faced by our ancestors. It is instructive to learn how they cope with them.

The size of baboon troops ranges from as few as 10 individuals to almost 200, most troops including about 40. The troop is a closed social system; interbreeding or exchange of members between troops is rare. However, a number of troops may feed in close proximity to one another or share the same water source without hostility. Baboons have no permanent home base, although many of them live out their lives within a few miles of where they were born and each troop has a rigidly defined territory beyond whose bounds no individual will venture. This territory may not represent an area to be defended against intruders so much as an area with which they are familiar and where they feel secure.

At night baboons seek the shelter and protection of trees. Morning finds them in the open, foraging for food, grooming one another in small groups, resting, engaging in occasional minor disputes, or — if they are young — playing (Figure 10.2). Females and young form the central core of the group. They are usually accompanied by a few older, dominant males and surrounded by adolescents. Young, aggressive males who have not yet risen in the hierarchy are usually on the periphery, where they serve as sentinels and protectors. The menacing posture of a strong male baboon often discourages a would-be predator without any show of violence. If necessary, the males fight fiercely, and few predators care to engage in battle with several aroused baboons. An isolated baboon, however, is often a doomed baboon. It may fall prey to a predator within hours of being separated from its troop. The situation was

**Figure 10–2** Baboons on the savanna. Some are playing, some foraging for food, but all are ready for instant action should danger arise. (Photograph by Irven DeVore.)

probably similar for primitive man. Life on the savanna has been compared to a baseball game: most of the time it is uneventful, but everything depends on successfully meeting the sudden challenge.

Chimpanzees, our nearest living relatives, offer an interesting contrast to baboons. Although they spend part of their time on the ground and may occasionally enter open terrain, they are primarily forest animals. Their territory is not sharply defined, their social relationships are free and easy, and their social groups are not permanent. They can afford to be relaxed. There is little danger in their lives.

Habitat affects the behavior of both baboons and chimpanzees. Social groups of forest-dwelling baboons are rather chimpanzee-like, while a group of chimpanzees, on leaving the forest, is pervaded by an air of nervousness and undergoes a baboon-like tightening of the ranks. In leaving the forest, our ancestors left a life of comparative safety and freedom and adopted a life that required constant vigilance and a high level of social organization.

Human social groups differ from other primate groups in several significant ways. One is that in human groups the family plays a major role as a biological, social, and economic unit. Another is that human social groups are open, and mates are customarily chosen from neighboring groups. Exchange of mates is a means of establishing higher orders of organization through alliances between groups — a phenomenon which has never been observed among other primates. But most important, the social organization of man has been freed from biological control. Man is not enslaved to traditional patterns; he can transcend even what he learns. A major difference between human culture and its prehuman antecedents is the ability of man intentionally to modify his socio-cultural systems, rendering them rapidly and sensitively responsive to the challenges of various environments.

But the ability to change social institutions may lie at the root of many of our problems as well as at the root of our extraordinary adaptability. Subhuman primate societies are genetically programmed; we look at their organization to get clues to our own nature unencumbered by the influence of culture. Primate groups generally contain between 20 and 50 members, and seldom more than 100. It is significant that for several million years the genus *Homo* and its Australopithecine forebears also lived in groups of about this size — for which they also presumably were genetically programmed. Our genetic constitution has not changed much in the relatively few years since we have forsaken foraging in small bands in favor of permanent settlement in increasingly larger groups. Is it possible that our genes are not compatible with the kinds of groups in which we now live? Was it only pressure on food and other resources that made primitive populations split when they surpassed a certain size? Can culture close the gap between our genetic endowment and our present environments? Recent emphasis on community action may be an unconscious attempt to return to the small-group way of life, and concern with the urban environment attests to our awareness that we are not adapted for some of the environments we have created.

COMMUNICATION.    The vocalizations of animals other than man are emotional outbursts elicited by an immediate situation. They consist of a system of stereotyped calls which are inflexible in their use and meaning even though they may be many in number. Animals also communicate through posture, gestures, and facial expressions. Monkeys and apes couple a limited variety of sounds with an enormous repertoire of meaningful expressions and gestures. Despite the limited range of vocalization, however, communication by sounds is exceedingly important to many primates, some of which seem to chatter incessantly. Complex patterns of vocal communication in man developed from earlier, genetically transmitted patterns of vocalization.

The number of messages that can be transmitted through a call system is limited to the number of calls. Calls mean such things as "food," or "danger," or "let's play," or "I'm hurt." It is postulated that true language began to evolve by the opening up of call systems so that parts of calls could be combined to create new messages. For example, if AB means food is present and CD means danger is present, AC might signify food and danger, AD food and no danger, and so on. With the opening of a call system, the young could no longer speak instinctively, although they could utter the basic calls. They would have to learn their language and how to use it.

Through language man has interposed a system of symbols between his sensory perceptions and his responses to them. There is no relationship between the sound of a word and what the word represents; the meaning is arbitrary and must be socially agreed upon. In true language a few basic, meaningless sounds are combined to form a large number of words which, in turn, can be combined in a virtually infinite number of ways to convey a limitless number of messages. Anyone who knows a language is able to say and to understand things he has never said nor heard before. The symbolic nature of human language frees our speech from restriction to emotional outbursts about present situations. With symbolic language we can speak about happenings in the past or the future, about imaginary objects or objects that are out of sight. Symbolic language is known to have evolved in only one other animal: the bee. The dance of the honeybee sheds no light on the evolution of human speech, however. It is of interest because it shows that symbolic language originated at least twice, in unrelated groups of animals: once as an instinctual, genetically determined behavior and once as a learned behavior. Communication by sound is also highly developed in whales and dolphins, marine mammals of considerable intelligence which live in a world dominated by auditory sensations. It is possible that their vast range and repertoire of sounds represents true language; but again, fascinating as the study of their communication is, it sheds no light on the evolution of human speech.

Use of symbolic language has a counterpart in the evolution of the primate brain. A monkey's brain contains few connections between auditory and visual centers, and it is therefore difficult for a monkey to associate a visual sensation with a sound. An ape's brain shows a more elaborate system of interconnections and integration of sensory information. A human brain, in addition to being complexly cross referenced, contains specialized areas for speech. As usual, however, the difference between us and the chimpanzees is more quantitative than qualitative. The chimpanzee has some capacity for symbolic communication, even though true speech is not possible. A chimp named Washoe has learned a vocabulary of more than fifty signs based on the standard American sign language for the deaf. At about the age of two, she began spontaneously to combine gestures into meaningful messages containing as many as five words. Another chimp named Sarah has learned a language based on plastic tokens of various forms and colors. Still another communicates by pressing combinations of buttons on a computer. It has thus been shown that chimpanzees are able to combine symbols in novel ways to express ideas, although there is no hint of grammar in their constructions. ("More drink, please" could as easily be "drink please more." A human child, in contrast, may speak nonsense — but he speaks it according to recognizable rules of grammar which he has not been taught.) Possibilities in this area of investigation are exciting. Some day a chimpanzee may even tell a psychologist, "I am lonely," or " I am frightened."

It is thought that evolution of language must have preceded or accompanied the making of all but the simplest tools, cooperative hunting, and establishment of home bases and kinship systems. It is difficult to imagine how plans for a hunt could be made without speech or how categories of relationship could be defined. Thus it is likely that *Australopithecus* spoke a primitive language 2 or 3 million years ago. Speech was but one of many aspects of culture that stimulated and was stimulated by the evolution of the human brain.

*TOOLS.*    The use of tools is an instinctive activity for many animals. The lowly larvae of the caddis fly construct shelters out of sand or pebbles in the streams where they live. Across the mouths of their shelters they build nets for straining out floating food particles. The wasp *Ammophila* hammers down the soil around the opening of its burrow with a pebble. Several kinds of ants use a sticky thread spun by their own larvae to fasten leaves together. Darwin described a finch that used cactus spines to pry insects from cracks in the bark of trees. The California sea otter uses stones to crack open the shells of mollusks on which it feeds.

Tool use among primates is on a psychologically higher level than it is in other animals. Stereoscopic vision, a high degree of intelligence and curiosity, and the structure of the hand permit the examination and manipulation of objects. Objects are perceived as things that can be taken from the environment for study, play, or other use. The implicit questions "what is it like?" and "what does it do?" led first to tool using and eventually to tool making.

Sticks and branches hold a particular fascination for young chimpanzees. A juvenile will spend long periods examining a stick and poking it at and into things. This innate behavior leads naturally to the use of sticks as tools. Foresight and planning occur when a chimpanzee breaks a twig from a bush, strips off a few leaves, and sets off in search of a termite mound, carrying the tool in its mouth. Perhaps it even prepares several tools at one time. If it finds a promising termite hole, it sticks in a probe, wiggles it around, and then withdraws it, licking off the catch with obvious enjoyment. In times of anger or excitement, chimpanzees pick up branches or break them from trees and wave them frantically, occasionally throwing them at one another. Captive chimpanzees use sticks to obtain objects that are out of reach.

Tool use and tool making by the chimpanzee are not restricted to sticks and branches. Some primates chew a mouthful of leaves and use the absorbent wad to soak up water from the crotch of a tree; or they may use a similar sponge to mop up the last bit of brain — a prized delicacy — from a skull. Chimpanzees wipe themselves with handfuls of leaves and scratch themselves with stones. Occasionally they use stones as weapons in aggressive encounters, or as hammers to open hard fruits. The spectrum of activities involving tools varies among groups, suggesting development of local chimpanzee "cultures."

In the wild, chimpanzees use only a part of their behavioral potential. When raised from infancy in human environments, they learn a great deal of very unchimpanzee-like behavior. They seem to enjoy learning, partly for the reward of human approval and partly for the apparent personal satisfaction that achievement brings. Several chimps have been avid painters, pursuing their hobby with no prodding from their human friends. Work with chimpanzees thus suggests that the potential for tool use, tool making, and learning a culture may have been present in the distant common ancestor of the chimpanzee and man.

## INTERACTION BETWEEN CULTURAL AND BIOLOGICAL EVOLUTION

Many questions about the evolution of man are chicken-and-egg type questions — for example, which came first, bipedalism or reliance on tools? Such questions are meaningless. There was feedback between physical evolution and emerging cultural patterns, each influencing the other. Man did not evolve trait by trait, physical advances alternating with cultural ones. Reinforced by natural selection and each other, physical and cultural evolution proceeded together.

Our early ancestors lived at the forest edge, where they spent much of their time on the ground eating foods that abounded in the open. The suggestion that the apes who were our ancestors were failures, kicked out of the trees by better-adapted forest apes, is overstated in this form because the aptitude for life on the ground had to accompany the opportunity—or necessity—for it. It is more likely that our ancestors came down from the trees in pursuit of food, and the better adapted they became for foraging on the ground, the less well adapted they were for life in the trees. In any case, as the climate changed and the savanna began to encroach on the forest, the ancestors of modern apes remained in the trees while our branch of the ape family adapted to the dangers and rigors of life on the savanna.

By the time our ancestors left the forest they were already on their way to becoming erect and bipedal. They used tools and relied heavily on vocal communication. Although basically vegetarian, they ate eggs, insects, fledgling birds, and lizards, just as many primates do today. Occasionally they devoured red meat when they came across a small animal or the remains of a lion kill.

As the climate became drier, edible vegetable foods grew scarce, especially toward the end of the dry season. Then the pre-men of the savanna turned to eating meat out of necessity, as an adaptive response to environmental change. The importance of meat eating cannot be overemphasized. It changed our ancestors physically, psychologically, and socially. In explaining the differences between *Australopithecus africanus* and *A. robustus*, anthropologists suggest that *robustus*, in his moister, less-challenging habitat with plentiful vegetable food, did not have to eat meat; he therefore did not have to hunt; and he did not change (see Chapter 5).

As far as we know, *Australopithecus* was the first erect biped. He not only used tools, but he made them. While tools were taking the place of teeth in offense and defense and for dividing food into pieces of manageable size, the bones of the head were being restructured, resulting in reduced size of teeth and jaws, reduction in bony structures which anchored chewing muscles, and more room for brains. At first, foraging bands of Australopithecines stayed together, each individual finding his own food and consuming it on the spot. But infants had to be carried, for they could no longer cling. With the advent of serious hunting came a differentiation of sex roles and establishment of home bases. Females and children began to remain together at the home base, perhaps gathering vegetable foods. Old, sick, or injured individuals could also remain behind. A sprained ankle or minor infection which could well have been fatal for another primate was merely an inconvenience for *Australopithecus*, who could rest in the relative safety of home until he became well.

At first, males caught only small animals, but they lived in constant sight of large herds of game and they observed the habits of both the game animals and other predators. Sometimes they killed a young or weak animal. Eventually they began to hunt large game in an organized way.

Cooperative hunting probably marked the beginning of carrying food back to the home base for distribution among all members of the group. Weapons and tools had to be produced for the hunt and for skinning and dividing the kill. Plans had to be made. The new life further favored natural selection for intelligence — for foresight, memory, and language. It required self control: postponement of immediate action and gratification for the sake of larger and longer-range benefits. *Australopithecus* was no longer completely at the mercy of his environment. He had begun to shape the events of his own life.

Increasingly, learned behavior included not only habits, roles, and strategies for dealing with the physical environment, but a system of values that influenced all behavior. The idea of standards emerged. There were standards for tool making and language; there were ideas of right and wrong, true and false, proper and improper behavior, past and future; there must have been a dim perception of the self. The permanent family may have begun to evolve at this time, owing to the trend toward constant sexual receptivity in the female and the periodic scarcity of food, which forced groups to fragment into smaller units. The smallest viable economic and biologic unit is an adult male, one or more adult females, and their children. Ideas of kinship would have to accompany the establishment of the family. These ideas imply a high level of conceptualization and words with which to express kinship relations.

Natural selection operated intensely on early bands of Australopithecines, hastening both physical and cultural evolution. When some groups began to hunt cooperatively, game became wary and more difficult to catch. Groups that did not improve their methods could not survive. Our ancestors no longer lived at peace with the other animals of the savanna. They had become predators more deadly than lions and leopards.

Climatic and geologic change created new north-south migration routes and new pressures for migration. It is not known with certainty who first made the trek from Africa into other parts of the Old World — *Australopithecus* or *Homo*, but whoever it was, he was a fellow of considerable intelligence and cultural achievement. He had a variety of tools, possibly including tools for making tools, which enabled him to use his muscular energy efficiently. Somewhere on the long journey out of Africa he probably began to use fire. He was ready to leave his ancestral home and establish himself in new environments.

## HUNTERS AND GATHERERS

Although each culture is a unique strategy for extracting energy from a specific habitat and for maintaining the social structure that insures effective use of the energy system, there are similarities among cultures based on foraging. The social organization of foraging societies is governed by the quest for food. It may vary with the season of the year, according to the major food source and method of obtaining it. The permanent social and economic unit is the family, with a number of related families forming a band. Neighboring bands may be loosely organized into tribes which share common traditions and language but have no central political authority. The size of a band is related to the availability of food and other resources, although when food is plentiful, other factors may be limiting, such as tensions within the group and the number of people that can live together governed only by customs of proper behavior toward kinsmen. The economy is one of sharing for the survival of the group.

Although human bands are politically autonomous, they form links with other bands through marriage. Marriage is an economic necessity for a man and a woman and a political necessity for a band, to minimize conflict and to promote cooperation between groups. It has been suggested that the practice of exchanging mates with neighboring bands began when men took up hunting. Pursuit of game must often have taken them into alien territory — an intrusion which certainly would have been resented unless some social ties existed. The most enduring social tie is a kinship relation.

The first hunters probably ran down their prey and bludgeoned it to death or killed small animals with their hands. Later, an assortment of projectile points and methods for delivering them to their targets was developed. The bow and arrow was invented by a fairly advanced *Homo sapiens*. It was used primarily in wooded terrain, where game was approached by stalking. The spear is a much more ancient weapon which is most effective in open terrain, where game is approached by running. In addition to the basic weapons, hunting techniques included a variety of nets, traps, snares, and fishing **weirs.** The partnership between man and dog probably began more than 15,000 years ago. Besides helping to locate, track, run down, kill, and retrieve game, the dog was induced to pull sleds of stone, skin, or wood, giving man his first source of overland transport other than his own feet. Tools useful in gathering and food preparation include the digging stick and many of the basic tools of the hunt. It has been suggested (see reference to Cohen) that all the tools of Stone Age man (except perhaps the digging stick) originated in connection with hunting.

*PREHISTORIC BIG GAME HUNTERS.*    Although the first scenes of cultural evolution took place on the African savanna, subsequent crucial events probably occurred in the Pleistocene snows of Europe and Asia. The actor was *Homo erectus,* big game hunter and user of fire. Fire kept cold, darkness, and predators at bay and drew people together for conversation and planning. With fire for offense and defense, established cave dwellers such as the giant cave bear (now extinct) could be driven from their lairs, and man could appropriate the best caves for himself. The oldest known hearths are from almost three quarters of a million years ago in Europe. There is also evidence of ancient hearths in China.

Big game hunting was more than laying a snare, setting a trap, or throwing a spear. It was the expression of values, technology, and social relationships with other hunters and with nonhunting members of the group. It required intimate knowledge of the ways of animals and some understanding of seasonal cycles, as well as carefully laid plans, cooperation, division of labor, and leadership. There is evidence from several parts of the world that *Homo erectus* engaged in massive animal drives, lighting brush fires or in other ways stampeding panicky animals over cliffs or into swamps. At various times his victims included large bison, elephants, wooly mammoths, ibexes, horses, and rhinoceroses. Hunting this type of animal implies still further differentiation of sex roles, a process that began during the days of small game hunting; it suggests new, closer bonds between males and perhaps also between the females waiting anxiously at home for the return of their mates.

**Figure 10–3** Prehistoric drawing from Altamira Caves. (Photograph courtesy of the Spanish National Tourist Office, New York.)

The challenge of big game hunting placed a premium on mental function. Centers continued to evolve for integrating messages from many areas of the brain, for coordinating responses to these many messages, and for inhibiting impulsive behavior. Self-control was all important in the life of the hunter. It was as necessary not to act at the wrong time as to act at the right time. Big game hunting was probably a major factor in the evolution of *Homo erectus* into *Homo sapiens.* Fossil evidence suggests that modern man evolved where there were herds of large animals. Elsewhere, primitive forms persisted with no signs of evolving into modern man.

Although *Homo erectus* appears to have used natural pigments for cosmetic purposes, the first signs of religion and art are connected with early *Homo sapiens.* Burial customs date back at least 75,000 years. Food and tools were placed in Neanderthal graves, presumably to be used in some kind of afterlife, and fossil pollen indicates that flowers were strewn on top of graves. Art originated somewhat later. Although the earliest known cave paintings are less than 40,000 years old, they are so advanced that it is impossible not to assume a history of art leading to them.

During the glacial periods in the north, all social institutions reveal the importance of the hunt. Mysterious animal cults grew up — the cult of the ibex and of the cave bear, for example. Bones of slaughtered animals were involved in rituals and ceremonial burials. Cave paintings invariably depicted animals, many of them trapped or wounded. Paintings were hidden deep in the caves in almost inaccessible nooks and crannies (Figure 10.3). Their purpose was probably magical or ritualistic, related to past or hoped-for future hunting successes. The life of the big game hunters, as far as we are able to reconstruct it, clearly shows how technology, rituals, beliefs, art, and social organization were geared to the hunt, which was the source of energy and life.

RECENT AND CONTEMPORARY HUNTER-GATHERERS. At the dawn of agriculture roughly 10,000 years ago, the human population of the world was probably on the order of ten million. All of these people obtained their food by foraging — by fishing, hunting large or small game, or collecting vegetable foods. They were widely distributed on all the continents. Today, with the world population nearly 4 billion, the remaining hunter-gatherers number only in the tens of thousands (Figure 10.4). In the past, people from advanced cultures have considered hunter-gatherers as something not quite human, an attitude evident in the writing of many explorers and pioneers. More recently we have begun to appreciate what simple cultures can tell us about our own cultural past and the origins of present social arrangements, as well as about human behavior in general. We also appreciate the near perfection of many of the cultural adaptations and the endless ingenuity of man as he adapts to different conditions.

If the habitat does not change, cultural adjustment can also be stable. Stability was probably the usual condition in preagricultural societies, al-

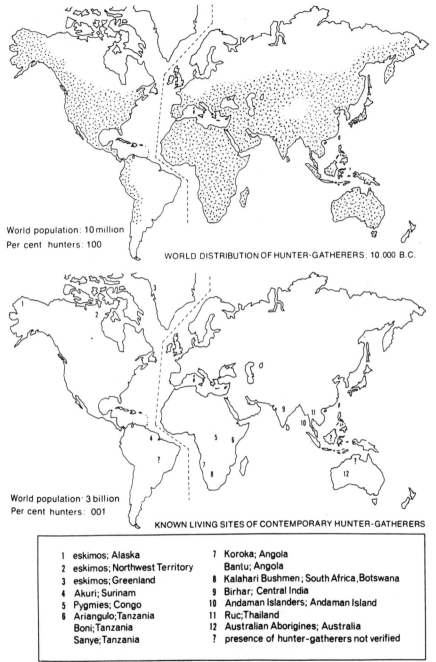

World population: 10 million
Per cent hunters: 100

WORLD DISTRIBUTION OF HUNTER-GATHERERS: 10,000 B.C.

World population: 3 billion
Per cent hunters: 001

KNOWN LIVING SITES OF CONTEMPORARY HUNTER-GATHERERS

| | | | |
|---|---|---|---|
| 1 | eskimos; Alaska | 7 | Koroka; Angola |
| 2 | eskimos; Northwest Territory | | Bantu; Angola |
| 3 | eskimos; Greenland | 8 | Kalahari Bushmen; South Africa, Botswana |
| 4 | Akuri; Surinam | 9 | Birhar; Central India |
| 5 | Pygmies; Congo | 10 | Andaman Islanders; Andaman Island |
| 6 | Ariangulo; Tanzania | 11 | Ruc; Thailand |
| | Boni; Tanzania | 12 | Australian Aborigines; Australia |
| | Sanye; Tanzania | ? | presence of hunter-gatherers not verified |

**Figure 10–4** Above: world distribution of hunter-gatherers at the dawn of agriculture, about 10,000 B.C. Below: known locations of the world's remaining hunter-gatherers, whose numbers total only a few tens of thousands. (From J. Pfeiffer, *The Emergence of Man*, Harper and Row, New York, 1969, p. 311.)

though there were periods of disequilibrium when culture and the environment did change. The hunter-gatherers who persisted into the nineteenth and twentieth centuries had lived in equilibrium with their environment for many generations — some of them, probably, for thousands of years. The following examples illustrate how all aspects of such a culture are related to the means of extracting energy from the habitat. They also show that change, when it does come, can have unexpected and far-reaching effects.

HUNTER-GATHERERS IN AUSTRALIA.   At the time of its colonization by Europeans near the end of the eighteenth century, Australia had a population estimated at 300,000 aboriginals. Without metals or any domesticated plants or animals, they led the kind of life that characterized man for all but his most recent history. The aboriginals occupied the entire 3 million square miles of the continent, each of the approximately 700 tribes commanding a rigidly defined territory. The size of a territory was closely related to the availability of food: in the desert, a tribe of 500 might wander over an area of 40,000 square miles, while in the moist coastal regions the same number of people would live semisedentary lives on no more than 150 square miles. The continent probably supported the maximum sustainable population without agriculture or grazing.

Although their technology was simple and political leadership essentially nonexistent, the aboriginals had a complex social organization based on age, sex, and kinship and a rich religious mythology with elaborate ceremonies and rituals. They also had encyclopedic knowledge of their territory and its resources — every spring, mudhole, or cranny where water might collect; every edible seed, root, or fruit; and every bird, frog, lizard, insect, or marsupial and its habits. A toddler could identify the track of a spider in the sand and tell in which direction it was walking.

Not only did the aboriginals have intimate practical knowledge of their territory, but everything was interwoven with magic and myth which gave meaning and a timeless quality to life. If a mother had to kill her newborn because she was still nursing an older child, she consoled herself by the faith that the soul of the baby would enter a future child. Signs of ancestors were everywhere, in inanimate objects as well as in living men and women. Heroes of the past had converted themselves to trees or other landmarks, and their life histories were easily read by the initiated in every feature of the land. The present was a copy of the past, and it was the duty of each individual to insure that the future would be a copy of the present. No wonder that sometimes only superficial contact with European culture was able to unhinge the web of beliefs, customs, and social relations that maintained the adjustment to the environment, leaving the aboriginals disoriented and demoralized. Perhaps it is with good cause that many people in the United States today harbor an uneasy feeling that if any one of our cherished institutions is undermined — whether it be the private automobile or economic growth — our entire culture would come apart at the seams. (Nor is it possible to abolish such evils as crime, poverty, racism, and sexism without fundamental changes in other aspects of our culture as well.)

The anthropologist Lauriston Sharp has described the disintegration of one tribal culture, that of the Yir Yoront, in terms of the impact of steel axes acquired from missionaries. Traditional tools of the Yir Yoront, like those of all aboriginals, were simple. Basic to all hunting and gathering, construction of shelters, and preparation of materials was the stone ax. Good quality axheads were obtained from distant quarries through a chain of trading partners in exchange for wooden spears tipped with the poison barb of a stingray. Trading partnerships established social links among aboriginal groups; trading of spears for axheads was a major event at ceremonial gatherings.

Only men made and owned stone axes, but women and children also used them in their daily activities. Rules of kinship strictly specified from whom and under what conditions an ax might be borrowed. Borrowing and lending of this vital tool was a constant reminder of the social order.

Perhaps the reason that introduction of steel axes into this culture had such far-reaching repercussions was that the ax was a fundamental part of the energy system, and as such, all institutions were related to it. When the Yir Yoront began to use steel axes, their trade relationships fell apart. Because social links between aboriginal groups depended on trading arrangements, the enthusiasm for ceremonial gatherings declined. With the acquisition of new axes depending on the whims of missionaries rather than on reliable social interactions, an element of uncertainty intruded into the order of things. Because women and children, as well as men, could obtain axes from missionaries, traditional sex roles and relations among kin were upset. But most insidiously of all, the steel ax undermined the core of religious belief. No myth could explain the steel ax or fit it into the traditions of the people. With this chink in the once impenetrable fortress of belief, it became possible to doubt many things. The mythology which had legitimized social customs and maintained order was no longer valid, and there was nothing to fill the void.

SOUTH AFRICAN BUSHMEN. The Bushmen who now live in the Kalahari Desert of southern Africa are the last of a culture that was once widespread on the African continent. Although it has been within fairly recent times that they were restricted to the desert, they are adept at living on the meager resources of the Kalahari — so adept, in fact, that hunting and gathering food occupies less than half of their time, and the remainder is spent resting or playing games, singing and dancing, and visiting friends from neighboring bands (Figure 10.5).

Like their aboriginal counterparts in Australia, the Bushmen have intimate knowledge of their territory and they take advantage of each seasonal

**Figure 10–5** A band of South African bushmen. These people, so used to the meager existence eked out of the Kalahari Desert, spend much time socializing with friends and neighboring bands. (Photograph courtesy of the American Museum of Natural History.)

water source and each quirk of animal behavior. Sharing, not only of food but of tools and other goods, is basic to Bushman life. If someone has a particularly good tool or beautiful ornament, he feels guilty until he has passed it on for another to enjoy. It is as if there were competition to be the most generous member of the band, and the major incentive for acquiring fine possessions is to be able to share them. Without strict social or political organization, Bushmen use sharing as a means of social control. If a person or family falls out of favor in the band, people simply stop sharing with the offender. Eventually the ostracized person or group will probably move to another camp.

For the Bushmen, dancing, especially the healing dance, lies at the core of religious and ceremonial life. And at the core of the healing dance is the trance of the healer. Almost anyone can become a healer, if he can dance his medicine to a boil so it can be transferred to others. The trance of the Bushman was once thought to be merely another savage oddity; but we now recognize that it strongly resembles many drug-induced states, and that it provides the same escape, altered sensory perceptions, and relief from fears and frustrations — a sort of safety valve — that members of other societies obtain through the use of drugs.

HUNTER-GATHERERS OF THE NEW WORLD. American Indians provide a treasury of information on cultural evolution and what may be called, by analogy with biological evolution, the adaptive radiation of cultures. The first immigrants to the New World, belonging to a race ancestral to modern Mongoloids, probably crossed the Bering land bridge between 35,000 and 45,000 years ago. Like their ice age counterparts in the Old World, they were big game hunters; in fact, it was pursuit of migratory herds that led them into North America. Evidence of the ice age hunters, indicating their remarkable cultural uniformity, is found throughout Canada and the United States and southward into Mexico. Figure 10.6 shows the major game hunted at different times, together with characteristic weapons of the period.

As the climate became warmer and drier following the last glacial retreat, big game hunters vanished along with their game. Many mammalian species became extinct in America, including some that survived in the Old World. A variety of new human cultures came into prominence as adaptations to the diverse environments and resources of the post glacial period. In dry areas people depended mainly on foraging for vegetable foods, supplementing their diets with fish, small game, and occasional larger game when it was available. In forested regions, more reliance was placed on game that remained in the area throughout the year. This was supplemented by fish, migratory waterfowl, and vegetable foods. Hundreds of plant species were used for food, beverages, smoking, medicines and drugs, dyes, poisons, and other products. Only in the far north did migratory herds continue to support the hunter. A new wave of immigrants, the Eskimos (who now resembled modern Mongoloids), also lived by hunting herd animals, sea mammals, and fish.

By the time the first European explorers came to the New World, the Indians had developed a bewildering range of cultures. Each of them was shaped in part by the environment and in part by the history and traditions of the local Indians. Although the environment did not determine the culture that developed, it did provide a combination of possibilities and limitations to which a group responded through its technology and social institutions. The process of adaptation was unconscious. Adaptation was not achieved through design but through generations of trial and error and adoption of solutions that — however strange they may seem — worked. Many of the technologic adaptations seem nearly perfect: toboggans, snowshoes, the kayak, the birchbark canoe. And, of course, the igloo — strong, durable, built from the only abundantly and reliably available material, to an

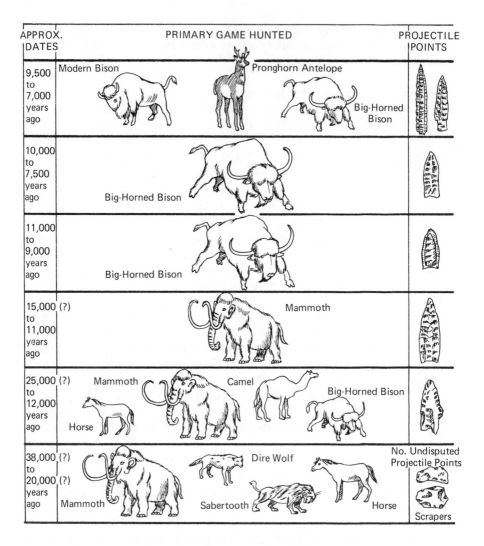

| APPROX. DATES | PRIMARY GAME HUNTED | PROJECTILE POINTS |
|---|---|---|
| 9,500 to 7,000 years ago | Modern Bison  Pronghorn Antelope  Big-Horned Bison | |
| 10,000 to 7,500 years ago | Big-Horned Bison | |
| 11,000 to 9,000 years ago | Big-Horned Bison | |
| 15,000 (?) to 11,000 years ago | Mammoth | |
| 25,000 (?) to 12,000 years ago | Mammoth  Camel  Big-Horned Bison  Horse | |
| 38,000 (?) to 20,000 (?) years ago | Mammoth  Dire Wolf  Sabertooth  Horse | No. Undisputed Projectile Points  Scrapers |

**Figure 10–6** Weapons used by prehistoric hunter-gatherers in the New World, and the major game they hunted. All but the pronghorn antelope and the modern bison have become extinct. (From Peter Farb, *Man's Rise to Civilization*, E. P. Dutton and Co., New York, 1968, p. 201.)

optimal dome-shaped design. Many social adaptations are incomprehensible, however, until it is understood how they play an integral role in the fabric of social relations that make the technology work.

The extremes of social and political organization among hunter-gatherers of the New World are exemplified by the Great Basin Shoshone and the Indians of the northwest coast. Many of the Shoshone lived where food was rarely abundant and supplies of particular foods were variable and unpredictable from season to season and from year to year. These Indians had no fixed territory because land was valueless unless it produced food, and confining a group to one locality would guarantee its starvation. The only permanent group was the family. When a particular food became plentiful, families in the vicinity would congregate to exploit it. There were cooperative hunts for rabbits, deer, antelope, and mudhens. But these groups were temporary. When the hunt was over, they dispersed; for while hunting favors congregation, gathering is best done by individual families. The same families that engaged in a rabbit hunt could not plan on coming together again because there was no guarantee when — or even if — rabbits would again be abundant in that place; meanwhile the quest for survival would very likely cause wide scattering of the families involved. Meager resources, primitive technology, and lack of social organization beyond the level of the family interacted to prevent development of a more complex culture. (Although there was no need for political leaders when families were independent, political war leaders did arise when some Shoshones obtained Spanish horses and took to a life of raiding white settlements.)

Greater variety and concentration of resources in the northwest coastal region supported a relatively dense population of sedentary foragers living in permanent villages. Food was so abundant that the word "harvesting" describes the method of obtaining it better than the word "foraging," although there were periods of scarcity which played an important part in the organization of social and economic life. The economy was based on preservation and storage of surplus food for periods of scarcity and on redistribution of food and durable goods through trade, gift-giving, and elaborate celebrations. Politically, the Indians were organized into a series of chiefdoms, with each chief in charge of collecting and redistributing wealth but otherwise having little authority and no power. The system made it possible for groups of people to specialize in activities such as ocean fishing, river fishing, hunting, or gathering vegetable foods or mollusks. If supplies of one resource failed, the economic system insured that other resources would be distributed equitably. Chiefdoms of this type constitute the most complex level of socio-political organization known to have arisen from a subsistence base of hunting and gathering. Its development requires a wealth and variety of resources, the ability and motivation to amass at least temporary surpluses, and possibly a relatively dense population.

## CHANGING LIFESTYLES OF AGRICULTURISTS

The last retreat of the glaciers brought many changes which required new adaptations by human populations. People adapted according to their local resources and traditions. In the far north many were able to continue their customary ways. In much of Eurasia and what is now the United

## THE NAVAJOS: SURVIVING THE WHITE MAN

*The white Europeans who spread across the North American continent in the last few centuries all but wiped out the many Indian cultures in their path. Some tribes, like the Luiseno of California, are actually extinct; many other dispirited groups have barely managed to survive. But the Navajos, or* dine *(The People), as they have always called themselves, have not only survived but even prospered, relatively speaking. How did it come about that they are now the largest and wealthiest tribe in the United States?*

*Certainly the white invaders did not treat the Navajos more gently than they did other tribes, although perhaps the People were lucky that white domination did not overtake them until the middle of the nineteenth century. In 1863 Colonel Kit Carson, under orders to stop the Navajos from raiding New Mexican settlements, burned Navajo crops and orchards, slaughtered their livestock, and herded most of the starving People off on the long walk to Fort Sumner. Perhaps the Navajos were also lucky that after four years of exile, misery, and bare subsistence, they were finally allowed to return to a reservation on their ancestral lands, parts of Arizona, New Mexico, and Utah. But during most of the following century, under the administration of the Bureau of Indian Affairs, the Navajos were either mistreated or neglected —starved, cheated, left unprotected from theft and murder, deprived of some of their best land, and left uneducated or forced to attend the prison-like mission schools.*

*After a century of this treatment, the wonder is not that the mean annual income of Navajos in 1970 was less than $700, or that in the same year unemployment on the reservation was 20 percent. The wonder is that the Navajos are doing so well. How have they managed to increase from a mere 8,000 a hundred years ago to their present population of over 133,500? How has it happened that the Navajo Reservation is now a self-governing concern of 110 million dollars per year?*

*A good part of the answer lies in the unusually adaptable culture of the Navajos, whose history has been one of rapid cultural evolution. The answer lies also perhaps, in what anthropologists call "hybrid vigor," resulting from the mixing of Navajo and Pueblo stock which occurred in the seventeenth and eighteenth centuries.*

*The ancestors of the Navajos were part of a linguistic and cultural group called the Athabascans, who migrated south from northwest Canada about a thousand years ago. When part of this group, still a simple hunting and gathering society, arrived in the Southwest, they encountered the much more sophisticated and prosperous Pueblo culture, and were greatly influenced by it. From the Pueblos they learned agriculture, weaving, and silversmithing, and* much of the Pueblo religious mythology. In contrast, the Apaches, part of the same Athabascan group, rejected borrowing from the cultures they came into contact with, and remained a hunting society.

But it is characteristic of the Navajos that they did not simply borrow an element of another culture—they transformed it into something uniquely Navajo. When they became weavers, they wove blankets so beautiful and strong that they are famous as blanket weavers among whites who know nothing else about Navajos. When they borrowed the rather pedestrian Pueblo religious myths, they turned them into vivid and poetic epics about superhuman beings riding on rainbows, armed with lightning. Later, when Navajos acquired livestock from the Spanish, they made herding the economic base of their society and the sheep a central symbol of their culture.

Judging from their history, the Navajos would have assimilated much more of white American culture by this time if they had been allowed to do so. But even under coercion and neglect, the Navajos have demonstrated an enthusiasm for new experience and an ambition to better their lot.

During World War II, many Navajos volunteered for military service as a means of gaining valuable knowledge about the white man's world. In contrast, the Zuni, another Southwestern tribe with many similarities to the Navajos, made every effort to avoid military service. And after the war, the returning Navajo veterans were welcomed back by their people, eager to share in what they had learned, while the few Zuni veterans were ridiculed and ignored by their tribe.

Another instance of Navajo initiative is the evolution of the Navajo Tribal Council. It was originally established by the Indian Bureau in 1923, solely to facilitate the leasing of reservation land by oil refineries. But the Navajos, even though they had had no experience with political community organization, gradually developed the Council into a representative political structure for the reservation. Today they govern themselves—state and federal laws, except for major crimes, do not apply inside the reservation. With their characteristic "hybrid vigor," the Navajos are intent on continuing to build a better life for themselves.

## SOURCES FOR *THE NAVAJOS*

PETER FARB, *Man's Rise to Civilization as Shown by the Indians of North America from Primeval Times to the Coming of the Industrial State* (New York: Dutton, 1968).

CLYDE KLUCKHOHN AND DOROTHEA LEIGHTON, *The Navaho* (Cambridge: Harvard University Press, 1946).

*The National Geographic*, December 1972, pp. 740–781.

JOHN UPTON TERRELL, *The Navajos* (New York: Weybright and Talley, 1970).

States, hunters shifted their attention from the great migratory herds to deer, rabbits, and smaller game which were available close to home at all seasons. But in the Near East were the first stirrings of what may have caused the most momentous cultural change in the history of our species: the invention of agriculture.

Some parts of the world seem to have experienced a population explosion about 10 or 12 thousand years ago. It is often said that this increase resulted from the invention of agriculture, but it is at least as likely that it was the other way around: increased population pressure stimulated the invention of agriculture, establishing positive feedback between cultivation and population. Mesopotamia had a variety of wild species suitable for domestication, and this is where the domestication of plants and animals was first accomplished.

When population threatened to outrun food supply and the most productive land was already occupied, people may have tried to extend the range of important plants. Or perhaps weeding came before sowing, if people tried to increase the yield of wild wheat and barley by removing less desirable species. In any case, the first attempts at cultivation were not intended to revolutionize lifestyles. As are most adaptations, they were conservative in purpose — an attempt to maintain the status quo.

Wheat and barley were the first plants to be domesticated, followed by peas and lentils. Gradually, the wandering hunting bands began to establish permanent villages on the best land, where crops could be grown without irrigation. Sheep and goats were domesticated, perhaps as an outgrowth of the practice of keeping young animals as pets; or young animals may have been captured with the intention of fattening them for slaughter, as is occasionally done by aboriginals today. After sheep and goats, cattle and pigs were domesticated.

Earliest agriculture did not modify the habitat very much, but it engendered major changes in the social order, creating a new human environment in the old habitat. Cultivation with the hoe or digging stick required new relationships among families for cooperation and regulation of competition. There was a notable change in sex roles and the status of women. The new economy was based on production and storage of surplus grain for seasons of scarcity. Agriculturists exchanged mobility and dietary variety for permanent settlements, dependability of food, and at times a rather monotonous diet.

Eventually agriculture did change the habitat. It brought an end to hunting where forests were cleared for farming. Although bands of hunters at first resisted with raids and conquests, cultural change was irrevocable. After the forests and the game were gone, there was no possibility of returning to the earlier way of life.

Chapter 9 introduced the problem of surplus — the seeming paradox that a complex culture cannot develop without a surplus of energy to support it, while in the absence of complexity there is neither the motivation to produce surplus nor the institutions for dealing with it. We can speculate on how production of surplus and the evolution of social institutions were interrelated in the farming villages of Mesopotamia. Geographically, resources were distributed unevenly. Fish and fowl were abundant in the swamps and rivers, dates and other fruits and vegetables on the moister land, and grain in drier areas. Water transport was easy, and farming villages began to trade their products with one another. A new cultural pattern began to emerge, one which spanned the range of social, economic, political, and religious life. Temporary surpluses which were used up during lean times were not surpluses in the true sense. But it would have been prudent to produce as much as was likely to be needed and then a little more, for insurance. Furthermore, the value of surplus as a means of exchange was evident: the more that was available for trade, the more other products could be obtained. But trading relationships with other villages required institutions for regulating commerce and distributing resources. Temples became warehouses as well as centers of religious activity, where a privileged class of individuals, commonly priests, handled the storage and redistribution of food. At the same time some of the surplus supported this privileged class, and an additional amount was required to support laborers who built and maintained the temples. Eventually, advances in technology were necessary if supply were to continue to meet demand. Large-scale systems of irrigation were constructed, which led to intensive management of water supply and food production and increased the power of the rulers. Ideas of property and inheritance developed; theft became a problem; warfare began; and a legal system was needed to settle property disputes and other grievances. Attacks on settled farmers by wandering hunters and pastoralists were an additional factor influencing settlement patterns: for the first time it became necessary for people to band together for their mutual protection against other people.

Agriculture was also invented in the New World, where early civilizations flourished in Mexico, the Yucatan Peninsula, and Peru. It probably arose independently in Egypt, as well. The habitats of Egypt and Mesopotamia differed from America with respect to climate, rainfall, the nature of river systems, topography, and the availability of building materials. Different species were available for domestication, and different techniques were used in their cultivation. In some respects, New World agriculture was superior to that of the Old. A greater variety of crops was planted, and maize was so thoroughly domesticated that it became unable to survive in the wild. Today there is no living wild relative of corn, but wild wheat and barley which are quite similar to cultivated types still grow in the Near East.

Animals played different roles in the Old World and the New. South and Central American Indians used llamas as beasts of burden and alpacas for their hair and skins. Transport by llama was inefficient, however, even though there were some excellent roads, for the animals balked at walking more than about 10 miles a day and could not carry more than 50 pounds. There were no animals that could be taught to pull wheeled vehicles; thus there was no use for the wheel, although some Indians knew about it and built wheeled toys and models. Use of domestic animals for meat and dairy products was insignificant; Indians obtained animal protein through hunting and fishing, or sometimes they ate their dogs. In the Old World, in contrast, domestic animals provided an important part of the diet, and some were used as draft animals. In addition, constant interaction between settled farmers and those whose lives depended on animals, the hunters and pastoralists, colored the history of the Old World until very recent times.

The four ancient civilizations that arose in Mesopotamia, Egypt, Peru, and Mexico grew from different technologies, different habitats, and people of different history and traditions. Nevertheless, all four were characterized by a functionally interrelated set of social institutions that involved class stratification; political and religious hierarchies that administered the territory; a complex division of labor including a mass of peasants, some craftsmen and servants, and various types of officials; a system of public works supported by taxation; and significant achievements in art, science, and writing. The details of basic adaptations represent adjustments to particular environmental conditions.

*SIMPLE AGRICULTURE.* Simple agriculture, sometimes called horticulture, is based on muscular energy and hand tools — chiefly the digging stick or hoe. It was practiced by many tribes of North American Indians and is still common in the tropics. Except under very favorable circumstances it does not support either a high density of population or a complex culture.

The Classic Mayan civilization provides an example of what may be the maximum cultural complexity possible based on simple agriculture and what may happen when a population overtaxes its resources through growth, maladaptive settlement patterns, and misuse of the soil. The details of the downfall of the Mayas are still shrouded in mystery; the situation was complex and the causes were multiple. Almost certainly, overpopulation and a failure of the food system played a role, although invasions from Mexico may have been the final blow to the weakened civilization.

The Mayas are renowned for their achievements in astronomy, mathematics, architecture, and the arts. They invented a calendar and writing. They also participated in a complex religious and ceremonial life, centering around elaborate pyramids and palaces, beautifully carved monuments, and enormous ceremonial centers. Toward the end of the Classic Period of Mayan civilization in the tenth century C.E.*, these ceremonial centers had

---

*C.E. Common Era; Christian Era; A.D.

become urban centers; and this may have been at the root of the cultural collapse.

The Mayas lived in a tropical rain forest and practiced the type of agriculture known as slash-and-burn. In this system a plot was cleared during the late fall and early winter, the dead wood being burned in the following dry season (Figure 10.7). The plot was then planted with a variety of crops, but chiefly maize. Slash-and-burn agriculture yields abundant harvests for one or two years. But weeding becomes increasingly difficult, and there is a rapid loss of humus through the action of microorganisms and the sun's rays. It then becomes necessary to let the plot lie fallow for up to 10 years or longer, while the forest regenerates and the structure and fertility of the soil are restored. The ecological implications of slash-and-burn agriculture are evident: an equilibrium can be established between man and his environment, but as soon as the period of cultivation is overextended and the fallow period cut short, the harvest will diminish and the soil may deteriorate almost irreparably.

The slash-and-burn system is usually associated with a dispersed settlement pattern because of the large amount of land (including that which is

**Figure 10–7** Slash-and-burn agriculture in the Amazon Basin. Rice is growing in the partially cleared land which was once jungle. (Photograph courtesy of the United Nations.)

fallow) required to support each person. If the Mayan population had remained dispersed as it was originally, it perhaps could have grown large without stress on the food system, although eventually dispersal would have been restricted by populations to the north. But the population of the ceremonial centers began to increase until they became urban centers with populations of up to 50,000, at a density well over 1,000 persons per square mile at the central core. The new settlement pattern was not adaptive in an environment which placed severe restrictions on the amount of food that could be produced with Stone Age technology and the distances over which it could be transported. With the Mayan environment and technology, the food system could support a maximum of about 200 persons per square mile. An area of 250 square miles (a circle with a radius of roughly 9 miles) would then be required to feed a population of 50,000. Peoples practicing slash-and-burn agriculture in the tropics today usually move their settlements when it becomes necessary to walk more than 3 or 4 miles to reach their gardens. It is not feasible to bring in food from great distances. The plight of the Mayas is clear. Increasing demands of population centers coupled with decreasing agricultural productivity on overexploited soils left the civilization vulnerable to a variety of internal and external pressures, including invasion and possibly a revolt of the peasants or a prolonged drought. In any case, there appears to have been disharmony between the energy system on the one hand and the complexity of the social system on the other. The collapse came quickly, when the civilization was at its peak.

*INTENSIVE AGRICULTURE.* Invention of advanced agricultural techniques gave man new mastery over nature. He could dig deeply into the soil, create new farming surfaces, and bring water to regions insufficiently watered by rain. No longer did social and cultural behavior of entire populations vary cyclically with the seasons. Great cities arose where urban dwellers could follow the same routine every day and eat the same assortment of foods 365 days a year. But when the commitment was made to intensive agriculture, the area no longer produced sufficient wild foods to support a population should crops fail. There was no going back.

Advanced systems of agriculture involve one or more of three innovations: use of the plow and draft animals, irrigation, and terracing. Any of these leads to more intensive use of land, greater productivity, and new social and political institutions. The initial stimulus for improved agricultural technology probably came from land shortages and population pressure. The population increase was due in part to a settled way of life. Infanticide was a common method of population control in foraging societies, because a woman who was constantly on the move could not nurse or care for more than one small child at a time. But with permanent villages and an availability of foods suitable for young children came a decline in the necessity for infanticide. Demographic characteristics of sedentary populations may have changed for other reasons as well (see Chapter 11).

Chapter 9 suggested that people practicing simple agriculture tend to disperse as long as arable land is available. But where land is limited, as it is on islands or in circumscribed river valleys, the only possibility lies in increasing agricultural productivity. A land squeeze undoubtedly provided a stimulus to war, which led to an increase in size and social stratification of political units. The vanquished — who under other circumstances would have relinquished their land and moved elsewhere — had to remain and pay tribute to their conquerors, because there was nowhere else to go. Strong political organization was necessary for control of new territory and subjugated peoples; warrior classes developed which required skilled military leaders; and the vanquished were kept as slaves. Such conquests did not really solve the land problem because the population density did not decrease, but they supplied the socio-political structure necessary for intensified agriculture. The large numbers of landless people provided labor for earth moving and construction projects — the building of terraces and construction and maintenance of irrigation systems — and also gave rise to a class of craftsmen whose handiwork was in growing demand. Thus wealthy and magnificent cultures emerged from what may have begun as a competition among simple farmers over land.

SETTLEMENT PATTERNS.    During the Middle Ages, people clustered around a powerful lord or lived in walled cities; cultivated fields surrounded the villages. This pattern was expedient because it afforded protection from ubiquitous marauders. It has persisted in most parts of the world until the present. In South and Central America land was owned by wealthy proprietors and worked by peasants whose houses surrounded the home of the owner. Southern plantations in the United States followed the same pattern before the Civil War. The people who work the collective farms of the USSR and China live in villages, as do the farmers of India. The familiar pattern of farms in the United States is exceptional. It developed from the environmental, historical, and social conditions on the new continent that favored homesteading — an unorthodox system in which farm families lived on their own land on well-separated farms.

CONTROL OF ENERGY SOURCES.    Strong central political authorities generally do not develop in horticultural societies because each farmer is in complete control of his source of energy — his own muscle power. But under intensive agriculture, no farmer is self-sufficient. Advanced agricultural societies are characterized by strong political authority, which directly controls the energy systems.

Plow agriculture, like any energy system, is much more than a technology for extracting energy from a habitat. It requires a complex of social and legal institutions to guarantee that all farmers will have access to labor, plows, and draft animals during the short plowing season. Use and misuse of livestock and breaking of agreements specifying plowing arrangements were a major preoccupation of early courts — in fact, the new agriculture and all it implied stimulated development of legal systems. The following excerpt is from the proceedings of an English court in the thirteenth century: "Robert le Coc complains . . . that the aforesaid Philip received a certain horse from him in a certain covenant, namely, that the aforesaid Philip should keep the aforesaid horse and pasture it and harness it in the plow. Moreover he says that Philip beat the aforesaid horse and bound a stone onto the ear of this horse, and he ought to render to the aforesaid Robert one day's work of plowing."

Where irrigation is practiced, the farmer is at the mercy of others for his water supply. The activities of farmers upstream must be regulated for the protection of those downstream. If water can be withheld at the discretion of a political authority, rulers have direct control over the lives of their subjects.

DEVELOPMENT OF COMPLEXITY. The advanced agriculturist is a specialist. He depends on others for part of his food and for tools and other goods; and others depend on him for food. Intensive agriculture is often commercial agriculture, in which there is specialization in crop production and the crop is sold or traded. Transportation and trade are essential for survival; there is positive feedback between development of trade, improvement of transportation, and the increase of wealth and diversity. Transportation also increases the number and kinds of contacts among people. While foragers dealt only with others whose lives were like their own, agricultural societies provide frequent contacts between farmers, laborers, craftsmen, merchants, religious and political leaders, and other specialists, as well as between people of different cultures. The rate of cultural diffusion grew rapid.

The first schools made their appearance in agricultural societies, for the culture could no longer be transmitted by simple oral tradition and the teaching of basic skills to children by parents. Poverty was another newcomer to the cultural scene. An economy based on sharing in a cultural environment with little or no occupational diversity gave way to conditions in which unemployment and poverty could run rampant. At the same time, care of the poor shifted from a family responsibility to a responsibility of local political and religious institutions. Such were the penalties and rewards of cultural advance.

## PASTORALISM AS AN ADAPTATION

Pastoralism is a way of life in which social organization and institutions are geared to the needs of large herds of animals for water, salt, forage, and protection. It is a way of obtaining energy from a habitat which can support

**Figure 10–8** A pastoralist encampment in Afghanistan. (Photograph courtesy of the United Nations.)

grazing animals but provides little food of direct use to humans. It frequently involves seasonal migration from lowland settlements to highland pastures, following the availability of water and forage. Many pastoralists also practice limited agriculture, raising a crop or two during the wet season; but basically the economy depends on the domestic animals which provide transportation, food, and materials for clothing and tools. Pastoralism should be distinguished from animal husbandry as practiced in advanced agricultural societies in which settled agriculturists provide food for their animals and crops are also grown intensively. The situation of an Asian camel herder who could not survive without his animals contrasts sharply with that of the midwestern livestock farmer in the United States who could live off his land perfectly well if he had to give up his cattle.

Pastoral cultures may arise from either foraging or agricultural backgrounds, as illustrated by certain of the Plains Indians of North America. These Indians are considered pastoralists because they relied on herds of horses in order to hunt bison. Their culture was forged from a variety of traditions, both foraging and agricultural, showing that when the possibilities for adaptation are limited, it is not surprising that similar technical and social solutions are found independently by different groups of people.

Pastoralists have adapted to many habitats. The Lapps and Mongolian peoples of the far north follow herds of reindeer (semidomesticated caribou), taking little responsibility for the care of their animals. The Turks and Mongols of Tartary raise complex herds of sheep, goats, cattle, horses, camels, and sometimes yaks, asses, and mules (Figure 10.8). Some pastoralists rely on herds of camels for food and transport. Swiss villagers traditionally drive their cattle to upland pastures during the summer and bring them back to permanent settlements in the valleys or lowlands during the winter.

Sedentary and pastoralist societies have been neighbors on the North American plains, in Mesopotamia, Africa, China, and eastern Europe. They have strongly affected each other culturally and historically. Pastoralists have been characterized as pugnacious, cooperative, independent, arrogant, and brave. Development of these traits is important in their way of life. Land and boundaries are unimportant to them, but pastures and water must be shared and protected. Their only worthwhile possessions are their animals, which must constantly be defended against theft and natural disaster. Groups of pastoralists frequently make war on one another and have terrorized settled people for thousands of years. Their lifestyle gives them the advantages of high mobility and ease of massing together in large groups or splitting into small groups while maintaining effective leadership. Rigorously trained and well-equipped armies of civilized societies have repeatedly been baffled when, on pursuing a horde of marauding pastoralists into the hills, they find that the enemy has dispersed and — vanished!

Pastoralist societies are highly specialized and are limited by environmental conditions in the level of complexity they can develop. In this sense they are a dead end in cultural evolution. Their main interest to us, aside from illustrating the adaptive flexibility of human culture, is their impact on cultural evolution through warfare and peaceful interactions with other societies.

## INDUSTRIAL SOCIETIES

Although the date and place of the beginning of the Industrial Revolution is often given as eighteenth century England, the Industrial Revolution (like the Agricultural Revolution) was really the culmination of the slow process of evolution. Chapter 9 identified several practices characteristic of elemental industrialization which were well developed in some societies 4,000 years ago. Advanced industrialization also depends on machines and the harnessing of inanimate energy to drive them. But machines and energy were also available many centuries before the Industrial Revolution began. What delayed it? The fact that industrialism, like hunting and agriculture, is more than a technology; it is a social, political, and economic organization and the expression of a people's goals and beliefs. The Industrial Revolution could not begin until society was ready for it.

THE HARNESSING OF ENERGY.   Table 10.1 presents a brief chronology of man's conquest of energy. Man had mastered the basic principles of machines more than a thousand years before the Industrial Revolution and could use wheels, gears, levers, and pulleys to augment the effectiveness of his muscular energy. Prototype machines of many descriptions had been invented by the Egyptians, the Chinese, the Arabs, the Cretans, and later the Greeks and Romans. But these peoples were not ready to exploit the new machines: the machines seem to have been merely models or toys.

It was not lack of energy that prevented widespread use of machines. There were no qualms about putting slaves or animals to work on treadmills and similar devices. Nor was man a stranger to the use of inanimate energy. The first windmills had appeared in the Moslem world about C.E. 650, they were used in China from the year 1000 on, and by the fourteenth century they had spread throughout Europe. The gigantic land reclamation projects of the Netherlands were accomplished by means of windpower during the sixteenth century. Waterwheels had been around even longer. They probably originated in the Near East in the fourth or third century B.C. and spread through Rome to the rest of Europe. By the twelfth century there were thousands of waterwheels all over western Europe. Although the steam engine has become the symbol of the Industrial Revolution, the revolution, based on waterwheels and windmills, was well underway by the time Watt's first engine was built. The steam engine was not even originally designed for use in industry; it was put to work pumping water in the mines, and only later was its application to factory work realized.

THE COMING OF THE INDUSTRIAL REVOLUTION.   History often suggests that the Middle Ages was a time of dismal stagnation. Curiosity was absent if not dead, and there was no progress. After this deep and dreamless sleep, people awoke in the bright morning of the Renaissance and shook themselves back to reality. But there were slow changes during the Middle Ages which prepared the way for the Renaissance and the Industrial Revolution. Water power was developed rapidly along the Rhine, the Danube, Italy's swift streams, and in the North Sea and Baltic lands. Water mills ground grain, sawed wood, pulped rags for paper, pumped water, crushed ore and otherwise furthered mining and metal working, and fostered the development of Europe's textile industry. Wind was more difficult to harness, although where conditions were favorable, it was the main source of power. Wind had driven sail boats since Stone Age times. The close of the Middle Ages saw the opening of an era of sailing and exploration that lasted for hundreds of years. And it was during the Middle Ages that man began to exploit the fossil fuels, both "sea coales" and oil shale, "the rocks that burn."

One of the major developments during the Renaissance was the rise of capitalism — the ultimate alchemy that transmuted everything into gold. Preoccupation with competition, personal gain, and insignificant luxuries

## TABLE 10.1

### Major Events in the Conquest of Energy

| | |
|---|---|
| 750,000-500,000 B.C. | Man begins to use fire |
| before 13,000 | Domestication of the dog |
| 9,000 | Beginnings of agriculture |
| 4,000 | Domestication of the horse |
| 3,500 | Invention of the wheel, probably in Mesopotamia |
| 3,000 | Man learns to smelt metal and make bronze |
| 1,000 | Beginning of iron technology |
| | Domestication of the camel |
| 300 | Waterwheels in Greece |
| 200 | Modern harness invented in China |
| 27 | Book by Vitruvius describes watermills, steam jets, and a variety of machines |
| C.E. 650 | First windmills |
| | Modern horse harness reinvented in Europe |
| 852 | Coal burned in an English monastery |
| 900 | Whale oil used for lighting |
| 1239 | Coal used as fuel by smiths and brewers |
| 1300 | First use of coal in home heating |
| 1404 | Giant cannon built in Austria |
| 1500 | Tide mills built in the Netherlands |
| | Windmills used for land reclamation in the Netherlands |
| 1606 | First known experimental steam engine built by Della Porta |
| 1673 | Huygens builds internal combustion engine run on gunpowder |
| 1693 | Leibnitz states the law of conservation of potential and kinetic energy |
| 1712 | Newcomen builds the first steam pumping engine |
| 1765 | Modern steam engine designed by Watt |
| 1820-1860 | Work of Oersted, Ampere, Faraday, and Maxwell in electricity |
| | Principles of thermodynamics worked out by Carnot and Clausius |
| 1857 | First oil well drilled in Pennsylvania |
| 1882 | First incandescent lighting, New York |
| 1895 | Roentgen discovers X rays |
| 1896 | Becquerel discovers radioactivity |
| 1898 | Tsiolkovski works out principles of rocket flight |
| 1903 | First flight of Wright brothers |
| 1920 | First scheduled public radio broadcast, Pittsburgh |
| 1926 | Goddard fires first rockets with liquid propellant |
| 1941 | First jet plane flight |
| 1942 | Fermi starts first atomic reactor in Chicago |
| 1945 | First nuclear explosion, Alamogordo, New Mexico |
| | Uranium bomb dropped on Hiroshima; plutonium bomb on Nagasaki |
| 1952 | First hydrogen bomb explosion |
| 1954 | Launching of first atomic powered submarine, *Nautilus* |
| | First nuclear power plant put into service near Moscow, USSR |

| 1957 | Sputnik I, first artificial satellite |
| | First commercial nuclear power plant in United States, in Shippingport, Pennsylvania |
| 1969 | Man lands on the moon |

displaced traditional values and the saints, angels, and demons that had cast their shadows on the medieval world. The technology of weapons was also pursued with vigor. Developments in energy use, iron technology, and explosives were united in Austria in 1404 to produce the first giant cannon on record — a monster weighing almost five tons. In 1450 near Caen, Normandy, 4,000 Frenchmen and two cannons faced 7,000 Englishmen and demolished them. The body count: 12 French, 5,600 English. Two years later, with cannons, the Turks conquered Constantinople.

Another factor conducive to the Industrial Revolution was a changing pattern of land use. During the seventeenth century, sheep-raising noblemen in both England and continental Europe began an unprecedented land grab that threw many tens of thousands of agricultural workers off what had been the common land. At first the dismayed English government restricted the paupers to their local parishes, on poor relief. Later, when factories began to proliferate, the paupers flocked to the cities, just as the agricultural poor do today. The empire on which the sun never set provided an insatiable market for the pottery of Five Towns, the textiles of Manchester, and the miscellaneous hardware of Birmingham.

Most people bitterly opposed the changes that were occurring. Innovation had been fought for centuries by individuals, craft and trade guilds, and governments. New patent applications were routinely denied when they threatened old ways, and people were put to death for defying convention. It was not the technological change that seemed threatening as much as the inevitable social change that accompanied it. People tend to welcome technological innovation without realizing that their social institutions will have to make adjustments to it. Today many of us harbor the absurd hope that technology will enable us to maintain the status quo, even though the lesson from cultural evolution is that every technological change engenders corresponding social adaptations and adjustments. As a result of cumulative changes in all aspects of culture, then, the Industrial Revolution began in England but a few centuries ago, and its reverberations are still being felt around the world.

*TODAY'S WORLD OF COMPLEXITY AND CHANGE.* In the complex, high-energy society of today, we have the illusion that we have freed ourselves from the exigencies of our environment. People in Iceland today eat vine-ripened tomatoes grown in greenhouses heated with hot water from geothermal reservoirs. This is the extent to which technology has freed man from the limitations of his habitat.

But there are signs that Western industrialized cultures must change their course in order to survive. Future-oriented studies speak predictively or imaginatively about the postindustrial society, and about the ethical and spiritual evolution that is occurring even now among many groups in our society. The following sections consider some aspects of highly industrialized societies in terms of both problems and achievements. This is where we are now; it is not an attempt to peer into the future or to prescribe for the future.

ENERGY.　Averaged over his lifetime, a person derives about 2,200 kilocalories of energy per day from the food he eats, representing a power output about equal to that of one 100 watt light bulb. Some of the world's people still exist at that level. But in the United States the per capita use of energy is more than 100 times the energy of the food that is eaten. Each of us uses energy at the rate of one hundred 100 watt light bulbs, rather than one. We convert this energy to heat, light, motion, sound, and things, and into a bewildering array of social institutions. The energy crisis has forced us to take a painful look at our use of energy, and it is apparent that considerable reductions can be made. But eliminating waste and minimizing inefficiency would reduce our rate of energy use by at most 25 to 50 percent — and even this reduction would result in marked social and economic change. A great deal of energy must be expended to maintain a complex culture — there is no way to escape this requirement. We have seen from comparative study of a range of biological ecosystems and human cultures that there is a direct relationship between complexity and the availability of energy.

Political institutions control our energy systems today just as in the past they controlled irrigation waters and the apportionment of draft animals and plows. The newest form of energy, nuclear energy, has been a jealously guarded and nurtured political ward since the moment of its inception. The future will see even more stringent controls over the energy system, which will be felt sharply in every aspect of our lives.

LAND USE.　When all the people of the world were foragers, land was used more extensively than it is today, even though population density was low. There was essentially no specialization in land use: people derived their food and materials for tools and shelter directly from the land on which they lived. With agriculture came changing settlement patterns and specialization in land use, culminating in the formation of cities and regional specialization in crops.

Industrialization has been accompanied by unprecedented urbanization (see Chapters 11 and 12), and regional specialization in land use has increased sharply. Some areas which once supported human populations at a simple level of technology and social organization are now virtually uninhabited — a situation resulting partly from environmental change, partly from the extinction of simple cultures, and partly from the appropriation of these lands for purposes other than human habitation.

Early cities usually developed in coastal regions and along waterways because transportation and trade were essential to their survival. Today there is continuing concentration of people along water. This is due only partly to the fact that the existing population centers tend to attract people for reasons which no longer have anything to do with the historical advantages of the location. Another major factor in the concentration of people along coasts and waterways is the need for large amounts of water in industrial processes and for the generation of electricity. Competing demands for coastal land have created such critical problems that both the United States and Great Britain have passed comprehensive legislation concerning use of coastal resources. At the same time, land policy in general is under study because of the often conflicting requirements of industry, agriculture, mining, forestry, recreation, conservation, transportation, fishing, electric power, and other special interests.

Meanwhile, about half the people in the world live on only 5 percent of the land. Rural population continues to decrease both as a percentage of total population and, in some areas, in terms of absolute numbers. Despite plans for multiple uses of the land, it appears that specialization is intensifying. A few counties in California supply most of the artichokes that are consumed in the entire United States, and similar specialization occurs in the production of many other crops. One strategy for meeting the energy needs of the future is to devote a portion of the southwestern desert to the collection of solar energy and its conversion to electricity or to the production of hydrogen fuel, or a combination of both. The hydrogen would be transported by pipeline throughout the country as natural gas is today, and the electricity would be transmitted via national grids of ultra high voltage transmission lines.

TRANSPORTATION AND COMMUNICATION.    Our ancestors were limited in their travels to distances they could cover on foot; they could transport only what they could move with their own muscle power; and communication was a simple matter of one person talking to another. Industrialized societies, in contrast, depend on complex systems of transportation and communication. A failure in either system, whether it be a strike of garbage collectors or of telephone operators, can be paralyzing.

Between one fifth and one quarter of the energy used in the United States today is used by the transportation sector of the economy. The constant movement of massive quantities of goods from one place to another is but another measure of specialization in modern society. The natural gas that cooks a roast in New York may have come nonstop through a pipeline from Texas. Unit trains carry coal from the mine directly to the power plant.

Food and manufactured goods move from their centers of production to all parts of the nation. In colonial America, each village, huddled around the waterwheel and the grist mill, had to be self-sufficient. Today no segment of the population is self-sufficient. In fact, the nation is not self-sufficient. Survival depends on transportation and trade.

About half the energy used for transportation is used by the private automobile. We can get into our automobiles and within a few minutes be miles from home, among people we have never seen before and will never see again. Perhaps the place is strange to us, as well. And we delude ourselves if we think we lead settled lives: 20 percent of the people in the United States change their place of residence each year. Our extraordinary mobility creates situations which contrast sharply with the experiences of our ancestors. In primitive societies most contacts were between people well known to each other in their daily lives, and a person might not meet more than a few hundred individuals in his lifetime. The only common reason for leaving one's home territory was marriage. It seems probable that we are biologically and psychologically designed to be closely associated with a home territory and to have only a limited number of personal relationships with other people. But our culture demands that we be constantly on the move, experiencing such an overwhelming number of contacts with other people that we are forced to keep almost all of them at an impersonal level. Many problems are related to this maladaptive feature of our culture, to which transportation has contributed significantly.

Until the invention of the telegraph, communication was inseparable from transportation. Now, however, much of what formerly required transport of people or informational materials can be accomplished through modern means of communication. To the extent that a telephone call can substitute for a business trip or a television appearance for a political barnstorming tour, for example, this tradeoff represents a potentially large saving in energy.

The significance of communication in modern society is self-evident. Communications span the range from satellite TV, which brings people vividly in touch with events all over the world, to the hotline between Moscow and Washington and direct telephone dialing between all parts of the United States. This type of communication is an integral part of our culture, but it presents some problems for which we have not yet found solutions. We are bombarded daily with more information than we can handle, and we are confronted with a mass of human problems that strains our capacity to care. Advances in communication were intended to help us deal with the complexity of our culture; they have added to it, as well.

AUTOMATION.    The first electronic computer was built during the second World War to compensate for a shortage of mathematicians. It was intended simply to prepare ballistic tables, supplanting an army of mathematicians sitting at desk calculators. It is a dramatic example of how a technological innovation, designed to permit us to continue doing customary things, forces adaptations and adjustments in all aspects of culture. While designed to deal with existing complexity, it has become inextricably entwined in our daily lives and has permitted a further increase in complexity.

The computer is but the most recent machine to which we must adjust. The team of man and computer represents an extension of intelligence byond the capacity of the human brain. It has brought us to a new level of control over our energy systems and the physical environment, and is revolutionizing our social institutions and relationships with other people.

ARCHAIC SOCIAL ORGANIZATION.    The social and technological aspects of our culture are clearly out of harmony with one another. Most of our political and social institutions were designed for and by an agricultural society, and they are poorly adapted for dealing with problems of a highly industrialized society. It should be evident that further technological change is unlikely to solve the existing problems and is almost certain to create new ones. There are signs of both the immediate and long range maladaptiveness of our culture. Even if the social and political aspects of our society can catch up with our technology and the result is compatible with our biological and psychological limitations, we face in the long term the problems of growth, pollution, and exhaustion of resources.

Legal systems evolved from simple mediation through various systems for enforcing the norm and providing counsel. Our system is designed for settling disputes between individuals; but increasingly the opposing parties are not people at all but abstract corporate entities, "the environment," or even "society" at large. Lost in a maze of jurisdictional disputes and a search for precedents where no precedent exists, the courts find it increasingly difficult to handle the problems which confront them.

Other institutions and traditions are equally outmoded. Our notions of kinship and the family, which pervade customs related to taxation, inheritance, divorce, and economic responsibility, do not correspond very well with reality. It would be more realistic, for example, to recognize residential units and decrease our emphasis on biological and marital — or ex-marital — relationships. Changing sex roles in industrialized society have not been fully accommodated. We rail at our language, which stubbornly reflects relationships and social structures that no longer exist: "chairperson" trips awkwardly from the tongue, and one wonders how to pronounce "Ms." Education has come under attack, largely because in the midst of social disorientation and cultural change we no longer know what we are educating our children for. Traditional religions no longer fulfill their unifying role, and there is no satisfactory substitute. Science showed signs of becoming the new religion, but it proved inadequate and is now viewed by many with suspicion. Nor has any political or social philosophy, ecological ethic, or goal for individual self-realization or collective fulfillment been able to integrate our technology, behavior, and beliefs in the way that religion did in the past.

## THE SPECIES AS AN ADAPTIVE UNIT

In the past, the individual hunting band succeeded or failed. The band was the adaptive unit; what happened to one group in Africa was irrelevant to what happened to another in Australia. The trend in cultural evolution has been to increase the size and scope of the adaptive unit until today our problems of adaptation confront us on a global scale, and it appears to be our entire species that will experience success or failure rather than isolated segments of it. We have a global population crisis, global pollution, threats of global war, and prospects of global hunger; and we also have a proliferating set of world organizations that deal with these problems. Our attempts at world order so far have not produced a well-integrated system. But we have the World Court and a large body of international law, and some kind of world government seems inevitable unless disaster befalls us — again, on a global scale. So far, *Homo sapiens* has been enormously successful with his unique strategy of adapting through cultural, rather than genetic, change. The decisions we make now and within the next few decades will determine the outcome of his story.

## REFERENCES

COHEN, Y., ED. 1968. *Man in Adaptation: The Biosocial Background.* Chicago: Aldine Publishing Co.

COHEN, Y., ED. 1968. *Man in Adaptation: The Cultural Present.* Chicago: Aldine Publishing Co.

CONSTANDSE, A. 1964. *Rural Sociology in Action.* FAO Agricultural Development Paper No. 29. Rome: Food and Agriculture Organization.

EYRE, S., AND G. JONES. 1966. *Geography as Human Ecology.* New York: St. Martin's Press.

FARB, P. 1968. *Man's Rise to Civilization.* New York: E. P. Dutton & Co.

GARLICK, J., AND R. KEAY. 1970. *Human Ecology in the Tropics.* New York: Pergamon Press.

HALPERN, J. 1967. *The Changing Village Community.* Englewood Cliffs, N.J.: Prentice-Hall.

MUMFORD, L. 1971. *Technics and Civilization.* New York: Harcourt Brace Jovanovich.

NELSON, L. 1969. *Rural Sociology.* Minneapolis: Univ. of Minnesota Press.

PFEIFFER, J. 1969. *The Emergence of Man.* New York: Harper & Row.

SMITH, T. 1970. *Principles of Inductive Rural Sociology.* Philadelphia: Davis.

VAN LAWICK-GOODALL, J. 1971. *In the Shadow of Man.* Boston: Houghton Mifflin Co.

WHARTON, C., JR., ED. 1969. *Subsistence Agriculture and Economic Development.* Chicago: Aldine Publishing Co.

# · 11 ·

NORMAN D. LEVINE

# Demography and Human Population Dynamics

Nowhere is the interplay of biological, cultural, and environmental factors in human ecology so evident as in the study of populations. Here, too, the past is clearly relevant to the present. This chapter is about the size, distribution, composition, and growth of human populations — a field of inquiry known as *demography*. In the demographer's "life tables," statistics on birth and death and illness (natality, mortality, and morbidity) lurk clues to both the past and the future. The analysis of demographic data provides important information in many fields, including history, politics, economics, genetics, public health, anthropology, and sociology. But most important for our purposes, the numbers of people alive at various times and in various places, their rates of birth and death and their distribution by age, and the main causes of their death tell a great deal about the relationships of those people to their environment.

Demographic information must be obtained in different ways for different periods of time. Only during the last two decades has reasonably accurate and complete statistical information become available for the whole world. Even now there are errors and uncertainties, but these are accounted for by "corrections" to the data (to allow for known inadequacies), or are expressed in the statistical **confidence limits** of the results. When you consider that of twenty-three drifters killed in Yuba City, California, in 1971, only one was ever reported as missing, it is not surprising that many people who live and die in the streets of Calcutta are not included in any census — or that we can often only guess at the numbers of people in hunting and gathering tribes, pursuing an ancestral way of life remote from modern civilization. In addition, although efforts are being made to standardize census data and methods of collecting them, cultural differences

265

remain. For example, it may be improper to speak of the dead, and in some cultures dead infants are rapidly "forgotten" if they did not reach some minimum age.

For the period from the sixteenth century to the mid-twentieth century, there is a great deal of information from censuses and other records, but it is available only for certain parts of the world. In 1532 the London Bills of Mortality were started so that the Court and the wealthier people in London could be warned to depart for the country during outbreaks of bubonic plague. At first the Bills merely listed the numbers of deaths from plague and "other causes," but in 1629 they were expanded to include total numbers christened and buried for each sex. Still later, christenings and burials were listed by parish, and a large number of causes of death were identified. In 1665, for example, 97,306 people were buried, of whom 68,596 had died of plague. Sixty-two other causes of death were listed, some of which we can recognize and some of which we can only guess at. After plague the most important causes of death were ague and feaver (malaria, at least in part) (5,257), consumption and tissick (probably tuberculosis) (4,808), teeth and worms (2,164), convulsion and mother (2,036), spotted feaver and purples (1,929), and griping in the guts (1,288). Among minor causes of death were frighted (23), blasted (5), and distracted (5).

The Bills of Mortality were far from complete. For one thing, they included no Dissenters or other non-Church people. For another, the diagnoses were often inaccurate and unreliable. Nevertheless, a London businessman named John Graunt pointed out that for all their failings, one could learn quite a lot by analyzing birth and death records. Graunt (1620–74) is given credit for developing vital human statistics. Among his many observations based on the Bills of Mortality were that male births exceeded female births, that the death rate was relatively high in infants and children (and, therefore, that age affects mortality rate), that urban death rates were higher than rural, that there was a net migration from the country to the city, and that birth rate and population increase were higher in the country than in the city. Then in 1693 the astronomer Edmund Halley compiled a series of life-tables in which he calculated the probable expectation of life at each age. The first life insurance companies established in London in the eighteenth century used Halley's tables.

Another pioneer in the study of population was the English economist, sociologist, and clergyman Thomas Malthus (1766–1834). Malthus pointed out that population increases at a geometric (exponential) rate, while food supply increases more slowly. Consequently, poverty and distress are the unavoidable lot of mankind. At first Malthus said that war, famine, and disease are the only restraints on population growth. Later, however, he added "moral restraint." Malthus had a great impact on later theorists — including those who tried to prove him wrong. In particular, as we have seen, Darwin's theory of natural selection and survival of the fittest was influenced by the ideas of Malthus (Chapter 4).

Elsewhere, the first true censuses were taken in 1655 by the French and British in their Canadian colonies. These were followed by counts in Iceland in 1703, in Sweden in 1748, and in Denmark in 1769. The United States took its first census in 1790, and Great Britain in 1801. Around the turn of the nineteenth century France also began to keep vital records.

The ancient Hebrews were perhaps the first to attempt to "number the people." After that time records were kept by many groups of people for many purposes. Church records documented ceremonial events: christenings, baptisms, marriages, funerals. Other records were kept for military purposes or for taxation. All these are useful to the demographer if their biases, limitations, and intended functions are kept in mind. They tell very little, however, about human populations in the world at large. Demographers concerned with these early times must base their work on historical and literary accounts, fragmentary records, knowledge of social and economic life, and educated guesses about the most plausible rates of birth and death and levels of population. For the demographer interested in prehistoric times, the situation is even murkier. His evidence is based on archeological finds, which may not be representative, and on analogy with "primitive" cultures existing today.

It is important to remember the nature and uncertainty of demographic data in reading the discussion that follows. In addition, the degree of confidence in various estimates has various meanings. For example, it is possible to say that the birth rate for a particular population at some time in the past was 24 per 1,000, and that this is correct within a factor of two. In other words, the birth rate was between 12 per 1,000 and 48 per 1,000. But this statement is of no use at all, because almost all birth rates fall between these limits, and the few that lie outside are not far outside. On the other hand, most demographers would be happy to be able to estimate the world's population at some time in the past to within a factor of two; in many cases they may be only within a factor of five. With this in mind, we can look at how our species has increased from a rather rare tropical and subtropical species of the Old World to one numbering almost 4 billion living individuals and occupying much of the land area of the earth.

## GROWTH OF THE HUMAN POPULATION

From their origin in Africa, where they probably never numbered more than 150,000 or 200,000, our ancestors migrated in small groups over the course of thousands of years until they reached other continents. *Homo erectus* was widely but sparsely distributed throughout Asia, Africa, and parts of Europe. He lived, as *Australopithecus* had before him, in small bands of perhaps twenty to fifty individuals. Occasionally these bands came together for a cooperative hunt and massive kill of large animals. For the most part, however, they probably remained separate; and some of them, in the extremes of the range or in relatively unfavorable areas, may have lived for many years without meeting a neighboring group. As man extended his range he also slowly increased his numbers, but the increase was halting. Periodically a band would grow large and split, one part going in search of new territory. Sometimes disaster struck in the form of disease or a natural catastrophe or conflict with another band, and an entire group would perish. Life was short and extremely hazardous. Birth and death rates were high. There is no reason to suppose, however, that either acute or chronic hunger was commonplace any more than it is among hunters and gatherers of today — whose good health and nutrition are often noted by observers. Nor was ill health the rule. Although disease might wipe out a band now and then, epidemic disease as we know it now was to become a phenomenon of later times. The greatest danger was accident and injury, with consequent infection.

While the birth rate probably remained near its maximum of about 50 per 1,000, cultural advances caused a decline in the average death rate, which made a slow rate of population growth possible. These cultural advances included establishment of permanent home bases, where the old, the sick, and the injured could remain safely, and improved weapons and techniques of hunting. Expansion into new territory also permitted population growth. The result was that, by the time of the beginnings of agriculture some 10,000 years ago, there were an estimated 5 million people on earth. They were irregularly scattered over about 20 million square miles — roughly one third of the land area of the earth. Depending on the resources available, and the technology existing, a minimum of 1 square mile was required to support each person. So although the earth would hardly have seemed crowded in those days, it had probably reached between one-quarter and one-third of its carrying capacity for *Homo sapiens*.

With the invention of agriculture, life became safer, the amount of land required to support a person decreased from a square mile or more to a few acres, death rates declined further, and the rate of population growth accelerated. Between 8000 B.C. and the beginning of the Christian era, the world's population increased from 5 million to between 200 and 300 million. But new problems began to emerge as a result of new technology and a new way of life. When the great urban civilizations arose — first in Mesopotamia, later in Egypt, Crete, India, and China — the lives of many people depended on a successful harvest. And if the harvest failed, as it periodically did, many lives were lost. The Bible records numerous famines, as do the records of China and other civilizations. Epidemics of contagious diseases that thrive under conditions of crowding, poverty, and poor nutrition began to occur. But although local populations rose and fell and civilizations grew, flourished, and decayed, the global trend in population was ever upward. Wherever he lived, man's numbers became adjusted to his capacity for procuring or producing food, and he was becoming increasingly adept at both. But sometimes he outgrew his food supply or exploited his environment too far, or natural events conspired against him. Then populations plummeted and great empires fell.

By 1650 the population had grown to around half a billion, despite the toll exacted by almost continuous war, periodic famine, and devastating epidemics. The first outbreak of bubonic plague appeared during the sixth century. Later a more virulent form of the disease spread into Europe,

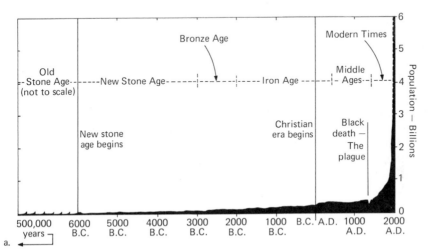

a.

**Figure 11–1a** Growth of the human population. It took three million years for man's numbers to reach 1 billion in 1800. The next five billion will be added in only 200 years, by the year 2000, at projected rates of growth. (From Greenwood and Edwards, *Human Environments and Natural Systems*, Duxbury Press, North Scituate, Mass., 1973, p. 20.)

**Figure 11–1b** Growth of population in the United States, 1790 to 1970. The recent escalation in rate of growth is evident here. (From "Toward an Equilibrium Population" by Alice Taylor Day and Lincoln H. Day, in *Patient Earth* by John Harte and Robert H. Socolow, p. 209. Copyright © 1971 by Holt, Rinehart and Winston, Inc. Reprinted by permission of Holt, Rinehart, and Winston, Inc.)

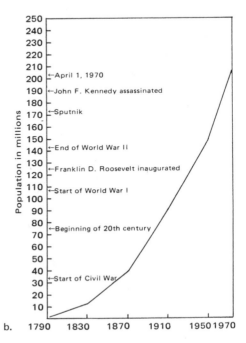

where wave after wave of the dread Black Death wiped out half or more of the people in stricken cities. Between 1348 and 1700 sporadic outbreaks of the plague killed an estimated quarter to a third of the inhabitants of Europe. In addition to disease, invasions and war frequently wiped out entire cities and demolished indigenous civilizations. The Etruscans and Scythians are known only from archeology and early histories; Carthage literally disappeared after the Punic Wars. As many as a third of the inhabitants of Germany and Bohemia may have died as a result of the Thirty Years' War during the first half of the seventeenth century. Still the population increased. By 1800 it was about 1 billion, by 1900 about 1.6 billion, and in 1970 it was 3.6 billion.

The history of growth in human population is shown graphically in Figure 11.1a, and that of the United States population in Figure 11.1b. The time that has elapsed since 1790 represents less than one tenth of 1 percent of human history, yet since that time more than a quarter of all the people who ever lived have been born. Some of the causes, results, and implications of this growth will be discussed in the following sections. The role of improved standards of living and the conquest of disease through medicine will be discussed in Chapter 14.

## THE MATHEMATICS OF GROWTH

Growth is increase. It usually occurs in one of three ways: at a constant rate, at a rate which changes by a constant amount in each unit of time, or at a rate which changes with time by an amount which depends on the size of the growing thing. There are examples of each type of growth in everyday life. The first is illustrated by the way the bathtub fills up when you plug the drain and turn on the water, or by the way your savings grow if you squirrel away a given amount in a coffee can each week. The second is illustrated by the acceleration of a falling object: disregarding effects of friction and viscosity, the rate of descent increases 32 feet per second during each second of the fall, regardless of how fast the object is traveling or how long it has been on its way. The third type of growth is by far the most common in the biological world and human affairs. It characterizes the growth of most individual organisms and populations of organisms at one time or another, as well as many institutions of human culture. It is *exponential* growth, the classic example of which is the compound interest offered by the savings and loan company, and which human populations have been experiencing at one rate or another for many years. Exponential growth rates are usually expressed as the percentage increase per unit time — for example, 2 percent per year.

It is most meaningful to think of exponential growth in terms of the length of time required to double the amount you started with. Table 11.1

**TABLE 11.1**
**Doubling Times at Various Rates of Increase**

| Annual Percent Increase | Doubling Time, Years |
|:---:|:---:|
| 0.001 | 70,000 |
| 0.01 | 7,000 |
| 0.05 | 1,400 |
| 0.1 | 700 |
| 0.3 | 240 |
| 0.7 | 100 |
| 1.0 | 70 |
| 2.0 | 35 |
| 3.0 | 24 |
| 5.0 | 14 |
| 7.0 | 10 |
| 10.0 | 7 |

shows the doubling times for various rates of growth. The results of exponential growth are shocking. Many examples, some real, some facetious, dramatize what happens when growth proceeds unchecked. Doubling every 20 minutes, a laboratory culture of the bacterium *Escherichia coli* increases from an initial inoculum of about 100 living cells in a liter of medium to 3,000 cells after 3½ hours, 50,000 cells after 5 hours, more than 25 million after 8 hours, and 100 billion after 12 hours. Then the rate of cell death catches up with the rate of cell division. After remaining constant for about a day, the number of living cells begins to fall, slowly at first, then faster and faster, until after another day most of the cells are dead. Computer models of human population growth and resource exhaustion project (not predict) a similar fate for man (see reference to Meadows et al.). The only hope for *Homo sapiens* lies in his ability, unlike *E. coli*, to do something about his growth before it is too late. The important thing to remember about exponential growth is, no matter how long it has been going on, one doubling period before the world has reached its carrying capacity for *Homo sapiens*, it is only half way to its limit. This is why we are warned that we have only a few decades to reverse trends which have been in progress for centuries.

A second look at the historical increase in population, with reference to Table 11.1, suggests that up until the invention of agriculture the average annual rate of population increase was only 0.002 percent, with a doubling time of 35,000 years. Between then and A.D. 1650 the average doubling time dropped to 1,500 years, representing a growth rate of 0.05 percent per year. The next doubling took place in only 200 years — and the next in 80, and the next (estimated for 1975) in 45. At the current growth rate of 2 percent per year, the population will double again in 35 years. Thus, not only are human populations undergoing exponential growth, but exponential growth at a constantly accelerating rate!

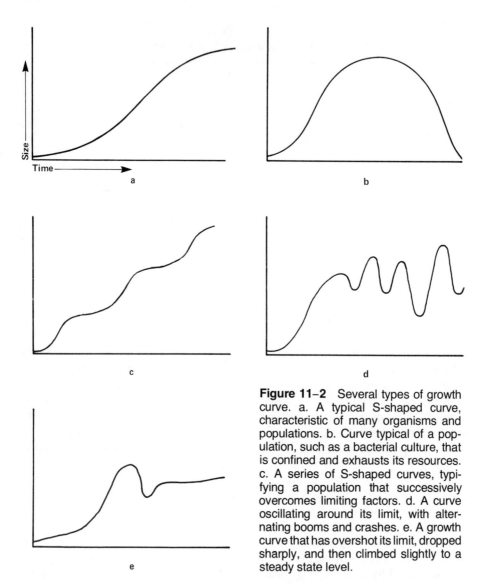

**Figure 11-2** Several types of growth curve. a. A typical S-shaped curve, characteristic of many organisms and populations. b. Curve typical of a population, such as a bacterial culture, that is confined and exhausts its resources. c. A series of S-shaped curves, typifying a population that successively overcomes limiting factors. d. A curve oscillating around its limit, with alternating booms and crashes. e. A growth curve that has overshot its limit, dropped sharply, and then climbed slightly to a steady state level.

Figure 11.2 shows some of the things that can happen to an exponential growth curve when it is deflected from its steep ascent. Figure 11.2a is the typical growth pattern of an organism, or of a population that expands into a new territory. Size increases slowly at first, then rapidly, and then slowly again until it reaches its maximum and remains constant. Exponential growth characterizes immature organisms and young populations, but the mature organism or the established population in equilibrium with its environment reaches a steady, no-growth state.

The population of *E. coli* confined in the closed system of a culture flask followed a growth curve like the one in Figure 11.2b. This is one type of curve that the computer predicts for a population of *Homo sapiens* that does not control its increase in numbers or consumption of resources. Sometimes, as a growth curve approaches its natural limit, it levels off for a while, only to undergo another exponential spurt that is followed by another plateau, another spurt, and so on. There is some evidence that this has occurred in the past growth of human populations, as innovations in agriculture and technology sequentially removed natural limits. This process cannot continue indefinitely, however. There are some limits that cannot be overcome. A growth curve with a series of plateaus is shown in Figure 11.2c.

Figure 11.2d shows a curve that is, in anthropomorphic terms, trying to avoid its inevitable ceiling by oscillatory behavior. Population studies of organisms in relatively simple ecosystems like the arctic tundra or northern forests reveal such a pattern, which illustrates either a Malthusian relationship with predators or the food supply, or unidentified physiologic or psychologic controls. Early human populations may have fluctuated in this manner, although the general trend was toward increase. Finally, Figure 11.2e shows a growth curve that has overshot its limit, dropped sharply, then risen again and leveled off at a value that could be sustained indefinitely. This may be an optimistic prediction of what our species can anticipate, as there are many who believe that the earth's present population is already larger than the maximum population that can be supported in the long term at a comfortable standard of living for all. In any case, growth will stop one way or another, and the steady-state world will be very different from the world we know now.

## DISTRIBUTION OF HUMAN POPULATIONS

The nearly 4 billion people living today are distributed very unevenly over the land surface of the earth. Some of the reasons for this have to do with the physical environment — with climate, soil, topography, possibilities for transport, and the distribution of resources. However, if the people of the world were to be redistributed optimally with respect to these factors, the new pattern would be quite different from the existing one. This is because historical events and culture have also played an important role in determining where people live.

An overall view of the present distribution of population can be seen in Figure 11.3. Almost half the world's people are concentrated on 5 percent of the land, while more than half the land supports only 5 percent of the people. There is a marked tendency for population distribution to follow continental and national boundaries. Thus there are four major areas of very high density,

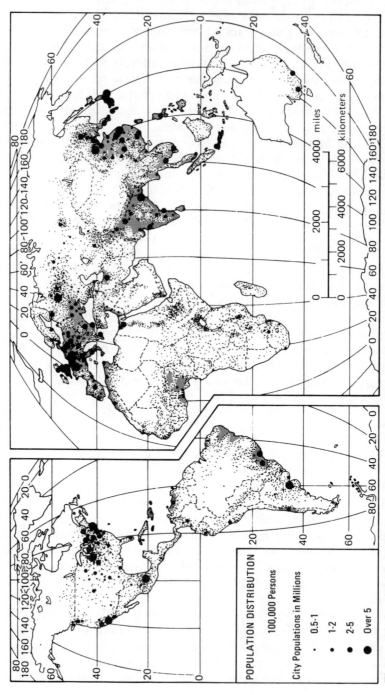

**Figure 11–3** World population distribution (Adapted from Brock and Webb, *A Geography of Mankind,* 2nd ed., New York, McGraw Hill book Co., 1973.)

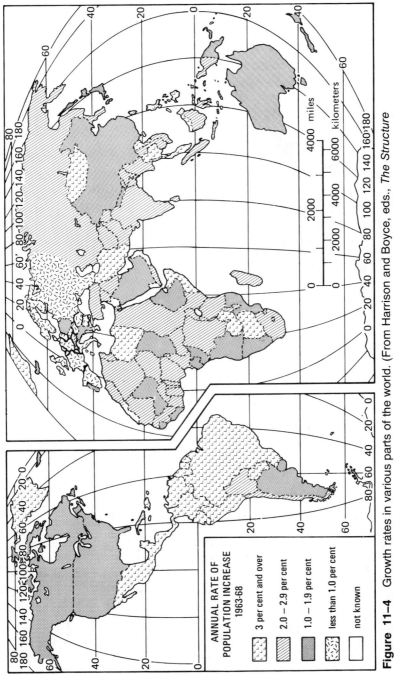

**Figure 11-4**  Growth rates in various parts of the world. (From Harrison and Boyce, eds., *The Structure of Human Populations*, Clarendon Press, Oxford, 1972, p. 27.)

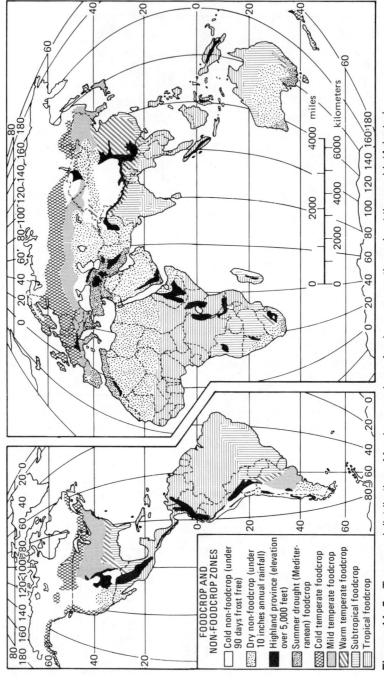

**Figure 11–5**  Types and distribution of foodcrop and non-foodcrop zones throughout the world. (Adapted from *A World Map of Food Crop Climates*, Food Research Institute Studies, Stanford University, Vol. 1, No. 3, Nov. 1960.)

FOODCROP AND
NON-FOODCROP ZONES

☐ Cold non-foodcrop (under
   90 days frost free)

Dry non-foodcrop (under
10 inches annual rainfall)

Highland province (elevation
over 5,000 feet)

Summer drought (Mediter-
ranean) foodcrop

Cold temperate foodcrop

Mild temperate foodcrop

Warm temperate foodcrop

Subtropical foodcrop

Tropical foodcrop

in which more than 60 percent of the population lives on 10 percent of the land. Two of these clusters, with more than 40 percent of the world's people, are the agricultural-rural areas in eastern and southern Asia. The other two, with roughly 20 percent of the people and 80 percent of the wealth, are the urban-industrial areas of Europe and northeastern North America.

Figure 11.4 shows the annual rate of population growth in various parts of the world. Note that there is no consistent relationship between growth and present population density. When these pictures of the world's populated areas are compared to the distribution of the world's major climatic zones (see Chapter 2, Figure 2.3), it can be seen, again, that there are only occasional relationships between actual distribution of population, rates of growth, and the degree to which the region is hospitable or hostile to human life. Finally, Figure 11.5 shows the types of agriculture that are possible in the various regions of the world.

*ENVIRONMENTAL FACTORS IN DISTRIBUTION OF POPULATION.* Despite the fact that ours is the most flexible of animal species in adapting to different environments, certain environments are preferred and certain environmental factors are necessary. Thus Antarctica, with twice the area of the United States, has no permanent human inhabitants. Other sparsely populated areas are the arctic, the North African and Asian deserts, the interior of Australia, and regions of high mountains. When we think of the great expanses of uninhabited land, it is important to remember that, although technology has weakened the bonds between man and his environment, formidable obstacles still remain to life in very hot, cold, dry, or high lands. If these now "empty" lands were occupied, it might place severe strains on the global economy and on the ability of productive agricultural regions to supply them with food.

In addition to climate, soils are also important determinants of population distribution. The great early civilizations arose in areas of fertile volcanic soils and rich flood plains; later, certain grasslands of temperate climates provided rich agricultural land. More will be said about the problems of food production in relation to climate, soil, and population in Chapter 13.

With the development of technology, some areas became important population centers because of their proximity to resources that were in widespread demand. Locations of these centers were also influenced by the availability of a cheap means of transport, which usually was a waterway. Thus mining and logging centers grew up.

Although in the past the distribution and density of population has been influenced by availability of resources, it is important to remember that what is perceived as a resource depends on the existing level of technology and on the needs and desires of the people. The great oilfields of the world were recognized as a priceless resource only within the last century, and most metal deposits were valueless until the principles of **metallurgy** were developed. Perhaps some resources for our future may come from seawater or common rock.

*HISTORICAL FACTORS IN DISTRIBUTION OF POPULATION.* Since the ancestral home of all of us was apparently in Africa, the current distribution of people throughout the world must be explained in terms of migrations to new territory and subsequent events. It is possible that some migrations were spurred by curiosity and the quest for adventure, but that would be difficult to prove. The best evidence is that migrations have been due to population pressure and local environmental deterioration, sometimes expressed as a search for a "better life."

Population pressure is generated when members of a group feel that their population density is too high in terms of either available resources or more subtle psychological and social factors. The concepts of density and overpopulation are relative. Densities that may be unbearably high for one culture and level of technology may be too low to support another. It would be hard for a Manhattan-dweller, for example, to imagine how the members of an isolated hunting tribe could feel that their group of eighty had grown too large!

There have been many times in the history of our species when the food resources of the home territory failed or were exhausted and the tribe had to move on. Sometimes the tribe moved in on its neighbors, and then conflict resulted. At other times virgin territory was exploited. When new and favorable territory was entered, population growth tended to be rapid until the available space and resources were fully utilized. Widespread climatic and geographic changes were factors necessitating or facilitating prehistoric human migration at some times, and inhibiting it at others.

Many migrations and invasions of historic as well as prehistoric times may have been prompted by population pressure. It is difficult to see why high priority was placed on gaining new lands unless the space and resources in the old lands seemed inadequate. Population pressure clearly lay behind the elaborate land reclamation projects undertaken in the Netherlands beginning in the sixteenth century.

Perhaps the most significant migration of recent times has been the migration to the New World, which began in the sixteenth century. It permitted economic as well as territorial expansion, first for the crowded nations of Europe which were already feeling the effects of depleted resources after centuries of maintaining growing populations, and later for Asian nations.

International migration continues today. But now instead of encountering groups of people ready to defend their homeland by war, the migrants are more likely to encounter increasingly rigid immigration laws. By drawing a network of political boundaries over the globe and protecting them by complicated rules and regulations, we have considerably influenced the pattern of migration in the last century.

Migration also continues to occur within nations. Some people are relocated by their governments or their employers; others move by choice. In the United States there are complex seasonal and long-term patterns of migration superimposed on one another. There is a net migration from east to west, from cold to warm, from country to city, and from city to suburbs. In addition, there is the yearly trek of migrant farm workers north with the spring, and another to follow the fall harvest.

Sometimes the distribution of population can be explained on the basis of past economic activities. The contrast between Haiti and the Dominican Republic illustrates this. There are almost twice as many people in Haiti as in the Dominican Republic, living on about half as much land, yet the Dominican Republic is favored by better soil. The explanation for the discrepancy lies in history. During the colonial period, the French established enormously profitable coffee plantations in Haiti, which required an unusually large number of workers. After the plantation economy fell, the workers remained, to reproduce at their customary high rate and bring Haiti to its sorry condition today. Under the Spanish much of the Dominican Republic was devoted to sugar plantations, a much less labor-intensive enterprise. Racial, language, cultural, and political barriers have prevented an equalizing of population density on the island.

When an area attracts or builds up a large population because of some environmental advantage, the population tends to remain concentrated there even if the environmental advantage later disappears. The port of New York today is intrinsically no better than those in many other coastal cities. What gave New York her greatest advantage over competitors was the opening of the Erie Canal in 1825, linking her with the continental interior. Today New York no longer has a transport advantage over other cities, but because of the temporary advantage granted her by the canal, she has been able to maintain her high position among cities of the United States.

Social policy also influences migrations, both positively and negatively. In Latin America today, unprecedented numbers of people are flocking to the cities, with the result that great areas of farmland have been abandoned. Half the population of Uruguay, for example, lives in the capital city. One reason for this is that agriculture is particularly difficult in much of Latin America, and crop failures are common. Fewer and fewer farmers are willing to take the risk of remaining on their farms. Despite the burgeoning population, many Latin American governments encourage immigration to maintain the agricultural system, but most foreigners are reluctant to perform duties that the natives have refused. The exception seems to be the Japanese, who are migrating in large numbers to Latin American farms. This

## MIGRANT LABORERS: LIFE ON THE MOVE

*Most of us who live in the United States in the 1970s are recorded and registered and kept track of by public and private agencies from all sides, sometimes much more so than we would like. But migrant laborers, the people who earn their living by following the harvest, are absent from the records that follow the rest of us. It is possible and even quite likely that a migrant child's birth could go unrecorded; that he would not attend any school long enough to acquire a permanent educational record; that he would grow up without ever getting a driver's license, or registering to vote; that he would work all his life without a Social Security number; that he would never have a bank account or a credit card; and that, his life ended, he would not be recorded as having died.*

*It is not surprising, therefore, that no one knows exactly how many migrant laborers there are in the United States—the estimate is about a million, counting dependents. But* where *they live is not at all difficult to find out: they live wherever there are crops to harvest by hand. They live in Florida, or Texas, or California during the winter, working in citrus or vegetables. In the spring they begin their dreary trek northward, up the East Coast to New York State and some-times as far as Maine, or through the Midwest to Wisconsin and Michigan, or up California to Utah and Idaho. When the summer harvests are over, they come south again, usually with no more money than they started with and often deeper in debt.*

*In our age of technological triumph over nature, migrant workers are as de-pendent on the success of crops as any medieval peasant. If a harvest is bad, their earnings are low—and since the* average *migrant family earns about $2,000.00 per year, "low" wages for a migrant laborer are not even subsistence. Besides, they have no financial last resort. Because they are constantly on the move, migrants do not qualify for unemployment insurance or other government relief programs. A person who earns only six dollars from a back-breaking day picking strawberries certainly needs financial assistance, but migrant laborers have generally been ig-nored by government anti-poverty programs.*

*A life of such poverty could not be easy in any case, but migrant workers suffer from further problems. First of all, the migrants are politically power-less. Usually they cannot even vote. Many are not able to pass state literacy requirements, and hardly any live long enough in one place to meet residency requirements. Furthermore, they lack a community—the basis for effective polit-ical organization. And migrant workers badly need political power. The minimum wage provisions of the Fair Labor Standards Act and the social*

is in accord with the policies of all governments concerned — the Japanese, who consider emigration along with birth control and abortion as a means of limiting population, and the Latin Americans, who want farmers. It remains to be seen whether the new immigrants will remain content to stay.

*welfare benefits of the 1935 Social Security legislation do not include them. They must struggle to bargain collectively, a right which has been guaranteed to nonagricultural workers for decades.*

*Living in substandard, unsanitary housing on greasy, starchy, nutritionally inadequate food, migrants have a shorter life expectancy than the general population, and a higher infant mortality rate. They suffer from many maladies almost unknown in North America—chronic malnutrition, parasitic diseases, untreated congenital defects, and infectious diseases against which other children are routinely immunized. But medical care is practically nonexistent, as transients do not qualify for public health services.*

*Education offers no escape from the cycle of poverty and helplessness in which migrants are trapped. A child who spends two weeks in this school, six weeks in that, three weeks in the next does not learn much. In addition, most migrant children of school age labor in the fields beside their parents during peak harvesting times. The families need every cent a child can earn, and laws restricting child labor are either nonexistent for agriculture or not enforced.*

*The weather, the crops, the whims of the grower or the crew boss—the migrant worker is totally at their mercy. Where migrants are needed to harvest crops, they are tolerated; anywhere else, they are literally run out of town. Since most migrants are of ethnic minorities—black, Puerto Rican, Mexican-American—they are rejected for their race or origin as well as for their occupation. Caught in a vicious cycle of perpetual travel, grinding labor, poverty, and powerlesness, do migrant workers have any prospects for change? Actually, two factors seem likely to do away with the migrants' wretched lifestyle, sooner or later.*

*First, farm laborers are finally beginning to organize and thus gain a small measure of political power. For example, Cesar Chavez's United Farm Workers' union, although it does not include nearly a majority of migrant workers, has made some important gains in wages and working conditions—to say nothing of self-respect.*

*Second, as the workers organize, the growers mechanize. Ironically, by forcing the growers to pay better wages and provide better working conditions, farm workers are making it more profitable for growers to replace their unskilled labor with machines. When modern technology has taken over the last farm, what will become of the migrant workers? It is not certain that change will be for the better, but there is no doubt about the grimness of their present lives. As one migrant father of six put it, "The only thing we can decide , . . is whether we'll stay alive or whether we won't."*

*FUTURE GLOBAL DISTRIBUTION OF POPULATION.* It is important to remember that projections are not the same as predictions. A prediction is the best educated guess of what is likely to happen, taking into account all available information and considering the relative probability of various events — and then leaving a large margin of uncertainty to allow for the unexpected. Prediction is a risky business. Projection, on the other hand, has an unimpeachable mathematical and theoretical basis — whether or not it has anything to do with real life. A series of projections can be made, taking various contingencies into account, but your choice of which projection to believe renders the projection a prediction, lent an aura of mathematical respectability by the computer. The United Nations and demographers of many nations make projections of future population growth, assuming either that present trends will continue or that trends will change in various ways. The projection of population doubling from 4 billion to 8, 16, 32, 64, 128 . . . infinity is clearly absurd. We know that this cannot happen. What gives us concern is what may happen instead.

An example of a population projection which assumes that the growth rate will continue unaltered is shown in Table 11.2. If the population of the world were to increase at a rate of 1.7 percent per year, by the year 2400 there would be an impossible 5330 billion people on earth, living at an average density of almost 100,000 per square mile over every inch of land on the surface of the earth. While this rate of growth cannot be maintained in the long run, short-term predictions expect an even higher rate for at least the rest of this century. Table 11.3 shows the anticipated increase in populations of developed and undeveloped nations between 1970 and 2050. It is unlikely that the developed nations will be able to support their increased populations at the standard of living that is taken for granted today. But more important still, populations in developed nations will only double in the projected time frame, while those of the undeveloped nations will almost quadruple. A more extreme projection gives the results shown in Table 11.4. Thus the political tensions of today may seem minor compared to those that will be generated in the next century by an ever-growing proportion of "have-nots" glaring across political boundaries at the shrinking proportion of "haves."

URBANIZATION. So far we have considered the distribution of population according to large-scale geographic, climatic, or political regions. But population is unevenly distributed on a small scale, also. Not only is there the obvious dichotomy between population density in "the city" and in "the country," but people are not distributed at an even density within these contrasting regions. Chapter 12 discusses the structure and function of the city, and some of the historical situations that have called cities into being. In this section we are concerned with the global migration of people into the cities, a phenomenon called *urbanization*.

The first true cities arose in Mesopotamia between 5,000 and 6,000 years ago. Since that time, the process of urbanization has continued almost without interruption, although for the most part it has been slow. It has not affected all parts of the world at the same time or to the same degree. But

**TABLE 11.2**
**Projected World Population at Annual Growth Rate of**
**1.7 Percent**

| Year | Population, in Billions |
|------|------------------------|
| 1975 | $3.9 \times 10^9$ |
| 2000 | $5.9 \times 10^9$ |
| 2050 | $13.9 \times 10^9$ |
| 2100 | $32.5 \times 10^9$ |
| 2200 | $177.9 \times 10^9$ |
| 2300 | $974.0 \times 10^9$ |
| 2400 | $5,330.4 \times 10^9$ |

**TABLE 11.3**
**Provisional Estimates of Future United States and World**
**Populations (in Millions)**

| | 1970 | 1985 | 2000 | 2050 |
|---|------|------|------|------|
| United States (official estimate) | 205* | 251 | 304 | 470 |
| United Nations ("medium" variant) | | | | |
|     Total for developed countries | 1,082 | 1,256 | 1,441 | 2,040 |
|     Total for undeveloped countries | 2,510 | 3,490 | 4,688 | 8,320 |
| World total | 3,592 | 4,746 | 6,129 | 10,360 |

* In 1972 the actual population of the United States was about 209 million (Taeuber, C. 1972. Population trends of the 1960s. Science 176:773–777).
From Keyfitz, N. 1969. United States and world populations. *In* National Academy of Sciences-National Research Council. *Resources and man.* Chap. 3, pp. 43–64. Freeman, San Francisco.

**TABLE 11.4**
**Population Projections for the Year 2070 Based on Current Demographic Trends**

| | Type of Population | | |
|---|---|---|---|
| | High birth and death rates (tropical Africa; parts of Asia) | High birth rate, low death rate (Asia and Latin America) | Low birth and death rates (Europe, North America, Oceania, Japan, USSR) |
| Total population circa 1970, in billions | 0.5 | 2.0 | 1.0 |
| % increase per year | 2 | 3 | 0.7 |
| Doubling time, years | 35 | 23 | 100 |
| Doublings per century | 3 | 4 | 1 |
| Total population circa 2070, in billions | 4 | 32 | 2 |

From N. Keyfitz and W. Flieger. 1971. *Population—Facts and Methods of Demography.* W. H. Freeman and Company, San Francisco.

**TABLE 11.5**
**Urban vs. Rural Population in the United States**

| Year | Percentage Urban | Rural | Total Population (Thousands) |
|------|------|------|------|
| 1790 | 5.1 | 94.9 | 3,929 |
| 1850 | 15.2 | 84.8 | 23,192 |
| 1900 | 39.6 | 60.4 | 75,995 |
| 1960 | 69.9 | 30.1 | 179,323 |
| 1970 | 73.5 | 26.5 | 203,166 |

From Pocket Data Book, USA 1971, U.S. Dept. of Commerce, Bureau of the Census; and Historical Statistics of the United States, Colonial Times to 1957. U.S. Dept. of Commerce, Bureau of the Census.

usually, whenever and wherever there was a surplus of agricultural products, and transport facilities were available, urban communities developed. (There are some notable exceptions to this, however. The early civilizations of Egypt and Central America, for example, advanced though they were in many ways, apparently did not build cities.)

The rate of urbanization began to rise rapidly at the beginning of the Industrial Revolution in Europe. Since then urban populations have continued to grow, largely at the expense of rural populations. Table 11.5 shows the trend of urbanization in the United States during the last two centuries. Similar trends are occurring throughout the world. In 1800 the percentage of the total population living in urban areas of more than 100,000 people was only about 2 percent; today it is more than 20.

Although urbanization is occurring in almost all nations, the causes and results of migration to the cities are not the same for industrialized and nonindustrialized nations. In western Europe and the United States, urbanization has traditionally been associated with economic development. The same is true of Japan. In the nonindustrialized nations, however, urbanization is a very recent phenomenon, caused largely by shipments of agricultural products from the wealthier nations. In the hope of receiving a share of the food, tens of thousands of rural poor flock to the ports where shipments arrive. There is no industry and there are no jobs for the unskilled in these dense cities. The situation has been poignantly described by Nathan Keyfitz and the Ehrlichs (see references).

Many people are concerned that the city, as it has developed in the last tenth of a percent of man's life on earth, is an environment to which man is not biologically adapted, and to which he cannot become adapted through the usual slow evolutionary processes for many more years. They point out that although cultural adaptation is a potent factor, it can operate only within biologically determined limits. Thus it should come as no surprise that there are many signs of man's maladaptation to urban life. The first of these, the appearance of epidemics of new contagious diseases, was ameliorated in time by culture, as we shall see in Chapter 14. More recently, however, the high incidence of mental disease and emotional disorders has caused concern, as have increasing crime rates and civil disorder. In addition, new diseases of modern life have appeared, replacing smallpox and plague. These are all signs of man's failure to adapt to the environment his culture has created.

When we consider cities of the future, it is hard to draw the line between serious planning and science fiction. There is talk of underground

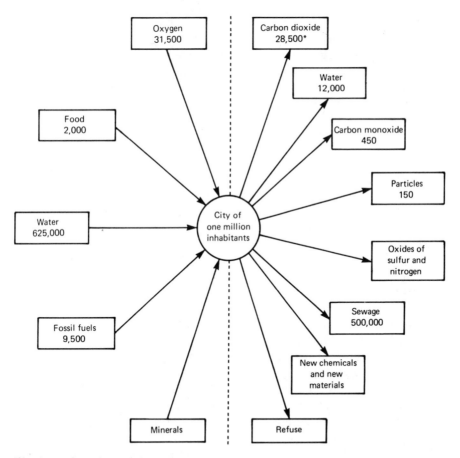

*Numbers, where given, are in tons per day.

**Figure 11–6** The metabolism of the city. (From S. Boyden in Harrison and Boyce, eds., *The Structure of Human Populations*, Clarendon Press, Oxford, 1972, p. 430.)

cities, and cities constructed on top of or at the bottom of the sea, or on polar ice caps. The projected population density of these cities is higher than the density on Manhattan Island today. It is probably within our technological ability to construct such cities, but it is not certain that the resources of our planet could maintain them. The city is not self-supporting. It depends on photosynthesis on the farms for food and on nuclear and fossil fuels for other energy. If the analogy is not pressed too far, the city can be compared to a gigantic animal that consumes stupendous quantities of food, oxygen, and water and excretes equally stupendous quantities of waste. Unlike the animal's excreta, however, the city's contains many products unlike the products of any biological organism. Some are acutely poisonous to other organisms and to the city-animal itself; others do not enter natural recycling processes. Furthermore, unlike the animal, the city demands energy in addition to food and many materials that must be gouged out of the earth. The "metabolism" of the city-animal is shown in Figure 11.6.

It is thought that some early civilizations, for example the Mayan, deteriorated because their centralized populations overtaxed the ability of the land to support them. The impact of a billion or two urban Antarcticans on the resources, agricultural capacity, and biogeochemical cycles of our planet is left for the reader to imagine.

## BIRTH AND DEATH RATES AND THE DEMOGRAPHIC TRANSITION

Increase or decrease in populations is mathematically described by the "demographic equation":

$$P_1 = P_0 + (B - D) + (I - E),$$

in which $P_1$ is the population at the final time in the interval under consideration; $P_0$ is the population at the initial time; B is the number of births that occurred in the interval; D is the number of deaths; I is the number of immigrants; and E is the number of emigrants.

We have seen that migration, represented by the term (I - E), can be very important locally and regionally. It accounts for the relative decrease of rural populations and the absolute decrease in some areas of New England. With only a few exceptions, however, (like emigration from Ireland during the potato famine or immigration to the newly formed state of Israel), migration has much less influence on a nation's population than the relationship between births and deaths — the (B − D) term in the equation. Globally, of course, both I and E are zero, as there has not been any migration to or from the earth. In the remainder of this chapter we will disregard the effects of migration and concentrate on demographic phenomena related to births and deaths.

*BIRTH RATE.* The actual number of births over a period of time is not as useful in describing demographic trends in a population as the birth rate, which is usually expressed as the number of births per 1,000 people per year. A number which describes the actual situation in a population even more exactly is the fertility rate, or the number of births per year per 1,000 women in their child-bearing years (ages 15 to 44.).

The maximum birth rate for our species is about 50 per 1,000. It is thought that this rate has prevailed throughout most of man's existence. Very high birth rates, between 40 and 50 per 1,000, still characterize most of the nonindustrialized societies of the world. In Western industrialized societies, however, birth rates have dropped markedly in the last two centuries, falling at times to as low as 14 or 15 per 1,000. A similar decrease has occurred in Japan, but much more rapidly and much more recently.

*DEATH RATE.* The overall death rate (called the *crude death rate* because it does not take into account factors of age, sex, or cause) is expressed as number of deaths per 1,000 people per year. Table 11.6 shows the crude death and birth rates of fourteen countries, their infant death rates, and their rates of natural increase (births minus deaths, disregarding migration).

**TABLE 11.6**
**Crude Death Rates, Crude Birth Rates, Infant Death Rates and Natural Increase for Selected Countries, 1966 or 1967**

| Country | A Crude Death Rate (per 1000) | B Crude Birth Rate (per 1000) | C Infant Death Rate (per 1000) Live Births) | D Natural Increase (per 1000) (Column B− Column A) |
|---|---|---|---|---|
| Argentina | 8.8 | 22.5 | 58.3 | 13.7 |
| Colombia | 9.4 | 35.7 | 80.0 | 26.3 |
| Czechoslovakia | 10.0 | 15.6 | 23.7 | 5.6 |
| France | 10.8 | 16.8 | 17.1 | 6.0 |
| Ghana (1960) | 24.0 | 49.5 | 156.0 | 25.5 |
| India (1951–1961) | 22.8 | 41.7 | 139.0 | 18.9 |
| Israel | 6.6 | 24.8 | 25.3 | 18.2 |
| Japan | 6.7 | 19.3 | 19.3 | 12.6 |
| Taiwan | 5.5 | 28.5 | 20.2 | 23.0 |
| Thailand (1965) | 7.1 | 36.4 | 31.2 | 29.3 |
| United Arab Republic | 14.3 | 39.3 | 83.2 | 25.0 |
| United Kingdom | 11.2 | 17.5 | 18.8 | 6.3 |
| United States | 9.4 | 17.9 | 22.1 | 8.5 |
| USSR | 7.6 | 17.5 | 26.0 | 9.9 |
| World (1960–1966) | 16.0 | 34.0 | Not Available | 18.0 |

From Pocket Data Book, USA 1969, U. S. Dept. of Commerce, Bureau of the Census.

As an indicator of demographic trends, the crude death rate is even less satisfactory than the crude birth rate. More meaningful measures of mortality are in terms of age-specific death rates, or age- and sex-specific rates. For this purpose, ages are usually given in five-year intervals, with mortality expressed as deaths per 1,000 individuals per year in each age bracket. If the cause of death is also specified, the rate is given in terms of deaths per 100,000 individuals per year.

Although birth rates have remained fairly constant and high throughout man's history, death rates have fluctuated widely in response to war, disease, famine, and natural catastrophes, alternating with periods of peace and well-being. In general, however, death rates have been slightly lower than birth rates and have decreased through time. If this had not been true, overall population growth would not have occurred as we know it did.

THE DEMOGRAPHIC TRANSITION.    Death rates in Europe began to fall during the seventeenth century. At first this resulted in a rapid increase in population, but social and economic factors soon effected a concomitant decrease in birth rate, which slowed the rate of population growth. The result of two centuries of adjustment to lowered death rates may be seen in Western industrialized society today, which is characterized by both low birth rates and low death rates. This shift from high rates of natality and mortality to low, passing through an intermediate stage of low death rate and high birth rate, has been called the *demographic transition*.

The low death rates of Western society were brought about slowly by a combination of factors, including improved nutrition, better sanitation, economic advancement leading to a higher average standard of living, and new medical knowledge. Within the last generation, however, a similar decrease in death rate has been experienced in nonindustrialized societies, not as a result of the factors that affected Europe and North America, but almost directly as the result of the conquest of a few specific diseases. Most important of these is malaria. The social and economic conditions which produced the demographic transition in industrialized nations are absent in these societies. The consequences have been tragic. The precipitous decline in death rates has not been accompanied by a decrease in birth rates, and populations have soared. Until these people understand their predicament and its causes, it is doubtful whether programs and preachments and the mere availability of birth control assistance will solve the problem.

## POPULATION STRUCTURE AND METHODS OF POPULATION CONTROL

Historically, societies have controlled their numbers in a variety of ways. The factor contributing most importantly to the lowered birth rate in Europe during the last two centuries was the customary late age for marriage, and the relatively large numbers of women who never married at all. A man simply did not marry until he could support his wife in appropriate style. In hard times this meant that he did not marry until he was in his 30s or 40s, and his wife was likely to be in her 30s. Since women in their 20s have the highest fertility rate, this custom of marrying late had a pronounced effect on the number of children a woman bore.

Some primitive societies condemn sexual intercourse while a woman is nursing a child; and since nursing may continue for up to three years, children are spaced at intervals of as many as four years and the total size of a family is limited. Other ancient methods of population control are abortion, coitus interruptus, and infanticide. Many peoples have killed "excess" babies of one sex or another. Most often the unwanted infants are girls, because girls are economically "useless." An important side effect of eliminating nonproductive members of society, is, of course, to limit the number of child-bearing members. Finally, throughout time, war has been a most effective means of reducing populations. It has been said that in current times this is no longer true; but if there should be an all-out nuclear war, world population would most certainly be drastically reduced — perhaps permanently.

The modern arsenal of birth control methods includes a large number of contraceptive devices, hormonal contraceptives, abortion, and sterilization. None of these is absolutely foolproof and safe, and cheap and delightful as well, but any one of them is cheaper and safer and more delightful than having an unwanted child. The technological part of the solution to population problems is at hand. The most formidable obstacles — cultural acceptance and implementation of birth control programs — remain.

AGE STRUCTURE OF A POPULATION.    In each population the relationship between fertility rate and age-specific mortality rate results in a characteristic distribution of population according to age. This distribution is usually shown as a *population pyramid*, several examples of which are presented in Figure 11.7. The purpose of these diagrams is not to show the most recent demographic data, but to illustrate the various types of age structure that occur. Figure 11.7a shows the population structure of the small island of Mauritius in the Indian Ocean. Mauritius, like many unindustrialized nations, has a high birth rate and a declining death rate. The population pyramid that represents this situation is roughly triangular, with pinched-in sides and an expanded base. Paradoxically, the usual effect of lowered mortality is to *decrease* the average age of the population, because it is primarily infant and childhood mortality that is reduced. The large proportion of children in a population like this is a severe social and economic burden. Children require food and education, and they provide nothing in return. The societies which have the largest proportion of children are least able to feed and educate them adequately.

Figure 11.7b shows the age structure of India before declining death

a.

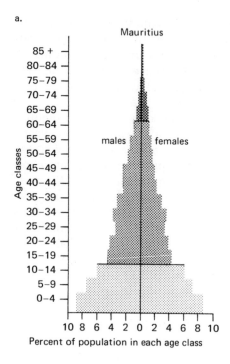

b.

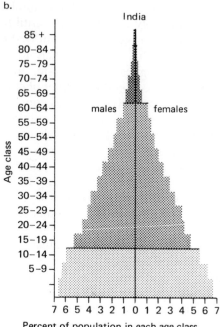

c.

**Figure 11–7** Some population pyramids. a. Age structure of population of Mauritius, a rapidly growing country, in 1959. Young people predominate. (From *Population, Resources, and Environment: Issues in Human Ecology*, Second Edition, by Paul R. Ehrlich, and Anne H. Ehrlich, W. H. Freeman and Company, copyright (c) 1972.) b. Age structure of population of India in 1951. The sides of the pyramid are not "pinched" in as they are in (a) because the declining death rate has not yet had an appreciable effect. (Ibid, p. 29.) c. U.K. in 1959. This is an old population, with a growth rate near zero. Note the excess of women over men in the older age groups. (Ibid, p. 26) d. Japan in 1960. The profile's narrowed base results from a sharp decrease in birth rate. (Ibid, p. 28.) e. The U.S. in 1960. The pinched region of the profile represents individuals born during and just after the Depression. The pyramid base widens rapidly. These are the individuals who are reproducing now. (Ibid, p. 30.)

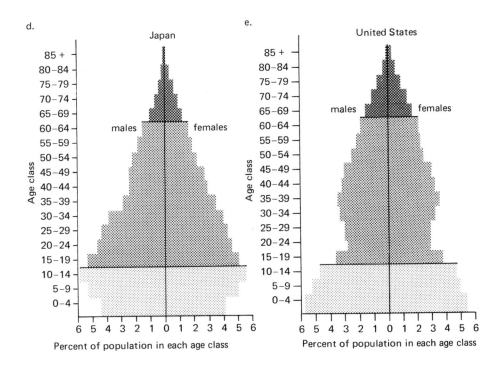

d.

Japan

e.

United States

rates had modified the triangular shape of the pyramid. The triangular shape characterizes nations with both high birth rates and high death rates. A stable population with a low birth rate and low death rate and a near-zero rate of growth, that of the United Kingdom, is shown in Figure 11.7c. This relatively old population is primarily a result of the birth rate, not the death rate, as might be expected. Note that there are proportionately only about half as many children in the United Kingdom as in Mauritius, but many more people past the age of 65. Now it is evident why comparison of crude death rates may be misleading. An old population like that of the United Kingdom may have a higher death rate than a very young population, but since old people have a higher death rate than young ones, a look at the age structure explains the apparent contradiction.

The pyramid shown in Figure 11.7d represents a declining population, that of Japan. The narrowed base is caused by a sharp decrease in birth rate. Finally, a somewhat more complex situation is illustrated by the pyramid of the United States, shown in Figure 11.7e. The top portion is typical of a population with fairly low birth and death rates, the constriction in the middle results from the decrease in birth rate during the Great Depression, and the broadened base represents the post-World War II baby boom. In addition, there is a slight deficit of males who were of fighting age during World War II.

*SEX STRUCTURE OF A POPULATION.* A closer look at the pyramids in Figure 11.7 reveals differences in relative numbers of males and females in various age groups. Percentages of males are shown on the left and percentages of females on the right in each diagram. The primary sex ratio, or ratio of males to females at the time of conception, is unknown; but it is usually thought to be about 1.6 to 1. Throughout gestation the mortality of male fetuses is consistently higher than the mortality of female fetuses; at birth, however, the sex ratio is about 106 to 100, the exact number varying somewhat among populations. In some societies the sex ratio is artifically modified through selective infanticide. Generally, however, the death rate for males is slightly higher than that of females, until at some time in middle life when the number of living females exceeds the number of males. The lack of symmetry in sex composition is shown most clearly in Figure 11.7c.

*CHARACTERISTICS OF STABLE AND STATIONARY POPULATIONS.* If fertility rates and age- and sex-specific mortality rates remain constant over a long period of time, a population reaches a state of unchanging age and sex distribution. This is called a stable population. Such a popula-

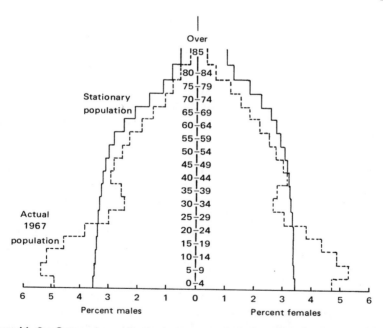

**Figure 11–8** Comparison of actual age structure of U.S. population in 1967 (broken line) with the age structure of a stationary population having the same birth and death rates (solid line). The broad base of the pyramid showing actual population indicates that the U.S. is a long way from achieving zero population growth (see text). (From "Toward an Equilibrium Population" by Alice Taylor Day and Lincoln H. Day, in *Patient Earth* by John Harte and Robert H. Socolow, p. 213. Copyright © 1971 by Holt, Rinehart and Winston, Inc. Reprinted by permission of Holt, Rinehart and Winston, Inc.)

**TABLE 11.7**
**United States Population Projections**

| Number of Children per Woman | Population (in Millions) | |
|---|---|---|
| | 1980 C.E. | 2000 C.E. |
| 3.11* | 237 | 321 |
| 2.78* | 232 | 301 |
| 2.45* | 228 | 281 |
| 2.11*,** | 226 | 266 |
| 2.11** | 221 | 250 |
| 1.52* | 214 | 229 |
| 1.52 | 209 | 214 |

 * Assumes net in-migration of 400,000 per year.
 ** 2.11 children per woman will result in each generation exactly replacing itself.
 The total U.S. population was 206 million on 31 December 1970 and 207.9 million on 31 December 1971.
 From ZPG National Reporter 4(5):15 (May 1972) based on U.S. Bureau of the Census Current Population Reports (Series P-25, No. 448).

tion may or may not be growing. In the special case where birth rate equals death rate and the growth rate is zero, the population is described as *stationary. Perfectly stable or stationary populations exist only as theoretical models,* but some actual populations approximate stability closely enough to make the concept a useful one. The optimum strategy for the long-term survival of our species and its continued success would be to achieve a stationary world population safely below the carrying capacity of the planet. "Consumption" of resources would stop, because almost everything would have to be recycled. The concept of carrying capacity is fuzzy, however, because it varies with one's ideas about the quality of life. Presumably, however, we are talking about a world at peace in which everyone can lead a life that is comfortable and creative.

If all the nations of the world were to declare right now that their goal was such a stationary population and to take necessary steps in that direction, it would be a long time before the goal could be reached. The situation in the United States is a case in point. Figure 11.8 compares the actual age-sex pyramid for the population in 1967 with the stationary distribution that would prevail with the same birth and death rates. The actual population is younger than the theoretical stationary one. The results of this are shown in Table 11.7, which shows United States population projections based on various average numbers of children per woman. The table shows that population growth will continue into the twenty-first century even if the number of children per woman drops as low as 1.52 — well below the number required for each generation to replace itself in numbers. The children who will produce the babies that increase the populations of the future have already been born, and even if their fertility rate is very low, world population will continue to grow. The demographic transition in Europe took several centuries, and even so it has not resulted in stationary European populations.

If the world should head toward a stationary population, there would be constant changes in age composition until the stationary state were attained — changes that would have important economic and social consequences. The ratio of children to adults would change, as well as the age distribution of adults in the labor force. These changes could be disruptive, if the deadline for true "zero population growth" were set for the too-near future. On the other hand, continued growth is certain to be at least as disruptive. In short, the ideal population policy is neither obvious nor the same for each nation, nor will it be developed and implemented with less than an extraordinary amount of wisdom and restraint. Whatever the future trends in the growth and distribution of human populations are, they will profoundly influence the relationships between man and his environment. Total population size is clearly related to demands for agricultural land and other resources. But the distribution of population between urban and rural areas, and perhaps the expansion of human populations into uninhabited or sparsely inhabited areas, will also have significant ecologic effects. Thus demographic studies are basic to the study of human ecology.

## REFERENCES

BOUGHEY, A. S. 1968. *Ecology of Populations.* New York: Macmillan.

DAVIS, K. 1969. *Basic Data for Cities, Countries, and Regions.* World Urbanization 1950–1970, vol I. Population Monograph Series No. 4. Berkeley: Univ. of Calif. Press.

EHRLICH, P., AND A. EHRLICH. 1970. *Population, Resources, Environment: Issues in Human Ecology.* San Francisco: W. H. Freeman and Co.

FREEDMAN, R., ED. 1964. *Population: The Vital Revolution.* Anchor Book No. A 423. New York: Doubleday.

HARDIN, C., ED. 1969. *Population, Evolution, and Birth Control.* 2nd ed. San Francisco: W. H. Freeman and Co.

KEYFITZ, N. 1969. United States and world populations. *Resources and Man,* NAS-NRC. San Francisco: W. H. Freeman and Co. Pp. 43–65.

KEYFITZ, N., AND W. FLIEGER. 1968. *World Population: An Analysis of Vital Data.* Chicago: Univ. of Chicago Press.

MEADOWS, D. H., D. L. MEADOWS, J. RANDERS, AND W. W. BEHRENS III. 1972. *The Limits to Growth.* New York: Universe Books.

MUDD, S., ED. 1964. *The Population Crisis and the Use of World Resources.* San Francisco: W. H. Freeman and Co.

NATIONAL ACADEMY OF SCIENCES-NATIONAL RESEARCH COUNCIL. 1969. *Resources and Man.* San Francisco: W. H. Freeman and Co.

SAUVY, A. 1969. *General Theory of Population.* New York: Basic Books.

SMITH, T. L., AND P. E. ZOPF, JR. 1970. *Demography: Principles and Methods.* Philadelphia: Davis.

SPIEGELMAN, M. 1968. *Introduction to Demography.* 2nd ed. Cambridge: Harvard Univ. Press.

U.S. DEPARTMENT OF COMMERCE, BUREAU OF THE CENSUS. 1969. *Pocket Data Book, USA 1969.* Washington, D.C.: U.S. Govt. Printing Office.

U.S. DEPARTMENT OF COMMERCE, BUREAU OF THE CENSUS. 1961. *Historical Statistics of the United States: Colonial Times to 1957.* Washington, D.C.: U.S. Govt. Printing Office.

WRONG, D. H. 1968. *Population and Society.* 3rd ed. New York: Random House.

# · 12 ·

ALBERT Z. GUTTENBERG*

# The Urban System

We have viewed the study of human ecology from several vantage points: from that of man's relationship to the climate, resources, and other living organisms in his environment, that of evolutionary and developmental biology, and that of the development and interplay of culture and social organization with the biological aspects of ecology. The picture is not yet complete. To many social scientists, the primary concern of human ecology today is the urban environment, and "human ecology" means the structure and function of cities and the activities and interrelationships of people within cities.

Cities are said to be out of control today. They spread malignantly across the landscape. They merge and form supercities. They make the air foul and the waters loathsome. Worst of all they gobble up honest farmers and turn them into soulless atoms.

The image of the cancerous city is not unfounded, although it probably owes as much to our present national mood as to the "facts." The negative imagination is rampant today and nothing escapes its attention. Let us assume, however, that our cities are out of control. The first step in regaining control is to understand them in positive terms. That is we must understand what they do *for* men rather than what they do *to* them.

The city is not a disease, nor is it a haphazard or accidental phenomenon. It is an intricate socio-economic mechanism whose parts bear a necessary and understandable relationship to each other. It is also, to be sure, a place where grave social problems manifest themselves, but in this fact there is no cause for discouragement. The modern Western city began as an association of free men, and to this day the capacity for self-direction remains one of its fundamental attributes.

* This chapter was written as well as authored by Albert Z. Guttenberg.

Since cities are a mixture of impersonal social and economic forces and free human will, theoretical interest in the city is divided between scientists and social reformers — between those who want to know what a city is and how it works and those who want to use it to create a just and prosperous social order. Especially today, the study of the urban system must encompass both these interests. On the one hand, it must approach the city as a scientific object; on the other hand, it must concern itself with social ideals lest it remain a mere scholastic exercise unrelated to living issues. To maintain this balanced approach is the task of the present chapter. The American city will first be considered in its broader economic and social context. The second part of the chapter is devoted to a closer study of the structure of the city and the relationship of this structure to questions of human welfare.

## THE CITY AS AN ECONOMIC COMMUNITY

There is considerable disagreement as to what constitutes the essential characteristics of a city. One writer has listed no less than fifteen approaches to definition, each one based on a different criterion. A statement which seems least open to dispute is that a city is a densely populated, closely built-up area whose inhabitants are employed mainly in nonagricultural pursuits (Thomlinson, 1969).

As a community of people not directly engaged in agriculture, a city must worry about its food supply. This may be one reason why the first cities appeared in river valleys, such as those of Egypt and Mesopotamia, where ecologic conditions, soil, and climate were favorable to the production of an agricultural surplus. The earliest cities secured their food by having it grown outside the walls, by the imposition of a tax, or by outright brigandage practiced on the surrounding rural population. With advancing civilization, however, the importance of trade as a source of food and other necessities increased. Classical Europe was full of thriving cities which owed their existence mainly to the vigorous trade carried on among different parts of the Roman Empire. When the trade routes were disrupted by the Islamic conquests, most of the urban communities shriveled and died. Only with commercial revival in the Middle Ages did urban life slowly revive and Europe once again become a region of interdependent cities (Pirenne, 1956).

The onset of industrialism with its division of labor and its mass markets merely accentuated the economic interdependence of cities. In the modern world no city is sufficient unto itself. Every city is part of a larger economic order, regional, national or international, in which it performs a specialized role. Urban America is essentially a network of interdependent economic communities. There are cities which serve as centers for mining or agricultural areas. There are manufacturing cities, recreational cities, educational

## GARY, INDIANA

*Besides being the catchy refrain to a familiar song from the Broadway show* Music Man, *Gary, Indiana, is a city associated with the name United States Steel. U.S. Steel planned and built Gary to serve the steel industry and to accommodate its workers. While other industrial cities, such as Pittsburgh and Detroit, evolved gradually in America's history, Gary was built in three and a half years. Its rapid development reflected the push of the steel industry to meet the needs of an expanding national economy.*

*U.S. Steel selected a geographically ideal site for its plants: the Indiana dunes on the shore of Lake Michigan. Gary was located near Chicago, the nation's fastest growing distributor of finished steel products, and it had access to the raw materials needed for the production of steel: iron ore from the Lake Superior region, limestone from Michigan and Indiana, and coal from Ohio, Illinois, and West Virginia. Gary's location on the lake and its proximity to several railroad lines meant also that goods could easily be transported by water or by rail.*

*But if this was an ideal site for the steel industry, it was ideal for people, too. The picturesque dunes provided a natural source of beauty and recreation. The amenities of the lakeshore were a welcome contrast to the clamor and toil of industrial activity. The advantages of Gary's location, however, were seen primarily in terms of the industry's needs. The lakefront was used for steel plants and subsidiary factories, forming a barrier between the lake and residential areas.*

*The Gary Land Company, organized by U.S. Steel to plan and develop the town, began construction in 1906. In 1909 the dunes were replaced by steel mills, railroad yards, and factories. The Indiana wilderness became a boom town to which thousands of immigrants came in search of jobs. Indeed, jobs*

cities, and governmental cities. Of course, we are speaking here not of exclusive occupations, but rather of those economic functions which provide the cities' principal employment — their main jobs in the national economy, as it were. Needless to say, many cities perform more than one of these functions for their regions, for the nation, or for the world (Ratcliff, 1949).

*ECONOMIC ORDER AND NATURAL ORDER.* As a member of a larger economic order, every city is subject to the vicissitudes of that order. Just like a man, a city can lose its job. Early last century the invention of the steamboat brought decline to once-flourishing Lexington, Kentucky, as business moved to the river towns. In the present century, as textile firms migrated south to take advantage of cheaper labor, New England cities shriveled. Most recently, when recession struck the aerospace industry, unemployment lines formed in Seattle.

*were plentiful, but the town offered little else. Dwellings were exposed to air pollution from the smokestacks of blast furnaces and to the noise and movement of heavy industrial traffic.*

*The company assumed that Gary would expand along an east-west axis close to the mills. Thus its land holdings were concentrated in the northern part of the city, where development was carefully regulated to control the spacing of houses, sanitary conditions, and the like. Unexpectedly, however, the city grew southward beyond the limits of the company's tract. Here speculators were free to buy land and construct cheap housing, unrestricted by regulations governing development. The overcrowded shacks of the south side soon deteriorated into a slum, ridden with the ills of prostitution, gambling, and crime.*

*Gary had been envisioned as "the very citadel of economy and efficiency in steel production." In the process of achieving this goal, its planners had overlooked some of the more human factors that make a city worth living in. Gary's cultural growth lagged far behind its industrial progress, and political corruption became commonplace. The failure of Gary to serve the total needs of its citizens raises serious questions about new cities planned by industry. Historically cities have evolved around a multitude of functions, which, through competition, ensured a balance of interests. Can an industry with narrowly defined goals effectively satisfy the long-term needs of people? Perhaps city planners of the future can learn a lesson from the experience of Gary.*

*Sources: Graham Romeyn Taylor, "Creating the Newest Steel City," The Survey, 22(1909): 20–36; Taylor, "Satellite Cities: Gary," The Survey, 29(1913) 781–798; Gary Redevelopment Commission, "Gary, Indiana, Community Renewal Program," final report, no date (courtesy of the Gary Public Library).*

Such events underscore the unity of economic life, but they also help to explain why American cities have strong competitive tendencies. In the nineteenth century many cities vied with each other to attract railroads, fearing that to be by-passed was to wither and die. Even today this struggle for a job continues. Witness the efforts of cities to lure lucrative industries within their boundaries by offering tax favors.

The critical role of the larger economy in the history of urban America is manifested most clearly in the impact of changing economic technology on the fortunes of cities. Perhaps the most impressive example here has been the almost uninterrupted migration of rural populations cityward, owing to the mechanization of agriculture. Only for a brief time during the Great Depression has this in-migration been reversed.

Among the economic forces that affect the size, internal structures, and environmental qualities of cities, none has had a greater impact than changing power technology. Many have expatiated on this subject, but no one has ever stated it with greater conciseness (or optimism) than the great conservationist, Gifford Pinchot:

> Steam brought about the centralization of industry, a decline in country life, and the weakening of family ties. Giant [electric] power may bring about the decentralization of industries, the restoration of country life, and the upbuilding of small communities. . . . Men can use steam only where it is generated. That is why steam has concentrated vast numbers of people in industrial cities. In a steam-driven civilization the worker must go to the power, but in an electrically-driven civilization the power shall be delivered to the worker. Steam makes slums. Electricity can replace them with garden cities (Pinchot, 1925).

Slums have not disappeared, but true to Pinchot's prophecy, electric power, the devices of telecommunication (telephone, radio and television) and, above all, the internal combustion engine have been converting our central cities from production centers to centers of consumption, specialized services, and administration, with a corresponding change in the behavior, habits, attitudes, and expectations of city populations.

If a city's job and changing fortunes depend on the city's place within the broader economic order, then it is only logical to ask what determines this economic order. One factor is certainly the natural order or environment. To a considerable extent, the size, functions, location, and spacing of cities are related to the distribution of natural resources as well as to other characteristics of the natural environment. For example, it would be impossible to imagine the City of Miami Beach apart from its coastal location and subtropical climate. Other cities are no less tied to their natural settings, although the relationship is not always as obvious. One reason why Pittsburgh became a great steel production center is its proximity to extensive coking-coal beds. Breaks in trade routes are also important in determining the location of cities. On a trade route wherever a change in the means of transportation (as from rail to ship) is required, a human settlement is likely to spring up.

*CENTRAL PLACE THEORY.* We must not suppose, however, that the variable distribution of natural resources is sufficient to explain the existence, size, functions, and spacing of cities. Even if the whole world consisted of a flat, undifferentiated plain, with all natural resources equally distributed, we would probably still find cities of different sizes and functions scattered over the earth's surface according to a fairly regular pattern. The basis for this assertion is called *central place theory*. A city, in addition to whatever other functions it performs, is also a central place; that is, it exists to provide goods and services for a surrounding market area. Cities, however, differ in the extent of their market areas according to the types of goods and services they provide. In any region, certain cities are the production sites for goods and services requiring many customers and very large

**TABLE 12-1**
**Central Functions Typical of Levels in the Hierarchy**
**of Central Places, Southwestern Iowa, 1960**

*(A) The Village-level functions*

| | |
|---|---|
| Gas and service station | Meeting hall |
| Automobile repair | Hardware |
| Bars | Farm materials |
| Restaurants | Farm sales |
| Grocery | Farm implements |
| Post Office | Oil fuel bulk station |
| Local government facility | Barber |
| Church | Beauty shops |

*(B) The Town-level functions*

| | |
|---|---|
| Furniture | Doctors |
| Appliances | Dentists |
| Variety | Building services |
| General clothing | Building materials |
| Drugstores | Radio-TV sales and service |
| Banks | Movers and haulers |
| Insurance agents | Funeral home |
| Real estate | Veterinarian |
| Telephone exchange | Automobile accessories |
| Cleaners | Farmers' cooperatives |

*(C) The City-level functions*

| | |
|---|---|
| Women's clothing | Newspaper publisher |
| Men's clothing | Office of labor union |
| Shoes | Sales of new automobiles |
| Jewelry | Sales of used automobiles |
| Florist | Specialized automobile repairs |
| Supermarket | Automobile wrecking |
| Bakery | Cleaners and laundry (operator) |
| Liquor store | Self-service laundry |
| Other medical practice (e.g. op- | Shoe repairs |
| tometrists, etc.) | Plumbing |
| Lawyer | Fixit |
| Hotel | Movies |
| Motel | Indoor amusements (billiards, etc.) |
| County government | Drive-in eating places |

Source: From Tables IV–VI in Berry, Barnum and Tennant, "Retail Location and Consumer Behavior," *Regional Science Association Papers*, Vol. 9 1962, pp. 77–78 as summarized in Table 7.5, *The North American City*, (Yeates and Garner, Harper & Row, 1971), p. 177.

market areas for their economic production. The same region will also contain smaller settlements — the production sites for goods and services requiring fewer customers and smaller market areas to maintain them. The result is a hierarchy of central places and market areas (Table 12.1).

*URBAN LAND USE AND SPATIAL STRUCTURE.* As with the national system of cities, so with the individual city — the economic facts of life are all-pervasive. In a sense, the land-use structure of the city is but the "lengthened shadow" of its economic structure. Consider what happens when trade or manufacturing replaces subsistence farming as the dominant form of economic life. Where before each farm family was meeting most of its own needs just as any other family, we now find many families specializing in some part of the common commercial or industrial tasks. Corresponding to the functional division of labor, there arises a *spatial separation of functions.* Places where the traded commodities are made, assembled, or stored tend to separate from places where they are displayed and sold, and from the residences where some of them are consumed. As the basic industries prosper, *ancillary functions* make their appearance and find their own locales — banking, insurance, record-keeping. Secondary services such as restaurants, hotels, and repair shops spring up for the convenience of those engaged in the main business of the community. Roads become more important as a means of maintaining contact among the separating activities and functional groups. Public services of all kinds — policing, fire control, water supply, and waste disposal — are now required.

Other characteristics of the developing city appear, such as a variety of lifestyles and value-systems, reflecting the role of each subgroup in the underlying economic order. The growing city becomes a center of opportunity. People of every type and condition of life are attracted, settling in their own neighborhoods with their own institutions, setting the stage for social conflict and social change. Competition for land, and consequently, a land market develop. There have been several attempts to generalize the resulting overall spatial pattern of the city (Figure 12.1). Thus the sociologist Ernest Burgess stressed the tendency of different types of urban activities to distribute themselves in *concentric zones* at various distances from the city center. Homer Hoyt, the land economist, concentrating on residential rental levels, noted the tendency of high and low rental districts to push out from the center along major transportation routes in separate wedges or *sectors.* On the other hand, the geographers Chauncy Harris and Edward Ullman suggest that the city does not necessarily grow or even orginate from a single center but possibly from many independent centers or *nuclei*, such as a university, a port, or a factory district (Harris and Ullman, 1945). None of these generalizations, however, has been accepted as necessarily valid for all times and all cities.

*ECONOMIC BASE THEORY.* The distinction between basic and non-basic or ancillary economic activities noted above has been an influential one in urban planning. More than 50 years ago the American planner, Frederick Law Olmstead, wrote: "Productive occupations may be roughly divided into those which can be called primary, such as the marine shipping

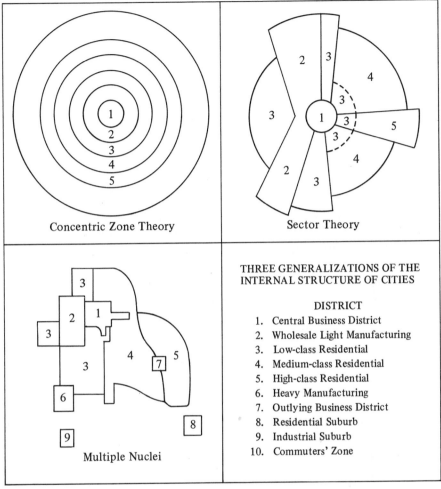

Concentric Zone Theory

Sector Theory

THREE GENERALIZATIONS OF THE
INTERNAL STRUCTURE OF CITIES

DISTRICT

1. Central Business District
2. Wholesale Light Manufacturing
3. Low-class Residential
4. Medium-class Residential
5. High-class Residential
6. Heavy Manufacturing
7. Outlying Business District
8. Residential Suburb
9. Industrial Suburb
10. Commuters' Zone

Multiple Nuclei

**Figure 12–1** Generalizations of internal structure of cities. The concentric-zone theory is a generalization for all cities. The arrangement of the sectors in the sector theory varies from city to city. The diagram for multiple nuclei represents one possible pattern among innumerable variations. (From *The Annals of the American Academy of Political and Social Science*, 1945. Vol 242, p. 113.)

business of the port . . . and those occupations which may be called ancillary, such as those devoted directly or indirectly to the service and convenience of the people engaged in the primary occupations" (quoted in Blumenfeld, 1967, p. 333).

Some planners, geographers and economists have seen in this distinction between "basic" and "non-basic" employment a powerful conceptual device for yielding insights into a city's present and future structure. They reason that it is the nature of the "basic industries" and the ratio between the two types of employment which ultimately determine a local community's land requirements, its required level of municipal costs and services, and its standard of living and quality of life. *Economic base theory* also seems to provide a certain rationale for local economic planning. Basic employment is defined as that employment which produces goods and services for export, while non-basic employment serves only the local market. The larger the basic component of the local economy, the more favorable, presumably, its balance of trade with other communities; therefore, the more wealth will flow into the exporting community's public and private coffers. One implication is that cities should build up their basic employment, since an unfavorable balance of payments leads to unemployment, population loss, and impoverishment. For all its apparent usefulness, economic base theory is far from receiving general acceptance. It has been taken to task sharply by some planners both for the difficulties it presents in actually distinguishing between basic and non-basic industries, as well as for fostering a narrow, mercantilistic spirit in local planning.

## THE CITY AS AN ENVIRONMENT

Despite the importance of economic forces, a city is not merely an economic mechanism. People live their lives in the midst of this mechanism, so the city is also a physical and social environment. The value of the urban environment, however, is a matter of continual controversy.

This controversy has its basis partly in the ordering of human needs. In most of us the aesthetic sense is secondary to the instinct for survival. Hungry people pay scant attention to environmental amenities — they are too busy securing their daily bread. But once their hunger is assuaged, the world appears to them in quite a different light — no longer as the scene of a perilous or backbreaking struggle for existence, but as a noble setting for human life.

So with the city. People have flooded to American cities from every quarter of the globe in search of economic opportunity, and those who have done well are now eager to enjoy the rewards of their labors. Consequently, the city appears under a double aspect — as a place to make a living and as a place to live well. These motives frequently collide. Shall our city be planned as a consumer's paradise, or must we still curb our desires for fulfillment in the interest of more jobs, cheaper food, or a lighter tax burden?

Since the 1960s when pollution was first widely perceived as an urgent problem, we have been bombarded with dire warnings. The capacity of the natural environment — the earth, the air, the waters — to absorb pollutants produced by our industrial civilization and to break them down into less-harmful substances, is fast approaching its limit. One authority, Glenn R.

Hilst, divides the effects of urban pollution into three general categories: (1) the effect on the physical health of the populace; (2) the effect on the people's mental health; and (3) the effect on other organisms and inanimate objects. The dismal list is now familiar.

To indicate the mounting assault on our health and senses from solid wastes alone, Hilst gives the following example: ". . . if the citizen and industries contribute equally, and if the average density of these solid wastes is one pound per cubic foot, . . . our typical city would generate a garbage heap ten feet high and one-half mile long in the course of a single year" (Hilst, 1970).

There is no reason to question the seriousness of the threat which such statements are meant to indicate. However, the quest for the good life — especially for the good urban life — is more than a quest for clean air, pure water, safe and pleasant surroundings. In addition to these there are other values involved in the perennial search for "environmental quality." They can hardly be considered without first inquiring into how Americans have traditionally regarded their cities as a social environment.

About 35 years ago, Louis Wirth, a sociologist at the University of Chicago, wrote a famous essay in which he defined a city as "a relatively large, dense and permanent settlement of socially heterogeneous individuals." Moreover, according to Wirth, the city is not just a place, it is also a way of life. In the city, he said, human relationships are anonymous, transitory, superficial:

> Characteristically, urbanites meet one another in highly segmental roles. They . . . are dependent upon more people for the satisfaction of their life needs than are rural people . . . but they are less dependent on particular persons. . . . The reserve, the indifference and the blasé outlook which urbanites manifest in their relationships may be regarded as devices for immunizing themselves against the personal claims and expectations of others (Wirth, 1938, p. 494).

The complaint implicit in Wirth's definition of the city was not a new one even in his day. Americans have always conceived of their society as essentially rural and are deeply troubled by the rise of the hurly-burly city. Indeed city-hatred is said to have a special place in American social thought. Evidence for this claim can be found in many terms applied to the city which, when viewed collectively, seem to betray an anti-city bias. Thus there are the terms which suggest the odious or menacing nature of urban expansion ("tryannopolis," "exploding metropolis," "sprawl"); terms which suggest what the spreading city leaves in its wake ("slurbs," "blight"); nostalgic terms recalling lost rural conditions ("neighborhood," "open space,"); and incantations to restore the ancient balance of nature ("conservation," "the ecology").

Americans have loathed the dirt and disorder of the urban environment, but above all, they have feared its presumed demoralizing effect on national life. In 1803 Thomas Jefferson warned against the social and political dangers inherent in a nation dominated by cities: "When we get piled up upon one another in large cities, as in Europe," he said, "we shall become corrupt as in Europe, and go to eating one another as they do there." In 1896 William Jennings Bryan, the great populist leader, expressed the credo of millions of Americans when he challenged the primacy of the urbanized East in his famous "cross of gold" speech: "— the great cities rest upon our broad and fertile plains. Burn down your cities and leave our farms and your cities will spring up again as if by magic; but destroy our farms and grass will grow in the streets of every city in America."

Populist rhetoric failed to stem the tide of urbanization, but Americans had other means at their disposal. In 1908 President Theodore Roosevelt created a Country Life Commission to search out and strengthen the bases of rural virtue. Experimental communities were founded for the purpose of creating a happy blend of town and country life. The vision was also confirmed in the findings of contemporary social scientists. Sociologist Lester F. Ward discerned a twofold process which he described "as, on the one hand, *the ruralization of city populations,* and on the other hand, *the urbanization of country populations.*" He further went on to say:

> Both are due to the general fact that rural conditions can only be appreciated through culture, while, in the present state of society, culture can only be acquired at the centers of population. The modern facilities of transportation and intercommunication are giving rural populations a taste of what culture and a higher intellectual standard of living mean, and they are gravitating cityward in search of it. At the same time . . . all the agencies of city life that secure mental friction and inspire intellectual, scientific and artistic development, are producing a distaste for the artificial conventionalities of city life and a yearning for that solid communion with nature which can only be realized by rural life. (Quoted in Henry C. Taylor, *The Story of Agricultural Economics.* Ames, Iowa: The Iowa State College Press. 1952. Pages 44–45).

Out of such stirrings amplified by the Great Depression, the well-known community building program of the New Deal period eventually grew. Its purpose was to reunite in individual "subsistence" communities those fundamental human values and activities torn asunder by the twin forces of industrialization and urbanization: work and leisure, man and nature, city and country, agriculture and industry. The program failed, but the impulse survives; witness the present-day commune movement among younger people. In a sense, even the tremendous suburbanization of the past 75 years reflects an effort to ruralize the city and citify the countryside. And yet, owing to the hurried, pell-mell character of decentralization, we have always seemed to be pushed further from our goal.

One of the most strenuous efforts to combine the best of urban and rural life was the Garden City movement, the ancestor of the modern New

Town movement. The founder of this movement was an Englishman, Ebenezer Howard, who as a young man had spent some time homesteading in Nebraska. Howard returned to his native land inspired with ideas of social reform, some of them acquired in America, but with a practical determination to put them into effect. In 1898 he published his famous proposal in a book entitled, *Garden Cities of Tomorrow, A Peaceful Path to Reform.* As the eminent American planner and social critic Lewis Mumford wrote, "Howard's prime contribution was to outline the nature of a balanced community and to show what steps are necessary to bring it into existence" (Mumford in Howard, 1965, p. 33). In Howard's own word, the Garden City was to be a "marriage" of the best in town and country.

The must lucid exposition of the Garden City is still to be found in Howard's book, but his associates have left us an excellent short definition: "A Garden City is a town — planned for industry and healthy living — of a size that makes possible a full measure of social life but no larger — surrounded by a permanent rural belt — the whole of the land being in public ownership or held in trust for the community. . . ." (Purdom, 1925).

The first English Garden City, Letchworth, was begun by Howard and his associates in 1903 and was followed in 1919 by a second town, Welwyn. The idea was slow in catching on in the United States. Generally speaking, Americans have preferred to shore up their sagging cities through urban renewal and zoning rather than to accept the outright loss of central land values implicit in the Garden City idea. This is not to say that the idea was entirely neglected. In the 1920s the architects Clarence Stein and Henry Wright were experimenting with new community forms through the application of science and technology. The outcome was Radburn, New Jersey, America's first attempt at a Garden City or New Town.

Radburn had definite social objectives. It was planned to foster community life, to put the automobile in its place, and "to supply recreational facilities adequate to the changing ratio between work and leisure in modern life" (Lubove, 1963). Consequently, and with some justification, it has been called an experiment in applied sociology. Many of Radburn's features were incorporated into the three Greenbelt towns built by the Resettlement Administration in the late 1930s — the houses turned inward to form a superhouse, the separation of foot and wheel traffic, and the interior park. These bold efforts provided dramatic examples for the future, but they scarcely spoke to the most urgent need of the day — economic recovery. The chief effect of the New Deal on existing American cities was through various pump-priming measures to create employment: the construction program of the Public Works Administration; the mortgage insurance provisions of the Federal Housing Authority which accelerated suburban development; and the loans to local public housing agencies by the United States Housing Authority, an agency created by the U.S. Housing Act of 1937 (Wagner-Steagall Act).

The Housing Act of 1937 also enabled a modest amount of slum clearance, but the national commitment to public urban redevelopment began in earnest only with the act of 1949 which authorized local authorities to acquire substandard urban tracts and to rebuild them in accordance with local plans, using Federal monies on a matching basis. In subsequent years this initial act was amplified and augmented by numerous Federal and state programs and enactments. As a result, the cores of many cities were "renewed," but this hardly sufficed to relieve the plight of the slum-dweller or to reverse the outward flow of money and population to the suburbs. Moreover, since the early 1960s the program has faced stiffening opposition from the cities' black populations because of their suspicion, not always unfounded, that urban renewal is really a covert form of "Negro removal" (Canter, 1970).

The 1970s promise to be the decade of the New Town. For diverse reasons a chorus of approval for this latest American venture can be heard on all sides. The reasons include not only the difficulty and expense of continued inner-city renewal, but also the desire to give suburbanization a more acceptable form, perhaps even opening the suburbs to nonwhites. Additional interest is displayed by the ecology crusade with its aim of a clean and healthful environment, and by developers who see the speculative opportunities. And yet there are those who, with the best of motives, fail to share the general enthusiasm. A case could be made against the New Town based on a deeper sense of what ails the American people.

John Silber, the American philosopher and educator, has said that ours is "an instantaneous culture." We live in an age that "rejects history" (Silber, 1971). We have instant food, instant travel, instant communication. Now we are told that with our lavish resources we can have instant cities. Herein lies our problem. Our very ability to pull up stakes and escape to a bright new town undermines our commitment to the old cities. Therefore, as one political scientist, Norton Long, has put it, the urban crisis is more than a matter of flooded cellars, traffic jams, foul air and falling real estate values, for these are but symptoms, all of which can be traced to a single cause — a failure in our sense of civic responsibility. Preferring consumership to citizenship, we regard our cities as disposable items to be abandoned and replaced as soon as they wear out or in some other respect fail to conform to our desires.

## THE ELEMENTS OF URBAN STRUCTURE

A first step in reviving the sense of responsibility to our cities is to arrive at an understanding of urban structure, for only within the context of structure do the limits and opportunities of constructive social action become apparent.

In a sense, however, "urban structure" is too broad a term. More appropriate is the concept of "relevant structure," since what is important in the structure of a city depends on the needs and aspirations of the people of the city, and this, in turn, is very much a matter of the times in which they live. For many ancient cities, it was military defense that counted. For the Rome of Pope Sixtus V, it was the holy processional. For nineteenth century Pittsburgh it was steel production. The modern American, however, regards his city as neither a fortress, nor a church, nor a factory, but as a larger home to be arranged for the convenience of all its members. The instinct of the age is to understand the city as a method of organizing urban space to provide all the people with access to all kinds of facilities. What follows is an attempt to interpret urban structure in the light of that cardinal objective.

ACCESS TO FACILITIES.    To begin, let us suppose that in a certain territory no city as yet exists and that our purpose is to build one. Suppose, further, that the people of the territory, future citizens, are fairly evenly scattered throughout the area. Finally, let us imagine that these people exist in an exceedingly primitive state, almost entirely without the necessities of life. Our first concern would be to provide them with all the facilities which they will need in order to live in both the biological and cultural sense.

Basically there are only two ways of accomplishing such a task. One way is to distribute all facilities locally, that is, to the scattered points where people live. Thus at many places in the future urban field there would be a complete set of required facilities — shops, work places, schools, churches and the like (small dots, Figure 12.2a). The alternative method would be to concentrate all facilities at one or two large centers (larger dots) and then transport the people (lines) to these centers to meet their daily needs (Figure 12.2b). In this case all the people become commuters.

In reality neither of these two methods is sufficient to meet the needs of the population. In the first case, not all facilities could be distributed in small quantities throughout the residential field because 1) either they are tied to some natural resource or fixed environmental feature as, for example, fisheries to waterfronts; or 2) because they are so expensive that we could not afford to divide them into miniature units for local distribution. For example, it would be difficult to break up a great university into units in the same way that elementary schools are distributed to serve different neighborhoods.

On the other hand, suppose we tried to rely on transportation to a few great centers as the sole means of giving the people access to needed facilities. We would soon find that many people could not be served because they have to remain close to home throughout the day, either because of their age and stage of life (the very young and the very old), or because their social roles require them to remain close to home (mothers with young children).

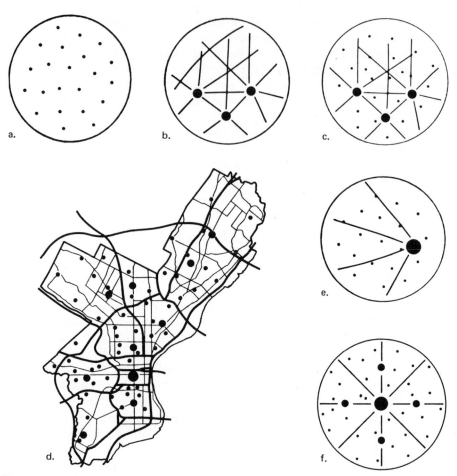

**Figure 12–2** The elements of structure. a. Certain facilities are used so often, or are so important to the public welfare, that they must be distributed throughout the city so as to be within easy reach of all. Facilities in this category are small parks and playgrounds, neighborhood schools and shopping centers, neighborhood clinics and community centers. b. Other facilities—large parks, high schools, and sports stadia—can be distributed only in the sense of being made accessible to the people through efficient transportation. c. The anatomy of a city—urban structure—results from a combination of both methods of distributing facilities. d. The anatomy of Philadelphia. e. Total distance between people and certain city-wide facilities is reduced by consolidating these facilities at one center in the urban field (central business district). f. Overall distance between people and facilities is further reduced by locating this center at the hub of the transportation system. (A, B, C, D, F, from *J. of the Amer. Inst. of Planners*, Vol. 26, No. 2, 1960. D from The Philadelphia Comprehensive Plan, Philadelphia City Planning Commission. 1960.)

Obviously both methods must be employed. Some needs may be satisfied by localized facilities while others must be met by transporting people to large centers. Consequently, combining Figures 12.2a and 12.2b gives us a more realistic picture of urban structure (Figure 12.2c).

This analysis, to be sure, is oversimplified, yet it enables us to identify the major functional parts of a city in relation to a single community goal or objective, that of providing people with access to needed facilities. These major parts are: 1) the locally distributed facility, such as the neighborhood school, store, or playground, 2) the non-distributable facility, such as the high school or sports stadium to which people have to be transported, and 3) the transportation routes which bring them to these places.

It is important to note that two of the elements — the locally distributed facility and transportation — have complementary roles. That is, as facilities become more widely distributed, the need for transportation capacity diminishes. For example, the advent of television has reduced the need for many trips by foot or car to the movie houses. In other words, the equipment for a certain kind of entertainment has been distributed more widely.

This example might lead us to speculate that in the future (assuming uninterrupted technological advance and rising incomes) all facilities will be virtually privatized (the ultimate in distribution), causing the structure of the city to approximate the situation depicted in Figure 12.2a. Everyone would have what he wants at his doorstep. As a practical matter, however, the level of public and private poverty will no doubt always remain high enough so that some facilities will have to be shared. Geography will also contribute to the same result. A community may have a municipal beach, but not everyone can have a beach in his own back yard (even though many attempt this with swimming pools). For such reasons urban structure will continue to be a compromise between the forces of concentration and the forces of distribution.

Not only does Figure 12.2c represent the anatomy of the city, but it also gives us in schematic form the basis for a city plan as illustrated in Figure 12.2d, a diagram from the 1960 Comprehensive Plan for Philadelphia. Current American standards and capabilities require that certain facilities be distributed throughout the city so as to be within easy reach of all. Small parks and playgrounds, schools, neighborhood shopping centers, and fire and police stations fall into this category. Other facilities such as beaches, sport stadia, or large department stores can be distributed only by being made more accessible through transportation planning.

URBAN FORM.    Cities exist to meet human needs, an objective met in part through the local distribution of some facilities. Nevertheless, a certain amount of friction always remains in the urban system as considerable time and energy must be spent in traveling to meet needs that cannot be satisfied locally (Haig, 1927). The problem then, an especially important one in this era of energy shortage, is how this remaining or *residual distance* can be reduced to the lowest possible degree.

Residual distance may be reduced, first of all, through adjustments in the overall spatial pattern or form of the community. Consider again Figure 12.2c. The obvious effect in this situation is much commuting between place of residence and the great community centers. But consolidate all facilities at one great center, as in Figure 12.2e, and the distance to be covered will decrease. It will decrease even further if the consolidated facilities are placed at the center of population (Figure 12.2f). As compared with the others, the arrangement in Figure 12.2f allows a considerable saving in community time and energy. In short, reducing residual distance requires that one center in the urban field be preeminent in size and location. This gives functional significance to the central business district of the community and to the radial form of the metropolis.

Residual distance can also be reduced through improvements in the transportation system (Haig, 1927), thereby making peripheral parts of the community more accessible. This effect can be achieved by building additional transportation routes, by extending and improving existing routes (widening them, for example), and by operational changes in the form of well-designed and well-regulated traffic control systems to facilitate smooth traffic flow. Finally, the substitution of telecommunication (radio, telephone, television) for transportation also contributes to the reduction of residual distance, although by other than physical means (Meier, 1962).

*HIERARCHY.* Urban structure, as we have shown, is the product of a compromise between those social and economic forces which tend toward the widest possible spatial distribution of facilities and those which tend toward their closest spatial concentration. Some people (the very young, the very old, the poor) cannot travel very far to facilities. The facilities they require must, so to speak, go to them. On the other hand, there are limits on the extent to which some facilities can be distributed. Certain types, in order to exist at all, require the patronage of very large numbers of people. For this reason there are comparatively few of them and they must be located at the most accessible points in the community. These are the types of facilities which typically come together to form one large facility center ("downtown" or a large regional shopping center). Examples are hotels, banks, theaters, fancy restaurants. Other facilities such as convenience food

**Figure 12–3** The hierarchical aspect of urban structure—the whole and the part. a. Urban structure is hierarchical. b. For each set of facilities a service area. c. For each service area a center. d. Highways differentiated in design and capacity according to the centers they serve. e. A hierarchy of communities based upon successively wider interests and fostering a progressively wider sense of place. (A from *J. of Amer. Inst. of Planners*, Vol 26, No. 2, 1960. B, C, D, E from Philadelphia Comprehensive Plan, Philadelphia City Plan. Commission, 1960.)

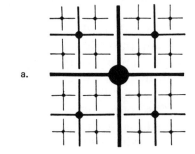
a.

stores, bars, or gas stations need comparatively fewer people to support them, and it is these that are able to distribute themselves closer to the residences of their users. Between these two extremes are centers of various sizes with service areas of different ranges (Figure 12.3). Thus there emerges a natural *hierarchic design*.

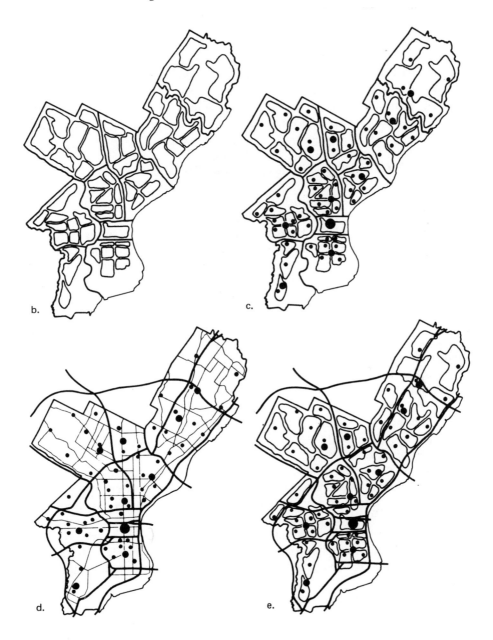

Figure 12.3a is an idealized rendering of the hierarchic tendency in urban structure. It says: for each level in the hierarchy there is a set of appropriate facilities; for each set of facilities there is a service area; for each service area there is a center; highways differ in design and capacity according to the importance of the centers they serve. Finally, there exists a hierarchy of communities based on successively wider interests and fostering a progressively wider sense of place.

Of course, the boundaries between communities indicated in Figure 12.3a must not be regarded as walls. Human social groups at any level in the hierarchy are too complex, their activities too fluid for them to be neatly contained within a single set of boundaries. Nevertheless, the hierarchic *tendency* is a definite fact of social and economic life, and, if its limitations are kept in mind, it provides a useful model for the planning of the physical city.

*THE WHOLE AND THE PART.*   Potential conflict is built into urban structure just as firmly as is order. To understand why, let us again consider the three basic elements of urban structure. The locally distributed facility becomes the basis for local organization of human activities. The non-distributed facility and the transportation element, on the other hand, become the bases for more-than-local organization (city-wide). These different levels of community generate opposed points of view with respect to every inch of land in the city. Such conflicts are aggravated when the local residents constitute a distinct social group with its own customs, institutions and lifestyle. The famous ethnic neighborhoods of the past come to mind here — the "little Italys," the Jewish ghettos, "Chinatown." Negro ghettos of the present day are of the same nature, although the segregation is less voluntary.

For the local community its neighborhood is "home." For the broader community the same territory is part of its own domain, a geographic resource for which it may have its own "superior" uses. The importance of this difference in outlook can hardly be overstated. It was an attempt to locate a hospital on local "turf" which sparked the devastating Newark, New Jersey riot of 1967.

Because of such conflicts, some advocates of local control now demand unlimited neighborhood sovereignty. They regard any attempt to regulate local affairs as an act of imperialism on the part of another neighborhood, usually the Central Business District. But neighborhood nationalism is hardly the means of relieving the social stresses inherent in urban structure. Rather, land-use arrangements are required which will permit both local and supra-local functions to coexist in the same area. Here urban planning can play a useful role.

Almost 50 years ago a generalized solution to the problem was proposed by the social reformer Clarence Perry in the New York Regional Plan.

The Neighborhood Unit, as he called it, was conceived as a framework for rational planning in residential areas. The social purpose of the unit was to provide a safe and healthful environment for family life. The neighborhood, which would be protected from the hazards of traffic and other disturbing influences, would contain facilities for primary group living, such as the elementary school and the playground. In the 1940s and 1950s, the Neighborhood Unit idea was denounced by some influential planners as an instrument of class and race exclusiveness, even though others pointed out that its discriminatory uses did not necessarily invalidate the technical concept itself.

*DENSITY.* In addition to form and hierarchy, there is a third dimension of urban structure — *density.* By density we mean the crowdedness of land, the intensity with which it is occupied by people or structures. Density is an important factor in determining the quality of urban life. In his book, *Design With Nature*, Ian McHarg suggests that high density in Philadelphia is associated with such personal and social disorders as syphilis, heart disease, alcoholism, and juvenile delinquency. This apparent connection with human well-being leads us to consider what causes density or, rather, what causes variations in density. In Figure 12.4, X represents one kind of facility and Y another. If a person (or business firm) needs access to X only, he would locate there. But what about the person who needs access to both X and Y? Now the question is whether the several possible location requirements of a single individual are compatible.

Figure 12.4 shows that the locational needs of our hypothetical individual are not beyond compromise. He can reconcile them to some extent by locating at a point where access to both facilities is adequate, but where access to neither of them is optimal. If X is one facility and Y another, then there is likely to be a point B from which both are accessible in proportion to the individual's needs. In this simple example, the relationship of B to X and Y constitutes a good part of its value as a location to the establishment or individual in question.

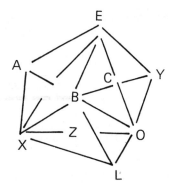

**Figure 12–4** Hypothetical framework for locational choice. If X is one point of opportunity and Y another, there is likely to be a point B from which both are accessible in proportion to the needs of the person (or business enterprise) who seeks them. (From *J. of Am. Inst. of Planners*, Vol. 26, No. 2, 1960.)

If all persons had the same needs and preferences, then all would try to locate at one point — for example, the point B. But all persons do not have the same needs and preferences, a fact which accounts for the value of all points and for the populating of the whole field. Nevertheless, the whole field is not evenly populated, for although every point is valuable to some people, not all are valuable to the same number of people. There are three general reasons for this. First, social forces operate to create like needs and interests in many persons. Second, because of their locations, certain points in the urban field offer better opportunities for access to the rest of the field (Haig, 1927). Such points are able to satisfy diverse locational interests. Third, there are certain points in the urban field which are inherently valuable because of their special natural or cultural qualities.

In the course of time and history, one area in a community acquires a fame far exceeding that of any other location. Here occurred the events which may have shaped the community or even the nation, and which have made it, in a sense, sacred ground. Here, too, are the famous shops, galleries, theaters, restaurants and grand residences which thrive on the high name of the place at the same time that they add to it their own lustre. People throng to it from all directions, and roads are built to facilitate their travel. Thus it becomes in the truest sense the community's chief central place and its symbolic home. Examples are Central Boston, Manhattan, Chicago's Loop, and Philadelphia's Central City. Adversity may engulf them and render them ugly and disorderly for a time, but it can never permanently deprive them of their greatness.

Where one place is supreme, every other point in the community acquires a value which is some fraction of the value of the chief place, the amount depending on how well it is able to substitute for the chief place. The better it can substitute, the more desirable it becomes as a place of business or residence; hence it tends to be more intensively occupied by households, establishments, and structures. Since places differ in their ability to substitute for the center, they differ also in their density.

**Figure 12–5** Density—its basis in urban structure. a. Density tends to decline with distance from the Central Business District (point O). b. The basis of density is accessibility to all facilities in the city as a group as well as to particular facilities. Accessibility is greater at the major center and subcenters . . . c . . . along major transportation routes and near expressway interchanges and mass transit stations . . . d . . . and declines with distance from all access-privileged points. e. The density pattern of a city is the complex resultant of all density-producing factors. (a from *J. of Am. Inst. of Planners*, Vol. 26, No. 2. 1960. b, c, d, e from Philadelphia Comprehensive Plan, Philadelphia City Planning Commission, 1960.)

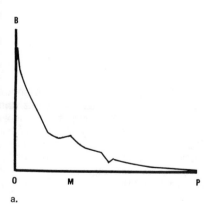

As a rule, as one leaves the metropolitan center, ease of access to the center declines, and with it substitute or *referred value* also declines (Figure 12.5a). In fact, a metropolitan region may be said to end (point P, Figure 12.5a) where it is no longer possible to substitute for the center (point O). That is, the time and expense required to reach the center for daily or

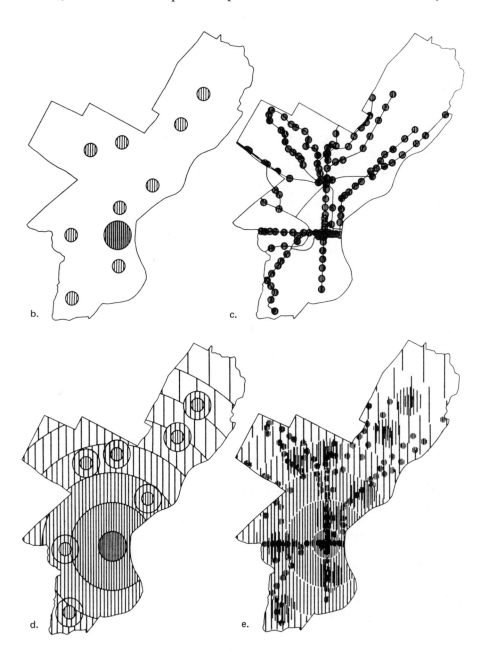

weekly functions are so great that they render the trip prohibitive. The rise or fall of referred value with distance from the center is the basic *value density gradient* which underlies all forms of the *physical density gradient*.

The general slope of the value gradient depends primarily on transportation efficiency in substituting more peripheral for more central location (Haig, 1927). Hypothetically, every point in the urban field has a density potential determined by its distance from the center when a given level of transportation efficiency prevails. Under this hypothesis, actual deviations from the potential are of two kinds. *Positive deviations* (higher than expected densities) are induced by some transportation advantage, such as an expressway interchange, which gives quicker general access from a point (point M, Figure 12.5a) than from immediately surrounding points. Otherwise, a subpeak is caused by the presence of subcenters (clusters of distributed facilities capable of performing at least some of the functions of the chief center or other important community centers). *Negative deviations* (lower than expected densities) are induced by unfavorable site conditions, such as swampy terrain, or by public actions, such as the creation of parks, which suppress normal development in favor of amenity considerations.

*SPECIALIZED AREAS.* The value gradient is a major determinant of both the kind and the amount of land use in any given area. Units of different kinds of activity, as well as different units of the same kind, compete for a site. Normally, the site goes to that unit whose use of it will result in the highest return (Haig, 1927). As activities differ in their ability to use different sites, that is, in their ability to survive at different time-distances from the center, they become spatially sorted. Broad areas which contain either one kind of activity (residential, commercial, industrial), or one quality (high-income residential), or a typical mix of activities (hotels, offices, shops), or no activity at all originate in this way. These may be called areas of *specialized density*. They are rich or poor in particular kinds of activity.

To understand specialized areas we must consider not only the general force of rent but also the functional requirements of particular establishments. Establishments performing similar functions will have similar locational needs; therefore, they will tend to locate near each other. Or by locating near each other the establishments of a single industry may benefit through production economies which none of them could achieve if they stood alone. For example, they may develop around them a common pool of employees or suppliers. Or they may use transportation facilities provided by the public or by a railroad.

But not all specialized areas contain establishments c: a single type. Some areas are specialized in the sense that they contain a stable mix of linked establishments of different types. There is a tendency for certain establishments to locate near each other because they are in some way functionally related. Two establishments are linked when they complement or supplement each other's work, as in the case of a restaurant which feeds the workers of a nearby factory. Another case would be two firms, one of which uses the other's wastes or by-products as the main raw material for its own product.

Residential establishments (households) are also linked, although here the linkage is more properly called social than functional.

*DENSITY AND RESIDENTIAL AMENITY.* We have seen how variations in referred value underly all forms of physical density. But the relationship between the value gradient and physical density is by no means simple or direct. Whether or not high value (rent) at a given distance from the center is translated into high residential density depends on the economic power of the establishments involved, that is, on the wealth of the households. Obviously, poor households can afford less space at a given rent than well-to-do households. The tremendous pressure to which the poor are subjected in central areas and the suffering it entails are well known. Squeezed into meager quarters, they pay the price in terms of disease and personal demoralization. The history of social reform in general and of community planning in particular is, to a considerable extent, the story of attempts to relieve central congestion. Such attempts necessarily require changes in urban structure, which we shall touch on in the following section. But, although both reformers and social scientists have made much of the evil effects of congestion on human life, it is only fair to note that density in itself is not a sufficient measure of the quality of a residential area. The importance of density varies in relation to the needs of people as well as in relation to other environmental characteristics. If the quality of a residential area were simply a result of its density, we could say that any apartment house area is always lower in residential quality than any area of single homes. Clearly, there are other factors involved, such as the design of houses, their age, the type of equipment they contain, the income of the residents, the public services provided in the neighborhood, and the neighborhood itself. Another variable affecting the quality of a residential area is the life situation of the residents relative to the type of dwelling. High-rise buildings are clearly less suited for families with children to supervise than they are for childless families.

*URBAN GROWTH AND ITS CONSEQUENCES.* It would be inappropriate to close even this brief account of the elements of urban structures without some reference to the changes that occur when an American city grows. To understand these changes properly, we must set them against a background of population movement which has characterized this nation for many years — the increasing concentration of the population in metropolitan areas. With rising agricultural productivity, energies formerly bound up in the production of food and fiber are released for urban employment. As a result, the population of metropolitan areas is increasing at a much faster rate than the population of the nation as a whole. Rapid urbanization is a worldwide phenomenon, but in the United States the greatest population growth is in the suburbs.

Urban growth means increase in the size of the city as well as adjustment of urban structure to the increased size. More specifically, growth entails the gradual adjustment of urban structure to a larger territorial scale, the relocation of major facilities and centers to serve a human and industrial population capable of wider dispersal.

In the recent past growth has so often been praised as an unqualified good that its relation to personal and social disorder tends to elude us. As explained earlier, every point in a city derives its social and economic value primarily from its position in the total structure. When the structure expands, population movements ensue as many people and establishments seek to improve their position in the expanding structure or at least to regain lost vantage points. In the process of expansion, therefore, the fate of individuals as well as of whole subcommunities of the metropolitan region is involved.

Among the subcommunities which suffer the consequences of growth is the central city of the metropolitan area. As the result of adjustment to a larger scale, its boundaries cease to coincide with the boundaries of the total functional community (Figure 12.6). As illustrated in Figure 12.6a, a service vacuum caused by excessive distance of population from the existing center is eventually filled by a newer center arising outside the central city. The influence of the new center ranges deep into the service area of the old, bringing about the reorientation of additional large numbers of people. The newer center, of course, may also arise within the boundaries of the central city (Figure 12.6b). From the standpoint of the metropolitan consumer, either development is acceptable since the difference between the two locations may be only a matter of a few miles. But to the political subcommunities of the metropolitan region vying with one another for tax ratables, it appears as a major difference in location.

Thus the forces of metropolitan growth and change include three factors: 1) technological advances, such as the modern expressway, which make possible the organization of urban life on a vastly wider geographic scale than previously; 2) numberless private decisions to relocate in response to the expanding urban framework; and 3) political fragmentation of the metropolitan community. The last warrants further comment in view of the conscious maneuvers of the politically independent suburb to bring about a shift of wealth and power in its own favor. This is a common objective, even though it may be stated in far more ingenuous terms as "a workable tax economy" to be achieved by means of "limited and balanced growth." The land-use meaning of limited growth is large-lot zoning and low density; the

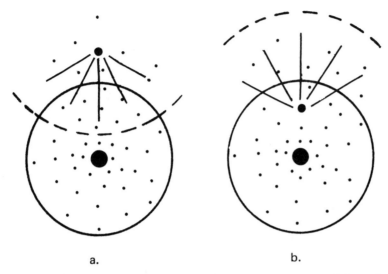

a.                                    b.

**Figure 12–6** Structural adjustment to growth—two cases. a. New activity centers may develop inside or outside the city boundaries. Here new growth centers have arisen outside the city and have cut deep into the service areas of older centers. b. The situation depicted here—new centers within the boundaries—may be more salutary from the standpoint of municipal solvency as well as jobs and services for minority groups. (A and B from *J. of Am. Inst. of Planners*, Vol. 26, No. 2, 1960.)

social meaning is exclusion of the poor and underprivileged; the fiscal meaning is low service costs. Balanced growth, on the other hand, means the selection of "clean," revenue-producing industries, such as research firms, and the rejection of low-income, service-demanding (hence revenue-consuming) families. However stated, the effect is to make of the political boundary of the central city a line separating the costs from the benefits of urban growth (Guttenberg, 1964).

Unplanned urban growth also contributes to environmental deterioration. Here the first image that comes to mind is of tacky suburban subdivisions, bulldozed trees, exposed topsoil, and overflowing septic tanks. We are not nearly so ready to see the connection between urban growth and inner-city decay, yet the connection definitely exists. Since growth means a farther-flung population to be served, the existing central districts are no longer entirely convenient places from which to serve them. Losing their normal time-distance relationships to a dispersing population, they become dislocated. Dislocated, the core of the city undergoes the ordeal of economic and social succession. Its original activities and its population begin to leave for new suburban locations. For those who remain behind, the process is a costly one, accompanied by the personal, social, and environmental disorder commonly termed blight. Thus suburban sprawl and the decay of the core, although separated by many miles, are but two sides of the same coin.

The plight of black residents is especially prominent in this dynamic setting. As the jobs move out to the suburbs, the Blacks often remain in the central ghettos, held there by their poverty as well as by such discriminatory legal practices as exclusionary zoning. Thus they are deprived of easy access to work opportunities which are shifting away from them.

Urban growth has also, in a special sense, impoverished the new suburbanite, black and white. It has estranged him from the life of the central city, yet he has not escaped its responsibilities and problems. For, as the middle class retreats to the suburbs, it must maintain contact with its besieged central political and economic institutions. For this purpose the expressways and the commuter lines knife their way through the ghettos. As one observer has noted, the suburbs get the stations and the ghettos get the tracks.

*REGAINING CONTROL OF OUR CITIES.* Clearly, Norton Long's assessment of what ails urban America is confirmed. Our cities have not failed us. We have failed them, preferring consumership to citizenship. As a result the metropolitan community is increasingly divided into two hostile camps. If it is ever to function again as a social and economic unit, strong remedies are required: metropolitan government, firm open-occupancy laws, tax reforms.

At the same time, it is apparent that only a revival of the local civic spirit can provide the will and energy for the required reforms. The nation waits expectantly for a prototype, an example. As Long has observed, the first metropolitan area that experiences a rebirth of local responsibility and "succeeds in creating a political form and a philosophy and leadership to go with it will ensure . . . the emergence of a great new age of cities in the United States" (Long, 1965).

## REFERENCES

ALEXANDER, C. 1965. A city is not a tree. *Architectural Forum* 1965:58–62.

ADVISORY COMMISSION ON INTERGOVERNMENTAL RELATIONS. 1968. *Urban and Rural America: Policies for Future Growth.* Washington, D.C.: U.S. Govt. Printing Office.

ALONSO, W. 1964. *Location and Land Use.* Cambridge, Mass.: Harvard Univ. Press.

BLUMENFELD, H. 1967. *The Modern Metropolis.* P. D. Spreiregen, ed. Cambridge: MIT Press.

BOLLENS, J. C., AND H. C. SCHMANDT. 1970. *The Metropolis.* New York: Harper & Row.

BOURNE, L. S., ED. 1971. *Internal Structure of the City.* New York: Oxford Univ. Press.

BURGESS, E. W. 1925. The growth of the city. In *City*, R. E. Park, ed. Chicago: Univ. of Chicago Press.

CANTER, D. 1970. How Negro removal became black renewal. *City.* 1970:55–59.

CHAPIN, F. S., JR. 1965. *Urban Land Use Planning.* Urbana: Univ. of Illinois Press.

CHAPIN, F. S., JR. 1966. *Household Activity Systems.* Chapel Hill: Center for Urban & Regional Studies, Univ. of North Carolina.

CHINITZ, B., ED. 1964. *City and Suburbs.* Englewood Cliffs, N.J.: Prentice-Hall.

CONKIN, P. K. 1959. *Tomorrow a New World: The New Deal Community Program.* Ithaca: Cornell Univ. Press.

CUNNINGHAM, J. V. 1965. *The Resurgent Neighborhood.* Notre Dame, Ind.: Fides Publishers.

DOWNS, A. 1968. Alternative futures in the American ghetto. *The Appraisal Journal.* Pp. 486–530.

EDITORS OF FORTUNE. 1957. *The Expanding Metropolis.* New York: Doubleday Anchor Books.

EKIRCH, A. E. 1963. *Man and Nature in America.* New York: Columbia Univ. Press.

EWALD, W., JR. 1967. *Environment for Man.* Bloomington: Univ. of Indiana Press.

FISHER, R. M., ED. 1955. *The Metropolis in Modern Life.* Garden City, N.Y.: Doubleday & Co.

GALLION, A. B., AND S. EISNER. 1963. *The Urban Pattern.* Princeton, N.J.: Van Nostrand.

GANS, H. J. 1962. *The Urban Villagers.* Glencoe, N.Y.: Free Press.

GIEDION, S. 1967. *Space, Time, and Architecture.* Cambridge: Harvard Univ. Press.

GLAAB, C. N., AND T. A. BROWN. 1967. *A History of Urban America.* New York: Macmillan.

GOODMAN, P., AND P. GOODMAN. 1960. *Communitas.* New York: Vintage Books.

GUTHEIM, F. 1963. Urban space and urban design. In *Cities in Space,* L. Wingo, ed. Baltimore: Johns Hopkins Press.

GREER, S. 1962. *The Emerging City.* New York: Free Press.

GUTKIND, E. A. 1962. *The Twilight of Cities.* Glencoe, N.Y.: Free Press.

GUTTENBERG, A. Z. 1964. The tactical plan. In *Explorations into Urban Structure,* M. M. Webber, et al. Philadelphia: Univ. of Penn. Press.

GUTTENBERG, A. Z. 1960. The general concepts of the comprehensive plan. In *Philadelphia Comprehensive Plan.* Philadelphia: Philadelphia City Planning Commission.

GUTTENBERG, A. Z. 1960. Urban structure and urban growth. *Journal of the American Inst. Plan.* 26(2):104–110.

HAIG, R. M. 1927. *Major Economic Factors in Metropolitan Growth and Arrangement.* Vol. I of *Regional Survey of New York and its Environs,* New York, N.Y.: Regional Plan Association.

HANSEN, W. B. 1961. An approach to the analysis of metropolitan residential extension. *Reg. Sci. Journal.* 3(1)37–55.

HARRIS, C. D., AND E. L ULLMAN. 1945. The nature of cities. *Ann. of Am. Acad. of Pol. and Soc. Sci.* 242:3.

HILST, C. R. 1970. Pollution: another dimension of urbanization. In *Urban America: The Expert Looks at the City,* D. Moynihan, ed. Voice of America Forum Lectures.

HOYT, H. 1939. *The Structure and Growth of Residential Neighborhoods in American Cities.* Washington, D.C.: U.S. Govt. Printing Office.

HOWARD, E. 1965. *Garden Cities of Tomorrow.* Cambridge: MIT Press.

ISAACS, R. 1948. The neighborhood theory: an analysis of its adequacy. *Journal of Am. Inst. Plan.* 14(2):15–23.

JACOBS, J. 1969. *The Economy of Cities.* New York: Random House.

JACOBS, J. 1961. *The Death and Life of Great American Cities.* New York: Random House.

JEFFERSON, T. 1903. *Writings of Thomas Jefferson.* Washington, D.C.: Thomas Jefferson Memorial Assoc. 2:228–30.

JOINT ECONOMIC COMMITTEE, CONGRESS OF THE UNITED STATES. 90TH CONGRESS, 1ST SESSION. 1967. *Urban America: Goals and Problems.* Washington, D.C.: U.S. Govt. Printing Office.

KAIN, J .F. 1965. *The Effect of the Ghetto on the Distribution and Level of Nonwhite Employment in Urban Areas.* Santa Monica, Cal.: Rand Corp.

KOTLER, M. 1969. *Neighborhood Government.* Indianapolis and New York: Bobbs-Merrill.

KRAMER, J., ED. 1972. *North American Suburbs.* California: The Glendessary Press.

LEVIN, M. R. 1971. *Exploring Urban Problems.* Boston: The Urban Press.

LONG, N. 1965. Citizenship or consumership in metropolitan areas. *Journal of the American Inst. Plan.* 31(1):2–6.

LUBOVE, R. 1963. *Community Planning in the 1920s.* Pittsburgh: Univ. Pittsburgh Press.

LYNCH, K. 1960. *The Image of the City.* Cambridge: The Technology Press & Harvard Univ. Press.

MCHARG, I. 1969. *Design with Nature.* New York: Natural History Press, Am. Mus. Nat. Hist.

MCLUHAN, M. 1964. *Understanding Media.* New York: Signet Books.

MEIER, R. L. 1962. *A Communications Theory of Urban Growth.* Cambridge: MIT Press.

MUMFORD, L. 1961. *The City in History: Its Origins, Its Transformations and Its Prospects.* New York: Harcourt, Brace & World.

NATIONAL ADVISORY COMMISSION ON CIVIL DISORDERS. 1968. *Report of the National Advisory Commission on Civil Disorders.* Washington, D.C.: U.S. Govt. Printing Office.

NATIONAL COMMISSION ON URBAN PROBLEMS. 1968. *Building the American City.* House Document No. 91–34, 91st Congress, 1st Session. Washington, D.C.: U.S. Govt. Printing Office.

PERIN, C. 1970. *With Man in Mind.* Cambridge: MIT Press.

PERRY, C. A. 1929. The neighborhood unit, *Neighborhood and Community Planning.* Vol. VII of *Regional Survey of New York and its Environs*, New York, N.Y.: Regional Plan Association.

PINCHOT, G. 1925. Message to the General Assembly of the Commonwealth of Penna, February 17. *Legislative Journal—Senate*, 126th Session of the General Assembly, Vol. 8, No. 13, p. 501.

PIRENNE, H. 1956. *Medieval Cities: Their Origin and the Revival of Trade.* Garden City, N.Y.: Doubleday.

PURDOM, C. B. 1925. *Building Satellite Towns.* London: Dent.

RATCLIFF, R. U. 1949. *Urban Land Economics.* New York: McGraw-Hill.

REPS, J. 1965. *The Making of Urban America.* Princeton, N.J.: Princeton Univ. Press.

SCOTT, M. 1969. *American City Planning Since 1890.* Berkeley: Univ. Calif. Press.

SENNETT, R. 1970. *The Uses of Disorder.* New York: Knopf.

SILBER, J. 1971. An age rejects history. *Washington Post*, May 30.

STRONG, A. L. 1971. *Planned Urban Environments: Sweden, Finland, Israel, The Netherlands, France.* Baltimore: Johns Hopkins Press.

THOMLINSON, R. 1969. *Urban Structure.* New York: Random House.

THOMPSON, W. 1965. *A Preface to Urban Economics.* Baltimore: Johns Hopkins Press.

WHITE, M. AND L. WHITE. 1962. *The Intellectuals and the City.* Cambridge: Harvard Univ. Press.

WILSON, J. Q. 1966. *Urban Renewal: The Record and the Controversy.* Cambridge: MIT Press.

WIRTH, L. 1938. Urbanism as a way of life. *Am. Journal Sociol.* 44:1–24.

WHYTE, W. H. 1968. *The Last Landscape.* New York: Doubleday and Co.

YEATES, M. H. AND B. J. GARNER. 1971. *The North American City.* New York: Harper & Row.

# PART FOUR

# Man's Confrontation
# with his Environment

# · 13 ·

JOSEPH KASTELIC

# Feeding the Human Population

In the last analysis, life can be viewed as a ceaseless web of energy conversions which follow well-known principles of energy conservation and transformation. Many ecologists describe an ecosystem in terms of the energy that flows into and out of it and from one trophic level to another. To an animal or microorganism, of course, energy means food. An organism's relationship to its food supply and the food supply of others, whether that organism is an earthworm or a man, is therefore a focal point in ecology.

Chapters 9 and 10 discussed how changes in the methods of procuring food and the new relationships to the environment that accompanied these changes were fundamental to the rich variety of human cultures that evolved. This chapter will focus on the influences of man's food-procuring activities on the various ecosystems of which he is a part, and on some aspects of human nutrition and diet and their tangle of relationships with culture and the environment.

## FOOD SYSTEMS

The way in which people obtain their food is related to their social customs, technology, and physical environment. The social and technological aspects of the food system depend, in turn, on the way in which people perceive their resources and envision ways of using them. Some of the American Indians in the Great Basin, located between the Rocky Mountains and the western coastal ranges, recognized that when mounted on horses obtained from the Spanish, they could become efficient hunters of buffalo. Others, seeing horses as direct competitors for limited food supplies, ate the horses.

Chapter 3 discussed some of the ways in which populations of plants and animals are controlled in size. It is not common in nature for a population to reach the point where food becomes the factor limiting further growth. Before that happens, increased disease, predation, territorial disputes, or behavioral and physiological changes resulting in decreased fertility are likely to intervene. Through culture, however, our species has evaded many of the usual controls, with the result that availability of food has played and will continue to play a major role in determining the size of the human population, unless voluntary social controls become effective.

*ENERGY INPUTS INTO THE ACQUISITION OF FOOD.* It is possible to relate what is known about the growth and distribution of human populations to the technology for obtaining food. For hunting and gathering societies, the amount of land required to support a person varies from a fraction of a square mile to several square miles or more depending on the available resources. At one extreme, some islands and coastal areas where food is richly and continuously abundant can support populations of ten or fifteen per square mile. At the other extreme, in the most inhospitable parts of their generally inhospitable range, the Shoshone Indians of the Great Basin lived at a density of one person per 50 or 100 square miles.

Clearly, the energy value of food obtained by foraging must exceed the energy expended in obtaining it. Under the most favorable conditions, the ratio of energy gained to energy expended can be as high as 10 to 1. But even in the bleak and limited environment of the North American Great Basin, the Shoshone Indians, because of the simplicity of their culture, had abundant leisure time after their requirements for food had been met. They existed at the minimum level of human organization, the family — self-sufficient unit of a man, a woman, and their children. Their tools were few, consisting chiefly of simple baskets, digging sticks for harvesting edible roots, and clubs and nets for hunting rabbits. Several families might come together for a rabbit hunt, but these alliances were temporary because no one could predict when or where conditions would next be favorable for another such endeavor. Because of fluctuations in rainfall and frequent droughts, no one food supply was dependable. But each Shoshone family was intimately acquainted with its terrain and knew exactly when, where, and under what conditions various food supplies would become available. They harvested about 100 species of plants as well as rabbits, grasshoppers, pronghorn antelope, and fish, in season. The limitations of their environment and the simplicity of their technology and social organization prevented them from elaborating a complex culture which would have required additional time and energy. As a result, in contrast to the common notion that people of hunting and gathering societies lead exhausting and precarious lives, the Shoshone enjoyed a great deal of leisure time.

The Shoshone's energy needs were hardly more than the 2,500 calories or so it took to maintain his body. Lacking the technology to store or preserve food, he had no incentive to accumulate more than enough to meet his

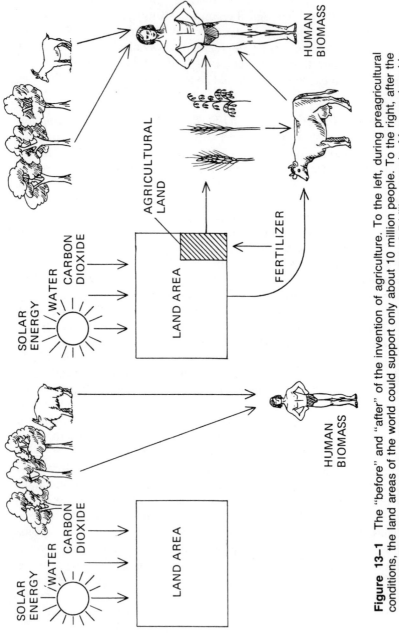

**Figure 13–1** The "before" and "after" of the invention of agriculture. To the left, during preagricultural conditions, the land areas of the world could support only about 10 million people. To the right, after the dawn of agriculture, 10 percent of this same land area now supports 3.5 billion people. Man receives his food both directly from agricultural produce and indirectly from animals who have been fed agricultural produce. Of course some animal food comes from the land area not under agriculture, and some of man's food comes from other sources such as the oceans. (Adapted from *Scientific American*, Sept. 1970, pp. 162–163.)

immediate needs; he could not cope with surplus. Contrast this with modern America, where the energy used by each person is approaching 100 times the energy he consumes as food. The excess energy supports not the people, but their culture.

A pastoral way of life may support fifteen or twenty people per square mile. Because of limitations of the environment and the amount of land required for grazing domestic animals, population densities remain low and cultures are simple. Pastoralism is an adaptation to semiarid open country or grasslands which cannot be cultivated. It often requires cyclic migrations from lowlands to highlands, or from rainy season settlements to dry season retreats. Population pressure can lead to accumulation of excessively large herds of animals and consequent over-grazing — with the disastrous results that have occurred in parts of Africa and India, where large areas that once supported pastoral societies have been converted to barren desert. There is very little surplus energy available in a pastoral way of life, but the possession of herds of grazing animals makes life possible in environments that otherwise could support only very small human populations.

Before the invention of agriculture, the land areas of the world could support only about 10 million people. Now, with agricultural systems based on solar energy and the energy of man and his domestic animals, 10 percent of this same land area can support 3.5 billion people, or about 25 to 200 people per square mile, depending on the environment and level of technology (Figure 13.1). Under the most favorable conditions, the yield from simple agriculture based on rice and water buffalo or cattle is 50 calories for every calorie expended by man, and the population density exceeds 600 per square mile. The animals provide power, meat, milk, hides, horn, and fertilizer, and they do not compete with man for food. At the other end of the scale, various systems of shifting agriculture yield between 10 and 20 calories for every calorie of work. When the proportion of the land that must lie fallow at any given time is considered, it turns out that in some cases the populations supported by shifting agriculture may not exceed those supported by foraging, and comparable amounts of labor are performed in the two systems. The difference, then, is not in the extent to which resources are exploited, but in a preference for one way of life or the other.

With simple industry and trade, populations can exist at a density of about 200 to 250 people per square mile. Here the level of exploitation of resources is significantly increased, and machines perform some of the work of man. Modern industry, integrated with efficient transportation and industrialized agriculture, supports populations whose maximum densities are determined locally, at least in the short run, by factors other than the availability of food. Thus the population of Manhattan has reached a density of some 75,000 people per square mile. The coming of industrialized agriculture, however, has brought a fundamental change in the energy relationships between man and his food supply. Instead of yielding net energy, the industrialized food system is a major *consumer* of energy! On the farm alone, between 2 and 5 calories are expended for every calorie gained; and when the total food system is considered, as it must be in any complete reckoning of the amount of energy modern Americans use in feeding themselves, the ratio of energy input to energy output approaches 10 to 1. The energy required merely to manufacture fertilizer for an acre of agricultural land may, for some crops, exceed the energy value of the harvest.

There are many ways of viewing the relationships between energy, land area, and population density, and the reader must be wary in interpreting statistics. The fact that the actual labor performed by one farmer may yield 400 calories for every calorie expended says very little except that agriculture, American style, is very efficient in terms of *human labor on the farm*. The high density of population in cities does not negate the fact that about 2 acres of agricultural land and 3 acres of grazing land are presently devoted to feeding each American. Thus the average population density on land utilized for the support of the population is about 130 per square mile — a level which can also be sustained by a much simpler system. And not only is the urban ecosystem closely coupled to the industrialized agricultural system, but both are coupled to the ecosystems which as yet have been modified to only a minor extent by man. The growing problems of pollution, agricultural productivity, and the availability of energy are creating serious doubts about the long-term stability of our present food system.

Discounting the energy actually used for photosynthesis, Figure 13.2 summarizes the relationships between energy input and energy gained for various methods of procuring food. Superimposed on the illustration is a graph showing the energy subsidy for the U.S. food system, from 1910 to 1970. This includes not only energy used on the farm, but energy used in the processing, distribution, storage, and preparation of food, and in the manufacture of related equipment and materials. The system must be considered as a whole, because the whole is involved in our breakfast of frozen orange juice from Florida, bacon from a midwestern meat packer, cereal from Nebraska, coffee from Colombia and perhaps eggs and milk from not *too* far away — purchased at the supermarket 4.7 miles away, stored in a frost-free refrigerator-freezer, and prepared on an instant-on gas or electric stove. Figure 13.3 shows a portion of the graph plotted on a different scale, comparing the energy subsidy to the food system with the actual food energy consumed by the American people.

There is a great deal of speculation, some of it disguised as science fiction, about the carrying capacity of the earth under conditions of intense industrialization. At present the major food problem is one of distribution; there is enough food to go around. But we do not know how long our finite resources can sustain this level of production or how much production can be increased through advances in agricultural science. The problem is com-

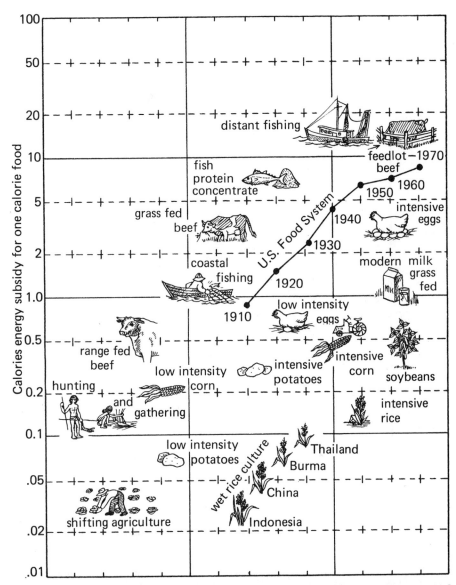

**Figure 13–2** Energy subsidies for various food crops, with energy inputs into the U.S. food system (1910–1970) for comparison. "Advanced" agriculture is energy-intensive, with many calories being expended for each calorie of food that reaches the table. Shifting agriculture (slash-and-burn), in contrast, yields between 20 and 50 calories of food for each calorie expended. Consideration of this diagram should lead us to question the desirability of exporting the food system and eating habits of the U.S. to the hungry nations. (From C. Steinhart and J. Steinhart, Energy: *Sources, Use, and Role in Human Affairs*, Duxbury Press, N. Scituate, Mass., 1974, p. 84.

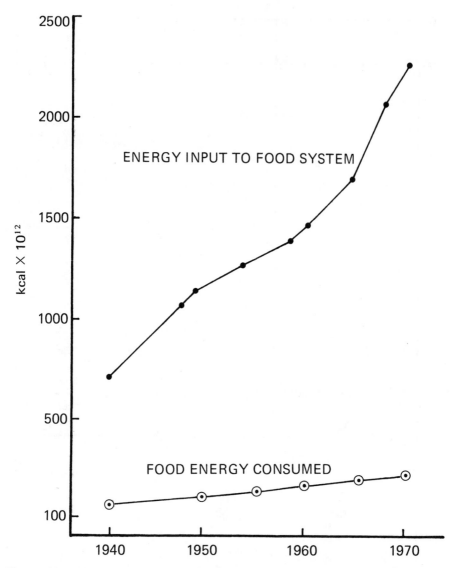

**Figure 13–3** Energy use in the food system, 1940–1970, compared to caloric energy content of the food consumed. (From C. Steinhart and J. Steinhart, *Energy: Sources, Use, and Role in Human Affairs*, Duxbury Press, N. Scituate, Mass., 1974, p. 76.)

pounded, of course, by continuing population growth. In addition, the more rapidly the nonindustrialized nations become industrialized, the more rapidly will problems of pollution and resource depletion mount.

*WORLD PRODUCTION OF FOOD: POSSIBILITIES FOR EXPANSION.* The great period of exploration and discovery which began in the Middle

Ages is over. It had to end some day, but since the time and circumstances of that end could not be foretold, it was easy to act as if it would go on forever. Today we are familiar enough with our planet to know that no hidden paradise awaits a twentieth century Marco Polo, and we can estimate, with varying accuracy, the amounts of all resources that remain. But although we can no longer pin our hopes on continual discovery of land and resources, it is difficult to shake off the belief that there is no limit to the new opportunities technology can offer. The ecological "facts of life," however, show that belief in the omnipotence of technology is as illusory as the earlier belief in the infinity of the earth and its resources.

There are three ways in which we can try to feed the growing number of human beings on earth: open up new agricultural and grazing lands, increase the productivity of the lands already in use, and develop new sources of food. The long-term success of any of these depends on the size of the population we are trying to support and on our ability to design self-sustaining systems for which there is a nondepletable source of energy and in which materials are recycled. This is the only way in which ecological balance can be maintained.

Theoretically, there is still room for expansion in some parts of the world, particularly in moist tropical lowlands. Chapter 2 discussed the amounts of land presently in use and potentially available for crops and grazing. It pointed out that the best land is already in use, and serious deficiencies must be overcome if virgin lands are to become productive. For some lands, even if technical problems were overcome, the necessary energy subsidy and resource requirements would be too enormous to make the yield worthwhile. The situation is analogous to that in which we mine lower and lower quality ore: before we actually "run out," the economic and ecologic price of continued exploitation will probably become too great. In the United States, other land uses are encroaching so rapidly on agricultural land that projections for California, for example, indicate that in less than 50 years half of that state's agricultural land will have been converted to nonagricultural uses. It is doubtful that, in opening new lands, we can run fast enough to stay where we are.

There are sound reasons for not rushing to open up vast new areas for crops or grazing, even if economic obstacles could be overcome. One of these is that agriculture, especially as practiced in industrialized nations, depends on the activities of unmanaged ecosystems for the cycling of wastes and other materials. The capacities of some of these systems are already overtaxed, and further reduction in their size would intensify the problems. Another reason for caution in expanding into new lands is that most of the potentially arable land is in regions for which present agricultural techniques are poorly suited, and new methods have not yet been adequately developed and tested. Finally, biologists point out the humble origins of our high-yielding crops of today and emphasize the importance of maintaining reservoirs of wild species from which new and valuable domesticates may be developed. Of the approximately 80,000 known species of edible plants, only about fifty are actively cultivated on a large scale, and a mere dozen comprise 90 percent of the world's crops. It does not seem a vain hope that we may be able to find new species that can help the world's food problem more than the wringing of another bushel per acre from corn. But if we destroy the remaining unmanaged ecosystems, this opportunity will be lost forever. Numerous research programs are directed toward developing agricultural methods suited to the moist tropics; but for other parts of the world, the best hope seems to be to increase the productivity of lands already in use.

DOMESTIC ANIMALS.     There are about as many large domestic animals as people in the world, and more domesticated fowl. An estimate of the livestock and poultry population of the world is given in Table 13.1. There are regional specializations in food animals: sheep in Australia, camels in Asia, water buffalo in China, and so on. Populations of mules and horses, draft animals which are not commonly used for meat and milk, are relatively small and will probably decrease further; but attempts are being made to intensify production of other animals.

Almost two thirds of the domestic animals are in nonindustrialized countries, but these countries produce only about a quarter of the world's meat, milk, and eggs. Animal diseases are one of the most serious limitations to animal production in developing countries, where a partial catalog of epidemiologic horrors includes rinderpest, contagious bovine pleuro-

TABLE 13.1
**Estimates of World Poultry and Livestock Populations**

| Animal | Number, in Millions |
|--------|--------------------|
| Total livestock | 3,270 |
| Cattle | 1,051 |
| Sheep | 1,026 |
| Pigs | 576 |
| Goats | 367 |
| Horses | 65 |
| Mules | 15 |
| Asses | 42 |
| Buffalo | 116 |
| Camels | 12 |
| Total poultry | 5,400 |
| Chickens | 5,000 |
| Ducks and geese | 300 |
| Turkeys | 100 |

Source: United Nations, 1969. FAO Production Yearbook Vol. 23

pneumonia, hemorrhagic septicemia, foot and mouth disease, African horse sickness, African swine fever, hog cholera, Newcastle disease, fowl plague, trypanosomiasis, East Coast fever, and a variety of parasitic, nutritional, and genetic diseases. Some of these have reservoirs in wild species and are transmitted by insect vectors. If the major animal diseases could be brought under control, animal production undoubtedly would be increased from 25 to 50 percent.

The method of feeding animals determines whether they will compete with man for food. In the United States where about half of the harvested agricultural land is planted with feed crops and more than three quarters of all our grain is fed to animals (as well as by-products like wheat germ from the milling of flour!), there is rising sentiment in favor of "eating lower on the food chain." In addition to the extravagant use of our own agricultural land, each year we import enough fish meal and fish protein concentrate from Peru to eliminate a large part of the protein malnutrition problem of South America; this, too, is fed to domestic animls. But it is not necessary to feed poultry and livestock in this grand manner; we have done it largely because until now it has been economically rewarding. In many countries the pig is a scavenger and keeps the premises clean; it consumes very little food that is fit for man. In some areas of the world, **ruminant animals** such as the ox and sheep are the only practical means of utilizing noncultivable lands for food production. Their grazing harvests grasses and other vegetation that could not otherwise be harvested, and they can graze rocky or wooded hillsides that cannot be plowed. With present technology, slightly more than 60 percent of the agricultural land in the world is considered to be best suited to grazing.

Animals can utilize a wide variety of agricultural and industrial wastes and by-products, much of which are now being wasted. Cattle and sheep thrive on a diet consisting solely of starch, cellulose, and sugar, with urea or urea and ammonium salts as the only source of nitrogen. Chickens wandering free to forage for insects and weed seeds may not produce 250 eggs per year, but neither do they compete with man for food, and whatever food they contribute is a net gain in energy rather than a net loss. It appears that *if* the serious animal diseases can be controlled, forage crops and range management techniques improved, and the wastes and by-products of the food system recycled through livestock and poultry as feed, then domestic animals may play a larger role in world food production — and in pollution control and resource conservation, as well.

WILD ANIMALS.   Many people still obtain all or most of their animal protein from wild animals. Eskimos live largely on caribou and seals; the reindeer, a semidomesticated caribou, is eaten in Siberia. For most people in affluent America, hunting is a sport, not a strategy for survival; but large numbers of game birds and animals are consumed, and pheasant, quail, venison, and rattlesnake meat can be purchased at gourmet grocery stores. The controlled cropping of wild game has been proposed for sub-Saharan Africa, but so far it has not been practiced on a significant scale. Instead, throughout much of Africa, hundreds of thousands of wild animals have been killed in order to reduce reservoirs of livestock disease and to permit the development of conventional livestock farming. The yield of meat from wild animals may, under certain circumstances, exceed the yield from conventional livestock operations. In one area of Rhodesia, for example, the number of animals that could be harvested annually without reducing the population in the long term was calculated and harvested by shooting. The yield of meat was estimated to be some 20 percent higher than the yield from the same area if it were fenced, provided with roads and water improvements, and stocked with cattle. Native animals have many advantages over domestic livestock, including physiologic variability — some never need to drink water, others have highly adapted foraging and digestive capabilities, and still others almost never succumb to local diseases. Yet the great herds of grazing animals are rapidly vanishing from the African savanna, just as 50 million bison were reduced to 6,000 in North America. It is not at all clear that domestic cattle are an improvement over the American bison, or that substitution of more energy-intensive cattle farming for the lightly managed natural system would be a gain for Africa.

CROPS.    Most of the people in the world subsist on a monotonous diet composed primarily of one of the major grains. This is not a phenomenon of the recent population explosion. Since the beginning of agriculture, there has been a heavy dependence on grain; bread has been the staff of life. Table 13.2 shows the principal food crops of the world. Note that the major grains comprise roughly three quarters of the total.

Thus the major efforts to increase world food production to date have been directed toward development of superior varieties of grain (Figure 13.4). Varieties traditionally grown in the nonindustrialized nations are adapted to the local vicissitudes of climate and soil, but as a result of their adaptation to marginal growing conditions, maximum yields are low. New, high-yielding varieties have been selected to take maximum advantage of light, water, fertilizers, and modern management practices. Translated into practical terms, this means that many of the new grain varieties require irrigation in places where traditional crops did not, and almost all the new crops require extensive fertilization.

It is generally agreed that the best plan for increasing the world's food supply is to continue to intensify management of cropland already under cultivation. Cultural and ecologic implications of this are profound and pervasive. The Green Revolution means industrialized agriculture: modern machinery, mining and manufacture of fertilizers, management of water resources, chemical pest control, transportation networks, storage and distribution facilities. Industrialized agriculture demands instant changes in ways of life that have persisted for centuries — the *Green* Revolution requires a *social* revolution on an immense scale.

There is no reason to limit our attention to grains, even though historically they have been of prime importance. Other crops have been, and can be, of considerable importance. The population of Ireland grew rapidly after the introduction of the potato; and it crashed even more dramatically with the potato famine of the mid-nineteenth century. For the future, the position of soybeans may be crucial. Soybeans possess the best amino acid balance (see the section on nutrition) and highest protein content of any widely grown crop. This has long been known to the Japanese, who make soybeans a staple of their diet, and to beef feedlot operators. Note, from their position on Figure 13.1, that soybeans yield about 2 calories of food energy for each calorie of energy subsidy. For grains, the Green Revolution may have gone about as far as it can go, at least in theory; but we can probably find other crops of great promise, if we look for them.

**TABLE 13.2**
**The Principal World Food Crops[1]**

| Food Crop[2] | Percent of Total Food Production on Area Cropped in the World | Production Million Metric Tons | Tons of Protein[3] (in Millions) |
|---|---|---|---|
| Wheat | 22.1 | 144 | 25 |
| Rice | 12.7 | 153 | 12 |
| Corn | 11.4 | 110 | 20 |
| Millet and sorghum | 10.1 | 46 | — |
| Barley | 6.6 | 41 | — |
| Oats | 5.0 | 45 | — |
| Rye | 3.3 | 21 | — |
| Oil seeds | 7.2 | 41 | 20 |
| Roots and tubers | 5.0 | 204 | — |
| Pulses (legumes) | 4.9 | 21 | 8 |
| Fruits and vegetables | 3.7 | — | — |
| Sugar | 1.5 | 230 | — |
| Beverage crops | 1.0 | — | — |
| | 94.5 | | |

Remainder, fibers,
rubber, and tobacco.

[1]People eat many thousands of plant and animal products. A recent compilation lists about 4,000 foods eaten by Africans alone. The amounts of most foods eaten are very small, and the food may be available for only short periods during the year, and then only in certain restricted geographic areas. These crops are produced on about 70 percent of the world's total cropped land.

[2]Excluding forage and fodder crops.

[3]The world supply of animal protein is between 20 and 25 million metric tons, of which fish constitute about 12 percent.

**Figure 13–4** An African scientist makes a varietal cross by hand pollination of wheat. (Photograph courtesy of the Rockefeller Foundation.)

We depend on plants for our lives, whether we eat them directly or first convert them to ham and eggs. Increasingly, the plants we eat are made from oil, as has been eloquently pointed out by ecologist Eugene Odum. Because of the dependence of modern agriculture on fossil fuels, and because supplies of fossil fuels are running out, we will take a closer look, in a later section, at a few specific agricultural systems in industrialized and nonindustrialized nations.

FOOD FROM THE WATER. While fishing is one of the oldest of man's industries, it has only recently begun to evolve along the lines of terrestrial-based food production systems. Basically, fishing is still hunting, or at best herding, most fishing methods depending on hopeful or indiscriminate capture. The use of trawls, large nets, and improved devices for locating schools of fish has increased the efficiency of the hunt, but has not increased the productivity of the seas. The maximum sustainable harvest of any species must be at a rate less than the rate at which stock is replaced. If the rate of harvest exceeds the rate of replacement, the size of the stock declines. This seems so obvious as not to require mentioning; yet when catches decline, the fishing industry responds with intensified efforts.

The productivity of the seas is limited by the primary productivity of aquatic plants which, in turn, is limited by the depth to which light can penetrate and by the availability of mineral nutrients. The most productive regions are along the continental shelves and in bays and estuaries where fresh and salt water mix. (Because many species of fish evolved in fresh water, they return to river estuaries to spawn.) Exceptionally high productivity is possible where there is an upwelling of nutrients from deep waters, as there is in the rich anchovy fishery off the coast of Peru. Relative to coastal regions, the open sea is a desert. However, coastal waters are also subject to pollution from land-based industry and agriculture, from sewage, and from the refining, transport, and offshore production of petroleum. Understanding of marine ecology has tempered the optimism which only a few years ago promised almost unlimited food from the sea.

About 80 percent of our aquatic food consists of marine fish. The rest is primarily fresh-water fish and invertebrates (chiefly mollusks and crustaceans). Whales and sea turtles, although the individual animals are large, contribute little to the overall food supply. Herring, pilchards, anchovies, and related forms comprise about 45 percent of the world fish catch. Next come cod, haddock, hake, and their relatives, chiefly bottom-dwellers, which provide some 15 percent of the catch. Another 15 percent consists of flatfishes, rosefishes, sea perch, mullets, and jacks. Tuna and mackerel provide about 7 percent. The most favored food fish tend to be high in the food chain — perhaps in the fourth or fifth trophic level. In Chapter 3 we saw that even though the higher-order predators may be quite large, their numbers and total mass are small relative to the species on which they feed. We could harvest much more food if we would switch our preference from carnivorous tuna to herbivorous carp. Alternatively, we could harvest the aquatic plants themselves; but, like grass, these generally require a great deal of processing to render them palatable or even digestible, and it is preferable to let an herbivorous animal transform them to high quality food for us.

Already the large whales have been hunted nearly to extinction, and failing to learn from experience, we are now increasing our efforts to capture the smaller whales. A number of major fisheries have either declined significantly or are showing signs of stress. These include the East Asian sardine, California sardine, Northwest Pacific salmon, Scandinavian herring, Barents Sea cod, Newfoundland cod, menhaden, British Columbia herring, Bering Sea flatfishes, and yellowfin tuna in the eastern Pacific. The decreased catch may or may not indicate that the sustainable yield has been exceeded; but it does mean that there is little hope of the yield being increased without ultimate depletion of the species. If we increase our catch of smaller fish, we are competing with the larger fish for their food. Yet this is precisely what we are doing. As Paul Ehrlich describes it, by analogy with the chicken farming industry, we plan to "eat up all the feed, all the eggs, all the chicks, and all the chickens simultaneously, while burning down the henhouses to keep . . . warm."

Because we may already be hunting fish as intensively as we can without permanently reducing the supply, it has been suggested that rather than devoting our resources to the building of bigger and better traditional

## FISH FARMING

*State fairs have long been renowned for recognizing successful green thumbs. Thanks to science and some creative experimentation, fish cultivation may soon capture some gardening blue ribbons. With an initial investment of $200.00, the backyard farmer who once grew tomatoes can be the proud owner of a plastic geodesic dome which will protect his yard-size fish factory. Ideally, such a backyard pond should produce enough fish to feed five. Besides reducing food bills, the project would encourage each family or group to become an ecologic unit able to produce sufficient protein for its members.*

*Backyard ponds are a spin-off of the worldwide preoccupation with satisfying protein demand through increasing fish supplies. Because population increases geometrically, the problem of feeding a hungry world magnifies daily. This year 75 million more people will have to be fed. Certain innovations or "discoveries" could increase the food supplied by the land—but it is doubtful that the land alone will ever satiate mankind's appetite. Seventy-one percent of the earth is covered by water—the natural habitat of fish. To many the water has become a panacea for man's food shortages.*

*Asia, with its historical problems of meat scarcity and expanding population, has been forced to cope with protein shortages much sooner than the West. For nearly eight centuries some Asian nations have depended on fish farming to increase natural fish supplies. Such intervention can take many forms—from nurturing eggs and young "fry" through their most vulnerable stage of development, to monitoring a mollusk's total life cycle. Rivers, lakes, and shallow areas of the ocean are farmed. Whatever the means, the end remains the same: more fish protein for a hungry world.*

fishing fleets, we should be developing methods for farming the sea. This seems to make sense, although at present such managed aquatic systems provide only a small fraction of the total food obtained from the sea. The fish farms must be located in coastal areas, where they are subject to all the problems of pollution and competing uses that threaten natural systems. Nevertheless, some attempts have brought promising results, especially as they are a means of utilizing and recycling certain wastes that otherwise would pollute the environment. A fish farm, like a land-based farm, is a simplified ecosystem with relatively few species, which must be maintained by an energy subsidy from man. But high yields can be obtained by controlling disease and predation, by fertilization with sewage or other wastes, and in some cases by utilizing waste heat discharged from electric power plants.

NOVEL SOURCES OF FOOD.    Hydroponics, the art of growing plants in water instead of soil, has been enthusiastically studied by scientists for many years, but the use of this method for commercial food production is

*In America, turning midwestern beef farmland into fish farmland is a relatively new but successful technique. The land is divided into pond sectors and then flooded. Species such as catfish are then placed in these manmade ponds. From then on their every flip is watched and analyzed.*

*A fish farmer faces unusual challenges since fish are very sensitive animals. Changes in water temperature, salinity, acidity, muddiness, toxicity, light and water depth can affect them positively or negatively. Some fish refuse to mate when watched. A knowledgeable farmer will supply "secluded" spots such as cylindrical milk cans for those fish who crave privacy. Fish growth also depends on monitoring the amount of food a fish eats. This is easy to do when a fish eats floating pelleted food. Some fish prefer to eat other living fish. Changing a fish's dietary habits takes about five weeks and is accomplished in four progressive steps: live fish to frozen fish to dried fish to pelleted fish.*

*Another novel experiment in fish culture focuses on two world problems: a need for protein and a plethora of garbage. Garbage is fed to algae which in turn is fed to shellfish. The results have been astounding. The fish thrive, the garbage disappears and a nearly perfect ecosystem emerges. The garbage is diluted with sea water and undergoes several treatments so that mineral wastes are oxidized. Even though shellfish tend to be easily polluted by viruses, bacteria, and traces of metal, the experimentally grown shellfish show no signs of adverse effects because of their diet. Researchers are currently trying to determine if the algae have an innate ability to kill bacteria. The success of this project could present man with a psychological dilemma. Man may balk at eating food grown on his own wastes. Perhaps the ultimate fate of this experiment lies in the hands of Madison Avenue. The success of recycled fish hard sell may determine the fate of a hungry and dirty world.*

limited because of the cost involved. Furthermore, the nutrients used to feed the plants must be combined and processed in an exacting manner and supplied to the plants in carefully regulated, time-spaced quantities.

Yeast has long been used as a source of vitamins and amino acids. Yeasts are bacteria-like, single-celled organisms that can readily be grown in a variety of culture media. In the United States yeasts of the genus *Torula* are frequently grown on spent sulfite liquor, a product employed in the manufacture of paper. In this way a useful product, yeast, is obtained, and a pollution problem is alleviated. Yeasts are also grown in whey, a by-product of the production of cottage cheese. This process, again, solves a disposal problem.

The annual world production of yeast is about 250,000 tons, a significant amount of which is used as animal feed. The quantity of yeast that can be produced is limited by the availability of industrial wastes suitable for culture media, but increased amounts of such wastes may be anticipated as more effort is made to abate stream pollution.

Protein can also be produced by the fermentation of petroleum. Fermentation processes have the advantages of speed of production, economy of materials, and adaptability to continuous-flow processes. Furthermore, organisms can be selected to yield any desired percentage of protein or fat. In the fermentation of petroleum, organisms can be selected that will preferentially attack only certain types of hydrocarbons, thus refining the oil by removing undesirable fractions. However, many technical problems must be solved before this method of producing protein becomes economically practical. At present the chief interest in petroleum-eating organisms lies in the cleaning up of oil spills.

Vitamins and amino acids are also manufactured by industrial fermentation and chemical processes. In 1966 the production of vitamins in the United States was about 9,000 metric tons, while the output of amino acids was about 5,000 metric tons. These materials, however, are not major sources of food, but are used only to correct nutritional imbalances. Production of these and other nutritional supplements usually requires a large energy subsidy. (Note, for example, the position of fish protein concentrate in Figure 13.2.)

*SYSTEMS OF AGRICULTURE.*    While the earliest traces of the transition to agriculture are associated with the Near East, in Mesopotamia and Egypt, there is evidence that agriculture originated independently in several parts of the world. A variety of agricultural systems were worked out through trial and error. It is difficult to guess how many attempts failed, although we have some well-documented examples from experiences of the last century. As in all evolutionary processes, agricultural systems that were well adapted to prevailing conditions survived and were perpetuated. Today, from our technological society, we look a bit superciliously at the "primitive" practices of "primitive" agriculturalists; but we fail to see that in many cases they are doing about as well as it is possible to do under the circumstances, and we should be sure we know what we are doing before we tamper with systems that have worked well for centuries. Often, when ancient methods of agriculture have failed, it has been because population pressure forced man to try to get more than the system could offer. There were also many mistakes. It is thought that soil erosion and deterioration were already major problems in many areas by the time of Christ.

The ancient Egyptians and Mesopotamians were masters in agricultural techniques. They produced an abundance of food by exploiting the natural fertility of river flood plains. They developed a variety of innovations in plant and animal domestication and the controlled use of water for irrigation.

An advanced agriculture was also practiced, somewhat later, by the Indians of South America. With only the most primitive of tools, these people built irrigation canals to collect melt water at the feet of high mountain glaciers. The canals wended carefully calculated zigzagging paths down the terraced mountainsides, where several dozen crops were planted to take advantage of the different conditions at different altitudes. Guano, the nutrient-rich excrement of sea birds, was used as fertilizer. High in the mountains, where conditions were too harsh for crops, flocks of llamas and alpacas grazed. Today this productive system has largely been abandoned in favor of the intensive monoculture of cash crops — in the name of economic progress.

Another highly successful form of agriculture, practiced in ancient Mexico, took advantage of the rich sediments at the bottom of large shallow lakes. Small island plots were built in the lakes and were tended from boats on the water. Again, a great variety of crops were planted, and there were several harvests in a year. The lakes were drained by the Spanish conquerors, and all that remains of this productive system is now only a tourist attraction: the famous "floating gardens" of Mexico City.

In some parts of the world, less favored by climate and soil, agriculture has never been highly productive, but the system that evolved was probably the best that could be expected. Slash-and-burn agriculture originated in Asia and Africa and is still practiced there and in parts of South America. Following age-old practices, plots of land are prepared for planting by the carefully controlled burning of trees, brush, and scattered branches to insure deposits of ash and the killing of shallowly rooted vegetation. The ash returns nutrients which will be utilized by the crops. Cereals are generally planted, and often a tuberous crop like the sweet potato, with varying numbers of minor crops. Sometimes pigs are kept as scavengers and as a source of meat. Weeding is a never-ending chore. When regrowth of natural vegetation and exhaustion of soil fertility force abandonment of the plot after 2 to 4 years, a new area is cleared and burned, and the forest and soil regenerate in the old plot. After a fallow period of 10 to 50 years, an area can be cultivated once again. Like any method, this works only as long as man does not overexploit the environment. Population pressure may force shortening of the fallow period and prolonging of cultivation to the point where the structure and fertility of the soil can no longer be maintained. The moist tropics are a tantalizing prospect for future agricultural ventures because of their year-round sunshine and abundant rainfall; but their soil is of about the poorest quality on earth — shallow, deficient in nutrients, and with undesirable physical properties.

The most productive nonindustrial farming system is rice growing. Rice, the principal food of 60 percent of mankind, has been grown in many humid tropical and subtropical regions for at least 5,000 years. While some rice is grown in the uplands, most is planted in fields of standing water. It is therefore ideally suited for cultivation in flood plains and river deltas. Seasonal flooding provides the water needed to flood man-made water impoundments which can be diked for alternating irrigation and drainage. The deposition of silt carried by flood water helps to maintain the fertility of the soil, insuring good rice yield over long periods of continuous cropping. In some areas, fish are grown in the fields during the period when the fields are flooded. Work may be provided by cattle or water buffalo, which at the same time supply fertilizer and additional food.

MODERN AGRICULTURE. In the Western world there have been major changes in agriculture during this century. They have resulted from advances in the physical and biological sciences, from industrial development and improved transportation, and, most of all, from the input of a huge energy subsidy in the form of fossil fuel.

Many new varieties of food plants have been introduced. Hybrid seed has transformed the production of corn, cotton, sorghum, and many other crops. Certain disease-resistant strains of plants have been developed, increasing use of inorganic fertilizers has improved crop yields, and scores of chemical agents are available for the control of weeds, insects, and microorganisms. The increase in yield that has resulted is shown for rice and wheat in Figure 13.5.

The new crops are much more uniform genetically than traditional varieties. They have been intentionally selected for uniformity in size, growth rate, time required to reach maturity, size and quality of yield, and response to environmental conditions. The miracle grains produce no miracles unless they are grown under optimum conditions. Unlike their unmiraculous but genetically heterozygous ancestors, they are uniformly vulnerable to unexpected stresses — freakish weather conditions, or outbreaks of a new type

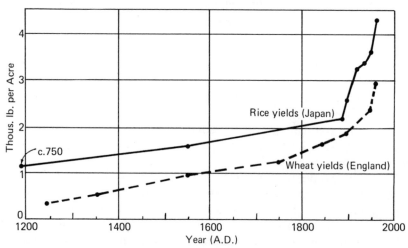

**Figure 13–5** Increase in the rice yields of Japan and the wheat yields of England as a credit of improved agricultural techniques. Yields of both crops have doubled during the 20th century.

of predator or disease. Plant breeders recognize the dangers of decreasing the variability of the gene pool. For this reason they are attempting to maintain stocks of as many varieties of seeds as possible.

The practice of growing single crops in intensive culture also encourages outbreaks of pests and disease. The deadly arsenal of poisons on which modern agriculture depends is necessary because most natural control mechanisms have been eliminated in the simplified agricultural ecosystem. In a complex system, epidemics of any sort are rare; it is virtually impossible for the population of one species to get out of control. But in the complex, lightly managed or unmanaged system, people must share the productivity of the earth with other creatures. The consistent goal of agriculture has been to appropriate all that productivity for man.

Hybridization of poultry stocks, blood typing, and novel mating systems have also revolutionized egg, poultry, milk, and meat production. With automated devices for feeding poultry and livestock, a few persons can feed thousands of animals. In addition, mechanical devices are used in poultry egg production to feed and water the laying hens and to collect, sort, clean, and package eggs on a continuous preprogrammed basis. Automation has so transformed dairy farming that many farmers no longer know how to milk a cow.

While human and animal labor were primary sources of improvement in early American agriculture, we now use large capital investments in materials and equipment and relatively little labor. The horse population of the United States was some 25 million in 1920; it has now decreased to about 3 million, and the horses that remain are largely pleasure animals. During the same time, the farmland devoted to production of feed for horses declined from 32 million hectares to about 2 million. The coming of the tractor released large areas for production of crops for human consumption.

When strong economic incentives for increasing farm production are absent, agriculture expands very slowly. This was clearly demonstrated in the United States during 1920–1935, when agricultural products were priced very low. Then rising prices and larger food markets stimulated the improvement of production methods, so that total agricultural output in the United States is now greater than at any time in the past. The agricultural output per worker has increased sharply since 1945, not only because each farm operator has had more capital and land, but also because he has found it to his advantage to use improved seed, more fertilizers, and plant protectants. More timely planting, weed control, and mechanical harvesting have contributed to improved yields per acre and lower unit production costs. These developments are largely responsible for the trend toward urbanization, which has been discussed in Chapters 11 and 12. Large numbers of ex-farmers are still employed in the industrialized agricultural system, however, whether they realize it or not. They produce the fuels and raw materials that power the farms and build their machines; or they work in the industries that produce fertilizers, chemical control agents, tools, and farm machinery; or they drive the trucks that haul the food (and garbage!); or they work in the food-processing industries, or the grocery stores. The farmer used to be self-sufficient. Now he is as dependent on the integrity of the industrialized economy as any apartment dweller in Manhattan.

Modern agricultural practices have been adopted in other countries, most notably Japan, Taiwan, Mexico, Israel, Argentina, Canada, Australia, and most of western Europe. In Europe and Japan, where agricultural land has long been at a premium, the emphasis is on maximum yield per acre rather than maximum yield per farmer.

The result of emphasis in the United States on the reduction of human labor on the farm is illustrated in Figure 13.6, which shows the changes in numbers of agricultural and nonagricultural workers during the last century and a half. That our agricultural system may be efficient only in use of human farm labor, but not in use of resources, is suggested by Figure 13.7. This illustration shows the position of selected countries with respect to the average income per person and the amount of arable land per person. In the area marked I are the nations with low per capita income and only a small amount of farmland per person. In area II are some nations that are relatively well off economically, but have just as little farmland as the poor nations in area I. Area III contains another group of poor nations in which the amount of farmland varies from adequate to abundant. In area IV are the richer nations with large amounts of arable land per person. Note the position of the United States, and the relatively extravagant amount of farmland that is available for each of us. With growing population pressure, agricultural pollution, and energy shortages, it is likely that ecological fac-

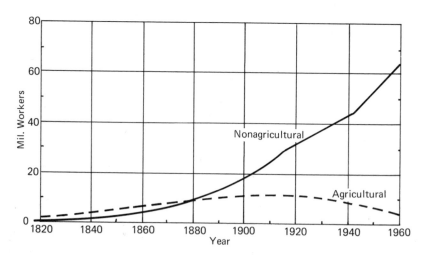

**Figure 13–6** Changes in the numbers of agricultural and nonagricultural workers in the United States during the last century and a half. The steady reduction in human labor is obvious.

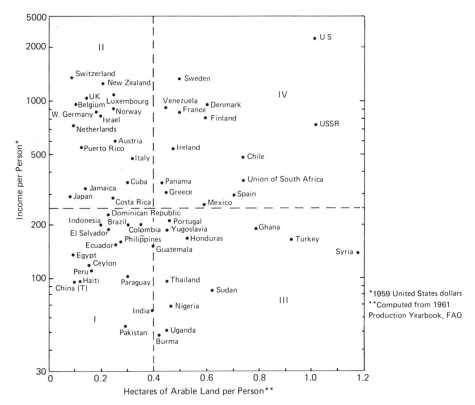

**Figure 13–7** Distribution of selected nations with respect to average income per person and amount of arable land per person. (Note that the income scale is logarithmic.) Of the nations shown, only Syria and the USSR equal or surpass the U. S. in amount of farmland per person.

tors and conservation of resources will begin to affect our agricultural practices more, and purely economic considerations less.

*AGRICULTURE AND ECOLOGY.* The way in which people obtain their food is at the very root of their relationship to their environment. Chapter 3 discussed the role of dominant species of plants and animals in determining the character of an ecosystem, and briefly described man's rise to dominance. Agricultural and industrial man has progressively simplified the ecosystems of which he is a part, altering energy flows and the energy balance, interrupting the interrelationships among species that result in a stable system, and creating large amounts of wastes that cannot be assimilated or recycled by natural processes. Some aspects of agricultural pollution will be discussed in Chapter 15. Here we will mention a few implications for agriculture of the awesome responsibility that accompanies our role as the dominant species on earth.

We must question the future role of energy subsidy in food production. In many cases the food-poor nations are also energy-poor. Even where fossil fuels have been abundant in the recent past, there is a sudden realization that supplies everywhere are running out. It might be a cruel hoax to introduce the internal combustion engine and all it implies into socio-agricultural systems which, however low their productivity, at least have demonstrated that they work in a time frame of centuries. The largest return comes from the early increments of energy input — perhaps not the very first, the curve may be sigmoid, but the advantage of one small tractor over none at all is tremendous, while the advantage of several large ones over one small may be much less. In the United States we reached the point of diminishing returns some time ago and probably ought to *decrease* the energy input. But a few horsepower per acre are of obvious advantage in nations that have no energy subsidy now. The Ehrlichs (see references) argue that proposed nuclear-agricultural-industrial complexes can provide local (although perhaps only temporary) relief; but they are very unlikely to be the ultimate solution to the world food problem, especially in the absence of rigorous population control. The same is true of fertilizers. There is no shortage of nitrogen, because its source, the atmosphere, is for practical purposes unlimited. (It requires a great deal of energy, however, to manufacture nitrate fertilizers.) The critical element may be phosphorus. A recent work group of The Institute of Ecology predicted that useful supplies of phosphate rock will be exhausted in 60 years. It has also been estimated that in order to double the world's yield of crops, we will have to increase the application of fertilizers *between five and sixfold.*

The metaphor "spaceship earth" has captured our imagination, but it is not yet literally true. In a spaceship the tiny ecosystem is totally managed by man. It approaches the theoretical ideal of self-contained renewal and recycling, designed for and by ourselves. Earth is not like that, although one of the most disturbing aspects of modern life is the realization that it may become that way. On earth there are still processes that run by themselves, beyond our control; there are still places where our intrusion and interference have been minimal. Our lives depend on those processes and places. But as it is clear that the intensity of our exploitation of earth is going to increase, we will have to take over more of the controls that nature once handled for us. In agriculture this may mean stable closed systems, in which water, nutrients, and organic matter are completely recycled, with energy from the sun, or perhaps from nuclear fission or fusion. With our present technology and understanding we cannot yet design or run such a system.

## NUTRITION AND DIET

A green plant has very simple nutritional needs: water, carbon dioxide, and inorganic nutrients in a suitable form. The organic matter in the soil plays no direct role in plant nutrition; its value is related to its effect on the physical and chemical properties of the soil. Organic matter affects the structure of the soil, its ability to retain water and nutrients, and the nature and number of soil-dwelling organisms; but organic compounds do *not* provide "food" for green plants.

Nutrients requirements of other organisms vary over a broad spectrum of substances. A few chemosynthetic and photosynthetic microorganisms are as independent, biosynthetically, as green plants. Others require only a few specific vitamins, or growth factors. Still others are able to build the bewildering array of molecules that compose any living organism, as long as they have inorganic nutrients and a source of chemical energy in the form of an organic compound of carbon. The majority of organisms lack the ability to synthesize many vital compounds. They therefore require a variety of preformed molecules, which they generally obtain from their food but in some cases from the activities of other organisms living symbiotically with them. Thus microorganisms living in the digestive tract often synthesize vitamins that are utilized by the host.

Higher animals, including man, have specific requirements for particular organic molecules, in addition to their general need for inorganic elements and organic compounds to provide energy. These requirements are modified by genetic and environmental factors, and by the stage of the life cycle and state of health (see Chapters 6 and 7). There is no one perfect food that supplies all the requirements of man, except for human milk, which suffices for a short time after birth. The identification of required nutrients, elucidation of their biochemical and physiologic roles, and determination of their quantitative requirements and dietary sources under various circumstances are the concerns of the science of human nutrition.

It is often asked whether we are "naturally" herbivorous, carnivorous, or omnivorous. It is anatomically obvious that we are not designed to survive on leaves and grass; we literally have neither the teeth nor the stomachs for it, and neither do any of our primate relatives. Nor do we and the other primates have the specialized attributes of a true carnivore. Our anatomy and physiology, as well as archeological remains and the feeding habits of our nearest primate relatives, indicate that from the earliest times men and ape-men have consumed a wide variety of animal and vegetable foods. The earliest cultural artifacts bear witness to man the hunter. The diet of primitive man was selected from available fruits, nuts, seeds, fleshy roots and tender leaves and stems; insects; eggs; and whatever small animals he could catch, including fish, frogs, and reptiles, as well as mammals. This menu sounds very similar to the list of foods recommended today for a well-balanced diet. The body can make limited physiological adjustments to diets deficient in some nutrients. Human expansion into diverse environments has been accompanied by restrictions in the type of foods available, as illustrated by the largely carnivorous diet of people living in the Far North. Probably natural selection has led to some degree of adaptation to restricted diets, but in general we still require and enjoy the wide variety of foods that our remote ancestors did.

The required nutrients are classified as carbohydrates, proteins, and fats, which are needed in large quantities to provide energy and materials for growth and maintenance, and vitamins and minerals, required in smaller amounts for proper metabolism and skeletal structure. The following sections summarize the nature and functions of these materials and some relationships between diet and health in different cultures.

*CARBOHYDRATE NUTRITION.* Carbohydrates are molecules composed of carbon atoms to which hydrogen atoms (H) and hydroxyl groups (OH) are attached in approximately equal numbers. They include sugars, starch, glycogen, cellulose, and gums. Carbohydrates are the first stable products of photosynthesis and provide both chemical energy for cellular metabolism and the carbon "skeletons" from which other compounds are synthesized by the plant.

In our bodies, carbohydrates are also the source of energy which keeps us alive. About 90 percent of the food we eat is "burned;" only some 10 percent is used for growth and maintenance. This is why the amount of food eaten is commonly estimated in calories — a unit of energy. One gram of carbohydrate yields slightly more than 4 calories of energy. (The food calorie is the "large calorie," which is really 1000 calories or 1 kilocalorie.)

The metabolism of carbohydrates is linked through many biochemical pathways to the metabolism of proteins and fats, so that any of these can serve as energy sources. In addition, excess dietary carbohydrate is converted to fat and stored, various sugar molecules provide the skeletons for synthesis of amino acids and other compounds, and complex carbohydrates are broken down into simple sugars, most of which are readily converted to glucose. Glucose is the major fuel for most cells of the body, and the only one for some. A constant supply is required under all conditions. Chapter 8 discussed the mechanism by which the concentration of glucose in the blood is regulated. A deviation of only a few percent from the norm can have serious consequences.

Only a small amount of carbohydrate is stored, as such, in the body. Table 13.3 shows the carbohydrate content and caloric needs of a hypotheti-

**TABLE 13.3**
**Carbohydrate Content and Caloric Needs of an "Average" Man**

Carbohydrate stored as muscle glycogen......................................245 grams
Carbohydrate stored as liver glycogen..........................................108 grams
Sugar in blood and extracellular fluid ...............................................14 grams

Total carbohydrates in body....................................370 grams

Caloric equivalent of 370 grams of carbohydrate = 1500 calories
Caloric requirement (sedentary occupation) = 2800 calories per day

cal average 70 kilogram (154 pound) man. Note that the energy value of all the carbohydrates in the body at any time is only enough to supply the energy required for about half a day. Note also that in order to supply his caloric needs from carbohydrates alone, our "average" man would have to eat nearly 700 grams of carbohydrate. This is more than ten times the amount of protein recommended for a balanced diet. In most diets varying proportions of energy are supplied by fats. A high protein-low caloric diet, however, is inefficient and wasteful, because protein cannot be utilized for growth and maintenance until the caloric needs of the body have been met. For this reason it is suggested that protein be omitted from "survival rations," and that protein or amino acids never be administered unless accompanied by carbohydrates.

Using protein to supply the body's energy is analogous to burning protein to heat your house. You *can* heat your house that way, but there are cheaper and better ways to do it. Similarly, the necessity of the vast quantities of ham and eggs and beefsteak that athletes are encouraged to consume may be questioned. Caloric requirements increase sharply with exercise, but protein requirements remain essentially the same. The crusade against consumption of "empty calories," which has reached political and almost religious proportions, is partially based on a fallacy (although, as we shall see, there are sound reasons for re-evaluating the quality of the American diet). We require a large number of "empty" calories every moment of our lives.

Table 13.4 shows the energy typically expended in various types of activity, in terms of calories per hour per kilogram of body weight. The actual caloric requirement of an individual varies with age, sex, size, activ-

**TABLE 13.4**
**Caloric Requirement for Various Activities, Calories Per Hour Per Kilogram of Body Weight**

| Activity | Calories |
|---|---|
| Sleeping | 0.9 |
| Sitting | 1.4 |
| Standing | 1.5 |
| Typing | 2.0 |
| Sweeping | 2.4 |
| Walking slowly | 2.9 |
| Walking moderately fast | 4.3 |
| Sawing wood | 6.9 |
| Swimming | 7.1 |

Caloric value of foods:
| | |
|---|---|
| Carbohydrates | 4 calories per gram |
| Fats | 9 calories per gram |
| Proteins | 4 calories per gram |

ity, climate, and metabolic rate. Children and adolescents require relatively huge amounts of energy, not, as is commonly supposed, because they are more active than adults (although this is a contributing factor), but because a great deal of energy is used in growth. The efficiency of converting what Sammy eats into Sammy is roughly 10 percent; the rest is burned in the process.

*PROTEIN NUTRITION.*    Proteins are large molecules composed of one or more chains of amino acids. They exist in many structural forms, in almost infinite chemical variety. Among them are *enzymes,* which facilitate the biochemical reactions within cells. They also form antibodies and some hormones, and they constitute a large fraction of mucus and milk. Hair and nails are a type of protein called *keratin,* while *collagen* is the main supportive protein in skin, tendon, bone, cartilage, and connective tissue. When boiled, collagen yields gelatin.

When dietary protein is digested, it is broken down into its constituent amino acids, which are then utilized in the synthesis of human proteins. Protein and amino acids are not stored in the body. Amino acids that are not used for protein synthesis are either metabolized to yield energy, converted to fats and stored, or excreted. Thus it is important that a sufficient supply of amino acids be available to the body at all times, in the proportions in which they are required for protein synthesis.

Of the twenty amino acids from which proteins are built, eight cannot be synthesized by man to any significant extent. These are the eight "essential" amino acids which must be supplied by the diet. The reason they are not synthesized seems to be that the organic acids from which they are derived are not readily formed during the metabolism of carbohydrates, for if the appropriate carbon skeleton is provided, the amino group can be added readily enough.

In small amounts, some amino acids are involved in the synthesis of compounds other than proteins. Tyrosine, for example, is a precursor of the hormone thyroxin; the vitamin niacin can be synthesized from tryptophan; histidine is converted to histamine (a regulatory compound in the blood); and methionine acts as a "methyl donor" in a wide variety of biochemical reactions involving the transfer of methyl groups. Glycine combines with some toxic substances to convert them to a harmless form in which they can be excreted. In addition, there are a number of biologically active polypeptides — short chains of amino acids. Some of these are antibiotics.

Because a protein molecule cannot be assembled unless all the necessary amino acids are available to the protein-synthesizing machinery, it follows that a particular balance of amino acids in the diet is required for the optimum utilization of dietary proteins. This applies to nonessential amino acids as well as essential ones, because although the body can synthesize many amino acids, this is an added metabolic burden and the synthesis may not occur at a rate which can compensate for the dietary imbalance. For this reason, there is a great deal of emphasis on the quality of dietary protein, as well as its quantity. In general, the amino acid composition of animal proteins more nearly resembles that of human proteins than the composition of plant protein does. Plant proteins tend to be deficient in one or more of the essential amino acids.

We do not know the ideal balance of amino acids for the human diet because of experimental difficulties in determining it. Egg protein appears to be the most nearly perfect protein food, showing superiority in feeding experiments even to mixtures of amino acids which theoretically *should* provide a better balance. For this reason the adequacy of the amino acid content of a protein is usually expressed using egg protein as a standard. The amino acid content does not tell the whole story, however. Not all amino acids in a protein are available to the body, some being tied up in chemical linkages that are resistant to digestive enzymes. In addition, some amino acids are destroyed or rendered unavailable during storage, processing, or cooking of the food.

One might think that if a diet containing, say, 50 grams of protein per day supplied only half the required amount of some amino acid but adequate amounts of all others, the deficiency could be corrected by doubling the intake of protein. This is not the case, pointing again to the importance of amino acid *balance*. In the hypothetical case just mentioned, better results are obtained by supplementing the diet with the amino acid that was deficient than by increasing the amount of protein. Thus diets containing large amounts of nutritionally inadequate protein may be inferior to ones with much smaller amounts of high quality protein. It is not true that if one eats "enough" corn or "enough" rice he will be adequately nourished.

It is possible to obtain the correct balance of amino acids in a diet consisting entirely of vegetable protein, if the proper foods are combined in each meal. Frances Lappé's book (see references) has abundant suggestions for how to do this. Between 30 and 40 grams of high quality protein per day is considered minimally adequate for an adult.

*FAT NUTRITION.*    Deposits of fat insulate the body against excessive loss of heat, protect vital organs from physical injury, and serve as storage depots for energy. In addition, derivatives of fats are integral structural parts of cell membranes.

When fats are digested, they are broken down into glycerol and various fatty acids. The fatty acids may be metabolized to yield energy or may recombine with glycerol to be stored in the body as fats. They may also form other compounds related to fats which are of physiologic importance, especially in brain and nervous tissue. Unlike carbohydrates, proteins, and most vitamins and minerals, fats can be stored in the body in enormous amounts.

The physical nature of fat is determined by the number of carbon atoms in the fatty acid chains and by the degree to which available bonds of the carbon atoms are saturated by combination with hydrogen. Fatty acids are synthesized in animals by the combination of two-carbon fragments derived from metabolism of carbohydrates and proteins. The resulting fats are highly saturated molecules. The unsaturated fatty acids in animal fats are largely derived from dietary sources. Thus the nature of the diet strongly influences the nature of animal fat. Three unsaturated fatty acids are known to be required by man because they are necessary constituents of cells and cannot be synthesized in sufficient quantities by the human body.

The amount of fat in human diets ranges from only a few percent to as much as 40 percent. Most nutritionists recommend that from a quarter to a third of the daily caloric intake be in the form of fats. In addition to being an excellent source of energy, fats render food more palatable and provide a feeling of satiety.

*VITAMIN NUTRITION.* The group of nutrients known as vitamins is composed of a variety of organic compounds, chemically unrelated to one another, which are necessary for normal metabolism. In general, when the role of a vitamin has been defined precisely, it has turned out that the vitamin plays a part in a particular enzymatic reaction or type of enzymatic reaction. In other words, vitamins function as cofactors or *coenzymes.* As such, they may constitute an integral part of the structure of the enzyme, or they may be only loosely or temporarily attached. The cofactor is sometimes identical to the vitamin. It may also consist of the vitamin in combination with other chemical groups, such as phosphate, or one of the nitrogen bases (the same nitrogen bases that occur in DNA).

Although a vitamin may contribute to the structure of only one or two cofactors, these cofactors may be active in a wide variety of metabolic pathways. This is why a vitamin deficiency usually has such generalized effects on health, in addition to whatever the highly specific deficiency symptoms may be.

It is not easy to quantify the vitamin requirements of man because of interactions among elements in the diet and in the environment and because of individual variations in their absorption and utilization. A few of the vitamins, notably the fat-soluble A, D, and E, but also vitamin C, can be stored. The rest must be present regularly in the diet. An excess one day does no good the next. In some cases, an excess of one vitamin alleviates the deficiency of another — but sometimes it exacerbates the condition. All this points, again, to the importance of a balanced diet which provides adequate amounts of all nutrients.

*MINERAL NUTRITION.* Inorganic elements and chemical groupings play a variety of roles in physiology and metabolism. Some are constituents of the skeleton and teeth. Others are involved in maintaining the acid-base balance of the blood, the normal balance and distribution of water, and the equilibrium in salt concentration between extracellular and intracellular fluids. Iron plays a key role in the transport and exchange of oxygen. Phosphate is a constituent of adenosine triphosphate (ATP), a compound which supplies energy for a great many enzymatic reactions, as well as of RNA and DNA, and of some types of protein and lipids.

There are many interactions among inorganic ions in the body. Sometimes one ion can partially substitute for another; sometimes an excess of one produces an apparent deficiency of another. Ions of similar size and charge can often substitute for one another chemically, but the physiologic activity of the resulting compound is altered. Selenium "looks like" sulfur to the cell, but when sulfur is replaced by selenium, the altered compound no longer fills the same metabolic role. Similarly, radioactive strontium and radium fit into the crystal lattice of bone, replacing calcium and bombarding the living bone cells with deadly ionizing radiation.

We obtain minerals from drinking water and food. Mineral content of both food and water is related to the amounts and chemical form of inorganic constitutents of the soil and underlying rock. Chapter 2 mentioned a few examples of poisoning or mineral deficiency resulting from the nature of the soil.

*NUTRITION AND HEALTH.*    In Great Britain in 1841, the life expectancy of a 50-year-old man was 20 more years. Today, more than a century and a quarter later, it is only 22 or 23 more years. The story is similar in other European nations and in the United States and Canada. This is not a very impressive testimonial to the success of modern medicine in dealing with the diseases and disabilities of adulthood. In fact, the prospects of health for an adult in industrialized societies seem to be worsening, as described in Chapter 14. In part, the failure to increase the life expectancy of an adult is explained by the unexplained mysteries of the life cycle — of development and birth, maturation, senescence and death — described in Chapter 7. In part, too, it may involve a failure to adapt biologically to the environments our culture has imposed on us, despite the aids of science and medicine. Increasingly, however, we begin to suspect there is a nutritional basis for many of the "new epidemic diseases" discussed in the next chapter. In the sections that follow, we will consider some diseases and consequences of malnutrition. Literally, malnutrition means bad nutrition. It does not necessarily imply starvation; it afflicts the affluent with their diet of steak and white bread and imported beer, just as it afflicts the more than 2 billion hungry people of the world.

SOME RELATIONSHIPS BETWEEN "MODERN FOODS" AND HEALTH.    Three features of the American diet have come under scrutiny by physicians, scientists, and laymen: the nature and amount of fat, the highly concentrated and refined foods, and the host of additives and contaminants. The last of these will be considered in Chapter 15; it is basically a problem of *health* — much less one of nutrition. The first two, however, are directly related to both nutrition and health.

There has been a precipitous increase in the incidence of atherosclerosis and coronary heart disease among people eating "modern foods." Evidence suggests that this increase is strongly related to diet, and not only to associated racial, cultural, and environmental influences — although these, too, are involved. Increased levels of cholesterol in the blood serum are associated with development of the disease. Cholesterol is a compound chemically related to fat; it is synthesized in the body in amounts usually exceeding the dietary intake by a factor of two or more and is essential for the proper functioning of brain and nervous tissue.

Scientists are still unraveling the tangle of relationships between diet, cholesterol, and atherosclerosis, but a few facts seem certain. One is that consumption of large amounts of saturated fats and fats consisting of short-chain fatty acids (such as those found in butter) relative to amounts of unsaturated and long-chain fatty acids leads to elevated levels of cholesterol. Note that this is *relative*, not *absolute* amounts of the kinds of fat. The role of essential fatty acids in decreasing serum cholesterol has been postulated to involve one or more of the following: Increasing rate of cholesterol metabolism and excretion, decreasing rate of its formation, decreasing its absorption from the intestines, or — by virtue of the nature of a diet high in essential fatty acids — decreasing its dietary intake. Diets high in carbohydrates and low in fiber are also implicated in the occurrence of elevated levels of serum cholesterol. The relationships are not yet completely clear, but diets high in fiber lead to decreased intestinal absorption of fatty acids and increased excretion of fats in the feces; and we have seen that saturated fatty acids are synthesized within the body from carbohydrates.

It might seem strange, at first, that people of many cultures in many environments have eaten large quantities of meat and animal fat for hundreds of thousands of years, and suddenly we indict animal fat as a major cause of the recent increase in atherosclerosis and coronary heart disease. It was pointed out, however, that diet influences the nature of animal fat, and this is true for the animals we eat as well as for ourselves. The fatty acid composition of wild animals and those foraging on open range is significantly higher in the unsaturated, essential fatty acids than is that of animals raised by the methods of industrialized agriculture. In addition, of course, we have purposely hydrogenated, or saturated, many other fats so that margarine is hard and peanut butter homogenous.

Obesity has become a national health problem. It is so commonplace that we hardly consider it remarkable. But why do people get fat? The rabbit nibbling in your back yard never gets fat, no matter how abundant the clover. Neither do people in primitive cultures, even when there is an abundance of food. Physiologists and psychologists have long tried to fathom the secrets of appetite, of feelings of hunger and satiety. They have probed the brain, identifying control centers for hunger and satiety; they have studied hunger contractions of the stomach; they have analyzed the chemistry of the blood; and they have investigated the role of emotions. There are many unanswered questions, but it is clear that there are homeostatic mechanisms which, under normal conditions, regulate the intake of food so that a constant and appropriate body weight is maintained. These mechanisms can be undermined by the modern highly concentrated diet, which may be extravagantly rich in the necessary nutrients but is nevertheless low in bulk and fiber content. Consider, for example, the average intake of sugar. It is now about 5 ounces per person per day. In the form of refined white sugar, probably dissolved in some beverage, this amount hardly makes you feel "full." But 5 ounces of sugar is the amount contained in 2½ pounds of sugar beets. If you had eaten sugar beets for sweetness, as your ancestors did, you certainly would know that you had eaten something after consuming 2½ pounds! Many health problems are associated with obesity, including diabetes, heart disease, hypertension, atherosclerosis, and, in general, a shortened life span.

An increase in tooth decay and dental and periodontal disease is also associated with the adoption of modern diets. This has been documented among many peoples in diverse cultures and geographic locations. In inhabitants of Iceland, the rugged Hebrides off the Scottish coast, Australia, Africa, the valleys of the Swiss Alps — problems in dental and skeletal development and health coincide with the introduction of refined sugar and flour and canned foods into the diet.

And still other problems are related to the high calorie-low bulk diet. The physiology of the large intestine is affected. The nature and number of bowel movements are changed; food remains longer in the large intestine. This is thought to contribute to the increasing incidence of **diverticulosis** and **diverticulitis,** hemorrhoids, varicose veins, blood clots in the vessels supplying the abdomen and legs, and a number of other problems of the bowel.

The movement back to "natural" foods is basically sound, although many people have been lured into food fads rather than diets based on what is now known about human nutrition. Many different diets can supply our nutritional needs. Many have been tested in the laboratory of evolution. Natives of the Yukon drank a sort of tea, rich in vitamin C, brewed from the terminal shoots of spruce trees, while later immigrants fell prey to scurvy, not having the dietary wisdom of those long adapted to the region. Others in the Far North value the adrenal gland as a "health food." It, too, is rich in vitamin C. The variety of native diets that support robust health is immense and fascinating: Australian aborigines eat small animals, insects, and wild plants; the diet in the Hebrides is sea food, oatmeal, and a few summer vegetables; some Africans live on blood, milk, grain, and green vegetables; high in the Swiss Alps people eat milk products, rye bread, and a few vegetables. These diets and many others have passed the test of time. The modern American diet seems to be failing that test in terms of the health of those who eat it.

Many diet-conscious Americans are now trying for nutritional over-kill. The basis for this is deep-rooted emotionally and is bound up with dissatisfaction with our present culture and a search for more meaningful goals and lifestyles. The return to "natural foods" is nutritionally sound, but most food fads are not. Once the body's needs for energy and specific nutrients — cofactors and building blocks — have been satisfied, an excess of some nutrient is unlikely to be beneficial. In some cases, it can be harmful, by creating an imbalance in the formerly balanced diet and the balanced metabolism established in relationship to that diet. Sometimes, too, an excessive amount of a nutrient is actually toxic.

UNDERNUTRITION AND HEALTH.    The dimensions of hunger in the world today are unprecedented. Famine has always been with us, but famines are local, acute crises which pass in time. Today hunger is widespread and chronic, and with increasing populations no lasting reprieve is in sight.

Proteins, vitamins, minerals, and hormones are the metabolic machinery of the body. *All* of these must be present in adequate amounts for the normal functioning of the body; all of them, or their biochemical precursors, must be supplied by the diet. If any is missing, health is generally impaired. In addition, there must be adequate fuel to keep the metabolic fires burning. More than 2 billion people in the world today subsist on diets deficient in both quantity and quality.

This is not an appropriate place to document the extent or all the effects of undernutrition, but we will mention a few. Figure 13.8 shows the per capita consumption of plant and animal proteins in forty-three selected countries. The minimum requirement for an adult is taken to be between 30

**TABLE 13.5**
**Per Capita Consumption of Animal Food in Selected Countries, Grams Per Person Per Day**

| Country | Meat | Fish | Milk | Total |
|---------|------|------|------|-------|
| New Zealand | 302 | 19 | 762 | 1083 |
| United States | 299 | 17 | 671 | 987 |
| France | 227 | 25 | 601 | 853 |
| United Kingdom | 205 | 26 | 595 | 826 |
| Argentina | 322 | 12 | 337 | 671 |
| Italy | 129 | 18 | 387 | 534 |
| Portugal | 74 | 61 | 166 | 301 |
| Japan | 37 | 89 | 123 | 249 |
| Taiwan | 74 | 41 | 17 | 132 |
| India | - | 3 | - | 3 |

Source: United Nations (1969) FAO Production Yearbook Volume 23

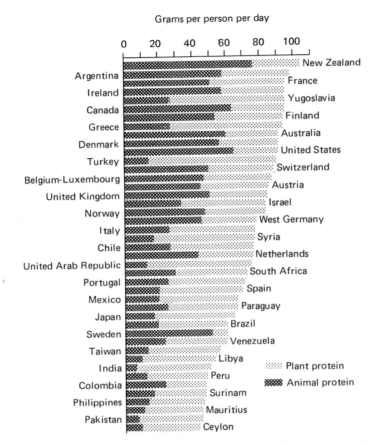

Grams per person per day

**Figure 13–8** Grams of plant and animal protein consumed daily per person in selected countries. The requirement for an adult is about 60 grams per day of good quality protein, which generally implies a substantial amount of protein of animal origin.

and 40 grams of high quality protein per day, with absorption and utilization of amino acids approaching 100 percent. Since perfect proteins are not eaten and utilized with perfect efficiency in real life, a more realistic estimate of the requirement is usually taken as 60 grams of good quality protein per person per day. As a first approximation, "high quality protein" means animal protein. The well-balanced combination of vegetable foods which the affluent can enjoy is just as far beyond reach for most hungry people as is roast beef. Figure 13.8, although it does not tell the whole story about the diet in any of the countries represented, does reveal the gross inequities in the distribution of protein in the world food supply. Roughly one quarter of the countries shown are deficient in both amount and quality of protein.

Table 13.5 takes a closer look at the types of animal foods consumed in ten of the countries shown in the figure. Note that this table gives grams of animal *food*, not animal *protein*. Fish, the most concentrated source of protein in the list, plays a more important role in protein nutrition than may appear at first glance.

Malnutrition has the most devastating effect on children, because in them the structures that must function for a lifetime are still being built. A particularly vulnerable period is the time of weaning, when due to lack of food or lack of nutritional understanding or both, a mother may try to support her child on a gruel of cornstarch and water. In some cultures the best food is traditionally reserved for adult males.

One consequence of undernutrition or malnutrition is increased susceptibility to a large number of infectious diseases, chiefly those caused by bacteria and protozoa. The epithelial surfaces of the body are the first line of resistance to infection. They include the outer part of the skin and the linings of the respiratory tract and digestive tract. Certain vitamins are specifically necessary for the health of these surfaces, and their deficiency leads to increased vulnerability to invasion by foreign organisms. After the foreign organism invades the body, it normally encounters the next line of defense — the immune system. If the protein-synthesizing machinery is not functioning properly, the appropriate antibodies cannot be produced and the already weakened host falls prey to the worst consequences of the disease. Many diseases that are mild in a well-nourished individual can run a fatal course in a victim of malnutrition. In the statistics the death may be chalked up to diarrhea, but its real cause is malnutrition.

An interesting exception to the above occurs in some virus diseases. A virus cannot carry out the metabolic processes necessary for its own perpetuation. It must suborn the protein- and nucleic acid-synthesizing machinery of its host. If that machinery is deranged as a result of poor nutrition, the virus may fail to thrive. The protective effect of nutritional deficiency was illustrated among prisoners in concentration camps during World War II. Viruses which produced only mild disease among the emaciated prisoners caused severe epidemics when released prisoners carried them back to the well-fed people at home.

The body makes many physiological adaptations to changes and inadequacies in the diet. It responds to chronic deficiency of calcium, for example, by an increased efficiency of absorption of calcium in the gut and its utilization and conservation in the body. Adaptation to the change from a diet high in calcium to one low in calcium is rapid in some individuals but may require many months in others. Eventually, however, the loss of calcium in the body's excretions equals the amount ingested — equilibrium is reached.

These adaptive mechanisms are part of what the great physiologist Cannon described as "the wisdom of the body." There are many examples. Enzymes requiring nicotinic acid as a cofactor, for instance, do not show equal reduction in activity during a deficiency of nicotinic acid. Some decrease sharply; others, not at all. It is usually the less critical functions that are lost first, while those fundamentally important to the life of the cell and the body are spared. As another example, one of the symptoms of kwashiorkor is sparse, brittle, and reddened hair. Hair is protein, and when survival is at stake, its synthesis is a profligate waste of scarce resources. Since hair is expendable, it is one of the first things to be sacrificed. (The condition of the hair and nails may often indicate that all is not well, before there are any other symptoms to arrest the attention.)

Diet affects patterns of metabolism and of health and disease in many ways, some of which we are just beginning to identify and understand. In the next chapter we will explore some other aspects of health and disease.

## REFERENCES

ALTSCHUL, A. M. 1966. *World Protein Resources.* Advances in Chemistry Series No. 57. Washington, D.C.: American Chemical Society.

BROWN, L. R. 1963. *Man, Land, and Food: Looking Ahead at World Food Needs.* Foreign Agric. Econ. Report No. 11. Washington, D.C.: U.S. Dept. Agric.

BROWN, L. R., AND G. W. FINSTERBUSCH. 1972. *Man and His Environment: Food.* New York: Harper & Row.

BORGSTROM, G. 1969. *Too Many: A Study of Earth's Biological Limitations.* London: Collier-Macmillan Ltd.

BURGESS, A., AND R. F. A. DEAN, ED. 1962. *Malnutrition and Food Habits.* New York: Macmillan.

CATON, D. D. 1970. *Growth in Demand for Feed Grains.* Foreign Agric. Econ. Report No. 63. Washington, D.C.: U.S. Dept. Agric.

CHANDLER, R. F., JR. 1968. The case for research. In *Strategy for the Conquest of Hunger.* Proceedings of a Symposium. New York: Rockefeller Foundation.

DESROSIER, N. W. 1961. *Attack on Starvation.* West Port, Conn.: Avi Publishing Co.

FURTH, F. E., ED. 1969. *Encyclopedia of Marine Resources.* New York: Van Nostrand, Reinhold.

HEEN, E., AND R. KREUZER, EDS. 1962. *Fish and Nutrition.* Technology Branch Fisheries Division FAO-UN. London: Fish News (Books) Ltd.

JANICK, J., R. W. SCHERY, F. W. WOOD, AND V. W. RUTTAN. 1969. *Plant Science: An Introduction to World Food Crops.* San Francisco: W. H. Freeman and Co.

LAPPE, F. M. 1971. *Diet for a Small Planet.* New York: Ballantine.

MATELES, R. I., AND S. R. TANNENBAUM, EDS. 1968. *Single-Cell Protein.* Cambridge: MIT Press.

MAY, J. M. 1961. *The Ecology of Malnutrition in the Far and Near East.* Studies in Medical Geography, vol. 3. New York: Hafner Publishing Co.

MAY, J. M. 1967. *The Ecology of Malnutrition in Northern Africa.* Studies in Medical Geography, vol. 7. New York: Hafner Publishing Co.

PATTON, W. C. 1970. How green is the green revolution. *BioScience.* 20:900.

SAUER, C. D. 1952. *Agricultural Origins and Dispersals.* New York: American Geographic Society.

WEBBER, H. H. 1968. Mariculture. *BioScience.* 18:940–45.

# · 14 ·

KENRAD E. NELSON

# The Ecology of Disease

For thousands of years people have wondered about the nature and cause of disease. To some, disease was a punishment for misdeeds, inflicted by an angered deity. This kind of thinking persists even today, even among people who "know better." "What did I do to deserve this?" is a common reaction to disease. Other people believed disease was caused by a chilling array of evil beings — witches, wizards, and various sorts of demonic spirits. Sometimes these spirits could be exorcised through appropriate rituals by qualified individuals — witch doctors, medicine men, rabbis, priests, or other holy men. Still other people believed, and still believe, that their fate is controlled by the stars.

The Greeks were the first to conceive of a universe governed by natural law, which was not capricious, and whose secrets could be fathomed by philosophical inquiry. Epidemics of disease were frequently related to a pestilential state of the air; but since even the most devastating epidemic left many people untouched, individual predisposition to disease determined who got sick and who did not. Today we realize that human sickness and health are intimately related to human ecology — to man's relationships to his physical, biological, and social environment. Furthermore, because people differ in their genotypic and phenotypic characteristics, they often have dissimilar responses to their environment.

Epidemiology is the study of disease's geographic distribution, its relative frequency in people with respect to their age, race, sex, socio-economic class, and habits, and its change in nature and frequency over time. A complete epidemiological study must also consider environmental factors like climate and human interactions with other organisms. In this chapter we will investigate the history of several epidemic diseases, their causes, characteristics, and their effects on different populations and on human

362

evolution itself. We will also discuss recent new types of epidemic disease and their relation to world health and human ecology.

Human variability makes it very difficult to define health and disease so that every individual can be classified unambiguously as "healthy" or "unhealthy." A physical or physiologic condition that is normal for one person may be a diseased condition in another. For example, a Peruvian native who is well adapted to his home on the high plateau would be considered "sick" at sea level. In order to compensate for the relatively lower oxygen pressure in his mountain atmosphere, the Peruvian has adapted with an increased number of circulating red blood cells. This increased red cell volume might lead to sluggish blood flow and even to small blood clots at sea level. In contrast, a person normally adapted to a sea-level environment who was abruptly transported to the Peruvian Andes would be likely to develop mountain sickness because his red cell mass was not yet adapted to the relative oxygen scarcity. It is clear that health cannot be defined without reference to the environment. But this in no way invalidates the concept of health, any more than the difficulty of classifying individuals by race invalidates the concept of race.

In this chapter we will use the word *disease* in a broad sense to include the spectrum of human infections, disorders, and defects. Changes in the causes of disease and death have accompanied man's physical and socio-cultural evolution. During the hunting and gathering stage of development, human population was probably too sparse to support major epidemic transmission of many diseases. Accidents and infections were most likely the main causes of death. With an agricultural way of life came larger stationary family and social groupings and intimate contact with a variety of domestic animals, factors which promoted the spread of disease through personal contact and the fecal-oral transmission of infectious agents. The introduction of agriculture created a whole new set of relationships among people, their domestic animals and cultivated plants, and wild species, which profoundly influenced patterns of disease.

When preindustrial cities arose, the frequency of contact among people increased further, encouraging the epidemic spread of such diseases as syphilis, tuberculosis, and typhus. Typhoid fever, dysentery, and cholera also appeared as a result of impure water supplies and inadequate sewage disposal systems. Plague became epidemic because of the proximity of diseased rats, germ-carrying fleas, and people. Later, with the development of large industrial cities characterized by crowded living and working conditions and pollution, the spread of epidemic disease was accelerated even more. In particular, tuberculosis and respiratory diseases flourished under these conditions.

Today many societies have passed from the rural "developing" stage to the urban "developed" stage. In this process disease patterns have changed once more. There has been a marked reduction in mortality associated with many of the classical infectious diseases, but at the same time there has been a steady increase in death rates associated with other diseases such as heart disease and cancer, and also in accidental deaths. We have also witnessed what has been described as an explosive adaptive radiation of pathogenic viruses that grow in human tissues. Many of these viruses are genetically unstable and mutate to new antigenic forms with great rapidity. This year's vaccine against influenza is likely to be ineffective against next year's virus.

## THE NATURE OF EPIDEMIC DISEASE

Some diseases are constantly present in a given population, occurring with a characteristic frequency. These are said to be *endemic*. Malaria, hookworm infections, and the common cold are endemic in various parts of the world. If the frequency of an endemic disease increases markedly, the disease has become *epidemic*. This happens periodically, for example, with diseases that are normally endemic, such as the cold, mumps, or chicken pox. Similarly, a small number of cases of a disease that has been very rare or not present in a population may be called an epidemic. Small clusters or epidemics of plague occur from time to time among American Indians living in the Southwest. When a disease affects a very large number of people, it is referred to as *pandemic*. Pandemics of plague, cholera, and, more recently, influenza have repeatedly devastated parts of the world.

Note that the definition of epidemic implies an *unusual* incidence of a disease, whatever the absolute number of individuals affected. Thus if the usual incidence is one case per 100,000 people, an increase to 10 per 100,000 would represent a small epidemic. People in the health professions are on the alert for any change in the occurrence of a disease. This is how the epidemic of **thalidomide babies** was detected. Note also that even the most severe epidemic rarely affects more than 20 percent or so of the population. Even though it seems as if "everyone" is sick, there almost always are many more unaffected people than affected ones. What is the cause of an epidemic? Who is affected and who is not? *Why?* These are the questions an epidemiologist must try to answer.

*THE DETERMINANTS OF DISEASE.*    All disease has more than one *causal factor*. Although a specific bacterium or other disease agent may be necessary for disease to occur, the presence of the agent alone is insufficient. In general, disease occurs upon interaction between an *agent* and a susceptible *host* in a propitious *environment*. Alterations in the frequency and severity of overt disease may be related to changes in the virulence of the agent, the resistance of the host, the nature of the environment, or any combination of these.

The biological goal of a **pathogenic organism,** like that of any organism, is survival. One successful evolutionary strategy for survival of the pathogen is evolution of a relationship that does not destroy the host — for when the host dies, large numbers of pathogens die, too. It seems likely that some serious diseases could become established at endemic or epidemic levels in human populations only after a certain concentration of human density had occurred in villages or small cities. Prior to this the human population was not sufficiently concentrated to support epidemic transmission of an extremely virulent mutant. With increased population density it became possible for a microorganism that caused a fatal disease to be disseminated to many other people by an infected person before his death. Thus it was increasingly possible for virulent mutants to thrive. With time, however, some agents may have lost virulence because of the survival advantage to less virulent mutants, and in some cases to natural selection favoring human hosts with greater degrees of resistance. Some changing relationships among agent, host, and environment will be described using the history of tuberculosis as a specific example.

It is commonly assumed that the main cause for the decreasing frequency of infectious and contagious disease during the past several decades has been the development and widespread use of antibiotics and vaccines. While these medical advances have certainly played a role, the decrease of communicable disease has been related to other factors as well. In fact, in some instances the role of the vaccine or antibiotic was secondary and minimal. Death rates from tuberculosis, for example, were very high in Europe and the United States during the eighteenth and nineteenth centuries, but they began to decline several decades before the discovery of the **tubercle bacillus** in 1882. If the changes in death rate from tuberculosis for different countries are compared for the period between 1800 and 1950, the patterns are seen to vary considerably from one country to another (Figure 14.1). While the decrease in death rate has been a general phenomenon, the time of its onset has varied, and in some cases the death rate was rising in one country at the same time that it was falling in another. Furthermore, the decline in death rate in such countries as the United States and Iceland, where the tuberculosis vaccine was rarely used, was equivalent to the decline in Scandinavia and Japan, where it was employed extensively.

What caused these declines if they were unrelated to anti-microbial therapy or vaccination? A look at the social and economic development of the various countries gives a clue. Those countries that were first to adopt an urban industrial culture, including Great Britain and the United States, had the earliest fall in death rates. Countries undergoing urbanization at a later time, such as Japan, Norway, Finland, Puerto Rico, and Chile, showed increasing rates during the early stages of urbanization and decreasing rates

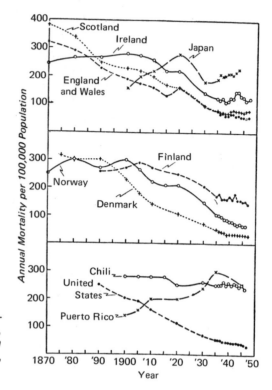

**Figure 14–1** Deaths from tuberculosis for several countries, 1870–1950. *(From Rene and Jean Dubos, The White Plague, Little, Brown and Co. Boston, 1952.)*

after urbanization had been largely accomplished. The many changes in environment and lifestyle related to urbanization and industrialization led to an increase in the natural resistance of most populations to death from tuberculosis.

The nature of this natural resistance and the means of acquiring it are not fully understood. It is possible that increased resistance includes the effects of natural selection, although the change certainly occurred too quickly to be explained solely on a genetic basis. In the crowded urban environment, an ideal setting for the airborne spread of pathogens, the population experienced an increased incidence of infection. Mere infection by a microorganism (its invasion of the body and multiplication in the body tissues) does not necessarily produce signs of disease, however; nor does the disease, if it occurs, follow the same course in all people. Thus those who survived the original infection with only mild disease or none at all became resistant to further infection, and they survived to pass their inborn (not their acquired) resistance on to successive generations.

The existence of genetic factors in resistance to tuberculosis has been demonstrated in studies of twins. There is a greater concordance in the occurrence, clinical type, and severity of tuberculosis among identical twins, who have the same genotypes, than among fraternal twins, who do not. This similarity persists even when identical twins are reared apart from one another under different environmental conditions. It is also thought that the Ashkenazic Jews have developed genetic resistance to tuberculosis. These people are descended from Jewish populations of the crowded European ghettos where the incidence of tuberculosis has been high for many generations. Mortality rates from tuberculosis are much lower among Ashkenazic Jews than among another group of Jews, the Yemenites, who come from a sparsely settled agricultural milieu where the incidence of tuberculosis has always been low. Even the relative genetic resistance of the Ashkenazic Jews was overcome, however, by the environmental conditions of extreme crowding and starvation in the Warsaw ghetto during World War II. Under these conditions morbidity and mortality from tuberculosis increased sharply.

Overall, however, the decline in rates of infection and death from tuberculosis has been too rapid to be explained primarily by natural selection. The drop has occurred in only a few generations, whereas normally many generations are required for natural selection to play a major role. It is not known precisely which environmental factors were most important in the general decline of death rates from tuberculosis and their increase with each major war. Crowding, malnutrition, and the frequency of other respiratory infections, all of which are associated with poverty, are probably involved. It is also possible that the virulence of the causative organism has decreased, although individuals from populations which are generally free from the disease still contract serious cases of tuberculosis when they are exposed.

NATURAL HISTORY OF A DISEASE.    Another important epidemiologic characteristic of a disease is its *natural history* (Figure 14.2), which has been described by Leavell and Clark:

> Any disease or morbid condition in man is the result of a dynamic process. From its earliest beginning, the dynamic process follows a more or less characteristic series of events in the environment and in man until the affected individual returns to normal, reaches a state of equilibrium with the disease, defect, or disability, or dies. Disease, therefore, is not a static condition but a process which follows a more or less natural history.

One person infected with the tubercle bacillus might quickly sicken and die, another might recover, whereas a third might have no illness at all, but only a positive skin test as evidence of infection. Besides quantitative differences in the severity of disease, there are also qualitative ones. Tuberculosis may affect the lungs, skin, bones, or occasionally other organs of the body.

Just as disease is not a static condition in an individual, the natural history of disease can change through time. When syphilis first spread through Europe in a massive epidemic in the late fifteenth and sixteenth

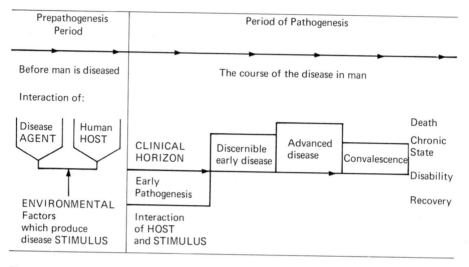

**Figure 14–2** The progression of the natural history of any disease process in man as conceived by Leavell and Clark. (From Leavell and Clark, *Preventive Medicine for the Doctor in his Community*, McGraw Hill, New York, 1965.)

centuries, it was called the "Great Pox" in contrast to the more benign "smallpox." In recent times syphilis has become a milder disease, frequently resolving spontaneously and rarely causing acute mortality. It is only in the late stage when symptoms involving the nervous or cardiovascular system appear that significant mortality results (Figure 14.3). In contrast, a 20 percent mortality rate has been associated with recent epidemics of smallpox in western Europe. Thus what was once considered the milder of the two diseases now bears the more serious prognosis. Again, this situation had nothing to do with development of antibiotics or vaccines. The ability to prevent smallpox by vaccination and to cure syphilis with antibiotics has been superimposed on natural trends in the natural history of the two diseases.

It is thought that human syphilis and related infections may have begun tens of thousands of years ago, when man was confined to tropical areas in sub-Saharan Africa. The first such infections may have been acquired through macerated or abraded areas of skin, and may have manifested themselves as diffuse skin infections. Later the early infection became localized primarily in the mouth and mucous membranes. It could now be spread by contact, a form of disease often called Bejel or endemic syphilis. This disease still occurs in areas of Africa, although its incidence is decreasing rapidly. With the evolution of cities in temperate areas and the greater density of population, the frequency and variety of sexual contact increased, and the pattern of transmission became predominantly venereal.

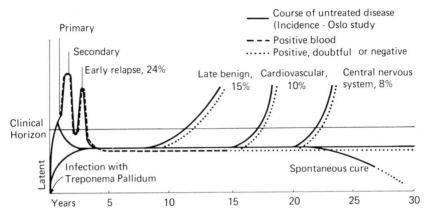

**Figure 14–3** The natural history of untreated syphilis. Symptoms of the disease tend to disappear spontaneously or sink below the level at which they can be detected clinically. About one quarter of cases will have a relapse within one or two years, however, and late symptoms will appear in about one third. The rest of the cases cure themselves spontaneously with no therapy. In the fifteenth and sixteenth centuries the outlook for a victim of syphilis was quite different, as a high mortality rate was associated with the primary and secondary stages of the disease. (From Rudolph H. Kampmeir, *The Late Manifestations of Syphilis: Skeletal, Visceral and Cardiovascular*, Medical Clinics of North America, Philadelphia, 1964.)

Data on attack rates for syphilis in the regular U.S. Army from 1821 to 1946 show a general downward trend, interrupted by increases during and following each armed conflict. There was no effective anti-syphilis treatment during most of this period. Although therapy with arsenic and mercury was introduced in 1910–1912, there is no evidence that this treatment was either widespread or effective enough to have had a marked effect on the incidence of the disease. Penicillin, a highly effective treatment was not available until the time of World War II. Clearly, the incidence of syphilis and the rapidity of its spread to new populations were related to a variety of social and environmental factors which were influencing many people's sexual and hygienic practices. At the same time, the natural history of syphilis and the prognosis for an individual who was infected were changing.

Poliomyelitis provides another example of the changing natural history of a disease. A century ago epidemics of polio were virtually unknown, although occasional sporadic cases had been described. Then in 1870–1880 in Norway and Sweden, small epidemics of polio began to appear. In the 1890s the first epidemics occurred in other parts of Europe, followed in a decade or two by epidemics in the United States. Since about 1930 this evolution from a rare endemic disease to one characterized by massive epidemics had also occurred in semitropical areas such as Puerto Rico, Jamaica, Malta, and Mauritius.

Another change in the natural history of "infantile paralysis" was an upward shift in ages of the individuals attacked. By 1950 most cases were occurring in children and adolescents rather than in infants. The name infantile paralysis was no longer appropriate. The disease ran a more severe and more often fatal course in its older victims.

The explanation for the increasing number of older children and adults contracting polio lies in changes in lifestyle that took place in the mid-twentieth century. Under the crowded and unhygienic conditions of earlier times, most people were exposed as infants to the polio virus, which is frequently shed in the feces of healthy persons. As infants they usually contracted very mild or totally asymptomatic forms of infection which conferred permanent immunity to the disease. As household crowding decreased and sanitation facilities improved, more and more infants were shielded from early mild infection. The consequence of this protection from "natural vaccination" was a greater risk of serious paralytic disease when an infection occurred later in life. Thus paralytic polio can be considered a disease of social and economic progress.

In the United States beginning in the early 1940s, poliomyelitis became a progressively more important health problem. Some 40,000 cases were reported in 1952. A precipitous decline occurred after introduction of the Salk vaccine in 1955 and the Sabin vaccine in 1961 (Figure 14.4). Now there are

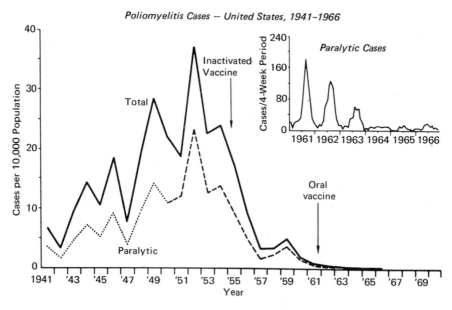

**Figure 14–4** Poliomyelitis cases by year in the United States, 1941–1966. Note the summer peaks in incidence of paralytic cases, as shown in the inset. (Courtesy of the Center for Disease Control, U.S. Polio Health Service, Atlanta, Ga.)

fewer than 100 cases a year, mostly among people who have not received the vaccine. Here, then, is a dramatic success story of the nearly complete conquest of a disease by use of a vaccine on a massive scale.

The former almost universal infection of infants with polio virus and their subsequent lifelong immunity masked the fact that adults, too, are highly susceptible to the disease and that its course is much more severe in them. A similar situation holds for measles and certain other "diseases of childhood." Under conditions of crowding and poverty, measles is a very serious disease of infants and young children. With improved standards of living it becomes a common disease of schoolchildren, in whom it generally runs a relatively mild course. In adolescents and adults it again becomes a dangerous and often fatal disease.

The occurrence and size of an epidemic are related to the number of susceptible individuals in a population and the number of carriers of the disease agent. Since measles virus is an agent that is very easily transmitted, epidemics in the United States have occurred about every two years in urban areas. This appears to be the length of time required to build up a large enough population of susceptible children to support an epidemic. With the recent availability of effective measles vaccines, the epidemiology of the disease has been altered to some extent. In middle-class urban and suburban areas, epidemics have become uncommon. When they do occur, immunization campaigns directed at schoolchildren in the first few grades usually abort their progression. In the inner city, infants and younger children are primarily affected, and epidemic progression is less dependent upon schoolchildren. The gruesome potential of measles is revealed only when it is introduced into a population which has not acquired immunity through prior infection. Among Indians and Eskimos of the Canadian arctic, measles is a dreaded disease. It is highly lethal in Asia, Africa, and South America, where it is superimposed on parasitic infestations, anemia, and malnutrition, and where it attacks nonimmune populations living under primitive conditions.

## EFFECTS OF EPIDEMIC DISEASE ON HUMAN POPULATIONS

Epidemics of disease have had a significant impact on human history, and probably even on human evolution. The outcome of many battles has been determined, not by military prowess, but by the ravages of infection on one side or the other. One of the most infamous epidemic diseases is bubonic plague. The plague has had three great periods of epidemicity: in the sixth century in the days of Justinian, in the fourteenth century with the devastating "Black Death" in Europe, and in the nineteenth and twentieth centuries with the widespread epidemics in China and India. It is thought that the disease was introduced into Asia by infected rats carried aboard ships. The following is one of many historical accounts of the plague:

> The remarkable account given by Procopius of the ravages of the disease at Constantinople in his *History of the Persian War* is typical of all historic outbreaks of bubonic plague down to the present day. . . . At the acme of the epidemic more than 10,000 people died each day and it became impossible to bury all the bodies. Even the Emperor Justinian himself appears to have developed a bubo [a swelling of a lymph node]. According to Procopius, half the inhabitants of the Byzantine Empire were dead by A.D. 565; while Gibbon considered that the total mortality might, without exaggeration be put at one hundred million! Doubtless this calamity played an important part in giving rise to the Dark Ages. The epidemics in Europe in the 14th–17th centuries were, if possible, even more dramatic. Hecker estimates that about a quarter of the inhabitants of Europe died, but in many parts of the continent the gross mortality must have far exceeded this proportion. One witness of the epidemic in Avignon in 1348 says that only a quarter of the population survived. In some parts of England, scarcely one-tenth of the inhabitants were left alive. England and Italy may have lost as much as half of their populations. (L. Hirst, 1953. *The Conquest of Plague.* Oxford Univ. Press.)

The social disruption caused by epidemics of this magnitude almost defies the imagination. Scenes of Bacchanalian celebration, of drunken dancing in the streets of plague-stricken towns, have been described. But in addition to the social effects, it is inconceivable that a disease that wiped out half or more of a local population in one swift stroke would not also alter the gene pool of the surviving population. The specific genotypes that were preferentially spared or destroyed by plague are not known. There have been attempts to explain current distribution of blood types with reference to plague epidemics of the past, but the results are inconclusive.

History provides other examples of diseases which have had dramatic effects on populations during their peak but then have waned equally dramatically. The spread of smallpox in the Western Hemisphere after it was introduced by the Spanish explorers is a classic example. In Mexico 3.5 million persons are said to have died from the disease within a decade or so. In 1841, 6 million of 12 million American Indians fell victims to smallpox. In Iceland more than a third of a total population of 50,000 died in a single year, 1707. In 1924 the United States witnessed an epidemic of 74,000 cases and 1,270 deaths. But then the heyday of smallpox was over. No indigenous cases have occurred in this country since 1947. In fact, the worldwide reservoir of smallpox cases has contracted at such a rate in the past few decades that the goal of the World Health Organization is no longer merely control but eradication of the disease. Smallpox is now localized in small areas in East Africa, India, Bangladesh, and Pakistan. Since the disease has a reservoir only in humans (that is, it does not infect any other animal populations), the use of vaccine, quarantine of cases, and other public health measures are highly effective means of control. If the human reservoir can be reduced to a low enough level, smallpox may eventually vanish from the scene. The smallpox virus will have become extinct.

Typhus, malaria, typhoid fever, yellow fever, and other epidemic diseases have also had decisive roles in human morbidity and mortality in the past. Although these diseases still exist in epidemic form in many parts of the world, they are gradually coming under control in the United States and western Europe. If the efforts of the World Health Organization and other interested groups are successful, many of the classic epidemic diseases will eventually be brought under worldwide control. The rate of this change will depend on such factors as the world political climate, the absence of war (cold and hot), and the economic resources and priorities for health expenditures of developing countries.

The outlook is not equally bright for all infectious diseases, however. Even in developed countries certain diseases — for example, influenza, syphilis, and viral hepatitis — have remained refractory. Pneumonia is still a major killer in almost all nations. A look at the number of hospital beds in the United States occupied by people with "infections" would suggest that the vaunted conquest of "infectious disease" might be illusory — that although some dread diseases have been or may soon be brought under control, infectious disease is still very much with us.

Although the technology for control of some epidemic infectious diseases is well developed, cultural and economic obstacles may delay the realization of actual control, just as they postpone the day of zero population growth. Before we can hope to control the most important of these diseases, the diarrhea-pneumonia complex, herculean efforts will be needed to improve the nutrition, housing, water supply, and waste disposal systems of developing countries.

Malaria is more amenable to rapid control than diseases that are spread by personal contact, through the air, or through contaminated food and water. Because it is transmitted by infected mosquitoes, temporary interruption of the transmission cycle over a wide area can have lasting effects in eradication of the disease. However, the development of insecticide resistance among mosquitoes has become an obstacle to control in some areas.

The abnormal hemoglobins which confer a high degree of immunity to malaria on individuals heterozygous for the abnormal genes provide the best documented example of how disease has affected the genetics of human populations. The geographic distribution of the gene for sickle-cell hemoglobin corresponds very closely with that of the falciparum form of malaria in Africa (Figure 14.5). Populations leaving malarious areas show a decreasing frequency of the sickle-cell gene in subsequent generations, be-

**Figure 14–5** Distribution of falciparum malaria (above) and of hemoglobin S and hemoglobin C (below) in Africa, Europe, and Asia. (From Arno G. Motulsky, "Metabolic Polymorphisms and the Role of Infectious Diseases in Human Evolution," *Human Biology*, 32:28–52, 1960, published by Wayne State University Press.)

cause the heterozygote no longer has a selective advantage and the homozygote has a marked disadvantage, suffering from severe and often fatal anemia.

## RECENT TYPES OF EPIDEMIC DISEASE

During the last several decades in economically advanced countries, there has been a marked reduction in mortality from many of the classic infectious diseases. At the same time there have been increases in the death rates associated with other diseases, particularly heart disease, cancer (especially lung cancer), chronic bronchitis, and emphysema (Figure 14.6). Accidents, although they are not diseases, sometimes appear in "epidemics" and are amenable to analysis by the methods of epidemiology. They have assumed a greater role as a cause of mortality in industrialized countries, especially among people between the ages of 1 and 34 — a group that has received much of the benefit from the control of infectious diseases (Figure 14.7).

There has also been a shift in the type of infectious disease and the type of patient infected. Infections today are one of the chief causes of death among patients whose normal defense mechanisms are impaired as a result of some other disease process. Many people with cardiovascular disease die from pneumonia. Similarly, infections are a major cause of death among cancer and leukemia patients, whose natural defenses are weakened by their disease or suppressed by drugs. One of the principal limiting factors in the success of organ transplants is the occurrence of infections in a host who has received immunosuppressive drugs to protect the grafted organ from rejection. Malnutrition is perhaps the greatest ally of infectious disease, not only in the poor nations but in the United States as well.

At one time the major pathogens were organisms that existed in the external environment and invaded the host to produce such diseases as smallpox, typhoid, syphilis, and diphtheria. These are called *exogenous* organisms because they are not normally found in healthy individuals.

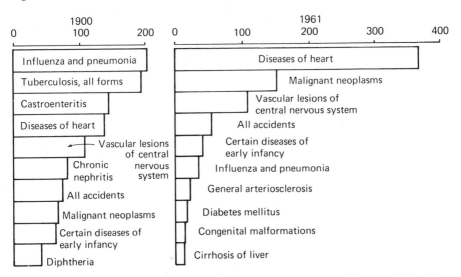

**Figure 14–6** Death rates for the ten leading causes of death: 1900 and 1961. (From "The Facts of Life and Death, selected statistics on the Nation's Health and People," Public Health Service Publication, No. 600, U.S. Government Printing Office, 1963, revised.)

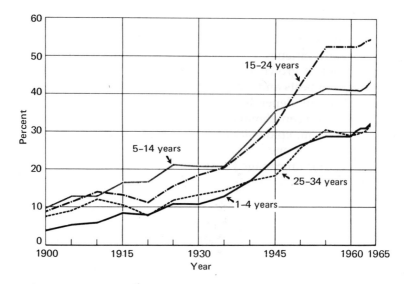

**Figure 14–7** Deaths from all accidents as a percentage of all deaths for persons aged 1–34 years: United States, 1900–1964. (Courtesy of the Division of Vital Statistics, U.S. National Center for Health Statistics.)

Today, however, another group of pathogens has assumed major importance. These are *endogenous* organisms that are commonly found associated with healthy people — in the gastrointestinal tract, on the skin, or in the mouth. Most of the time these organisms are held in check by the body's defenses. But when the immune system is depressed by illness, age, malnutrition, or drugs, these endogenous organisms become capable of causing illness. Official health statistics usually tend to record many deaths as due to cancer, heart disease, kidney disease, transplant rejection, or whatever the primary cause may be, when in fact an endogenous infection played the decisive role.

In many undeveloped and developing areas of the world, exogenous organisms are still the major killers. The major causes of mortality in these countries are infectious diarrhea (which may be caused by a variety of bacteria, protozoa, viruses, or parasitic worms) and respiratory infections such as measles and pneumonia. Where nutrition is poor, weaning from the breast is associated with a high risk of mortality from diarrhea. In Latin America in 1960, over 40 percent of all deaths occurred in children under 5 years of age, and from 60 to 70 percent of these deaths were attributable to diarrheal disease. In contrast, New York death rates from infectious diarrhea fell from 5,600 per 100,000 people in 1900 to 45 per 100,000 in 1961. The reasons for the decrease are improved sanitary facilities and hygiene, safer food and water supply, and better nutrition.

Modern medical treatment, particularly fluid replacement therapy, has reduced mortality from diarrhea in advanced countries, but antibiotics and vaccines have played relatively small roles. Antibiotics have little effect on the ultimate outcome of diarrheal disease. The vaccines available against typhoid and cholera are not usually used for children because they are not very effective in epidemic situations.

In the United States the rise of new epidemic diseases is related in part to the reduction of infant mortality and the increase in life expectancy. During the first half of this century, approximately 25 years were added to the life expectancy of newborn American infants. While the difference in life expectancy for black and white infants has decreased somewhat, the difference between the sexes has increased. These facts relate directly to the successful control of infectious and nutritional diseases in the past century and a half and to the epidemiologic characteristics of the new diseases. Infectious and nutritional diseases claimed their greatest toll among the young: in 1900 in the United States about 200 out of 1,000 newborn white infants were destined to die before their fifteenth birthday. By 1968 this figure had dropped below thirty. In contrast, the life expectancy for males at age 40 was only 4 years longer in 1968 than in 1900. This is because the decreased mortality among the young has been accompanied by an increased death rate among middle-aged and elderly people from the new epidemic diseases.

*HEART DISEASE.* Cardiovascular diseases, especially arteriosclerotic coronary heart disease, lead the list of diseases of increasing frequency in the United States (Figures 14.6, 14.8). In recent years about a third of all deaths in this country have been due to coronary heart disease, and about half of these occurred in individuals between the ages of 35 and 65. Epidemiologic studies of the worldwide distribution of coronary heart dis-

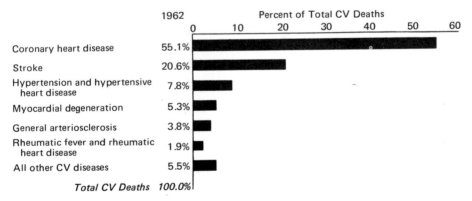

**Figure 14–8** Percentage breakdown of total cardiovascular deaths by specific cause, United States, 1962. (Reprinted by permission from *Lectures in Preventive Cardiology*, J. Stamler, published by Grune and Stratton, 1967.)

ease disclose that it is much more frequent in the United States and western Europe than in northern Africa, Japan, and other Asian countries.

Several studies have attempted to define the *risk factors* associated with coronary heart disease. Although no single exclusive cause has been identified, several factors appear to be involved. They include a high level of cholesterol in the blood (probably brought about by large amounts of fat in the diet), hypertension, diabetes, cigarette smoking, overweight, physical inactivity, familial history (genetic factors), and behavior pattern. The most consistent of these factors is the level of cholesterol in the blood. The incidence rates are lower in premenopausal women than in men or older women, even when serum cholesterol is high, suggesting that female hormones may inhibit development of the disease.

Recently, the association between behavior pattern and coronary heart disease has been evaluated. Friedman and Rosenman believe that the following types of behavior are likely to increase the risk of heart attack:

(1) intense, sustained drive to achieve self-selected but usually poorly defined goals,

(2) profound inclination and eagerness to compete,

(3) persistent desire for recognition and advancement,

(4) continuous involvement in multiple and diverse functions constantly subject to time restrictions (deadlines),

(5) habitual propensity to accelerate the rate of execution of many physical and mental functions, and

(6) an extraordinary mental and physical alertness.

This pattern, which they call Behavior Pattern A, seems to be associated independently from cholesterol or other risk factors with high rates of coronary heart disease. It also describes the typical "successful" American businessman, professor, or student.

Coronary heart disease is probably a disease of many causes. Much that is typical of modern American culture — rich diet and obesity, lack of healthful physical exercise, and a drive for "success" — may be related to the ascendancy of one of the most frequent causes of death.

CANCER AND EMPHYSEMA.    The other diseases that have shown striking increases in mortality in the United States in recent years are cancer, especially of the lung, and emphysema, with or without accompanying bronchitis. In 1962 about 16,000 deaths were attributed to emphysema or chronic bronchitis, in contrast to only 3,900 in 1952, a fourfold increase. Only about half of the increase in cancer deaths is related to the larger number and proportion of people in older age groups. The rest reflects the absolute increase in the probability of a person in the older age groups contracting the disease.

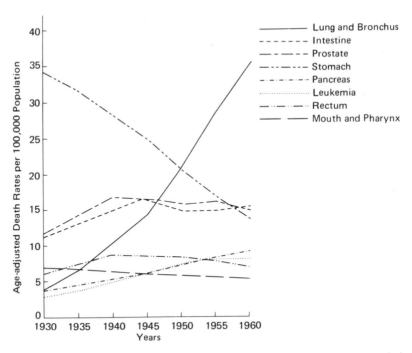

**Figure 14–9** Age-adjusted death rates per 100,000 white males, by selected sites of cancer, United States (1930–1960). From Lillienfeld, Pedersen, and Dowdy, *Cancer Epidemiology: Methods of Study*, Johns Hopkins Press, Baltimore, 1967.)

The lung cancer epidemic has primarily involved males (Figure 14.9). As much as 90 percent of the increase of lung cancer in males may be related to an increase in cigarette smoking during the past 40 years. Females, too, are smoking more frequently, and their incidence of lung cancer is also rising. An individual who smokes one pack of cigarettes a day has a relative risk of lung cancer about 3 or 4 times greater than that of a nonsmoker. The risk increases steadily. A three-pack-a-day smoker has a risk from 20 to 35 times higher than a nonsmoker. The risk among those who give up smoking eventually returns to the nonsmoker's level.

Although the lung cancer epidemic has been linked epidemiologically to cigarette smoking, exposure to other cancer-producing substances (*carcinogens*) has also been associated with the occurrence of cancer, including cancer of the lung. Constituents of polluted air are suspected, since death rates from lung cancer are lower among nonsmokers in rural areas than among nonsmokers in cities. The risk of lung cancer is about 5 times higher among nickel workers and considerably higher among asbestos workers. Mine workers, especially those mining uranium ores, inhale radio-active particles which may remain in their lungs, emitting harmful alpha radiation. Incidence of lung cancer is somewhat higher than average among miners. In view of the increasing environmental contamination with these materials, it would be valuable to establish **dose-response curves** for them as has been done with cigarette smoking. Unfortunately, such statistical studies depend on observation of large numbers of individuals. It is chronic exposure to low doses that is of most concern, and for this the data are very poor. The question of whether there is a threshold level below which exposure to radiation or a carcinogen has no effect is still hotly debated.

The first clear evidence for **chemical carcinogenesis** was reported by Percival Pott in 1775. He observed the frequent occurrence of an unusual tumor, cancer of the scrotum, in the chimney sweeps of London. About one out of ten chimney sweeps who held their jobs for several years would develop this tumor. During the 150 years after Potts' observations, a number of other occupational tumors were observed, including cancer of the bladder among workers in the aniline dye industry, bone cancers among watch-dial painters who accidentally ingested or inhaled radium, lung cancers among chromate workers, cancer of the nasal sinuses and of the lung in nickel miners, skin cancers in dentists who held the film by hand when x-raying their patient's teeth, and leukemia among radiologists.

Early in this century, scientists were successful in producing cancer in experimental animals by painting their skin with various chemicals. A wide range of compounds was found to have carcinogenic activity under the right circumstances. Among these were hydrocarbons, nitrosamines, carbamates, alkylating agents, radiomimetic agents, alkaloids, and the aflatoxins (compounds produced by mold growing on wet peanuts and corn). Even female sex hormones can induce tumors. The recent controversy over the safety of several types of birth control pills is in part related to this.

In general, the chemical carcinogens have no structural or pharmacological properties in common. Furthermore, impure mixtures of substances, such as crude tars, are frequently more active than equivalent or larger amounts of pure carcinogenic compounds. This observation led to an ingenious series of experiments in which mice were exposed to a single dose of a potent carcinogen, applied to an area of their skin. They failed to develop cancer. After a time the same area of skin was painted with croton oil, a material that alone is not carcinogenic. The mice treated in this way rapidly developed cancers. The interpretation was that croton oil functions as a *co-carcinogen*, enhancing the effect of the more potent substance. When the combined effect of two substances (or two variables of any kind) is greater than the sum of the two separate effects, the substances are said to act *synergistically*. Since the discovery of synergism between carcinogens, screening for carcinogenic materials in the environment has become extremely complex. We must now investigate not only pure substances, but determine what combinations of stimuli will provoke a cancer. Furthermore, not only interactions among chemicals are involved, but interactions among chemicals and variables like temperature, radiation, microorganisms and viruses, and, of course, the genetic constitution of the host and chronic conditions that might exist in him.

Additive or synergistic effects between carcinogens are well known. Asbestos workers who also smoke have unusually high rates of lung cancer. Similarly, a controversy arose in recent Congressional hearings on radiation exposure and the safety of uranium miners, when it was learned that those miners who developed lung cancer were almost invariably smokers. The reason that so many investigations of the causes of cancer have produced conflicting results may well be that, in searching for a single cause, scientists have overlooked or misinterpreted the effects of interacting factors.

In the case of lung cancer, it should be apparent that search for "the" carcinogen in cigarette smoke is search for a will-o'-the-wisp. A number of purified materials in cigarette smoke can induce skin cancer in mice and other animals; in combination, they are even more carcinogenic. In addition, dangerous inorganic materials, including arsenic and certain radioactive elements, may be present.

Racial and international comparisons of cancer mortality are of considerable epidemiologic interest because they may provide clues to genetic or environmental factors related to the incidence of cancer. In Japan stomach cancer is much more frequent in males than lung cancer (Figure 14.10). The incidence of stomach cancer is highest among Japanese living in Japan, lower in Japanese living in Hawaii, and lowest — but still higher than average — among Japanese living in the United States. The most obvious conclusion is that both racial (genetic) and environmental factors are involved — that the Japanese people are inherently susceptible to this form of cancer, but influences in their native environment exacerbate the situation. It is impossible to assign relative weights to "genes" and "the environment," however, because it is impossible to determine how significant a portion of their environment Japanese migrants carry with them in the form of their lifestyle. The positive correlation between stomach cancer and blood type A was mentioned in Chapter 6; what other genetic factors may be involved is not known.

In Egypt, bladder cancer is common among peasants who work in the irrigated fields along the Nile River. These people are also frequently infected with a fluke, *Schistosoma haematobium*, that lives in this water. The fluke can penetrate the skin or gain entrance into the body in drinking water. It invades the bloodstream, eventually causing chronic inflammation of the urinary bladder. After years of this chronic condition, changes characteristic of cancer of the bladder frequently appear. Part of the life cycle of this parasite takes place in one of a number of species of snails. Control of the disease, like control of malaria, involves eradication of the invertebrate host. Recently, however, the situation has become worse instead of better.

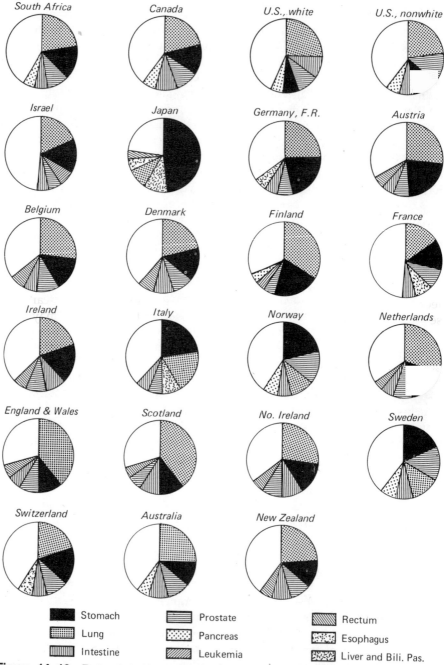

**Figure 14–10** Ratio of deaths from malignant neoplasms affecting five leading sites. Data for males in 22 selected countries, 1964–1965. (From *Cancer Mortality for Selected Sites in 24 Countries*, no. 5 (1964–1965), Dept. of Public Health, Tohoku University, Japan, 1959.)

There has been a population explosion among snails in the new lands irrigated by water from the Aswan Dam. The increase in snails has been accompanied by epidemics of schistosomiasis (the disease caused by the fluke); and because of the association between schistosomiasis and bladder cancer, a future epidemic of bladder cancer should cause no surprise.

Although no virus has been proved to cause cancer in humans, and experimental proof is impossible because of moral constraints on human experimentation, a number of viruses are able to produce tumors in animals. Some of these *oncogenic* viruses have been isolated from humans, and some have been shown to be oncogenic in a wide range of species, including primates. It is likely, therefore, that viruses will eventually be irrefutably linked with some human cancers. One candidate is a herpes virus called the E-B virus, which has repeatedly been isolated from tissues of children who have died from a peculiar type of tumor, Burkitts' lymphoma. This disease is the chief cause of death among children and adolescents in some central African tribes. It occurs primarily at certain altitudes and under certain climatic conditions which suggest that a mosquito may be involved in its transmission. In fact, the geographic distribution of the tumor is very similar to that of malaria and some other mosquito-borne diseases. It has not yet been proved that the virus is the actual cause of the tumor and not merely an opportunist that infects the patient whose defenses are already weakened, but the case against the virus is building up strongly.

Patients who receive organ transplants have an increased risk of developing cancer. There are two theories to explain this, both of which relate to the use of immunosuppressive drugs to prevent rejection of the transplant. One is that a latent oncogenic virus that had been held in check by the host's defense mechanisms becomes able to grow and stimulate the formation of a cancer after the activity of the immune system is depressed. The other theory holds that cancer cells begin to develop many times in the life of each of us. These cells may possess antigens unlike any found in normal cells. In a person whose immune system is functioning normally, these cancer cells are recognized as foreign and are destroyed. When the ability to distinguish "self" from "not-self" is impaired, cancer cells can flourish. Neither theory has yet been proved.

Viruses with oncogenic properties for lower animals have also been isolated from human tissues. It is possible that under usual conditions these viruses cause only mild symptoms of infection or none at all, but that under certain circumstances — simultaneous exposure to some pollutant, drug, or carcinogen, for example — a cancer reaction could be provoked.

Finally, it has frequently been observed that cancer "runs in families." It is difficult to isolate the component of this tendency that is actually genetic, and not related to culture, lifestyle, and common environmental influences. However, cancer is unusually common among siblings of leukemic children, and relatives of lung cancer patients have an increased risk of developing this disease whether or not they are smokers. The increased risk does not

## CROSS-CULTURAL PSYCHIATRY

*"Physicians consider that when the cause of a disease is discovered, the cure is discovered."*

*Cicero*

Many physical diseases which afflicted man during Cicero's time have either been eliminated or controlled. Unfortunately, the same mental ailments which prevented first century B.C. man from functioning to his fullest are still haunting twentieth century man. Yet despite this long history, few causes or cures have been found. Records show that approximately 19 million people are afflicted with some form of mental illness. In America alone this amounts to one in every ten people.

In contrast to these grim statistics, the field of mental health is exploding with ideas, research, cross-disciplined studies, and experimentation. In addition to searching for cures, professionals are now more than ever seeking causes. The field of cross-cultural psychiatry is one area which hopes to supply some "cause" pieces to this extraordinarily complex puzzle called mental illness.

Cross-cultural psychiatry represents a merging of four disciplines: psychiatry, anthropology, psychology, and sociology. It attempts to compare mental disorders, ignoring socio-political boundaries. The importance of such a comparison is manyfold. First, through such a comparison the role, if any, that culture plays in mental disorder may become obvious. Second, factors which are impossible to vary within a culture vary naturally across cultures (for instance, family structure, societal role expectations, success modules, and sociological organization). By changing these variables, perhaps the role each plays in mental organization and disorganization will become readily evident. Third, cross-cultural studies force the exploration of mental illness to be more epidemiological. Such an approach requires definitions, procedures, evaluations, and goals to be well delineated and objective. For too many years mental illness has been victimized by subjectivity masked in professional jargon. Hopefully, cross-cultural psychiatry will force a complacent medical community do do some self-analysis.

One of the major stumbling blocks for the psychiatrist is defining mental disorders cross-culturally. For example, in the early thirties "evidence" was found to support the view that schizophrenia was only peculiar to Western

extend to spouses, indicating a genetic rather than an environmental cause. The association between blood type A and stomach cancer at least makes plausible the theory that other genetically determined characteristics are also associated with the probability of developing specific types of cancer.

*MENTAL ILLNESS.* Although a detailed discussion of mental illness is beyond the scope of this book, some of its epidemiologic aspects should at least be mentioned. It has long been realized that not only the incidence but societies. Through further study, however, researchers found that the difference was not the result of culture but of linguistics and symptom manifestation, and the importance of a culture-free diagnosis of an individual began to emerge. A recent experiment, however, demonstrated just how far we still are from such diagnosing. Patient interviews were taped and then played to American and British psychiatrists. The British doctors regularly diagnosed the patients as having "affective psychosis," while the American diagnosis was "schizophrenia." Currently, there is an attempt to standardize ratings through an Inpatient Psychiatric Rating Scale. Hopefully, this scale will remove transcultural differences in diagnosis and reliable figures will emerge.

Another problem that cross-cultural psychiatry has yet to solve is the different societal attitudes toward symptoms. For instance, in some cultures hallucinations are looked upon as religious phenomenon and even admired. In others, hallucinations represent "sick" behavior. In some cultures loneliness or inactivity is plauded, while in others it is regarded scornfully. The question of what is normal and what is abnormal is not easy to determine within a culture, but across cultures it becomes infinitely more complex.

Despite these various difficulties, cross-cultural psychiatry has reaped some rewards. In the comparison of literate and non-literate societies, data has emerged that indicates a low incidence of depression and suicide in non-literate societies. When hostility was evident, it was found to be inner-directed in the more complex society and outer-directed in the more primitive one. Again, the lack of standardized evaluations makes for cautious conclusions. Another survey has indicated that there is a relationship between symptom manifestation and culture. Rural patients were found more prone to delusions of grandeur, while urban patients suffered from depersonalization symptoms. Asians seemed more predisposed to delusional jealousy, while Christians and Muslims manifested delusions of destructiveness.

Such survey summarizing could continue ad infinitum. Because designing and executing experiments is complex and expensive, cross-cultural psychiatry cannot yet boast long lists of eye-opening correlations. The horizon, however, looks promising. Perhaps cross-cultural psychiatry's most significant contribution will lie in the area of prevention. By establishing what role each sociocultural variable plays in the scenario of mental illness, man, through a deliberate change in the environment, will be able to "cure" one of society's most perplexing ills—mental disorder.

---

also the forms of mental disorder vary with culture. Epidemics of "dancing mania," once common, are no longer encountered. The kind of "hysteria" to which Freud devoted so much attention is now rare. The classic manifestations of schizophrenia described in psychiatry texts of half a century ago are disappearing, although new manifestions have appeared and schizophrenia remains a widespread and serious disorder. Diseases once more common in one sex or the other are now appearing with increasing frequency in the opposite sex. It has been postulated that psychosomatic processes related to the changing way in which the two sexes perceive their roles may lie at the root of this change.

In the broadest sense we already know that age, marital status, socio-economic class, social attitudes, and roles in the family and the community are powerful determinants of mental illness. The prevalence of mental disorders, however, and the high rates of crime and civil disorder, suggest that we should pay more attention to man's psychological adaptation or maladaptation to the environment.

## DISEASE, GENETICS, AND RACE

Not all diseases that have a genetic component are related to race, but many of them are. Each racial group is characterized by a certain pattern of disease, determined by a combination of genetic, social, cultural, and geographic influences. The bulk of the population of most races is still localized geographically, and geographic and climatic factors strongly influence the nature and occurrence of disease. But when migrants show the same tendencies to contract some diseases and be resistant to others, genetic and cultural factors are also implicated. If racial differences persist when individuals of the same age, sex, and socio-economic class, living in similar environments, are compared, the evidence for real, genetically-determined racial differences becomes strong.

Table 14.1 shows comparative death rates for whites and nonwhites in the United States from a few selected causes. For some of these, like homicide, it is clear that the difference between the groups is due to social conditions. For others there is probably a significant genetic component underlying the differences. Current knowledge of the relationships among genetics, race, and disease is summarized by Damon (see references).

There are many genetically caused disorders whose mode of inheritance is known. The frequencies of some of these vary markedly from one racial group to another. For example, the Ashkenazic Jews show relatively high frequencies of Tay-Sachs disease (amaurotic family idiocy), stub thumbs, Niemann-Pick disease (a disturbance of lipid metabolism accompanied by enlargement of the liver and spleen, anemia, and, in some cases, severe mental retardation), Gaucher's disease (a splenic anemia), and a number of other disorders. The incidence of phenylketonuria, in contrast, is unusually low. Among Koreans lack of the enzyme catalase and a form of night blindness are common. Africans have a low frequency of cystic fibrosis, hemophilia, and phenylketonuria, and a high frequency of abnormal hemoglobins. (We have seen, however, that some of the more common abnormal hemoglobins are maintained through their selective advantage in conferring resistance to malaria, and that their frequency decreases when malaria is no longer a threat.)

**TABLE 14.1**
**Death Rates from Selected Causes for Whites and Nonwhites in the United States, 1965 (per 100,000 population in the specified group)**

| Cause | Mortality Rates Whites | Mortality Rates Nonwhites | Ratio of Mortality Rates White/Nonwhite |
|---|---|---|---|
| Suicide | 11.9 | 5.0 | 2.38 |
| Leukemia | 7.4 | 4.1 | 1.80 |
| Arteriosclerotic heart disease | 303.8 | 175.8 | 1.73 |
| Urinary cancer | 7.5 | 4.6 | 1.63 |
| Lymphosarcoma | 8.1 | 5.1 | 1.59 |
| Breast cancer | 14.6 | 9.5 | 1.54 |
| Peptic ulcer | 5.6 | 3.8 | 1.47 |
| Respiratory cancer | 27.7 | 20.6 | 1.34 |
| Digestive cancer | 49.6 | 41.8 | 1.19 |
| Motor vehicle accidents | 25.3 | 25.8 | 0.98 |
| Stroke | 102.3 | 114.7 | 0.89 |
| Genital cancer | 20.5 | 23.3 | 0.88 |
| Cirrhosis of the liver | 12.5 | 14.6 | 0.86 |
| Diabetes mellitus | 16.7 | 20.1 | 0.83 |
| Accidents, excluding motor vehicle | 28.9 | 41.2 | 0.70 |
| Pneumonia | 28.9 | 44.2 | 0.65 |
| Hypertensive heart disease | 24.7 | 55.3 | 0.45 |
| Tuberculosis | 3.4 | 9.3 | 0.37 |
| Syphilis | 1.0 | 2.8 | 0.36 |
| Homicide | 3.0 | 24.6 | 0.12 |

From A. Damon, 1971. Race, Ethnic Group, and Disease. In *The Biological and Social Meaning of Race*. R. Osborne, ed. W. H. Freeman and Company, San Francisco. P. 62.

Although specific mutant genes can be linked with certain diseases, many, perhaps most, diseases for which there is a genetic predisposition involve the action and interaction of more than one gene. Perhaps the best way to unravel the relationships in these cases is to search for physiologic and biochemical differences in individuals or races and to try to explain varying incidences of disease on this basis. A number of racial differences are listed in Table 14.2. Many of them are related to the interaction of a number of genes, with perhaps some environmental influence as well. Others, like color blindness and lactase deficiency, are caused by a single gene.

Some of these physiologic and biochemical variations among the races suggest possible explanations for racial variations in disease prevalence. For example, the higher bone density of Negroids may be related to the lower incidence of hip and spinal fractures among elderly blacks, and differences in prenatal skeletal development are probably related to decreased incidence of congential hip malformations. The correlation between physiological and biochemical characteristics of the races with the incidence of specific diseases is fruitful ground for further research.

TABLE 14.2
Some Racial Differences in Physiologic and Biochemical Norms

| Trait | In Relation to Caucasoids | |
|---|---|---|
| | Negroids | Mongoloids |
| Birth weight | − | − |
| Skeletal and dental maturation at birth | + | |
| Neurological maturation at birth | + | |
| Neonatal motor development | + | |
| Auditory and visual acuity | + | |
| Blood pressure | + | − |
| Bone density | + | − |
| Color blindness | − | − |
| Fibrinolysin activity (dissolving fibrin in blood clots and inactivation of fibrinogen | + | |
| Inactivation of isoniazid (a drug used to treat tuberculosis) | | + |
| Keloid formation (small growths on skin, probably in response to trauma) | + | |
| Lactase deficiency (milk intolerance) in adult | + | + |
| Skin resistance, electrical | + | |
| Ability to taste phenylthiocarbamide | + | + |
| Twinning, dizygotic (fraternal) | + | − |

Plus sign (+) indicates greater than; minus sign (−) indicates less than.
Source: A. Damon. 1971.

## OTHER ENVIRONMENTAL FACTORS AND DISEASE

Before the campaign of 1946–1950 to eradicate the mosquito *Anopheles darlingi* from the densely populated coastal areas of British Guiana, there was a high incidence of malaria in the population. Control of the mosquito permitted development of new areas for much-needed housing and industry. The victory over malaria proved to be short-lived, however. Economic development reduced and displaced much of the former livestock population, on which another mosquito, *Anopheles aquasalis*, fed. Forced to change its habits or perish, *A. aquasalis* shifted its attention to man, and new outbreaks of malaria began.

Similarly, outbreaks of viral encephalitis are thought to have begun about the time large areas of lowlands were opened for agriculture. Wild birds and small mammals are the natural hosts for these viruses, which are transmitted by mosquitoes. Infected birds experience only mild disease or none at all. When their natural habitat was destroyed, many wild birds began to feed in the cultivated lands. This altered many relationships among birds, mosquitoes, wild mammals, poultry, and man, resulting in introduction of the virus into species closely associated with man and from them to man himself.

Around the turn of this century, Dr. H.T. Ricketts elucidated the cause and epidemiology of a form of "black measles" that was indigenous to persons living in the Snake River Valley in Idaho and Montana. The agent was discovered to be an intracellular organism spread by the bite of an infected tick *(Dermacentor andersoni)*. The disease was named Rocky Mountain Spotted Fever, which was descriptive of its clinical symptoms and location. In the past few decades Rocky Mountain Spotted Fever has become much more common in the Appalachian Mountains and southern United States than it is in the West. In this new endemic location the organism has infected a new vector, the American dog tick *(Dermacentor variabilis)* which has a much more intimate association with man than *D. andersoni*. Furthermore, the rising population density in the eastern United States, with the encroachment of suburban housing tracts on the Appalachian foothills, has also increased the disease frequency among people living in this area.

These are but a few of many examples of how environmental changes caused by human activity have led to changes in the complex relationships between man, his environment, and disease. We have already discussed the changed patterns of disease related to cultural evolution. Man the hunter and gatherer came into intimate contact with many wild species, and he may have shared a large number of diseases with them. Man the agriculturalist and pastoralist had fewer close contacts with wild animals; but now he developed a new set of relationships with a large number and variety of domesticated animals, and disease patterns shifted. In modern industrialized cities man has only occasional contact with other species of animals. The few types of animals he keeps as pets are under the same close medical scrutiny and protection from contact with wild animals as man himself.

A disease or infection that may be transmitted from animals to man is called a *zoonosis*. Some pathogenic organisms and parasites have complex life cycles involving early development in one host and maturation in another. The disease agent may be transmitted from one host to another by still another animal, the *vector*, which may or may not play an essential role in its life cycle — other than to transmit it from host to host. The vector is often an arthropod — for example, a fly, mosquito, tick, mite, or flea. Severe epidemics may occur when environmental conditions are particularly favorable to the vector, as when an unusually wet season provides widespread breeding grounds for mosquitoes. The culture of rice had to be abandoned in some provinces of Turkey because no other means of mosquito control was effective. One of the most effective means of controlling vector-borne diseases has been to destroy the vector or its habitat.

Relationships between environmental factors and disease are not always either predictable or obvious. Subtle changes in the ecosystem can have unforeseen and drastic effects on the human population. Recently, DDT was used in an area of Bolivia in an attempt to control malaria-transmitting mosquitoes. The DDT also killed a large number of local cats. Death of the cats was soon followed by an epidemic of Bolivian hemorrhagic fever, a typhus-like disease spread by a population of small rodents no longer held in check by the cats.

Under different environmental conditions, different sectors of the population may be exposed to disease agents. In urban areas, for example, the virus causing St. Louis encephalitis is carried by a mosquito vector that frequents homes. Consequently, a large proportion of those contracting the disease are older persons. In rural areas, however, the virus is transmitted by a species of mosquito that does not often enter the home. Here young children, who encounter the mosquito while playing outdoors, are most often infected with the St. Louis encephalitis virus.

One zoonotic disease, salmonellosis, has increased dramatically in the past three decades among persons in developed countries. This increased incidence is related to modern methods of agriculture, food processing, and marketing. While *Salmonella* organisms can be spread through the feces, they also have an important natural reservoir in domestic animals such as poultry, cattle, swine, or dogs. Humans may often acquire infection by ingesting contaminated eggs, meat, meat products, or other foods prepared from infected animals. "Nonedible" protein such as fish meal and leftover material from the slaughterhouse is often added to animal feed. Much of this animal feed is contaminated with salmonellae, resulting in a food-borne disease that is maintained in animals. The modern agricultural practice of crowding animals together in the feedlot and on the way to slaughter has also increased the animal reservoir by direct infection from one animal to another. In addition, the use of small amounts of antibiotics in animal feed as a growth stimulant may have substantially increased the number of infections in animals, since the normal antibiotic-sensitive bacteria in their intestinal tracts help keep exogenous *Salmonella* in check. This practice of feeding antibiotics to animals is so widespread that nearly half of all antibiotics currently produced in the United States are used for this purpose. Finally, massive centralized processing of foods creates special hazards. A glass of eggnog or a meringue pie is likely to contain eggs from dozens or even hundreds of farms. A small amount of contamination with pathogenic *Salmonella* bacteria might be distributed to thousands of dinner tables and under the proper circumstances might produce a large epidemic of disease. When most food was processed and consumed on a single farm, massive outbreaks of food poisoning due to *Salmonella* were very unusual.

Many of the pollutants we are introducing into the environment have sometimes surprising and often widespread effects on various ecosystems. They also have adverse effects on man, either directly or indirectly as a result of their effects on other organisms or the physical environment. We are experiencing epidemics of lead poisoning, mercury poisoning, deaths related to smog, and many other problems related to pollution. These will be discussed in Chapter 15.

Clearly, the survival of our civilization depends, among other things, upon avoidance of what ecologist Barry Commoner has termed the "ultimate blunder" — nuclear war. If such a catastrophe were ever to happen, the ravages of disease would probably overshadow all the immediate effects of the explosion and fallout. Shelters to protect against blast damage and radioactive fallout would be virtually worthless in the face of such an assault on the ecosystem. Fortunately, ecologic effects are being considered increasingly often and seriously by politicians and other policymakers; but what is perceived as political necessity or practical expediency is still likely to foster decisions that overvalue short-term political or economic gains at the expense of long-term ecologic values.

## REFERENCES

ARMELAGOS, G. J., AND J. R. DEWEY. 1970. Evolutionary response to human infectious disease. *Bio-Science.* 20:271–274.

BLUMBERG, B. S. 1962. *Proceedings of the Conference of Genetic Polymorphisms and Geographic Variations in Disease.* New York: Grune & Stratton.

COMMONER, B. 1963. *Science and Survival.* New York: Viking Press.

DAMON, A. 1971. Race, ethnic group, and disease. In *The Biological and Social Meaning of Race.* R. Osborne, ed. San Francisco: W. H. Freeman and Co.

DUBOS, R., AND J. DUBOS. 1952. *The White Plague: Tuberculosis, Man, and Society.* Boston: Little, Brown & Co.

DUFFY, J. 1953. *Epidemics in Colonial America.* Baton Rouge: Louisiana State Univ. Press.

FLEMING, W. C. 1964. Syphilis through the ages. Symposium on Syphilis and Other Venereal Diseases. *Medical Clinics of North America.* 48:587–612.

FORBES, T. R. 1970. Life and death in Shakespeare's London. *American Scientist.* 58:511–520.

GORDON, J. E., I. CHITKARA, AND J. B. WYON. 1963. Weanling diarrhea. *American Journal of Medical Science.* 246:345–377.

HIRST, L. F. 1953. *The Conquest of Plague.* London: Oxford Univ. Press.

HUDSON, E. H. 1965. Treponematosis and man's social evolution. *American Anthropologist.* 67:885–901.

KILBOURNE, E. D., AND W. G. SMILLIE. 1969. *Human Ecology and Public Health.* Toronto: Macmillan.

LEAVELL, H. R., AND E. G. CLARK. 1965. *Preventive Medicine for the Doctor in His Community.* New York: McGraw-Hill.

LERNER, M., AND O. W. ANDERSON. 1963. *Health Progress in the United States: 1900–1960.* Chicago: Univ. of Chicago Press.

LILLIENFELD, A. M., E. PEDERSEN, AND J. E. DOWD. 1967. *Cancer Epidemiology: Methods of Study.* Baltimore: Johns Hopkins Press.

LIVINGSTONE, F. B. 1971. Malaria and human polymorphisms. *Ann. Rev. of Genetics.* 5:33–64.

MOTULSKY, A. C. 1960. Metabolic polymorphisms and the role of infectious diseases in human evolution. *Human Biology.* 32:28–63.

NEEL, J., M. SHAW, AND W. SCHULL, EDS. 1963. *Genetics and the Epidemiology of Chronic Diseases.* Public Health Service Pub. No. 1163. Washington, D.C.: U.S. Dept. of Health and Welfare.

PAUL, J. R. 1966. *Clinical Epidemiology*. Chicago: Univ. of Chicago Press.

POLGER, S. 1964. Evolution and the ills of mankind. In *Horizons in Anthropology*, S. Tax, ed. Chicago: Aldine Publishing Co.

PRYOR, W. A. 1970. Free radicals in biological systems. *Scientific American*. 223:70–83.

ROSENMAN, R. H., M. FRIEDMAN, R. STRAUSS, M. WURM, D. JENKINS, H. B. MESSINGER, R. KOSITCHEK, W. HAHN, AND N. T. WETHERSSEN. 1966. Coronary heart disease in the western collaborative study. *Journal of the American Med. Assoc.* 195:86–92.

SIGERIST, H. E. 1962. *Civilization and Disease*. Chicago: Univ. of Chicago Press.

STAMLER, J. 1967. *Lectures on Preventive Cardiology*. New York: Grune and Stratton.

# · 15 ·

NORMAN D. LEVINE

CAROL E. STEINHART

# Pollution and the Quality of the Human Environment

For each living thing there is an optimal environment or range of environmental conditions which embraces the web of functional relationships among organisms and their physical surroundings. Within limits, all organisms can adjust to environmental change; and in time some organisms, through the process of mutation and natural selection, become adapted to conditions their ancestors could not have tolerated. But despite their ability to adjust and adapt, a suitable environment is the first requirement for all living things, and man is no exception.

Environments of the modern world pose a twofold threat to human well-being. First, the modern environment contains manmade elements which are directly poisonous or otherwise harmful to us; second, rapid, drastic, and perhaps irreversible changes are underway which threaten to overwhelm many of the natural systems on which we depend and to outrun our capacity for adaptation. These manmade elements which threaten our physical and mental health and the integrity of our support systems may collectively be called *pollution*.

## THE NATURE AND ORIGIN OF POLLUTION

Pollution is the accumulation of wastes or by-products which occurs when wastes are discharged into the environment faster than they can be degraded, assimilated, or dispersed by natural processes. Although there are examples of "natural" pollution, including that from volcanic eruptions and natural oil seeps, the concept usually connotes human activity.

The production of wastes is inextricably tied with the conversion of energy, which we use to bring about changes in the material aspects of our environment. No process of energy conversion is or ever can be entirely efficient; all produce unwanted and sometimes unexpected by-products and side effects. Similarly, there are by-products in the conversion of materials from one form to another. In the past we have not recycled materials as nature does nor have we tried to control the side effects of energy use. The net result, then, of our use of energy is to convert resources to an equal or greater volume of waste. Today no one needs to be convinced of the necessity to recycle materials. What may escape attention, however, is that even recycling requires energy (which, for natural processes, is provided by the sun), and that the use of energy inevitably exacts penalties of its own. And in the end, all the energy we use is degraded to heat, which itself has a wide range of environmental effects.

The scope and magnitude of our pollution problems are the combined result of the size of the human population, our failure to recycle materials, and the scale on which we manipulate the material and energy resources of the earth. In the end, the carrying capacity of the earth for our species may be determined more by its ability to process human wastes than by its capacity to produce food.

When there were relatively few people on the earth and they had only the energy of their own muscles, human activities were integrated into the ecosystems of which people were a part, and human wastes were recycled along with other materials through the many biological, chemical, and physical cycles of the earth. Man was unable to pollute his environment. Pollution became a plague of increasing frequency and severity as man became a dominant species — as he harnessed new energy sources and developed technology. In the beginning, pollution was localized and small-scale. If pollution and depletion of resources occasionally led to epidemics, hunger, or even cultural collapse, the problem affected only isolated populations and restricted areas. Today, however, as Chapter 10 pointed out, the entire human species is becoming the adaptive unit, and the many separate human environments are merging into one — this planet. In addition, a citizen of the United States or another affluent nation consumes more resources and contributes more massively to pollution than a citizen of a poor nation; and all nations, rich and poor, find their problems growing as their more disadvantaged citizens strive to improve their standard of living. Our national parks would not be crowded, even with our present population, if efforts to achieve social justice had not brought automobiles and paid vacations to most of us. The poverty-stricken do not pollute very much.

Pollutants are classified according to their physical and chemical natures. They include such unwanted side effects and products as heat, noise, radioactive elements, dust and other particles, hydrocarbons, carbon dioxide, pesticides, and toxic metals and chemicals. Pollution is also considered in terms of what is polluted — air, water, soil, or food. For preventing pollution or controlling it at its origin, the polluter must be identified. Agriculture, industry, mining, power plants, transportation, domestic and municipal wastes, and the production and refining of petroleum are all major sources of pollutants and pollution. The references listed at the end of this chapter contain information on the amounts and sources of various pollutants and on technology and institutional arrangements for control of pollution. Our concern here will be with the ecologic effects of pollution, especially as it affects man and his possible futures.

## BIOLOGICAL EFFECTS OF POLLUTION

An organism may be affected by pollution either directly or indirectly, through changes in its environment. Conversely, biological effects of pollution lead to changes in the habitat, because most of the chemical processes in an ecosystem are driven by the metabolism of living organisms. Existing species have had a long time in which to adapt — to evolve a biochemical balance within themselves which is compatible with external conditions. Thus any change is more likely to be harmful than beneficial, whether it be a mutation within the organism or a new substance in the environment. We are introducing many pollutants with which living organisms have had no evolutionary experience and against which they have no defense.

*WASTE HEAT.* Production of waste heat is inevitable, and we will have to learn to deal with it as long as large numbers of people continue to use huge amounts of energy. Until recently, the quantity of heat released at a particular place was small compared to the total energy flow in the area, and the total amount of energy used by man was negligible compared to global energy flow. Both situations are changing rapidly.

No matter where or how waste heat is disposed of, it eventually ends up in the atmosphere, from which it is radiated into space. But before it is lost from the earth, this heat — which is a form of energy, with the capacity to bring about change — can accomplish much mischief.

Electric power plants are the most notorious producers of waste heat, although large amounts are also released in urban areas as a result of transportation and space heating and by industrial processes requiring heat. Limited by the laws of thermodynamics and the practical realities of materials and design, many of these processes have already nearly attained their maximum possible efficiency. Whatever gains in efficiency are still possible will rapidly be canceled by continued growth in the use of energy. Thus the best we can do is to find uses for waste heat wherever possible and ulti-mately to discharge it where and in a way in which it will do the least harm.

Waste heat discharged directly to the atmosphere has no direct biologi-cal effects, although, as we will discuss later, it may cause local climate modification. The problem of most immediate concern is thermal pollution of water. In industrial processes and in the generation of electricity, waste heat is conventionally transferred to cooling water which, after passing through the system once, is discharged to the source some 10° to 25°F warmer than when it began. This warm water has major effects on physical, chemical, and biological processes.

The rate of chemical reactions, including those that occur in living or-ganisms, is approximately doubled for each rise in temperature of 18° F. As the rate of metabolic reactions increases, so does the demand for oxygen. (Field measurements show, however, that the increase in rate of oxidation may be only 20 or 30 percent per 18° F, because temperature may not be the only factor limiting metabolic rate.) While the oxygen requirement increases with temperature, the solubility of oxygen and other gases in water decreases so that there is less oxygen available to meet the increased demand. At 85° F water can dissolve only half as much oxygen as it can at 32° F.

Metabolism is the total of all chemical reactions occurring in living cells, including both constructive and destructive processes. Although all reac-tions proceed faster as temperature increases, they do not all increase at the same rate, and destructive processes often predominate. At high tempera-tures enzymes are inactivated and the balance among chemical reactions in the cell is disrupted. Furthermore, surrounding each cell is a membrane which regulates the exchange of materials between the cell and its environ-ment and on which many chemical reactions take place. The properties of this membrane are altered by high temperatures, sometimes leading to dis-organization and death of the cell. These are the direct effects of high tem-peratures on living cells.

Most heat is transferred from water to the atmosphere through evapora-tion, although some is transferred through radiation and conduction. In-creased temperature increases the rate of evaporation, leading to higher concentrations of dissolved salts if evaporation exceeds precipitation. The salts may be harmful to aquatic life.

Each organism has a characteristic temperature range in which it can survive and, within this range, a much smaller temperature range that favors optimal growth. The temperature range is determined not only by the direct effects of temperature on the organism but by the nature of the plant and animal communities that thrive in that range. The presence or absence of food, parasites, pathogens, competitors, or predators may determine the ability of an organism to survive at a particular temperature. Some types of game fish vanish from warm water not because they themselves cannot live there, but because the organisms which they eat cannot.

The optimum temperature for an organism is usually toward the higher end of the temperature range in which it can survive. The upper end of the natural temperature range in a body of water may be so close to the lethal temperature for many organisms that an added increment of waste heat is an unbearable stress. For this reason, the effects of waste heat vary with the season of the year and with shorter-term weather conditions. Waste heat is most likely to be beneficial in cold climates and harmful in hot ones. In addition, rapid fluctuations in temperature, such as occur when cooling water is intermittently discharged, can be more harmful than a constant temperature above or below the optimum.

Temperature influences the behavior of organisms, from the tiniest planktonic creatures to the great game fish. There is a daily vertical migration of tiny, surface-feeding animals (zooplankters) in response to diurnal temperature changes. The effects on this behavior by various strategies for disposing of waste heat are unknown. Migratory behavior of some fish is also triggered by temperature. If animals are caused to migrate by exposure to a discharge of warmed water, several kinds of potential trouble await them at their destination. They may find conditions unfavorable for spawning. Temperatures may be too low for development of eggs and survival or growth of the young. Or, appropriate food may not be available.

In general, plant and animal species of value to people thrive at lower temperatures than nuisance species. An outstanding example of this is the blue-green algae. Diatoms, basic elements of many food chains, flourish at temperatures between 59° F and 77° F. Green algae, also important in food chains, thrive in warmer water at 77° to 95° F. Blue-green algae can grow within this entire temperature range, and beyond. At lower temperatures they usually cannot compete successfully with diatoms and green algae, but as temperatures increase, so do the blue-greens. Blue-green algae are not part of the food chains of most organisms we wish to encourage. They flourish in the absence of predators at the expense of green algae and diatoms, indirectly driving away animals that prey on the greens and diatoms. When the blue-greens die, their decomposition by microorganisms further depletes the oxygen supply, which has already been diminished by increased temperature.

Many population studies have shown that if two species are competing for the same environmental niche, one tends eventually to displace the other. This is what happens in the contest between the blue-green algae and the greens and diatoms. Once the blue-greens have become established in a region of warm water, they have the opportunity to colonize waters relatively unaffected by thermal discharges. What begins as a rather small and local shift in the balance among species can have far-reaching effects. The replacement of one group of species by another followed by deterioration of the habitat often resembles acceleration of the natural aging, or eutrophication, of an aquatic ecosystem (see Chapter 3). The rate of change is further accelerated by addition of nitrates, phosphates, and organic carbon from agricultural runoff and sewage.

Not all effects of waste heat are undesirable. Up to a point, an increase in temperature can result in more rapid development of eggs and faster growth of fish of all ages. There have been schemes to use waste heat in nurseries for fish and shellfish. Some waters that are too warm for trout and too cold for bass or catfish might be transformed into excellent fishing grounds by thermal discharges from a power plant. There are many reports of improved fishing in the vicinity of such discharges. If a power plant operates intermittently, however, or is shut down for refueling or repairs, the fish that depend on it for heat may suffer. We must learn many things about the effects of heat on aquatic life before we can predict what the effects of thermal discharge in a particular place may be. Current concern is well founded, because, while the environment has so far been able to assimilate our waste heat, continued growth in use of energy will rapidly exceed its capacity to do so.

RADIOACTIVITY.　The potential hazards of radioactivity became known in connection with development and testing of nuclear weapons and the threat of nuclear war. Today, however, we realize that even the peaceful atom may not be peaceful after all, and this realization accompanies a growing commitment among industrialized nations to the development of nuclear energy. Not only is the nuclear power plant a source of radioactive pollutants. Equal or greater problems arise from the mining, transport, processing, and ultimate disposal of nuclear fuels and radioactive wastes.

THE NATURE OF RADIOACTIVITY.　The chemical identity of an element is determined by the number of positively charged particles (protons) in its nucleus. Each element, however, may exist in a variety of forms, called *isotopes*, according to the number of uncharged particles (neutrons) in its nucleus. Some isotopes of an element may be radioactive, while others are stable. An isotope is identified by its *mass number*, which is the total number of protons and neutrons in the nucleus. The mass number is written as a superscript to the left of the symbol for an element as $^{235}U$, which would be read "uranium-235". Nuclei of a radioactive isotope are unstable and undergo spontaneous change, or decay, to form nuclei of a different chemical element. In the process of this transformation, the nucleus emits particulate or electromagnetic radiation, or both. The *particulate radiation* of most significance consists of positive or negative electrons (beta rays), alpha particles (composed of two protons and two neutrons, identical with nuclei of helium), or neutrons. The *electromagnetic radiation* consists of gamma rays, which carry even more energy than X-rays. All these forms of radiation can interact with the atoms and molecules of living cells, imparting energy to them and creating charged particles (ions). For this reason they are called *ionizing radiation*.

There are more than a thousand different radioactive isotopes, many of them manmade. With each isotope is associated a characteristic time called the *half-life*, a statistical property giving the time required for half the atomic nuclei to decay. After one half-life has elapsed, half of the original nuclei remain; after two half-lives, one quarter; after three half-lives, one eighth, and so on. The half-life varies tremendously from isotope to isotope. For example, half the nuclei of polonium-212 decay in less than a millionth of a second, while the half-life of thorium-232 is ten billion years. In evaluating the hazards of radioactivity, it is important to consider the half-lives the isotopes involved, because they determine whether the problem is a short-range or a long-range one.

Radiation and radioactivity are measured in special units, only three of which need concern us here. A *curie* (named in honor of Marie and Pierre Curie, who discovered radium) is the quantity of a radioactive isotope equivalent in activity to one gram of radium, in which there are $3.7 \times 10^{10}$ nuclear disintegrations per second. Radiation itself is measured in units which represent the amount of energy that radiation imparts to matter. The standard unit of dosage is the *rad*. One rad corresponds to the absorption of 100 ergs (about 24 billionths of a calorie) of energy per gram of matter. Standards for exposure to radiation are defined in *rems*, which are essentially equivalent to rads, except for high energy alpha radiation.

HOW RADIATION DAMAGES LIVING CELLS.    Particles emitted from radioactive nuclei carry more than a million times the energy of the same particles at rest, or in normal motion. Charged particles lose this energy bit by bit in collisions with atoms. Most of the collisions are with electrons, which are driven away from the influence of the nuclei which controlled them, leaving behind positively charged ions and broken chemical bonds. The ions have different chemical properties from the atoms or molecules that gave rise to them. If enough ionizations occur, the function of an entire cell can be disrupted. This is how radiation damages living things.

An average charged particle ionizes on the order of one hundred thousand atoms before coming to rest. The heavier the particle, the shorter is its disruptive path. An alpha particle travels only $1/10$ as far as a proton, which, in turn, travels only $1/60$ as far as an electron. Since an alpha particle, a proton, and an electron can ionize the same number of atoms if they have the same initial energy, the trail of an alpha particle, while shortest, will be the most intensely devastated. For this reason, alpha particles are exceedingly dangerous when they arise from a source within the body — in the bones or lungs, for example — but virtually harmless if created only a few centimeters outside the body.

Although they bear no charge, gamma rays also interact with orbital electrons. They transfer such large amounts of energy in each collision that electrons escape with enough energy to cause further ionizations, creating secondary tracks of ionization.

Neutrons usually interact with nuclei. A collision between a neutron and a nucleus may knock the nucleus away from one of its electrons with enough force to form an ion. When a neutron is captured by a nucleus, emission of particles, gamma rays, or both follows. Nuclei of some isotopes (specifically, the nuclear fuels) undergo fission when they capture a neutron. Other nuclei are rendered radioactive by the absorption of a neutron.

GENERAL EFFECTS OF RADIATION.     Exposure of the whole body to a concentrated dose of more than 600 rads brings death in a few weeks from irreparable damage to bone marrow, lymph nodes, and spleen. A dose this size causes an average of more than a million ionizations in each cell of the body. With an acute dose of between 100 and 600 rads, the same types of changes occur but recovery is increasingly likely as the dose becomes lower. Doses of 100 rads or more would be experienced only in nuclear war, in a major nuclear accident, or in radical radiation therapy. Large acute or chronic doses of ionizing radiation are deadly to all forms of life (Figure 15.1).

The causal relationship between radiation and cancer and leukemia is

**Figure 15–1**   Aerial view of the Biology Gamma Forest where the effects of long-term chronic exposure of ecological systems to ionizing radiation are being studied. The trees in the center died after exposure to gamma radiation in the amount of 20 hrs. per day for 6 months. After several years, this experiment hopefully will yield information on longer term genetic effects of ionization. (Photograph courtesy of the Brookhaven National Laboratory.)

well documented although incompletely understood. Cancers have been produced in adults by single or extended doses of 100 rads. Doses to the fetus of only 5 rads have been implicated in the development of bone cancer. There was an increased incidence of leukemia among early radiologists and among survivors of Hiroshima and Nagasaki. Workers painting radium dials in the years before World War II moistened and shaped their brushes on their tongues. The radioactive material they ingested in this way collected in their bones, where it caused a high incidence of cancer. Deposits of radioactive iodine in the thyroid can cause cancer of this organ. Inhalation of **radon** and its radioactive "daughters," successive stages in the disintegration of uranium, has led to a high rate of lung cancer among uranium miners (Table 15.1). Chronic exposure to radiation also results in a shortening of the lifespan which cannot be attributed to any particular cause of death. It has been compared to the acceleration of the aging process, and is probably due to cumulative minor damage to cells in all parts of the body.

If radiation causes ionizations in the hereditary material (DNA) of a sperm or an egg cell, a mutation can result. Mutations are likely to cause abnormality or death of organisms developing from affected cells. The defects are inheritable and may be passed on to future generations, if the bearer of the mutation survives. Not all genetic damage is as dramatic as a stillbirth, abortion, or gross defect. Many mutations — perhaps most — are subtle and at present impossible to detect. They may predispose an organism to certain diseases, or render it generally less fit than one not carrying the mutation.

THE CONTROVERSY OVER STANDARDS FOR EXPOSURE TO RADIATION. Some of the radiation to which we are exposed is natural, arising from cosmic rays, solar radiation, and radioactive elements in the earth. It varies between 80 and 150 millirads per person per year. (A millirad is $10^{-3}$ rad.) It varies both with the latitude and the altitude at which a person lives and with the composition of the rocks beneath him and the house around him. The fact that man has always lived in this level of radiation does not mean that it is without effect. On the contrary, it is reasonable to assume (even though we cannot measure it) that some fraction of the cancers, genetic defects, and diseases of aging from which man has always suffered is caused by the natural radiation around and in him, and that any increase in exposure will bring about a corresponding increase in radiation-induced disabilities.

Exposure to radiation in medical diagnosis and therapy adds, on the average, 65 millirads per person per year. Although exposure from a single diagnostic X-ray has been reduced through improved equipment and technique, overall medical exposure is increasing because of increased reliance on radiologic methods. Benefits from medical exposure are generally considered to exceed the risks, and the exposure is voluntary.

Much of the controversy about radiation standards for the general

**TABLE 15.1**
**Decay of $^{238}U$**

| Element | Radiation | Half-life |
|---------|-----------|-----------|
| Uranium-238 ↓ | alpha | $4.5 \times 10^{10}$ years |
| Thorium-234 ↓ | beta | 24 days |
| Proactinium-234 ↓ | beta | 1.1 minutes |
| Uranium-234 ↓ | alpha | $2.4 \times 10^5$ years |
| Thorium-230 ↓ | alpha | $8.0 \ 10^4$ years |
| Radium-226 ↓ | alpha | $1.6 \times 10^3$ years |
| Radon-222 ↓ | alpha | 3.8 days |
| Polonium-218 ↓ | alpha or beta | 3.0 minutes |
| -Lead-214 or | beta | 27 minutes |
| ↳Astatine-218 | alpha | 2 seconds |
| Bismuth-214 ↓ | beta or alpha | 20 minutes |
| -Polonium-214 or | alpha | $1.5 \times 10^{-4}$ seconds |
| ↳Thallium-210 | beta | 1.3 minutes |
| Lead-210 ↓ | beta | 22 years |
| Bismuth-210 ↓ | beta or alpha | 5.0 days |
| -Polonium-210 or | alpha | 140 days |
| ↳Thallium-206 | beta | 4.2 minutes |
| Lead-206 | stable | stable |

The radioactive disintegration series beginning with uranium-238 is one of several that occur in nature. The first five members of this series do not contribute significantly to the hazards from mines and mining. Radium, however, poses a double threat. It gives rise to the gas radon, which escapes from rocks and pervades the atmosphere of the mine. Most of the radon which is inhaled is exhaled again; but some of it decays to polonium-218, which remains in the lungs to decay further. Radium itself is dangerous if it enters water supplies or food chains. Because it has chemical properties similar to those of calcium, it is selectively deposited in bone, where it emits destructive alpha rays.

population and for workers who receive occupational exposure centers around whether there exists a threshold dose below which no damage occurs. The problem is to establish dose-response curves which describe the relationship between the dose and its effect (Figure 15.2). For a few effects, like the development of cataracts, a fairly definite threshold has been established. Certain other types of damage occur only when the radiation has more than some minimum amount of energy. Several factors, including nutritional status and oxygen concentration, influence the extent of damage. The body has mechanisms which we are only beginning to understand by which it repairs radiation damage, but an acute dose overwhelms the capacity for repair. This is probably why a given dose becomes less harmful as it is spread out over time. It also helps to explain why cells that are growing, dividing, or metabolizing rapidly are more sensitive than inactive cells, and why a fetus is more sensitive than an adult. The active, growing, dividing cell does not have time to repair itself before the damage is expressed.

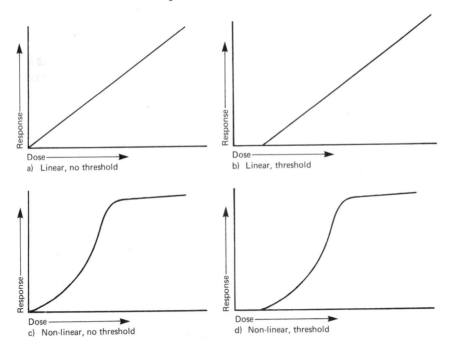

**Figure 15-2** Various types of dose-response curves. a. Response is proportional to dose, and for the smallest dose there is a measurable response. b. Response is proportional to dose, but there is a threshold value for the dose below which no response is detected. c. Response not proportional to dose. In this case the curve follows a typical S-shaped pattern with a period of slow increase followed by a period of exponential increase which levels off at a plateau value. d. Similar to (c), but there is a threshold value below which no response is detected.

Although a linear relationship between dose and response has been established for doses exceeding 20 or 25 rads, extrapolation of this curve to low or attenuated doses is risky, for the reasons mentioned above. But it is chronic, low level exposure, for which data are scarce and inconclusive, that concerns us most. Many radiation biologists believe that for cancer induction there may be a practical threshold if not an absolute one. This is because a latent period occurs between the time of exposure and the development of a cancer, and the latent period increases as the dose rate and the dose decrease. When it becomes longer than a normal lifespan, you will die of something else before your cancer develops. For genetic effects, however, no such practical threshold can exist. Experiments with lower animals generally confirm the idea that there is no threshold for genetic effects.

At present, the United States standards for maximum exposure to manmade radiation are set at an average of 0.17 rem per person per year for the general population, with a maximum of 0.5 rem per year for an individual. Medical exposure is excepted from these limits. Although the permissible doses of manmade radiation approximate those from natural sources, there is widespread concern that the standards are not strict enough. There is also the question of whether we will be able to meet the standards if we come to rely almost totally on nuclear energy, as we seem to be planning to do.

It is misleading, however, to compare the total exposure to manmade radiation with the exposure to natural radiation, because the **radioisotopes** involved are not the same. Some radioisotopes released by man do not occur in nature at all. The dangerous iodine-131 is one of these. Plutonium-239 is another. It is not as if we walk around in some general level of radiation which human activities promise to raise by a factor of two or so. We are exposing ourselves to brand new hazards, and each isotope poses a unique problem. For example, radioactive krypton, a chemically inert gas, is considered practically harmless and has been intentionally vented to the atmosphere (although the rate of release of krypton-85 has now become so high that steps are being taken to control it). Similar amounts of iodine-131, however, accumulating in their target, the thyroid gland, would long since have become intolerable.

THE FATE OF RADIOACTIVE WASTES DISCHARGED TO THE ENVIRONMENT.    The half-lives of radioisotopes and the rate at which they are released are only two factors related to their ultimate concentration or dispersal in the environment. For gaseous emissions, prevailing wind and precipitation patterns must be considered. For isotopes in liquid effluents, the characteristics of the body of water receiving them are important. Radioactivity from one power plant using the cooling capacity of a swiftly flowing river might have no significant effect on the environment. But what about the second plant on the same river? Or the tenth? The situation with lakes is especially complex.

Lakes are fed by some rivers and drained by others. Each lake has its characteristic flushing time, which is the time required for a complete renewal of its water. The flushing time of Lake Erie is about 3 years. Lake Michigan, on the other hand, has a flushing time of many decades — perhaps as much as a century — and that of Lake Superior has been estimated to be as much as 1,000 years. While radioisotopes discharged into Lake Erie are soon washed out again, it is clear that those discharged into Lake Michigan or Lake Superior can accumulate to dangerous levels. It is also possible, because of circulation patterns of the water, for radioisotopes to collect in certain regions of a lake.

Radioisotopes may be concentrated biologically in the food chain, with the result that predators at the top of the food chain (including man) are most likely to be affected. We will say more about this process in a later section. In any case, standards must be set with more than the immediate safety of man in mind. When we think of protecting man, we mean protecting individual people, not the species in general. With other species, however, the concern is for survival of populations, and the fate of an individual matters relatively little. Thus individuals may be damaged while populations adapt and survive. Chronic exposure to radioactivity will probably increase the mutation rate in most or all organisms, leading to increased variation and possibilities for adaptation, as well as to larger numbers of genetic defects. Increased mutation rates among some types of organisms would have profound implications for man. Consider, for example, viruses, bacteria, insects, and rodents — which, with their short life cycles and high reproductive potential, are already adapting faster than we can devise ways to control them.

*AIR POLLUTION.* The conversion of energy has material byproducts, as well as heat. When these by-products become airborne in sufficient concentrations to be troublesome, we have air pollution. The byproducts are inevitable. Our only options involve the proportions of the various substances produced and the ways in which we deal with them — remembering that "solutions" to air pollution problems frequently create problems of water pollution or solid wastes. (Of course, we could also try to use less energy — the most sensible but perhaps least likely course of action.)

The atmosphere has tremendous capacity for diluting, dispersing, and eventually destroying a large variety of substances that we discharge into it. But this capacity is not infinite, as air pollution in most of the world's major cities attests. Furthermore, although the largest concentrations of pollutants remain near their source, deterioration of air quality is no longer confined to the cities. Carbon dioxide and particulate matter have increased everywhere, and carbon monoxide levels are generally higher in the Northern Hemisphere (where most fuel is burned) than in the Southern Hemisphere.

Weather satellites have detected bands of polluted air circling the globe around the latitudes of the United States, Europe, and Japan. At present these occur only during periods of very stable circulation patterns; they are usually broken up by the mixing of air over the oceans. But even the occasional formation of zones of intercontinental air pollution should be taken as a serious warning of things to come.

About 80 percent of all air pollutants are generated by the burning (and steps that lead to the burning) of fossil fuels, and most of the rest comes from burning something else. Table 15.2 lists the major air pollutants, and Figure 15.3 summarizes their sources. The United States contributes roughly one third of the world's air pollutants, corresponding with its use of slightly more than one third of the world's energy. The total amount of these pollutants released in the United States increased 12 percent between 1966 and 1970, a frightening trend.

Most pollutants have a half-life in the atmosphere of from a few hours to a few weeks, although small particles in the upper atmosphere may persist for many years. Thus most types of air pollution with which we are now familiar will disappear with the passing of the era of burning fossil fuels. More significantly, successful measures to reduce air pollution should have almost immediately obvious effects.

As in the case of radioactivity, the setting of standards for air quality is surrounded by controversy over whether thresholds exist in the relationship between concentration of pollutant and response, and over the level at which cost for reducing the risk becomes excessive. In these respects each pollutant must be considered individually. The situation is further complicated because some poisons, particularly lead and other heavy metals, are cumulative and may also be concentrated in the food chain, and because most air pollutants eventually end up in the soil, water, or food supply, in some form. There is a series of thresholds for some pollutants — for exam-

**TABLE 15.2**
**Major Air Pollutants, 1970**

| | Amount (in million tons) | |
| Pollutant | United States | World |
| --- | --- | --- |
| Carbon monoxide | 100 | 280 |
| Sulfur oxides | 37 | 146 |
| Hydrocarbons | 32 | 88 |
| Nitrogen oxides | 21 | 53 |
| Particulate matter | 28 | 110 |
| TOTAL | 214 | 677 |

Source: Greenwood, N., and Edwards, J. 1973. *Human Environments and Natural Systems.* Wadsworth, Belmont, Calif., p. 138.

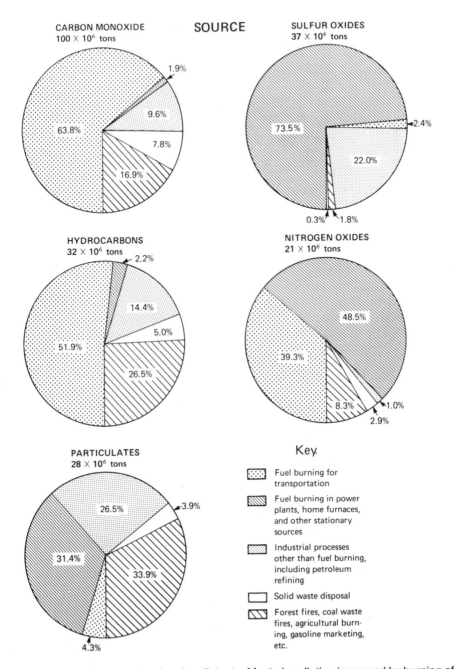

**Figure 15–3** Sources of major air pollutants. Most air pollution is caused by burning of fossil fuels, and the rest is largely caused by the burning of something else or by the production of fuels for burning. (From Greenwood and Edwards, *Human Environments and Natural Systems* Duxbury Press, North Scituate, Mass., 1973, p. 139.)

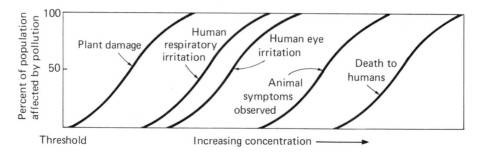

**Figure 15–4** Thresholds for various types of damage caused by exposure to sulfur dioxide. Plants are a sensitive indicator of air pollution by sulfur dioxide: about 75 percent of plants will be showing signs of damage before the first human symptoms appear. (From Greenwood and Edwards, *Human Environments and Natural Systems*, Duxbury Press, North Scituate, Mass., 1973, p. 155.)

ple, sulfur dioxide (Figure 15.4). Plants are most sensitive to sulfur dioxide. At somewhat higher levels, human respiratory irritation and eye irritation become apparent. At still higher concentrations symptoms are observed in other animals; and finally, at the highest concentrations observed, excess human deaths are attributed to the effects of sulfur dioxide. Table 15.3 shows the effects on human health of some common air pollutants. In Europe, Japan, and the United States the effects of air pollution on health are real and well documented, and are conservatively estimated to cost between 2 and 4 billion dollars in health care annually.

Discovery of the relationship between microorganisms and disease, a simple cause and effect, illuminated the nature of infectious disease and strongly influenced the methods of epidemiology. For many health problems of today, however, there is no single cause, as the preceding chapter explained. A wide range of genetic, environmental, nutritional, and other cultural factors is involved. Pollutants may interact synergistically with each other, so that the combined effect of several substances is greater than the sum of their individual effects. Chronic irritation of the respiratory tract, for example, may enhance the effect of carcinogens. Pollution may also enhance susceptibility to infectious disease or disease commonly associated with stress. We may never be able to apportion the guilt among the various factors involved, and it is important to remember this when listening to conflicting accusations — "It is diet," "No, it is stress," or "No, it is pollution." It is all of them, but pollution, and especially air pollution, plays a major role.

The adverse effects of air pollution are not confined to people living in cities. Veterinarians report that animals in zoos are experiencing health problems that are also apparently related to air pollution. Outside of the cities, in many parts of the world, citrus groves, truck garden crops, alfalfa, corn, tobacco, and evergreen and deciduous forests have also fallen victim to air pollution. Acid rains cause extensive agricultural and property damage

**TABLE 15.3**
**Some Common Air Pollutants—Where They Come From, What They Do**

| Pollutant | Major Sources | Effect |
|---|---|---|
| Aldehydes (organic compounds with a −CHO group) | Thermal decomposition of fats, oils, or glycerol | Irritate nasal and respiratory tracts |
| Ammonia ($NH_3$) | Chemical processes; fertilizers | Irritates upper respiratory passages |
| Arsine ($AsH_3$) | Industrial processes involving compounds containing arsenic | Destroys red blood cells; damages kidneys; causes jaundice |
| Carbon monoxide (CO) | Incomplete combustion of fossil fuels and other organic matter | Binds to hemoglobin in blood, reduces its oxygen-carrying capacity; heart and respiratory system must work harder |
| Chlorine ($Cl_2$) | Chemical processes, especially bleaching of cotton and flour | Attacks mucous membranes of eyes and respiratory tract; causes edema of lungs |
| Fluorine ($F_2$) | Manufacture of phosphate fertilizers | Severe eye irritation, skin burns, irritation of respiratory tract; weakening of bones and ligaments |
| Hydrocarbons | Transportation; petroleum production and processing; gasoline marketing; evaporation of volatiles from spilled oil | Take part in formation of smog, which injures repiratory system; some are carcinogens |
| Hydrogen cyanide (HCN) | Fumigation; blast furnaces; metal plating; chemical industry | Nerve poison; produces dry throat, blurred vision, headache |
| Hydrogen fluoride (HF) | Petroleum refining; glass etching; aluminum and fertilizer production | Irritates all mucous membranes; causes severe burns to skin and eyes |
| Hydrogen sulfide ($H_2S$) | Chemical industry; petroleum refining | Unpleasant odor; nausea; irritates eyes and throat |
| Lead | Burning leaded gasoline | Cumulative effects on all body systems, especially nervous system |
| Nitrogen oxides ($NO_x$) | Combustion of fossil fuels at high temperatures | Anoxia (lack of oxygen); inhibit action of cilia so that inhaled particles can reach the lungs; inflammation of lungs; pulmonary edema |
| Pesticides and herbicides | Aerial spraying | Wide range, depending on the poison |
| Phosgene ($COCl_2$) | Manufacture of dyes and chemicals | Irritation of eyes; choking, pneumonia or pulmonary edema; death |
| Pholychlorinated biphenyls (PCBs) | Vaporize from storage containers; burning plastics; emitted from smokestacks | Highly toxic; possibly carcinogenic |

**TABLE 15.3 continued**

| Pollutant | Major Sources | Effect |
|---|---|---|
| Radioactive isotopes | Nuclear power plants; nuclear explosions | Ionizing radiation (see text); mutations, cancer |
| Sulfur oxides (SOx) | Combustion of coal and oil, industrial processes; petroleum refining | Headache, vomiting; irritating to respiratory tract; increases death rate from respiratory ailments; chronic and acute asthma, bronchitis, emphysema |
| Suspended particles | Incinerators; manufacturing; combustion of coal; open burning; poor agricultural and mining practices; forest fires, volcanoes | Eye irritation; emphysema; may be carcinogenic |

in some areas. They result from the solution of the oxides of nitrogen and sulfur in atmospheric water, and their subsequent precipitation. The chemistry of this process is very simple. For example, $H_2O + SO_2 \rightarrow H_2SO_3$ (sulfurous acid). Nitrates washed out of the air by precipitation may be a significant source of excess nutrients in bodies of water near urban areas. Thus air pollution becomes a source of water pollution.

The processes by which the atmosphere cleanses itself lead to pollution of still other kinds. Large particles settle out as dust and soot. Chemicals and small particles settle or are washed out in rain, contaminating soil and water and finding their way into living things. The most notorious example of this is radioactive fallout from nuclear explosions, but there is analogous fallout of many materials. One of them is the gas fluorine, a by-product in the manufacture of fertilizer. Fluorine is adsorbed onto foliage and in this form may injure grazing animals. Figure 15.5 shows a cow that has suffered severe skeletal damage as a result of eating grass covered with fluorine. In addition, a large part of the pesticides and hydrocarbons washed out of the air may ultimately pollute the sea.

WATER POLLUTION. Water has been considered the universal sink for disposal of all kinds of wastes. It was once confidently assumed that running water purified itself and that the ocean was so vast it could assimilate all the wastes we cared to dump into it. But today the fact that we have overtaxed the ability of water to purify itself and have fouled the oceans in many ways is amply documented. In some ways water pollution is a relative term: water that is polluted for drinking may not be polluted for irrigation, and water that is thermally polluted for trout may be ideal for catfish. Paradoxically, water that is safe for drinking may be unfit for some industrial processes because of its dissolved minerals. But difficulties in defining

**Figure 15–5** This cow has suffered damage to teeth and skeleton from eating fluorine-covered grass. The gaseous fluorine, a byproduce of the fertilizer industry, was absorbed onto the forage. (From Greenwood and Edwards, *Human Environments and Natural Systems*, Duxbury Press, North Scituate, Mass., 1973, p. 150.)

water pollution do not make the phenomenon disappear any more than difficulties in defining race make the reality of race disappear. A useful definition might be that water pollution is the unfavorable alteration of ground water or water in lakes, rivers, estuaries, or seas through changes in levels of radiation, the flow of energy, chemical or physical constitution, or the abundance and nature of living organisms. We are then left, of course, with deciding what is "unfavorable."

Many of the natural cycles on which we depend are mediated by organisms in aquatic ecosystems, and we hope to increase our harvest of food from the water. Meanwhile, in the United States we use about 400 billion gallons of water per day, supplied through controlled water systems. More than half of this is used by industry, including the electric power industry; about 40 percent is used for agriculture; and less than 10 percent is for domestic use. All this water is returned to the environment altered in some way, and the messages we get from nature in the form of massive fish kills, rivers that catch fire, and so on indicate that many of these alterations are exceedingly "unfavorable," by any definition. We do not yet know how unfavorable they may be, and this is cause for much debate. To some, danger is not real until it has been demonstrated: although the bacterial count in many municipal water supplies is higher than the limits set by public health standards, there is no danger because we have not yet had devastating epidemics of water-borne diseases. To others, however, there is more danger in the unknown than in the known: we do not know which portions of the biosphere can be tampered with or sacrificed without seriously disrupting the human environment, but we seem determined to find out.

The broadest division of water pollutants classifies them as conservative pollutants, which are not altered by biological processes occurring in natural waters, and nonconservative pollutants, which are. Conservative pollutants for the most part are inorganic chemicals which are diluted in the receiving water but are not changed appreciably in quantity. Thus they tend to accumulate somewhere. They may also be concentrated in food chains, and herein lies their most immediate danger. Nonconservative pollutants are primarily organic materials which are altered by a variety of aerobic and anaerobic processes. Even a "biodegradable" waste, however, leaves inorganic end products — bicarbonates, nitrates, sulfates, phosphates — which can themselves cause further pollution problems. A primary pollutant is one which is actually discharged to the environment; it may be altered in the environment to form a secondary pollutant.

Sources of water pollution span the range of human activities. Mining leads to acid mine drainage when rocks that have lain undisturbed through geologic ages are broken up and exposed to the oxygen of the air, with subsequent solution of oxidized material in streams or groundwater. Many minerals that are insoluble in more nearly neutral water dissolve in acid water from mines, thus increasing the salt concentration to levels that may be toxic for aquatic life. Mining also produces pollution by sediments and radioactive material. Thermal pollution comes from the generation of electric power and other industrial processes requiring the use of cooling water. Agriculture contributes herbicides and pesticides, excess nutrients, and infectious agents. Municipal sewage contains excess organic and inorganic nutrients and infectious agents; even when organic matter has been broken down, nitrates and phosphates remain, and some viruses stubbornly resist ordinary efforts at purification. Industry produces a bewildering array of organic and inorganic wastes, many of which are acutely toxic to living things. Table 15.4 shows some major water pollutants, their principal sources, and their biological effects.

All aquatic ecosystems are threatened. Some ecologists have already written off the Great Lakes — largest reservoir of fresh water in the world. Catches of shellfish have been drastically reduced in all coastal regions of the United States. There is an overall decrease in the number of species of plants and animals found off the coast of California, accompanied by an

**TABLE 15.4**
**Some Common Water Pollutants—Where They Come From, What They Do**

| Type of Pollutant | Pollutant | Major Sources | Effect |
|---|---|---|---|
| Heat | Waste heat | Generation of electricity; industrial processes requiring cooling water | Decreases solubility of oxygen; speeds up metabolism, increasing biochemical oxygen demand; changes the composition of the biological community |
| Sediments | Soil, silt | Mining, forestry, agriculture | Clogs lakes and streams; alters properties of lake or stream bottom and types of bottom-dwelling organisms; can adsorb infectious agents or toxic chemicals, preventing their dilution and removal; increases costs of treating water supplies; decreases algal growth by reducing penetration of light |
| Radiation | Radioactive isotopes | Mining; generation of nuclear power | Cancer; mutations; death of cells or organisms |
| Minerals | Acid | Mining; industrial wastes | Kills organisms not adapted to living in acid water; increases solubility of many minerals |
| | Excess salts | Irrigation; artificial lakes, reservoirs, or cooling ponds —anything causing excess of evaporation over precipitation; mining; industrial wastes | Lethal to fresh water organisms; render water unfit for irrigation, domestic use, and many industrial purposes |
| | Toxic metals | | |
| | Lead | Burning leaded gasoline; smelting of lead; pesticides; plumbing | Cumulative cell poison with widespread physiological effects on digestive, nervous, reproductive, and circulatory systems; toxic to plankton |
| | Mercury | Industrial wastes; fungicides | Highly toxic, especially when converted to methylmercury by microorganisms; affects nervous system |

**TABLE 15.4 continued**

| Type of Pollutant | Pollutant | Major Sources | Effect |
|---|---|---|---|
| | Arsenic, antimony, beryllium, zinc, nickel, cadmium, silver, copper, chromium, and others | Pesticides; herbicides; mining; industrial wastes | Toxic; may be carcinogenic (such as organic arsenic herbicides); information on long-term, low-level effects lacking |
| Infectious agents | Viruses, bacteria, protozoa | Agricultural wastes; domestic sewage | Agents of water-borne diseases of people and animals: hepatitis, dysentery, cholera, typhoid, and others |
| Excess nutrients | Organic nutrients | Agricultural wastes and domestic sewage; food processing industry | Increase biochemical oxygen demand; encourage bacterial growth; can lead to anaerobic conditions, death of fish, and production of foul odors |
| | Nitrate ($NO_3^-$) | Agricultural runoff; nitrogen oxides precipitated from atmosphere; inorganic end product of sewage treatment | Hastens natural process of eutrophication by encouraging excessive algal growth and growth of aquatic weeds; may be toxic to livestock and children after conversion to nitrite ($NO_2^-$) by intestinal microorganisms—nitrite interacts with hemoglobin, reducing the oxygen-carrying capacity of the blood |
| | Phosphates ($PO_4^\equiv$, $HPO_4^=$, $H_2PO_4^-$) | Mining; agricultural runoff; detergents and industrial wastes; inorganic end product of sewage treatment | Hasten natural process of eutrophication by encouraging excessive algal growth and growth of aquatic weeds; lead to increased biochemical oxygen demand when dead algae decay |
| Biocides | Chlorine | Water treatment | May be mutagenic; sometimes fatal to fish and plankton |
| | Agents of chemical warfare | Accidents and disposal, especially ocean dumping | Variety of nerve poisons and other materials toxic to people and aquatic animals; some are mutagenic or teratogenic. |

| | | |
|---|---|---|
| Herbicides (2,4-D; 2,4,5-T; organic arsenates; derivatives of urea and triazine) | Agriculture; military use | Possibly mutagenic, carcinogenic, or teratogenic; potential threat to aquatic photosynthesizing plants |
| Pesticides DDT (and its breakdown products) | Agriculture; forestry; mosquito control | Affects sex hormones of rats and birds; decreases thickness of egg shells; affects activity of a number of liver enzymes; causes abortions in sea lions and decreased hatchability of fish eggs and survival of fry; carcinogenic for rats; inhibits photosynthesis by phytoplankton; toxic to many fish and shellfish; lethal to predatory birds and mammals; concentration in human fat is positively correlated with death from a number of causes including cerebral hemorrhage, portal cirrhosis of the liver, and several forms of cancer |
| Other chlorinated hydrocarbons | Agriculture; forestry | Many effects similar to those of DDT |
| Organic phosphates (parathion, malathion, and others) | Agriculture; forestry; domestic use | Nerve poisons; vomiting, diarrhea, convulsions, respiratory failure; affects cumulative |
| Carbamates | Agriculture; forestry | Nerve poisons; may be fatal to bees and fish; may be teratogenic |
| Miscellaneous organic chemicals  Petroleum and petroleum products | Production, refining, transport, end use, and disposal of petroleum and petroleum products | Lethal to some aquatic organisms by coating them and inhibiting respiration or feeding; some constituents are toxic; some constituents are carcinogenic; diverse physical and physiological effects on birds; increases biochemical oxygen demand; produces unpleasant flavors in fish and shellfish; interferes with reproduction in some invertebrates |
| Phenols, cresols, and other aromatic compounds | Industrial wastes; petroleum refineries | Toxic to many forms of aquatic life |

increase in species generally associated with polluted water. Even remote scenic lakes, such as Lake Tahoe, show signs of an increasing rate of eutrophication that has been induced by man. Most ominous of all, perhaps, are the reports of explorers Jacques-Ives Cousteau and Thor Heyerdahl that ocean waters thousands of miles from land are coated with oil and miscellaneous floating debris; and Cousteau reports a sharp decline in marine life, with the extinction of numerous species in the last 50 years. The problem of water pollution has clearly reached global proportions.

*NOISE POLLUTION.* Noise has come to be considered a form of pollution, although it is not an identifiable material product as other pollutants are. High levels of noise have been definitely associated with hearing loss. Noise is also thought to be a factor in diseases related to stress, including ulcers and hypertension. It is very difficult, however, to isolate the effects of noise from other aspects of industrialized culture, and so far the evidence is only suggestive. Excessive noise increases irritability and decreases efficiency of performance; it produces physiologic changes similar to those related to other forms of anxiety and stress. In any case, the constant drone of cars and trucks, aircraft, assorted household motors, chain saws, and other everyday sounds can hardly be thought to enhance the quality of life.

*SOLID WASTES: POLLUTION OF LAND AND SOIL.* Our lifestyle depends on the massive conversion of resources to waste — several billion tons of it each year. Most of our solid wastes are merely dumped on the land, where they are unsightly and can lead to pollution of air, water, and soil. Some wastes are burned, almost invariably creating air pollution and leaving a residue with about one-tenth the mass of the original material, which is still a solid waste to be disposed of. Some materials are dumped at sea, where they are an immediate or potential source of water pollution. Some are used to fill in wetlands — a tragic sacrifice of highly productive ecosystems. It is difficult or impossible to imagine a completely satisfactory way to dispose of solid wastes in the quantities in which we produce them. With our joint problems of population, pollution, and resource exhaustion, one course of action that makes ecologic sense is *not* to "dispose" of wastes, but to use them. Recycling or otherwise using wastes is uneconomical only because reckoning of the true cost of not using them is incomplete.

Efforts at reclaiming land that has been mined are incomplete and unsatisfactory. Despite attempts at legislative control, some 3 billion tons of waste rock and **mill tailings** are still dumped near mine sites each year. In some cases this is a cruel waste of the material being mined. For example, rock containing between 4 and 8 percent phosphorus is now stripped away in order to reach richer underlying ores, and the phosphate it contains cannot later be reclaimed. But within the lifetimes of some of us, we will be searching for rocks containing no more than 8 percent phosphorus, for higher-grade sources will have been exhausted. In addition to the waste involved in mining, heaps of rock and mill tailings are easy prey for erosion by wind and water. Dust and long-burning fires pollute the air. Streams become loaded with silt, dissolved minerals, and radioactive isotopes. The land is ugly and no longer productive.

There are more than 2 billion tons of agricultural wastes each year. About one quarter of this is of plant origin (such as corn stubble); the rest is from animals, chiefly manure and dead animals. Modern agricultural practices have created this problem by interrupting the cycles and destroying the interrelationships that kept earlier systems in balance. The droppings of animals no longer fertilize the fields which provide the animals with food. Instead, animals are crowded together in feedlots, producing situations like that in Kansas, where about 5.5 million cattle and 1.3 million hogs cover some 200 feedlots with sewage equivalent to that from 70 million people. Chickens no longer peck for food in the barnyard (incidentally providing a measure of insect control); a single intensive chicken farm may contain 200,000 birds which produce as much solid waste as a city of 20,000 people. These wastes produce intolerable odors and may pollute water and soil with infectious agents. They are also a major source of excess nutrients in water supplies.

There is nothing subtle about the tons of manure that farmers pay dearly to have trucked away, but these wastes are not the most dangerous residues of our agricultural system. More threatening in terms of permanent ecologic damage and difficulty of solution is the buildup of persistent biocides in the soil. Already, in some places, populations of earthworms and other soil invertebrates have been drastically reduced, and microorganisms of the soil have also been affected either directly from the effects of the biocides or indirectly through changes in the biological community of the soil. The soil is more than an inert substratum in which plants are anchored (see Chapter 2); it is a complex material whose nature depends on the activities of many living organisms. Changes in the fauna and flora of the soil lead some ecologists to predict ominously that the fertility of agricultural soil may be permanently destroyed if heavy applications of persistent biocides continue.

About three-quarters of a billion tons of solid wastes come each year from residential, commercial, institutional, and industrial sources. This includes the litter that is thoughtlessly strewn wherever people are, in an amount that would cover a superhighway from New York to San Francisco to a depth of one foot. It also includes the 7 million automobiles that are junked each year. It includes rapidly growing amounts of virtually permanently radioactive wastes, enough to kill every living thing on earth. And of course it includes the familiar trash and garbage of everyday life —newspaper, discarded packaging materials, tin cans, bottles and bottle caps, worn-out furniture and appliances, tree trimmings, street sweepings — in fact, most of the gargantuan production of our industrialized society appears relatively quickly as solid waste (Figure 15.6). Most of the dumps which receive municipal refuse are unsightly and unsanitary. Open burning pollutes the air; solution of toxic materials in rainwater pollutes the soil. Even the 6 percent of disposal sites that qualify as acceptable sanitary landfills may not be so sanitary after all: persistent poisons are buried, sometimes to be reexposed at a later time; toxic materials are leached from the wastes; and the very process of biodegradation of some wastes may produce pollutants.

*POLLUTANTS IN FOOD AND THE FOOD CHAIN.* The concentration of harmful materials in food chains in the progression from primary producers to herbivores to carnivores and higher order carnivores has been dramatically publicized. Plants themselves may concentrate pollutants to some extent because the water that is constantly drawn into their roots contains many substances in solution which are left behind when the water evaporates from the leaves of the plant. Similarly, filter-feeding aquatic organisms may accumulate high levels of pollutants because of the large amounts of

**Figure 15–6** A typical dump where the solid wastes of everyday life accumulate at a frightening rate. (Photograph by Marshall Hendrick.)

water they filter. At higher levels of the food chain, about 90 percent of the organic matter is converted to energy at each step; but some pollutants are not disposed of in this way, and thus they become more concentrated. Using the oversimplified ten to one ratio and assuming that all the pollutant persists from one trophic level to the next, you can see that 1,000 pounds of plants will produce 100 pounds of herbivores which will produce 10 pounds of primary carnivores and 1 pound of secondary carnivore — but the secondary carnivores will contain all the pollutant originally present in the 1,000 pounds of plants. Remember, too, that the top predators are relatively few in number and slow to reproduce. They can ill afford the consequences of the poisons that they eat.

People generally eat plants and herbivores and are thus not the major victims of the effects of concentration of pollutants in the food chain. Most highly prized game fish, however, are second or third order carnivores, and this is why fish may be dangerously contaminated with a variety of poisons from DDT to heavy metals to radioisotopes.

Many other materials have been introduced into the foods we eat. These introduced materials, which may be considered pollutants in the sense that they have been added to the natural food, include almost innumerable food additives as well as antibiotics and hormones used to increase the yield and growth rate of poultry and livestock. In many cases, whether they are actual or potential health hazards in the amounts consumed remains unknown.

## POLLUTION AND CLIMATE

Matter and energy are constantly exchanged between air, land, and water and carried to all parts of the globe by two great circulating systems, the atmosphere and oceans. Thus water is polluted by spilled oil; volatile fractions of the oil evaporate and pollute the air; the tarry residue washes ashore to deface beaches; hydrocarbons are washed out of the air by rain to pollute the sea once more; and much of the residue on land may also find its way back to the sea. Radioisotopes emitted into the air may eventually contaminate soil and water many miles from where they were discharged. Almost everything that pollutes the air and land eventually reaches the sea.

The processes that spread pollution around the globe are the same processes that determine weather and climate, and they may be modified by pollution. To understand how this is so, it is necessary to know something of the nature of the atmosphere.

*THE ATMOSPHERE.* The atmosphere is an unconfined mixture of gases moving ceaselessly above the earth. We divide it into a series of layers, each of which is characterized by certain physical properties and

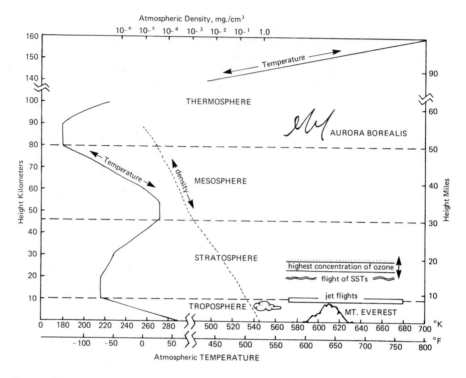

**Figure 15–7** The structure of the atmosphere. The activities of man are affecting the composition and circulation of all regions of the atmosphere. (From C. Steinhart and J. Steinhart, *Energy: Sources, Use, and Role in Human Affairs*, Duxbury Press, North Scituate, 1974, p. 248.)

related phenomena (Figure 15.7). The boundaries between these layers are neither sharp nor invariable, but rather, they are regions of transition. The layer nearest the ground is the *troposphere*, seat of most of the phenomena collectively called "the weather." Ordinarily, there is extensive vertical mixing of air in the troposphere, and temperature decreases fairly uniformly with height. Of the total mass of the atmosphere, about 90 percent is in this layer.

Vertical mixing of air in the troposphere, brought about by the rising of warm air from the ground and the sinking of cool air from above, usually assures that pollutants will be diluted and carried away. But under some conditions a layer of relatively warm air may overlie a layer of cool air at ground level. This situation is known as a temperature inversion. The cool air and any pollutants it may contain are trapped below the warm air, and the result may be one of the dangerous smog episodes that keep schoolchildren in from recess and cause excess deaths and illness from respiratory problems. The Los Angeles area is notoriously prone to develop long-lasting temperature inversions. Figure 15.8 shows the areas of the United States that are most susceptible to air pollution because of meterologic conditions. Areas already suffering from chronic air pollution are also shown.

The transition between the troposphere and the *stratosphere* is marked by a low point in the vertical temperature gradient, after which the temperature begins to rise. There is very little water vapor in the stratosphere, although **cirrus clouds** sometimes form in the lower part of it. How the stratosphere influences weather and climate is not understood very well.

Above the stratosphere the temperature declines sharply with increasing height until it reaches a minimum about 50 miles above the earth. This region of decreasing temperature is called the *mesosphere,* and above it lies the *thermosphere.* The thermosphere is characterized by rapidly increasing temperatures which may reach 2,500° F and by bands of ionized gases and free electrons (hence the other name for this region, the ionosphere). Major belts of ionized gas occur at heights of about 60 miles and 150 miles. They are responsible for the **aurora borealis.** Changes in the upper atmosphere are related to long-term climatic phenomena, but we do not know much about the relationship.

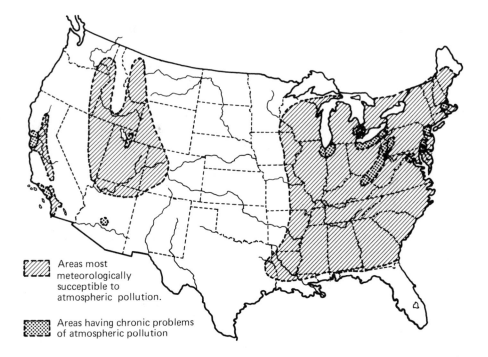

Areas most meteorologically succeptible to atmospheric pollution.

Areas having chronic problems of atmospheric pollution

**Figure 15–8** Areas of the U.S. affected by or susceptible to air pollution. Smog could become a chronic problem in the lightly shaded areas if population growth and industrial development continue. (From Greenwood and Edwards, *Human Environments and Natural Systems*, North Scituate, Mass., 1973, p. 147.)

**TABLE 15.5**
**Composition of the Atmosphere**

| Substance | Percent by Volume |
|---|---|
| Nitrogen | 78.09 |
| Oxygen | 20.95 |
| Argon | 0.93 |
| Carbon dioxide | 0.034 |
| Neon | $1.8 \times 10^{-3}$ |
| Helium | $5.2 \times 10^{-4}$ |
| Krypton | $1.1 \quad 10^{4}$ |
| Hydrogen | $5.0 \times 10^{-5}$ |
| Xenon | $8.0 \times 10^{-6}$ |
| Ozone | $1.0 \times 10^{-6}$ |

Variable constituents: water, in solid, liquid, and gaseous state, averaging about 0.6 percent; solid particles, including dust, pollen spores, and salts; carbon monoxide, nitrogen oxides, sulfur oxides, gaseous hydrocarbons, and other organic and inorganic molecules.

The dry atmosphere to a height of about 50 miles is a mixture of nitrogen and oxygen with small amounts of other gases, as shown in Table 15.5. In addition, the troposphere always contains water vapor in amounts varying from only traces in polar and desert regions to as much as 4 percent in the moist tropics. The troposphere also contains salts, primarily chlorides and sulfates, whipped into the air by the action of the wind on the sea. Pollen, spores, bacteria, dust from the surface of the earth, dust from volcanic eruptions, dust, chemicals, and smoke from the activities of man, and hydrocarbons produced by plants are all part of the troposphere, and all participate in the phenomena of the weather.

*INTERACTIONS OF SOLAR RADIATION WITH THE ATMOSPHERE.* Although solar radiation spans much of the **electromagnetic spectrum,** more than 90 percent of it is of wavelengths between 0.4 and 4.0 microns, corresponding to visible and infrared regions of the spectrum (Figure 15.9a). Solar energy in wavelengths less than about 0.2 microns is absorbed and converted to heat by oxygen in the thermosphere. Longer ultraviolet wavelengths, up to 0.3 microns, penetrate into the mesophere and stratosphere before they are absorbed by ordinary molecular oxygen and ozone. By the time solar radiation reaches the lower stratosphere, about 3 percent of it, the shortest wavelengths, has been absorbed. Most of this has been converted directly to heat, but a part has caused ionization of gases or dissociation of molecules into atoms.

About 35 percent of the energy of wavelengths longer than 0.3 microns is reflected from the atmosphere and the surface of the earth. The ratio of reflected energy to energy received is called the *albedo.* The albedo of clouds ranges from a few percent for light cirrus clouds to more than 80 percent for dense **cumulus clouds.** On the average, it is about 50 to 60 percent. Since the average cloud cover of the earth is about 50 percent and the albedo of the clouds is 50 percent, we see that roughly 25 percent of the energy striking the atmosphere is reflected back into space by clouds. Any change in cloud cover would immediately affect the amount of energy received by earth. Similarly, a change in the distribution of clouds would affect the distribution of incoming solar energy.

Ten or twenty percent of **incident solar energy** is absorbed in the atmosphere, chiefly by water vapor and carbon dioxide (Figure 15.9b, c). Radiation that finally reaches the surface of the earth is either reflected or

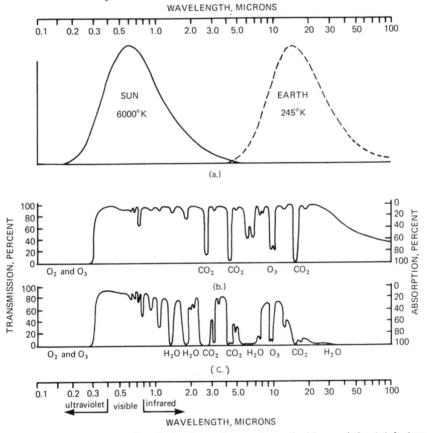

**Figure 15–9** Absorption of radiation by water, carbon dioxide, and the total atmosphere. a. Spectral distribution of energy radiated by the sun and the earth. b. The portion of a beam of solar radiation that reaches the top of the troposphere. Most of the absorption has occurred in the short wavelengths, due to ozone and carbon dioxide. c. The portion of a beam of solar radiation that reaches the earth's surface. Absorption in the troposphere is due primarily to water. (From C. Steinhart and J. Steinhart, *Energy: Sources, Use, and Role in Human Affairs*, Duxbury Press, North Scituate, Mass., 1974, p. 253.)

absorbed. That which is absorbed is converted to heat and either stored, reradiated as long wavelength radiation, transferred back to the atmosphere by conduction or **convection,** or used to evaporate water and stored as latent heat of vaporization. A very small part of it participates, as light, in photochemical reactions, including the most important photochemical reaction of all — photosynthesis.

The radiative characteristics of a body depend on its temperature. Because the earth is relatively cool, its radiation is largely confined to the less energetic, longer wavelength region of the spectrum between 5 and 100 microns (Figure 15.11a). More than 90 percent of the energy radiated by the surface of the earth is of wavelengths that are absorbed by water vapor and carbon dioxide; much of it is absorbed or reflected back to earth by clouds (Figure 15.9, b, c). The transparency of the atmosphere to incoming visible light coupled with its opacity to outgoing infrared creates the greenhouse effect, which warms the surface of the earth. The effects of various constituents of the atmosphere on solar radiation are summarized in Table 15.6. Anything we do to change the amounts of these constituents will affect earth's energy balance and consequently the climate.

CIRCULATION OF THE ATMOSPHERE AND OCEANS.    The atmosphere is a great heat engine that runs on solar energy, moving the surplus of energy that falls in the equatorial zone to the poles, where there is a deficit. The oceans are another such heat engine, running on the same principle and interacting with the atmosphere.

In general, warm air rises at the equator and moves toward the poles, where it is cooled, sinks, and moves back toward the equator again. The rotation of the earth makes things more complicated, causing bands of prevailing winds: the polar easterlies, the westerlies of middle latitudes, and the trade winds near the equator. Further modifications in atmospheric circulation occur because of the irregular distribution of continents and oceans and of the location and topographic features of land masses.

Ocean currents are established by differences in temperature and density of water and are modified by the prevailing winds. Some 20 to 25 percent of the energy carried from equatorial regions to the poles is carried by ocean currents. In addition to the heat directly redistributed by the oceans, almost 20 percent of the energy carried poleward is in the form of latent heat in water vapor, most of which evaporates over the oceans. This heat is released in the atmosphere when rain or snow falls.

Thus climates of the earth are determined not only by amounts of energy received from the sun and radiated back from earth, but by the way in which energy is distributed between the equator and the poles. When the distribution is fairly uniform, global climates are mild. When circulation between the equator and the poles is restricted, an ice age results. We do not have to blot out the sun to change the climate, or warm the earth by the

**TABLE 15.6**
**Interaction of Atmospheric Components With Solar and Terrestrial Radiation**

| *Substance or Material* | *Effect* |
|---|---|
| Ozone ($O_3$) | Absorbs radiation of wavelengths shorter than 0.3 microns and converts it to heat. Reradiates this heat energy toward earth and into space, warming the stratosphere. |
| Water vapor | Absorbs radiation strongly in the range of 5 to 8 microns and greater than 18 microns. The average water vapor content of the atmosphere is about $1.3 \times 10^{19}$ grams, which stores $9 \times 10^{15}$ kilowatt-hours of energy as latent heat of vaporization. The average annual rainfall of $1.1 \times 10^{17}$ gallons ($4 \times 10^{20}$ grams) releases $3 \times 10^{17}$ kilowatt-hours of energy into the atmosphere. This is 5000 times the world's annual energy use by man. |
| Clouds | Absorb between 2 and 30 percent of incoming radiation and reflect between 20 and 85 percent, depending on the type of cloud and the angle of the radiation. Absorb long wavelength radiation from earth's surface and reradiate it back toward earth and out to space. |
| Carbon dioxide ($CO_2$) | Absorbs radiation between 0.7 and 18 microns (most strongly between 12 and 16 microns). Reradiates it toward earth and space. |
| Oxygen ($O_2$), nitrogen ($N_2$), and minor atmospheric gases | Generally transparent to both solar and terrestrial radiation, although radiation of short wavelengths causes dissociation and ionization of molecules. They scatter radiation in a symmetrical way which depends on the wavelength of the radiation and the size of the molecule; this is why the sky looks blue. |
| Oxides of nitrogen and sulfur, hydrocarbons, carbon monoxide | Negligible direct interation with radiation. Many of these gases undergo photochemical reactions which involve ozone and/or which produce smog. |
| Particles (smoke, smog, dust, salts, pollen, spores, etc.) | Scatter and absorb solar and terrestrial radiation throughout the infrared. Increase the albedo of the atmosphere in general (although they may make clouds "dirty" and decrease their albedo). Act as nuclei for cloud formation and condensation of rain and snow. |

sheer magnitude of our production of waste heat. We can do, and perhaps are doing, many more subtle things to change the winds, the rains, and the snows.

CLIMATIC CHANGE. Modern man evolved during an ice age, a period of violent activity on earth — of mountain building, earthquakes, and volcanic eruptions. He has never known the earth as geologists believe her to have been throughout most of geologic time. In "normal" times, the earth is calm and mild. Polar seas are free of ice and polar climates are similar to those of middle latitudes today. There are vast expanses of continental lowlands covered by warm, shallow seas. The Pleistocene ice age embraces alternating periods of growth and recession of glaciers, called glacial and interglacial stages. Scientists are not certain whether the period in which we now live is the end of the Pleistocene ice age or merely one of its interglacial stages. Conceivably, the answer to this question could hinge on the activities of man.

The concept of a stable climate becomes uncertain when we ask, stable over what period? World and local climates have undergone many fluctuations since the last glacier receded 11,000 or 12,000 years ago. Many explanations have been invoked to account for these changes which, except possibly for the most recent cooling trend, had nothing to do with the activities of man. None of the explanations is completely satisfactory. Climatic change has been a major, if not *the* major, force in evolution and in the rise and fall of human cultures. If conditions had remained ideal for the dinosaurs, there would probably be no men today to worry about man's influence on the climate. There is no reason to suppose that our present climate will prevail. The question that concerns us, then, is what is the "natural" trend and how are we influencing it.

MAN'S INFLUENCE ON CLIMATE.    *Homo erectus pekinensis* began to change the climate when he first carried fire to his cave. He changed the climate immediately about himself from cold and damp to warm and dry. Since that time man's influence on local climate has grown until the cumulative impact of local changes threatens to cause global changes. But here we are on shaky theoretical and observational ground, because of the number of variables involved and the complexity of their interactions. It is very difficult to determine the relative contributions of man and of forces beyond human control, but the significance of our role makes it imperative that we try.

Some of the climatic repercussions of waste heat and pollution are related to the uneven distribution of human inputs into the environment. Consideration of Table 15.7 should convince us that we are not about to heat up the globe with our waste heat production. The rate of world energy use, which is essentially equivalent to world production of heat, is about $7 \times 10^9$ kilowatts. This is insignificant compared to the $9 \times 10^{13}$ kilowatts of solar power that reaches earth's surface, or the latent heat added to the atmosphere at a rate of $4 \times 10^{13}$ kilowatts through evaporation of water, or the energy of the winds flowing at a rate of about $4 \times 10^{11}$ kilowatts. Even a local thunderstorm releases energy equivalent to that of many hydrogen bombs. But man's use of energy is heavily concentrated in urban and industrialized areas, which comprise only a tenth of 1 percent of the earth's surface. In some of these areas man's output of waste heat has reached about 10 percent of the input of the sun. This value of 10 percent is not likely

**TABLE 15.7**
**Comparison of Manmade and Some Natural Flows of Energy**

| Energy Flow | Rate, in Watts per Square Meter |
|---|---|
| Average solar radiation at earth's surface | about 170 |
| Energy used to evaporate water, average rate | 79 |
| Average energy output of urban industrial areas | 12 |
| Average net photosynthetic production on land | 0.13 |
| Average heat flow from interior of the earth | 0.054 |
| World use of energy (1970), distributed evenly over the continents | 0.047 |
| World use of energy (1970), distributed evenly over the entire earth | 0.013 |

to increase very much, but the number and size of urban areas producing heat at this level will. (However, in cities which have very cold winters, such as Moscow and Fairbanks, man may approach or surpass the sun's rate of energy input to the local environment.)

We do not need to be told that cities modify local climate; our bodies can feel the difference between a city and surrounding rural areas or forest. Table 15.8 summarizes the ways in which cities change local energy balance and also the climatic effects of these modifications. Of this list, particulate and gaseous air pollutants and waste heat have by far the greatest impact.

The climatic effects of cities are well documented. But when we try to determine the effects of pollution on global climate, the sequence of cause and effect is seldom obvious. The problem is compounded by our uncertainty about the magnitude and direction of the natural trend in world climate. We do, however, understand the basic dynamics of the atmosphere, and we know how individual factors modify the amount, distribution, and flow of energy. We are beginning to understand the many ways in which these factors interact. We know that by adding dust, smoke, carbon dioxide, and a variety of chemicals to the atmosphere, we change its reflective, absorptive, and radiative properties (Table 15.6). So we can formulate hypotheses about climatic change and test them by computation. When climatic variables are represented by mathematical equations arranged for solution by a computer (as, for example, the rate of increase in atmospheric carbon dioxide and the relationship between concentration of carbon dioxide and surface temperature), we have a mathematical simulation or model of climatic change. These models, imperfect as they are, are the best way we now have to learn about the tangle of relationships which govern climate and the behavior of the atmosphere. As one meteorologist put it, ". . . we can eventually say what features or combinations of features *could have* produced the changes. . . . As to what features *did* produce [them] we shall still have the privilege of arguing."

**TABLE 15.8**
**Climatic Effects of Urbanization**

Urbanization produces many changes that affect energy balance. The albedo of the surface is increased due to the reflectivity of buildings and pavement. In snowy areas, however, there may be a compensating decrease in albedo due to dirty snow and snow removal. Accompanying the change in albedo is a change in heat storage capacity of the surface. Buildings and other obstacles to wind flow create increased atmospheric turbulence near the surface. There is decreased evaporation and transpiration of water and increased runoff of precipitation. Burning of fuel produces air pollution, both gaseous and particulate, and waste heat. These changes are related to the following observed climatic effects:

Typical differences of urban climates from surrounding rural areas
Cloudiness
    5–10% more cloud cover
    100% more winter fog
    30% more summer fog
Precipitation (effect may be more pronounced downwind from urban area, at times)
    5–10% more (total)
    5% more snow
Relative humidity
    2% less (winter)
    8% less (summer)
Radiation striking surface
    15–20% less
    30% less ultraviolet in winter
    5% less ultraviolet in summer
Temperature
    0.5°–1.0° C higher annual mean
    1°–2° C higher winter minimum
Winds
    20–30% lower mean annual wind speed
    10–20% decrease in extreme gusts
    5–20% increase in calms

Different models may lead to conflicting results and paradoxes. It has been suggested, for example, that an ice age could be started by an increase in solar radiation, which would lead to increased evaporation of water, increased cloudiness, increased rain and snow, and decreased temperatures. Most people, however, do not believe that a hotter sun would cause a colder earth. With some reservations, then, we will look at a few of the observed and predicted changes in variables affecting the climate and at their potential influence on the climate.

CARBON DIOXIDE. There are about $2.5 \times 10^{18}$ grams of carbon dioxide in the atmosphere. Each year we release an increasing amount through combustion of fossil fuels. In 1950 it was $6.4 \times 10^{15}$ grams, by 1965 it had doubled to $12.7 \times 10^{15}$ grams, and the estimate for 1980 is that it will have doubled again to $26.0 \times 10^{15}$ grams.

The first systematic measurements of carbon dioxide concentration were begun in 1958. The mean annual concentration seems to be growing everywhere at a rate of about 0.2 percent per year, with the highest levels reported from Point Barrow, Alaska, and the lowest from Antarctica. In general, values in the Northern Hemisphere are higher than those in the Southern Hemisphere — as might be expected, since most of the fossil fuel is burned in the north. The difference suggests a time lag of about 18 months in the mixing of air between the arctic and the antarctic.

Almost half of the carbon dioxide added to the atmosphere by man remains there. The remaining half must be taken up by the oceans or the biosphere; there is nowhere else for it to go. The biosphere is only a temporary sink, because increased photosynthetic production leads to increased breakdown of organic material by herbivores and decomposers, releasing the carbon dioxide again. It is generally assumed, for the purpose of designing climatic models, that about half of each increment of carbon dioxide added to the atmosphere will continue to be removed; but most natural processes do not remain so nicely linear. We assume this one will only because we do not know how it is likely to change.

Simplified models of global climate predict that a doubling of carbon dioxide concentration would increase the average surface temperature by about 2° C, while the stratosphere would become cooler. The actual increase in carbon dioxide that is predicted for the year 2000 would cause a warming of about 0.5° C. This model takes into account that absolute humidity will probably increase as temperature increases and that infrared absorption by the additional water vapor will contribute to the warming effect. As usual, the entire picture is not this simple. We do not know, for example, whether the increased humidity will produce more clouds. The temperature increase will probably be greater toward the poles than in the tropics, because as the snow cover recedes, the albedo of the surface will decrease and more solar energy will be absorbed. A decreased temperature differential between the equator and the poles has implications for global patterns of atmospheric circulation. It is possible that the Arctic Ocean would become and remain essentially free of ice. In this case, patterns of oceanic circulation would also be profoundly changed. On the other hand, if the increased content of water vapor in the atmosphere leads to an increase in cloud cover of only 0.6 percent, the cooling effect of the clouds could cancel the warming effect due to carbon dioxide.

We could stop the atmospheric increase of carbon dioxide by turning to sources of energy other than fossil fuels. In reality, however, no matter what progress is made in the technology of nuclear and solar energy, man will probably be burning large amounts of fuel for at least several centuries to come. After we perceive carbon dioxide to be causing a problem, it may be too late to do anything about it. Once a trend toward climatic change has started, halting the increase of carbon dioxide is unlikely to stop it because of the way in which the effects of decreasing snow and ice cover and altered patterns of circulation reinforce each other through positive feedback.

PARTICULATES.    Apart from sudden increases in the particulate content of the atmosphere following major volcanic eruptions, there appears to be a global trend toward an increase of particles. This conclusion is based largely on measurements of solar radiation reaching the earth's surface and on the assumption that decreases in solar radiation are due to increased scattering and reflection by atmospheric particles. In cities there has been a well-documented decrease in solar radiation of 15 to 20 percent during the last 50 years. Observations are neither consistent enough nor of long enough standing in nonpolluted areas to come to firm conclusions, but evidence suggests that in the Northern Hemisphere solar radiation has been reduced by about 5 percent, even in areas of "clean air." Measurements over the North Atlantic suggest a doubling in the number of particles between 0.02 and 0.2 microns in diameter. Because these data were collected in an area undisturbed by human activity, they may represent an overall trend in the Northern Hemisphere. There are few reliable observations for the Southern Hemisphere, but the concentration seems to be smaller there, as would be expected, because the major sources of manmade particles are concentrated in the north.

Models of climatic effects of particles must take into account the particles' horizontal and vertical distribution, their size, and the way in which they interact with light. Because information of this sort is inadequate, predictions from climatic models are tenuous at best. The most that can be said with confidence is that an increase in particles will increase the albedo of the atmosphere and will probably tend to cool the surface of the earth. How much our production of particulate matter will influence the climate remains a vital but unanswered question. It is comforting to note, however, that with a shift to nuclear or solar energy and with stringent pollution controls and attention to agricultural and mining practices, almost all manmade atmospheric particles could be eliminated. Because the lifetime of particles in the atmosphere is relatively short, unlike the lifetime of excess carbon dioxide, the problems of air pollution by particulates will not linger to haunt generations of people who may no longer be polluting the air.

MODIFICATION OF THE UPPER ATMOSPHERE. Potential changes in the composition of the upper atmosphere are related to the effects of jets flying in the upper troposphere and lower stratosphere, supersonic transport aircraft (SSTs) flying in the stratosphere, and rockets, which penetrate all layers of the atmosphere.

Jet aircraft flights may increase sixfold by 1990, and more, if SSTs do not begin operation as expected. There is no doubt that condensation of water vapor emitted from these aircraft (causing the well-known **"contrails"**) will increase the cloudiness of the upper troposphere. The effect will be most pronounced in heavily traveled air corridors near major jet airports. The primary effect of increased cloudiness will be to increase the albedo of the atmosphere, although it is difficult to estimate how large the effect will be, or how it will affect the surface of the earth. It is also possible that ice crystals from the upper troposphere will fall into clouds below, seeding them, and causing precipitation to occur sooner that it otherwise would.

Concern about the effect of SSTs involves their emissions of water vapor, carbon dioxide, and particles. The best experience we have to go on, related to modification of the stratosphere, is the known effects of major volcanic eruptions. Injection of volcanic dust into the stratosphere causes a rise in stratospheric temperature of as much as 6° or 7° C. Increased volcanic activity also appears to be associated with decreased surface temperatures. A strict analogy cannot be made between volcanic emissions and the emissions of SSTs, however, because SSTs will operate within a narrow range of altitude and primarily in a few heavily traveled air corridors in the Northern Hemisphere. Volcanic debris is more widely distributed by latitude and longitude and throughout all vertical layers of the atmosphere.

The greenhouse effect of stratospheric water vapor and carbon dioxide is expected to be very small, and insignificant relative to the effect from the burning of fossil fuel. Because the stratosphere is very dry, it is expected that additional water vapor will cause increased cloudiness only in the coldest regions. The idea that the ozone layer will be destroyed by increased photochemical reactions involving ozone, water vapor, and other emissions has been carefully studied and discredited, because the aircraft will fly below the most concentrated ozone layer and because computer models indicate that water vapor has the greatest effect on ozone concentration at altitudes higher than those where most ozone is found. In conclusion, many who have studied the problem most thoroughly say they do not think that stratospheric flights of SSTs will cause any serious problems, but they are extremely reluctant to try the experiment and find out.

The higher we go in the sky, the shakier our theoretical and observational bases for prediction become. Because there is so little matter in the upper regions of the atmosphere, each rocket and each explosion of a nuclear bomb in the atmosphere can cause a significant change in the composition of the mesosphere and thermosphere. We know that we are changing the chemistry and perhaps the circulation of the very high atmosphere, but we do not know what the effects of this change may be.

SIGNIFICANCE OF CLIMATIC CHANGE.    When we think of modifying the climate, we often think in melodramatic terms of another ice age, with all living things fleeing in advance of the glaciers. Or we think of melting the polar ice and flooding all our coastal cities. These would be but the final results of our activities. Many other changes would come before we froze or drowned. A slight but persistent change in temperature or humidity can tip the balance in favor of organisms pathogenic to plants, animals, or man, or of vectors (such as the mosquito) that spread those organisms. The result could be severe epidemics of diseases and pests that formerly were held in check by climatic conditions. Major epidemics of crops and forest trees have often been associated with just such changes. Or the major winds could shift their course, as there is some evidence that they are doing. They could fail to bring rain at the usual season or bring disastrous rains at the time of harvest, and the resulting crop losses would bring starvation to additional millions of people. We have always been slow to adjust agricultural practices to changes in climate.

Nor are climatic changes necessarily for the worse. If we really thought they were, we would be foolish to engage in research on practical applications of weather and climate modification (although it would be foolish on other grounds to undertake massive experiments of this nature*). The explanation for many of our fears is related to the idea mentioned earlier in this chapter — that danger lies in the unknown. And after the unknown becomes known, it may be too late to do anything about it.

## POLLUTION, CULTURE, AND THE FUTURE

We have shown that biological evolution is conservative in its mindless striving to enable organisms and species to continue doing what they have always done — but a little better. The first vertebrates that successfully struggled across the land were not trying to become terrestrial; they were trying to get back to the water. Much of cultural evolution has been the same. To many people even today, cultural change means changes that will permit the American way of life to continue, changes that will bring a higher material standard of living to even more people. Our national policy is to develop technology for producing gasoline from coal, so that we may continue our transportation system based on the private automobile, and in many other ways to maintain the status quo. Without realizing that *we* are the polluters, not "they," we look for pollution control not through a change in lifestyle but through a technological fix, so that our lifestyle will not have to change. But we have seen how a cultural adaptation leads to many cultural adjustments which accumulate until a lifestyle does change. Pollution has already changed our lives, and either failure or attempts to deal with it will inevitably change them further.

*TECHNOLOGICAL SOLUTIONS.* Our thinking tends to be linear, cause-and-effect thinking. This type of thinking is our cultural and perhaps also our biological heritage, and it naturally gives rise to the search for technological solutions to problems. Since pollution is not the basic problem

---

* It would seem at first to be an unmitigated good, for example, to break up or detour the hurricanes that ravage our southern coastal states. On second look, it appears that doing so might modify patterns of rainfall along the entire Atlantic seaboard, with results not quite as welcome as the successful conquest of tropical storms.

with our relationship to our environment but merely a symptom that something is wrong, alleviating pollution might lull us into a false belief that the problem itself is going away. Nevertheless, no sensible person could argue that concerted efforts at pollution control are not desirable. We need the technological fix to buy time for reexamining our goals for the world, our nation, and our individual lives, and for adjusting them if necessary so that they are compatible with the limits imposed by nature.

If we continue on our present course, our use of energy in the year 2000 will be three times the level of 1970 (Figure 15.10). This is an average estimate, based on estimates of population and GNP (gross national product) that fall in the middle of the range of projections. Most of this energy will be used to do more of the same kinds of things we have been doing, although a small but growing part of it (perhaps up to 10 percent) will be used in pollution control.

What of the levels of pollution associated with projected energy use? Figure 15.11 shows the situation for several pollutants and various combina-

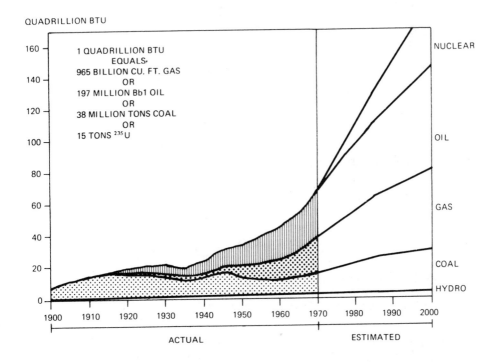

**Figure 15–10** U.S. energy consumption in the twentieth century. (From Environmental Protection Agency, Office of Research and Development, *Alternative Futures and Environmental Quality*, U.S. Government Printing Office, Washington, D.C., 1973, p. 95.)

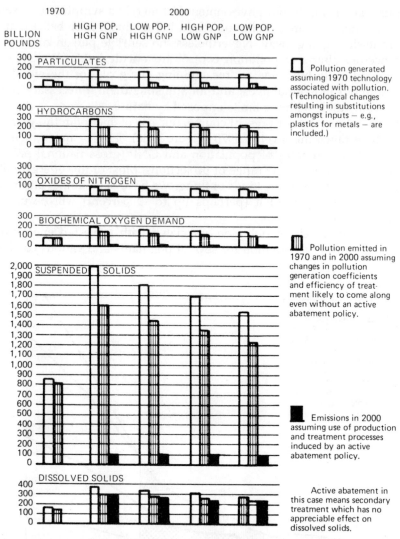

**Figure 15–11** Pollution generated and emitted under alternative assumptions. (From Environmental Protection Agency, Office of Research and Development, *Alternative Futures and Environmental Quality*, U.S. Government Printing Office, Washington, D.C., 1973, p. 73.)

tions of population, GNP, and efforts at control. The bar representing "active abatement policy" is based on the Environmental Protection Agency's recommended emission standards for 1975 and assumes that these standards will be met. The cost of this level of control is estimated to be about 2 percent of the GNP projected for the year 2000. Such pollutants as radioactive materials, heavy metals, and persistent biocides, however, are conspicuously missing from this list, and the outlook for their control is less promising.

There are a great many schemes for turning wastes into resources, some of which have already been put into practice in Europe or Japan and appear to be on the horizon for the United States. These include the pollution-free burning of municipal wastes for the generation of electricity, the production of methane (natural gas) from sewage or agricultural wastes, the use of waste heat for space heating, for fish and shellfish nurseries, for defogging airports, or for increasing the rate of decomposition of sewage, the incorporation of fly ash into construction materials, and the use of wastes from agriculture and the food processing industry for animal feeds. Redesign of municipal water supply and sewage systems would simplify water management. It is not necessary, for example, to flush the toilet with water that meets the standards of purity for drinking. Many valuable materials for the chemical industry and other industries can be salvaged from **effluents** of all kinds. As only one example, if we could salvage the sulfur from the coal and oil we burn, it would not only solve a major pollution problem, but it would furnish all the sulfur we need. In agriculture we could reestablish some of the nutrient cycles we have interrupted and once again balance agricultural ecosystems. By returning agricultural wastes to the soil, we alleviate two problems: one is the disposal of agricultural wastes and the other is pollution from runoff of inorganic fertilizers. This would decentralize meat and milk production and make them more expensive, but if we do not do it, pollution costs will make them more expensive anyway.

Some pollution problems may be fairly easy to solve, while others may remain intractable. One of the intractable variety seems to be emissions from the internal combustion engine. Control of carbon monoxide and hydrocarbons is incompatible with control of nitrogen oxides, because present design requirements for one lead to increased emission of the other. Present efforts are directed at controlling carbon monoxide and hydrocarbons, which may be the lesser of the two evils, with the result that emission of nitrogen oxides is increasing.

A more serious problem with pollution control is related to growth. If we decrease automobile emissions by a factor of two and then double the number of automobiles, we have not gained very much. The same is true, of course, for any source of pollution. We may take pride in holding back 90 percent of the pollutants in an effluent, but 10 percent of a very large amount is still a large amount. Growth can rapidly cancel out any improvements that technology can bring in the control of pollution. In any case, pollution control which relies on a technological fix can never be total. There is a fundamental physical limit because no technology is perfect, and there is also an economic limit. At some point, by anyone's criteria, the cost of additional pollution control is greater than the benefit.

In the past, waste disposal has been based on spreading out the wastes

## SOLID WASTE: A NEW RESOURCE

*This year's "Pepsi generation" will discard 65 billion beverage containers. Most of these bottles and cans will be laid to rest in the city dump, contributing significantly to the 200 million tons of garbage America generates yearly. Garbage, or solid waste as it has been labelled recently, is fast becoming the quicksand of modern society. The search for solutions to the problem has begun. Man needs a life raft to prevent him from drowning in his own wastes.*

*Recycling has emerged as the lifesaver — a panacea for our garbage ills. Recycling is not really a new concept, however. Using things more than once or for multipurposes was common practice until affluence and packaging became synonymous with consumer. Barrels were made to hold anything from water to pickles; beer was carted home in a jug; even the twentieth century "returnable" bottle was often refilled forty times. The 1960s saw the birth of throwaway beverage containers. Their advantages are obvious — cleanliness and convenience. Their disadvantages are becoming more obvious — contribution to litter, adding to an already overtaxed waste disposal system, and wasteful use of diminishing material and energy resources. This last point is dramatically illustrated by Dr. Bruce Hannon of the University of Illinois: "The annual energy now diverted into supplying beer and soft drinks in throwaway cans and bottles would supply* all *the electrical needs of Pittsburgh, Boston, Washington, D.C., and San Francisco for* one *year."*

*Although beverage containers currently make up only 7 percent of the solid waste in the United States, they are the fastest growing portion of municipal waste. The problems which arise with throwaway beverage containers typifies the problems encountered in other types of waste recycling. There are three solutions to the beverage container problem: (1) reuse the container in its present form as a beverage container; (2) use the material as a portion of the ingredients combined to make "new" material; (3) crush the container and change its form and use.*

*By applying these solutions to throwaway beverage cans, we see that using the can in its present form as a container really is not applicable. Steel cans are currently used in their present form, however, to help extract copper from ore. Copper is dissolved in solution and passed over discarded steel beverage cans. The tin replaces the copper, and the copper emerges as a deposit on the surface of the can. Solution number two is practiced both with steel and aluminum cans. The discarded metal is used in the making of new steel and aluminum cans. Making scrap steel perform well in an oxygen furnace, however, remains a challenge for the metallurgist. Aluminum, on the other hand,*

and depending on natural systems either to destroy or dilute them. Now we realize that by spreading them around we have not made them go away, but have merely coupled large numbers of ecosystems, causing general instead because of the incredible energy needed to make it from virgin materials, readily lends itself to reuse. Many aluminum companies have enthusiastically set up aluminum reclamation centers to encourage recycling and to save money. The major stumbling block with any of these solutions is the sorting and transporting. In many cases the cost for transporting scrap is four times as high as it is for virgin material. More favorable rail rates might add impetus to these forms of can reuse.

Bottles are easier to dispose of than cans. First of all, a bottle can be made returnable, thus increasing its use and life. For a returnable bottle to be profitable, it must be refilled six times. The current average is fifteen times, but some urban areas average only four times. If all throwaways were banned, the consumer would have to adjust to returning bottles. Such consumer cooperation is a must for successful bottle recycling. Consumers, although they usually state a preference for returnables, inevitably choose throwaways even though the price is higher. The second solution — using the bottle's glass in making new glass — is currently quite common. Most new glass contains 30 percent "cullett" or "old" glass. The only problem here is separating the colors and imperfections in the glass so that a new batch is not "contaminated." Some experts contend that old glass can make up as much as 50 percent of new glass. If so, the supply is abundant.

Both cans and bottles lend themselves to the third solution — crushing. Cans and bottles can be crushed and ground to create a very coarse sand. Such sand is readily usable as land fill for eroding shorelines. In addition, bottles can be crushed and used as road surfacing material. "Glasphalt" may soon replace "asphalt."

Recycling is less a search for novel ideas and more an economic jigsaw puzzle. In most cases recycled goods cost more than those made from virgin sources. (Aluminum is an exception.) If virgin materials were to increase in price or become scarce, or if energy costs were to accelerate, reuse as such might be more attractive. In some cases determining whether new materials or used materials are more economical is a question of choosing whatever figures support your point of view. It is hard to assess the dollar-and-cents advantages of less air pollution.

Man will have to recycle. The motivating force will be economic — either dumping land will be too expensive or materials and energy will be too expensive. The question thus becomes not "if" but "how." Garbage is one of the few things in today's world that is free. All it needs is some pioneer to exploit it. Perhaps the first step would be a reevaluation of garbage. Rather than an albatross, it should be regarded as a resource — a resource that is being misused.

of localized pollution. A better plan now appears to be to concentrate effluents, rather than to dilute them. We may have to uncouple ecosystems from one another, rather than couple them. Thus some people envision closed agricultural systems in which all nutrients and even water are recycled. We can still count on natural systems to handle nonconservative pollutants, if we do not overtax them. But the process of gouging minerals out of the depths of the earth and spreading them on the surface where they enter water supplies and embark on their one-way trip to the sea — creating pollution all along the way — must stop.

SOCIAL SOLUTIONS.    The technological fix has its place but also its limitations; technology can solve only technological problems, not social ones. The problems of today, of which pollution is but one manifestation, require social solutions.

Our culture is strained by powerful new knowledge which shakes our perceptions of reality and conflicts with our traditions. In the face of it, we are forced to invent a new culture. In order to do this in consonance with our awakening understanding of our place in nature, we have to replace our traditional straight-line thinking with pattern thinking. We can no longer isolate a simple cause and effect, oblivious of the rest of the universe, because what is really involved is the ever-changing relationship between everything and everything else. Unaided, our minds simply cannot handle the complexity of the situations in which we are now involved, but the computer will become an increasingly important extension of our minds, handling the new type of pattern thinking which we need to do.

The new knowledge tells us that an extension of the past and present is not an appropriate prescription for the future. For probably the first time in cultural history, we must systematically plan cultural changes which are really intended to change things. We have usually sought alternatives on the supply side to meet our needs. Now we must begin to explore alternatives on the demand side — to provide social solutions. For example, there is no question that the transportation system of today will undergo radical changes. The future will not see more and bigger automobiles run on synthetic gasoline manufactured from coal. It will see efficient, low-polluting mass transit, with the automobile — if it still exists — banned from the central city. But this will change more than our habits in transportation; it will change the entire fabric of our lives.

The relative value of goods and services and of amenities is related to what has been described as the hierarchy of human needs (Figure 15.12). This concept is not accepted by everyone, largely because there is no one hierarchy that applies to all cultures. A hierarchy could be devised for each culture, however, and the point is that the goals and priorities of a culture change according to where it is in terms of satisfying the needs of its people. In the starving nations the goal is the conquest of hunger; a starving person does not care about "sense of accomplishment and achievement of full capability," as stated at the apex of the triangle in Figure 15.12. The actual order or description of levels in the hierarchy may vary, but the hierarchical

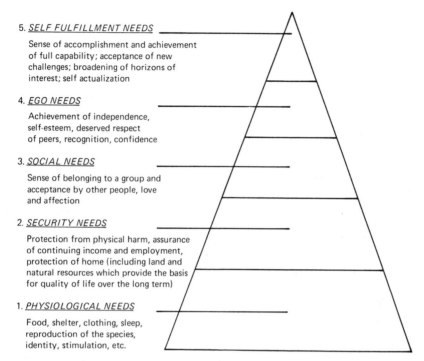

**Figure 15–12** Hierarchy of human needs. (From Environmental Protection Agency, Office of Research and Development, *Alternative Futures and Environmental Quality*, U.S. Government Printing Office, Washington, D.C., 1973, p. 107.)

structure suggests that after most of the needs at a low level have been met, a need at the next higher level tends to produce the primary motivation for an individual or a society.

There is growing conviction these days that we are entering a postindustrial stage of cultural evolution. Many basic changes already seem to be underway, among which a publication of the Environmental Protection Agency identifies the following (see references):

.. From primary and secondary industries (agriculture-manufacturing) to tertiary and quaternary industries (service, knowledge activities).

.. From goods to services.

.. From goods' services produced by muscle power to those produced by machines and **cybernetics.**

.. From the materialistic to the sensate.

.. From "things" to experiences.

.. From physiological to psychological needs.

.. From scarcity to abundance and eventually to superabundance.

.. From a few stark choices to a bewildering array of choices.

.. From durability to disposables and planned obsolescence and back to recyclables, reclaimables.

.. From self-interest motivation to a broader social and humanitarian outlook.

.. From independence and self-sufficiency to interdependence.

.. From individual freedom to voluntary restraints to mandatory restraints.

.. From Puritan hard-work ethic to leisure as a matter of right.

.. From Darwinian self-survival to humanistic security.

.. From atomistic to large-scale, pluralistic institutions.

.. From national to multinational and "one-world" scale operations.

.. From decentralization to centralization and eventual globalization.

.. From irrational chaos to creative, long-range planning.

These changes have already begun. But our disharmony with the environment has been evolving for a long time — since the massive animal drives of the big game hunters and the first extensive burning of forests — and the new knowledge and pattern thinking are very new. The final solution to the problem of man's disharmony with his environment may require cultural changes that we cannot yet even imagine. Thoughtful people object to the term environmental crisis not because our present problems are not many and immense, but because the word crisis implies that everyone is sitting around impotently awaiting the outcome. We hope we are not in that situation. We hope we can take sustained, rational, and creative action to direct cultural evolution in a way that will restore our harmony with our environment.

## REFERENCES

AMERICAN CHEMICAL SOCIETY. 1969. *Cleaning Our Environment: The Chemical Basis for Action.* Washington, D.C.: American Chemical Society.

ARTHUR, D. R. 1969. *Man and His Environment.* New York: Elsevier.

BLAU, S. D., AND J. RODENBECK, EDS. 1971. *The House We Live In: An Environment Reader.* New York: Macmillan.

BRADY, N. C., ED. 1967. *Agriculture and the Quality of Our Environment.* Washington, D.C.: Am. Ass. Adv. Sci. Pub. 85.

EDITORS OF FORTUNE. 1969. *The Environment: A National Mission for the Seventies.* New York: Harper & Row.

ENVIRONMENTAL PROTECTION AGENCY. 1973. *Alternative Futures and Environmental Quality.* Washington, D.C.

FOREMAN, H., ED. 1972. *Nuclear Power and the Public.* Anchor Books. Garden City, N.Y.: Doubleday & Co.

GARVEY, G. 1972. *Energy, Ecology, Economy.* New York: W. W. Norton and Co.

GEESAMAN, D. 1971. Plutonium and the energy decision. *Science and Public Affairs, Bulletin of the Atomic Scientists.* 27(7):33–36.

GOFMAN, J. 1971. Nuclear power and ecocide: an adversary view of new technology. *Science and Public Affairs, Bulletin of the Atomic Scientists.* 27(7):28–32.

GOLDMAN, M. I. 1970. The convergence of environmental disruption. *Science.* 170:37–42.

GOLDMAN, M., ED. 1967. *Controlling Pollution: The Economics of a Cleaner America.* Englewood Cliffs, N.J.: Prentice-Hall.

GRAVA, S. 1969. *Urban Planning Aspects of Water Pollution Control.* New York: Columbia Univ. Press.

GREENWOOD, N., AND J. EDWARDS. 1973. *Human Environments and Natural Systems.* Belmont, Cal.: Wadsworth Publishing Co.

HANKS, T. W. 1967. *Solid Waste/Disease Relationships: A Literature Survey.* Cincinnati: U.S. Dept. of Health, Educ. and Welfare.

HARTE, J., R. SOCOLOW, AND J. GINOCCHIO. 1971. Radiation. In *Patient Earth*, J. Harte and R. Socolow, eds. New York: Holt, Rinehart, and Winston.

JACKSON, W., ED. 1971. *Man and the Environment.* Dubuque, Iowa: Brown.

KNEESE, A. V., AND B. T. BOWER. 1968. *Managing Water Quality: Economics, Technology, Institutions.* Baltimore: Johns Hopkins Press.

KRENKEL, P. A., AND F. L. PARKER, EDS. 1969. *Biological Aspects of Thermal Pollution.* Proceedings of the National Symposium on Thermal Pollution. June 3–5, 1968. Nashville, Tenn.: Vanderbuilt Univ. Press.

KRYTER, K. D. 1970. *The Effects of Noise on Man.* New York: Academic Press.

LEDERBERG, J. 1971. Squaring an infinite circle: radiobiology and the value of life. *Science and Public Affairs, Bulletin of the Atomic Scientists.* 27(7):43–45.

LINDROP, P., AND J. ROTBLAT. 1971. Radiation pollution of the environment. *Science and Public Affairs, Bulletin of the Atomic Scientists.* 27(7):17–24.

MARX, W. 1971. *Man and His Environment: Waste.* New York: Harper & Row.

MASS. INST. TECHNOL. 1970. *Man's Impact on the Global Environment: Assessment and Recommendations for Action.* Report of the Study of Critical Environmental Problems (SCEP). Cambridge: MIT Press.

MASS. INST. TECHNOL. 1971. *Inadvertent Climate Modification.* Report of the Study of Man's Impact on Climate (SMIC). Cambridge: MIT Press.

MATTHEWS, W., W. KELLOGG, AND G. ROBINSON, EDS. 1971. *Man's Impact on the Climate.* Cambridge: MIT Press.

MATTHEWS, W., F. SMITH, AND E. GOLDBERG. 1971. *Man's Impact on Terrestrial and Oceanic Ecosystems.* Cambridge: MIT Press.

MELLANBY, K. 1967. *Pesticides and Pollution.* London: Collins.

PAULSEN, D., AND R. DENHARDT, EDS. 1973. *Pollution and Public Policy.* New York: Dodd, Mead & Co.

PERRY, J. 1967. *Our Polluted World: Can Man Survive?* New York: Watts.

PITTS, J. N., JR. AND R. L. METCALF, EDS. 1969. *Advances in Environmental Sciences and Technology.* Vol. I. New York: Wiley-Interscience.

PURDOM, P. W., ED. 1971. *Environmental Health.* New York: Academic Press.

RUDD, R. L. 1964. *Pesticides and the Living Landscape.* Madison: Univ. Wisconsin Press.

SMALL, W. E. 1970. *Third Pollution: The National Problem of Solid Waste Disposal.* New York: Praeger.

STEINHART, C., AND J. STEINHART. 1972. *Blowout: A Case Study of the Santa Barbara Oil Spill.* Belmont, Cal.: Wadsworth Publishing Co.

STRAUSS, W., ED. 1971. *Air Pollution Control.* Part I. New York: Wiley-Interscience.

STROBBE, M. A., ED. 1971. *Understanding Environmental Pollution.* St. Louis: Mosby.

TAMPLIN, A. 1971. Issues in the radiation controversy. *Science and Public Affairs, Bulletin of the Atomic Scientists.* 27(7):25–27.

VAN TASSEL, A. J., ED. 1970. *Environmental Side Effects of Rising Industrial Output.* Lexington, Mass.: D. C. Heath.

VELZ, C. J. 1970. *Applied Stream Sanitation.* New York: Wiley-Interscience.

VERNBERG, F. J., AND W. B. VERNBERG. 1970. *The Animal and the Environment.* New York: Holt, Rinehart & Winston.

WARNER, A. W., D. MORSE, AND T. E. COONEY, EDS. 1969. *The Environment of Change.* New York: Columbia Univ. Press.

WILBER, C. G. 1969. *The Biological Aspects of Water Pollution.* Springfield, Ill.: Thomas.

WILLRICH, T. L., AND N. W. HINES, EDS. 1967. *Water Pollution Control and Abatement.* Ames: Iowa State Univ. Press.

WILSON, B. R., ED. 1968. *Environmental Problems: Pesticides, Thermal Pollution, and Environmental Synergisms.* Philadelphia: Lippincott.

WOLMAN, A. 1969. *Water, Health, and Society.* Bloomington: Indiana Univ. Press.

# · Epilogue ·

NORMAN D. LEVINE

# The Future of Man

My niece recently asked me, "Is it true that we'll all be dead in 25 years?" I reassured her, but the idea that something is ultimately going to make life impossible on earth is a common one today. Either the **greenhouse effect,** resulting from the burning of fossil fuels, will make the world too warm for man, or the SST will release so much water vapor that the earth will be continually covered by clouds, or environmental pollution will prevent oceanic plankton from manufacturing oxygen, or lead or mercury or some other pollutant will poison us, or the polar ice will melt and inundate our coastal cities, or the sun will turn into a **nova** or send out a superflare and burn us all to a crisp, or. . . . The list of potential catastrophes is enormous, and while most are impossible and the remainder improbable, speculation on the future of man continues to be an intriguing subject.

Although few prophecies are valid — unknown factors vitiate them — we do know that the eventual and inevitable fate of man is extinction. Evolution is still occurring, and species are continually changing. Man — *Homo sapiens*, that is — is perhaps 500,000 years old. In another 500,000 years, today's man will no longer exist; he will have evolved into a new, and hopefully a wiser, species.

But this forecast concerns the far distant future. We are interested in more immediate events. As an arbitrary date, suppose we consider the year 3000 C.E. How will our culture adapt itself to the changes foreshadowed in the previous chapters?

Of course, a thousand years from now is a long time, at least for us. It is forty human generations or fourteen to fifteen lifetimes. If we think back to the year 1000 C.E., which marked about the beginning of the High Middle Ages, we can see how far we have come. People then had practically none of the comforts that we enjoy. They shivered in winter, roasted in summer, had few clothes, bathed seldom if ever, ate a monotonous and restricted diet, labored hard physically, carried around a rich fauna of lice, fleas, and intestinal parasites, and died early of disease or injury. Infant mortality was high, and, of course, most people were illiterate.

In 1000 C.E. no one could have predicted what life would be like today. And no one today can truly know what it will be like in the future, although a recent prediction by Meadows et al. (1972) concluded that the limits to growth on this planet would be reached sometime within the next 100 years, resulting in a sudden and uncontrollable decline in both population and industrial capacity. Overshoot and collapse, in other words.

The mere existence of such an unfavorable prediction — and there are many besides the Meadows' — ensures that it will not come to pass; people will move to counteract. Present trends will not continue.

## THE ROLE OF SCIENCE

Science has only recently become the overriding feature of civilization. It is now a profession, not a leisure-time avocation or obsession for gentlemen. We are consciously changing things, consciously looking for improvements. But science by itself is neutral. All it does is give us information, and while man uses that information to achieve his ends, he cannot always know the results. It is this fact that has enabled Meadows et al. to predict overshoot and collapse. Their views remind us that we cannot ignore the human factor in the use of information gained from science.

## MAN'S IMPACT ON THE EARTH

Originally, man was but one of several predators or omnivores living on the face of the earth. He had little more effect on his environment than any of the many species with which he shared it. He was part of the balance of nature. However, his brain changed all that. Nature is no longer in balance, and the cause is man.

At first man did little to his surroundings, but as he multiplied and learned more, he began to modify his environment. Little clearings appeared in the forest, and then larger ones. Crops were planted, and eventually whole countrysides became checkered with growing monocultures. Forests were felled, roads were built, hills were terraced, soil was stripped away to get at what lay beneath, earth and minerals and animals were transferred from one place to another, rivers were run backwards, canals were dug, some animals and plants were destroyed and others encouraged. From the moon, the earth may look no different today than it did centuries ago, but a close-up view shows hardly a place on its surface where the hand of man has not left an imprint. History traces that imprint over the last thousand years; I shall make an attempt to predict what may happen in the next.

FOOD.   It is extremely difficult to estimate how many people the earth can feed. Over half of the world's population today is malnourished, but this is due mainly to poor distribution rather than to insufficient production. Assuming that we could solve the maldistribution problem (an improbable assumption), the number of people that could be fed would still depend upon several factors, none of which can necessarily be anticipated.

One factor relates to the amount of land used for food production. At present the net amount is decreasing, primarily in the more developed countries. A great deal of good land is being taken out of production by mining, highways, and expanding cities, and more is being temporarily removed (in the United States, at least) by a governmental policy of idling land because we are producing too much. However, more land can be made available by fertilization and still more by irrigation. Fertilization depends in large part upon fixation of nitrogen from the air, and the supply of nitrogen is essentially inexhaustible. Irrigation, however, depends upon an abundance of fresh water, and this supply is definitely limited. As a result, we are starting to turn to desalination of seawater, a process which will become increasingly economic as time goes on. Icebound lands could also be cultivated if enough heat were provided, perhaps by covering the land with glass or plastic to form huge greenhouses, or by transferring heat from the tropics to the arctic, or by generating heat from nuclear power, or by a combination of these methods.

A second factor relates to the development of new or more productive varieties of food plants or animals, as we presently depend upon an extremely small number of these. Agriculture has already been improved many times in this area through hybridization and genetic selection. Improvement could be continued by introducing new food animals or plants to various areas. As the cattle of Africa are not particularly productive, it has been suggested that the **lechwe** would utilize forage much better than the ox; it is large and has broad feet which allow it to graze where the ox cannot. Reindeer could be raised in the Western Hemisphere; after all, their wild form, the caribou, is already there.

A third factor deals with the human part of the food web. Eating animals rather than plants is highly inefficient. Although algae and grass aren't as palatable as fish and beef, starvation is not an acceptable alternative. In case of need, it shouldn't be too difficult, technologically speaking, to extract the nutrients from grass and make them into an acceptable food, leaving the cellulose for other purposes, such as making sugar. Marine and freshwater algae, too, could be used like land vegetation, turning eutrophication of inland waters into an asset.

WATER.   Fresh water is already in short supply in some parts of the world, and while our need for it is ever-increasing, the introduction of pollutants has decreased its availability. Seawater itself can be thought of as heavily polluted water, polluted with salts. However, future technological improvements in the process of desalinization should provide plenty of fresh water from the ocean for all human needs.

MINERALS AND OTHER NONRENEWABLE RESOURCES. Some minerals are essentially inexhaustible, while others are not. We can divide nonrenewable resources into three groups, depending on their abundance. Sand, gravel, and rock will always be available. Limestone can be mined either from the earth or from coral islands. Magnesium, iodine, bromine, and salt can be obtained from the ocean, and there seems to be an adequate supply of sulfur from one source or another. Iron and aluminum are also abundant.

An intermediate group includes copper, cobalt, nickel, vanadium, zinc, titanium, and lead. Presumably there can be sufficient quantities if enough energy is available for their mining.

A third group includes the scarce minerals, such as mercury, tungsten, tantalum, tin, molybdenum, silver, gold, platinum, palladium, and lanthanum. Many of these are valuable in their own right, while others are necessary for certain alloys. Conservation, the discovery of substitutes, and recycling should make most of these still available by 3000 C.E.

ENERGY. The key to more food, water, and minerals is abundant, cheap energy, which should be available by 3000 C.E. I suspect that we shall have nuclear fusion by then, but if not, nuclear breeder reactors or solar energy might be sufficient for our needs.

One thing should be made clear about the "if" that is energy. If we do not master breeder, fusion or solar technology *within the next few decades* while we still have fossil fuels to burn up and to supply our needs, there may well be no such technologies in 3000. It takes energy to produce energy, and we must get the long-term sources of energy operating now or there will be nothing to build them from. I think that we will, and my predictions are based on this assumption.

WEATHER AND CLIMATE. Earth has witnessed many profound climatic changes, some of them within the history of our species. Today, while we scheme to alter the weather locally, we realize that human activity is inadvertently modifying climate on a global scale. How much and in what direction we do not know with certainty, but we are tampering with the elements from which climate is determined. Even now we can *change* the climate, although we cannot *control* it. However, in a thousand years we shall undoubtedly possess this power. Not only shall we be able to predict weather accurately, but we shall be able to modify it to our own advantage. Control of the circulation of the air above the earth will be extended to control of the circulation of water in the oceans, and both of these will affect the weather.

POLLUTION.    Pollutants will probably not be a major problem in the future. Many of them are present now because we are wasteful in our extraction of minerals and other nonrenewable resources. Eventually, however, we shall be able to extract metals from lower and lower quality ores, and recycling will become routine. Garbage will be a resource, not an inconvenient liability. Sewage will be an important fertilizer. Petroleum will have been all but forgotten, and coal will be too precious as a source of organic compounds to be burned. The heat which now causes thermal pollution will be used to heat houses and for many other purposes. It will not be necessary to store fission products in salt mines or elsewhere until they no longer give off radiation, for we shall make use of them for many purposes, including heat and metal sources. In short, man will have tidied up his environment; he will no longer live on the dungheap of his effluvia.

POPULATION.    At present the human population of the earth is estimated to be 3.6 billion and is doubling every 35 years. At this rate the population would reach 37 million billion in 3000 C.E. This number is an impossibility, of course. Despite this potentiality, I think that the world population will be smaller in 3000 C.E. than it is now. My guess is 1 billion.

The quality of the people is as important as their quantity. Many **eugenicists** claim that man is deteriorating, and this may well be true of his physical qualities. Steadily occurring mutations are accumulating in the human gene pool, and every advance in medical science that makes it possible for people with severe genetic defects to survive and reproduce increases the number of such defects in the population. It is possible, however, that with curtailment of population, artificial selection might well be practiced, just as it is for dairy cattle and other domestic animals and plants, and that future offspring will be selected for intelligence and freedom from physical defects.

Another aspect of population concerns its distribution. At present most people live in the temperate zone. But the continental climate is too cold for comfort in the winter and too hot in the summer. Why, then, do we concentrate here? Is it because of the mental stimulus provided by the changing seasons, as some people think, or is it because food plants grow best in the temperate zone, and people tend to live near their supply of food? Certainly it would be more comfortable to live in the subtropics. Perhaps the present migration to Florida, California, and Hawaii is an index of future trends.

It is evident that man is becoming more and more urbanized. If the current pattern were to continue uninterrupted, it would be less than a century before everyone lived in the cities. It is much more likely, however, that the trend toward urbanization will decrease and that the proportion of our urban population will level off. But the point at which it will occur depends upon many things—upon total population, upon farming practices and the number of people needed to run the farms, and upon customs — whether farmers want to live on their farms or commute to them from the city.

My prediction for 3000 C.E. is that 95 percent of the population will live in the cities, that most will live in the subtropics, that the number of births per family will be limited (possibly by law), and that parents will be carefully selected by the state to meet certain physical, mental, and genetic standards. The average man will be superior to the average man today.

What animals and plants will there be in another thousand years? According to the International Union for the Conservation of Nature and Natural Resources, the average life of a mammalian species before man emerged was close to 600,000 years and that of a bird species over 2 million years. But man has changed all that. Thirty-six of the 4,226 species of mammals living in 1600 C.E. have become extinct, and at least 120 more are in danger of extinction. Ninety-four of the 8,685 species of birds living in 1600 C.E. have become extinct, and some 187 more of these are in danger of extinction. We preserve some species and destroy or ignore others. Those which are able to adapt to the man-altered environment survive and multiply, but those which cannot die out or become rare.

Some species of wild animals will surely become extinct in the next thousand years. Certainly this will be true of the larger and more conspicuous ones. Extinction is the normal result of evolution. Only about 1 percent of all the species that have existed are still with us. Without evolution there would be no man, and there would be none of the animals whose demise some of us deplore.

*HEALTH.*    Will man live longer in 3000 C.E. than now? Will he suffer the same diseases? The average length of life has increased, but this is due more to a decrease in infant mortality than to an increase in maximum survival. Seventy years is still the usual life expectation, although some people live a decade longer, and a very few live more than 100 years. The body wears out and degenerative diseases take over. Because the average length of life will undoubtedly increase in the next thousand years, so will the prevalence of these diseases. Organs will give out, will lose their functioning power. Organ transplantation is being hailed as a solution, but every time one man receives a heart, another must die. Artificial prosthetic devices seem more promising. We already have an artificial kidney, and by 3000 an artificial heart should be as common as an artificial leg is today. Perhaps eventual understanding of cell renewal will help us defeat the aging process.

*GOVERNMENT AND POLITICAL SYSTEMS.*    It is often said that if one wants to know what the future will be like, he should read science fiction. In their treatment of political systems, almost all science fiction stories point toward a single world government. The number of sovereign governments in the world *has* been steadily decreasing. After World War I the idea of self-determination was stressed, but all parts of the world are so interrelated that no group can be allowed to do what it wants regardless of what effects its actions may have on its neighbors. Self-governing tribes and city-states were appropriate in the past, but today, when we can go to any part of the globe in 24 hours, and when communication is instantaneous, these forms of government are obsolete. The trend today is toward union, as indicated by the European Common Market, and it is my guess that the trend will continue. A few small independent governments may survive, but they will exist only on sufferance, for the convenience of the dominant government(s), or as "pets."

*ECONOMIC SYSTEMS.* The nations that dominate the earth are those with the greatest resources. These are the source of power. Resources may be natural, such as coal or iron or oil, or they may be the result of education or industrialization, or they may be a combination of these. For example, western Europe had coal and iron conveniently together; England industrialized and scoured the world for raw materials that it could use for its manufacturers; Switzerland had little in the way of natural resources, but it had education, manufacturing skill, and imaginative people, and it became a source of specialties like watch-making, banking, and hotel-keeping. The United States became the most powerful nation in the world because of its vast resources.

Monopoly is a source of power, too. If one nation or one group has the sole supply of some needed commodity, it can, within limits, set its own price and it can be very influential. But as resources run out, so does influence.

What will the situation be in 3000? What region of the world will be dominant? Resources run out, and their nature changes as our needs change. What will be the important minerals in 3000? Where will they be? Regions which today depend on oil for their clout will no longer be able to do so. Regions with an excess of food will have power only as long as there are regions with a deficiency. If solar energy becomes especially important, then deserts and tropical regions where insolation is greatest will become dominant. However, if our main source of energy is fusion, then coastal regions with ready access to the hydrogen in water will be more powerful. Valid prediction at this point is impossible.

*LANGUAGE.* The number of the world's languages will decrease, mainly because of the inevitable disappearance of primitive groups with individual dialects and because of the consolidation of governments. As a result, communication between peoples will be easier.

The grammar and spelling of the remaining languages will change and become simpler. Inflections and diacritical marks will disappear, and spelling will become uniform. The trends which are so evident in English today will continue. What our language will be like in another thousand years is impossible to guess, but surely such multiple pronunciations as we have for combinations like *-ough* will no longer exist.

*RELIGION.* Despite the fact that advanced thinkers have no use for religions, religions will still be with us in 3000 C.E. Man needs a higher power on which to lean, and he will invent one if it does not exist. He needs a religion in order to explain the incomprehensible, and some things will always be incomprehensible.

Perhaps there will be a new religion, such as the ethical, non-miraculous one that Julian Huxley tried to introduce. It is much more likely, however, that there will be new offshoots of the old religions. The spiritual needs that a 3000 C.E. human ecology might demand will depend upon the type(s) of society existing then. Dissatisfaction might breed a new messianic religion, or contentment might breed one which emphasizes ethics and denigrates the supernatural, or one or more of our present religions might persist with more or less change.

*PROBLEMS.* It may sound as though I am predicting a utopia, but I am doing no such thing. Even if man achieves equilibrium with his environment, he will still have himself to contend with. Man is aggressive, he wants to dominate, he wants his way. Most men want to impose themselves and their ideas on their fellows. If they cannot do so, they want to get rid of the opposition. This attitude is what brings on conflicts and wars. Perhaps there will no longer be national wars in 3000 C.E., but there will certainly be conflicts of one sort or another.

There will still be the racial problems that stem from the me-thee dichotomy. The individual ("I") identifies with some people but not with others; he divides the world into similar and dissimilar, friendly and unfriendly. Primitive tribes speak of themselves as "the people" as opposed to everyone else; the Greeks divided everyone into Greeks and barbarians (who said ba-ba and could not be understood). This attitude persists today. Every nation, ethnic group, and race considers itself first, and all others next. The brotherhood of man is still an idealist concept.

Are we in for a series of boom-and-bust cycles, overshoot and collapse, or for some sort of dynamic equilibrium? I suspect that we shall have both, that the first will be followed by the second. Perhaps the latter will also come during the next thousand years. Hopefully, we shall be more knowledgeable about guiding our destinies by that time. The most solid prediction that I can make for 3000 C.E. is that man will still be around — better off than he is now, but still beset with problems.

# REFERENCES

ANDERSON, P. K., ED. 1971. *Omega: Murder of the Ecosystem and Suicide of Man.* Dubuque, Iowa: Brown.

BERNAL, J. D. 1965. *Science in History.* 3rd ed. New York: Hawthorn.

COLE, L. C. 1968. Can the world be saved? *BioScience.* 18:679–684.

COMMONER, B. 1963. *Science and Survival.* New York: Viking Press.

FADIMAN, C., AND J. WHITE, EDS. 1971. *Ecocide . . . and Thoughts Toward Survival.* Santa Barbara, Calif.: Center for the Study of Democratic Institutions.

HANDLER, P., ED. 1970. *Biology and the Future of Man.* New York: Oxford Univ. Press.

KAHN, H., AND A. J. WIENER. 1967. *The Year 2000: A Framework for Speculation on the Next Thirty-Three Years.* New York: Macmillan.

SINGER, S. F., ED. 1971. *Is There an Optimum Population?* An AAAS Symposium, Boston, Dec. 1969. New York: McGraw-Hill.

TAYLOR, G. R. 1970. *The Doomsday Book.* New York: World.

WALLIA, C. S., ED. 1970. *Toward Century 21.* New York: Basic Books.

WELLS, H. G. 1936. *The Shape of Things to Come.* New York: Macmillan.

WOLSTENHOLME, G. E., ED. 1963. *Man and His Future.* Boston: Little, Brown & Co.

# · Glossary ·

*Absolutism.* The idea that the government shall exercise complete and unrestricted power.

*Acellular.* Not composed of cells.

*Alluvial soils.* Soils deposited by sedimentation from flowing water.

*Amphibians.* Frogs, toads, salamanders and other vertebrates that live part of their life in water (as tadpoles) and part on land.

*Anaerobes.* Microbes that do not use free oxygen for respiration.

*Anaerobic respiration.* Respiration without free oxygen.

*Antigen-antibody response.* Formation of antibody by the body in response to the presence of an antigen; the antibody combines with the antigen and precipitates it.

*Arboreal.* Tree-inhabiting.

*Asymmetric.* Nonsymmetrical; not showing a center, axis, or plane of symmetry.

*Atmosphere.* The air; the gaseous envelope surrounding the earth.

*Aurora borealis.* The northern lights; a luminous display over the North Pole.

*Australoids.* The aboriginal human inhabitants of Australia.

*Binomial system of nomenclature.* In biology, the system of naming plants or animals whereby they are given a scientific name (in Latin) composed of two words; the first word is the genus name and the second word is the species name.

*Biosphere.* That part of the earth and its atmosphere where life exists.

*Cartilage.* A translucent, firm, skeletal material composed of a type of connective tissue, used by vertebrate animals for internal support.

*Caucasoids.* The type of human being inhabiting Europe, North Africa, the New World and India, mostly light-skinned.

*Cerebral cortex.* The outer layer of the cerebrum (part of the brain).

*Chaparral.* A growth of low, dense trees and bushes, such as occurs in the southwestern United States.

*Chemical carcinogenesis.* Production of cancer by a chemical or chemicals.

*Cholesterol.* A white, fatty crystalline alcohol, $C_{27} H_{45} OH$, that is found in bile, egg yolk, and especially nerve tissue.

*Circadian rhythms.* Rhythms that occur at about daily intervals.

*Cirrus clouds.* Clouds composed of ice crystals, having the form of thin white filaments or narrow bands and occurring about 20,000 to 40,000 feet above the earth.

*Concubinage.* The living together of a man and a woman without formal marriage.

*Confidence limits.* In statistics, a pair of numbers that indicate a specified probability that a certain population is included within them.

*Coniferous.* Pertaining to cone-bearing trees such as pine trees.

*Convection.* Transfer of heat by movement of a gas or liquid.

*Cropping.* Producing or harvesting a crop.

*Crustaceans.* Any of a large class of arthropods, principally aquatic and commonly covered with a horny shell, such as crabs, lobsters, and barnacles.

*Cumulus clouds.* Puffy, cottony clouds which occur about 3,000 to 20,000 feet above the ground.

*Cybernetics.* The study of human control functions and of mechanical or electric systems designed to replace them.

*Deciduous.* Shedding its leaves; used in referring to trees or shrubs.

*Diatoms.* Primitive, microscopic, single-celled green plants occurring in water and having cell walls composed of silicon dioxide.

*Diploid.* Having two sets of chromosomes; the normal situation in vertebrate body cells.

*Diverticulitis.* Inflammation of a diverticulum (a blind tube or sac branching off from a canal or cavity); the diverticulum may be natural, such as the human appendix, or abnormal, such as a diverticulum from the esophagus.

*Diverticulosis.* An infection of a diverticulum.

*Dorsal.* Having to do with the back.

*Dose-response curves.* Curves which show the responses of some organism to different doses or amounts of a substance.

*Dynamic equilibrium.* A situation which appears constant but which is due to continual interchange between two opposing forces.

*Electromagnetic spectrum.* The gamut of electromagnetic waves of different wavelengths, from gamma rays through ultraviolet light, visible light and heat waves to radio waves.

*Entrepreneurism.* The system under which some person undertakes, organizes, or manages each enterprise.

*Environmental heat sink.* Something that absorbs heat in or from the environment.

*Estrous cycle.* A series of changes in the sexual and other organs of female mammals from one heat period (estrus) to another.

*Estuary.* The region where a river flows into the sea, where fresh and salt water mix.

*Eugenicist.* A person who specializes in the science of improving the qualities of the human race.

*Fauna.* Animals of a particular region, considered as a whole.

*Fiefdom.* The situation by which land is held in fee from a feudal lord or owner.

*Follicle.* A small cavity, sac or gland, such as a portion of an ovary.

*Gestation.* The period during which a fetus is held in the uterus; pregnancy.

*Glomerular filtration rate.* The rate at which fluids are filtered through the kidney, eventually emerging as urine.

*Gonads.* Sexual organs; ovaries or testes.

*Gradient.* A gradual change from one level to another.

*Greenhouse effect.* The trapping of heat by a lengthening in the wavelength of incident radiation such as occurs in a greenhouse.

*Haploid.* Having one set of chromosomes, such as occurs in mammalian sperm or egg cells.

*Hemoglobin.* The red coloring matter of blood; it combines with oxygen which it carries from one place to another.

*Hemophilia.* A tendency to bleed, caused by failure of the blood to coagulate properly.

*Herbaceous.* Characteristic of herbs, i.e., of nonwoody flowering plants.

*Homologous chromosomes.* A pair of chromosomes which carry the same or similar genes, one member of the pair being derived from each parent.

*Horticulture.* The science or art of cultivating flowers, fruits, vegetables, or ornamental plants.

*Hybridization.* The process of crossing plants or animals of different breeds or species.

*Hydrosphere.* The parts of the earth's surface that are more or less permanently covered by water.

*Incident solar energy.* The energy from the sun that strikes or impinges on an object.

*Infantilism.* The persistence in the adult of childish anatomic, physiologic or psychologic characteristics.

*Interstices.* Intervening spaces, especially between small objects.

*Intervertebral discs.* Discs between the vertebrae of the back.

*Invertebrate.* An animal that does not have vertebrae (a backbone).

*Ionization.* The production of an electric charge on an atom or group of atoms by loss or gain of one or more electrons.

*Ion.* An atom or group of atoms which bears an electric charge.

*Isotopes.* Atoms of the same element with different atomic weights; U-235 and U-238 are both isotopes of uranium.

*Jaundice.* A condition characterized by yellowness of the eyes and skin, due to the presence of yellow bile pigments in the blood and tissues.

*Lactation.* Production of milk by the mammary gland.

*Lechwe.* An African antelope, *Onotragus leche.*

*Lipid.* A fatty or similar substance.

*Lipid sheath.* A sheath composed of fatty substances around a nerve.

*Lithosphere.* The part of the earth consisting of rocks and metals, from the earth's crust (except for the soil) all the way to its core.

*Metallurgy.* The science or art of working with metals.

*Meteorite.* A mass of stone or metal which has fallen onto the earth from outer space.

*Microflora.* Microscopic plants.

*Mill tailings.* The residue of unwanted by-products produced by a mill.

*Mongoloid.* A member of a racial division of mankind which includes the Chinese and Japanese.

*Monoculture.* Cultivation of a single species rather than several species mixed together; a cornfield is a monoculture of corn.

*Motile.* Moving or able to move.

*Negroid.* A member of a racial division of mankind which includes the Negroes, with a more or less black or brown skin.

*Notochord.* A rod-like cord of cells forming a dorsal internal support for primitive chordates and vertebrate embryos.

*Nova.* A star that suddenly becomes thousands of times brighter than before.

*Nucelus.* A membrane-bound structure within a cell that contains the genetic material of the cell.

*Nucelotide.* One of the building blocks of the nucleic acids, consisting of a phosphate, a sugar, and a nitrogen-containing base.

*Order of magnitude.* A statement regarding size. An order of magnitude is a factor of ten. The number 230 is greater than 23 by one order of magnitude and greater than 0.23 by three orders of magnitude.

*Oxidation.* The combination of oxygen with some substance, or the loss of electrons.

*Pathenogenic organism.* An organism or virus which causes disease.

*Peat.* A highly organic soil containing more than half combustible matter.

*Photoperiod.* The period during the day when a plant or animal is exposed to light.

*Photosynthesis.* Production of carbohydrate from water and carbon dioxide by the action of a substance such as chlorophyll, using sunlight for energy.

*Plankton.* The floating organisms, usually microscopic, in a body of water.

*Plasma.* The noncellular part of the blood.

*Prosimians.* Primitive primates belonging to the suborder Prosimii; this suborder includes the lemurs and lorises.

*Protozoa.* One-celled animals, such as *Paramecium, Amoeba* and the malaria parasite.

*Psychosomatic factors.* Factors resulting from the influence of the mind on the body.

*Radioisotope.* A radioactive isotope, often used in medical diagnosis and therapy.

*Radon.* A chemical element, No. 86, resulting from the breakdown of radium.

*Reef.* A ridge of rocks, sand, or coral near the surface of the water.

*Riffle.* A ripple on the surface of a stream; a rapid.

*Rotifer.* An animal of the phylum Rotifera; these are microscopic animals that have a hair-like feeding apparatus on the anterior end that looks in action like a pair of rotating wheels.

*Ruminant animals.* Mammals that have a rumen or paunch; cattle and sheep are ruminants.

*Sedimentation.* Settling out of solid materials from water or some other liquid.

*Shale.* A rock formed by the consolidation of clay.

*Shaman.* A medicine-man; a priest-doctor.

*Sigmoid growth curve.* An S-shaped curve depicting the way organisms grow or multiply.

*Steppe.* An extensive plain, ordinarily without trees.

*Symbiotic microorganisms.* Microorganisms which live in a mutually beneficial relationship with another organism, such as the nitrogen-fixing bacteria in the root nodules of leguminous plants.

*Thalidomide baby.* A baby born with shortened limbs due to its mother's use of the tranquilizer thalidomide when pregnant.

*Thermodynamics.* The science concerned with the conversion of heat into mechanical energy or work (and vice versa).

*Totalitarian state.* A nation governed by a single political party which does not recognize or tolerate other parties.

*Trachea.* The windpipe.

*Tubercle bacillus. Mycobacterium tuberculosis,* the bacterium which causes tuberculosis.

*Vaginal epithelium.* The layer of cells lining the vagina.

*Vascular plant.* A plant with a system of tubular vessels for transporting sap.

*Vertebra.* One of the bones forming the spinal column.

*Vital capacity.* The greatest amount of air that can be expelled from the lungs after a maximum inspiration.

*Watershed.* A drainage area.

*Weir.* An obstruction, such as brush or boards, placed across a stream to raise the water level.

# · Index ·